14th Workshop on Cognitive Modeling and Computational Linguistics (CMCL 2025)

Albuquerque, New Mexico, USA
3 May 2025

ISBN: 979-8-3313-1916-8

Printed from e-media with permission by:

Curran Associates, Inc.
57 Morehouse Lane
Red Hook, NY 12571

Some format issues inherent in the e-media version may also appear in this print version.

Printed with permission by Curran Associates, Inc. (2025)

For permission requests, please contact the Association for Computational Linguistics at the address below.

Association for Computational Linguistics
209 N. Eighth Street
Stroudsburg, Pennsylvania 18360

Phone: 1-570-476-8006
Fax: 1-570-476-0860

acl@aclweb.org

Additional copies of this publication are available from:

Curran Associates, Inc.
57 Morehouse Lane
Red Hook, NY 12571 USA
Phone: 845-758-0400
Fax: 845-758-2633
Email: curran@proceedings.com
Web: www.proceedings.com

CMCL 2025

The 14th edition of the Workshop on Cognitive Modeling and Computational Linguistics

Proceedings of the Workshop

May 3, 2025

This workshop has been supported by National Institute for Japanese Language and Linguistics (NINJAL), Japan.

NINJAL
National Institute for Japanese Language and Linguistics

Introduction

Welcome to the 14th edition of the Workshop on Cognitive Modeling and Computational Linguistics (CMCL 2025)!

CMCL continues to be one of the leading workshops at the intersection of Cognitive Modeling, Computational (Psycho-)Linguistics, and Natural Language Processing. Building on the success of the CMCL 2024 edition, we are delighted to gather once again this year to explore the latest advancements in this vibrant interdisciplinary field.

This year, we received 47 submissions in total, including 35 regular archival submissions and 12 non-archival submissions. We accepted 22 archival papers, resulting in an acceptance rate of 22/35=62.9%, which remains consistent with the previous year (63.9%). We also accepted 9 non-archival papers, out of 12 non-archival submissions. The program covers a wide array of topics, encompassing main topics such as real-time sentence processing, alongside advanced themes like language disorders, neuroscientific comparison of humans and language models, and the integration of speech data/models. This diversity reflects the growing engagement in our field and the increasing importance of understanding human/language through computational methods.

We appreciate the Program Committee members for their timely and constructive reviews, which were instrumental in shaping the program. We also extend our gratitude to our invited speakers, Dr. John Hale and Dr. Tessa Verhoef, for enriching this year's program with their expertise and inspiring talks. Given that the number of proposals for ACL workshops has increased in recent years, it is also important to express our gratitude to the ACL workshop chairs for selecting CMCL as one of workshops in NLP top-conferences.

Lastly, we are immensely grateful to our sponsor, National Institute for Japanese Language and Linguistics (NINJAL). Their generous support enables us to host the participation of our invited speakers in this year's CMCL.

Thank you for joining CMCL 2025. We look forward to an engaging and stimulating exchange of ideas!

The CMCL 2025 Organizing Committee

Organizing Committee

Organizers

Tatsuki Kuribayashi, Mohammed bin Zayed University of Artificial Intelligence
Giulia Rambelli, University of Bologna
Ece Takmaz, Utrecht University
Philipp Wicke, Ludwig Maximilian University
Jixing Li, City University of Hong Kong
Byung-Doh Oh, New York University

Program Committee

Invited speakers

John Hale, Johns Hopkins University, University of Georgia, and DeepMind
Tessa Verhoef, Leiden Institute of Advanced Computer Science

Program committee

Giorgia Albertin, University of Bologna
Anna Bavaresco, University of Amsterdam
Luca Capone, University of Pisa
Ludovica Cerini, University of Pisa
Luca Dini, University of Pisa
Filip Ilievski, Vrije Universiteit Amsterdam
Alessio Miaschi, Institute for Computational Linguistics A. Zampolli"(CNR-ILC), Pisa
Martina Miliani, University of Pisa
Andrea Pedrotti, Institute of Information Science and Technologies of the National Council of Research (ISTI-CNR)
Alice Suozzi, University of Venice
Giorgia Albertin, University of Bologna
Raquel G. Alhama, University of Amsterdam, University of Amsterdam
Afra Alishahi, Tilburg University
Masayuki Asahara, National Institute for Japanese Language and Linguistics, Japan
Anna Bavaresco, University of Amsterdam
Ted Briscoe, Mohamed bin Zayed University of Artificial Intelligence
Emmanuele Chersoni, The Hong Kong Polytechnic University
Marianne De Heer Kloots, University of Amsterdam
Aniello De Santo, University of Utah
Andrea Gregor De Varda, University of Milan - Bicocca
Vera Demberg, Universität des Saarlandes
Luca Dini, University of Pisa
Jakub Dotlacil, Utrecht University
Micha Elsner, Ohio State University
Abdellah Fourtassi, Aix Marseille Univ
Diego Frassinelli, Ludwig-Maximilians-Universität München
Richard Futrell, University of California, Irvine
John T. Hale, Johns Hopkins University, University of Georgia and DeepMind
Tim Hunter, University of California, Los Angeles
Filip Ilievski, Vrije Universiteit Amsterdam
Shinnosuke Isono, National Institute for Japanese Language and Linguistics and University of Tokyo
Anna A Ivanova, Georgia Institute of Technology
Cassandra L Jacobs, State University of New York, Buffalo
Jaap Jumelet, University of Groningen
Kristina Kobrock, Universität Osnabrück
Tom Kouwenhoven, Leiden University
Agnese Lombardi, University of Pisa
Alessio Miaschi, Institute for Computational Linguistics A. Zampolli"(CNR-ILC), Pisa
James A. Michaelov, Massachusetts Institute of Technology

Sathvik Nair, University of Maryland
Yohei Oseki, University of Tokyo
Ludovica Pannitto, University of Bologna
Sandro Pezzelle, University of Amsterdam
Roi Reichart, Technion, Israel Institute of Technology
Rachel Ryskin, University of California at Merced
Lavinia Salicchi, The Hong Kong Polytechnic University
William Schuler, Ohio State University, Columbus
Cory Shain, Massachusetts Institute of Technology
Taiga Someya, The University of Tokyo
Sean Trott, University of California, San Diego
Ryo Ueda, The University of Tokyo
Shaonan Wang, Chinese Academy of Sciences
Ryo Yoshida, The University of Tokyo

Table of Contents

Non-archival papers

The LLM Language Network: A Neuroscientific Approach for Identifying Causally Task-Relevant Units
Badr AlKhamissi, Greta Tuckute, Antoine Bosselut and Martin Schrimpf

Modeling Pragmatic Accommodation: A [Rational, Irrational] Speaker in a [Wonky, Normal] World
Muxuan He, Elsi Kaiser and Khalil Iskarous

Spontaneous Speech Variables for Evaluating LLMs Cognitive Plausibility
Sheng-Fu Wang, Laurent Prevot, Jou-an Chi, Ri-Sheng Huang and Shu-Kai Hsieh

Event Order Recognition in BERT: Evidence from Temporal Connectives
Hannah S. Rognan and Shohini Bhattasali

Logical forms complement probability in understanding language model (and human) performance
Yixuan Wang and Freda Shi

Syntactic Learnability of Echo State Neural Language Models at Scale
Ryo Ueda, Tatsuki Kuribayashi, Shunsuke Kando and Kentaro Inui

A Preliminary Analysis of the Predictive Power of Surprisal in Reading Chinese
Hongao Zhu, Muxiaoqiao Xu, Siyuan Song, Yikang Liu, Yuxia Wang and Hai Hu

Humanlikeness of LLMs in Mental Lexicon
Bei Xiao, Xufeng Duan and Zhenguang Cai

FiSMiness: A Finite State Machine Based Paradigm for Emotional Support Conversations
Yue Zhao, Qingqing Gu, Xiaoyu Wang, Teng Chen, Zhonglin Jiang, Yong Chen and Luo Ji

Program

Saturday, May 3, 2025

09:00 - 09:10 *Opening Remarks*

09:10 - 10:10 *Invited talk by Dr. John Hale*

10:10 - 10:50 *Session 1: Oral Presentations*

Capturing Online SRC/ORC Effort with Memory Measures from a Minimalist Parser
Aniello De Santo

Quantifying Semantic Functional Specialization in the Brain Using Encoding Models of Natural Language
Jiaqi Chen, Richard Antonello, Kaavya Chaparala, Coen Arrow and Nima Mesgarani

10:50 - 11:10 *Break*

11:10 - 12:20 *Session 2: Poster Presentations*

ParaBLoCC: Parallel Basic Locative Constructions Corpus
Peter Viechnicki and Anthony Kostacos

Profiling neural grammar induction on morphemically tokenised child-directed speech
Mila Marcheva, Theresa Biberauer and Weiwei Sun

Spontaneous Speech Variables for Evaluating LLMs Cognitive Plausibility
Sheng-Fu Wang, Laurent Prevot, Jou-an Chi, Ri-Sheng Huang and Shu-Kai Hsieh

Exploring the Integration of Eye Movement Data on Word Embeddings
Fermín Travi, Gabriel Aimé Leclercq, Diego Fernandez Slezak, Bruno Bianchi and Juan E Kamienkowski

Logical forms complement probability in understanding language model (and human) performance
Yixuan Wang and Freda Shi

A Preliminary Analysis of the Predictive Power of Surprisal in Reading Chinese
Hongao Zhu, Muxiaoqiao Xu, Siyuan Song, Yikang Liu, Yuxia Wang and Hai Hu

Saturday, May 3, 2025 (continued)

SPACER: A Parallel Dataset of Speech Production And Comprehension of Error Repairs
Shiva Upadhye, Jiaxuan Li and Richard Futrell

Towards a Bayesian hierarchical model of lexical processing
Cassandra L Jacobs and Loïc Grobol

Modeling Chinese L2 Writing Development: The LLM-Surprisal Perspective
Jingying Hu and Yan Cong

Beyond Binary Animacy: A Multi-Method Investigation of LMs' Sensitivity in English Object Relative Clauses
Yue Li, Yan Cong and Elaine J. Francis

When Men Bite Dogs: Testing Good-Enough Parsing in Turkish with Humans and Large Language Models
Onur Keleş and Nazik Dinctopal Deniz

Transformers Can Model Human Hyperprediction in Buzzer Quiz
Yoichiro Yamashita, Yuto Harada and Yohei Oseki

12:20 - 13:40 *Lunch break*

13:40 - 14:40 *Invited talk by Dr. Tessa Verhoef*

14:40 - 15:40 *Session 3: Oral Presentations*

Unzipping the Causality of Zipf's Law and Other Lexical Trade-offs
Amanda Doucette, Timothy J. O'Donnell and Morgan Sonderegger

Creolization versus code-switching: An agent-based cognitive model for bilingual strategies in language contact
Charles John Torres, Weijie Xu, Yanting Li and Richard Futrell

Cross-Framework Generalizable Discourse Relation Classification Through Cognitive Dimensions
Yingxue Fu

Saturday, May 3, 2025 (continued)

15:40 - 16:00 *Break*

16:00 - 17:10 *Session 4: Poster Presentations*

The LLM Language Network: A Neuroscientific Approach for Identifying Causally Task-Relevant Units
Badr AlKhamissi, Greta Tuckute, Antoine Bosselut and Martin Schrimpf

Modeling Pragmatic Accommodation: A [Rational, Irrational] Speaker in a [Wonky, Normal] World
Muxuan He, Elsi Kaiser and Khalil Iskarous

Linguistic Blind Spots of Large Language Models
Jiali Cheng and Hadi Amiri

From Punchlines to Predictions: A Metric to Assess LLM Performance in Identifying Humor in Stand-Up Comedy
Adrianna Romanowski, Pedro H. V. Valois and Kazuhiro Fukui

Event Order Recognition in BERT: Evidence from Temporal Connectives
Hannah S. Rognan and Shohini Bhattasali

Syntactic Learnability of Echo State Neural Language Models at Scale
Ryo Ueda, Tatsuki Kuribayashi, Shunsuke Kando and Kentaro Inui

Distinct social-linguistic processing between humans and large audio-language models: Evidence from model-brain alignment
Hanlin Wu, Xufeng Duan and Zhenguang Cai

Are Larger Language Models Better at Disambiguation?
Ziyuan Cao and William Schuler

An Empirical Study of Language Syllabification using Syllabary and Lexical Networks
Rusali Saha and Yannick Marchand

Humanlikeness of LLMs in Mental Lexicon
Bei Xiao, Xufeng Duan and Zhenguang Cai

Saturday, May 3, 2025 (continued)

	Investigating noun-noun compound relation representations in autoregressive large language models Saffron Kendrick, Mark Ormerod, Hui Wang and Barry Devereux
	FiSMiness: A Finite State Machine Based Paradigm for Emotional Support Conversations Yue Zhao, Qingqing Gu, Xiaoyu Wang, Teng Chen, Zhonglin Jiang, Yong Chen and Luo Ji
17:15 - 17:55	*Session 5: Oral Presentations*
	"Is There Anything Else?": Examining Administrator Influence on Linguistic Features from the Cookie Theft Picture Description Cognitive Test Changye Li, Zhecheng Sheng, Trevor Cohen and Serguei V. S. Pakhomov
	What to Predict? Exploring How Sentence Structure Influences Contrast Predictions in Humans and Large Language Models Shuqi Wang, Xufeng Duan and Zhenguang Cai
17:55 - 18:10	*Closing Remarks*

Linguistic Blind Spots of Large Language Models

Jiali Cheng **Hadi Amiri**
University of Massachusetts Lowell
{jiali_cheng, hadi_amiri}@uml.edu

Abstract

Large language models (LLMs) are the foundation of many AI applications today. However, despite their remarkable proficiency in generating coherent text, questions linger regarding their ability to perform fine-grained linguistic annotation tasks, such as detecting nouns or verbs, or identifying more complex syntactic structures like clauses in input texts. These tasks require precise syntactic and semantic understanding of input text, and when LLMs underperform on specific linguistic structures, it raises concerns about their reliability for detailed linguistic analysis and whether their (even correct) outputs truly reflect an understanding of the inputs. In this paper, we empirically study the performance of recent LLMs on fine-grained linguistic annotation tasks. Through a series of experiments, we find that recent LLMs show limited efficacy in addressing linguistic queries and often struggle with linguistically complex inputs. We show that the most capable LLM (Llama3-70b) makes notable errors in detecting linguistic structures, such as misidentifying embedded clauses, failing to recognize verb phrases, and confusing complex nominals with clauses. Our results provide insights to inform future advancements in LLM design and development.

1 Introduction

Large Language Models (LLMs) have revolutionized NLP by achieving remarkable performance on a wide range of tasks and applications, including zero-shot inference (Weller et al., 2020; Brown et al., 2020); solving math problems (Wei et al., 2022); representing human emotions (Li et al., 2024); and serving as planners (Huang et al., 2022), conversational agents (Ouyang et al., 2022), or text-to-code convertors (Sun et al., 2023). Nevertheless, despite recent studies (Shen et al., 2021; Yu et al., 2023; Chen et al., 2024) aiming to understand Transformers (Vaswani et al., 2017) as the building block of LLMs, there is a lack of systematic evaluation of their ability in performing fine-grained linguistic annotation tasks.

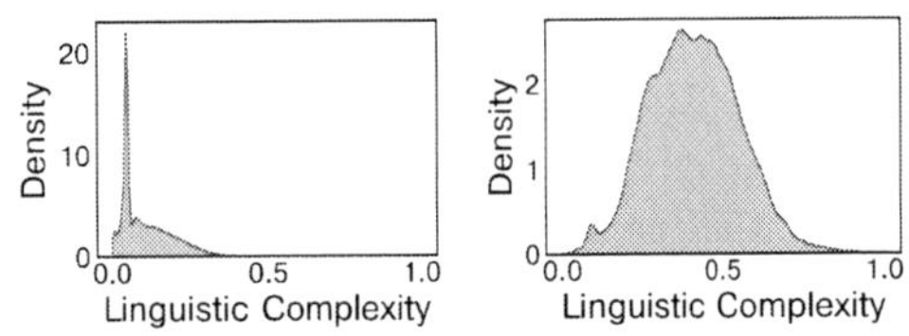

(a) Penn Treebank (b) CoNLL 2000

Figure 1: Distribution of linguistic complexity in two widely-used NLP datasets. The plots show **(a)**: a strong skew toward linguistically simple examples in the Penn Treebank and **(b)**: a concentration around moderate complexity in CoNLL 2000, which highlights an over-representation of easier or medium-difficulty samples in the datasets.

Recent work studied LLMs from different linguistic perspectives, including grammar learning with small models (Huebner et al., 2021), effect of pre-training on learning linguistic properties like the depth of parse tree or verb tense (Alajrami and Aletras, 2022), the role of individual neurons in POS tagging and chunking tasks (Durrani et al., 2020), and the effect of prompt design for detecting linguistic properties (Blevins et al., 2023). However, existing evaluations are based on NLP datasets where linguistically "easy" examples (see Section 2) are overrepresented. For instance, Figure 1 shows histograms of the linguistic complexity of samples in two widely-used NLP datasets: Penn Treebank (Marcus et al., 1993) and CoNLL 2000 (Tjong Kim Sang and Buchholz, 2000). The skewed distribution toward linguistically easy or medium examples can artificially inflate performance on NLP tasks[1] and prevent true

[1]This phenomenon has challenged the NLP community across natural language inference (NLI), POS tagging, and parsing tasks, where models show human-level performance, while lacking cognitive ability to address these tasks. For example, recent work by Sinha et al. (2021) shows that BERT

Proceedings of the Workshop on Cognitive Modeling and Computational Linguistics, pages 1–17
May 3, 2025

evaluation of models in NLP. We mitigate this bias by reducing the effect of overrepresented examples, i.e., categorizing samples based on their linguistic complexity and uniformly sampling data from distinct groups for a more reliable assessment.

We investigate the following research questions: (1): *how accurately can recent LLMs detect complex linguistic structures in input text?* (2): *which linguistic structures represent the blind spots of recent LLMs–meaning the most challenging for them?* (3): *how does the performance of LLMs vary across different levels of linguistic complexity of inputs?* We answer these questions by designing an empirical study for LLMs. The contributions of this paper are in examining recent LLMs's ability to detect specific linguistic structures across varying levels of linguistic complexity, providing meaningful insights into their limitations and biases, and highlighting potential avenues for future improvements.

Experimental results show that recent LLMs have limited efficacy in addressing linguistic queries, particularly struggling with complex linguistic structures such as complex nominals and T-units. In particular, Llama3-70b and GPT-3.5 are the most capable models among evaluated LLMs, while still making mistakes on simple linguistic queries. In addition, the performance of all evaluated LLMs often substantially fluctuates as sample complexity varies.

2 Background

Linguistic Complexity: quantifies the variability and sophistication in productive vocabulary, grammatical structures, and fluency in text data. It has been extensively investigated in psycholinguistics literature (Wolfe-Quintero et al., 1998; Zareva et al., 2005; Lu, 2010; Housen et al., 2019; Biber et al., 2020); and examined in quantifying language proficiency (Yannakoudakis et al., 2011; Lu, 2012), readability assessment and text simplification (Feng et al., 2009; Xu et al., 2015; Xia et al., 2016; Lee et al., 2021), and improving NLP tasks (Wei et al., 2021).

Lexical Complexity: is concerned with lexical *density*, *sophistication*, and *variation*. Lexical density is often quantified by the extent of information-carrying words in inputs. Lexical sophistication measures the proportion of *sophisticated* or infrequent words in texts. Lexical Variation refers to the diversity of vocabulary in text. Examples include type-token ratio (Templin, 1957) and its variations including *D-measure* (Malvern et al., 2004), which determines lexical variation of text by finding the curve that best fits the actual relationship between types and tokens in input text.

Syntactic Complexity: determines variability and sophistication in grammatical structures. A sentence like "*the mouse ate the cheese*" can be converted to its well-formed yet complex counterpart "*the mouse the cat the dog bit chased ate the cheese*," which forces readers to suspend their partial understanding of the sentence by encountering subordinate clauses that substantially increase the cognitive load of the sentence. Syntactic complexity measures the length of production units at the clausal, sentential, or T-unit levels; the amount of subordination, e.g. number of clauses per T-unit; the amount of coordination, e.g. number of coordinate phrases per clause or T-unit; and the range of surface and particular syntactic and morphological structures, e.g. frequency and variety of tensed forms (Wolfe-Quintero et al., 1998; Ortega, 2003).

Linguistic Knowledge of LLMs Blevins et al. (2023) designed *structured* prompting to assess the linguistic capabilities of LLMs. They provided each LLM with fully labeled demonstrations, and a query sentence and its partially tagged version. Each predicted label was appended to the partially tagged query along with the next word to iteratively tag the full query. They found that GPT-3.5 is robust to arbitrary label selections and ignores labels conflicting with its prior knowledge, indicating that the models can learn general linguistic knowledge during pre-training, rather than simply memorizing the data. Alajrami and Aletras (2022) empirically compared linguistically-motivated (e.g. masked language modeling (Devlin et al., 2019)) and non-linguistically motivated (e.g. masked first character prediction (Yamaguchi et al., 2021)) pre-training objectives for BERT on linguistic probing tasks (Linzen et al., 2016; Warstadt et al., 2020). They found the two objectives achieve similar performance. Clark et al. (2019) showed that attention heads in transformers attend to boundary tokens, positional offsets, and whole sentence; while Voita et al. (2019) showed that attention heads mainly handle positions, syntax, and rare words. Dur-

is invariant to random word order permutation in case of NLI, which can be attributed to the high prevalence of linguistically easy samples in NLI datasets (Elgaar and Amiri, 2023b).

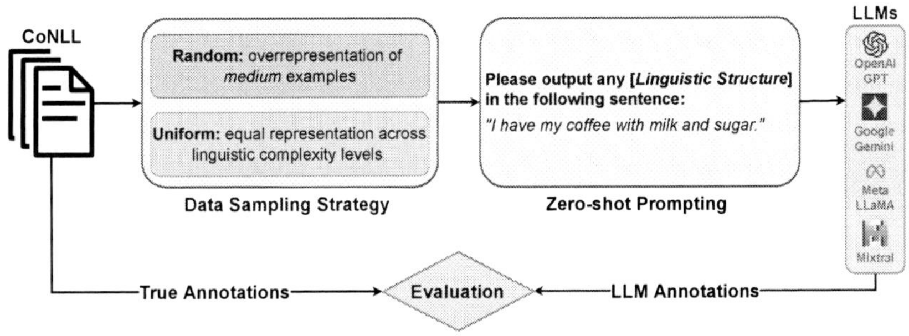

Figure 2: Workflow for finding linguistic blind spots of LLMs. As illustrated in Appendix A, GPT and other LLMs have good knowledge of our target tasks and the relevant terminology used in the prompts. [*Linguistic Structure*] in the prompts indicate any of the lexical or syntactic structures listed in Appendix C.

rani et al. (2020) compared linguistic knowledge learned by LMs at neuron level. They narrowed down neurons to a specific subset, located in lower hidden layers for lexical knowledge and in higher layers for semantic knowledge. Finally, Sharma et al. (2023) found that learning non-linguistic knowledge (e.g. numerical skills) sacrifices the linguistic knowledge of LLMs, and Ettinger (2020) found that BERT underperforms on commonsense, pragmatic inference, and negation tasks.

3 Finding Linguistic Blind Spots

We evaluate LLMs on recognizing specific linguistic structures (see below). For this purpose, we use gold linguistic annotations, lexical complexity analyzer from (Lu, 2012), and syntactic complexity analyzer from (Lu, 2012) to quantify linguistic complexity of samples. We note that the estimations provided by these tools have perfect agreement (based on Cohen's Kappa) with estimations provided by more recent linguistic complexity analysis tools (Lee et al., 2021; Lee and Lee, 2023).

Linguistic Structures: we consider different levels of granularity: **word-level structures** like nouns, verbs, adjectives, adverbs, prepositions, conjunctions, numerals, determiners, punctuation, particles, and words that cannot be assigned a part-of-speech (POS) tag; **phrase-level structures** like noun phrases (NP), verb phrases (VP), adjective phrases (ADJP), adverb phrases (ADVP), conjunction phrases (CONJP), complex nominals (CN); and **sentence-level structures** like clauses (C), dependent clauses (DT), T-units (T), and complex T-units (CT). Appendix C lists these structures.

Data Sampling Strategy The overrepresentation of easy and medium examples shown in Figure 1 suggests that the linguistic capability of LLMs may have been overestimated in existing literature (Blevins et al., 2023; Yang and Tu, 2022; Shen et al., 2018). For fair evaluation across the linguistic complexity spectrum, we divide samples into eight groups of increasing linguistic complexity, determined using (Lu, 2010, 2012), and uniformly at random sample from each group, leading to a total number of $8 \times 125 = 1$k samples, denoted as $\mathcal{U}$. For comparison, we also randomly select 1k samples from the dataset, which shows similar distribution to the original distribution, denoted as $\mathcal{R}$.

Prompting Strategies: we use zero-shot prompting to assess LLMs' ability to identify individual linguistic structures in input text in a question-answering format, see Figure 2. We also investigate other prompting techniques, such as manually optimizing instructions, chain-of-thought (CoT) prompting (Wei et al., 2022) and structured prompting (Blevins et al., 2023). However, in a small scale experiment, the alternative approaches did not result in consistent performance improvement over the zero-shot approach. This could be because LLM's current pretraining does not fully capture the complex syntactic and semantic information of inputs required for fine-grained linguistic annotation. Instead, they might rely heavily on surface-level patterns, which limits the impact of more advanced prompting strategies.

4 Experimental Setup

Dataset & Evaluation: We use the CoNLL 2000 (Tjong Kim Sang and Buchholz, 2000) subset of the Penn Treebank corpus (Marcus et al., 1993) (Wall Street Journal (WSJ) sections 15, 16, 17, 18, 20), which provides ground truth POS tags and syn-

LLM	Sampling	P	R	F1
Llama3-70b	$\mathcal{R}$	**31.3**	**30.8**	**29.2**
Llama3-70b	$\mathcal{U}$	**28.2**	**27.5**	**26.1**
Llama3-8b	$\mathcal{R}$	24.0	26.8	23.2
Llama3-8b	$\mathcal{U}$	21.8	24.0	20.8
GPT-3.5	$\mathcal{R}$	21.6	26.1	21.2
GPT-3.5	$\mathcal{U}$	20.4	23.5	19.5
Llama2-70b	$\mathcal{R}$	13.4	21.4	14.7
Llama2-70b	$\mathcal{U}$	11.8	18.4	12.8
Mixtral-8x7b	$\mathcal{R}$	11.0	25.4	13.0
Mixtral-8x7b	$\mathcal{U}$	10.2	22.5	11.8
Mistral-7b	$\mathcal{R}$	7.4	15.2	8.0
Mistral-7b	$\mathcal{U}$	6.9	13.5	7.5
Llama2-7b	$\mathcal{R}$	7.0	9.8	7.4
Llama2-7b	$\mathcal{U}$	7.0	9.7	7.3
Gemini	$\mathcal{R}$	1.2	1.2	1.0
Gemini	$\mathcal{U}$	1.2	1.2	1.1

Table 1: Average performance in identifying linguistic structures. We compute precision, recall, and F1 for each sample, and average them across all samples to assess LLM performance in detecting linguistic structures.

tactic annotations. We use standard pre-processing to convert POS tags to Universal POS tags (Blevins et al., 2023). Following previous work (Blevins et al., 2023), we compute precision, recall, and F1 score for each sample, and average them across all samples to evaluate LLM performance in recognizing linguistic structures.

Large Language Models: We use several robust LLMs including GPT-3.5 (Ouyang et al., 2022) (`gpt-3.5-0613`), Gemini-Pro 1.0 (Team et al., 2023), Llama3 (7B, 13B, 70B) (Touvron et al., 2023), Llama2 (7B, 13B, 70B), and Mistral (7B, 8x7B) (Jiang et al., 2023, 2024).

5 Main Results

5.1 Deficient Linguistic Performance of LLMs

Tables 1 show significant performance differences between LLMs when tasked with identifying linguistic structures across different sampling strategies. Despite outperforming other LLMs by a large margin, Llama3-70b, Llama3-8b, and GPT-3.5 have considerably low performance in identifying linguistic structures. Among the evaluated LLMs, Llama3-70b performs the best, with average precision, recall, and F1 score of 31.3, 30.8, and 29.2 on randomly selected samples ($\mathcal{R}$), and 28.2, 27.5, and 26.1 on uniformly selected samples ($\mathcal{U}$). However, these results are substantially lower than that of traditional models with significantly smaller sizes (Manning et al., 2014).

In addition, Gemini, Llama-2 and Mistral show poor performance across all settings, indicating that many linguistic structures are indeed a blind spot for these LLMs. Larger scales of Llama2 and Mistral show slightly better performance, but still limited compared to GPT-3.5 and Llama3. These models often recognize the entire sentence as a phrase, can't distinguish between noun phrases (NPs) and verb phrases (VPs), and show poor performance in detecting clauses. Surprisingly, Gemini lacks the ability to identify linguistic structures, with an average F1 score close to 0. Through manual analysis, we find that Gemini often misinterprets linguistic queries with harmful content, see Section 6.2.

5.2 Task Complexity

We find all evaluated LLMs show stronger capability in detecting simpler linguistic structures (e.g. word-level) than more complex structures (e.g. sentence-level). Specifically, GPT-3.5 achieves an average F1 scores of 37.5 ($\mathcal{U}$) and 34.4 ($\mathcal{R}$) on word-level structures, but close to zero F1 on phrase-level and sentence-level structures, see Table 2. For some complex structures including verb phrase (VP), complex nominal (CN), dependent clause (DC), T-unit (T), and complex T-unit (CT), all LLMs have close to zero F1 score. This might be because these complex structures require a model to detect simpler structures (e.g. POS tags) and build on them in a compositional manner to correctly identify the more complex ones. Our results show that LLMs can accomplish simpler linguistic tasks but fail to perform complex ones, which mainly require knowledge about compositionality.

GPT-3.5 Performance: As shown in Table 2, word-level structures such as nouns, verbs, and punctuation are generally better annotated by GPT-3.5, while phrase-level and sentence-level structures, particularly verb phrases (VP), clauses (C), and complex T-units (CT), have significantly lower performance. These high-level structures are indeed blind spots for existing LLMs, due to their complexity and linguistic understanding required to accurately identify them. Overall, GPT-3.5 tends to perform better on $\mathcal{R}$ than on $\mathcal{U}$ across most word-level and phrase-level structures. Specifically, on randomly selected samples, GPT-3.5 achieves average F1 scores of 37.5, 4.0, and 0.0 on word-level, phrase-level, and sentence-level structures respectively. On $\mathcal{U}$, GPT-3.5 achieves lower average F1 scores of 34.4 for word-level structures, 4.2 for phrase-level structures, and remains at 0.0 for sentence-level structures. These results indicates the model's relative strength in handling word-level structures but its significant limitation on more complex structures.

Structure	Sampling	P	R	F1
Word-level Structure				
PUNC	$\mathcal{R}$	82.5	77.4	77.4
PUNC	$\mathcal{U}$	86.1	79.5	80.9
NOUN	$\mathcal{R}$	71.6	65.6	66.1
NOUN	$\mathcal{U}$	67.6	64.3	62.9
VERB	$\mathcal{R}$	61.4	61.4	55.9
VERB	$\mathcal{U}$	53.9	51.0	47.7
DET	$\mathcal{R}$	56.4	56.2	50.7
DET	$\mathcal{U}$	50.3	47.9	43.4
ADP	$\mathcal{R}$	48.7	60.1	50.2
ADP	$\mathcal{U}$	42.0	47.7	41.6
ADJ	$\mathcal{R}$	26.5	43.7	29.1
ADJ	$\mathcal{U}$	22.7	32.9	23.1
ADV	$\mathcal{R}$	25.1	37.0	26.6
ADV	$\mathcal{U}$	25.8	33.4	25.8
PRON	$\mathcal{R}$	18.0	35.1	20.1
PRON	$\mathcal{U}$	17.0	32.7	18.8
PRT	$\mathcal{R}$	8.5	34.7	12.7
PRT	$\mathcal{U}$	8.1	30.8	11.6
CONJ	$\mathcal{R}$	30.3	30.9	29.1
CONJ	$\mathcal{U}$	28.8	28.8	27.0
NUM	$\mathcal{R}$	31.5	29.8	29.7
NUM	$\mathcal{U}$	30.3	28.6	28.6
Average	$\mathcal{R}$	38.6	44.8	37.5
Average	$\mathcal{U}$	36.2	40.2	34.4
Phrase-level Structure				
ADVP	$\mathcal{R}$	6.0	22.8	8.1
ADVP	$\mathcal{U}$	6.5	20.4	7.9
NP	$\mathcal{R}$	11.5	14.0	11.8
NP	$\mathcal{U}$	12.3	14.1	12.2
ADJP	$\mathcal{R}$	1.2	5.9	1.8
ADJP	$\mathcal{U}$	1.7	5.8	2.1
VP	$\mathcal{R}$	2.2	3.3	2.3
VP	$\mathcal{U}$	2.7	3.6	2.7
CONJP	$\mathcal{R}$	0.0	0.0	0.0
CONJP	$\mathcal{U}$	0.0	0.0	0.0
CN	$\mathcal{R}$	0.0	0.1	0.0
CN	$\mathcal{U}$	0.0	0.0	0.0
Average	$\mathcal{R}$	3.5	7.7	4.0
Average	$\mathcal{U}$	3.9	7.4	4.2
Sentence-level Structure				
C	$\mathcal{R}$	0.1	0.3	0.1
C	$\mathcal{U}$	0.0	0.1	0.1
DC	$\mathcal{R}$	0.0	0.0	0.0
DC	$\mathcal{U}$	0.0	0.1	0.0
T	$\mathcal{R}$	0.0	0.0	0.0
T	$\mathcal{U}$	0.0	0.0	0.0
CT	$\mathcal{R}$	0.0	0.0	0.0
CT	$\mathcal{U}$	0.0	0.0	0.0
Average	$\mathcal{R}$	0.0	0.0	0.0
Average	$\mathcal{U}$	0.0	0.0	0.0

Table 2: Linguistic annotation performance of GPT-3.5 across different linguistic structure groups. We compute precision, recall, and F1 for each sample, and average them across all samples to assess LLM performance in detecting linguistic structures.

5.3 Linguistic Complexity

Performance Drop on Complexity-Balanced Samples: We observe significant differences in LLMs' performances on $\mathcal{R}$ and $\mathcal{U}$, as determined by a t-test at 95% confidence interval. All evaluated LLMs (GPT-3.5, Gemini, Llama3, Llama2, Mistral) show significant decrease in performance on uniformly selected samples ($\mathcal{U}$) compared to randomly selected ones ($\mathcal{R}$). The only exceptions are Gemini and Llama2-7B, which is likely due to their already low performance on both $\mathcal{R}$ and $\mathcal{U}$. For GPT-3.5, the performance drops from an F1 score of 21.2 to 19.5, with significant p-value of $1e$-7. We note that although the performance consistently and significantly decreases across models from R to U, the absolute drop is small to modest. This may be due to the already low overall performance ceiling on these tasks, where even small differences are meaningful; the models' relative robustness to certain types of linguistic complexity, despite persistent weaknesses on edge cases and harder structures; or the prevalence of easier (word-level) structures compared to more complex (phrase- or sentence-level) ones in the set of linguistic structures we investigate.

Linguistic Complexity Fluctuation: We find that LLMs' performance fluctuate with increasing linguistic complexity of inputs, as shown in Figure 3 for GPT-3.5; see performance of other LLMs in Appendix B Figures 9–15. Specifically, the performance of GPT-3.5 improves initially but then declines on structures like verbs, nouns, pronouns, adjectives, and adverbs as linguistic complexity increases, with F1 scores ranging from 0 to 50. This suggest that expert-defined linguistic complexity (Lu, 2010, 2012) may not align with how LLMs view complexity, which is an underexplored topic. Interestingly, for other structures like punctuation (PUNC), we observe the opposite performance trend. This is likely due to the unique nature of these linguistic structures as punctuation marks typically follow more predictable and less complex rules compared to other linguistic structures like verbs or nouns. In addition, performance trend vary substantially across different LLMs and scales. For instance, Llama3-70b consistently shows an inverted U-shaped ($\bigcap$) performance pattern, while

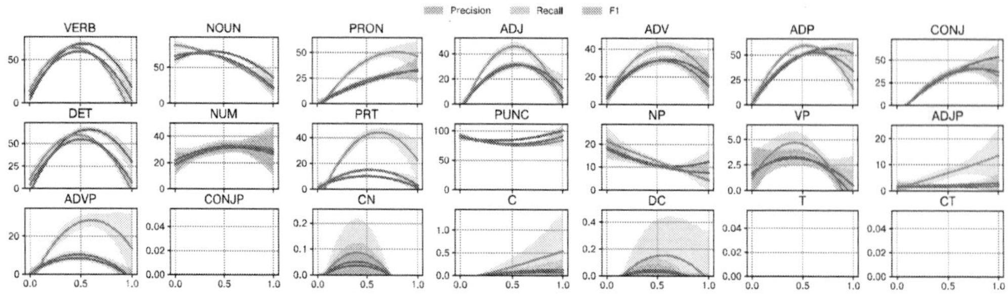

Figure 3: Performance of GPT-3.5 on texts of increasing linguistic complexity. GPT-3.5 achieves close to zero performance on CONJP, T, and CT. Figures 9-15 in Appendix B show results of other LLMs.

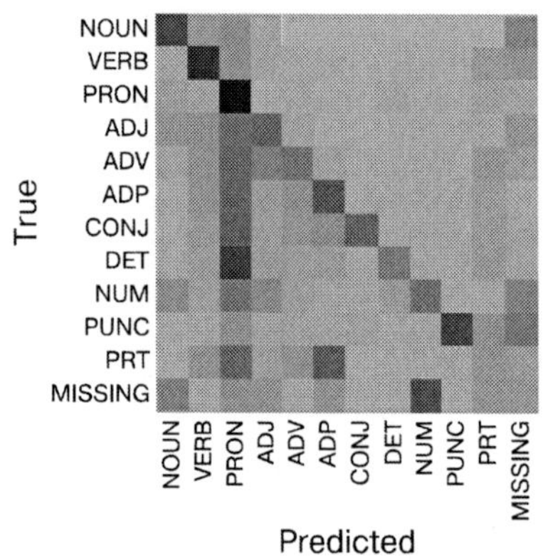

Figure 4: Confusion matrix of POS tagging on GPT-3.5. Darker indicates larger value. Diagonal/off-diagonal elements represent correct/wrong predictions respectively.

Llama2-70b have unique trends on noun and punctuation, which indicate model-specific challenges with different linguistic structures.

POS Tag Errors in GPT-3.5: Figure 4 shows a confusion matrix that assess the POS tags generated by GPT-3.5 Most of the errors stem from the model's failure to detect specific tags, denoted as "MISSING." The higher occurrence of MISSING cases is likely due to the increased complexity and linguistic knowledge required for these tasks–the need to identify and label all instances of linguistic structures in inputs. In addition, GPT-3.5 often confuses different POS tags with pronouns. This could be because pronouns often appear in diverse contexts where their function can be easily confused with other POS tags, such as determiners or nouns. In addition, GPT-3.5 (and other LLMs) tend to rely on surface-level patterns rather than deep linguistic understanding. Pronouns frequently co-occur within sentences, and the model may overgeneralize their patterns to other words.

Entity	NOUN	VERB	ADJ	ADV	ADP	CONJ	DET
# Dup.	334	370	93	156	526	400	635
# Succ.	0	1	0	0	5	1	2

Table 3: GPT-3.5 performance on samples that contain multiple instances of the same linguistic structure. Dup. indicates number of such texts (out of 1K) for each structure and Succ. indicates cases where *all* instances of the same POS tag are retrieved.

5.4 Multiple Structures and False Positives

When a samples contains multiple occurrences of the same linguistic structure, such as nouns, LLMs often struggle to retrieve all instances of of those structures. Table 3 shows that GPT-3.5 consistently fails to identify *all* nouns in any of the 334 samples containing more than one noun. This limitations extends beyond open-class words to closed-class tags such as prepositions (ADP), conjunctions (CONJ) and even determiners (DET).

We also observe that when a particular linguistic structure is absent in a given sample, LLMs still frequently make inaccurate predictions of its presence. Specifically for GPT-3.5, we find that in 6,892 out of 21,000 queries (33.9%), GPT-3.5 generates false positive predictions. Figure 5 shows the distribution of such errors across POS tag categories. The results show that GPT-3.5 often predict the existence of numerals (NUM), conjunctions (CONJ) and pronouns (PRON) when they are not present in the inputs. We conjecture that this behavior is due to biases in training data where certain words or structures co-occur frequently and the model learns to predict the presence of these words or structures based on relevant patterns in the training data, even when they don't exist in the input. For instance, if a sentence discusses quantities, the model might predict numerals. Therefore, false positive predictions

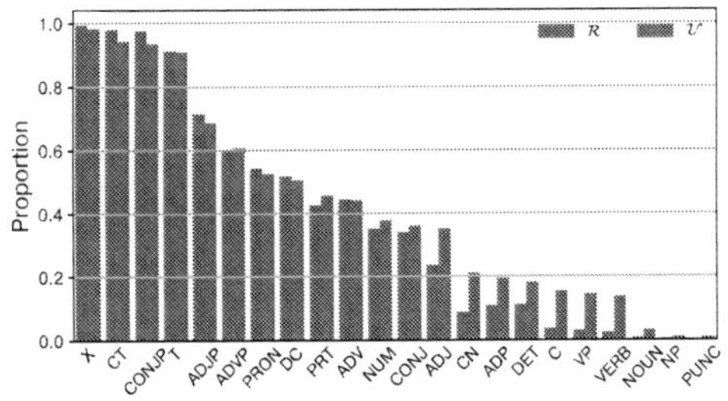

Figure 5: Distribution of false positive predictions by GPT-3.5 for absent linguistic structures in input. All evaluated LLMs show very similar distribution

for linguistic structures is common. In addition, all LLMs achieve higher recall than precision, especially all scales of LLaMA (see Table 1), again indicating that LLMs tend to retrieve more false positives than false negatives.

5.5 Model Capacity

We observe that models with higher capacity show slightly better performance. We evaluate the effect of model capacity, measured by the number of parameters, in performing fine-grained linguistic annotation tasks by comparing two scales of Llama3, Llama2, and Mistral, see Table 1. All models show improved or maintained linguistic performance as their capacity increases. However, it's noteworthy that the performance advantage may not be significant enough compared to the increase of scale. Specifically, using a 10 times larger Llama3 and Llama2 only boosts F1 score by 5.8 and 5.0, and 7.3 and 5.5 on randomly and uniformly sampled data respectively. The performance gain is also smaller on uniformly sampled inputs across all LLMs, due to the diverse inputs with various linguistic complexity, which outweighs model scale.

5.6 Dense model vs. Sparse model

Scaling up LLMs with Mixture-of-Experts (MoE) (Shazeer et al., 2017) in a sparse manner is a more efficient approach than dense scaling. We find that MoE can effectively boost LLM performance, see Mixtral 8x7b vs. Mistral-7b in Table 1. The performance of the MoE-based model–Mixtral 8x7b–is also comparable to that of Llama2-70b, a dense model of similar scale. This suggests that sparsity in LLMs is not a key or limiting factor in their fine-grained linguistic annotation ability.

6 Discussion

6.1 Limitations and Failure Cases

We identify significant limitations in the performance of the evaluated LLMs when responding to linguistic queries. Since GPT-3.5 is one of the most capable models with instruction-following capabilities in the evaluated LLMs, we mainly focus on its limitations. GPT-3.5 may **fail on linguistically easy examples**. For instance, it does not detect any of the 34 nouns that appear in the easiest linguistic examples in our dataset. GPT-3.5 (and most evaluated LLMs) may occasionally **skip tokens** in their responses. For example, they may skip tagging nouns or punctuation in inputs, which reduces their overall performance. They also **generate ill-formatted outputs**, including missing tags or corrupted parse trees. This is unexpected given that GPT-3.5 have a good knowledge about the definition of the linguistic tasks and required format; see Appendix A, Figures 6–8. GPT-3.5 (and most evaluated LLMs) may **generate biased outputs**. We find that the evaluated LLMs are biased to output common tokens and concepts, such as nouns and pronouns, while neglecting uncommon ones. Table 4 provides several example outputs. The first two show the tendency of GPT-3.5 to misclassify familiar structures such as nouns as adjectives or adverbs (first row) or verbs (second row). In addition, in may skip generating tags, see highlighted words "The" and "from" in Table 4. Note that the third example also shows GPT-3.5 mislabels many tokens, frequently replacing the correct POS tags with "PRON" or other incorrect tags.

6.2 Quality of Alignments

The LLMs we consider for this study have instruction-following capabilities. However, their performances in following linguistic-related instructions vary considerably. We find that GPT-3.5 tends to follow instructions better than other LLMs evaluated in our experiments. On the other hand, LLaMA-2 and LLaMA-3 generate irrelevant outputs including auxiliary text and special characters such as "\" and ">", even if we explicitly prompt them not to generate such characters. We note that the base model of GPT-3.5 has been fine-tuned on code data, which helps the model understand structured and instructional input. In addition, reinforcement learning from human feedback (RLHF) (Stiennon et al., 2020) is a more effective method to align LLMs for following instructions than fine-

Type	Expected output	Output by GPT-3.5
Easy example	He-PRON remains-VERB chief-ADJ executive-NOUN officer-NOUN .-PUNC	He-PRON remains-VERB chief-ADJ executive-ADJ officer-ADV .-PUNC
Confusion	The-DET consensus-NOUN calls-VERB for-ADP a-DET 0.5-NUM %-NOUN increase-NOUN in-ADP September-NOUN personal-ADJ income-NOUN and-CONJ a-DET 0.3-NUM %-NOUN gain-NOUN in-ADP consumption-NOUN .-PUNC	The-PRON consensus-NOUN calls-VERB for-PRON a-PRON 0.5-ADJ %-PUNC increase-VERB in-PRON September-NOUN personal-MISSING income-MISSING and-PRON a-PRON 0.3-ADJ %-PUNC gain-VERB in-PRON consumption-NOUN .-PUNC
Skip token	The-DET department-NOUN has-VERB collected-VERB over-ADV $-PUNC 6.5-NUM million-NUM from-ADP brokers-NOUN so-ADV far-ADV and-CONJ recommended-VERB more-ADJ than-ADP 30-NUM of-ADP them-PRON for-ADP criminal-ADJ prosecution-NOUN .-PUNC	The department-NOUN has-PRON collected-VERB over-PRON $-PRON 6.5-PRON million-PRON from brokers-NOUN so-PRON far-PRON and-PRON recommended-VERB more-PRON than-PRON 30-NOUN of-PRON them-PRON for-PRON criminal-PRON prosecution-PRON .-PUNC

Table 4: Summary of inaccurate, low quality and erroneous linguistic content generated by GPT-3.5.

tuning with conversation data (Zheng et al., 2023) and instruction tuning (Chung et al., 2022). In addition, GPT-3.5 has a much larger number of parameters, much larger capacity, than our other evaluated LLMs.

We find that Gemini rejects 24,630 prompts due to safety concerns related to sexual content, hate speech, harassment. Since we prompt Gemini to perform linguistic tasks, we conclude Gemini misinterpret linguistic queries with harmful contents, and it may have been superficially aligned (Zhou et al., 2023) to restrict its ability when processing sensitive words in the prompt. It is also over-aligned in terms of security-related content, leading to degenerated and undesired behavior.

Furthermore, we find that small scales of LLaMA-2 and Mistral do not follow instructions. They sometimes simply echo back the input sentence without linguistic annotation, responding they don't understand what the task is, or ask for the input to be processed. We hypothesize that this is strongly correlated with the distribution of instruction-tuning data, where linguistic instructions do not appear frequently.

6.3 Differences among Prompting Strategies

Prompting format and strategies differ in how they elicit knowledge from LLMs. However, we find that on identifying linguistic structures, adding in-context examples (Brown et al., 2020), CoT (Huang et al., 2022) or ReAct (Yao et al., 2023) provide only trivial performance gain over the plain prompt (0.05, 0.02 and 0.03 in F1 score respectively). We hypothesize that identifying linguistic structures, especially the complex ones, requires fundamental understanding of syntax and semantics, while CoT and ReAct focus on eliciting reasoning capabilities of LLMs, which is not sufficient.

6.4 Potential Solutions

Addressing the above limitations and biases requires developing effective data curation and training strategies using a linguist-in-the-loop process. Linguistically equitable and diverse datasets with balanced presence of linguistic structures (that specifically avoid overrepresentation of linguistically easy samples) are essential for NLP and for analyzing and understanding LLMs from a linguistic perspective. In what follows, we provide several avenues for investigating the above limitations.

Direct Training: Fine-tuning LLMs with targeted challenging examples, like those carrying complex sentence structures, or augmenting data to increase exposure to challenging examples can improve LLM's performance on fine-grained linguistic annotation tasks (Nguyen et al., 2024). The resulting computational costs can be alleviated through Parameter-Efficient Fine-Tuning techniques (Hu et al., 2022; Su et al., 2023).

Better Instructions: Designing linguistic instructions with sufficient context information to improve contextual understanding can potentially guide the model in handling complex structures. However, it would be challenging to generalize instructions to all linguistic structures and LLMs.

Curriculum Learning: LLM's performance on challenging linguistic structures could be improved by gradually training through a linguistic curriculum (Elgaar and Amiri, 2023a). A curriculum is a planned sequence of learning materials (a training paradigm) and an effective one can make learning efficient and effective for humans (Nishimura, 2018; Tabibian et al., 2019) and computers (Bengio et al., 2009). Curriculum learning techniques can present progressively increase the complexity of the linguistic structure of training samples, e.g. starting with easier structures before more complex ones to potentially improve LLM's performance on fine-grained linguistic annotation tasks.

Retrieval Augmented Generation: Incorporating documents with relevant linguistic knowledge retrieved from trustworthy sources can complement LLMs' knowledge (Lewis et al., 2020). For example, definitions of complex syntactic structures such as clauses and T-units can be retrieved to support more accurate analysis and generation. However, care must be taken to mitigate potential biases introduced within retrieval models (Ziems et al., 2024; Cheng and Amiri, 2025).

Tool Learning: LLMs can be trained to use tools (Schick et al., 2023), either by updating their parametric knowledge or interacting with tools directly. Training LLMs to use external linguistic tools, such as those discussed in this work (Lu, 2010, 2012; Lee et al., 2021; Lee and Lee, 2023), can potentially improve LLMs' capabilities on fine-grained linguistic tasks by complementing their internal representations with structured linguistic knowledge.

Human-in-the-Loop: Using a linguist-in-the-loop approach can provide a valuable feedback for refining model outputs. Expert input can help correct linguistic errors, mitigate biases, and guide the model toward more accurate and interpretable language understanding (Parrish et al., 2021).

7 Conclusion

We empirically study the ability of recent LLMs in annotating linguistic structures at different levels of linguistic complexity. Our study determines how accurately recent LLMs can detect complex linguistic structures in input text, which linguistic structures represent the blind spots of recent LLMs (the most challenging for LLMs), and how the performance of LLMs varies across different levels of linguistic complexity of inputs. Our findings show a tendency to overestimate the linguistic capabilities of LLMs in previous research, which mainly stems from the prevalence of linguistically easy examples in NLP datasets. To address this gap, we uniformly sample data from different linguistic complexity groups, to improve the reliability of evaluating LLMs' performance. Among all evaluated LLMs, Llama3-70b, Llama3-8b, and GPT-3.5 show relatively better performance in responding to linguistic queries–though overall performance remains low. We outline several potential solutions to address these limitations.

Limitations

Although we carefully developed and experimented with different prompting strategies, prompting cannot fully replace methods that directly analyze model's probability distributions over outputs (Hu and Levy, 2023; Kuribayashi et al., 2024). In addition, we did not investigate the ability of LLMs on a wider range of linguistic queries. For examples, linguistic structures related to *discourse complexity* (Feng et al., 2010; Guinaudeau and Strube, 2013; Bedi et al., 2015), which determines the complexity of higher-level structures and flow of language beyond individual phrases or sentences, need to investigated. Finally, understanding why a closed-source LLM produces a specific output can be challenging. This is a key challenge for deeper understanding of LLMs through theoretically-motivated linguistic probing techniques (Linzen et al., 2016; Warstadt et al., 2020; Hu et al., 2020), and limits our ability in providing insights into their potential weaknesses.

References

Ahmed Alajrami and Nikolaos Aletras. 2022. How does the pre-training objective affect what large language models learn about linguistic properties? In *Proceedings of the 60th Annual Meeting of the Association for Computational Linguistics (Volume 2: Short Papers)*, pages 131–147, Dublin, Ireland. Association for Computational Linguistics.

Gillinder Bedi, Facundo Carrillo, Guillermo A Cecchi, Diego Fernández Slezak, Mariano Sigman, Natália B Mota, Sidarta Ribeiro, Daniel C Javitt, Mauro Copelli, and Cheryl M Corcoran. 2015. Automated analysis of free speech predicts psychosis onset in high-risk youths. *npj Schizophrenia*, 1(1):1–7.

Yoshua Bengio, Jérôme Louradour, Ronan Collobert, and Jason Weston. 2009. Curriculum learning. In *Proceedings of the 26th Annual International Conference on Machine Learning*, ICML '09, page 41–48, New York, NY, USA. Association for Computing Machinery.

Douglas Biber, Bethany Gray, Shelley Staples, and Jesse Egbert. 2020. Investigating grammatical complexity in l2 english writing research: Linguistic description versus predictive measurement. *Journal of English for Academic Purposes*, 46:100869.

Terra Blevins, Hila Gonen, and Luke Zettlemoyer. 2023. Prompting language models for linguistic structure. In *Proceedings of the 61st Annual Meeting of the Association for Computational Linguistics (Volume 1: Long Papers)*, pages 6649–6663, Toronto, Canada. Association for Computational Linguistics.

Tom Brown, Benjamin Mann, Nick Ryder, Melanie Subbiah, Jared D Kaplan, Prafulla Dhariwal, Arvind Neelakantan, Pranav Shyam, Girish Sastry, Amanda Askell, Sandhini Agarwal, Ariel Herbert-Voss, Gretchen Krueger, Tom Henighan, Rewon Child, Aditya Ramesh, Daniel Ziegler, Jeffrey Wu, Clemens Winter, Chris Hesse, Mark Chen, Eric Sigler, Mateusz Litwin, Scott Gray, Benjamin Chess, Jack Clark, Christopher Berner, Sam McCandlish, Alec Radford, Ilya Sutskever, and Dario Amodei. 2020. Language models are few-shot learners. In *Advances in Neural Information Processing Systems*, volume 33, pages 1877–1901. Curran Associates, Inc.

Angelica Chen, Ravid Shwartz-Ziv, Kyunghyun Cho, Matthew L Leavitt, and Naomi Saphra. 2024. Sudden drops in the loss: Syntax acquisition, phase transitions, and simplicity bias in MLMs. In *The Twelfth International Conference on Learning Representations*.

Jiali Cheng and Hadi Amiri. 2025. Equalizeir: Mitigating linguistic biases in retrieval models. In *Proceedings of the 2025 Conference of the North American Chapter of the Association for Computational Linguistics*. Association for Computational Linguistics.

Hyung Won Chung, Le Hou, Shayne Longpre, Barret Zoph, Yi Tay, William Fedus, Yunxuan Li, Xuezhi Wang, Mostafa Dehghani, Siddhartha Brahma, Albert Webson, Shixiang Shane Gu, Zhuyun Dai, Mirac Suzgun, Xinyun Chen, Aakanksha Chowdhery, Alex Castro-Ros, Marie Pellat, Kevin Robinson, Dasha Valter, Sharan Narang, Gaurav Mishra, Adams Yu, Vincent Zhao, Yanping Huang, Andrew Dai, Hongkun Yu, Slav Petrov, Ed H. Chi, Jeff Dean, Jacob Devlin, Adam Roberts, Denny Zhou, Quoc V. Le, and Jason Wei. 2022. Scaling instruction-finetuned language models.

Kevin Clark, Urvashi Khandelwal, Omer Levy, and Christopher D. Manning. 2019. What does BERT look at? an analysis of BERT's attention. In *Proceedings of the 2019 ACL Workshop BlackboxNLP: Analyzing and Interpreting Neural Networks for NLP*, pages 276–286, Florence, Italy. Association for Computational Linguistics.

Jacob Devlin, Ming-Wei Chang, Kenton Lee, and Kristina Toutanova. 2019. BERT: Pre-training of deep bidirectional transformers for language understanding. In *Proceedings of the 2019 Conference of the North American Chapter of the Association for Computational Linguistics: Human Language Technologies, Volume 1 (Long and Short Papers)*, pages 4171–4186, Minneapolis, Minnesota. Association for Computational Linguistics.

Nadir Durrani, Hassan Sajjad, Fahim Dalvi, and Yonatan Belinkov. 2020. Analyzing individual neurons in pre-trained language models. In *Proceedings of the 2020 Conference on Empirical Methods in Natural Language Processing (EMNLP)*, pages 4865–4880, Online. Association for Computational Linguistics.

Mohamed Elgaar and Hadi Amiri. 2023a. HuCurl: Human-induced curriculum discovery. In *Proceedings of the 61st Annual Meeting of the Association for Computational Linguistics (Volume 1: Long Papers)*, pages 1862–1877, Toronto, Canada. Association for Computational Linguistics.

Mohamed Elgaar and Hadi Amiri. 2023b. Ling-CL: Understanding NLP models through linguistic curricula. In *Proceedings of the 2023 Conference on Empirical Methods in Natural Language Processing*, pages 13526–13542, Singapore. Association for Computational Linguistics.

Allyson Ettinger. 2020. What BERT is not: Lessons from a new suite of psycholinguistic diagnostics for language models. *Transactions of the Association for Computational Linguistics*, 8:34–48.

Lijun Feng, Noémie Elhadad, and Matt Huenerfauth. 2009. Cognitively motivated features for readability assessment. In *Proceedings of the 12th Conference of the European Chapter of the ACL (EACL 2009)*, pages 229–237, Athens, Greece. Association for Computational Linguistics.

Lijun Feng, Martin Jansche, Matt Huenerfauth, and Noémie Elhadad. 2010. A comparison of features for automatic readability assessment. In *Coling 2010: Posters*, pages 276–284, Beijing, China. Coling 2010 Organizing Committee.

Camille Guinaudeau and Michael Strube. 2013. Graph-based local coherence modeling. In *Proceedings of the 51st Annual Meeting of the Association for Computational Linguistics (Volume 1: Long Papers)*, pages 93–103, Sofia, Bulgaria. Association for Computational Linguistics.

Alex Housen, Bastien De Clercq, Folkert Kuiken, and Ineke Vedder. 2019. Multiple approaches to complexity in second language research. *Second language research*, 35(1):3–21.

Edward J Hu, yelong shen, Phillip Wallis, Zeyuan Allen-Zhu, Yuanzhi Li, Shean Wang, Lu Wang, and Weizhu Chen. 2022. LoRA: Low-rank adaptation of large language models. In *International Conference on Learning Representations*.

Hai Hu, Kyle Richardson, Liang Xu, Lu Li, Sandra Kübler, and Lawrence Moss. 2020. OCNLI: Original Chinese Natural Language Inference. In *Findings of the Association for Computational Linguistics: EMNLP 2020*, pages 3512–3526, Online. Association for Computational Linguistics.

Jennifer Hu and Roger Levy. 2023. Prompting is not a substitute for probability measurements in large language models. In *Proceedings of the 2023 Conference on Empirical Methods in Natural Language Processing*, pages 5040–5060, Singapore. Association for Computational Linguistics.

Wenlong Huang, Pieter Abbeel, Deepak Pathak, and Igor Mordatch. 2022. Language models as zero-shot planners: Extracting actionable knowledge for embodied agents. In *Proceedings of the 39th International Conference on Machine Learning*.

Philip A. Huebner, Elior Sulem, Fisher Cynthia, and Dan Roth. 2021. BabyBERTa: Learning more grammar with small-scale child-directed language. In *Proceedings of the 25th Conference on Computational Natural Language Learning*, pages 624–646, Online. Association for Computational Linguistics.

Albert Q Jiang, Alexandre Sablayrolles, Arthur Mensch, Chris Bamford, Devendra Singh Chaplot, Diego de las Casas, Florian Bressand, Gianna Lengyel, Guillaume Lample, Lucile Saulnier, et al. 2023. Mistral 7b. *arXiv preprint arXiv:2310.06825*.

Albert Q Jiang, Alexandre Sablayrolles, Antoine Roux, Arthur Mensch, Blanche Savary, Chris Bamford, Devendra Singh Chaplot, Diego de las Casas, Emma Bou Hanna, Florian Bressand, et al. 2024. Mixtral of experts. *arXiv preprint arXiv:2401.04088*.

Tatsuki Kuribayashi, Yohei Oseki, and Timothy Baldwin. 2024. Psychometric predictive power of large language models. In *Findings of the Association for Computational Linguistics: NAACL 2024*, pages 1983–2005, Mexico City, Mexico. Association for Computational Linguistics.

Bruce W. Lee, Yoo Sung Jang, and Jason Lee. 2021. Pushing on text readability assessment: A transformer meets handcrafted linguistic features. In *Proceedings of the 2021 Conference on Empirical Methods in Natural Language Processing*, pages 10669–10686, Online and Punta Cana, Dominican Republic. Association for Computational Linguistics.

Bruce W. Lee and Jason Lee. 2023. LFTK: Handcrafted features in computational linguistics. In *Proceedings of the 18th Workshop on Innovative Use of NLP for Building Educational Applications (BEA 2023)*, pages 1–19, Toronto, Canada. Association for Computational Linguistics.

Patrick Lewis, Ethan Perez, Aleksandra Piktus, Fabio Petroni, Vladimir Karpukhin, Naman Goyal, Heinrich Küttler, Mike Lewis, Wen-tau Yih, Tim Rocktäschel, Sebastian Riedel, and Douwe Kiela. 2020. Retrieval-augmented generation for knowledge-intensive nlp tasks. In *Advances in Neural Information Processing Systems*, volume 33, pages 9459–9474. Curran Associates, Inc.

Ming Li, Yusheng Su, Hsiu-Yuan Huang, Jiali Cheng, Xin Hu, Xinmiao Zhang, Huadong Wang, Yujia Qin, Xiaozhi Wang, Kristen A. Lindquist, Zhiyuan Liu, and Dan Zhang. 2024. Language-specific representation of emotion-concept knowledge causally supports emotion inference. *iScience*, 27(12).

Tal Linzen, Emmanuel Dupoux, and Yoav Goldberg. 2016. Assessing the ability of LSTMs to learn syntax-sensitive dependencies. *Transactions of the Association for Computational Linguistics*, 4:521–535.

Xiaofei Lu. 2010. Automatic analysis of syntactic complexity in second language writing. *International journal of corpus linguistics*, 15(4):474–496.

Xiaofei Lu. 2012. The relationship of lexical richness to the quality of ESL learners' oral narratives. *Mod. Lang. J.*, 96(2):190–208.

David Malvern, Brian Richards, Ngoni Chipere, and Pilar Durán. 2004. *Lexical diversity and language development*. Springer.

Christopher Manning, Mihai Surdeanu, John Bauer, Jenny Finkel, Steven Bethard, and David McClosky. 2014. The Stanford CoreNLP natural language processing toolkit. In *Proceedings of 52nd Annual Meeting of the Association for Computational Linguistics: System Demonstrations*, pages 55–60, Baltimore, Maryland. Association for Computational Linguistics.

Mitchell P. Marcus, Beatrice Santorini, and Mary Ann Marcinkiewicz. 1993. Building a large annotated corpus of English: The Penn Treebank. *Computational Linguistics*, 19(2):313–330.

Dang Nguyen, Jiuhai Chen, and Tianyi Zhou. 2024. Multi-objective linguistic control of large language models. In *Findings of the Association for Computational Linguistics: ACL 2024*, pages 4336–4347, Bangkok, Thailand. Association for Computational Linguistics.

Joel Nishimura. 2018. Critically slow learning in flashcard learning models. *Chaos*, 28(8):083115.

Lourdes Ortega. 2003. Syntactic complexity measures and their relationship to l2 proficiency: A research synthesis of college-level l2 writing. *Applied linguistics*, 24(4):492–518.

Long Ouyang, Jeffrey Wu, Xu Jiang, Diogo Almeida, Carroll Wainwright, Pamela Mishkin, Chong Zhang, Sandhini Agarwal, Katarina Slama, Alex Gray, John Schulman, Jacob Hilton, Fraser Kelton, Luke Miller, Maddie Simens, Amanda Askell, Peter Welinder, Paul Christiano, Jan Leike, and Ryan Lowe. 2022. Training language models to follow instructions with human feedback. In *Advances in Neural Information Processing Systems*.

Alicia Parrish, William Huang, Omar Agha, Soo-Hwan Lee, Nikita Nangia, Alexia Warstadt, Karmanya Aggarwal, Emily Allaway, Tal Linzen, and Samuel R. Bowman. 2021. Does putting a linguist in the loop improve NLU data collection? In *Findings of the Association for Computational Linguistics: EMNLP 2021*, pages 4886–4901, Punta Cana, Dominican Republic. Association for Computational Linguistics.

Timo Schick, Jane Dwivedi-Yu, Roberto Dessi, Roberta Raileanu, Maria Lomeli, Eric Hambro, Luke Zettlemoyer, Nicola Cancedda, and Thomas Scialom. 2023. Toolformer: Language models can teach themselves to use tools. In *Thirty-seventh Conference on Neural Information Processing Systems*.

Mandar Sharma, Nikhil Muralidhar, and Naren Ramakrishnan. 2023. Learning non-linguistic skills without sacrificing linguistic proficiency. In *Proceedings of the 61st Annual Meeting of the Association for Computational Linguistics (Volume 1: Long Papers)*, pages 6178–6191, Toronto, Canada. Association for Computational Linguistics.

Noam Shazeer, *Azalia Mirhoseini, *Krzysztof Maziarz, Andy Davis, Quoc Le, Geoffrey Hinton, and Jeff Dean. 2017. Outrageously large neural networks: The sparsely-gated mixture-of-experts layer. In *International Conference on Learning Representations*.

Sheng Shen, Zhewei Yao, Douwe Kiela, Kurt Keutzer, and Michael Mahoney. 2021. What's hidden in a one-layer randomly weighted transformer? In *Proceedings of the 2021 Conference on Empirical Methods in Natural Language Processing*, pages 2914–2921, Online and Punta Cana, Dominican Republic. Association for Computational Linguistics.

Yikang Shen, Zhouhan Lin, Athul Paul Jacob, Alessandro Sordoni, Aaron Courville, and Yoshua Bengio. 2018. Straight to the tree: Constituency parsing with neural syntactic distance. In *Proceedings of the 56th Annual Meeting of the Association for Computational Linguistics (Volume 1: Long Papers)*, pages 1171–1180, Melbourne, Australia. Association for Computational Linguistics.

Koustuv Sinha, Prasanna Parthasarathi, Joelle Pineau, and Adina Williams. 2021. UnNatural Language Inference. In *Proceedings of the 59th Annual Meeting of the Association for Computational Linguistics and the 11th International Joint Conference on Natural Language Processing (Volume 1: Long Papers)*, pages 7329–7346, Online. Association for Computational Linguistics.

Nisan Stiennon, Long Ouyang, Jeffrey Wu, Daniel Ziegler, Ryan Lowe, Chelsea Voss, Alec Radford, Dario Amodei, and Paul F Christiano. 2020. Learning to summarize with human feedback. In *Advances in Neural Information Processing Systems*.

Yusheng Su, Chi-Min Chan, Jiali Cheng, Yujia Qin, Yankai Lin, Shengding Hu, Zonghan Yang, Ning Ding, Xingzhi Sun, Guotong Xie, Zhiyuan Liu, and Maosong Sun. 2023. Exploring the impact of model scaling on parameter-efficient tuning. In *Proceedings of the 2023 Conference on Empirical Methods in Natural Language Processing*, pages 15062–15078, Singapore. Association for Computational Linguistics.

Shuo Sun, Yuchen Zhang, Jiahuan Yan, Yuze Gao, Donovan Ong, Bin Chen, and Jian Su. 2023. Battle of the large language models: Dolly vs LLaMA vs vicuna vs guanaco vs bard vs ChatGPT - a text-to-SQL parsing comparison. In *Findings of the Association for Computational Linguistics: EMNLP 2023*, pages 11225–11238, Singapore. Association for Computational Linguistics.

Behzad Tabibian, Utkarsh Upadhyay, Abir De, Ali Zarezade, Bernhard Schölkopf, and Manuel Gomez-Rodriguez. 2019. Enhancing human learning via spaced repetition optimization. *Proc. Natl. Acad. Sci. U. S. A.*, 116(10):3988–3993.

Gemini Team, Rohan Anil, Sebastian Borgeaud, Yonghui Wu, Jean-Baptiste Alayrac, Jiahui Yu, Radu Soricut, Johan Schalkwyk, Andrew M Dai, Anja Hauth, et al. 2023. Gemini: a family of highly capable multimodal models. *arXiv preprint arXiv:2312.11805*.

Mildred C. Templin. 1957. *Certain Language Skills in Children: Their Development and Interrelationships*, ned - new edition edition, volume 26. University of Minnesota Press.

Erik F. Tjong Kim Sang and Sabine Buchholz. 2000. Introduction to the CoNLL-2000 shared task chunking. In *Fourth Conference on Computational Natural Language Learning and the Second Learning Language in Logic Workshop*.

Hugo Touvron, Thibaut Lavril, Gautier Izacard, Xavier Martinet, Marie-Anne Lachaux, Timothée Lacroix, Baptiste Rozière, Naman Goyal, Eric Hambro, Faisal Azhar, Aurelien Rodriguez, Armand Joulin, Edouard Grave, and Guillaume Lample. 2023. Llama: Open and efficient foundation language models.

Ashish Vaswani, Noam Shazeer, Niki Parmar, Jakob Uszkoreit, Llion Jones, Aidan N Gomez, Ł ukasz Kaiser, and Illia Polosukhin. 2017. Attention is all you need. In *Advances in Neural Information Processing Systems*.

Elena Voita, David Talbot, Fedor Moiseev, Rico Sennrich, and Ivan Titov. 2019. Analyzing multi-head self-attention: Specialized heads do the heavy lifting, the rest can be pruned. In *Proceedings of the 57th Annual Meeting of the Association for Computational Linguistics*, pages 5797–5808, Florence, Italy. Association for Computational Linguistics.

Alex Warstadt, Alicia Parrish, Haokun Liu, Anhad Mohananey, Wei Peng, Sheng-Fu Wang, and Samuel R. Bowman. 2020. BLiMP: The benchmark of linguistic minimal pairs for English. *Transactions of the*

Association for Computational Linguistics, 8:377–392.

Jason Wei, Kelly Finn, Emma Templeton, Thalia Wheatley, and Soroush Vosoughi. 2021. Linguistic complexity loss in text-based therapy. In *Proceedings of the 2021 Conference of the North American Chapter of the Association for Computational Linguistics: Human Language Technologies*, pages 4450–4459, Online. Association for Computational Linguistics.

Jason Wei, Xuezhi Wang, Dale Schuurmans, Maarten Bosma, brian ichter, Fei Xia, Ed H. Chi, Quoc V Le, and Denny Zhou. 2022. Chain of thought prompting elicits reasoning in large language models. In *Advances in Neural Information Processing Systems*.

Orion Weller, Nicholas Lourie, Matt Gardner, and Matthew E. Peters. 2020. Learning from task descriptions. In *Proceedings of the 2020 Conference on Empirical Methods in Natural Language Processing (EMNLP)*, pages 1361–1375, Online. Association for Computational Linguistics.

Kate Wolfe-Quintero, Shunji Inagaki, and Hae-Young Kim. 1998. Second language development in writing: Measures of fluency, accuracy, and complexity. *Honolulu, HI: University of Hawai'i, Second Language Teaching & Curriculum Center.*

Menglin Xia, Ekaterina Kochmar, and Ted Briscoe. 2016. Text readability assessment for second language learners. In *Proceedings of the 11th Workshop on Innovative Use of NLP for Building Educational Applications*, pages 12–22, San Diego, CA. Association for Computational Linguistics.

Wei Xu, Chris Callison-Burch, and Courtney Napoles. 2015. Problems in current text simplification research: New data can help. *Transactions of the Association for Computational Linguistics*, 3:283–297.

Atsuki Yamaguchi, George Chrysostomou, Katerina Margatina, and Nikolaos Aletras. 2021. Frustratingly simple pretraining alternatives to masked language modeling. In *Proceedings of the 2021 Conference on Empirical Methods in Natural Language Processing*, pages 3116–3125, Online and Punta Cana, Dominican Republic. Association for Computational Linguistics.

Songlin Yang and Kewei Tu. 2022. Bottom-up constituency parsing and nested named entity recognition with pointer networks. In *Proceedings of the 60th Annual Meeting of the Association for Computational Linguistics (Volume 1: Long Papers)*, pages 2403–2416, Dublin, Ireland. Association for Computational Linguistics.

Helen Yannakoudakis, Ted Briscoe, and Ben Medlock. 2011. A new dataset and method for automatically grading ESOL texts. In *Proceedings of the 49th Annual Meeting of the Association for Computational Linguistics: Human Language Technologies*, pages 180–189, Portland, Oregon, USA. Association for Computational Linguistics.

Shunyu Yao, Jeffrey Zhao, Dian Yu, Nan Du, Izhak Shafran, Karthik R Narasimhan, and Yuan Cao. 2023. React: Synergizing reasoning and acting in language models. In *The Eleventh International Conference on Learning Representations*.

Yaodong Yu, Sam Buchanan, Druv Pai, Tianzhe Chu, Ziyang Wu, Shengbang Tong, Benjamin David Haeffele, and Yi Ma. 2023. White-box transformers via sparse rate reduction. In *Thirty-seventh Conference on Neural Information Processing Systems*.

Alla Zareva, Paula Schwanenflugel, and Yordanka Nikolova. 2005. Relationship between lexical competence and language proficiency: Variable sensitivity. *Studies in Second Language Acquisition*, 27(4):567–595.

Lianmin Zheng, Wei-Lin Chiang, Ying Sheng, Siyuan Zhuang, Zhanghao Wu, Yonghao Zhuang, Zi Lin, Zhuohan Li, Dacheng Li, Eric. P Xing, Hao Zhang, Joseph E. Gonzalez, and Ion Stoica. 2023. Judging llm-as-a-judge with mt-bench and chatbot arena.

Chunting Zhou, Pengfei Liu, Puxin Xu, Srini Iyer, Jiao Sun, Yuning Mao, Xuezhe Ma, Avia Efrat, Ping Yu, Lili Yu, et al. 2023. Lima: Less is more for alignment. *arXiv preprint arXiv:2305.11206*.

Caleb Ziems, William Held, Jane Dwivedi-Yu, and Diyi Yang. 2024. Measuring and addressing indexical bias in information retrieval. In *Findings of the Association for Computational Linguistics: ACL 2024*, pages 12860–12877, Bangkok, Thailand. Association for Computational Linguistics.

A GPT's Knowledge on Target tasks

As illustrated in Figures 6–8, we asked relevant questions from GPT 3.5 about the target linguistic tasks of this study. The responses clearly indicate that GPT 3.5 have knowledge about the universal dependencies dataset and the universal POS tag set, the CoNLL 2000 shared task and its format, and the Penn Treebank dataset and the format of its syntactic structures.

B Detailed Results

B.1 Performance of all LLMs

We present the performances of all LLMs in Figure 9–15.

B.2 Performance across linguistic complexity spectrum

We present the performance-sample complexity plot for all models in Figure 9-Figure15. These results suggest that LLM's linguistic capability largely depends on the linguistic complexity of their inputs, and existing work may have overestimated the linguistic capability of LLMs. However, it's crucial to note that linguistic complexity as understood by humans and machines may differ significantly. Indeed, there are particular linguistic structures where model performance surprisingly escalates with increasing complexity. Understanding the reason for such model behaviors require understanding their learning dynamics and is the subject of our future work.

C Linguistic indices

Table 5 presents the 45 linguistic indices in our study.

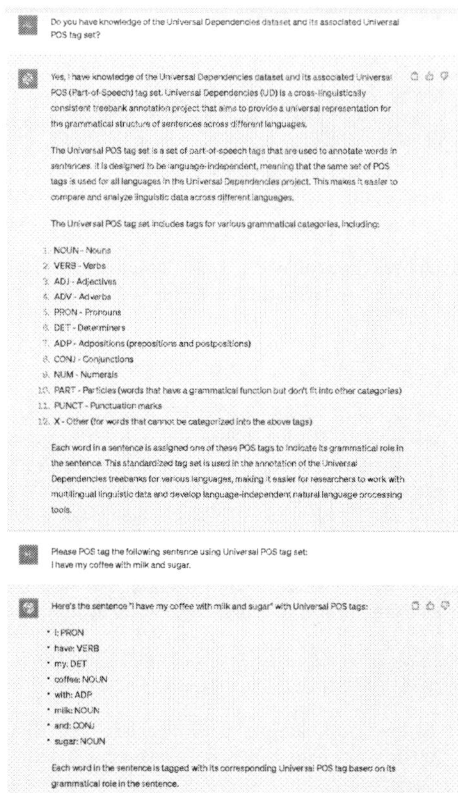

Figure 6: GPT's responses to our questions about universal dependencies dataset and its associated universal POS tag set.

Granularity	Name	Notation
Word	Nouns	Num_NN
Word	Verbs	Num_VB
Word	Adjectives	Num_JJ
Word	Adverbs	Num_RB
Word	Prepositions/Subordinates	Num_IN
Word	Coordinating Conjunction	Num_CC
Word	Determiner	Num_DT
Phrase	Noun Phrases	Num_NP
Phrase	Verb Phrases	Num_VP
Phrase	Adjective Phrases	Num_ADJP
Phrase	Adverb Phrases	Num_ADVP
Phrase	Preposition Phrases	Num_PP
Phrase	Conjunction Phrases	Num_CONJP
Phrase	Quantitative Phrases	Num_QP
Phrase	Complex Nominal	Num_CN
Sentence	T-Units	Num_T
Sentence	Complex T-Units	Num_CT
Sentence	Clause	Num_C
Sentence	Dependent Clause	Num_DC
Sentence	Fragment Clause	Num_FC

Table 5: Linguistic indices we use in the study.

Figure 7: GPT's responses to our questions about the CoNLL 2000 shared task and its format.

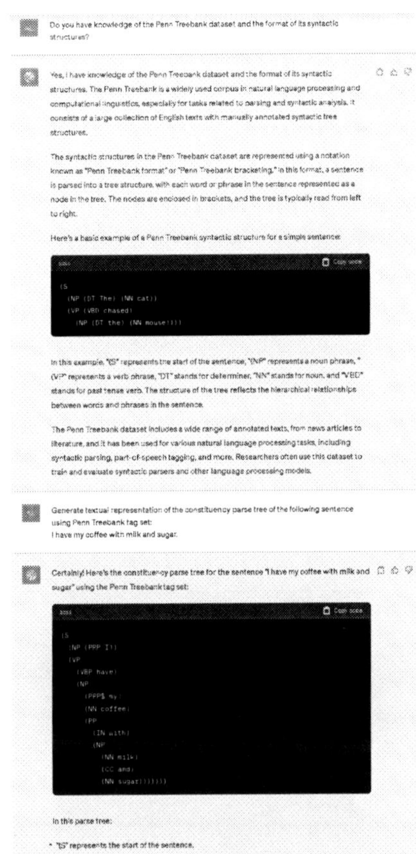

Figure 8: GPT's responses to our questions about the Penn Treebank dataset and the format of its syntactic structures.

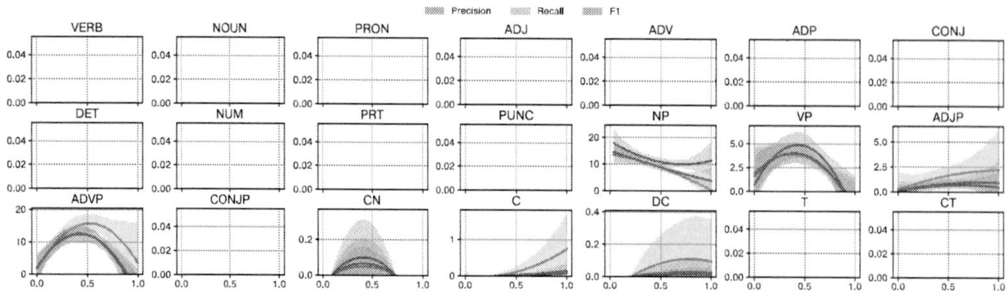

Figure 9: Performance of Gemini with respect to linguistic complexity.

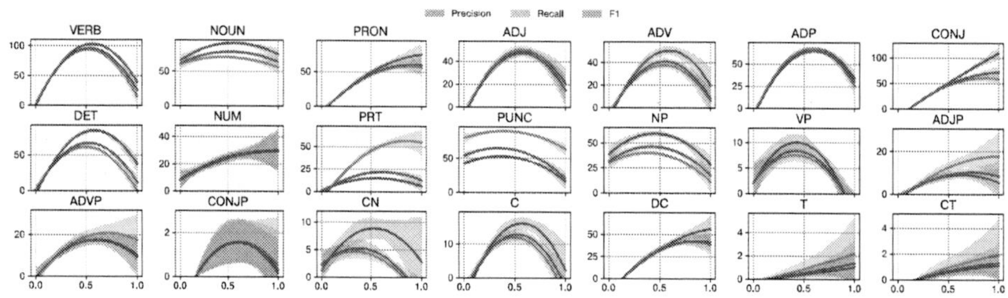

Figure 10: Performance of LLaMA3-70b with respect to linguistic complexity.

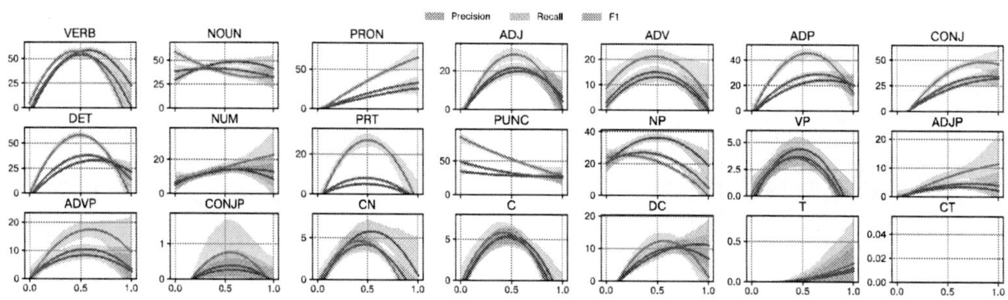

Figure 11: Performance of LLaMA2-70B with respect to linguistic complexity.

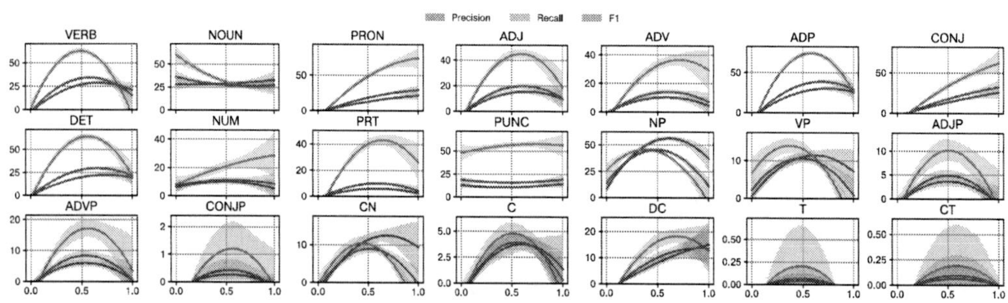

Figure 12: Performance of Mixtral-8x7B with respect to linguistic complexity.

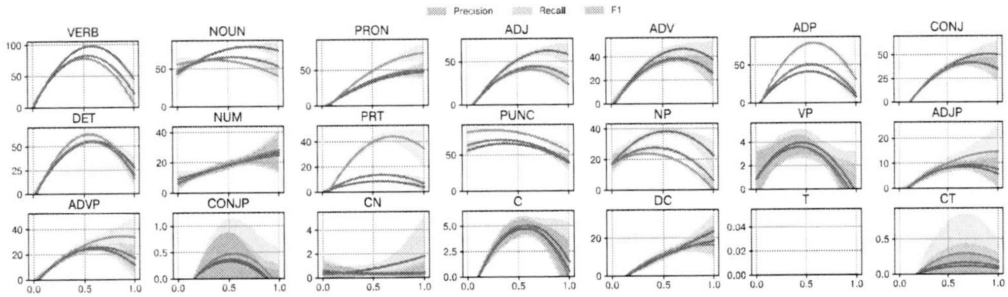

Figure 13: Performance of LLaMA3-8B with respect to linguistic complexity.

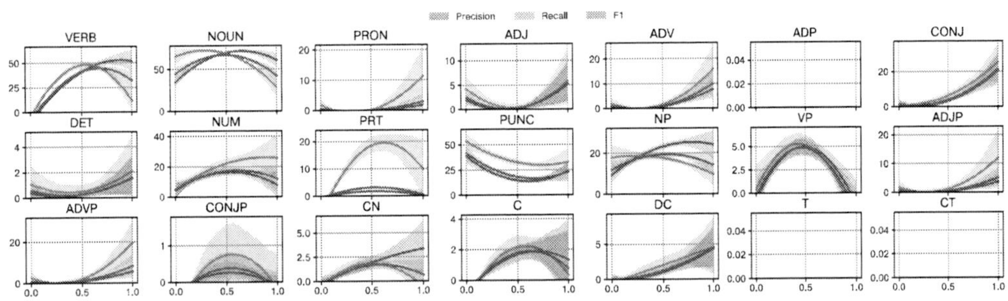

Figure 14: Performance of LLaMA2-7B with respect to linguistic complexity.

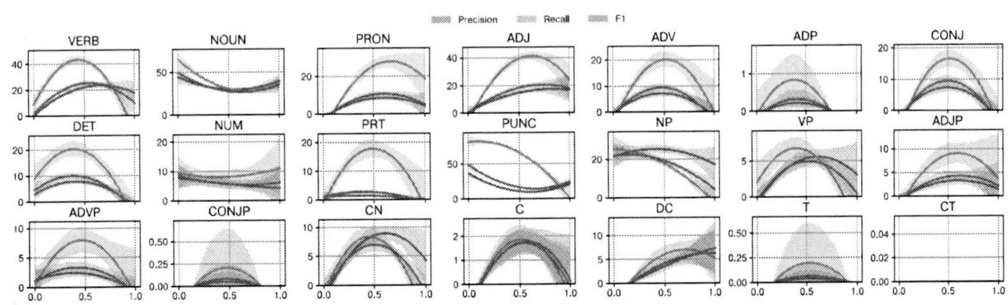

Figure 15: Performance of Mistral-7B with respect to linguistic complexity.

ParaBLoCC: Parallel Basic Locative Constructions Corpus

Peter Viechnicki and Anthony Kostacos
Johns Hopkins University
{pviechn1,akostac1}@jh.edu

Abstract

We introduce ParaBLoCC, the Parallel Basic Locative Construction Corpus, the first multilingual compendium of this important grammatico-functional construction, and particularly the first such corpus containing semantically equivalent BLCs in source/target language pairs. The data —taken from bitext corpora in English paired with twenty-six typologically diverse languages —are likely to prove useful for studying questions of cognitive underpinnings and cross-linguistic usage patterns of spatial expressions, as well as for improving multilingual spatial relation extraction and related tasks. The data are being made available at https://github.com/pviechnicki/parablocc.

1 Introduction: Definition and Importance of Basic Locative Constructions

Basic Locative Constructions (BLCs) are a sentence type identified through the specific pairing of syntactic form and usage purpose (Sadock and Zwicky, 1985). BLCs —identified notably by Levinson and Wilkins (2006) —are statements used to answer questions of the form, *Where is the figure object in relation to the ground object?*[1] Cross-linguistically, BLCs are taken to be ubiquitous – no languages have been reported which are unable to answer such a question. Languages do vary in choice of syntactic forms used to express BLCs (Fortis, 2010). In English, canonical syntax for BLCs is `[NP Copula PP]`: 'The figure object is over/on/under/behind the ground object.' In other languages, BLC syntactic form may be very different, for example in KwaKwala, BLCs are expressed through locative suffixes (Rosenblum, 2015).

[1]We follow (Talmy, 1983) in referring to *figure* and *ground;* other terms for the same concepts are *theme* and *relatum,* or *trajector* and *landmark.*

2 Importance of BLCs for Cognitive Science and Linguistics

BLCs have been considered important tools for several decades by cognitive scientists who have used them to elicit cross-linguistic properties of spatial expressions. The prominence of BLCs in studies of spatial cognition was enabled by Bowerman and Pederson's (1992) Topological Relations Picture Series, a set of 71 spatial scene cartoons, each depicting a spatial relation between a figure and ground. A number of studies have used controlled elicitation with BLCs to shed light on psycholinguistic topics: for example BLCs have been used to explore core versus peripheral spatial references (Landau et al., 2016); evidence from spatial relations for the Sapir-Whorf hypothesis (Tseng et al., 2016); language acquisition patterns in infancy (Lakusta et al., 2021); and supposed 'natural concepts' in the spatial domain (Levinson and Meira, 2003).

Relatively few studies have looked at usage patterns of BLCs in uncontrolled settings; to our knowledge only (Viechnicki et al., 2024) have done so. The ParaBLoCC corpus aims to allow such work to proceed, by making available a large corpus of English BLCs paired with parallel text from a typologically diverse set of twenty-six languages. The data are publicly available at https://github.com/pviechnicki/parablocc.

3 Related Research

BLCs differ from two closely related expression types: geospatial expressions and spatial relation triples, both of which have more extensive corpora available. Geospatial expressions in text, which have been studied in the context of georeferencing techniques, are commonly defined as spatial relations whose ground object is located out of doors and is not mobile, and whose spatial relation is expressed within a geospatial coordinate

Proceedings of the Workshop on Cognitive Modeling and Computational Linguistics, pages 18–23
May 3, 2025

reference system (Stock et al., 2021). BLCs, by contrast, may reference ground objects of any size, interior/exterior status, and mobility. Spatial relation triples – often discussed in the context of techniques for extracting such relations from text, e.g. (McNamee et al., 2020); (Hassani and Lee, 2017) – are a superset of BLCs. Spatial relation triples include both locative and path expressions, whereas BLCs are restricted to static constructions. Spatial relations also include a wide variety of syntactic forms in whichever language is being studied, whereas BLCs are typically restricted to a single canonical syntactic form, such as `[NP Copula PP]` in English.

Our work in extracting a parallel corpus of BLCs is similar in spirit to other recent efforts to use web-scale usage data to inform theoretical linguistic or psychological research. For example, Hale and Stanojevic (2024) use data from five languages to investigate syntactic universals; and Beekhuizen et al. (2017) use parallel usage patterns from thirty languages to study cognitive properties of indefinite pronouns. This work is therefore part of the larger trend that has been called the 'quantitative turn' in linguistic research (Kortmann, 2021).

4 ParaBLoCC Corpus Characteristics and Data Preparation

4.1 Corpus Characteristics

Data in the ParaBLoCC corpus comprise parallel English and target-language sentence pairs ('bitext') from twenty-six languages. The twenty-six languages were chosen to maximize genetic and areal diversity as well as availability of bitext material. Bitext sentences are harvested from the Opus Machine Translation Portal (Tiedemann et al., 2023), and similar sources, from a wide variety of domains. Numbers of parallel sentence pairs for each language plus domains are shown in Table 1. ParaBLoCC thus contains paired BLCs in English and one of the target languages, for example:

> EN: 'He is still in Serbia.'::HU: 'Szerbiában maradt.'

Table 1: Languages, domains, bitext pairs, and BLCs occurring (plus rate per 1000 bitext sentence pairs) in ParaBLoCC corpus. Domains: a: Bible-UEDIN; d: QED; e: TEDTalks2020; f: Bible-Literal; g: GlobalVoices; h: OpenSubtitles; j: Europarl; k: UN V1 16; m: IWSLT2016; n: Flores200; o: NLLBv1; p: GoURMET; q: CCaligned; s: SETTIME2; t: Tico19; u: Tanzil; v: ntrex128.

Language	Domains	Bitext Pairs (m)	BLCs (k) *(per 1000)*
Bantu			
Swahili	d,e,g,n,o,q,t,v	21.2	135 *(6.4)*
Finno-Ugric			
Finnish	a,d,e,h,j	25.9	132 *(5.1)*
Hungarian	a,d,e,g,h,j	38.4	169 *(4.4)*
Indo-European			
Catalan	d,e,f,g,h,i	7.6	81 *(10.7)*
Czech	a,d,e,h,j	35.5	178 *(5.0)*
Dutch	a,d,e,g,h, j,n,o,q,v	157.5	1924 *(12.2)*
French	a,d,e,g,h,m	36.6	197 *(5.4)*
German	a,d,e,g,h,j	20.0	101 *(5.1)*
Greek	a,d,e,g,h, j,n,o,q,s,v	99.8	740 *(7.4)*
Italian	a,d,e,g,h,j	32.0	159 *(5.0)*
Polish	a,d,e,g,h, j,n,o,v	129.3	1211 *(9.4)*
Russian	a,d,e,g,h,k	35.3	165 *(4.7)*
Spanish	a,d,e,g,h,j, k	55.5	266 *(4.8)*
Swedish	a,d,g,h,j	15.6	80 *(5.2)*
Niger-Congo			
Igbo	d,e,f,n,o,q,v	5.6	32 *(5.7)*
Other, Isolate			
Japanese	d,e,h,n,o,q,v	66.5	511 *(7.7)*
Korean	a,d,e,g,h,n,o,q	28.9	204 *(7.1)*
Quechumaran			
Aymara	d,g,o,q	1.0	9 *(8.9)*
Quechua	d,o	2.2	23 *(10.7)*
Semitic			
Amharic	a,d,g,n,o,p,t	15.7	147 *(9.4)*
Arabic	a,d,e,g,h,k	39.7	149 *(3.8)*
Hebrew	a,d,e,g,h,n,q	34.6	150 *(4.3)*
Tigrinya	d,n,o,q,t	1.1	6 *(5.9)*
Sino-Tibetan			
Chinese	a,d,e,g,h, k,n,o,q,t,v	64.6	926 *(14.3)*
Turkic			
Turkish	a,d,e,g,h, o,p,q,s	99.0	825 *(8.4)*
Uzbek	d,e,n,o,u,v	28.9	245 *(8.5)*

4.2 Parallel BLC Data Preparation

BLCs are selected from the available bitext for each language using a three-stage filtration procedure: 1. lexical filtering, followed by 2. syntactic filtering, followed by 3. spatial sense filtering.

The lexical filter selects sentence pairs whose English sentence contains a locative spatial expression drawn from a reference list of fifty expressions: twenty-nine common English locative spatial prepositions ('above', 'between', 'on', etc) and twenty-one spatial nominals ('in back of', e.g.). Our reference list contains all non-archaic forms from The Preposition Project (Litkowski and Hargraves, 2007), plus spatial nominals. See Appendix A for the complete list. Data files in the ParaBLoCC archive record which lexical item matched each English sentence.

The syntactic filter selects parallel sentences whose English dependency parse structurally matches one of the syntactic parse templates found in English Basic Locative Constructions. We parse the bitext and the BLC templates with the Stanford Core NLP parser (Manning et al., 2014), then perform subgraph matching through depth-first search. In practice, all syntactic patterns for BLCs with the fifty spatial expressions can be expressed using eight unique dependency parse subgraphs. ParaBLoCC data files annotate each bitext sentence with the number of the matching spatial expression subgraph template.

The third and final filtration stage selects only sentences whose lexical match from the first filtration state has a spatial sense in context, vice a temporal or other sense. Many of the lexical items from our reference list are highly polysemous – in fact at least twenty common English prepositions have six or more spatial and non-spatial senses (Litkowski and Hargraves, 2021). We train a 'glossbert'-style neural word sense disambiguation model (Huang et al., 2019) as a binary classifier and infer spatial/non-spatial sense for each ParaBLoCC English sentence. Model architecture is shown in Figure 1. The spatial sense classifier is trained with 8,111 sentences exemplifying the senses extracted from The Preposition Project dictionaries (Litkowski and Hargraves, 2021). The model uses the ADAM optimizer, batch size of 16, and is trained for 10 epochs.

4.3 Spatial Sense Filter Performance

We assess the performance of the spatial sense filter using held-out validation data from the aforecited Preposition Project and 200 hand-labeled in-domain sentence pairs (Table 2).

While performance of the spatial filter is not as high as state-of-the-art word sense disambiguation (WSD) models tested on less challenging test sets

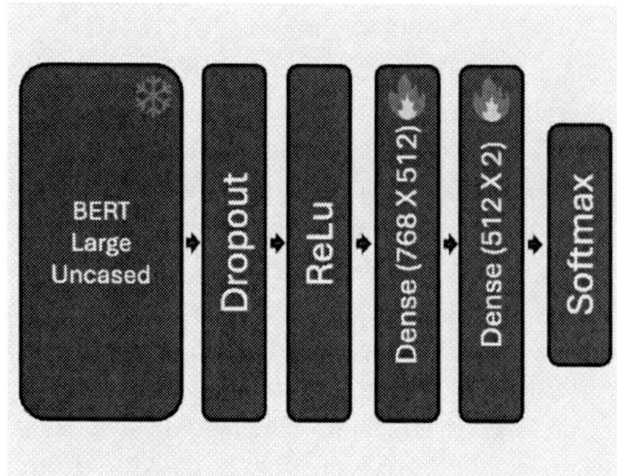

Figure 1: Model architecture for spatial sense disambiguation classifier, based on (Huang et al., 2019).

Table 2: Spatial Sense Classifier Performance: recall, precision, and macro-averaged F1.

	Precision	Recall	F1
Validation Set	.69	.70	.66
In-Domain Set	.56	.80	.66

(Yigzaw and Assefa, 2024), we consider spatial sense disambiguation problem to be particularly challenging and the current model to be adequate for the large-scale filtration task at hand, while recognizing the challenges described in §5.

4.4 BLC Occurrrence Rates

The mean observed rate of BLC occurrence per thousand original sentences, taken across ParaBLoCC languages, is 7.2 (see Table 1). While domain differences may explain some extreme values, we continue to investigate outliers to rule out processing errors resulting in artificially low or high values. Extrapolating from our small set of hand-labeled validation sentences, we believe the ParaBLoCC estimate of 7.2/1000 is three times less than the true BLC occurrence rate, measured at twenty per thousand. See §5 for discussion of the reasons for the underestimate.

5 Sources of Error in ParaBLoCC

The ParaBLoCC data contain noise from two main sources. First due to errors in harvesting target-language sentences from the web, some ParaBLoCC entries will contain target sentences which are not exact semantic equivalents of the source BLC, or which contain other types of bitext alignment errors. In spite of improvements in identifi-

Table 3: BLC Detection Error Analysis and Error Modes

Metric	Value
BLC Detection Rate	.095
False Positive Rate	.016
False Positives	.016
Syntax Errors	-
Spatial Sense Errors	.016
False Negatives	.018
Syntax Errors	.012
Spatial Sense Errors	.006

cation of parallel text for harvest (cf. Paracrawl, (Bañón et al., 2020)), source-target sentence pair mismatches are common in the corpora from which ParaBLoCC draws: recent estimates of error rates in bitext corpora vary from as low as 24% to as high as 76% of sentence pairs (Kreutzer et al., 2022).

A second source of errors in the ParaBLoCC entries comes from BLC detection errors, either Type 1 (false positives) or Type II (false negatives). Those errors in turn can be grouped into errors from the syntactic matching filter and errors from the spatial sense disambiguation filter. (It is assumed that lexical matching errors are negligible, since matching is deterministic.)

To assess the accuracy and sensitivity of the BLC labels in the ParaBLoCC corpus, we used a hand-labeled reference set of 1,000 ParaBLoCC sentences which passed the lexical filter, from sixteen of the included languages.[2] The authors independently coded the sentences and discarded any where we did not agree. Inter-annotator agreement was $\kappa = .55$ —in the 'moderate' range. BLC detection error rate and Type I and II errors are reported in Table 3. The observed BLC detection rate in ParaBLoCC is estimated at .095, quite low with a balance of false positives and false negatives. The false positive rate is .016. Post-hoc analysis of error modes shows that the spatial sense filter did not perform well on longer sentences, particularly those with multiple clauses, which are common in the ParaBLoCC corpus. We leave improvements to the spatial sense filter for future work.

6 Likely uses of ParaBLoCC

We created the ParaBLoCC data to appeal to a wide variety of scholars interested in spatial language, and by making them available we hope to encourage additional study in this area. The primary utility of the data are to allow study of usage patterns for parallel spatial expressions in twenty-six genetically and typologically diverse languages. Through automated alignment and span detection, silver labels for BLCs in the target languages can be extracted and studied themselves or used for downstream tasks.

Likely secondary uses for the ParaBLoCC data will be to enable work on multilingual aspects of spatial relation extraction (Rawsthorne et al., 2023). Until very recently, text corpora annotated for spatial relation triples were limited to the most high-resource numbers of languages, though this situation is starting to improve (Wang et al., 2023) so the multilinguality of ParaBLoCC should be welcome. The data can be used to improve current models of geospatial expression resolution (Wang et al., 2024). Finally we expect multilingual image caption models (Ramos et al., 2023) will benefit from the parallel data collected by ParaBLoCC.

7 Limitations

We acknowledge several limitations of the ParaBLoCC corpus. The selection of languages is limited to those with adequate bitext availability. In practice, this limits us from collecting BLCs in languages whose spatial expression systems are most formally distinct from English and European languages. For example, languages with only absolute reference frames, lacking intrinsic or relative frames (Fortis, 2010), are conspicuously absent from ParaBLoCC.

Granularity of annotation is another limitation of ParaBLoCC. Because of the method of collecting and labeling the sentence pairs in the corpus, text spans representing BLCs are not overtly annotated in either source language (English) or target language. Explicit span annotations for BLCs would provide additional training and test data veracity. Furthermore, ParaBLoCC would ideally provide semantic role annotations for sub-spans of source and target-language BLCs as `<figure>`, `<ground>`, and `<spatial relation>`. While stochastic methods of labeling subspans of BLCs have been demonstrated (Viechnicki et al., 2024), they are noisy. Explicit annotation of this nature would allow more in-depth analysis of the kinds of syntactic variation found in BLCs 'in the wild.' We leave annotation improvements to future community efforts.

[2] am, ar, ay, cs, de, es, fi, hu, ig, ko, nl, qu, sw, ti, uz, zh

8 References

References

Marta Bañón, Pinzhen Chen, Barry Haddow, Kenneth Heafield, Hieu Hoang, Miquel Esplà-Gomis, Mikel L. Forcada, Amir Kamran, Faheem Kirefu, Philipp Koehn, Sergio Ortiz Rojas, Leopoldo Pla Sempere, Gema Ramírez-Sánchez, Elsa Sarrías, Marek Strelec, Brian Thompson, William Waites, Dion Wiggins, and Jaume Zaragoza. 2020. ParaCrawl: Web-scale acquisition of parallel corpora. In *Proceedings of the 58th Annual Meeting of the Association for Computational Linguistics*, pages 4555–4567, Online. Association for Computational Linguistics.

B. Beekhuizen, J. Watson, and S. Stevenson. 2017. Semantic typology and parallel corpora: Something about indefinite pronouns. *CogSci.*

M. Bowerman and T. Pederson. 1992. *Topological relations picture series*, chapter 1.2. Max Planck Institute for Psycholinguistics, Nijmegen.

Jean-Michel Fortis. 2010. Space in language. *Leipzig Summer School 2010 Part 1.*

John T. Hale and Miloš Stanojević. 2024. Do LLMs learn a true syntactic universal? In *Proceedings of the 2024 Conference on Empirical Methods in Natural Language Processing*, pages 17106–17119, Miami, Florida, USA. Association for Computational Linguistics.

K. Hassani and W. Lee. 2017. Disambiguating spatial prepositions using deep convolutional networks. *Proceedings of the AAAI Conference on Artificial Intelligence*, 31.

Luyao Huang, Chi Sun, Xipeng Qiu, and Xuanjing Huang. 2019. GlossBERT: BERT for word sense disambiguation with gloss knowledge. In *Proceedings of the 2019 Conference on Empirical Methods in Natural Language Processing and the 9th International Joint Conference on Natural Language Processing (EMNLP-IJCNLP)*, pages 3509–3514, Hong Kong, China. Association for Computational Linguistics.

B Kortmann. 2021. Reflecting on the quantitative turn in linguistics. *Linguistics*, 59:1207–1226.

Julia Kreutzer, Isaac Caswell, Lisa Wang, Ahsan Wahab, Daan van Esch, Nasanbayar Ulzii-Orshikh, Allahsera Tapo, Nishant Subramani, Artem Sokolov, Claytone Sikasote, Monang Setyawan, Supheakmungkol Sarin, Sokhar Samb, Benoît Sagot, Clara Rivera, Annette Rios, Isabel Papadimitriou, Salomey Osei, Pedro Ortiz Suarez, Iroro Orife, Kelechi Ogueji, Andre Niyongabo Rubungo, Toan Q. Nguyen, Mathias Müller, André Müller, Shamsuddeen Hassan Muhammad, Nanda Muhammad, Ayanda Mnyakeni, Jamshidbek Mirzakhalov, Tapiwanashe Matangira, Colin Leong, Nze Lawson, Sneha Kudugunta, Yacine Jernite, Mathias Jenny, Orhan Firat, Bonaventure F. P. Dossou, Sakhile Dlamini, Nisansa de Silva, Sakine Çabuk Ballı, Stella Biderman, Alessia Battisti, Ahmed Baruwa, Ankur Bapna, Pallavi Baljekar, Israel Abebe Azime, Ayodele Awokoya, Duygu Ataman, Orevaoghene Ahia, Oghenefego Ahia, Sweta Agrawal, and Mofetoluwa Adeyemi. 2022. Quality at a glance: An audit of web-crawled multilingual datasets. *Transactions of the Association for Computational Linguistics*, 10:50–72.

L. Lakusta, Y. Hussein, A. Wodzinski, and B. Landau. 2021. The privileging of 'support-from-below' in early spatial language acquisition. *Infant Behav Dev.*

B. Landau, K. Johannes, D. Skordos, and A. Papafragou. 2016. Containment and support: Core and complexity in spatial language learning. *Cognitive Science: A Multidisciplinary Journal.*

S. Levinson and S. Meira. 2003. 'natural concepts' in the spatial topologial domain–adpositional meanings in crosslinguistic perspective: An exercise in semantic typology. *Language*, 79:485–516.

S Levinson and D. Wilkins. 2006. *Grammars of Space: Explorations in Cognitive Diversity*. Language Culture and Cognition. Cambridge University Press.

Ken Litkowski and Orin Hargraves. 2021. The preposition project. *Preprint*, arXiv:2104.08922.

Kenneth C. Litkowski and Orin Hargraves. 2007. SemEval-2007 task 06: Word-sense disambiguation of prepositions. In *Proceedings of the Fourth International Workshop on Semantic Evaluations (SemEval-2007)*, pages 24–29, Prague, Czech Republic. Association for Computational Linguistics.

Christopher D. Manning, Mihai Surdeanu, John Bauer, Jenny Finkel, Steven J. Bethard, and David McClosky. 2014. The Stanford CoreNLP natural language processing toolkit. In *Association for Computational Linguistics (ACL) System Demonstrations*, pages 55–60.

Paul McNamee, James Mayfield, Cash Costello, Caitlyn Bishop, and Shelby Anderson. 2020. Tagging location phrases in text. In *Proceedings of the Twelfth Language Resources and Evaluation Conference*, pages 4521–4528, Marseille, France. European Language Resources Association.

Rita Ramos, Bruno Martins, and Desmond Elliott. 2023. Lmcap: Few-shot multilingual image captioning by retrieval augmented language model prompting. *Preprint*, arXiv:2305.19821.

Helen Mair Rawsthorne, Nathalie Abadie, Eric Kergosien, Cécile Duchêne, and Éric Saux. 2023. Automatic nested spatial entity and spatial relation extraction from text for knowledge graph creation: A baseline approach and a benchmark dataset. In *Proceedings of the 7th ACM SIGSPATIAL International Workshop on Geospatial Humanities*, GeoHumanities '23, page 21–30, New York, NY, USA. Association for Computing Machinery.

Daisy Rosenblum. 2015. *A grammar of space in Kwakwala*. Ph.D. thesis, University of California Santa Barbara.

Jerrold Sadock and Arnold Zwicky. 1985. Speech act distinctions in syntax. In Tim Shopen, editor, *Language, Typology, and Syntactic Description*, volume 1, pages 155–196. Cambridge University Press, Cambridge.

K. Stock, C. Jones, S. Russell, M. Radke, P. Das, and N. Aflaki. 2021. Detecting geospatial location descriptions in natural language text. *International Journal of Geographical Information Science*, 36(3).

Leonard Talmy. 1983. How language structures space. In Herbert L. Pick and Linda P. Acredolo, editors, *Spatial Orientation: Theory, Research, and Application*, pages 225–282. Springer US, Boston, MA.

Jörg Tiedemann, Mikko Aulamo, Daria Bakshandaeva, Michele Boggia, Stig-Arne Grönroos, Tommi Nieminen, Alessandro Raganato, Yves Scherrer, Raul Vazquez, and Sami Virpioja. 2023. Democratizing neural machine translation with opus-mt. *Preprint*, arXiv:2212.01936.

Christine Tseng, Alexandra Carstensen, Terry Regier, and Yang Xu. 2016. A computational investigation of the sapir-whorf hypothesis: The case of spatial relations. In *Proceedings of the 38th Annual Meeting of the Cognitive Science Society, CogSci 2016*, Proceedings of the 38th Annual Meeting of the Cognitive Science Society, CogSci 2016, pages 2231–2236. The Cognitive Science Society. Publisher Copyright: © 2016 Proceedings of the 38th Annual Meeting of the Cognitive Science Society, CogSci 2016. All rights reserved.; 38th Annual Meeting of the Cognitive Science Society: Recognizing and Representing Events, CogSci 2016 ; Conference date: 10-08-2016 Through 13-08-2016.

Peter Viechnicki, Kevin Duh, Anthony Kostacos, and Barbara Landau. 2024. Large-scale bitext corpora provide new evidence for cognitive representations of spatial terms. In *Proceedings of the 18th Conference of the European Chapter of the Association for Computational Linguistics (Volume 1: Long Papers)*, pages 1089–1099, St. Julian's, Malta. Association for Computational Linguistics.

W. Wang, J. Li, W. Ku, and H. Wang. 2024. Multilingual spatial domain natural language interface to databases. *GeoInformatica*.

Zixiang Wang, Jian Yang, Tongliang Li, Jiaheng Liu, Ying Mo, Jiaqi Bai, Longtao He, and Zhoujun Li. 2023. Multilingual entity and relation extraction from unified to language-specific training. *Preprint*, arXiv:2301.04434.

R. Yigzaw and B. Assefa. 2024. State-of-the-art approaches to word sense disambiguation: A multilingual investigation. *Communications in Computer and Information Science*.

A Appendix: Prepositions and Spatial Nominals used in Lexical Filtration Step

English Spatial Expressions used in lexical filtration stage.

A.1 Prepositions

`above, across, against, along, alongside, amid, amidst, among, around, at, atop, before, behind, below, beneath, between, by, down, in, inside, near, off, on, over, toward, towards, under, underneath, with`

A.2 Spatial Nominals and Spatial Phrases

`out of, in back of, in the front of, on the top of, on top of, in front of, to the right of, to the left of, right of, left of, north of, south of, east of, west of, in the middle of, on the bottom of, next to, outside of, in the back of, on the left of, on the right of`

Capturing Online SRC/ORC Effort with Memory Measures from a Minimalist Parser

Aniello De Santo
Dept. of Linguistics, University of Utah
aniello.desanto@utah.edu

Abstract

A parser for Minimalist grammars (Stabler, 2013) has been shown to successfully model sentence processing preferences across an array of languages and phenomena when combined with complexity metrics that relate parsing behavior to memory usage (Gerth, 2015; Graf et al., 2017; De Santo, 2020b, a.o.). This model provides a quantifiable theory of the effects of fine-grained grammatical structure on cognitive cost, and can help strengthen the link between generative syntactic theory and sentence processing. However, work on it has focused on *offline* asymmetries. Here, we extend this approach by showing how memory-based measures of effort that explicitly consider minimalist-like structure-building operations improve our ability to account for word-by-word (*online*) behavioral data.

1 Introduction

Formally specifying hypotheses about how grammatical structure drives processing cost makes it possible to connect long-standing ideas about cognitive load in human language processing with representational assumptions in theoretical syntax — thus adding to the interpretability of theories of sentence comprehension, and to the plausibility of particular syntactic analyses/theories of syntactic representations (Bresnan, 1978; Berwick and Weinberg, 1982; Kaplan and Bresnan, 1982; Hale, 2001, 2011).

In this sense, recent studies have argued that the behavior of a parser for Minimalist grammars (Stabler, 1996) can link structural complexity to memory usage. In particular, this takes the form of a specific implementation of Stabler (2013)'s top-down parser, coupled with complexity metrics measuring how a tree traversal algorithm recruits memory resources (Kobele et al., 2013). This model makes fully specified commitments to (a) the nature of the structures built during the parsing process, (b) the time-course of the structure building operations connecting linear input to hierarchical representations, and (c) a psychologically plausible theory of how cognitive resources are linked to parsing operations to derive measures of sentence difficulty. Thanks do these commitments, this approach offers an insightful, empirically grounded reframing of past theories trying to bridge the study of competence and the study of performance (e.g., the Derivational Theory of Complexity; Miller and Chomsky, 1963; Fodor and Garrett, 1967; Berwick and Weinberg, 1983; De Santo, 2020b).

From an empirical perspective, computational modeling work in this framework has proved successful in accounting for a number of processing preferences across a variety of phenomena cross-linguistically (Gerth, 2015; Graf et al., 2017, a.o.). Most of this work has focused on deriving estimates of *offline* (over a whole sentence) effort, which then has been used to qualitatively evaluate categorical contrasts between minimally different sentence pairs. However, if we aim to probe the cognitive plausibility of a Minimalist Grammar model, it is important to understand its ability to capture fine-grained sentence comprehension processes, beyond broad, sentence-level complexity profiles (Demberg and Keller, 2008; Li and Hale, 2019).

In this paper, we extend this approach by extracting a metric of word-by-word effort from memory-usage measures defined in previous work on offline effects. We then evaluate this complexity metric based on its ability to capture difficulty profiles in self-paced reading from a large scale dataset. As this model implements theories of effort grounded in memory load, we also compare its predictions to those of a metric (surprisal) estimating word predictability (Hale, 2001).

2 MG Parsing and Cognitive Effort

We adopt a model combining a parser for Minimalist Grammars with metrics measuring memory usage. In the rest of this section we outline the core intu-

Proceedings of the Workshop on Cognitive Modeling and Computational Linguistics, pages 24–35
May 3, 2025

itions behind this approach to sentence difficulty. While it is possible to implement alternative cognitive models incorporating Minimalist Grammar parsers, we refer to the specific set of choices made here as the **MG model** for ease of discussion.

2.1 A Brief introduction to MGs

Minimalist Grammars (MGs; Stabler, 1996) are a mildly-context sensitive, transformational formalism incorporating ideas from the Minimalist Program (Chomsky, 1995). An MG grammar consists of a sets of lexical items associated with a non-empty string of syntactic features and two core transformational operations — Merge and Move. Merge is a binary operation encoding subcategorization, while Move is a unary operation allowing for a movement approach to long-distance, filler-gap dependencies. Importantly for us, the central data structure of MGs is a *derivation tree*, explicitly encoding the sequence of Merge and Move operations required by a given sentence (Michaelis, 1998; Harkema, 2001; Kobele et al., 2007). Derivation trees differ from more commonly known phrase structure trees in that moving phrases remain in their base position, and thus the final, linear word order of a sentence is not directly reflected in the order of the leaf nodes in the tree (see Figure 1a).

Since MGs are able to exemplify the structurally rich analyses of modern generative syntax, they can contribute to the development of models of sentence processing that provide insights into the connection between fine-grained syntactic structure and offline processing behavior. This is the intuition behind a line of computational modeling work which, starting with Kobele et al. (2013), has shown that a top-down parser for MGs (Stabler, 2013) is successful in predicting offline processing difficulty contrasts.

2.2 MG Parsing

Stabler (2013)'s parser is adapted from a standard recursive-descent parser for CFG, accounting for the mismatch between the order of lexical items in a derivation tree and the linear surface order. Broadly, the parser scans the nodes from top to bottom and from left to right. Given the way Move is implemented however, simple left-to-right scanning of the leaf nodes yields an incorrect word order. In order to keep track of the derivational operations affecting linear order, the MG variant follows the standard approach of predicting nodes downward (toward words) and left-to-right only until a Move node is predicted. At that point, the pure top-down strategy is discarded, and the parser instead follows the shortest path towards predicting the moved item's base position (a *string-driven* strategy). After a position for the mover has been found, the parser continues from the point where the the top-down strategy had been paused (Figure 1b).

The memory stack associated to the parser plays a fundamental role in this: if a parse item is hypothesized at step i, but cannot be worked on until step j, it must be stored for $j - i$ steps in a priority queue. For instance, consider the derivation tree in Figure 1a for the sentence *Who do the Gems love __?*. Here, the node for *do* is predicted at step 3 but it is only flushed out of the parser's stack at step 10. This is because a movement dependency for *who* has been postulated at Spec,CP. Upon encountering *who* in the input string and predicting a movement operation, the parser cannot integrate the mover into the structure until a base position for it has been predicted and confirmed (at step 8 and 9). While doing so, the parser will predict intermediate structure (e.g., a position for an auxiliary in C, which could be occupied by *do*), but it will not match that prediction against the linear input until the search for *who* has been resolved.[1]

Stabler's algorithm seems to capture some core properties of human language processing strategies: it works incrementally, and it is *predictive* — it makes hypotheses about how to build the upcoming syntactic structure that need to be confirmed based on the input (Marslen-Wilson and Tyler, 1980; Tanenhaus et al., 1995; Phillips, 2003; Demberg and Keller, 2009, a.o.). As in other aspects of cognition, prediction also plays a crucial role in language processing. In the MG model, this is reflected by the fact that the predictive abilities of the string-driven top-down approach guide how the parser recruits memory resources. However, the psycholinguistic literature traditionally refers to prediction in the context of *ambiguity resolution* — the task of choosing between multiple, alternative structural hypotheses available to the parser during processing (Traxler and Pickering, 1996; Wagers and Phillips, 2009; Chambers et al., 2004; Hale, 2006). This predictive aspect has been shown to have a significant role in determining processing cost (Traxler and Pickering, 1996; Wagers and Phillips, 2009; Chambers et al., 2004), and to be modulated by past experience (Ellis, 2002; Hale, 2006; Levy, 2013).

[1]The reader in referred to (De Santo, 2020b, Chp. 2) for a deeper discussion of the differences in stack-usage between a string-driven traversal and a classic top-down traversal.

In this respect, Stabler's parser can be equipped with a search beam discarding the most unlikely predictions. Here though, we follow Kobele et al. (2013) in ignoring the beam and assuming that the parser is equipped with a perfect oracle, which always makes the right choices when constructing a tree. Essentially, the MG model adopts deterministic parsing strategy. This idealization is clearly implausible from a psycholinguistic point of view, but has a precise purpose: to ignore the cost of choosing among several possible predictions and focus on the specific contribution of structure-building strategies to processing difficulty. However, the MG model has enough flexibility to allow for the implementation and evaluation of theories of ambiguity resolution and reanalysis (Chen and Hale, 2021; De Santo and Lee, 2022; Ozaki et al., 2024). We come back to this possibility in Section 5.

2.3 Parsing Effort and Tenure

Kobele et al. (2013) introduces a tree annotation schema to make Stabler (2013)'s tree traversal strategy easy to follow (Figure 1a). Each node in a tree is annotated with the step at which it was first conjectured by the parser and placed in memory (superscript, *Index*), and the step at which it is considered completed and flushed from memory (subscript, *Outdex*). Index and Outdex thus fully encode the relation between a node and stack-states. We can then use them to link the parser's traversal strategy, syntactic structure, and memory usage. In turn, this allows us to derive predictions about sentence difficulty, based on how the structure of a derivation tree affects memory (Rambow and Joshi, 1994; Gibson, 2000; Kobele et al., 2013; Gerth, 2015).

The MG model distinguishes several cognitive notions of memory usage (Graf et al., 2017). Of interest to us is a measure of how long a node is kept in memory through a derivation (TENURE). Tenure for each node is computed considering the moment a node was first postulated into the structure (i.e., placed in the memory stack of the parser) and the moment such prediction was confirmed (i.e., the node could be taken out of memory). In practice, a node's Tenure can be computed as the difference between its index and its outdex. Considering again the annotated MG tree in Figure 1a, Tenure for *do* is $Outdex(do) - Index(do) = 10 - 3 = 7$.

As mentioned, past work has then formalized this notion in metrics of *offline* processing difficulty — for instance measuring maximum Tenure (MAXT), which ties processing difficulty to differences in grammatical structure over a whole derivation. Specifically, MAXT has been used to derive categorical processing contrasts, by comparing maximum Tenure values for derivation trees corresponding to pairs of sentences with stark asymmetries in reported offline processing preferences. For instance, Graf and Marcinek (2014) show that MAXT makes the right difficulty predictions for phenomena such as right embedding vs. center embedding, nested dependencies vs. crossing dependencies, as well as a set of cross-linguistic contrasts involving relative clauses. Following work has then strengthen the empirical support for Tenure based metrics, further demonstrating their ability to qualitatively capture offline contrasts across languages and constructions (Gerth, 2015; Graf et al., 2017; Liu, 2018; De Santo, 2019, 2020a). Evaluating this model on online patterns of effort seems then the natural next step in the enterprise. In what follows, we leverage word-by-word Tenure values as already computed by the MG model to derive online predictions.

3 Evaluating Tenure Online

Building on previous successes of the MG model in capturing offline contrasts, we ask whether structure-building effort as captured by Tenure improves estimates of word-by-word reading time patterns. We show that Tenure as computed by the model can be directly leveraged to derive predictors of processing difficulty. We then evaluate Tenure against surprisal measures extracted from two different neural architectures, as an implementation of expectation-based complexity metrics.

3.1 Reading Time Data

The relative comprehension difficulty of object-extracted (ORC; 2) over subject extracted (SRC; 1) relative clauses is well-attested both in English and cross-linguistically (Lau and Tanaka, 2021).

1. The Pearl who welcomed the Diamond.

2. The Pearl who the Diamond welcomed.

Additionally, while this difficulty has been partially linked to the lower frequency/predictability of ORCs (Chen and Hale, 2021; Vani et al., 2021), expectation-based approaches have been argued to fall short in accounting for the overall pattern of relative complexity. Instead (or additionally), a subject preference in RCs can be associated to the impact of memory-related processes/demands (Gibson and Wu, 2013; Levy, 2013; McCurdy and Hahn, 2024).

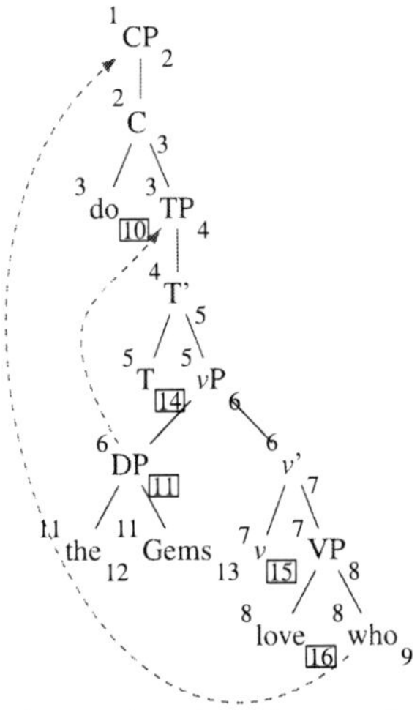

	Who	do	the	Gems	love
Tenure	1	7	1	2	8

(a)

Step	Parse Action
1	*CP* is conjectured
2	*CP* expands to *C'*
3	*C'* expands to *do* and *TP*
4	*TP* expands to *T'*
5	*T'* expands to *T* and *vP*
6	*vP* expands to *DP* and *v'*
7	*v'* expands to *v* and *VP*
8	*VP* expands to *love* and *who*
9	***who*** is found
10	***do*** is found
11	*DP* expands to *the* and *Gems*
12	***the*** is found
13	***Gems*** is found
14	***T*** is found
15	***v*** is found
16	***love*** is found

(b)

Figure 1: In (a): Example of an MG derivation tree for *Who do the Gems love?* with annotated parse steps as index/outdex at each node. Below it, Tenure values for pronounced lexical items computed for a node i as $\mathit{Outdex}(i) - \mathit{Index}(i)$. Boxed nodes are those with Tenure > 2. Unary branches indicate movement landing sites. In (b): Actions of a string-driven recursive descent parser for *Who do the Gems love?* as exemplified by the derivation tree in (a).

In this sense, *offline* SRC/ORC asymmetries have been extensively probed with the MG Model, with MAXT deriving the empirically reported subject advantage across languages and syntactic analyses (Graf et al., 2017; De Santo, 2021a,b; Del Valle and De Santo, 2023; Fiorini et al., 2023). Subject/Object asymmetries in RCs are then a natural venue to investigate whether structure-based complexity metrics like Tenure offer quantitative insights into online patterns of effort during sentence processing.

Thus, we use as target behavioral data the reading times (RT) for the SRC/ORC items in the Syntactic Ambiguity Processing Benchmark (SAP; Huang et al., 2024).[2] The SAP benchmark is a recent dataset of self-paced RTs from 2000 participants, covering a wide-range of complex syntactic phenomena in English. This large scale dataset has been explicitly designed in order to provide a quantitative benchmark for the evaluation of theories of sentence processing over a variety of well-studied phenomena. We focus here on the RC items in the dataset. The benchmark offers word-by-word RTs for 24 RC sets, comprising of lexically matched SRCs and ORCs taken from a classic study in the literature (Staub, 2010). Relevantly, the SAP data have already been used to probe the limited ability of expectation-based metrics (e.g., surprisal) to account for the relative difficulty of ORCs over SRCs in English.

3.2 Word-by-Word Tenure

We compute word-by-word Tenure values from derivations built for each one of the RC sentences in the benchmark. For each item, gold-standard MG derivations are built following standard generative assumptions for the main clause of each sentence, and a wh-movement analysis for the structure of RCs (Chomsky, 1977, see Figure 2). Then, derivations are annotated via Graf et al. (2017)'s implementation of Stabler (2013)'s MG parser.[3] As discussed above, Tenure is computed as $\mathit{Outdex}(i) - \mathit{Index}(i)$ for each pronounced node i in a tree (Figure 1a).

4 Model Fitting and Results

As a reminder, we want to probe whether word-by-word Tenure improves model fit to the self-paced RT data made available for English SRCs/ORCs in the SAP (Huang et al., 2024) benchmark, beyond established expectation-based predictors. Following Huang et al. (2024), in this paper we present analy-

[2]https://osf.io/b6rqh/

[3]https://github.com/CompLab-StonyBrook/mgproc

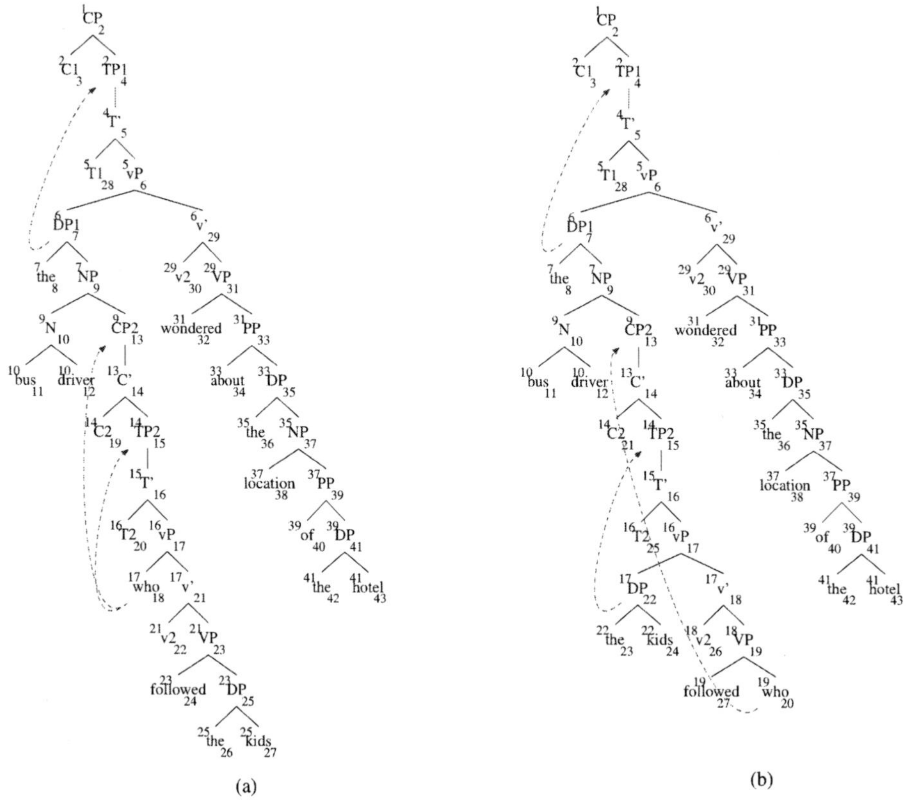

Figure 2: Annotated derivation trees for one of the subject (a) and an object (b) RCs in the dataset, modeled according to a wh-movement analysis of RCs.

ses using raw RTs, avoiding the logarithmic transformation common in the self-paced reading literature.[4] As Huang et al. (2024) argue, while this transformation reduces the right skew of RTs collected through self-paced reading, it does so by violating some theoretical assumptions about the relationship between RTs and prediction-based complexity metrics (e.g., surprisal, but also possibly Tenure).[5]

First, we fit a baseline frequentist linear mixed-effects model to the RTs, with several (scaled) lexical control predictors as computed by Huang et al. (2024):

$$\begin{aligned} RT \sim & WordPosition(i) \\ & + logfreq(i) * length(i) \\ & + logfreq(i-1) * length(i-1) \\ & + logfreq(i-1) * length(i-2) \\ & + (1|participant) + (1|item) \end{aligned}$$

These include the position of a word in a sentence, its length and unigram frequency, and the interaction between the two. Predictors for the two preceding words are also included to account for spill-over effects common in self-paced reading (Mitchell, 2018; Vasishth, 2006).

We use surprisal as our expectation-based metric (Hale, 2006; Levy, 2008; Wilcox et al., 2023). We fit two models adding to the baseline model specified above surprisal values computed with an LSTM (Gulordava, 2018) and with GPT-2 small (Radford et al., 2019). Again, surprisal predictors are included both at the current word and at the two preceding words. We also include a random slope for surprisal by participant. Finally, we fit two models adding word-by-word Tenure (for the current word and the two preceding words) to the two surprisal models, including additional random slopes for Tenure by participant.

We select the best fitting models using AIC and BIC criteria (Akaike, 1973; Schwarz, 1978; Chakrabarti and Ghosh, 2011). Consistently with previous results, surprisal models improve fit over

[4] R scripts and data available at https://osf.io/8amqp/

[5] Analyses using log-transformed RTs are nonetheless available in our analyses scripts.

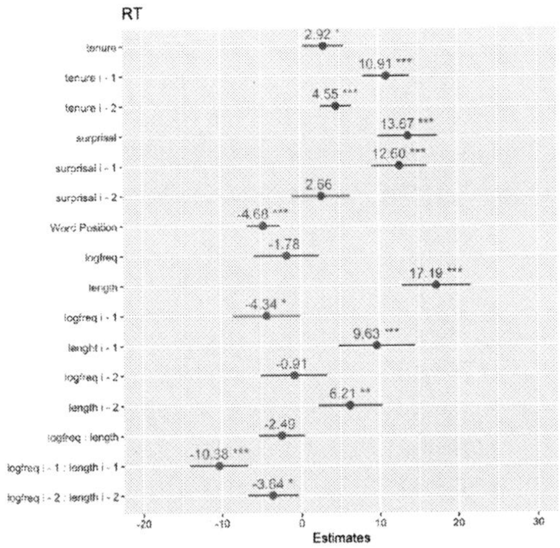

Figure 3: Estimates of coefficients for the best fitting model (GTP Surprisal + Tenure).

the baseline model (Table 1), with the GPT-2 surprisal model performs better than the LSTM model. Adding Tenure to the surprisal-only models further improves fit for both the LSTM and GPT models, showing the modeling advantage of taking memory into account explicilty. The overall best performing model was the *GPT-surprisal + Tenure* model (Table 1), consistently with GPT-2 surprisal providing a better fit than LSTM surprisal and with the structural advantage provided by Tenure. In particular, we found that Tenure of both the current word and the preceding two words is associated with significantly slower RTs independently of surprisal (Table 2 and Figure 3).

	df	AIC	BIC
Baseline	14	977122.5	977250.8
LSTM Surprisal	19	976309.1	976483.1
GPT Surprisal	19	976301.9	976475.9
LSTM Surprisal + Tenure	23	974174.8	974385.5
GPT Surprisal + Tenure	**24**	**974106.3**	**974326.2**

Table 1: Model Comparison.

5 Discussion

By combining a Minimalist grammar parser with a cognitively grounded complexity metric, the model adopted in this paper implements algorithmically theories of sentence comprehension that explicitly link comprehension difficulty to how building complex hierarchical structure affects memory usage. As discussed earlier in the paper, this approach has been successful in capturing qualitative contrasts in offline comprehension for an encouraging array of sentence processing phenomena cross-linguistically. Here, by leveraging the existing definition of Tenure, we were able to extend the evaluation of this modeling approach to quantitative word-by-word measures, providing an explicit link to the processes involved in online sentence comprehension. Importantly, Tenure does not simply measure the "raw" number of parse actions to estimate difficulty (cf. Brennan et al., 2016; Stanojević et al., 2023). It related effort to a notion of memory usage directly related to how the mismatch between the structure of the tree and the surface form of the string is navigated by the parser. By taking derivational steps seriously, Tenure ties effort to parse objects that have to be maintained "active" during the parse (e.g., partially hypothesized phrases/projections).

Our results show that predictors linking structure-building operations to memory usage improve our ability to model word-by-word RTs, beyond the contribution of expectation-based surprisal measures — adding support to the cognitive relevance of transparent structure-building measures. In particular, we found a significant positive correlation between Tenure at the current word and RTs, as well as strong effects of Tenure at the previous two words. Lingering effects of Tenure at the preceding words are compatible with known delays in RTs measured via self-paced reading. Future work could probe the plausibility of this hypothesis, and a more subtle understanding of the link between Tenure and online effort, by evaluating Tenure for similar constructions over different kinds of behavioral data (Schotter and Dillon, 2025; Boyce et al., 2020).

The recent development of broad coverage MG parsers (Torr et al., 2019) might also allow for a more fine-grained approach to the evaluation of this model's ability to capture the magnitude of the effects under study. In particular, the two-steps Bayesian approach to magnitude estimation suggested by Van Schijndel and Linzen (2021) and Huang et al. (2024) could help us leverage the modeling advantages provided by a broad coverage parser, while also retaining MGs' granular view into specific syntactic choices/details.

Similarly, building on previous offline MG results, here we only focused on the SRC/ORC asymmetry. A better understanding of the relevance of this model to theories of sentence comprehension will naturally come from evaluations over different constructions and different languages. In fact, cross-

	RT					
Predictors	*Estimate*	*Std. Error*	*df*	*t value*	*Pr(>|t|)*	
(Intercept)	404.178	5.359	45.273	75.423	<2e-16	***
Tenure	2.920	1.327	3758.499	2.200	0.027899	*
Tenure $i-1$	10.907	1.507	3223.985	7.236	5.75e-13	***
Tenure $i-2$	4.553	1.018	62441.736	4.475	7.65e-06	***
Surprisal	13.675	1.924	9708.665	7.108	1.26e-12	***
Surprisal $i-1$	12.603	1.762	10126.632	7.154	9.03e-13	***
Surprisal $i-2$	2.656	1.861	59141.060	1.427	0.153489	
Word Position	-4.682	1.058	60334.657	-4.426	9.60e-06	***
logfreq	-1.782	2.102	37139.995	-0.848	0.396547	
length	17.195	2.266	22649.688	7.588	3.38e-14	***
logfreq $i-1$	-4.337	2.149	24284.605	-2.018	0.043568	*
length $i-1$	9.626	2.487	14971.417	3.871	0.000109	***
logfreq $i-2$	-0.909	2.136	46859.397	-0.425	0.670483	
length $i-2$	6.207	2.073	32905.438	2.994	0.002757	**
logfreq:length	-2.488	1.470	52063.647	-1.693	0.090503	.
logfreq $i-1$:length $i-1$	-10.378	1.871	41785.471	-5.545	2.95e-08	***
logfreq $i-2$:length $i-2$	-3.642	1.620	46877.483	-2.249	0.024533	*

$^{***}p<0.001$; $^{**}p<0.01$; $^{*}p<0.05$

Table 2: Lmer summary for the best fitting model (GTP Surprisal + Tenure).

linguistic comparison is central to the evaluation of both structure-based and expectation-based complexity metrics in cognitive modeling (Wilcox et al., 2023; Kajikawa et al., 2024). As mentioned, previous MG parsing work has proved successful in capturing the subject advantage in RCs for languages varying across several interesting structural dimensions (e.g., head-directionality, pre-nominal vs. post-nominal RCs, etc; Graf et al., 2017; De Santo, 2020b; Fiorini et al., 2023, a.o.). An investigation of this preference on cross-linguistic RT dataset would thus be a promising next step for the application of the MG model to online data.

For English specifically, the SAP benchmark offers self-paced reading data for a variety of phenomena beyond SRC/ORC contrasts (e.g., RC attachment ambiguities). Most of these phenomena involve ambiguity resolution strategies which have been used to argue in favor of single-stage, prediction based approaches — of which surprisal is one instantiation (Hale, 2001; Levy, 2013; Hale, 2016). As for the SRC advantage discussed in this paper however, surprisal has been shown unable to fully capture the magnitude of these effects within and across constructions (Van Schijndel and Linzen, 2021; Huang et al., 2024). Interesting, while this paper's model assumes a deterministic oracle and thus does not factor in ambiguity resolution explicitly, it has been shown to predict RC attachment preferences purely based on structural complexity (Lee, 2018; Lee and De Santo, 2022). More crucially, without discarding the importance of expectation/prediction in sentence comprehension, the explicit structure-building mechanisms of the MG model give us a way to implement alternative theories of ambiguity resolution — for instance two-stage approaches that consider the effort involved in structural reanalysis (Frazier and Fodor, 1978; Gorrell et al., 1995; Sturt, 1997; Pritchett, 1988; Ozaki et al., 2024).

Relatedly, the linking theory implemented by Tenure is distinct from proposals that argue for expectation-based metrics modulated/informed by syntactic structure (Demberg and Keller, 2008; Roark et al., 2009; Oh et al., 2022; Arehalli et al., 2022). As discussed, the framework described in this paper does not just argue for the relevance of syntactic structure, but for a notion of effort grounded in the direct interaction of structure building operations and memory. With this in mind, the grammar formalism adopted here is compatible with multiple ways to condition probability distributions over structural representations (Hunter and Dyer, 2013; Torr et al., 2019). Because of this, the MG approach is also flexible enough to allow for the exploration of potentially complex interactions of memory, structure, and expectation beyond the simple computation of structure-informed metrics like surprisal (Futrell et al., 2020; Brennan et al., 2020; Chen and Hale, 2021).

More generally, deeper insights into the contribution of structure-building metrics to models of sentence comprehension will come from a broader comparison between Tenure and other memory-based metrics (Kaplan, 1975; Pulman, 1986; Kaplan, 2020; Gibson, 1998; Lewis et al., 2006; Boston, 2012). For instance, an informative next step in this enterprise would be to conduct an empirical evaluation of the different predictions made by Tenure and a complexity metric like Node Count, which counts the number of syntactic operations in a tree (Brennan et al., 2016; Nelson et al., 2017; Brennan et al., 2020; Li and Hale, 2019; Stanojević et al., 2023, 2021; Kajikawa et al., 2024). It would also be fruitful to compare our results to measures of memory load relying less on rich structural information (e.g., Dependency Locality Theory; Gibson, 1998).

Similarly, through the use of MGs this work has committed explicitly to syntactic representations as hypothesized by modern generative syntax. While we made the case that the computation of particular Tenure values is deeply tied to commitments about the shape of a syntactic derivation *and* the timing of how such a derivation is built, its definition is conceptually independent of specific representational/algorithmic choices. Therefore, Tenure could be ideal for a comparison of the behavioral predictions made by different (often expressively equivalent) syntactic formalisms such as, for instance, TAG and CCG (Demberg et al., 2013; Stanojević et al., 2023, a.o.).

Relatedly, among this approach's degrees of freedom is the tree-traversal strategy adopted by the parser. This paper has followed the majority of offline MG work in extracting Tenure by evaluating the stack-usage of a top-down parser. Whether similar, or better, modeling results could be derived via different parsing strategies is thus an open question (cf. Brennan et al., 2016; Stanojević et al., 2023). In this sense, left-corner parsing algorithms have been recently proposed for MGs, and have been shown to correctly capture some interesting offline processing contrasts (Hunter, 2019; Hunter et al., 2019; Liu, 2024). Left-corner parsing's combination of top-down prediction and bottom-up "greedy" integration has also independently been argued to be more plausible as a description of human comprehension processes (Resnik, 1992). Crucially, the complex status of a parse item in Liu (2024)'s implementation of Hunter et al. (2019)'s left-corner MG parser makes adapting a word-by-word definition of Tenure non-trivial. Working out what the exact computation of online Tenure over the stack items stored by Hunter et al. (2019)'s parser would thus be the essential next step to perform this type of comparisons.

Finally, the model's sensitivity to fine-grained grammatical assumptions implies that analytical choices have a significant impact on the derived Tenure values. Conscious of this feature of the model, in this paper we have committed to one syntactic analysis for the main construction of interest. However, previous offline work has shown that alternative analyses of RCs might result in different behavioral predictions, especially when evaluated cross-linguistically (Graf et al., 2017; De Santo and Shafiei, 2019; Lee and De Santo, 2022). In this sense, the granularity of online data and the clear linking hypothesis implemented by the MG model could contribute to psycholinguistic data (and theories) bringing insights into the evaluation of analyses in theoretical syntax (Rambow and Joshi, 1994; Kobele et al., 2013; De Santo and Lee, 2022; Prasad and Linzen, 2024). Future work could then exploit online behavioral data to distinguish competing syntactic proposals based on their psycholinguistic predictions, thus clarifying how/which aspects of sentence structure modulate processing difficulty.

6 Conclusion

Extending previous work on offline contrasts, this paper provides a first evaluation of a parser for Minimalist grammars and a memory-based complexity metric over word-by-word behavioral data. While previous work in this domain evaluated offline behavior qualitatively, we provide quantitative evidence for the success of the approach by showing that the MG-based metric Tenure is a strong predictor of SRC/ORC RTs from a large scale behavioral dataset, independently of expectation-based surprisal. While many questions remain open, these results strengthen previous offline work arguing for relevance of the combination of MGs and Tenure in investigating the interaction of generative syntax and psycholinguistic results. Furthermore, they provide additional support to a growing body of computational modeling work arguing for the role of structure-building operations in developing plausible cognitive models of human sentence comprehension.

References

H Akaike. 1973. nformation theory and an extension of the maximum likelihood principle. In *Proceedings of the Second International Symposium on Information Theory. BN Petrov and F. Cs' aki, editors. Akademiai Ki'ado, Budapest.*

Suhas Arehalli, Brian Dillon, and Tal Linzen. 2022. Syntactic surprisal from neural models predicts, but underestimates, human processing difficulty from syntactic ambiguities. In *26th Conference on Computational Natural Language Learning, CoNLL 2022 collocated and co-organized with EMNLP 2022*, pages 301–313. Association for Computational Linguistics (ACL).

Robert C. Berwick and Amy S. Weinberg. 1982. Parsing efficiency, computational complexity, and the evaluation of grammatical theories. *Linguistic Inquiry*, 13:165–291.

Robert C. Berwick and Amy S. Weinberg. 1983. The role of grammar in models of language use. *Cognition*, 13:1–61.

Marisa Ferrara Boston. 2012. *A COMPUTATIONAL MODEL OF COGNITIVE CONSTRAINTS IN SYNTACTIC LOCALITY*. Ph.D. thesis, Cornell University.

Veronica Boyce, Richard Futrell, and Roger P Levy. 2020. Maze made easy: Better and easier measurement of incremental processing difficulty. *Journal of Memory and Language*, 111:104082.

Jonathan R Brennan, Chris Dyer, Adhiguna Kuncoro, and John T Hale. 2020. Localizing syntactic predictions using recurrent neural network grammars. *Neuropsychologia*, 146:107479.

Jonathan R Brennan, Edward P Stabler, Sarah E Van Wagenen, Wen-Ming Luh, and John T Hale. 2016. Abstract linguistic structure correlates with temporal activity during naturalistic comprehension. *Brain and Language*, 157:81–94.

Joan Bresnan. 1978. A realistic transformational grammar. *Linguistic theory and psychological reality*, pages 1–59.

Arijit Chakrabarti and Jayanta K. Ghosh. 2011. Aic, bic and recent advances in model selection. In Prasanta S. Bandyopadhyay and Malcolm R. Forster, editors, *Philosophy of Statistics*, volume 7 of *Handbook of the Philosophy of Science*, pages 583–605. North-Holland, Amsterdam.

Craig G Chambers, Michael K Tanenhaus, and James S Magnuson. 2004. Actions and affordances in syntactic ambiguity resolution. *Journal of experimental psychology: Learning, memory, and cognition*, 30(3):687.

Zhong Chen and John T Hale. 2021. Quantifying structural and non-structural expectations in relative clause processing. *Cognitive Science*, 45(1):e12927.

Noam Chomsky. 1977. On wh-movement.

Noam Chomsky. 1995. *The Minimalist Program*. Cambridge, MA: MIT Press.

Aniello De Santo. 2019. Testing a Minimalist grammar parser on Italian relative clause asymmetries. In *Proceedings of the ACL Workshop on Cognitive Modeling and Computational Linguistics (CMCL) 2019*, June 6 2019, Minneapolis, Minnesota.

Aniello De Santo. 2020a. Mg parsing as a model of gradient acceptability in syntactic islands. *Proceedings of the Society for Computation in Linguistics*, 3(1):53–63.

Aniello De Santo. 2020b. *Structure and memory: A computational model of storage, gradience, and priming*. Ph.D. thesis, State University of New York at Stony Brook.

Aniello De Santo. 2021a. Italian postverbal subjects from a minimalist parsing perspective. *Lingue e linguaggio*, 20(2):199–227.

Aniello De Santo. 2021b. A minimalist approach to facilitatory effects in stacked relative clauses. *Proceedings of the Society for Computation in Linguistics*, 4(1):1–17.

Aniello De Santo and So Young Lee. 2022. Evaluating structural economy claims in relative clause attachment. In *Proceedings of the Society for Computation in Linguistics 2022*, pages 65–75.

Aniello De Santo and Nazila Shafiei. 2019. On the structure of relative clauses in Persian: Evidence from computational modeling and processing effects. In *Talk at the 2nd North American Conference in Iranian Linguistics (NACIL2)*, April 19-21 2019, University of Arizona.

Daniel Del Valle and Aniello De Santo. 2023. Processing french rcs with postverbal subjects in a minimalist parser. *Society for Computation in Linguistics*, 6(1).

Vera Demberg and Frank Keller. 2008. Data from eye-tracking corpora as evidence for theories of syntactic processing complexity. *Cognition*, 109(2):193–210.

Vera Demberg and Frank Keller. 2009. A computational model of prediction in human parsing: Unifying locality and surprisal effects. In *Proceedings of the Annual Meeting of the Cognitive Science Society*, volume 31.

Vera Demberg, Frank Keller, and Alexander Koller. 2013. Incremental, predictive parsing with psycholinguistically motivated tree-adjoining grammar. *Computational Linguistics*, 39(4):1025–1066.

Nick C Ellis. 2002. Frequency effects in language processing: A review with implications for theories of implicit and explicit language acquisition. *Studies in second language acquisition*, 24(2):143–188.

Matteo Fiorini, Jillian Chang, and Aniello De Santo. 2023. An mg parsing view into the processing of subject and object relative clauses in basque. In *Proceedings of the Society for Computation in Linguistics 2023*, pages 145–154.

Jerry A. Fodor and Merrill Garrett. 1967. Some syntactic determinants of sentential complexity. *Perception and Psychophysics*, 2:289–296.

Lyn Frazier and Janet Dean Fodor. 1978. The sausage machine: A new two-stage parsing model. *Cognition*, 6(4):291–325.

Richard Futrell, Edward Gibson, and Roger P Levy. 2020. Lossy-context surprisal: An information-theoretic model of memory effects in sentence processing. *Cognitive science*, 44(3):e12814.

Sabrina Gerth. 2015. *Memory Limitations in Sentence Comprehension: A Structural-based Complexity Metric of Processing Difficulty*, volume 6. Universitätsverlag Potsdam.

E Gibson. 2000. The dependency locality theory: A distance-based theory of linguistic complexity. *Image, Language, Brain*, pages 95–126.

Edward Gibson. 1998. Linguistic complexity: Locality of syntactic dependencies. *Cognition*, 68(1):1–76.

Edward Gibson and H-H Iris Wu. 2013. Processing chinese relative clauses in context. *Language and Cognitive Processes*, 28(1-2):125–155.

Paul Gorrell et al. 1995. *Syntax and parsing*, volume 76. Cambridge University Press Cambridge.

Thomas Graf and Bradley Marcinek. 2014. Evaluating evaluation metrics for minimalist parsing. In *Proceedings of the 2014 ACL Workshop on Cognitive Modeling and Computational Linguistics*, pages 28–36.

Thomas Graf, James Monette, and Chong Zhang. 2017. Relative clauses as a benchmark for Minimalist parsing. volume 5, pages 57–106.

K Gulordava. 2018. Colorless green recurrent networks dream hierarchically. *arXiv preprint arXiv:1803.11138*.

John Hale. 2001. A probabilistic earley parser as a psycholinguistic model. In *Proceedings of the Second Meeting of the North American Chapter of the Association for Computational Linguistics*.

John Hale. 2006. Uncertainty about the rest of the sentence. *Cognitive Science*, 30(4):643–672.

John Hale. 2011. What a rational parser would do. *Cognitive Science*, 35(3):399–443.

John Hale. 2016. Information-theoretical complexity metrics. *Language and Linguistics Compass*, 10(9):397–412.

Henk Harkema. 2001. A characterization of minimalist languages. In *International Conference on Logical Aspects of Computational Linguistics*, pages 193–211. Springer.

Kuan-Jung Huang, Suhas Arehalli, Mari Kugemoto, Christian Muxica, Grusha Prasad, Brian Dillon, and Tal Linzen. 2024. Large-scale benchmark yields no evidence that language model surprisal explains syntactic disambiguation difficulty. *Journal of Memory and Language*, 137:104510.

Tim Hunter. 2019. Left-corner parsing of minimalist grammars. *Minimalist parsing*, pages 125–158.

Tim Hunter and Chris Dyer. 2013. Distributions on minimalist grammar derivations. In *Proceedings of the 13th Meeting on the Mathematics of Language (MoL 13)*, pages 1–11.

Tim Hunter, Milos Stanojevic, and Edward Stabler. 2019. The active-filler strategy in a move-eager left-corner minimalist grammar parser. In *Cognitive Modeling and Computational Linguistics*, pages 1–10. Association for Computational Linguistics.

Kohei Kajikawa, Ryo Yoshida, and Yohei Oseki. 2024. Dissociating syntactic operations via composition count. In *Proceedings of the Annual Meeting of the Cognitive Science Society*, volume 46.

R Kaplan and Joan Bresnan. 1982. Grammars as mental representations of language. *The mental representation of grammatical relations, ed. Bresnan J.. MIT Press.[rEPS]*.

Ronald M Kaplan. 1975. *Transient processing load in relative clauses*. Ph.D. thesis, Harvard University.

Ronald M Kaplan. 2020. Computational psycholinguistics. *Computational linguistics*, 45(4):607–626.

Gregory M Kobele, Sabrina Gerth, and John Hale. 2013. Memory resource allocation in top-down minimalist parsing. In *Formal Grammar*, pages 32–51. Springer.

Gregory M. Kobele, Christian Retoré, and Sylvain Salvati. 2007. An automata-theoretic approach to minimalism. In *Model Theoretic Syntax at 10*, pages 73–82. J. Rogers and S. Kepser.

Elaine Lau and Nozomi Tanaka. 2021. The subject advantage in relative clauses: A review. *Glossa: a journal of general linguistics*, 6(1).

So Young Lee. 2018. A minimalist parsing account of attachment ambiguity in English and Korean. *Journal of Cognitive Science*, 19(3):291–329.

So Young Lee and Aniello De Santo. 2022. A computational view into the structure of attachment ambiguities in chinese and korean. In *Proceedings of NELS*, volume 52.

Roger Levy. 2008. Expectation-based syntactic comprehension. *Cognition*, 106(3):1126–1177.

Roger Levy. 2013. Memory and surprisal in human sentence comprehension. In *Sentence processing*, pages 90–126. Psychology Press.

Richard L Lewis, Shravan Vasishth, and Julie A Van Dyke. 2006. Computational principles of working memory in sentence comprehension. *Trends in cognitive sciences*, 10(10):447–454.

Jixing Li and John Hale. 2019. Grammatical predictors for fmri time-courses. *Minimalist parsing*, pages 159–173.

Lei Liu. 2018. Minimalist Parsing of Heavy NP Shift. In *Proceedings of PACLIC 32 The 32nd Pacific Asia Conference on Language, Information and Computation*, The Hong Kong Polytechnic University, Hong Kong SAR.

Lei Liu. 2024. Psycholinguistic adequacy of left-corner parsing for minimalist grammars. *Proceedings of the Society for Computation in Linguistics (SCiL)*, pages 275–280.

William Marslen-Wilson and Lorraine Komisarjevsky Tyler. 1980. The temporal structure of spoken language understanding. *Cognition*, 8(1):1–71.

Kate McCurdy and Michael Hahn. 2024. Lossy context surprisal predicts task-dependent patterns in relative clause processing. In *Proceedings of the 28th Conference on Computational Natural Language Learning*, pages 36–45.

Jens Michaelis. 1998. Derivational minimalism is mildly context–sensitive. In *International Conference on Logical Aspects of Computational Linguistics*, pages 179–198. Springer.

George A. Miller and Noam Chomsky. 1963. Finitary models of language users. In R. Luce, R. Bush, and E. Galanter, editors, *Handbook of Mathematical Psychology*, volume 2. John Wiley, New York.

Don C Mitchell. 2018. An evaluation of subject-paced reading tasks and other methods for investigating immediate processes in reading 1. In *New methods in reading comprehension research*, pages 69–90. Routledge.

Matthew J Nelson, Imen El Karoui, Kristof Giber, Xiaofang Yang, Laurent Cohen, Hilda Koopman, Sydney S Cash, Lionel Naccache, John T Hale, Christophe Pallier, et al. 2017. Neurophysiological dynamics of phrase-structure building during sentence processing. *Proceedings of the National Academy of Sciences*, 114(18):E3669–E3678.

Byung-Doh Oh, Christian Clark, and William Schuler. 2022. Comparison of structural parsers and neural language models as surprisal estimators. *Frontiers in Artificial Intelligence*, 5:777963.

Satoru Ozaki, Aniello De Santo, Tal Linzen, and Brian Dillon. 2024. Ccg parsing effort and surprisal jointly predict rt but underpredict garden-path effects. *Proceedings of the Society for Computation in Linguistics (SCiL)*, pages 362–364.

Colin Phillips. 2003. Parsing: Psycholinguistic aspects. In *International Encyclopedia of Linguistics*, 2 edition. Oxford University Press.

Grusha Prasad and Tal Linzen. 2024. Spawning structural priming predictions from a cognitively motivated parser. *arXiv preprint arXiv:2403.07202*.

Bradley L Pritchett. 1988. Garden path phenomena and the grammatical basis of language processing. *Language*, pages 539–576.

Steven G Pulman. 1986. Grammars, parsers, and memory limitations. *Language and Cognitive processes*, 1(3):197–225.

Alec Radford, Jeffrey Wu, Rewon Child, David Luan, Dario Amodei, Ilya Sutskever, et al. 2019. Language models are unsupervised multitask learners. *OpenAI blog*, 1(8):9.

Owen Rambow and Aravind K Joshi. 1994. A processing model for free word order languages. *Perspectives on Sentence Processing*.

Philip Resnik. 1992. Left-corner parsing and psychological plausibility. In *COLING 1992 Volume 1: The 14th International Conference on Computational Linguistics*.

Brian Roark, Asaf Bachrach, Carlos Cardenas, and Christophe Pallier. 2009. Deriving lexical and syntactic expectation-based measures for psycholinguistic modeling via incremental top-down parsing. In *Proceedings of the 2009 conference on empirical methods in natural language processing*, pages 324–333.

Elizabeth R Schotter and Brian Dillon. 2025. A beginner's guide to eye tracking for psycholinguistic studies of reading. *Behavior Research Methods*, 57(2):68.

Gideon Schwarz. 1978. Estimating the dimension of a model. *The annals of statistics*, pages 461–464.

Edward P Stabler. 1996. Derivational minimalism. In *International Conference on Logical Aspects of Computational Linguistics*, pages 68–95. Springer.

Edward P Stabler. 2013. Two models of minimalist, incremental syntactic analysis. *Topics in cognitive science*, 5(3):611–633.

Miloš Stanojević, Shohini Bhattasali, Donald Dunagan, Luca Campanelli, Mark Steedman, Jonathan Brennan, and John Hale. 2021. Modeling incremental language comprehension in the brain with combinatory categorial grammar. In *Proceedings of the workshop on cognitive modeling and computational linguistics*, pages 23–38.

Miloš Stanojević, Jonathan R Brennan, Donald Dunagan, Mark Steedman, and John T Hale. 2023. Modeling structure-building in the brain with ccg parsing and large language models. *Cognitive science*, 47(7):e13312.

Adrian Staub. 2010. Eye movements and processing difficulty in object relative clauses. *Cognition*, 116(1):71–86.

Patrick Sturt. 1997. Syntactic reanalysis in human language processing.

Michael K Tanenhaus, Michael J Spivey-Knowlton, Kathleen M Eberhard, and Julie C Sedivy. 1995. Integration of visual and linguistic information in spoken language comprehension. *Science*, 268(5217):1632–1634.

John Torr, Milos Stanojevic, Mark Steedman, and Shay Cohen. 2019. Wide-coverage neural a* parsing for minimalist grammars. In *57th Annual Meeting of the Association for Computational Linguistics*, pages 2486–2505. ACL Anthology.

Matthew J Traxler and Martin J Pickering. 1996. Plausibility and the processing of unbounded dependencies: An eye-tracking study. *Journal of Memory and Language*, 35(3):454–475.

Marten Van Schijndel and Tal Linzen. 2021. Single-stage prediction models do not explain the magnitude of syntactic disambiguation difficulty. *Cognitive science*, 45(6):e12988.

Pranali Vani, Ethan Gotlieb Wilcox, and Roger Levy. 2021. Using the interpolated maze task to assess incremental processing in english relative clauses. In *Proceedings of the annual meeting of the cognitive science society*, volume 43.

Shravan Vasishth. 2006. On the proper treatment of spillover in real-time reading studies: Consequences for psycholinguistic theories. In *Proceedings of the international conference on linguistic evidence*, pages 96–100.

Matthew W Wagers and Colin Phillips. 2009. Multiple dependencies and the role of the grammar in real-time comprehension. *Journal of Linguistics*, 45(2):395–433.

Ethan G Wilcox, Tiago Pimentel, Clara Meister, Ryan Cotterell, and Roger P Levy. 2023. Testing the predictions of surprisal theory in 11 languages. *Transactions of the Association for Computational Linguistics*, 11:1451–1470.

From Punchlines to Predictions: A Metric to Assess LLM Performance in Identifying Humor in Stand-Up Comedy

Adrianna Romanowski
International Christian University
adaromanowski@gmail.com

Pedro H. V. Valois
University of Tsukuba
pedro@cvlab.cs.tsukuba.ac.jp

Kazuhiro Fukui
University of Tsukuba
kfukui@cs.tsukuba.ac.jp

Abstract

Comedy serves as a profound reflection of the times we live in and is a staple element of human interactions. In light of the widespread adoption of Large Language Models (LLMs), the intersection of humor and AI has become no laughing matter. Advancements in the naturalness of human-computer interaction correlates with improvements in AI systems' abilities to understand humor. In this study, we assess the ability of models in accurately identifying humorous quotes from a stand-up comedy transcript. Stand-up comedy's unique comedic narratives make it an ideal dataset to improve the overall naturalness of comedic understanding. We propose a novel humor detection metric designed to evaluate LLMs amongst various prompts on their capability to extract humorous punchlines. The metric has a modular structure that offers three different scoring methods – fuzzy string matching, sentence embedding, and subspace similarity – to provide an overarching assessment of a model's performance. The model's results are compared against those of human evaluators on the same task. Our metric reveals that regardless of prompt engineering, leading models, ChatGPT, Claude, and DeepSeek, achieve scores of at most 51% in humor detection. Notably, this performance surpasses that of humans who achieve a score of 41%. The analysis of human evaluators and LLMs reveals variability in agreement, highlighting the subjectivity inherent in humor and the complexities involved in extracting humorous quotes from live performance transcripts. Code available at https://github.com/swaggirl9000/humor.

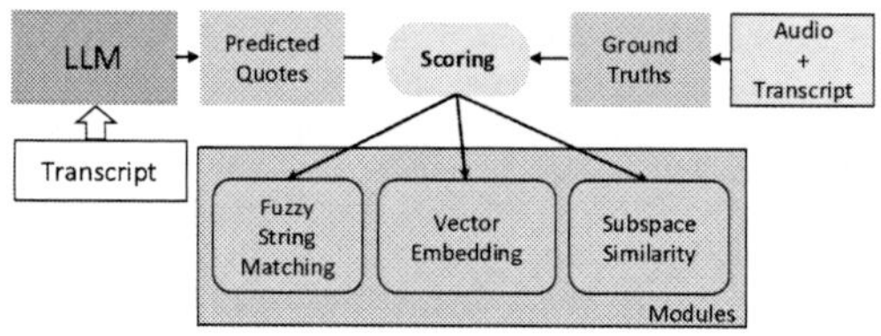

Figure 1: We propose a humor detection metric with three alternative scoring modules – fuzzy string matching, vector embedding, subspace similarity – and integrate them to assess a model's predictions with the ground truth, the stand-up comedy quotes that made the audience laugh.

1 Introduction

Humor plays a significant role in our daily lives and is a fundamental part of human interaction. Despite the rapid advancements in artificial intelligence and human-computer interactions, the field of computational humor lags behind. Improvement in the ability of machines to understand and generate humor has the potential to enhance the naturalness of exchanges with Large Language Models (LLMs). Prior research has demonstrated that humans interact with the personalities of computers similarly to the ways they respond to other humans. As AI systems continue to integrate into e-commerce, virtual reality, and take on personal assistant roles, the necessity for these systems to exhibit a certain level of social intelligence, which goes hand-in-hand with humor, becomes essential (Binsted et al., 2006).

The tasks of humor detection, evaluation, and generation are consistently a challenge for AI due to humor's reliance on irony, sarcasm, and cultural nuances. Research shows that models trained on diverse datasets, ranging from humorous tweets to funny news headlines to puns, can achieve strong performance on tasks. However, they often struggle with out-of-domain scenarios (Baranov et al., 2023) and tend to over rely on stylistic features such as punctuation and question words, rather than a deep semantic understanding (Lima Inácio et al., 2023).

Traditionally, research on humor detection was approached through binary classification tasks, using standalone jokes (Mihalcea and Strapparava, 2005) or occasional jokes within longer presentations (Hasan et al., 2019). In this paper, we propose

Proceedings of the Workshop on Cognitive Modeling and Computational Linguistics, pages 36–46
May 3, 2025 ©2025 Association for Computational Linguistics

a shift towards using datasets that capture humor within a narrative structure, specifically focusing on stand-up comedy transcripts for humor detection (Mittal et al., 2021; Turano and Strapparava, 2022). Stand-up comedy is a performance where comedians deliver jokes and funny monologues directly to a live audience. Regardless of the diversity in comedic styles, the overarching goal of any comedian remains consistent – to maximize audience laughter – creating a valuable resource for the perception of everyday humor (Daboin, 2022). In essence, stand-up comedy serves as both a data source and a pedagogical example for teaching AI the mechanics of humor, especially when the goal is to improve a model's ability to communicate in a way that feels intuitive and relatable to humans.

LLMs demonstrate notable proficiency across a broad spectrum of tasks, but their performance can fluctuate based on the task's nature. By developing a task-specific metric that focuses on humor detection, we offer a means of evaluation for a nuanced domain like comedy. The simplest method for measuring the capability of a model would be by counting the number of perfect matches. Taking subjectivity into consideration, it is unreasonable to expect perfection, even for humans. Thus, we offer a metric that provides a fair quantitative assessment that encompasses the subjectivity of humor with the probabilistic nature of LLMs.

Following Figure 1, our metric assesses a model's performance in humor detection in zero-shot prompting scenarios by comparing the similarity of predicted humorous quotes against the ground truth – the punchlines that elicited laughter from the audience. The model operates in a zero-shot setting, meaning it is not provided with examples or prior instructions before prompting. The metric offers a modularized approach with three different ways to output a score.

First, the most straightforward approach uses fuzzy string matching to compare the similarity of two lists of strings (Snasel et al., 2009), where each list consists of humorous quotes from a stand-up comedian's transcript. However, this quick, efficient method does not account for semantics and context, making it too punitive if a model makes a slight mistake when providing the quote.

Second, the vector embedding module captures semantic similarity between the vector representations of sentences, facilitating a more flexible assessment that emphasizes the underlying meanings of quotes rather than a strict word-for-word correspondence. (Reimers and Gurevych, 2019).

Third, while fuzzy string matching and vector similarities offer focused insights on a task, the last module provides a score that reflects the overall capability of a model in humor detection tasks using subspace representations. A subspace is generated for the model after it is prompted with several variations of an instruction and another subspace is generated for the ground truth. The alignment between these two subspaces reflects the structural similarity between the model's outputs and the ground truth for the transcript in a more general way.

By proposing three distinct scoring modules for assessment, our metric acknowledges the subjectivity of the task, granting the evaluator the flexibility to decide how punitive they want to be towards a model's responses. Fuzzy string matching offers a direct evaluation focusing on precision. Whereas, sentence embeddings are particularly useful when the model generates both a quote and accompanying explanation, allowing for an evaluation of contextual understanding and semantics. Subspaces introduce a novel approach that captures a model's overall ability, considering multiple possible responses for the task in a single score. Balancing these methods gives a well-rounded view of performance, ensuring that both accuracy and deeper semantic understanding are taken into account.

We employ this metric to evaluate the efficacy of several different prompts and various language models. Additionally, we conduct a human evaluation on the same dataset to provide a reliable comparison for model performance. The human-based assessment accounts for the inherent subjectivity of humor, offering a reliable context to gauge the relative performance of the problem at hand.

The main contributions of this paper are:

1. Introduce a flexible metric that is designed to consider the subjectivity of humor detection tasks, providing a fair measure for the performance of LLMs;
2. Assess the metric across various models and multiple prompt variations, applied to stand-up comedy transcripts;
3. Provide a quantitative assessment of human performance on the same humor detection task, alongside a calculation of agreement ratios between human and LLM-based humor detection, offering a basis for comparison.

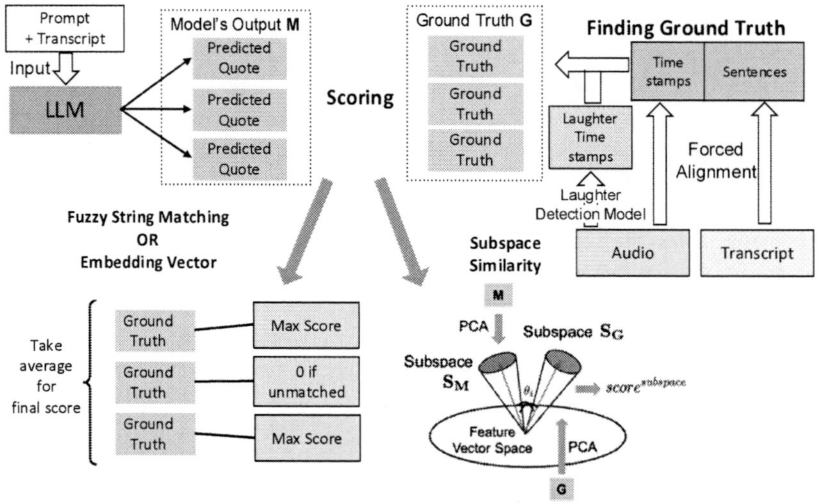

Figure 2: The humor detection metric evaluates a model's ability to identify funny quotes by comparing its outputs against the ground truth found through forced alignment and laughter detection. The metric offers three alternative scoring modules: 1) fuzzy string matching that assigns a score based on text similarity, 2) vector embeddings that compare semantic similarities, and 3) subspace similarity that analyzes the underlying patterns of a model on the task. Fuzzy string matching and the vector embedding modules operate under a similar scoring procedure, where the predicted quote is matched with ground truth quotes and assigned a similarity score, with unmatched quotes receiving a score of 0, and the average representing the final score. We integrate the metrics to assess a model's predictions with the the stand-up comedy quotes that made the audience laugh. Only one of these three modules is selected and used to generate the final metric score for evaluation.

2 Related Work

2.1 Computational Humor and Humor Theory

Humor is a widely recognized but conceptually complex phenomenon, with psychologists disagreeing on its precise definition. It encompasses three distinct constructs: sense of humor (an individual's tendency to laugh or amuse others), comedy (a stimulus that elicits laughter and amusement), and humor appreciation (the psychological response to humor). Collectively, these constructs form what we refer to as humor. Additionally, some researched describe humor as a subjective psychological reaction to comedic stimuli (Warren et al., 2021). Through a linguistic lens, three widely recognized theories explain the phenomena of humor: the Superiority Theory, humor arises from feeling superior to others; the Relief Theory, humor releases psychological tension; and the Incongruity Theory, humor stems from the sudden violation of expectations (Morreall, 2020). A common task in computational humor is humor detection, identifying whether a given text or media is intended to be funny. Bertero and Fung (2016) explore various classification algorithms to detect punchlines in the TV sitcom *The Big Bang Theory* and Purandare and Litman (2006) examine humor recognition in the TV show *Friends*, employing acoustic-prosodic and linguistic features for analysis. However, both studies rely on artificial laughter rather than authentic audience reactions. Platow et al. (2005) argues that canned laughter functions as a prompt to engage viewers and bolster weaker jokes, while real audience laughter serves as a more reliable indicator of natural humor, providing an accurate reflection of comedic effectiveness. The UR-FUNNY dataset avoids artificial laughter by using TED talks in order to provide an authentic representation of humor (Hasan et al., 2019). Stand-up comedy, with its immediate audience feedback, offers a unique advantage for humor research, as it mirrors the Incongruity Theory where comedians create an expectation through a set-up and subvert it with the punchline (Amin and Burghardt, 2020). Mittal et al. (2021)'s Open Mic dataset of stand-up performances was used to train models to assign a "funniness" score to script segments validated by human annotators.

2.2 LLM's in Humor Detection

In computational humor, there is a growing interest in evaluating the humor detection capabilities of LLMs. Research in this area has explored the ability of a model to assess the funniness of jokes, with findings indicating that ChatGPT can recognize humor when prompted, though its evaluation was limited to a set of top jokes (Jentzsch and Kersting, 2023). Subsequent tests with a larger set of comedic content showed that zero-shot prompting resulted in ChatGPT's humor ratings closely aligning with those of human evaluators (Góes et al., 2023). Baranov et al. (2023) examined humor detection across various comedic datasets using both fine-tuned models and two LLMs, ChatGPT and Flan-UL2, as zero-shot classifiers. While these models achieved high results, they did not outperform fine-tuned models. Crowd Score was introduced to classify jokes using LLMs as AI judges, by providing a personality profile with zero-shot prompting (Goes et al., 2022). To the best of our knowledge, there has been no research focusing on statistical metrics for evaluating the accuracy of zero-shot settings in LLMs for detecting humor.

2.3 Subspaces in NLP

Using word subspaces for text representation and the mutual subspace method framework for text classification extends on using word embeddings like word2vec (Shimomoto et al., 2018). While embeddings represent word semantics as vectors, word subspaces capture the intrinsic variability of features in a set of word vectors in order to preserve semantic relationships. Subspace representations leverage the geometric structure of embeddings to address the challenge of effective text classification with limited training data (Shimomoto et al., 2024).

3 Methodology

In this section, we will explain our proposed metric and its mathematical details. It is crucial to consider a metric that can evaluate the model's understanding of what makes a text humorous, despite the broad and subjective nature of humor.

3.1 Humor Detection Metric

Our metric utilizes three alternative approaches for scoring that capture the similarity of the model's answers to the ground truth. As shown in Figure 2, the model's score is computed in the following:

1. The model is prompted to extract humorous quotes from a stand-up comedian's transcript. These quotes are stored as a list of strings, with $M = \{m_1, \ldots, m_n\}$ being the set of quotes predicted to be funny by the model for a specific transcript.

2. The ground truth is determined from the transcript using a laughter detection model (Gillick, 2017) that extracts laughter time stamps from the accompanying audio recording (Mittal et al., 2021). Forced alignment allows for a mapping between sentences in the transcript and laughter time frames. Thus, let $G = \{g_1, \ldots, g_k\}$ be the set of ground truths for the same transcript.

3. We calculate how close M is to G by offering a scoring module that allows for the use of either fuzzy string matching, sentence embeddings, or subspace similarity.

The following contain explanations of each scoring module.

3.2 Fuzzy String Matching Module

Fuzzy string matching provides a straightforward approach for comparing text using Levenshtein distance (Levenshtein, 1966). For a given transcript, a similarity score, s^{fuzzy}, between every model output and ground truth is stored in a similarity matrix $\mathbf{S}^{fuzzy} \in [0, 1]^{n \times k}$:

$$\mathbf{S}_{ij}^{fuzzy} = \mathrm{s}^{fuzzy}(m_i, g_j). \tag{1}$$

Ideally, it is clear that the perfect score resembles an identity matrix, but in practice a ground truth can be matched with more than one prediction or to none. Therefore, the highest similarity score is selected for each ground truth to form a matrix that holds the best matches. In order to find the closest match, the maximum value is taken:

$$t_j = \max_{m_i \in M} \mathbf{S}_{ij}^{fuzzy}. \tag{2}$$

Notice that if a ground truth was not matched to any model output, t_j is automatically assigned a score of 0. In the case of overgenerating quotes, which can be used as a tactic to exploit the metric, a penalty p is applied if the number of predictions n exceeds the number of ground truths k:

$$p = \max(n - k, 0). \tag{3}$$

The final score is adjusted with the penalty and a scaling factor, $\alpha = 0.1$, and the average score is computed for the transcript:

$$score^{fuzzy} = \max\left(\frac{1}{k}\sum_{j=1}^{k} t_j - \alpha p, 0\right). \quad (4)$$

3.3 Vector Embedding Module

In the second module, we switch to using sentence embeddings that better reflect context and meaning. In some cases, LLMs may generate non-compliant responses in which the output would be an explanation of the humor rather than a direct quote. Since fuzzy string matching purely focuses on character-level changes, like insertions or deletions, it fails to capture the semantic nuances, and therefore would heavily penalize the model's predictions. Yuan et al. (2021) introduced BARTSCORE, a metric to evaluate the accuracy and effectiveness of generated text using BART, an encoder-decoder based model. We take a similar approach by using an embedding model from Sentence Transformers (Reimers and Gurevych, 2019), to apply a more flexible measure of similarity emphasizing the essence of a text.

The similarity score, s^{embed}, is now calculated using vectors of the quotes from M and G:

$$\mathbf{S}_{ij}^{embed} = s^{embed}(\mathbf{m}_i, \mathbf{g}_j), \quad (5)$$

where $\mathbf{m}_i$ and $\mathbf{g}_j$ are the vector representations of the model's predicted quote and ground truth quote that are currently being evaluated. The penalty and average are handled the same way as in the fuzzy string matching module to produce $score^{embed}$.

3.4 Subspace Similarity Module

Fuzzy string matching and sentence embeddings allow us to evaluate each LLM from its output strings, but we can also conduct a deeper analysis by evaluating the LLMs feature vector space directly. With that in mind, we leverage the structural similarity between two subspaces (Fukui and Maki, 2015) that can take into account the structure of the LLM feature vectors using multiple variations of instructions as input and the accompanying output for a transcript. Let $\mathbf{M} = \begin{bmatrix}\mathbf{m}_1 & \mathbf{m}_2 & \dots & \mathbf{m}_n\end{bmatrix}$ represent the collection of model outputs and $\mathbf{G} = \begin{bmatrix}\mathbf{g}_1 & \mathbf{g}_2 & \dots & \mathbf{g}_k\end{bmatrix}$ represent the ground truths for each variation of instruction for a transcript. By applying PCA to the set of vectors, $\mathbf{M}$ and $\mathbf{G}$, respectively, we obtain the bases, $\mathbf{S_M}$ and $\mathbf{S_G} \in \mathbb{R}^{d \times q}$ of subspaces, $\mathcal{S}_M$ and $\mathcal{S}_G$, where d is the dimension of the feature vectors and q is the dimension of the subspaces. We calculate the SVD, $\mathbf{S_M}^\top \mathbf{S_G} = \mathbf{U}\Sigma\mathbf{V}^\top$, where $diag(\Sigma) = (\kappa_1, \dots, \kappa_q)$, $\kappa_1 \geq \dots \geq \kappa_q$, represents the set of singular values, which are the cosines of the canonical angles θ_i. The similarity can then be defined

$$score^{subspace} = \frac{1}{r}\sum_{i=1}^{r} \kappa_i^2, \quad (6)$$

where r is the number of canonical angles used for score calculation.

By using subspaces, our metric allows us to simulate variations of the prompt while reducing penalization for minor variations, offering a comprehensive reflection of the model's performance.

4 Experiments

In this section, we evaluate several LLMs using the proposed metric, apply prompt engineering techniques to optimize model performance, and conduct a human-machine agreement task.

4.1 Experimental Settings

We use the Open Mic dataset (Mittal et al., 2021), which provides both audio and transcripts for several stand-up performances. To create a fair comparison, we randomly selected 51 transcripts with an average word length of 270 words and length of 106 seconds. We prompt each model with a transcript and the following instruction:

Prompt 1 (Standard Humor Detection Prompt) *Extract the key humorous lines and punchlines for this stand-up comedy transcript. Focus on the quotes highlighting the main comedic moments. List of quotes:*

The model outputs a list of quotes that it found humorous. All experiments ran in less than a day.

4.2 Model Comparison

We evaluate various models using Prompt 1 to gain deeper insight into our metric's assessments and explore the ability of LLMs in detecting humor. We use the instruct versions of Google's Gemma with 2-billion parameters, Google's Gemma 2 with 9-billion parameters, Meta's Llama 3.1 with 8-billion parameters, and Microsoft's Phi 3-Mini with 3.8-billion parameters. We continue experimentation with OpenAI's ChatGPT-4o, Anthropic's Claude

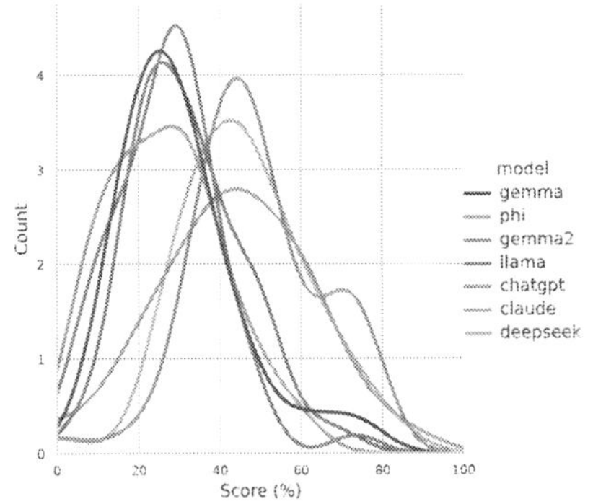

Figure 3: Distribution of scores with fuzzy string matching across several LLMs among 51 transcripts.

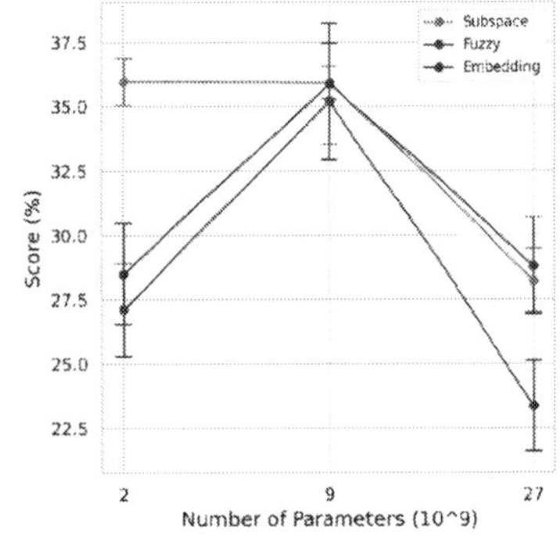

Figure 4: Evaluation of the Gemma 2-it family among model sizes using all three modules.

Model	Fuzzy	Embed	Sub
Gemma 2b-it	30.1	30.0	55.7
Gemma 2 9b-it	35.2	35.9	35.9
Phi 3-Mini 3.8b-it	26.4	25.8	33.6
Llama 3 8b-it	31.9	33.8	38.4
ChatGPT-4o	48.9	25.4	–
Claude 3.5 Sonnet	43.4	46.9	–
DeepSeek-V3	46	51.6	–

Table 1: Scores (%) across models against all three metric modules using 51 transcripts.

3.5 Sonnet [1], and DeepSeek-V3 [2] known for their advanced ability to engage in human-like interactions. These models have been employed in various studies, particularly in joke detection, generation, and evaluation using many-shot prompting (Jentzsch and Kersting, 2023; DeepSeek-AI et al., 2024). Figure 3 shows the average scores for each model found with fuzzy string matching and Table 1 shows results with all modules. Interestingly, ChatGPT performs well using fuzzy string matching but exhibits a significant decline in performance with semantic similarity metrics. This discrepancy suggests that while ChatGPT excels in identifying quotes with high lexical similarity, it struggles to capture deeper semantic relationships.

Given Gemma 2's high performance, we further evaluate the model across varying model sizes among all scoring modules. The results in Figure 4 suggest a potential relationship between the nature of the task and the architecture of the model. In general, models with higher parameter configurations tend to succeed in logical tasks, as opposed to subjective tasks (Chen and Varoquaux, 2024). Additionally, the 27-b parameter model exhibited more instances of misaligned outputs to the prompt, where it not only listed a quote but provided an explanation of why the quote was funny. Thus, this difficulty of capturing humor's nuances may account for the model's low scores.

4.3 Prompt Engineering

A model's performance on a task can be heavily dependent on the input they receive. Prompt engineering focuses on crafting inputs to elicit a desired response. For humor detection, we focus on maximizing the model's ability to retrieve humorous quotes and measure the performance throughout various prompt designs. All evaluations were done using the fuzzy string matching module.

In order to generate a list of prompts, we provided ChatGPT with a transcript and ground truth and asked, *"If I wanted a model to extract this list of quotes from the following stand-up comedy transcript, what would the best instruction be?"*. The results are shown at Prompts 2, 3 and 4.

Prompt 2 *When performed in front of a live audience, which jokes do you think made the audience laugh?*

Prompt 3 *What are the funniest punchlines from the transcript?*

Prompt 4 *Analyze the transcript and extract the quotes that are most likely to have made the audience laugh.*

An assessment of Gemma 2b-instruct can be seen in Table 2. Prompt 2 received the highest score and the remaining prompts had no positive change in performance.

[1]Experiments were conducted in December 2024

[2]Experiment was conducted in January 2025

A popular technique for prompt engineering is *The Persona Pattern*, where the model is given a role that guides it into focusing on specific details when generating an output (White et al., 2023). We sought to examine how the scores of Gemma 2b-instruct would be affected across personas. First, the model was assigned three distinct roles: a comedian, a comedy fan, and a comedy critic. The same instructional prompt (5) was employed across all roles. Table 2 indicates that personas do not make relevant changes to the scores.

Prompt 5 (Persona Pattern Prompt) *Pretend that you are a [insert role] reading the following stand-up comedy transcript.*

Although previous persona adoption showed no improvement, Goes et al. (2022)'s success in evaluating jokes with roles that specialize in categories of humor inspired a similar approach in this study. We instructed Gemma 2 9b-instruct to embody an individual who enjoys a specific type of humor following the template at Prompt 6. However, as seen in Table 3, the prompt with no specialization received the highest score, suggesting that humor-specialized prompts do not enhance performance.

Prompt 6 (Humor Preference Prompt) *You are a person who enjoys [insert humor type] humor.*

We prompt the model with the comedian whose transcript it was analyzing. This was implemented using Gemma 2b-instruct and ChatGPT-4o, which has previously showed the capability for celebrity impersonation (Yokoyama et al., 2024). Despite earlier success in mimicking famous individuals, Table 4 shows no improvements in humor detection, despite the comedians being quite well known.

Prompt 7 (Audience Demographic Prompt) *Pretend you are a [insert gender/race/age].*

Prompt engineering has been used to target specific audience demographics (Choi et al., 2024). In this study, we assign Gemma 2 with varying race, ages, and gender to investigate if scores change based on demographics. We assign a race of either Caucasian/White, Black/African American, Hispanic/Latino, or Asian. We chose the age ranges of teenager (13-18 years), young adult (18-34 years), adult (35-64 years), and elderly (65+). Lastly, we use a female or male persona. In Table 5, no specific demographic yields improvement compared to the baseline, but the young adult persona resulted in the closest performance, suggesting a marginal alignment with the model's inherent capabilities.

Prompt Engineering			
Original	Prompt 1	Prompt 2	Prompt 3
30.1%	27.4%	31.2%	28%
Persona Prompts			
Original	Comedian	Fan	Critic
30.1%	28.7%	27.9%	30.5%

Table 2: Average scores found using fuzzy string module for prompt engineering for Gemma 2b-instruct.

Humor Type Prompt			
Original	Aggressive	Dark	Deprecating
35.2%	32.7%	31.2%	32.0%

Table 3: Average scores found using fuzzy string module for different humor types as personas for Gemma 2 9b-instruct.

Stand-up Comedian Persona		
	ChatGPT-4o	Gemma 2b-instruct
Original	50.3%	27.1%
Persona	45.2%	26.0%

Table 4: Prompt engineering average scores using fuzzy string module for ChatGPT-4o and Gemma 2b-instruct when taking the role of the comedian whose transcript it was analyzing.

4.4 Human-Machine Agreement

Human evaluation remains one of the most valuable methods for assessing LLM performance, especially when examining a subjective output like humor. Thus, we asked 11 participants to perform the same task as the models on 6 transcripts from well-known comedians. The evaluators were naive raters across various cultural backgrounds, all within an age range of 20 to 30 years.

Following the approach of Hada et al. (2024), we compute the agreement between evaluators using Percentage Agreement (PA). Each person received the 6 transcripts, split into sentences, and was asked to mark each as funny or not. The scores in Table 7 indicate that humans achieved a relatively high PA across all transcripts, with an average of 86.7%. Even though participants were generally able to identify the same quotes, the absence of a perfect consensus emphasizes the subjectivity of the task. It is important to note that the PA could be

Race				
None	White	Black	Hispanic	Asian
35.2%	31.1%	28.7%	30%	26.9%

Age				
None	Teen	YA	Adult	Elderly
35.2%	32.8%	34.2%	31.7%	28.7%

Gender		
None	Woman	Man
35.2%	31.9%	33.3%

Table 5: Average scores found using fuzzy string module for audience demographic prompt for Gemma 2b-instruct.

Model	%
Gemma 2b-instruct	68.8
Gemma 2 9b-instruct	68.8
Llama 3 8b-instruct	61.1
Phi3-Mini 3.8b-instruct	66.9
ChatGPT-4o	28.7
Claude 3.5 Sonnet	65.0
DeepSeek-V3	58.9
Average	59.9

Table 6: Agreement scores between human evaluators and LLMs.

influenced by similar age ranges, leading to shared cultural references and senses of humor, potentially narrowing the diversity of interpretations.

We use the fuzzy string matching module to evaluate human answers against the ground truth. This revealed that humans receive a score of 40.7%. Interestingly, leading models ChatGPT, Claude, and DeepSeek, when measured with the same module, outperform humans. This disparity may arise because LLMs are inherently optimized for text-based tasks, focusing on linguistic and semantic cues without needing situational context. Mohamed and Bnini (2020) argues that humor in stand-up comedy often stems from incongruity, relying less on a performer's stage persona and more on linguistic mechanisms. In the absence of theatrical embellishments, models excel at language-centric tasks and are particularly adept at identifying puns and wordplay. In contrast, humans often rely on elements such as delivery, tone, and audience reactions, which are absent in written transcripts, potentially limiting their ability on the task. We hypothesize that the scores for humans may differ if the evaluators were tasked with focusing on textual properties rather than general context.

Transcript	%
Ali Wong	83.7
Anthony Jeselnik	90.1
Hasan Minhaj	85.4
Jimmy Yang	87.0
Joe List	88.5
John Mulaney	85.7
Average	86.7

Table 7: Agreement scores between the human evaluators on a specific comedian's transcript.

The human-machine agreement rate between each model and humans was found with PA. For humans, a quote was funny if majority of raters voted on it. The scores can be found in Table 6.

Gemma 1 and 2 have the highest agreement rates, meaning that humans and these models agreed most on the funniness of a quote. The average agreement rate reaches 59.9%, suggesting that while there is a notable level of alignment in humor detection, pinpointing the same quotes proves to be difficult. It is interesting to note that Gemma 2 and humans received similar scores with the metric's evaluation, suggesting a high level of similarity in how the model and humans assessed humor in a text-based format. Despite receiving a high score with the metric, ChatGPT has the lowest agreement rate, demonstrating that the agreement rate and metric scores do not have to match. ChatGPT's ability surpassing humans on the task is unrelated to the agreement rate.

5 Conclusion

In this work, we introduce a novel humor detection metric designed to score a model's output in relation to the ground truth of a text. The metric uses a scoring module in which the model can be evaluated using fuzzy string matching, sentence embeddings, or subspace similarity. We use a stand-up comedy dataset that offers unique narratives crafted with punchlines to maximize audience laughter. The ground truth is derived from laughter during the performance in which the entire atmosphere is conducive to comedy, emphasizing the limitations of text-based analysis. The task of identifying humor in a transcript appears to be a challenge, with even leading models, such as ChatGPT, Claude, and DeepSeek, barely receiving scores over 50%.

However, this difficulty is also evident among humans, who only received a score of 40.7% when assessed with the metric, revealing that leading models can outperform humans on the task.

In the future, we aim to apply the metric to evaluate a model's predicted quotes in a format distinct from text. Stand-up comedy is heavily influenced by elements not captured in written transcripts. We hypothesize that if a model were to extract quotes from a performance with muted laughter, the nature of the output would differ substantially. Moreover, this approach raises questions about the perception of humor among humans when they view stand-up without background laughter. By exploring live comedy performances, we hope to deploy our metric for humor detection on stand-up comedy videos.

6 Limitations

This study presents some limitations regarding the calculation of ground truth and the nature of humor analysis. First, the ground truth is derived from audio recordings where laughter is marked using timestamps. Since we assume that the sentence preceding the laughter is the humorous one, there is a possibility that the most humorous part of the joke was not accurately captured. Although we accounted for potential delays in laughter, some reactions may have been misattributed. Second, the ground truth does not differentiate between varying magnitudes of laughter. We used a laughter detection model with a minimum laughter length of 0.2 seconds and a minimum probability threshold of 0.5 (default values) (Gillick, 2017), which may have resulted in some laughter being missed. Thus, jokes that elicited subtler audience reactions might not have been accounted for. Lastly, our study relies on a text-based analysis of humor, which is a clear limitation when evaluating performances originally designed for live delivery. Future research could explore how incorporating non-textual elements—such as tone, timing, and body language—affects humor perception for both human evaluators and language models.

7 Ethical Statement

In this work, we use stand-up comedy audio recordings and transcripts, which may contain humor that some may find offensive or politically incorrect. The content was analyzed solely for research purposes, without endorsement of any particular viewpoint.

Acknowledgement

This work was supported by JSPS KAKENHI Grant Number JP23K28117.

References

Miriam Amin and Manuel Burghardt. 2020. A survey on approaches to computational humor generation. In *Proceedings of the 4th Joint SIGHUM Workshop on Computational Linguistics for Cultural Heritage, Social Sciences, Humanities and Literature*, pages 29–41, Online. International Committee on Computational Linguistics.

Alexander Baranov, Vladimir Kniazhevsky, and Pavel Braslavski. 2023. You told me that joke twice: A systematic investigation of transferability and robustness of humor detection models. In *Proceedings of the 2023 Conference on Empirical Methods in Natural Language Processing*, pages 13701–13715, Singapore. Association for Computational Linguistics.

Dario Bertero and Pascale Fung. 2016. Deep learning of audio and language features for humor prediction. In *Proceedings of the Tenth International Conference on Language Resources and Evaluation (LREC'16)*, pages 496–501, Portorož, Slovenia. European Language Resources Association (ELRA).

K. Binsted, A. Nijholt, O. Stock, C. Strapparava, G. Ritchie, R. Manurung, H. Pain, A. Waller, and D. O'Mara. 2006. Computational humor. *IEEE Intelligent Systems*, 21(2):59–69.

Lihu Chen and Gaël Varoquaux. 2024. What is the role of small models in the llm era: A survey. *Preprint*, arXiv:2409.06857.

Yoonseo Choi, Eun Jeong Kang, Seulgi Choi, Min Kyung Lee, and Juho Kim. 2024. Proxona: Leveraging llm-driven personas to enhance creators' understanding of their audience. *Preprint*, arXiv:2408.10937.

Alan Daboin. 2022. What's the deal with standup comedy? In *Aesthetic Literacy vol I: a book for everyone.*, pages 128–140. Mont Publishing House.

DeepSeek-AI, Aixin Liu, Bei Feng, Bing Xue, Bingxuan Wang, Bochao Wu, Chengda Lu, Chenggang Zhao, Chengqi Deng, Chenyu Zhang, Chong Ruan, Damai Dai, Daya Guo, Dejian Yang, Deli Chen, Dongjie Ji, Erhang Li, Fangyun Lin, Fucong Dai, Fuli Luo, Guangbo Hao, Guanting Chen, Guowei Li, H. Zhang, Han Bao, Hanwei Xu, Haocheng Wang, Haowei Zhang, Honghui Ding, Huajian Xin, Huazuo Gao, Hui Li, Hui Qu, J. L. Cai, Jian Liang, Jianzhong Guo, Jiaqi Ni, Jiashi Li, Jiawei Wang, Jin Chen, Jingchang Chen, Jingyang Yuan, Junjie Qiu, Junlong Li, Junxiao Song, Kai Dong, Kai Hu, Kaige Gao, Kang Guan, Kexin Huang, Kuai Yu, Lean Wang, Lecong Zhang, Lei Xu, Leyi Xia, Liang Zhao, Litong Wang, Liyue Zhang, Meng Li, Miaojun Wang, Mingchuan Zhang, Minghua Zhang, Minghui Tang, Mingming Li, Ning Tian, Panpan Huang, Peiyi Wang, Peng Zhang, Qiancheng Wang, Qihao Zhu, Qinyu Chen, Qiushi Du, R. J. Chen, R. L. Jin, Ruiqi Ge, Ruisong Zhang, Ruizhe Pan, Runji Wang, Runxin Xu, Ruoyu Zhang, Ruyi Chen, S. S. Li, Shanghao Lu, Shangyan Zhou, Shanhuang Chen, Shaoqing Wu, Shengfeng Ye, Shengfeng Ye, Shirong Ma, Shiyu Wang, Shuang Zhou, Shuiping Yu, Shunfeng Zhou, Shuting Pan, T. Wang, Tao Yun, Tian Pei, Tianyu Sun, W. L. Xiao, Wangding Zeng,

Wanjia Zhao, Wei An, Wen Liu, Wenfeng Liang, Wenjun Gao, Wenqin Yu, Wentao Zhang, X. Q. Li, Xiangyue Jin, Xianzu Wang, Xiao Bi, Xiaodong Liu, Xiaohan Wang, Xiaojin Shen, Xiaokang Chen, Xiaokang Zhang, Xiaosha Chen, Xiaotao Nie, Xiaowen Sun, Xiaoxiang Wang, Xin Cheng, Xin Liu, Xin Xie, Xingchao Liu, Xingkai Yu, Xinnan Song, Xinxia Shan, Xinyi Zhou, Xinyu Yang, Xinyuan Li, Xuecheng Su, Xuheng Lin, Y. K. Li, Y. Q. Wang, Y. X. Wei, Y. X. Zhu, Yang Zhang, Yanhong Xu, Yanhong Xu, Yanping Huang, Yao Li, Yao Zhao, Yaofeng Sun, Yaohui Li, Yaohui Wang, Yi Yu, Yi Zheng, Yichao Zhang, Yifan Shi, Yiliang Xiong, Ying He, Ying Tang, Yishi Piao, Yisong Wang, Yixuan Tan, Yiyang Ma, Yiyuan Liu, Yongqiang Guo, Yu Wu, Yuan Ou, Yuchen Zhu, Yuduan Wang, Yue Gong, Yuheng Zou, Yujia He, Yukun Zha, Yunfan Xiong, Yunxian Ma, Yuting Yan, Yuxiang Luo, Yuxiang You, Yuxuan Liu, Yuyang Zhou, Z. F. Wu, Z. Z. Ren, Zehui Ren, Zhangli Sha, Zhe Fu, Zhean Xu, Zhen Huang, Zhen Zhang, Zhenda Xie, Zhengyan Zhang, Zhewen Hao, Zhibin Gou, Zhicheng Ma, Zhigang Yan, Zhihong Shao, Zhipeng Xu, Zhiyu Wu, Zhongyu Zhang, Zhuoshu Li, Zihui Gu, Zijia Zhu, Zijun Liu, Zilin Li, Ziwei Xie, Ziyang Song, Ziyi Gao, and Zizheng Pan. 2024. Deepseek-v3 technical report. *Preprint*, arXiv:2412.19437.

Kazuhiro Fukui and Atsuto Maki. 2015. Difference subspace and its generalization for subspace-based methods. *IEEE Transactions on Pattern Analysis and Machine Intelligence*, 37(11):2164–2177.

Jonathan Gillick. 2017. Laughter detection. `https://github.com/jrgillick/laughter-detection`. Accessed: 2024-09-26.

Fabricio Goes, Zisen Zhou, Piotr Sawicki, Marek Grzes, and Daniel G. Brown. 2022. Crowd score: A method for the evaluation of jokes using large language model ai voters as judges. *Preprint*, arXiv:2212.11214.

Luis Fabricio Góes, Piotr Sawicki, Marek Grzes, Dan Brown, and Marco Volpe. 2023. Is GPT-4 Good Enough to Evaluate Jokes?

Rishav Hada, Varun Gumma, Adrian de Wynter, Harshita Diddee, Mohamed Ahmed, Monojit Choudhury, Kalika Bali, and Sunayana Sitaram. 2024. Are large language model-based evaluators the solution to scaling up multilingual evaluation? *Preprint*, arXiv:2309.07462.

Md Kamrul Hasan, Wasifur Rahman, AmirAli Bagher Zadeh, Jianyuan Zhong, Md Iftekhar Tanveer, Louis-Philippe Morency, and Mohammed (Ehsan) Hoque. 2019. Ur-funny: A multimodal language dataset for understanding humor. In *Proceedings of the 2019 Conference on Empirical Methods in Natural Language Processing and the 9th International Joint Conference on Natural Language Processing (EMNLP-IJCNLP)*. Association for Computational Linguistics.

Sophie Jentzsch and Kristian Kersting. 2023. Chatgpt is fun, but it is not funny! humor is still challenging large language models. *Preprint*, arXiv:2306.04563.

V. I. Levenshtein. 1966. Binary Codes Capable of Correcting Deletions, Insertions and Reversals. *Soviet Physics Doklady*, 10:707.

Marcio Lima Inácio, Gabriela Wick-pedro, and Hugo Goncalo Oliveira. 2023. What do humor classifiers learn? an attempt to explain humor recognition models. In *Proceedings of the 7th Joint SIGHUM Workshop on Computational Linguistics for Cultural Heritage, Social Sciences, Humanities and Literature*, pages 88–98, Dubrovnik, Croatia. Association for Computational Linguistics.

Rada Mihalcea and Carlo Strapparava. 2005. Making computers laugh: Investigations in automatic humor recognition. In *Proceedings of Human Language Technology Conference and Conference on Empirical Methods in Natural Language Processing*, pages 531–538, Vancouver, British Columbia, Canada. Association for Computational Linguistics.

Anirudh Mittal, Pranav Jeevan, Prerak Gandhi, Diptesh Kanojia, and Pushpak Bhattacharyya. 2021. "so you think you're funny?": Rating the humour quotient in standup comedy. *Preprint*, arXiv:2110.12765.

B. Mohamed and C. Bnini. 2020. Analyzing the incongruity theory of humor: George carlin's stand-up comedy as a case study. *International Journal of Sciences: Basic and Applied Research (IJSBAR)*, 54(5):22–33.

John Morreall. 2020. Philosophy of humor. In *The Stanford Encyclopedia of Philosophy*, fall 2020 edition. Metaphysics Research Lab, Stanford University.

Michael J. Platow, S. Alexander Haslam, Amanda Both, Ivanne Chew, Michelle Cuddon, Nahal Goharpey, Jacqui Maurer, Simone Rosini, Anna Tsekouras, and Diana M. Grace. 2005. "it's not funny if they're laughing": Self-categorization, social influence, and responses to canned laughter. *Journal of Experimental Social Psychology*, 41(5):542–550.

Amruta Purandare and Diane Litman. 2006. Humor: Prosody analysis and automatic recognition for F*R*I*E*N*D*S*. In *Proceedings of the 2006 Conference on Empirical Methods in Natural Language Processing*, pages 208–215, Sydney, Australia. Association for Computational Linguistics.

Nils Reimers and Iryna Gurevych. 2019. Sentence-bert: Sentence embeddings using siamese bert-networks. In *Proceedings of the 2019 Conference on Empirical Methods in Natural Language Processing*. Association for Computational Linguistics.

Erica K. Shimomoto, Edison Marrese-Taylor, Hiroya Takamura, Ichiro Kobayashi, and Yusuke Miyao. 2024. Subspace representation for text classification with limited training data. Manuscript.

Erica K. Shimomoto, Lincon S. Souza, Bernardo B. Gatto, and Kazuhiro Fukui. 2018. Text classification based on word subspace with term-frequency. *Preprint*, arXiv:1806.03125.

Vaclav Snasel, Aleš Keprt, Ajith Abraham, and Aboul Ella Hassanien. 2009. *Approximate String Matching by Fuzzy Automata*, volume 59, pages 281–290.

Beatrice Turano and Carlo Strapparava. 2022. Making people laugh like a pro: Analysing humor through stand-up comedy. In *Proceedings of the Thirteenth Language Resources and Evaluation Conference*, pages 5206–5211, Marseille, France. European Language Resources Association.

Caleb Warren et al. 2021. What makes things funny? an integrative review of the antecedents of laughter and amusement. *Personality and Social Psychology Review*, 25(1):41–65.

Jules White, Quchen Fu, Sam Hays, Michael Sandborn, Carlos Olea, Henry Gilbert, Ashraf Elnashar, Jesse Spencer-Smith, and Douglas C. Schmidt. 2023. A prompt pattern catalog to enhance prompt engineering with chatgpt. *Preprint*, arXiv:2302.11382.

Hibiki Yokoyama, Rikuto Tsuchida, Kosei Buma, Sho Miyakawa, Takehito Utsuro, and Masaharu Yoshioka. 2024. Aggregating impressions on celebrities and their reasons from microblog posts and web search pages. In *Proceedings of the 3rd Workshop on Knowledge Augmented Methods for NLP*, pages 59–72, Bangkok, Thailand. Association for Computational Linguistics.

Weizhe Yuan, Graham Neubig, and Pengfei Liu. 2021. Bartscore: Evaluating generated text as text generation. *Preprint*, arXiv:2106.11520.

Profiling neural grammar induction on morphemically tokenised child-directed speech

Mila Marcheva[1], Theresa Biberauer[2,3,4], and Weiwei Sun[1]

[1]Department of Computer Science & Technology, University of Cambridge, UK
[2]Department of Theoretical and Applied Linguistics, University of Cambridge, UK
[3]General Linguistics Department, Stellenbosch University, South Africa
[4]Linguistics Department, University of the Western Cape, South Africa
{mmm67,mtb23,ws390}@cam.ac.uk

Abstract

We investigate the performance of state-of-the-art (SotA) neural grammar induction (GI) models on a morphemically tokenised English dataset based on the CHILDES treebank (Pearl and Sprouse, 2013). Using implementations from Yang et al. (2021b), we train models and evaluate them with the standard F1 score. We introduce novel evaluation metrics—depth-of-morpheme and sibling-of-morpheme—which measure phenomena around bound morpheme attachment. Our results reveal that models with the highest F1 scores do not necessarily induce linguistically plausible structures for bound morpheme attachment, highlighting a key challenge for cognitively plausible GI.

1 Introduction

Functional morphemes are a key focus of current generative research in First Language Acquisition (FLA) due to their role in shaping the overall structure of language (Guasti, 2017; Dye et al., 2018; Biberauer, 2019). The computational task of grammar induction (GI) takes as input a corpus of unlabelled sentences and outputs the predicted hierarchical structure for these sentences based purely on the latent statistics of the corpus; see §2.2 for an overview of GI and Figure 3 for an example of induced structures. GI thus provides a lower bound on the types of grammatical structures that can be inferred from linguistic signal alone, particularly when appropriate acquisitional metrics are employed, and recent advances in GI (Kim et al., 2019) necessitate a reevaluation of its performance in the context of FLA. This paper is concerned with bridging the gap between the state-of-the-art (SotA) in GI and in FLA by evaluating the performance of neural GI models on morphemically tokenised English child-directed speech (CDS).

To provide a more cognitively realistic setup (see §3) we propose a modification to the input of SotA neural GI systems: we only use CDS, which we morphemically tokenise (see §3.2 and §3.3) in order to reflect the salience of functional morphemes in FLA (Shi, 2013). We select SotA neural grammar induction models: Compound Probabilistic Context-Free Grammar (C-PCFG; Kim et al., 2019), Neural PCFG (N-PCFG; Kim et al., 2019), and Tensor Decomposition PCFG (TN-PCFG; Yang et al., 2021b).

We evaluate the models using the standard measure – F1 score. Furthermore, we propose two original evaluation metrics—depth-of-morpheme and sibling-of-morpheme—specific to evaluating the attachment of functional morphemes (see §4.1). Our original evaluation metrics reveal that the models with highest F1 do not necessarily induce the most linguistically plausible structures.

2 Background

2.1 Functional morphemes

The distinction between lexical and functional items is fundamental in the study of human language structure (Dye et al., 2018). Functional items encode grammatically salient information and serve as the locus for the grammatical organisation of language, as per the *Borer-Chomsky Conjecture* (Borer, 1984; Baker, 2008). During the initial focus on lexical items exhibited in FLA (Brown, 1973; Shi and Werker, 2003), functional items serve as high-frequency "edge elements", which aid in segmentation of language input and in identifying the category of the lexical item they occupy predictable positions in relation to (Mintz, 2013; Biberauer, 2019). Thus, for example, *the* consistently signals the left-edge of a (definite) noun phrase while *-ed* consistently signals the right edge of a (past-tense) lexical verb. The edge significance approach is considered SotA in FLA (see i.a. Christophe et al. (2008) and Dye et al. (2018) for further discussion). By tokenising bound functional morphemes (see §3.3), we reflect their salience in FLA.

Proceedings of the Workshop on Cognitive Modeling and Computational Linguistics, pages 47–54
May 3, 2025 ©2025 Association for Computational Linguistics

Inflectional morphology, the productive combination of lexical and functional items, starts to emerge in child-produced speech in stages related to the overall vocabulary size and mean length of utternace (MLU) (Brown, 1973; Devescovi et al.; Ravid et al., 2020). English is a quite strongly isolating language, so most functional items appear as free morphemes (separate words), and there are few bound functional morphemes, which appear as affixes (see §3.3). In GI systems the bound functional morphemes are ignored because tokens are treated as atomic units. Our approach—morphemic tokenisation—addresses the loss of "edge" information that follows from this practice by splitting, for example, *runs* into the lemma *run* and the bound functional morpheme *-s* before training. This allows the system to learn the grammatical rules governing bound morphemes, which play a crucial role in syntax.

2.2 Neural grammar induction

Grammar induction (GI) is the task of finding the latent structure of a natural language, a grammar, based on a set of raw sentences from the language, a corpus. Most statistical attempts at GI rely on a sequence of POS tags as input (Carroll and Charniak, 1992; Klein, 2005; Perfors et al., 2011), and attempts to use raw text underperform (Klein and Manning, 2004). Using POS tags (or other derivatives of raw text) is unrealistic from an FLA point of view because it postulates the existence of a standalone POS induction system. Neural systems do not require such modification of the input and achieve SotA results (Kim et al., 2019).

The general principle in neural grammar induction systems is to parametrise probabilities of (phrase-structure) rules with neural networks. Dyer et al. (2016) lay the foundations for neural GI with the Recurrent Neural Network Grammar (RNNG), and more recent works include Neural PCFG (N-PCFG; Kim et al., 2019), Compound PCFG (C-PCFG; Kim et al., 2019), Neural Lexicalised PCFG (NL-PCFG; Zhu et al., 2020), Neural Bi-Lexicalised PCFG (NBL-PCFG; Yang et al., 2021a), Tensor Decomposition PCFG (TN-PCFG; Yang et al., 2021b), SimplePCFG (Liu et al., 2023). Character-based PCFG (Jin et al., 2021) has a similar motivation to ours: to utilise the information inside a word. However, we specifically target the smallest standalone linguistic unit, morphemes, instead of naively placing equal importance on all alphanumeric characters. Tsarfaty et al. (2020) provide preliminary support for the marriage of morphological information with neural unsupervised approaches.

3 Experimental setup

3.1 Systems

We perform experiments using C-PCFG, N-PCFG, and TN-PCFG. To optimise the computational resource requirements, we use the implementations of Yang et al. (2021a), and the C-PCFG and N-PCFG experiments rely on SimplePCFG (Liu et al., 2023). All of the systems work with a preset number of non-terminals (nt) and terminals (t). The number of nt and t in our experiments follows the previous experimental setup of Yang et al. (2021a).

3.2 Data

We use the CHILDES Treebank (CHITB; Pearl and Sprouse, 2013), which consists of child-directed speech (CDS) sentences with phrase structure annotations. We use all of the Brown-Adam data for testing because its annotations are most widely verified. The remaining sentences are randomly split between training and validation. Table 1 displays the number of sentences in each split. CDS differs from adult speech, and especially the Penn Treebank (PTB; Marcus et al., 1993), as shown in previous works (Gelderloos et al., 2020; Jones et al., 2023). In this specific instance, it is worth noting that: sentences of length one are common in CDS, but constitute trivial examples for the GI task, so we eliminate them; CHITB consists of a smaller vocabulary and shorter sentences than PTB; CHITB is not canonical (e.g. includes unfinished sentences).

	PTB			CHITB		
	№	S	T	S	T	MT
Train	2-21	39	912	140	643	676
Valid	22	1.7	40	24	129	136
Test	23	2.4	56	16	82	86

Table 1: Count in thousands of sentences (S), standard tokens (T) and morphemic tokens (MT) in PTB WSJ sections (№) and in CHITB.

3.3 Morphemic tokenisation

The data in CHITB comes standardly tokenised, and we additionally render it lowercase and remove punctuation. The procedure for morphemic tokenisation is as follows: 1) identify words with bound functional morpheme endings; 2) ensure the word is not an exception; 3) split the original word into a word lemma and a functional morpheme, using `en_core_web_lg` (Montani et al., 2020) and regular expressions; 4) save the lemma and functional morpheme.

The **bound functional morphemes** in English of interest in this work are listed below, followed by the percentage that they represent of the training tokens:

- present progressive *-ing*, 2.7%
- regular plural *-s*, 1.64%
- regular past tense *-ed*, 0.82%
- regular third person present tense *-s*, 0.49%

After morphemic tokenisation, the structure of the parse trees also needs to be appropriately modified to reflect the presence of the new tokens. We attach the bound functional morpheme as illustrated in Figure 1. A complete list of cases illustrated with syntactic trees is provided in Appendix A.

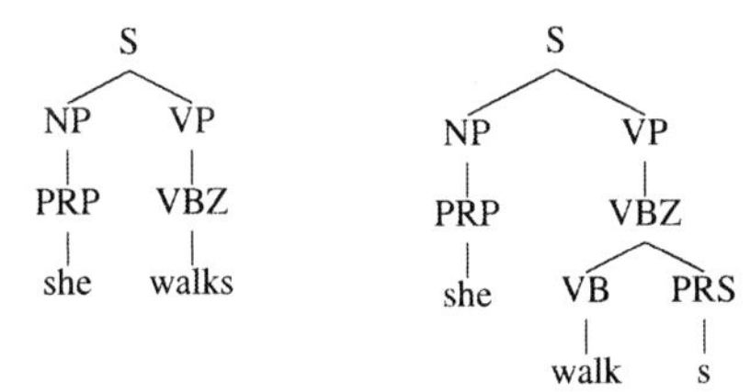

Figure 1: Regular third person present *-s*. (L) Original tree. (R) Rewritten tree post morphemic tokenisation.

The **exceptions** where morphemic tokenisation should not be applied depend on the language, and for English include: plural-only nouns (e.g. *trousers*), as these forms are monomorphemic; irregular forms of third person singular verbs (*is*, *has*, *goes*, *does*); and words which coincidentally end in *-ed* or *-ing* (e.g. *bed* or *sting*).

4 Results and analysis

The standard method of assessing GI is to use a sentence-level F1 score, which is calculated based on the gold annotations of the test set. We present the F1 scores for the different models in Table 2.

From Table 2 it is apparent that the morphemically tokenised data performs on par or better than the standardly tokenised data when using a large number of non-terminals and terminals. The highest F1 is achieved by N-PCFG (nt8192 t16384), where the standard tokenisation slightly outperforms the morphemic tokenisation. Overall systems with a higher number of non-terminals and terminals, which can capture more subtle variation

Model	Morphemic	Standard
Left-branching	14.17	14.83
Right-branching	71.94	73.77
Random trees	36.45	36.61
TN-PCFG (nt9000 t4500)	73.81	45.75
C-PCFG (nt2048 t4096)	68.79	59.86
C-PCFG (nt512 t1024)	41.99	72.95
N-PCFG (nt4096 t8192)	69.19	60.83
N-PCFG (nt8192 t16384)	**78.56**	**79.01**

Table 2: Sentence-level F1 for constituency parses for morphemic and standard tokenisation.

in the data, perform better. The right-branching baseline achieves an F1 score comparable and even higher than for some neural models. This trend is apparent for both standard and morphemic tokenisation because English has a right-branching pattern (Greenberg, 1963). The high performance of right-branching baselines for English is reported for C-PCFG (Kim et al., 2019, Table 1) and for TN-PCFG (Yang et al., 2021b, Table 1).

4.1 Functional morpheme evaluation

F1 is reliant on annotations, which for natural languages are prone to ambiguity because the target grammar may not necessarily be known. We devise annotation-independent evaluation metrics focused on the structure of attachment of functional morphemes.

4.1.1 Depth-of-morpheme

We assume that the nodes for bound functional morphemes are sibling nodes for the lexeme they combine with (see §3.3 and Figure 1). To establish whether a bound functional morpheme is correctly attached in the predicted tree, we check whether it is found at the same depth as the lexeme it forms a word with. If the depth differs, then the predicted subtree is incorrect in describing the functional morpheme attachment. We perform depth-of-morpheme evaluation on the models with highest F1: TN-PCFG (nt9000 t4500), N-PCFG (nt8192 t16384), and the right-branching baseline; the results are displayed in Table 3.

	TN-PCFG	N-PCFG	Right-br.
-ed	100	55.11	30.49
-ing	100	41.11	21.37
-s	95.11	95.95	40.88

Table 3: Percentage of bound functional morphemes attached at the correct depth. *-s* has two uses (§3.3).

N-PCFG has the highest F1, but appears not to be expressive enough to encode the examined linguistic phenomena: this is likely because it captures a higher frequency of simple cases. TN-PCFG makes no errors on *-ed* and on *-ing*. The right-branching baseline, although comparable in F1 score with the neural models, underperforms on the task of correctly attaching the bound functional morpheme. These insights highlight the importance of acquisitionally-focused evaluation, because standard NLP measures, such as F1, may obscure task-specific errors.

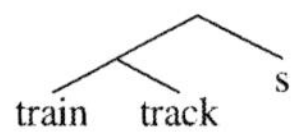

Figure 2: N-PCFG prediction for the structure of the morphemically tokenised phrase "train tracks". The induced structure implies the functional morpheme *-s* combines with the whole noun compound.

Note however that the binary nature of depth-of-morpheme also obscures patterns which may be of linguistic interest. For example, N-PCFG predicts that the plural noun morpheme *-s* attaches to the whole noun compound as displayed in Figure 2, and the depth-of-morpheme of *-s* is therefore incorrect (the expected pattern is for *-s* to attach to the single noun preceding it, as displayed in Figure 5). However, the induced structure might be of linguistic interest because the compounding of the nouns is not implausible. To gain deeper insight, depth-of-morpheme should be used in combination with sibling-of-morpheme, the metric introduced in the following section.

4.1.2 Sibling-of-morpheme evaluation

We next analyse the sibling of the bound functional morpheme in the predicted tree. The sibling is the span of the smallest tree immediately dominating the tree where the functional morpheme node appears; in linguistics, this notion is also referred to as a sister. For example, the sibling of *-ed* in Figure 3 is *knock* (as predicted by TN-PCFG) and the subtree spanning *one down* (as predicted by N-PCFG). The sibling predicted by TN-PCFG is linguistically plausible, whereas the one predicted by N-PCFG is not – not only does it group two words in a grammatically unlikely constituent, but it implies the functional morpheme does not combine with the verb.

To systematically look for patterns in the siblings of morphemes, we look at the siblings' semantic

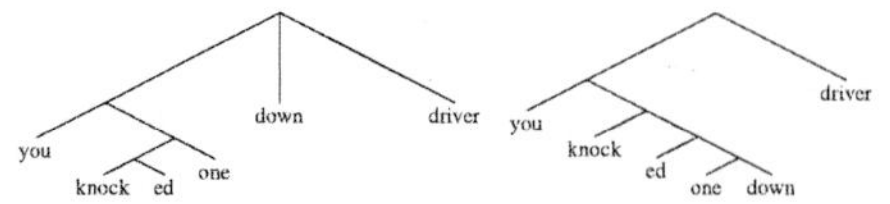

Figure 3: Predicted trees for the sentence "You knocked one down, driver."; TN-PCGF (L) and N-PCFG (R).

role labels (SRL)[1], obtained via SRL BERT[2] (Shi and Lin, 2019), and whether there is any relation to the *depth-of-morpheme* measure. For an overview of SRLs please consult Jurafsky and Martin (Chapter 21; 2025). Beyond standard SRLs we introduce two more labels: the "straddles boundary" category signifies that the sibling of the morpheme spans more than one semantic role and this kind of attachment is always incorrect, because it poses a grammatically incoherent constituency. The "all O" category, where all of the leaves in the sibling are labelled as (O)utside of a semantic role, applies to cases which may include a constituent boundary, or more rarely where a constituent was missed by the SRL model.

SRL	TN-PCFG		N-PCFG	
	Count	% Correct	Count	%Correct
Overall	1796	95.43	1796	78.12
ARG1	780	95.38	790	*91.65
ARG2	211	*91.94	210	*89.52
V	398	*99.75	118	*98.31
ARGM	63	95.24	72	77.78
all O	32	96.88	40	75.0
ARG0	27	92.59	26	*100
ARG3	3	100	3	100
ARG4	2	100	14	*14.29
strad. b.	6	*0	249	*0

Table 4: Comparison of SRL Tag Performance: TN-PCFG vs. N-PCFG. Statistically significant ($p < 0.05$) difference from the **Overall** marked with *.

Verbal instances are ones where the bound morpheme is attached to a verb identified by the SRL model (Figure 3 illustrates a verbal instance). In the verbal instance, the only correct label for the sibling of the morpheme is V. The TN-PCFG system correctly attaches all instances of *-ed* and *-ing* to a single lexeme with SRL V (also see Table 3), but N-PCFG makes errors where the bound morpheme is attached to lexemes tagged as direct object (ARG1), indirect object (ARG2), adjuncts (ARGM), and others.

[1]Other annotations (e.g. dependencies) may be used.
[2]`https://paperswithcode.com/lib/allennlp/srl-bert`

In the **non-verbal** instance, the morpheme attaches to a lexeme which is not identified as a verb by the SRL tagger, but we nonetheless look to find the functional role of the sibling in the sentence. Here there is no one correct SRL (see Appendix A for the full range of cases). Table 4 displays the percentage of morphemes which are found at the correct depth, grouped by the SRL of their sibling. We perform Fisher's Exact Test (Fisher, 1922) to identify SRLs for which the percentage of correct depth-of-morpheme differs significantly from the overall rate of correct depth-of-morpheme for that system. For TN-PCFG, indirect object (ARG2) siblings of functional morphemes co-occur with a significantly lower depth-of-morpheme correct percentage, especially in comparison with direct object (ARG1) and adjunct (ARGM) siblings, which follow the same as the overall rate and appear to pose less of a challenge for the model. The N-PCFG system has a very high number of siblings of morphemes which include a boundary, which lower the **Overall** depth-of-morpheme correctness for the system. This result again highlights that the system with the highest F1 does not necessitate the correct attachment of functional morphemes: N-PCFG (highest F1) often predicts that the functional morphemes attach to an implausible constituent.

5 Conclusion

We explore how morphemic tokenisation, an insight inspired by FLA, influences neural GI systems. We evaluate the GI systems with F1 score, and conduct further error analysis on the attachment of bound morphemes. Our findings reveal that high F1 scores do not always correspond to linguistically meaningful structures for functional morpheme attachment. In the future, we will apply this methodology to CDS from morphologically rich languages, such as the ones in SPMRL (Goldberg et al., 2014).

6 Limitations

Morphemic tokenisation follows a generativist perspective rather than a theory-neutral approach, so it may not align with non-generativist frameworks. The limitations of the novel evaluation metrics —depth-of-morpheme and sibling-of-morpheme— mainly stem from the fact that their utility depends on morphemically tokenised text. Additionally, there are cases where the binary result of depth-of-morpheme may not be informative enough (e.g. Figure 2), which is why the depth-of-morpheme metric should be used in combination with the sibling-of-morpheme metric.

English is currently the only language with an annotated CDS treebank of suitable magnitude, but our focus on English unfortunately further reinforces the dominance of English in NLP research. Since English is a largely isolating/weakly inflecting language with minimal inflectional morphology, a morphologically complex language would provide a more rigorous test for morphemic tokenisation, with greater potential benefits, but potentially also increased challenges. Future work will expand both the linguistic scope and the experimental design.

References

Mark C. Baker. 2008. The macroparameter in a microparametric world. In *The Limits of Syntactic Variation*, page 351–373. John Benjamins Publishing Company.

Theresa Biberauer. 2019. Children always go beyond the input: The maximise minimal means perspective. *Theoretical Linguistics*, 45(3–4):211–224.

Hagit Borer. 1984. *Parametric syntax : case studies in Semitic and Romance languages / Hagit Borer.* Studies in generative grammar ; 13.

Roger Brown. 1973. *A first language: The early stages.* Cambridge, MA: Harvard University Press.

Glenn Carroll and Eugene Charniak. 1992. Two experiments on learning probabilistic dependency grammars from corpora. Technical Report CS-92-16, Dept. of Computer Science, Brown University, Providence, RI.

Anne Christophe, Séverine Millotte, Savita Bernal, and Jeffrey Lidz. 2008. Bootstrapping lexical and syntactic acquisition. *Language and Speech*, 51(1–2):61–75.

Antonella Devescovi, Maria Cristina Caselli, Daniela Marchione, Patrizio Pasqualetti, Judy Reilly, and Elizabeth Bates. A crosslinguistic study of the relationship between grammar and lexical development. *Journal of Child Language*, 32(4).

Cristina Dye, Yarden Kedar, and Barbara Lust. 2018. From lexical to functional categories: New foundations for the study of language development. *First Language*, 39(1):9–32.

Chris Dyer, Adhiguna Kuncoro, Miguel Ballesteros, and Noah A. Smith. 2016. Recurrent neural network grammars. In *Proceedings of the 2016 Conference of the North American Chapter of the Association for Computational Linguistics: Human Language*

Technologies, pages 199–209, San Diego, California. Association for Computational Linguistics.

R. A. Fisher. 1922. On the interpretation of 2 from contingency tables, and the calculation of p. *Journal of the Royal Statistical Society*, 85(1):87.

Lieke Gelderloos, Grzegorz Chrupała, and Afra Alishahi. 2020. Learning to understand child-directed and adult-directed speech. In *Proceedings of the 58th Annual Meeting of the Association for Computational Linguistics*, pages 1–6, Online. Association for Computational Linguistics.

Yoav Goldberg, Yuval Marton, Ines Rehbein, Yannick Versley, Özlem Çetinoğlu, and Joel Tetreault, editors. 2014. *Proceedings of the First Joint Workshop on Statistical Parsing of Morphologically Rich Languages and Syntactic Analysis of Non-Canonical Languages*. Dublin City University, Dublin, Ireland.

Joseph Harold Greenberg. 1963. *Universals of language.* MIT press.

Maria Teresa Guasti. 2017. *Language acquisition*, 2 edition. A Bradford Book. Bradford Books, Cambridge, MA.

Lifeng Jin, Byung-Doh Oh, and William Schuler. 2021. Character-based PCFG induction for modeling the syntactic acquisition of morphologically rich languages. In *Findings of the Association for Computational Linguistics: EMNLP 2021*, pages 4367–4378, Punta Cana, Dominican Republic. Association for Computational Linguistics.

Gary Jones, Francesco Cabiddu, Doug J. K. Barrett, Antonio Castro, and Bethany Lee. 2023. How the characteristics of words in child-directed speech differ from adult-directed speech to influence children's productive vocabularies. *First Language*, 43(3):253–282.

Daniel Jurafsky and James H. Martin. 2025. *Speech and Language Processing: An Introduction to Natural Language Processing, Computational Linguistics, and Speech Recognition with Language Models*, 3rd edition, chapter 21: Semantic Role Labeling and Argument Structure. Online manuscript released January 12, 2025.

Yoon Kim, Chris Dyer, and Alexander Rush. 2019. Compound probabilistic context-free grammars for grammar induction. In *Proceedings of the 57th Annual Meeting of the Association for Computational Linguistics*, pages 2369–2385, Florence, Italy. Association for Computational Linguistics.

Dan Klein. 2005. *The unsupervised learning of natural language structure*. Stanford University.

Dan Klein and Christopher Manning. 2004. Corpus-based induction of syntactic structure: Models of dependency and constituency. In *Proceedings of the 42nd Annual Meeting of the Association for Computational Linguistics (ACL-04)*, pages 478–485, Barcelona, Spain.

Wei Liu, Songlin Yang, Yoon Kim, and Kewei Tu. 2023. Simple hardware-efficient PCFGs with independent left and right productions. In *Findings of the Association for Computational Linguistics: EMNLP 2023*, pages 1662–1669, Singapore. Association for Computational Linguistics.

Mitchell P. Marcus, Mary Ann Marcinkiewicz, and Beatrice Santorini. 1993. Building a large annotated corpus of english: the penn treebank. *Comput. Linguist.*, 19(2):313–330.

Toben H. Mintz. 2013. The segmentation of sub-lexical morphemes in english-learning 15-month-olds. *Frontiers in Psychology*, 4.

Ines Montani, Matthew Honnibal, Sofie Van Landeghem, Adriane Boyd, Henning Peters, Maxim Samsonov, Jim Geovedi, Jim Regan, György Orosz, Paul O'Leary McCann, Søren Lind Kristiansen, Duygu Altinok, Roman, Leander Fiedler, Grégory Howard, Wannaphong Phatthiyaphaibun, Explosion Bot, Sam Bozek, Mark Amery, Yohei Tamura, Björn Böing, Pradeep Kumar Tippa, Leif Uwe Vogelsang, Ramanan Balakrishnan, Vadim Mazaev, GregDubbin, jeannefukumaru, Jens Dahl Møllerhøj, and Avadh Patel. 2020. explosion/spaCy: v3.0.0rc: Transformer-based pipelines, new training system, project templates, custom models, improved component API, type hints & lots more.

Lisa S. Pearl and Jon Sprouse. 2013. Syntactic islands and learning biases: Combining experimental syntax and computational modeling to investigate the language acquisition problem. *Language Acquisition*.

Andrew Perfors, Joshua B. Tenenbaum, and Terry Regier. 2011. The learnability of abstract syntactic principles. *Cognition*, 118(3):306–338.

Dorit Ravid, Emmanuel Keuleers, and Wolfgang Dressler. 2020. *Emergence and early development of lexicon and morphology*, pages 593–633.

Peng Shi and Jimmy Lin. 2019. Simple bert models for relation extraction and semantic role labeling. *arXiv preprint*.

Rushen Shi. 2013. Functional morphemes and early language acquisition. *Child Development Perspectives*, 8(1):6–11.

Rushen Shi and Janet F. Werker. 2003. The basis of preference for lexical words in 6-month-old infants. *Developmental Science*, 6(5):484–488.

Reut Tsarfaty, Dan Bareket, Stav Klein, and Amit Seker. 2020. From SPMRL to NMRL: What did we learn (and unlearn) in a decade of parsing morphologically-rich languages (MRLs)? In *Proceedings of the 58th Annual Meeting of the Association for Computational Linguistics*, pages 7396–7408, Online. Association for Computational Linguistics.

Songlin Yang, Yanpeng Zhao, and Kewei Tu. 2021a. Neural bi-lexicalized PCFG induction. In *Proceedings of the 59th Annual Meeting of the Association for Computational Linguistics and the 11th International Joint Conference on Natural Language Processing (Volume 1: Long Papers)*, pages 2688–2699, Online. Association for Computational Linguistics.

Songlin Yang, Yanpeng Zhao, and Kewei Tu. 2021b. PCFGs can do better: Inducing probabilistic context-free grammars with many symbols. In *Proceedings of the 2021 Conference of the North American Chapter of the Association for Computational Linguistics: Human Language Technologies*, pages 1487–1498, Online. Association for Computational Linguistics.

Hao Zhu, Yonatan Bisk, and Graham Neubig. 2020. The return of lexical dependencies: Neural lexicalized PCFGs. *Transactions of the Association for Computational Linguistics*, 8:647–661.

A All cases of tree rewriting

All cases of tree rewriting are shown below in Figure 4, Figure 5, Figure 6, Figure 7, Figure 8, Figure 9. The original trees are on the left, and the rewritten trees are on the right. The trees are constructed as explained in §3.3.

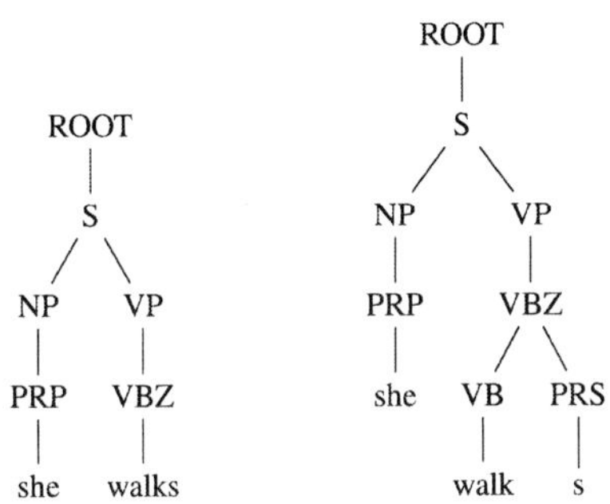

Figure 4: Regular 3rd person present *-s*.

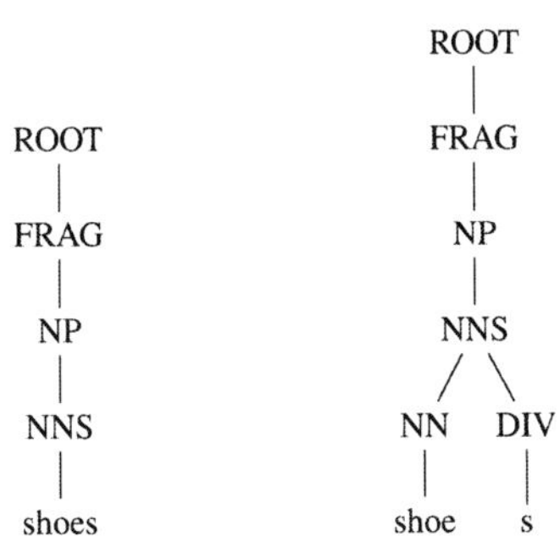

Figure 5: Regular plural -s.

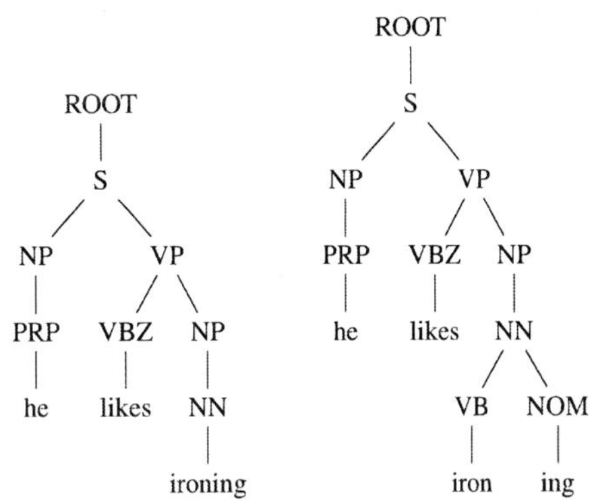

Figure 6: Nominal *-ing*

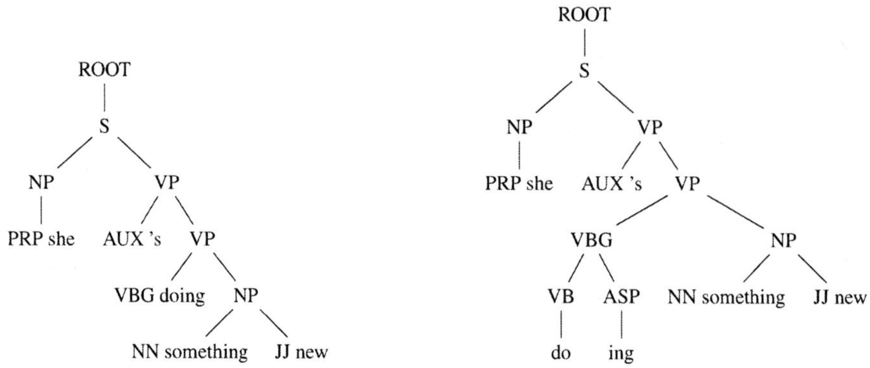

Figure 7: Progressive *-ing*.

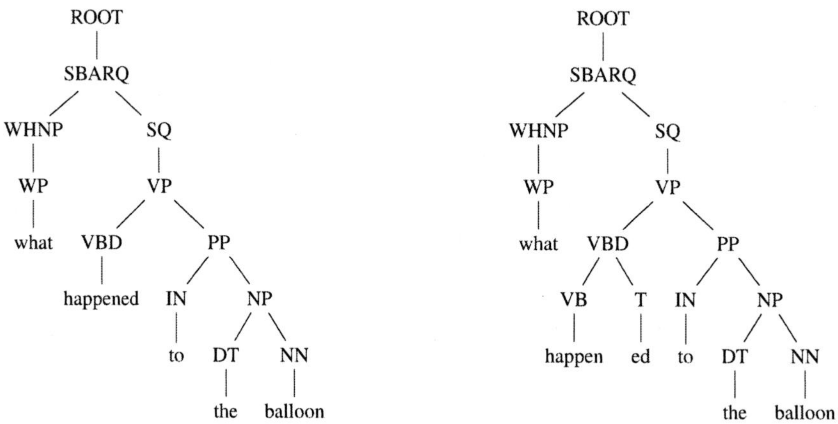

Figure 8: Regular past *-ed*.

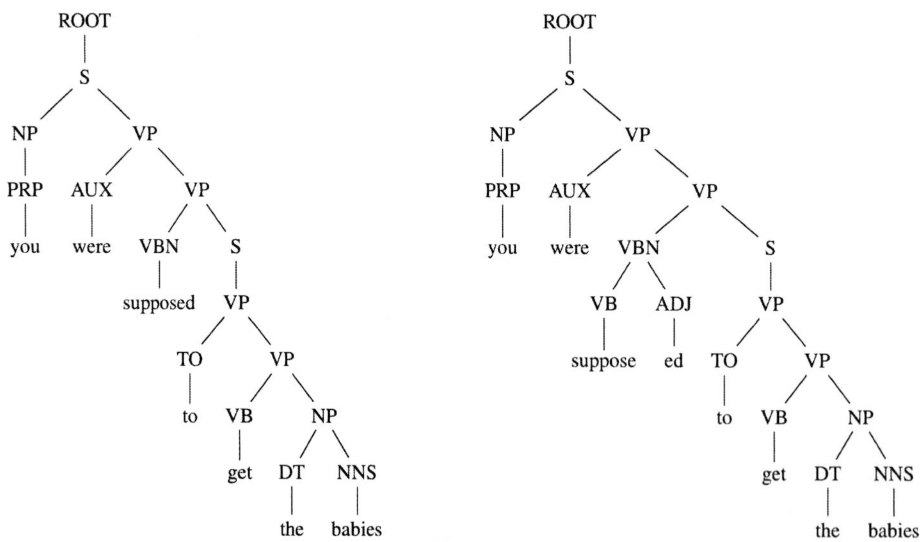

Figure 9: Adjectivial *-ed*.

Exploring the Integration of Eye Movement Data on Word Embeddings

Fermín Travi[1,2], Gabriel Leclercq[2], Diego Fernández Slezak[1,2], Bruno Bianchi[1,2], Juan E. Kamienkowski[1,2,3]

[1]Departamento de Computación, Facultad de Ciencias Exactas y Naturales, Universidad de Buenos Aires.
[2]Instituto de Ciencias de la Computación, Facultad de Ciencias Exactas y Naturales, Universidad de Buenos Aires.
[3]Maestría en Explotación de Datos y Descubrimiento del Conocimiento, Facultad de Ciencias Exactas y Naturales, Universidad de Buenos Aires.

Correspondence: ftravi@dc.uba.ar

Abstract

Reading, while structured, is a non-linear process. Readers may skip some words, linger on others, or revisit earlier text. Emerging work has started exploring the incorporation of reading behaviour through eye-tracking into the training of specific language tasks. In this work, we investigate the broader question of how gaze data can shape word embeddings by using text as read by human participants and predicting gaze measures from them. To that end, we conducted an eye-tracking experiment with 76 participants reading 20 short stories in Spanish and fine-tuned Word2Vec and LSTM models on the collected data. Evaluations with representational similarity analysis and word pair similarities showed a limited, but largely consistent, gain from gaze incorporation, suggesting future work should expand linguistic diversity and use cognitively aligned evaluations to better understand its role in bridging computational and human language representations.

1 Introduction

The field of natural language processing (NLP) is currently driven by artificial neural networks primarily trained on the task of predicting the next word in a given sentence (Radford et al., 2018, 2019). However, next-word prediction of written text is a pale reflection of how language is processed in the brain, as written text is the product of deliberate conscious processes, often edited, proofread, and restructured. This stands in stark contrast with the spontaneous generation of language in our everyday life.

Eye-tracking during reading has long been recognized as a central tool for unraveling language processing in the brain (Kliegl et al., 2006), with its earliest studies dating over a century ago (Huey, 1908). Recent advances have demonstrated how eye movement data from reading can be integrated into NLP applications, enhancing performance in various downstream language tasks through its incorporation into language models (Zhang and Hollenstein, 2024; Yang and Hollenstein, 2023; Hollenstein and Zhang, 2019; Klerke et al., 2016; Barrett et al., 2018). However, whether gaze information can influence the latent representations of language processing models to align more closely with human cognitive processing remains an unresolved question. Moreover, despite its long history in reading research, eye-tracking during reading datasets are not widely available, and most of this emerging research has focused exclusively on English, while similar studies utilizing eye-tracking data in Spanish have yet to be conducted.

Thus, we collected eye-tracking data during reading in Spanish and utilized the resulting gaze information to train simple language processing models. Our findings suggest that incorporating gaze information into word embeddings may offer modest but promising steps toward greater cognitive alignment. We argue that combining larger, linguistically diverse datasets with cognitively focused evaluation tasks will be critical for uncovering the potential of eye-tracking to bridge computational and human language representations.

2 Materials & Methods

2.1 Eye-tracking experiment

To collect eye movement patterns during natural reading, we selected twenty self-contained short stories (800 ($\pm$ 135) words long, average reading time of three minutes) written in Latin American Spanish. We cleaned and processed data from 76 participants (mean age 23.5 (IQR 4.8); 44 females, 32 males; mostly college students), resulting in 1,015 trials (Fig. A1). All details of the experiment can be found in Appendix A. Gaze measures were extracted from those words that were not the first or last words in a sentence or line and did not contain punctuation marks, dashes or numbers, resulting in

Proceedings of the Workshop on Cognitive Modeling and Computational Linguistics, pages 55–65
May 3, 2025 ©2025 Association for Computational Linguistics

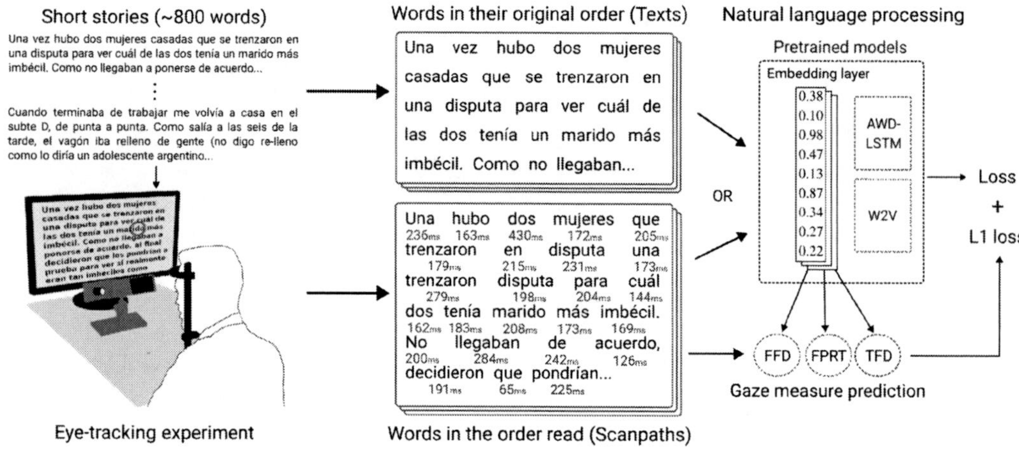

Figure 1: Gaze embedding pipeline. The stories read during the eye-tracking experiment were reconstructed following the reading order of the participants (Scanpaths). Gaze measures were extracted from all trials, discretized in ten bins for each individual, and a global average for each word was computed. These values were then predicted from the word embeddings as the output of a fully connected layer.

3,016 unique words (of 3,493) with gaze measures. The code used for the experiment and extracting gaze measures can be found at `https://github.com/NeuroLIAA/reading-et`.

2.2 Natural Language Processing

To test our hypothesis, we selected two different architectures: a word embedding model (Word2Vec in its skip-gram variation with negative sampling (Mikolov et al., 2013)), and a language model (AWD-LSTM (Merity et al., 2017), one of the latest variations of LSTMs), from which we extracted its embedding layer. These selections were based primarily on simplicity and ability to perform well without requiring extensive amounts of data. While Large Language Models could be applied with larger gaze datasets, these simpler models serve as an efficient proof of concept for our methodology. The hardware employed for training consisted of a personal computer: Intel i7-11700, 32GB RAM DDR4, and a GPU ASUS RTX 3060 12GB. The pre-training and fine-tuning consumed, respectively, 5 h and 0.5 h for the Word2Vec model and 50 h and 2 h for the LSTM model. The source code is available at `https://github.com/NeuroLIAA/gaze-word-embeddings`.

2.2.1 Baselines

As baseline training data, we employed a 2019 dump of Spanish Wikis hosted in Huggingface[1]. To reduce vocabulary size and noise, words that contained numbers, special characters, non-latin characters, were shorter than two tokens, or longer than twenty tokens, were filtered out. Resulting sentences shorter than four words and longer than forty were also removed. This yielded a total of approximately 22 million sentences. Vocabulary was composed of individual words that appeared at least twenty times. Pre-training for both Word2Vec and AWD-LSTM followed default hyperparameters (with an embedding size of 300 and batch size of 32 sentences) for five epochs.

2.2.2 Gaze embedding

To embed gaze, we used scanpath-generated text as input (extracted from the eye-tracking experiment described in §2.1) and fine-tuned the baseline with them, while also predicting gaze measures from word embeddings (Fig. 1). Scanpath-generated text was constructed by following the fixations from each trial in the experiment, yielding 1,015 different texts (named *Scanpaths*). Although it mostly overlapped with the text read, its word order was markedly distinct from written text, as human reading is a non-sequential process. If a word with a punctuation mark was fixed several times consecutively, or a regression was done inside the same sentence, all those words were stripped from the punctuation marks and put together as a single sentence. This totalled 44,748 sentences (612,299 words) after preprocessing. For a correct comparison, we also defined a corpus containing the original texts (from §2.1) repeated the same number of

[1]https://huggingface.co/datasets/large_spanish_corpus

		CKA	Correlations		
			SimLex	Abstract	Concrete
W2V	Baseline	**0.1434**	**0.4147**	**0.4814**	**0.3312**
	Scanpaths	0.1402*	0.2946*	0.3357*	0.3036*
	Scanpaths + GM	**0.1434**	0.3867*	0.3163*	0.3308
	Texts	0.1382*	0.3119*	0.2796*	0.2671*
	Texts + GM	0.1422*	0.4018*	0.2784*	0.3006*
AWD-LSTM	Baseline	0.1114	0.2301	0.2507	0.1238
	Scanpaths	0.1088*	0.2377*	0.2147*	**0.2199***
	Scanpaths + GM	0.1102*	**0.3537***	0.2261*	0.2122*
	Texts	0.1124*	0.3113*	**0.2715***	0.1741*
	Texts + GM	**0.1127***	0.3298*	0.2689*	0.1773*

Table 1: Mean CKA to word embeddings derived from SWOW-RP of 1,650 content words with gaze measures, and mean Spearman rank correlation of cosine distances between word pairs with human similarity judgments. The latter analysis was conducted across three datasets (SimLex, Abstract, and Concrete) with 216, 276, and 378 word pairs respectively. Random samplings of 1000 words and 100 word pairs were performed a hundred times with replacement. Baseline refers to models trained on the baseline corpus, Scanpaths are models fine-tuned on text as read by participants, and Texts are models fine-tuned on stimuli as is. GM refers to the addition of gaze measures to the training process. The asterisk indicates the distribution was significantly different from the baseline.

times, totalling 42,213 sentences (666,374 words, named *Texts*).

Gaze measures are usually classed as early (First Fixation Duration, FFD; First Pass Reading Time, FPRT) or late (Total Fixation Duration, TFD), depending on the stage of reading processing they reflect (Inhoff, 1984). Early measures are thought to be a reflection of primarily automatic word recognition and lexical access processes, whereas late measures tend to reflect more conscious, controlled, strategic processes. By forcing the word model to predict them (early measures for Word2Vec, late for AWD-LSTM), we intended to embed (cognitive) attention into it (Klerke et al., 2016; Barrett et al., 2018). Specifically, this was done by adding a fully connected layer that received the embedding of the input word and predicted its corresponding gaze measures. The resulting L1 loss was then added to the standard loss of the model (Fig. 1).

These measures were computed individually for each item and participant in the experiment. As the values of these measures vary between participants and items, we discretized them in ten quantiles for each participant. A word average was then obtained by computing the mean across participants and items. If the input word contained no gaze measure, its value was set to zero. It is important to note that these measures are not independent, as First Fixation Duration (FFD) is a part of First Pass Reading Time (FPRT), which is a part of Total Fixation Duration (TFD). We left out regression measures because they showed to be lowly correlated between subjects (Fig. A2). Fine-tuning was carried out for 50 epochs with the same hyperparameters as the baseline.

2.3 Evaluation framework

2.3.1 Association-based word embeddings

Our main reference point was based on a massive word association task in Rioplatense Spanish (*Small World of Words Rioplatense Spanish* (SWOW-RP)) (Cabana et al., 2024), primarily due to its size, as well as the well-studied link between word associations and semantic representations stored in memory (De Deyne et al., 2016). From these word associations, Cabana et al. (2024) derived graph embeddings that have been shown to be more closely related to human similarity judgments of word pairs than standard word embeddings.

We hypothesize that gaze-derived word embeddings are a closer match to word embeddings derived from SWOW-RP with respect to the baseline. To evaluate this, we employed centered kernel alignment (CKA) (Kornblith et al., 2019) on the resulting 1,650 content words with gaze measures. CKA is a similarity measure that quantifies the similarity between two sets of representations by comparing their Gram matrices in a reproducing kernel Hilbert space. Unlike traditional similarity metrics, CKA is invariant to orthogonal transformations and can effectively capture global structural similarities between high-dimensional representa-

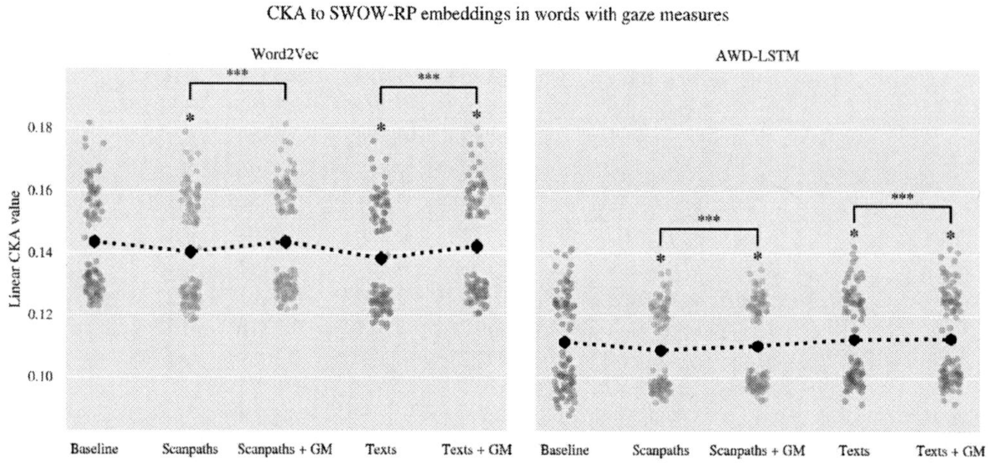

Figure 2: Distribution of the CKA values to the word embeddings derived from SWOW-RP presented in Table 1.

tions, making it particularly useful for comparing embedding spaces across different domains or models. Recent works in machine learning and cognitive science have leveraged CKA to analyze representational similarities in neural networks, comparing learned representations across different layers, architectures, and even modalities (Vulić et al., 2020b; Hao et al., 2023; Maniparambil et al., 2024). In the context of our study, CKA provided a robust method to assess the semantic alignment between gaze-derived and association-based word embeddings, allowing us to evaluate how closely these distinct representational spaces match. CKA similarity ranges between 0 and 1, from most dissimilar to most similar spaces. To mitigate potential outlier effects, we performed random samplings of 1,000 words with replacement a hundred times and report the mean and standard error to it.

2.3.2 Word pairs similarity judgments

A more classical way of evaluating word embeddings is to compute the Spearman rank correlation between the cosine distance of two words and their corresponding semantic similarity as defined by human participants (Mikolov et al., 2013). However, a limitation to this approach is the requirement for both words to have been fine-tuned. We made use of two different resources: Multi-SimLex ES (*SimLex*; 1,888 semantically aligned concept pairs, of which 216 possess gaze measures) (Vulić et al., 2020a) and a relatedness task for Rioplatense Spanish speakers collected by De Deyne et al. (2020) (3,321 conceptually abstract (*Abstract*) and 3,321 conceptually concrete (*Concrete*) word pairs, of which 276 and 378 possess gaze measures, respectively). In this case, we sampled 100 word pairs randomly with replacement a hundred times.

3 Results

We evaluated the impact of fine-tuning NLP models using text as read by participants in an eye-tracking experiment, compared to text in its original order, as well as the effect of predicting gaze measures from word embeddings during training. Both architectures successfully incorporated gaze measures into their embeddings: Word2Vec achieved a close-to-perfect correlation between predicted and true gaze values, while AWD-LSTM achieved a median correlation of 0.89 per batch. All reported p-values were computed using Wilcoxon signed-rank tests on bootstrapped distributions.

When comparing the alignment of these embeddings with those derived from SWOW-RP, differences emerged (Fig. 2). For Word2Vec, fine-tuning without gaze measures resulted in a slight decrease in alignment compared to the baseline (Table 1). However, the incorporation of gaze measures slightly improved their alignment and their distributions resulted significantly different from their counterparts without gaze measures (both $p < 0.0001$, ws. 0.0), although the addition of gaze measures to Scanpaths resulted in CKA values not significantly different to the baseline. In contrast, AWD-LSTM showed no decrease when fine-tuned with Texts relative to the baseline and a slight decrease when fine-tuned with Scanpaths. The addition of gaze measures barely increased the mean, but provided significantly different distributions ($p < 0.0001$, ws. 1189.0 for Texts and $p < 0.01$, ws. 1698.0 for Scanpaths).

The differing behavior between architectures when fine-tuning with Scanpaths or Text likely stems from their design: Word2Vec, employing a bag-of-words approach with moving windows, is less affected by syntax and may leverage the non-sequential patterns of human reading when capturing first-order relationships. Meanwhile, AWD-LSTM, pre-trained on syntactically structured sentences, is more sensitive to deviations from natural text order, such as those found in Scanpaths.

When analyzing the correlation between the cosine distance of word embeddings and human similarity judgments of word pairs with gaze measures, distinct trends emerged for the two models tested (Fig. B1). For Word2Vec, fine-tuning generally reduced correlation scores compared to the baseline across datasets, with the most pronounced drop observed in Abstract (Table 1). All correlations were significantly different to the baseline ($p < 0.0005$), with the exception of Scanpaths plus gaze measures in Concrete ($p > 0.5$, ws. 2448.0), as was the case in the CKA analysis. The inclusion of gaze measures to Scanpaths and Texts increased correlations in all datasets except for Abstract, as well as producing significantly different distributions ($p < 0.0001$). The fine-tuned variations of AWD-LSTM, on the other hand, improved correlations with respect to the baseline, except for Abstract as well. Correlations were once again significantly different to the baseline ($p < 0.001$) and the addition of gaze measures had a significant impact in SimLex, but not in Abstract nor Concrete.

In the case of word pairs not present in the stimuli, the mean remained relatively unchanged across datasets for both models (Fig. B2).

4 Discussion

In this work, we investigated the integration of gaze information into word embeddings of language processing models by means of feeding them text as read by human participants and incorporating gaze measures into the latent space. Our findings suggest that architectures like Word2Vec may better leverage the non-sequential patterns of human reading, while pre-trained language models like AWD-LSTM appear to be more negatively impacted by them. Moreover, the incorporation of early and late gaze measures, respectively, yielded modest improvements in most evaluation tasks, hinting at the potential for gaze measures to nudge the latent space toward greater cognitive alignment. However, further research should look deeper into the morphological or linguistic variables involved to fully understand and optimize this effect. One key limitation of our study lies in some aspects of the dataset: while the number of participants in our eye-tracking experiment was high (76), the number of unique words read was low (3,493). This constraints the size of the fine-tuning corpus (44,709 sentences) and the contextual variety it offers. As seen in analogous studies translating other cognitive modalities to deep learning models (Tang et al., 2023), future efforts should prioritize increasing the number of reading sessions per subject rather than expanding the participant pool. Additionally, tasks more closely tied to cognitive processes, such as cloze tasks (Bianchi et al., 2020), may provide a more suitable evaluation framework.

Finally, our study is the first to integrate Spanish eye-tracking data into language models, raising questions about the language-specificity of prior findings. Future work can build on this foundation to enhance the use of gaze data in aligning computational and human language representations.

5 Limitations

As discussed throughout the article, the present study is limited by the contextual diversity and number of unique words present in the eye-tracking experiment. Vocabulary size is small, which, in turn, constrains the size of the evaluation space. Future work will expand this experiment by including novel texts. The lack of linguistic resources in Spanish also makes it impossible to combine datasets.

Gaze measures were aggregated to obtain global averages, but there may be large individual variability across participants (see Fig. A2). In line with recent suggestions in functional magnetic resonance images (fMRI) (Kupers et al., 2024), future work will include several sessions per participant. Eye-tracking offers the advantage of enabling intensive sampling across a substantial number of participants.

References

Maria Barrett, Joachim Bingel, Nora Hollenstein, Marek Rei, and Anders Søgaard. 2018. Sequence classification with human attention. In *Proceedings of the 22nd Conference on Computational Natural Language Learning*, pages 302–312, Brussels, Belgium. Association for Computational Linguistics.

Bruno Bianchi, Gastón Bengolea Monzón, Luciana Ferrer, Diego Fernández Slezak, Diego E. Shalom, and Juan E. Kamienkowski. 2020. Human and computer estimations of predictability of words in written language. *Scientific Reports*, 10(1):4396. Publisher: Nature Publishing Group.

David H. Brainard. 1997. The Psychophysics Toolbox. *Spatial Vision*, 10(4):433–436. Place: Netherlands Publisher: VSP.

Álvaro Cabana, Camila Zugarramurdi, Juan C. Valle-Lisboa, and Simon De Deyne. 2024. The "Small World of Words" free association norms for Rioplatense Spanish. *Behavior Research Methods*, 56(2):968–985.

Hernán Casciari. 2021. *100 covers de cuentos clásicos*. Editorial Orsai S.R.L., Buenos Aires.

Simon De Deyne, Álvaro Cabana, Bing Li, Qiang Cai, and Matthew McKague. 2020. A cross-linguistic study into the contribution of affective connotation in the lexico-semantic representation of concrete and abstract concepts. In *Proceedings of the Annual Conference of the Cognitive Science Society*, volume 7.

Simon De Deyne, Amy Perfors, and Daniel J Navarro. 2016. Predicting human similarity judgments with distributional models: The value of word associations. In *Proceedings of COLING 2016, the 26th International Conference on Computational Linguistics: Technical Papers*, pages 1861–1870, Osaka, Japan. The COLING 2016 Organizing Committee.

Andrew Duchon, Manuel Perea, Nuria Sebastián-Gallés, Antonia Martí, and Manuel Carreiras. 2013. EsPal: One-stop shopping for spanish word properties. *Behavior Research Methods*, 45(4):1246–1258.

Zhiwei Hao, Jianyuan Guo, Kai Han, Yehui Tang, Han Hu, Yunhe Wang, and Chang Xu. 2023. One-for-all: bridge the gap between heterogeneous architectures in knowledge distillation. In *Proceedings of the 37th International Conference on Neural Information Processing Systems*, NIPS '23, Red Hook, NY, USA. Curran Associates Inc.

Nora Hollenstein and Ce Zhang. 2019. Entity recognition at first sight: Improving NER with eye movement information. In *Proceedings of the 2019 Conference of the North American Chapter of the Association for Computational Linguistics: Human Language Technologies, Volume 1 (Long and Short Papers)*, pages 1–10, Minneapolis, Minnesota. Association for Computational Linguistics.

E B Huey. 1908. *The Psychology and Pedagogy of Reading*. The Psychology and Pedagogy of Reading. Macmillan, Oxford, England.

Albrecht Werner Inhoff. 1984. Two stages of word processing during eye fixations in the reading of prose. *Journal of Verbal Learning and Verbal Behavior*, 23(5):612–624.

Sigrid Klerke, Yoav Goldberg, and Anders Søgaard. 2016. Improving sentence compression by learning to predict gaze. In *Proceedings of the 2016 Conference of the North American Chapter of the Association for Computational Linguistics: Human Language Technologies*, pages 1528–1533, San Diego, California. Association for Computational Linguistics.

Reinhold Kliegl, Antje Nuthmann, and Ralf Engbert. 2006. Tracking the mind during reading: the influence of past, present, and future words on fixation durations. *Journal of Experimental Psychology. General*, 135(1):12–35.

Simon Kornblith, Mohammad Norouzi, Honglak Lee, and Geoffrey E. Hinton. 2019. Similarity of neural network representations revisited. *CoRR*, abs/1905.00414.

Eline R. Kupers, Tomas Knapen, Elisha P. Merriam, and Kendrick N. Kay. 2024. Principles of intensive human neuroimaging. *Trends in Neurosciences*, 47(11):856–864.

Mayug Maniparambil, Raiymbek Akshulakov, Yasser Abdelaziz Dahou Djilali, Sanath Narayan, Mohamed El Amine Seddik, Karttikeya Mangalam, and Noel E. O'Connor. 2024. Do vision and language encoders represent the world similarly? *Preprint*, arXiv:2401.05224.

Stephen Merity, Nitish Shirish Keskar, and Richard Socher. 2017. Regularizing and optimizing LSTM language models. *CoRR*, abs/1708.02182.

Tomas Mikolov, Ilya Sutskever, Kai Chen, Greg S Corrado, and Jeff Dean. 2013. Distributed Representations of Words and Phrases and their Compositionality. In *Advances in Neural Information Processing Systems*, volume 26. Curran Associates, Inc.

Alec Radford, Karthik Narasimhan, Tim Salimans, and Ilya Sutskever. 2018. Improving Language Understanding by Generative Pre-Training.

Alec Radford, Jeffrey Wu, Rewon Child, David Luan, Dario Amodei, and Ilya Sutskever. 2019. Language Models are Unsupervised Multitask Learners.

Núria Sebastián Gallés, Antonia Martí, and Manuel Carreiras. 1998. *LEXESP: Léxico informatizado del español*. Ediciones de la Universidad de Barcelona, Barcelona.

Jerry Tang, Amanda LeBel, Shailee Jain, and Alexander G. Huth. 2023. Semantic reconstruction of continuous language from non-invasive brain recordings. *Nature Neuroscience*, 26(5):858–866. Publisher: Nature Publishing Group.

Ivan Vulić, Simon Baker, Edoardo Maria Ponti, Ulla Petti, Ira Leviant, Kelly Wing, Olga Majewska, Eden Bar, Matt Malone, Thierry Poibeau, Roi Reichart, and Anna Korhonen. 2020a. Multi-SimLex: A Large-Scale Evaluation of Multilingual and Crosslingual Lexical Semantic Similarity. *Computational Linguistics*, 46(4):847–897.

Ivan Vulić, Edoardo Maria Ponti, Robert Litschko, Goran Glavaš, and Anna Korhonen. 2020b. Probing pretrained language models for lexical semantics. In *Proceedings of the 2020 Conference on Empirical Methods in Natural Language Processing (EMNLP)*, pages 7222–7240, Online. Association for Computational Linguistics.

Duo Yang and Nora Hollenstein. 2023. PLM-AS: Pre-trained Language Models Augmented with Scanpaths for Sentiment Classification. *Proceedings of the Northern Lights Deep Learning Workshop*, 4.

Leran Zhang and Nora Hollenstein. 2024. Eye-tracking features masking transformer attention in question-answering tasks. In *Proceedings of the 2024 Joint International Conference on Computational Linguistics, Language Resources and Evaluation (LREC-COLING 2024)*, pages 7057–7070, Torino, Italia. ELRA and ICCL.

A Eye-tracking experiment

All participants were native Spanish speakers and had normal or corrected-to-normal vision. All of them were recruited from the university mailing lists and were compensated with the equivalent of 5 USD per one-hour session. Written informed consent in agreement with the Helsinki declaration was provided by each of them. The experiment was approved by the Comité de Ética del Centro de Educación Médica e Investigaciones Clínicas "Norberto Quirno" (CEMIC) (Protocol 435). Records were anonymized in compliance with ethical board approvals and contain no personal information.

A.1 Corpus

Fifteen of the twenty short stories were extracted from "100 covers de cuentos clásicos" (Casciari, 2021), while the other five were extracted from online Argentinian blog posts. The original stories of the former were written by several different authors and were subsequently simplified, translated (if needed) and re-written in Spanish by Hernán Casciari. This way, there is diversity in literary style, while maintaining both difficulty and slang constant. The titles, authors and fixation statistics can be found in Table A1.

The selection criteria for the short stories was based on minimizing dialogue, very short and very long sentences (less than six words and greater than 29 words, respectively), infrequent words (less than 100 appearances in the Latin American subtitles database EsPal (Duchon et al., 2013)), infrequent characters (¿; ?; ¡; !; "; "; —; «; (;)), not containing written dates, and being no shorter than 400 words and no longer than 1500 words.

A.2 Environment & Setup

The experiment was written in MATLAB 2015a, using Psychtoolbox-3 (Brainard, 1997). It was conducted in a dark room, employing the EyeLink 1000 (SR Research, Ontario, Canada) binocular eye-tracker at 1000Hz. The monitor had a resolution of 1920x1080 and participants were seated 55cm away from it, using a chin and forehead rest to stabilize their head. The stimuli were presented in Courier New with font size 24 and black color with a gray background, 55 pixels of line spacing, 280 pixels of left margin and 185 pixels of top margin, with a maximum of fourteen lines per screen. Using these parameters, the text was divided in screens (ranging from four to six, depending on its length), and participants were allowed to go backward and forward between screens.

At the beginning of the experiment, participants were instructed to read the texts carefully, as comprehension questions would be asked at the end of each of them. Each short story constitutes an item and a separate trial, with eye-tracking calibration preceding the presentation of the stimuli (Fig. A1). Items were sorted by their number of infrequent words and characters, and short and long sentences, in ascending order. They were subsequently divided in four blocks and each block was shuffled randomly for each participant. Following this order, the experiment was carried out in two sessions of ten trials (two blocks, approximately one hour of reading). After the comprehension questions, a word association task was presented, where words were displayed (one by one) and the participant was required to write the first word that came to mind. For this task, five words were chosen randomly from the 150 most frequent words that are not propositions, verbs, articles (according to the corpus LexEsp (Sebastián Gallés et al., 1998)), and were not present in stories. The same five words were always presented for a given item. The goal of this task is to remove any lingering bias that may have remained from reading the story. The following trial did not begin until the participant agreed to it.

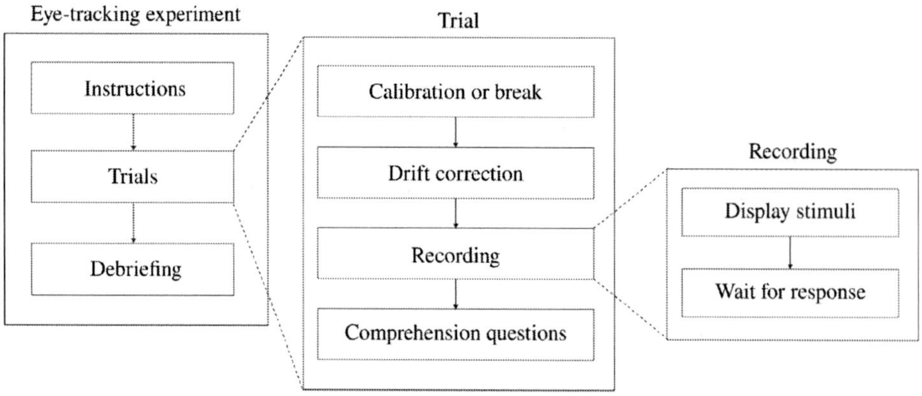

Figure A1: Depiction of the experiment setup, in which each trial consisted of a short story. The story was divided into screens and the participant was free to navigate forwards or backwards. At the end of each trial, the participant was required to answer comprehension questions about it.

A.3 Data processing

When processing a given trial, only fixations from the eye that had the least calibration error (as reported by the eye-tracker) were kept. Horizontal lines were drawn manually for each screen, indicating to what line of text each row of fixations belonged to. Very long and very short fixations (over 1000ms and under 50ms, respectively), as well as the first and last fixations in a screen, were automatically discarded. For a given word in a text line, its corresponding fixations are those whose x-coordinates fall within the word's surrounding blank spaces. Gaze measures were extracted from those words that were not the first or last words in a sentence or line and did not contain punctuation marks, dashes or numbers.

As the eye-tracker was used in binocular mode, fixations and saccades from both eyes were recorded. For data analysis, we only took into account the recordings from the eye that had the least calibration error as reported by the eye-tracker.

Each time a participant moved forward or backward to a different screen (pressed the right or left arrow), a message, with a timestamp, was logged by the eyetracker. These timestamps where utilized to divide the fixations by their corresponding screen. Some participants returned to a previous screen more than once, usually to get a better comprehension of the story so they could answer the questions accurately. In these cases, when the return was made by mistake (there are some fixations scattered across the screen in no particular order), the data is disposed of. However, when the return included re-reading some portion of the text, the data is kept, and the fixations are counted as regressions.

Once the data were curated and horizontal lines were drawn to decide to which text line each row of fixations corresponded to, fixation assignment to words followed. Given an item, this process is performed separately for each trial. As fixations are divided by screen, for each screen, text lines were first split into words by using blank spaces as separators. A subset of screen fixations is considered to belong to a given text line if their y-coordinate falls within the lower (included) and upper (excluded) bound of the corresponding horizontal lines.

In every screen, the first and last fixations are automatically discarded. Additionally, for each line, any regressive fixation between the first and the left-most is considered to be the result of oculomotor errors (i.e., *return sweep*) and is discarded. Fixations resulting from returning to the screen are numbered starting from the last fixation number on that screen. They are considered regressions if they fixate on the same words as the previous times. Fixations outside the scope of any word in the text are considered out of bounds.

B Non fine-tuned word pairs

When analyzing word pairs that were not present in the stimuli of the eye-tracking experiment (see 2.1), as expected, we found little to no change in the mean of the distributions (Fig. B2). In the case of Word2Vec, fine-tuning with Texts and its variation with gaze measures provided no difference whatsoever with respect to the baseline in all datasets. However, despite small changes to the

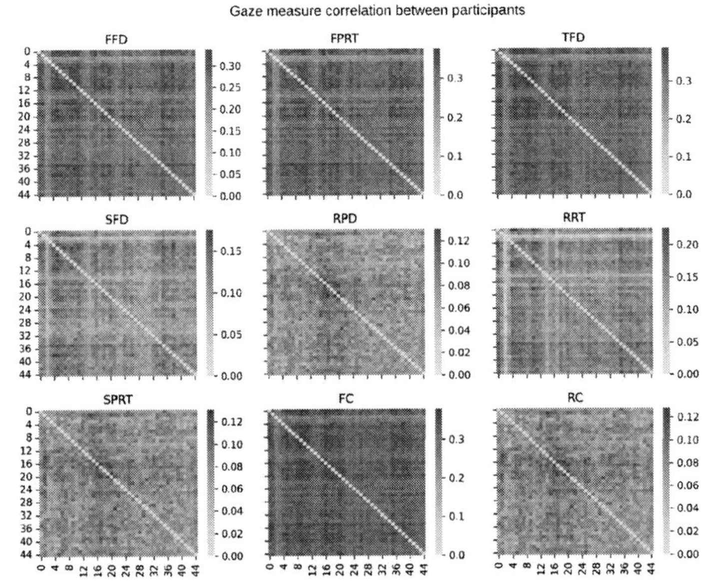

Figure A2: Correlation matrix for each gaze measure, averaged across items, between the 45 participants that read all items. Gaze measures were discretized in ten bins for each individual. FFD refers to First Fixation Duration; FPRT to First Pass Reading Time; TFD to Total Fixation Duration; SFD to Single Fixation Duration; RPD to Regression Path Duration; RRT to Re-Reading Time; SPRT to Second Pass Reading Time; FC to Fixation Count; RC to Regression Count.

mean, fine-tuning with Scanpaths provided significantly different values in all datasets compared to the baseline: in SimLex, the mean of the baseline was 0.4716 (s.e.m. 0.0086) and 0.4611 (s.e.m. 0.0087, $p < 0.0001$, ws. 275.0) for Scanpaths; in Abstract, 0.4389 (s.e.m. 0.0077) and 0.4190 (s.e.m. 0.0079, $p < 0.0001$, ws. 283.0); and, in Concrete, 0.4492 (s.e.m. 0.0083.0) and 0.4461 (s.e.m. 0.0083, $p < 0.0001$, ws. 1211.0).

With respect to AWD-LSTM, on the contrary, most variations provide significant differences in the distributions of the correlations with respect to the baseline in all datasets, with the exception of Scanpaths (with and without gaze measures) in Abstract ($p > 0.1$, ws. 2236.0 and 2423.5, respectively). When fine-tuning with Texts, with and without gaze measures, the mean of the distribution is slightly higher than the baseline: in SimLex, the mean of the baseline is 0.2991 (s.e.m. 0.0099) compared to 0.3076 and 0.3079 (s.e.m. 0.0098, $p < 0.0001$, ws. 442.0 and 413.0), respectively; in Abstract, 0.2594 (s.e.m. 0.0089) compared to 0.2728 (s.e.m. 0.0087, $p < 0.0001$, ws. 136.0 and 163.0); and, in Concrete, 0.2101 (s.e.m. 0.0098) compared to 0.2187 and 0.2192 (s.e.m. 0.0098, $p < 0.0001$, ws. 726.5 and 632.0). Scanpaths with and without gaze measures, on the other hand, slightly decreases the mean in SimLex (0.2877 and 0.2841, s.e.m. 0.01, $p < 0.005$, ws. 1067 and 1634, respectively) and in Concrete (0.1898 and 0.1952, s.e.m. 0.01, $p < 0.0001$, ws. 80.0 and 182.0, respectively).

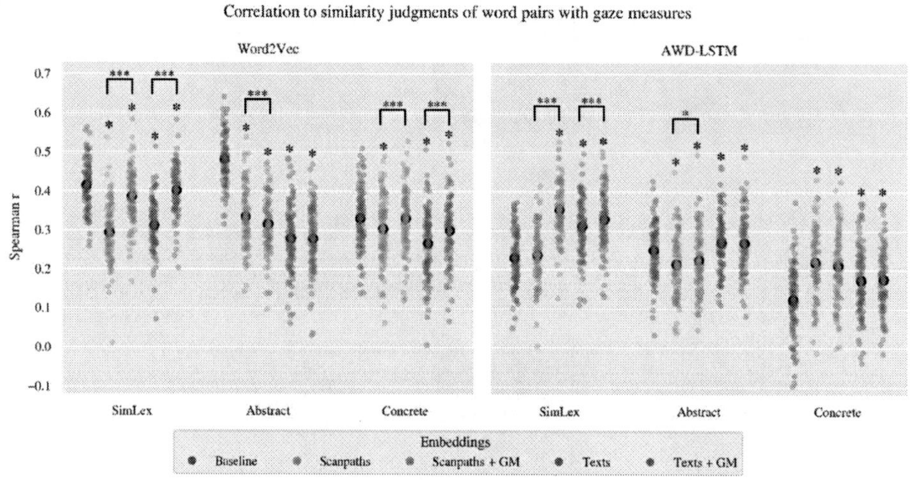

Figure B1: Distribution of the Spearman rank correlations of the cosine distances between word pairs that possess gaze measures with respect to human similarity judgments presented in Table 1.

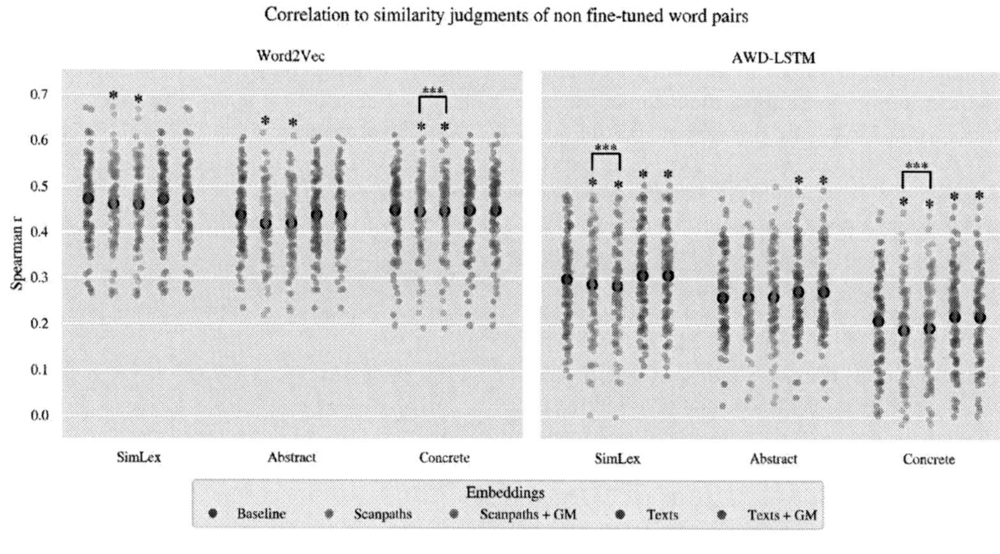

Figure B2: Spearman rank correlation of the cosine distance between word pairs that have not been fine-tuned (i.e., were not present in the stimuli of the eye-tracking experiment) with respect to human similarity judgments in three different datasets. 895, 1081, and 1431 word pairs were evaluated in total for SimLex, Abstract and Concrete, respectively, using random sampling with replacement of a hundred word pairs a hundred times. An asterisk above the strip plot indicates significance against the baseline. On the left are the results of the fine-tuning on Word2Vec and, on the right, on AWD-LSTM. Baseline refers to the models trained on the baseline corpus, whereas Scanpaths are the models fine-tuned on the text in the stimuli as read by the participants, and Texts are the models fine-tuned on the stimuli as is. GM refers to the addition of gaze measures to the training process.

Story	Author	Words	Fixations	Excluded fixations	Regressions	Skips
La noche de los feos	Mario Benedetti	544	25774	10290	8046	11234
Cómo funcionan los bolsillos	Valentín Muro	972	45815	11677	16176	19705
La máscara de la Muerte Roja	Edgar Allan Poe	572	26641	6805	9092	11974
Las fotografías	Silvina Ocampo	618	26686	8034	8580	12636
La salud de los enfermos	Julio Cortázar	667	34486	7596	12189	17953
Buenos Aires	Hernán Casciari	607	28813	6855	10368	12932
Wakefield	Nathaniel Hawthorne	693	31610	9034	10467	17397
Cómo funciona caminar en la nieve	Valentín Muro	1066	47302	10650	16245	20937
Ahora debería reírme, si no estuviera muerto	Angela Carter	606	25629	7124	7022	15558
El espejo	Haruki Murakami	628	29851	9597	9170	16788
Embarrar la magia	Facundo Alvarez Heduan	683	34749	12290	12143	14400
La lluvia de fuego	Leopoldo Lugones	640	30960	9236	10121	15979
Educar para escalar y bucear	Andrés Rieznik	599	27797	7472	9500	12621
El golpe de gracia	Ambrose Bierce	602	27629	7567	9540	14387
La gallina degollada	Horacio Quiroga	659	30188	8958	9825	15769
La canción que cantábamos todos los días	Luciano Lamberti	620	28299	7247	8418	15386
El almohadón de plumas	Horacio Quiroga	579	28063	9453	8301	15087
Una rosa para Emilia	William Faulkner	643	33946	8968	12007	16178
La de la Obsesión por la Patineta	Hernán Casciari	579	29200	8516	10044	13171
Total	-	**13218**	**623654**	**175481**	**206586**	**305949**

Table A1: List of stories employed in the eye-tracking experiment. Exclusion criteria for words (and their corresponding fixations) include being first or last in a sentence or screen line, or containing punctuation marks, dashes or numbers. Stories were divided in screens and participants were free to return to a previous screen. Fixations to words in a returning screen are counted as regressions.

Unzipping the Causality of Zipf's Law and Other Lexical Trade-offs

Amanda Doucette[1] **Timothy J. O'Donnell**[1,2] **Morgan Sonderegger**[1]
[1]Dept. of Linguistics, McGill University [2]Canada CIFAR AI Chair, Mila
amanda.doucette@mail.mcgill.ca timothy.odonnell@mcgill.ca
morgan.sonderegger@mcgill.ca

Abstract

There are strong constraints on the structure of a possible lexicon. For example, the negative correlation between word frequency and length known as Zipf's law of abbreviation, and a negative correlation between word length and phonotactic complexity appear to hold across languages. While lexical trade-offs like these have been examined individually, it is unclear how they interact as a system. In this paper, we propose causal discovery as a method for identifying lexical biases and their interactions in a set of variables. We represent the lexicon as a causal model, and apply the Fast Causal Discovery algorithm (Spirtes et al., 1995) to identify both causal relationships between measured variables and the existence of possible unmeasured confounding variables. We apply this method to lexical data including measures of word length, frequency, phonotactic complexity, and morphological irregularity for 25 languages and find evidence of universal associations involving word length with a high likelihood of involving an unmeasured confounder, suggesting that additional variables need to be measured to determine how they are related. We also find evidence of variation across languages in relationships between the remaining variables, and suggest that given a larger dataset, causal discovery algorithms can be a useful tool in assessing the universality of lexical biases.[1]

1 Introduction

Although lexicons vary significantly across languages, they exhibit striking regularity. For example, it is well documented that the most frequent words in a language tend to be the shortest (Zipf's law of abbreviation;[2] Zipf, 1935; Piantadosi, 2014), and that frequent words tend to be phonotactically simple (Mahowald et al., 2018). Some of these trade-offs appear to be linguistic universals while others, such as the relationship between frequency and morphological irregularity, are more debated and appear to display more variation across languages (Fratini et al., 2014; Yang, 2016; Wu et al., 2019; Doucette et al., 2024). Each of these trade-offs imposes limitations on the set of possible natural language lexicons. Although it is possible to construct a lexicon where, for example, the most frequent words are the longest, no human language follows this pattern.

Many of these trade-offs have been attributed to universal cognitive pressures. For example, a pressure for efficient communication may explain why frequent words tend to be short and phonotactically simple (Zipf, 1935; Mahowald et al., 2018; Piantadosi et al., 2011; Graff, 2012; Gibson et al., 2019; Levshina, 2022). Hay and Baayen (2003) attribute a tendency for frequent words to be morphologically irregular to a constraint on processing – it is more efficient to access these frequent irregulars as whole words, rather than parse them into component morphemes. However, a pressure for efficient communication could also imply the opposite pattern: It is more memory-efficient to store component morphemes in the lexicon, so irregulars should be *infrequent*. Another trade-off, a negative correlation between word length and phonotactic complexity demonstrated by Pimentel et al. (2020), has been attributed to a pressure towards uniform information density: A consistent rate of information requires shorter words to be more complex (Pellegrino et al., 2011; Coupé et al., 2019; Meister et al., 2021). However, Doucette et al. (2024) showed that this correlation becomes positive when only morphologically complex words are examined. Such complex and potentially contradictory results suggest a network of interacting pressures influencing the shape of a lexicon. A cognitive pressure that neatly explains one trade-off may be

[1]Code is available at https://osf.io/g8b35.

[2]Not the Zipf's law from Zipf (1949), which states that a word's frequency is inversely proportional to its frequency rank.

Proceedings of the Workshop on Cognitive Modeling and Computational Linguistics, pages 66–76
May 3, 2025 ©2025 Association for Computational Linguistics

contradicted by another. Because we are examining interactions among sets of variables, we will refer to the limitations on possible lexicons imposed by these trade-offs as *lexical biases*, independent of the *cognitive constraints* that may cause them. In order to study the cognitive constraints shaping the lexicon, we cannot only consider data representing a single trade-off in the lexicon. Instead, we need an understanding of what lexical biases exist, how they interact with each other, and whether and how they vary across the world's languages.

In this paper, we propose a method for identifying lexical biases and their interactions: causal discovery. Much of the previously described work on lexical biases implicitly suggests a causal relationship – that there is some process where words that become more frequent are shortened over time, for example. It is also possible that this type of direct causal process does not exist, and instead word length and frequency share some common cause – a *confounder*. The structural causal modeling framework introduced by Pearl (1995) is useful in assessing these types of causal structures. A causal model includes a set of random variables and the causal relationships between them, represented by a graph. We can represent the situation where a change in word length (WL) causes a change in frequency (FR) as $WL \longrightarrow FR$, and the situation where both share an unknown common cause (U) as $WL \longleftarrow U \longrightarrow FR$. These graphs represent data generating processes. In the first graph, a word length is sampled, then its frequency is determined based on that value. In the second graph, we sample a value of U, which determines the values of WL and FR. Causal discovery allows us to identify causal graphs consistent with a sample of observational data. Identifying a causal model of the lexicon through causal discovery allows us to examine the networks of lexical biases across languages and ultimately identify the cognitive constraints that underlie them.

Although many questions about language involve causality, causal analyses have only been applied to linguistic data in a few cases. For example, in identifying the causes of lenition (Priva, 2017; Priva and Gleason, 2020), examining causality in child language acquisition (Irvin et al., 2016; Spokoyny et al., 2016), in language change (del Prado Martín, 2014; Moscoso del Prado Martín and Brendel, 2016; Dellert, 2019, 2024), and in examining cross-linguistic trade-offs between case marking and word order (Levshina, 2021). Causal models have not yet been used to investigate lexical biases, which we do using causal discovery.

We apply this method to data described in Doucette et al. (2024): measures of word length, frequency, phonotactic complexity, and morphological irregularity in 25 languages. Through causal discovery, we are able to identify the well-known associations between word length and frequency, and word length and phonotactic complexity, as well as the association between word length and morphological irregularity identified by Doucette et al. (2024). However, we are also able to identify possible unmeasured confounding variables in each of these relationships, suggesting that the direct causal relationship implied by previous studies may not exist. Furthermore, we find evidence of variation in relationships between the remaining pairs of variables: an association only exists in approximately half of the languages in the sample, and where it does exist there is the possibility of confounding. These results demonstrate that in order to determine the causal structure of lexical biases, a larger set of variables need to be considered. Causal discovery allows us to both identify relationships between aspects of the lexicon and determine where more data is needed to make conclusions about causal structure.

2 Data

In this paper, we examine data from Doucette et al. (2024), which was used to study compensation relationships between word length, frequency, morphological irregularity, and phonotactic complexity. It contains 25 languages selected from UniMorph, a database of morphologically annotated corpora (Batsuren et al., 2022), with between 334 and 96,196 word forms per language (median 8,061), converted to IPA transcriptions using Epitran (Mortensen et al., 2018). We note that this data does not represent a random sample from each lexicon: UniMorph largely consists of words with multiple morphemes, with few monomorphemic words. We return to this point in the discussion.

In this data, word length is measured in number of phones, and frequency is calculated from Wikipedia as log count per million. The phonotactic complexity measure, defined by Pimentel et al. (2020), comes from a neural network model trained to estimate the probability of a word w given the rest of the language $\mathcal{L}$. Phonotactic complexity is a measure of bits per phoneme:

Edge type	Interpretation
X ⟶ Y	X causes Y, Y does not cause X
X o→ Y	either X causes Y, or an unobserved confounder causes both X and Y, but not both
X ⟷ Y	an unobserved confounder causes both X and Y
X o–o Y	One of the following holds: 1. X causes Y; 2. Y causes X; 3. an unobserved confounder causes X and Y; 4. both 1 and 3 hold; 5. both 2 and 3 hold
X - - - Y	no association between X and Y

Table 1: Partial Ancestral Graph (PAG) edge types and their interpretations.

$\log p(w \mid \mathcal{L})/|w|$. The morphological irregularity measure, from Wu et al. (2019), is a neural estimate of the predictability of the surface form of an inflected word from its lemma. A neural network is trained to predict an inflected form from a lemma ℓ, a set of morphological features σ, and the rest of the language with the target lemma removed $\mathcal{L}_{-\ell}$, and the morphological irregularity measure is $\log\left(p(w \mid \ell, \sigma, \mathcal{L}_{-\ell})/\left[1 - p(w \mid \ell, \sigma, \mathcal{L}_{-\ell})\right]\right)$.

3 Causal Graphs and Causal Discovery

In Pearl's (1995) structural causal modeling framework, a causal model is represented by a directed acyclic graph (DAG), $G = (\mathbf{V}, \mathbf{E})$, a tuple with a finite set of vertices $\mathbf{V}$ representing random variables, and a finite set of edges $\mathbf{E} \subseteq \mathbf{V} \times \mathbf{V}$ representing causal relationships. An edge $X \rightarrow Y$ implies that X directly causes Y. The value of any variable in a causal graph is completely determined by a function of its parents. In a DAG $X \rightarrow Y \leftarrow Z$, Y is caused by X and Z, and $Y = f(X, Z)$. There is a large literature on causal modeling, which we only partially and briefly summarize here. For more background, see Pearl et al. (2016) or Hernán and Robins (2024).

Causal discovery algorithms aim to recover the true graph G from a sample dataset. To do this, several assumptions about the relationship between a graph G and the joint probability distribution over its random variables $P(\mathbf{V})$ are needed. The graph G must satisfy the *Causal Markov Condition*: every variable is conditionally independent of its nondescendents given its parents. The probability distribution associated with G must decompose recursively as $P(\mathbf{V}) = \prod_{X \in \mathbf{V}} P(X \mid Pa(X))$, where $Pa(X)$ is the parents of X in G. We also need to assume *faithfulness*: that all independence relationships among the variables $\mathbf{V}$ are represented in G. In other words, the conditional independence relationships in the data are closely tied to the structure of the DAG G. Causal discovery algorithms identify conditional independencies in data, then construct a graph consistent with them.

There are many causal discovery algorithms, each with different assumptions (see Zanga et al. (2022) or Malinsky and Danks (2018) for a summary). Many assume *causal sufficiency*: that any cause of a variable in $\mathbf{V}$ is also contained in $\mathbf{V}$. If there are any unmeasured common causes in the data, an algorithm assuming causal sufficiency will not output a correct causal graph. For example, if we are trying to discover a true DAG $X \longrightarrow U \longleftarrow Y$, but do not have measurements of U, an algorithm assuming causal sufficiency will fail to recover the correct DAG. The unmeasured variable U is a confounder that can induce a spurious correlation between X and Y even though there is no causal relationship between X and Y.

It is likely that most lexical data is not causally sufficient: there are likely to be additional causes outside of the set of variables included in the data. Therefore, we use an algorithm that does not assume sufficiency: the Fast Causal Inference (FCI) algorithm (Spirtes et al., 1993, 1995), which takes a set of observations of random variables as input and ouputs a Partial Ancestral Graph (PAG), a causal graph with additional edge types in order to represent unmeasured confounders and uncertainty. In a PAG, directed edges $\longrightarrow$ and $\longleftarrow$ have the same meaning as in a DAG: they represent a direct causal relationship. A PAG represents the presence of an unmeasured confounder with a bidirected edge, $\longleftrightarrow$. For example, an edge $X \longleftrightarrow Y$ means there is some unmeasured variable that causes both X and Y, and that there is no direct causal relationship between X and Y. PAGs also add circle endmarks to edges, representing uncertainty. For example, X o–o Y corresponds to one of several possibilities: X causes Y, Y causes X, there is an unmeasured common cause of both X and Y, or there is both an unmeasured common cause and a direct causal relationship (i.e. $X \longrightarrow Y$ *and* $X \longleftrightarrow Y$). The interpretation of all possible edges in a PAG are listed in Table 1.

The FCI algorithm starts with a complete undirected graph, where all random variables are connected by undirected edges. Next, a series of conditional independence tests are conducted. An undirected edge A — B is removed if A and B are conditionally independent given some set of variables **C**. The resulting graph after no more edges can be removed is called a *skeleton*. The unorieted edges in a graph skeleton do not have a causal interpretation, but can be useful for examining statistical *associations* between the random variables. In the next step of the FCI algorithm, all edges in the skeleton begin as unoriented o–o edges. Edges are then oriented following a series of rules based on graph structure.

We use an implementation of the FCI algorithm and an implementation of the Fisher's Z conditional independence test from the R package `pcalg` (Kalisch et al., 2012). This conditional independence test assumes a Gaussian distribution, and requires a significance level. This assumption may not be reasonable, and we will return to it in the discussion. For each language in the dataset, we used a bootstrapping procedure to resample the data 1000 times. The FCI algorithm was run on each sample with a significance level of 0.01, and the proportion of edge types discovered for each pair of variables was recorded.

4 Results

For each language, the most frequently occurring edge type for each pair of variables in the bootstrap samples was selected to create a "most-likely graph" for that language. These are shown in Figure 1, where we can see that there is significant variation in the most-likely graphs discovered for each language – there are 18 unique graphs identified across 25 languages. At most three languages share the same graph. One of these groups, containing Chewa and Zulu, can be explained by typological relatedness, but the others have no clear explanation. The variation in these most-likely graphs may suggest that there is no universal set of lexical biases shared across languages. We return to this point in the discussion.

We also see that the graphs for many languages contain edges with circle marks (←o , o→ , o–o), which suggests that there is not enough information in the dataset to fully determine causal relationships. It is likely that there are unmeasured confounding variables. If we instead examine the graph skeletons discovered by FCI, we can examine associations between variables. In these undirected graphs, the presence of an edge implies an association between variables – a correlation that is not necessarily causal. In Figure 1, groups of languages sharing the same skeleton are outlined. When considering the graph skeletons, we see larger groups of languages emerge, suggesting less variation in lexical biases across languages. It is unclear why certain languages share the same skeleton structure. Many of the groups in Figure 1 are not typologically related, such as Polish, Dutch, Czech, French, and Ukrainian. A larger set of languages is needed to determine if there is any typological explanation behind these groupings.

To further examine these individual language graphs, we created a cross-linguistic most-likely graph by selecting the most frequently occurring edge type for each pair of variables from the graphs in Figure 1. This is shown in Figure 2. A most-likely skeleton, shown in Figure 3 was created by following the same procedure with the graph skeletons. To examine the distribution of edge types in the bootstrap sampling procedure, we plotted histograms for each pair of variables showing the proportion of bootstrap samples where types of edges were found across all languages. A right-skewed histogram implies that an edge was discovered in most languages, while a left-skewed histogram implies that no edge was discovered in most languages. Figure 4A shows the proportion of samples where an edge of any type was discovered (⟶ , ⟵ , ⟷ , o→ , ←o , o–o), Figure 4B shows the proportion where a directed edge was discovered (⟶ or ⟵), and Figure 4C shows the proportion of edges discovered with confounding variables (⟷) or with potential confounding variables (o–o , ←o , or o→).

4.1 Word Length and Frequency

Due to Zipf's law of abbreviation (Zipf, 1935), where word length and frequency are negatively correlated, we expect to find an association between word length and frequency. This is what we find: in Figure 3, we see that the most likely skeletons for all languages have an edge between these variables. In Figure 4, we also see that an edge was discovered in nearly all bootstrap samples for nearly all languages. However, directed edges (⟶ or ⟵) were not found in nearly all samples, as shown in Figure 4. Instead, as can be seen in Figure 4, nearly all bootstrap samples indicate the possible presence of an unmeasured confounding variable. In Figure 2, a o–o edge is most likely between word

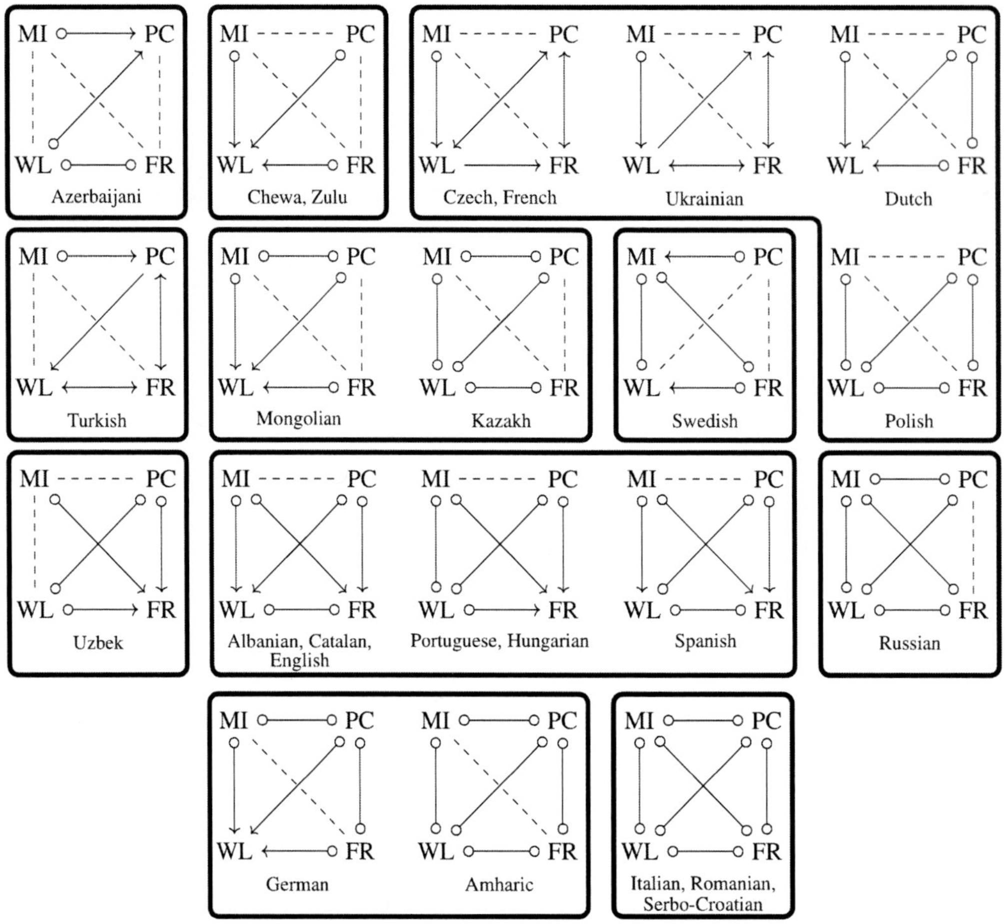

Figure 1: Most likely PAGs for individual languages. Languages with the same undirected graph outlined in black. MI: morphological irregularity; PC: phonotactic complexity; WL: word length; FR: frequency.

length and frequency, implying an association with unknown causal direction and possible confounding. This suggests that we are not able to infer the causality of this relationship from the variables in this dataset.

This is consistent with previous work where it has been argued that average surprisal, or predictability in context, correlates more strongly with word length than frequency does (Piantadosi et al., 2011), although other analyses have failed to reproduce this finding (Meylan and Griffiths, 2021; Pimentel et al., 2023). This dataset does not include a measure of average surprisal, but it is possible that surprisal is the unmeasured confounding variable, and causal discovery could help determine the relationship between frequency, word length, and surprisal given a dataset with measurements of average surprisal. Because word length correlates with surprisal, surprisal may also be a confounder in its relationships with morphological irregularity and phonotactic complexity. In order to make conclusions about causal relationships involving word length and frequency, more variables need to be measured than those included here.

4.2 Word Length and Phonotactic Complexity

In Figure 3, we also see that an edge was discovered between word length and phonotactic complexity in all languages, as predicted by Pimentel et al.'s (2020) finding that these variables are negatively correlated. The most frequently occurring edge type between word length and phonotactic complexity is ∘–∘ , implying that either word length is constrained by phonotactic complexity (PC ⟶ WL), phonotactic complexity is constrained by word length (PC ⟵ WL) or there is an unmeasured confounding variable (PC ⟷ WL). However, despite being the most frequent edge type between

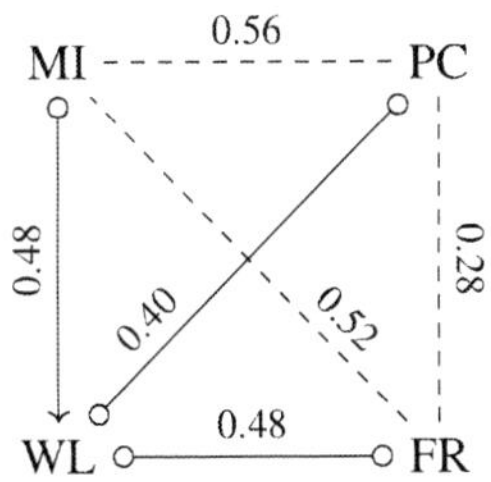

Figure 2: Most likely PAG across all languages, with proportion of languages where edge type occurred. MI: morphological irregularity; PC: phonotactic complexity; WL: word length; FR: frequency.

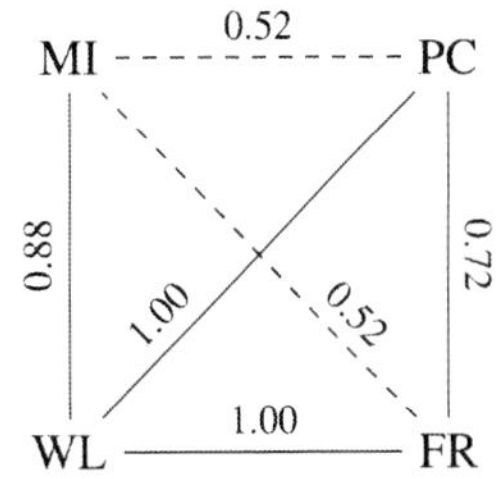

Figure 3: Most likely undirected graph skeleton across all languages, with proportion of languages where edge type occurred. MI: morphological irregularity; PC: phonotactic complexity; WL: word length; FR: frequency.

these variables, it occurs in less than half of languages, suggesting variation in the causal structure of this relationship. This can be seen in Figure 1, where there is little consistency in the type of edge between word length and phonotactic complexity. Figure 4 shows that a directed edge was found in very few samples, and that a possible confounder was identified in nearly all samples. Again, this shows that while an association between word length and phonotactic complexity may be universal, we do not have enough data to determine their causal relationship.

4.3 Word Length and Morphological Irregularity

Figure 3 and Figure 4 show that an edge was also discovered between word length and morphological irregularity in most languages, consistent with Doucette et al.'s (2024) finding of a negative correlation. Again, directed edges were discovered in very few samples and a possible confounder was discovered in most samples, as shown in Figure 4. In Figure 2, the most common edge type between word length and morphological irregularity is ←o , discovered in 12 of 25 languages. Like the relationship between word length and phonotactic complexity, an association between these variables is near-universal, but it is likely confounded by a variable outside of this dataset.

4.4 Frequency and Phonotactic Complexity

The remaining three pairs of variables display less consistency in whether or not an edge is present. For frequency and phonotactic complexity, the most likely scenario is that an edge does exist, shown in Figure 3. However, the most likely PAG shows no edge between these variables. Although the presence of an edge between these variables is slightly more likely than not, the type of edge varies across languages, as shown in Figure 1. Mahowald et al. (2018) found that a negative correlation between phonotactic complexity and frequency was robust after controlling for the effect of word length as a confounding factor. The FCI algorithm is able to identify confounding relationships, but this relationship does not appear as robustly as previously found, even in Doucette et al.'s (2024) analysis of the same data. This suggests that it may not be correct to conclude that there is an association between frequency and phonotactic complexity while only considering word length as a confounder. Once another factor like morphological irregularity is included, the relationship becomes less clear.

4.5 Frequency and Morphological Irregularity

While Wu et al. (2019) found a positive correlation between morphological irregularity and frequency, we found no association in about half of the 25 languages, as shown in both the most-likely skeleton in Figure 3. and the most-likely PAG in Figure 2. In Figure 4, we can see that for some languages, this edge occurred in almost no bootstrap samples, while for other languages, it occurred in nearly all samples. Very few languages fall in the center of the histogram, with the edge being discovered in some samples, but not others. This U-shaped histogram suggests that the existence of an association between morphological irregularity and frequency may be a point of variation across languages – some definitively have an association, while others do not.

The histogram for possible confounders in Figure 4 is similarly U-shaped. This suggests if an edge between frequency and morphological irreg-

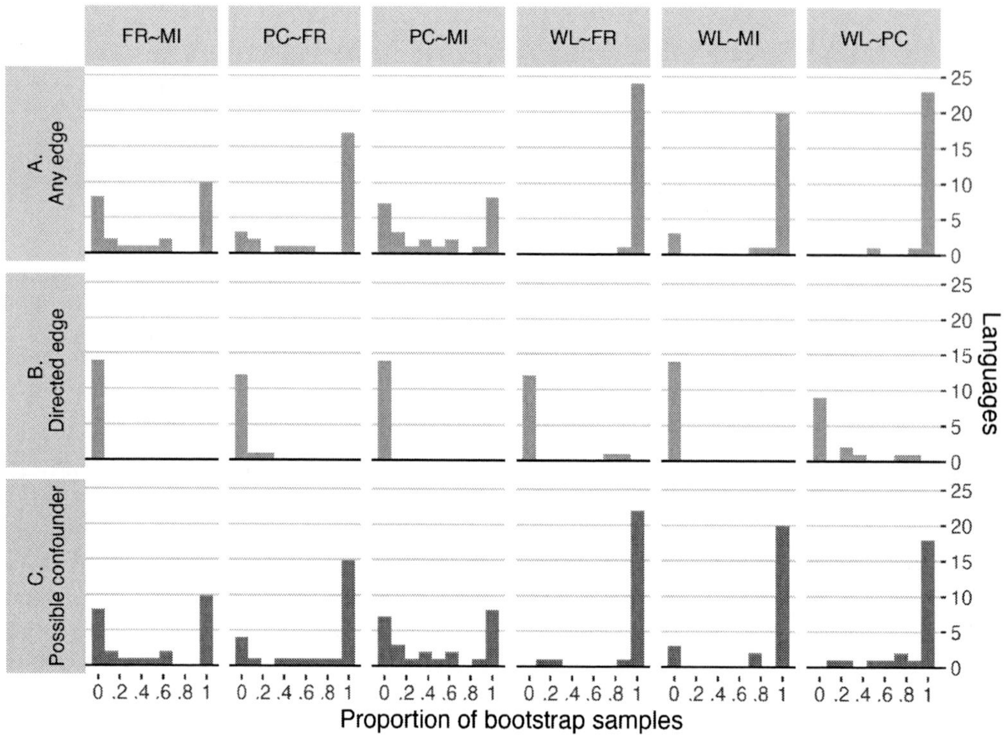

Figure 4: Histograms of proportion of bootstrap samples including edge types for each pair of variables. A: ⟶ ⟵ , ⟷ , o–o , o⟶ , or ⟵o ; B: ⟶ or ⟵ ; C: ⟷ , o–o , o⟶ , or ⟵o . MI: morphological irregularity; PC: phonotactic complexity; WL: word length; FR: frequency.

ularity exists for a language, it is likely to have a possible confounding variable. Like previously discussed pairs of variables, directed edges are rarely identified between frequency and morphological irregularity.

4.6 Morphological Irregularity and Phonotactic Complexity

We see a similar pattern in the histograms in Figure 4 for phonotactic complexity and morphological irregularity: Directed edges almost never occur, and the edge existence and possible confounder histograms are U-shaped, suggesting that languages vary in whether or not there is an associatino between these variables. This is consistent with previous findings that a relationship between morphological irregularity and phonotactic complexity may exist in some languages (Hay and Baayen, 2003; Burzio, 2002; Hay, 2003), but not others (Doucette et al., 2024).

5 Discussion

Although previous work on biases in the lexicon have implied that certain lexical trade-offs are cross-linguistic universals, our findings suggest that evidence of these universals may not be as strong as previously thought. For example, Zipf's law of abbreviation has been studied extensively, showing that a relationship between word length and frequency holds cross-linguistically. Previous work has shown a strong negative correlation across languages (Piantadosi, 2014), which indeed does hold in all 25 languages in our data. However, it is unclear if there is a direct *causal* relationship between frequency and word length. The FCI algorithm allows us to identify possible unmeasured confounding variables in a causal model. In our analysis, possible confounding in the relationship between word length and frequency is identified in nearly all languages. If only word length and frequency are considered, the causal model underlying Zipf's law cannot be identified. It is possible that surprisal is the confounding variable in this relationship, as suggested by Piantadosi et al. (2011), or it could be something else. Structural causal modeling and causal discovery provide a framework for testing this, which we leave to future work.

We also identified possible confounding in the relationships between word length and phonotactic complexity and word length and morphological irregularity. This potential confounding occurred consistently across languages, as it did in the relationship between word length and frequency. This suggests that there may be universal lexical biases involving either word length or some other cause of word length. Again, this could be surprisal. The confounding variable could also differ across languages, but the existence of an association between word length and these variables appears to be universal.

While relationships involving word length occur consistently across languages, we find strong evidence of variation in the other relationships examined. In approximately half of the languages in our sample, there is no association between frequency and morphological irregularity, frequency and phonotactic complexity, and morphological irregularity and phonotactic complexity. In the languages where associations do exist, there is a probable unmeasured confounder. This suggests that lexicons may vary in whether or not these relationships are constrained, and that a set of universal lexical biases may not exist. Previous work has claimed that these relationships are universal, but considering a larger set of variables with causal discovery shows that this may not be true. If the properties of a lexicon are the result of some universal cognitive pressure (towards efficient communication, for example), only minor variation would be expected, rather than qualitative variation in whether or not a trade-off exists. This suggests that strong claims about universality and causal structure in the lexicon may need to be reconsidered.

We also note that the notion of causality in the lexicon implies diachronic language change, while our data represents observations of lexicons at a single point in time. Although in the ideal case we would examine changes in lexicons across time to determine causality, a causal model of a synchronic lexicon still has a useful interpretation. Pearl (2019) argues that a causal model can be interpreted as constraints on a mathematical system. The lexical biases we examine are exactly that: although they are likely caused by some underlying cognitive constraint, they impose constraints on possible lexicons.

However, our results are not without limitations. We examine a larger number of variables than many previous studies of lexical trade-offs, but the four variables we investigate are still not causally sufficient. Several possible unmeasured confounders are identified, leading to a causal graph that is not fully specified. Although we are able to identify patterns in causal structure across languages, we are not able to make any strong claims about direct causal relationships – there is simply not enough data. Our analysis is also limited by the dataset, which mainly includes morphologically complex words. It is possible that morphologically simple words may follow a different pattern. Additional data is needed to assess this possibility, which we plan on investigating in future work. We also note that the independence test used by the FCI algorithm in our analyses assumes that data is normally distributed. While this may be a reasonable assumption, further work is needed to assess how non-normality impacts the output of FCI. The data for word length, frequency, and phonotactic complexity have roughly normal distributions, but in many languages the morphological irregularity measure has a bimodal distribution. Nonparametric conditional independence testing is an active area of research (Li and Fan, 2020; Kim et al., 2022; Bianchi et al., 2023), and there may be tests with assumptions that better fit lexical data. There are also many different causal discovery algorithms, each with different assumptions about the data, and it should be explored how different algorithms can affect results. We leave investigating these possibilities to future work.

6 Conclusion

In this paper, we have shown that causal discovery methods can help identify relationships between statistical properties of the lexicon, providing more information about these relationships than correlations or regression models of pairs or small sets of variables. Given a dataset with more variables measured, and more languages, causal discovery may make it possible to determine exactly how the lexicon of a language is constrained, and how these biases vary across languages. In future work, we plan on applying causal discovery to a larger dataset with more languages and more variables with the goal of identifying a more specified causal model.

Acknowledgements

We thank the Montreal Computational & Quantitative Linguistics Lab for helpful feedback. The first author was supported by funding from the Fonds de recherche du Québec - Société et culture (FRQSC). The third author acknowledges the support of the Natural Sciences and Engineering Research Council of Canada (RGPIN-2023-04873) and the Canada Research Chairs program. The second author also gratefully acknowledges the support of the Natural Sciences and Engineering Research Council of Canada (RGPIN-2018-06385) and the Canada CIFAR AI Chairs Program. This research was enabled in part by support provided by Calcul Québec and the Digital Research Alliance of Canada.

References

Khuyagbaatar Batsuren, Omer Goldman, Salam Khalifa, Nizar Habash, Witold Kieraś, Gábor Bella, Brian Leonard, Garrett Nicolai, Kyle Gorman, Yustinus Ghanggo Ate, Maria Ryskina, Sabrina Mielke, Elena Budianskaya, Charbel El-Khaissi, Tiago Pimentel, Michael Gasser, William Abbott Lane, Mohit Raj, Matt Coler, Jaime Rafael Montoya Samame, Delio Siticonatzi Camaiteri, Esaú Zumaeta Rojas, Didier López Francis, Arturo Oncevay, Juan López Bautista, Gema Celeste Silva Villegas, Lucas Torroba Hennigen, Adam Ek, David Guriel, Peter Dirix, Jean-Philippe Bernardy, Andrey Scherbakov, Aziyana Bayyr-ool, Antonios Anastasopoulos, Roberto Zariquiey, Karina Sheifer, Sofya Ganieva, Hilaria Cruz, Ritván Karahóğa, Stella Markantonatou, George Pavlidis, Matvey Plugaryov, Elena Klyachko, Ali Salehi, Candy Angulo, Jatayu Baxi, Andrew Krizhanovsky, Natalia Krizhanovskaya, Elizabeth Salesky, Clara Vania, Sardana Ivanova, Jennifer White, Rowan Hall Maudslay, Josef Valvoda, Ran Zmigrod, Paula Czarnowska, Irene Nikkarinen, Aelita Salchak, Brijesh Bhatt, Christopher Straughn, Zoey Liu, Jonathan North Washington, Yuval Pinter, Duygu Ataman, Marcin Wolinski, Totok Suhardijanto, Anna Yablonskaya, Niklas Stoehr, Hossep Dolatian, Zahroh Nuriah, Shyam Ratan, Francis M. Tyers, Edoardo M. Ponti, Grant Aiton, Aryaman Arora, Richard J. Hatcher, Ritesh Kumar, Jeremiah Young, Daria Rodionova, Anastasia Yemelina, Taras Andrushko, Igor Marchenko, Polina Mashkovtseva, Alexandra Serova, Emily Prud'hommeaux, Maria Nepomniashchaya, Fausto Giunchiglia, Eleanor Chodroff, Mans Hulden, Miikka Silfverberg, Arya D. McCarthy, David Yarowsky, Ryan Cotterell, Reut Tsarfaty, and Ekaterina Vylomova. 2022. UniMorph 4.0: Universal Morphology. In *Proceedings of the Thirteenth Language Resources and Evaluation Conference*, pages 840–855.

Pascal Bianchi, Kevin Elgui, and François Portier. 2023. Conditional independence testing via weighted partial copulas. *Journal of Multivariate Analysis*, 193:105120.

Luigi Burzio. 2002. Missing players: Phonology and the past-tense debate. *Lingua*, 112(3):157–199.

Christophe Coupé, Yoon Mi Oh, Dan Dediu, and François Pellegrino. 2019. Different languages, similar encoding efficiency: Comparable information rates across the human communicative niche. *Science Advances*, 5(9):eaaw2594.

Fermín Moscoso del Prado Martín. 2014. Grammatical change begins within the word: Causal modeling of the co-evolution of Icelandic morphology and syntax. In *Proceedings of the Annual Meeting of the Cognitive Science Society*, volume 36.

Johannes Dellert. 2019. *Information-theoretic causal inference of lexical flow*. Language Science Press.

Johannes Dellert. 2024. Causal inference of diachronic semantic maps from cross-linguistic synchronic polysemy data. *Frontiers in Communication*, 8.

Amanda Doucette, Ryan Cotterell, Morgan Sonderegger, and Timothy J. O'Donnell. 2024. Correlation does not imply compensation: Complexity and irregularity in the lexicon. In *Proceedings of the Society for Computation in Linguistics 2024*, pages 117–128.

Viviana Fratini, Joana Acha, and Itziar Laka. 2014. Frequency and morphological irregularity are independent variables. Evidence from a corpus study of Spanish verbs. *Corpus Linguistics and Linguistic Theory*, 10(2):289–314.

Edward Gibson, Richard Futrell, Steven P Piantadosi, Isabelle Dautriche, Kyle Mahowald, Leon Bergen, and Roger Levy. 2019. How efficiency shapes human language. *Trends in Cognitive Sciences*, 23(5):389–407.

Peter Graff. 2012. *Communicative efficiency in the lexicon*. Ph.D. thesis, Massachusetts Institute of Technology.

Jennifer Hay. 2003. *Causes and Consequences of Word Structure*. Routledge.

Jennifer Hay and Harald Baayen. 2003. Phonotactics, parsing and productivity. *Italian Journal of Linguistics*, 15:99–130.

M.A. Hernán and J.M. Robins. 2024. *Causal Inference: What If*. Chapman & Hall/CRC.

Jeremy Irvin, Daniel Spokoyny, and Fermín Moscoso Martın, del Prado Martín. 2016. Dynamical systems modeling of the child–mother dyad: Causality between child-directed language complexity and language development. In *Proceedings of the Annual Meeting of the Cognitive Science Society*, volume 38.

Markus Kalisch, Martin Mächler, Diego Colombo, Marloes H. Maathuis, and Peter Bühlmann. 2012. Causal inference using graphical models with the R package pcalg. *Journal of Statistical Software*, 47(11):1–26.

Ilmun Kim, Matey Neykov, Sivaraman Balakrishnan, and Larry Wasserman. 2022. Local permutation tests for conditional independence. *The Annals of Statistics*, 50(6):3388 – 3414.

Natalia Levshina. 2021. Cross-linguistic trade-offs and causal relationships between cues to grammatical subject and object, and the problem of efficiency-related explanations. *Frontiers in Psychology*, 12.

Natalia Levshina. 2022. *Communicative Efficiency*. Cambridge University Press.

Chun Li and Xiaodan Fan. 2020. On nonparametric conditional independence tests for continuous variables. *WIREs Computational Statistics*, 12(3):e1489.

Kyle Mahowald, Isabelle Dautriche, Edward Gibson, and Steven T. Piantadosi. 2018. Word forms are structured for efficient use. *Cognitive Science*, 42(8):3116–3134.

Daniel Malinsky and David Danks. 2018. Causal discovery algorithms: A practical guide. *Philosophy Compass*, 13(1):e12470.

Clara Meister, Tiago Pimentel, Patrick Haller, Lena Jäger, Ryan Cotterell, and Roger Levy. 2021. Revisiting the uniform information density hypothesis. In *Proceedings of the 2021 Conference on Empirical Methods in Natural Language Processing*, pages 963–980.

Stephan C. Meylan and Thomas L. Griffiths. 2021. The challenges of large-scale, web-based language datasets: Word length and predictability revisited. *Cognitive Science*, 45(6):e12983.

David R. Mortensen, Siddharth Dalmia, and Patrick Littell. 2018. Epitran: Precision G2P for many languages. In *Proceedings of the Eleventh International Conference on Language Resources and Evaluation*.

Fermín Moscoso del Prado Martín and Christian Brendel. 2016. Case and cause in Icelandic: Reconstructing causal networks of cascaded language changes. In *Proceedings of the 54th Annual Meeting of the Association for Computational Linguistics (Volume 1: Long Papers)*, pages 2421–2430.

Judea Pearl. 1995. Causal diagrams for empirical research. *Biometrika*, 82(4):669–688.

Judea Pearl. 2019. On the interpretation of do(x). *Journal of Causal Inference*, 7(1):20192002.

Judea Pearl, Madelyn Glymour, and Nicholas P Jewell. 2016. *Causal Inference in Statistics: A Primer*. John Wiley & Sons.

François Pellegrino, Christophe Coupé, and Egidio Marsico. 2011. A cross-language perspective on speech information rate. *Language*, 87(3):539–558.

Steven T. Piantadosi. 2014. Zipf's word frequency law in natural language: A critical review and future directions. *Psychonomic Bulletin & Review*, 21(5):1112–1130.

Steven T. Piantadosi, Harry Tily, and Edward Gibson. 2011. Word lengths are optimized for efficient communication. *Proceedings of the National Academy of Sciences*, 108(9):3526–3529.

Tiago Pimentel, Clara Meister, Ethan Wilcox, Kyle Mahowald, and Ryan Cotterell. 2023. Revisiting the optimality of word lengths. In *Proceedings of the 2023 Conference on Empirical Methods in Natural Language Processing*, pages 2240–2255.

Tiago Pimentel, Brian Roark, and Ryan Cotterell. 2020. Phonotactic complexity and its trade-offs. *Transactions of the Association for Computational Linguistics*, 8:1–18.

Uriel Cohen Priva. 2017. Informativity and the actuation of lenition. *Language*, 93(3):569–597.

Uriel Cohen Priva and Emily Gleason. 2020. The causal structure of lenition: A case for the causal precedence of durational shortening. *Language*, 96(2):413–448.

Peter Spirtes, Clark Glymour, and Richard Scheines. 1993. *Causation, Prediction, and Search*. Springer.

Peter Spirtes, Christopher Meek, and Thomas Richardson. 1995. Causal inference in the presence of latent variables and selection bias. In *Proceedings of the Eleventh Conference on Uncertainty in Artificial Intelligence*, page 499–506.

Daniel Spokoyny, Jeremy Irvin, and Fermín Moscoso del Prado Martín. 2016. Explicit causal connections between the acquisition of linguistic tiers: Evidence from dynamical systems modeling. In *Proceedings of the 7th workshop on Cognitive Aspects of Computational Language Learning*, pages 73–81.

Shijie Wu, Ryan Cotterell, and Timothy O'Donnell. 2019. Morphological irregularity correlates with frequency. In *Proceedings of the 57th Annual Meeting of the Association for Computational Linguistics*, pages 5117–5126.

Charles Yang. 2016. *The Price of Linguistic Productivity: How Children Learn to Break the Rules of Language*. MIT press.

Alessio Zanga, Elif Ozkirimli, and Fabio Stella. 2022. A survey on causal discovery: Theory and practice. *International Journal of Approximate Reasoning*, 151:101–129.

George Kingsley Zipf. 1935. *The Psycho-Biology of Language: An Introduction to Dynamic Philology*. Houghton Mifflin.

George Kingsley Zipf. 1949. *Human behavior and the principle of least effort: An introduction to human eoclogy*. Addison-Wesley Press.

Quantifying Semantic Functional Specialization in the Brain Using Encoding Models of Natural Language

Jiaqi Chen*
MRC Laboratory of Molecular Biology
jc2130@cam.ac.uk

Richard J. Antonello*
Columbia University
rja2163@columbia.edu

Kaavya Chaparala
Johns Hopkins University
kchapar1@jh.edu

Coen Arrow
University of Western Australia
coen.arrow@research.uwa.edu.au

Nima Mesgarani
Columbia University
nima@ee.columbia.edu

Abstract

Although functional specialization in the brain - a phenomenon where different regions process different types of information - is well documented, we still lack precise mathematical methods with which to measure it. This work proposes a technique to quantify how brain regions respond to distinct categories of information. Using a topic encoding model, we identify brain regions that respond strongly to specific semantic categories while responding minimally to all others. We then use a language model to characterize the common themes across each region's preferred categories. Our technique successfully identifies previously known functionally selective regions and reveals consistent patterns across subjects while also highlighting new areas of high specialization worthy of further study.

1 Introduction

The theory of functional specialization states that different brain regions have evolved to process different types of information. This is apparent at a high level – for instance, the occipital lobe is heavily involved in processing visual information, whereas the temporal lobe is implicated in processing auditory stimuli. There is also evidence to support the theory at a lower level where smaller regions of interest (ROIs) are active in processing even more specific information. Examples of such ROIs include fusiform face area (FFA), which is selective for facial features, or places in parahippocampal place area (PPA). These discoveries have relied on 'contrast' studies that observe how brain regions respond to specific categories. While successful contrast studies have been influential, this approach also depends heavily on educated guesses about where in the brain to look and what to look for.

In this study, we propose an intuitive technique to identify and quantify functional specialization across the brain. We show that our method can correctly identify ROIs previously observed to have high semantic functional specialization, and that it can additionally identify several new ROIs with high functional selectivity throughout cortex for further study. We further demonstrate that this method can be used to explicitly recover known selectivity properties of well-documented regions such as the location-selective retrosplenial cortex (RSC) and the body-selective extrastriate body area (EBA), as well as for its newly-proposed regions. We additionally explore the degree to which our method generalizes across individuals, demonstrating that our observations are largely consistent across three subjects.

2 Related Work

Functional specialization has been studied in settings like vision (Kamps et al., 2016; Julian et al., 2016; Taylor et al., 2007; Calvo-Merino et al., 2010; Leibo et al., 2015; Saleem et al., 2018; Howard et al., 1996), language (Fedorenko et al., 2011), auditory processing (Perani et al., 2010; Tervaniemi et al., 1999), and motor function (Wilson et al., 2014). Previous work identifying areas of high functional specialization typically focuses on locating lateral asymmetries (Wang et al., 2014; Zilles and Amunts, 2015). However regions can be functionally specialized without being asymmetric, as is the case for regions like retrosplenial cortex (Mitchell et al., 2018; Burles et al., 2017), parahippocampal place area (Epstein and Kanwisher, 1998; Epstein, 2005), occipital place area (Kamps et al., 2016; Dilks et al., 2013), and extrastriate body area (Astafiev et al., 2004).

Researchers have also uncovered more direct links between semantics and brain activity by developing encoding models to predict neural responses

*Equal contribution.

Proceedings of the Workshop on Cognitive Modeling and Computational Linguistics, pages 77–90
May 3, 2025 ©2025 Association for Computational Linguistics

from continuous linguistic features. Mitchell et al. (2008) showed that different semantic categories (e.g., tools versus animals) elicit distinct spatial activation patterns in the brain, and a model trained on corpus-derived semantic features could forecast fMRI responses to previously unseen words. Later investigations built on this approach by applying distributed semantic representations to more complex, real-world language inputs (Huth et al., 2016; Jain and Huth, 2018; Caucheteux et al., 2023; Antonello et al., 2023). Utilizing high-dimensional word embeddings or semantic spaces derived from modern LLMs, these encoding models can capture brain responses to entire sentences and stories and generalize to numerous concepts. In this work, we build upon recent studies that use encoding models to generate and test interpretable hypotheses about semantic selectivity in the brain (Singh et al., 2023; Antonello et al., 2024).

3 Methods

3.1 fMRI Data

We used publicly available functional magnetic resonance imaging (fMRI) data collected from 3 human subjects as they listened to 20 hours of English language podcast stories over Sensimetrics S14 headphones. The stories came from podcasts such as *The Moth Radio Hour*, *Modern Love*, and *The Anthropocene Reviewed*. Each 10-15 minute story was played during a separate scan. Subjects were not asked to make any responses, but simply to listen attentively to the stories. For encoding model training, each subject listened to roughly 95 different stories, giving 20 hours of data across 20 scanning sessions, or a total of ~33,000 datapoints for each voxel in the brain.

MRI data were collected on a 3T Siemens Skyra scanner at The University of Texas at Austin Biomedical Imaging Center using a 64-channel Siemens volume coil. Functional scans were collected using a gradient echo EPI sequence with repetition time (TR) = 2.00 s, echo time (TE) = 30.8 ms, flip angle = 71°, multi-band factor (simultaneous multi-slice) = 2, voxel size = 2.6mm x 2.6mm x 2.6mm (slice thickness = 2.6mm), matrix size = 84x84, and field of view = 220 mm. Anatomical data were collected using a T1-weighted multi-echo MP-RAGE sequence with voxel size = 1mm x 1mm x 1mm.

In addition to motion correction and coregistration (LeBel et al., 2022), low-frequency voxel response drift was identified using a 2nd order Savitzky-Golay filter with a 120 second window and then subtracted from the signal. The mean response for each voxel was subtracted and the remaining response was scaled to have unit variance.

All subjects were healthy and had normal hearing. The experimental protocol was approved by the Institutional Review Board at The University of Texas, Austin. Written informed consent was obtained from all subjects.

3.2 Topic Encoding Model

A topic model was pre-trained on the entire story data. Given a list of word sequences for every two-second interval of the podcasts, we used sliding windows of [2, 4, . . . , 20] seconds. We trained 10 separate topic models on a different sliding window length each and then merged the topics to yield the final topic model, which had $T_n = 463$ topics. The multi-scale topic model was used to ensure the topic model generalized well across varied semantic timescales. In total, this training took $\sim$50 CPU node-hours.

Each model was based on the BERTopic technique (Grootendorst, 2022). Each string was embedded using sentence embedding model "all-MiniLM-L6-v2". Uniform Manifold Approximation and Projection (UMAP) was used to reduce the embedding dimension. The reduced embeddings were then clustered using Hierarchical Density-Based Spatial Clustering of Applications with Noise (HDBSCAN) (McInnes et al., 2017).

Each cluster is associated with the the initial strings from each of the two-second intervals represented in the cluster. We manipulate these strings to extract a common semantic theme to describe the cluster. Initially, a bag-of-words is generated for each topic. The bags-of-words are then all concatenated into a single string and further reduced with class-based Term-Frequency Inverse-Document-Frequency (c-TF-IDF). The final representation reduction used KeyBERT(Grootendorst, 2020). The resultant meta-topics provide each cluster with a semantic theme common to all of its members.

The trained topic model encodes the story data, annotating the dataset using the general encoding methodology described in Antonello et al. (2021). Each 16 word phrase from the story dataset was fed through the topic model and was scored according to how likely each phrase is a member of each topic. The context length of 16 words was selected to bal-

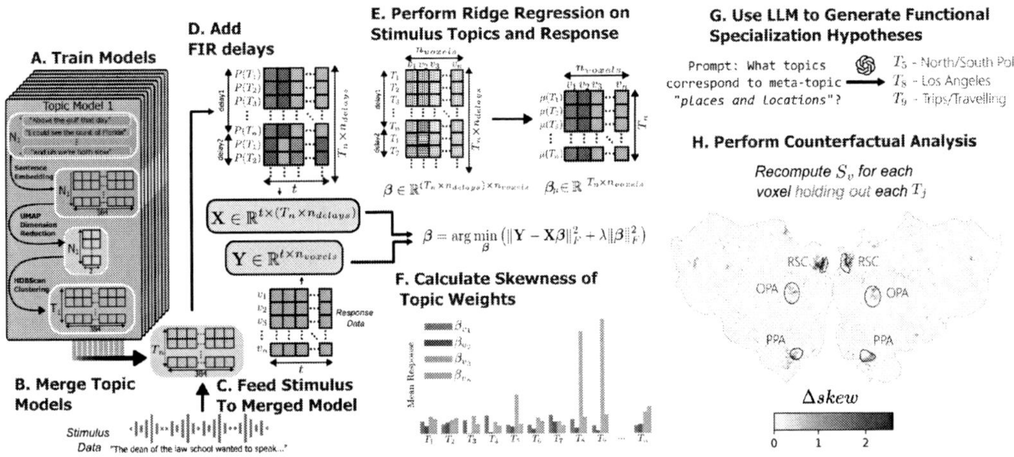

Figure 1: **Functional Selectivity Detection Pipeline**: Functional selectivity for a given meta-topic is generated using an automated pipeline. (A) 10 topic models are trained on strings of varying lengths derived from the stimulus dataset using a hierarchical clustering algorithm. (B) The topics generated are merged via cosine similarity, resulting in a single final topic model of T_n topics. (C) Story segments are fed into the newly generated merged topic model to build topic embeddings for the stimulus. (D) FIR delays are added to the topic embeddings, yielding our final stimulus matrix X. The BOLD response is temporally aligned with the time-delayed stimulus to produce our response matrix Y. (E) Bootstrapped ridge regression is used to generate weights β that map the stimulus to the voxelwise response. (F) We calculate the Pearson skewness of each voxel to find voxels with high functional selectivity. (G) An LLM is prompted to automatically determine which topics from the merged topic model correspond to a chosen meta-topic. (H) A counterfactual analysis is performed, where we observe which functionally selective voxels have their Pearson skewness reduced when the voxels from the corresponding meta-topic are excluded. The final flatmap shows the resulting drop in skewness for the "Places" meta-topic, demonstrating that the method correctly identifies RSC, OPA, and PPA as places-selective regions.

ance good performance of the model with a need to keep the topic labels relatively contemporaneous with the immediate content. These topic probabilities were then used as features for the encoding model. These features were then downsampled using Lanczos downsampling and finite impulse response (FIR) delays of 2, 4, 6 and 8 seconds were applied to model the hemodynamic response function (HRF) of the BOLD signal. A linear projection from these downsampled, time-delayed features to the measured BOLD response was then trained using bootstrapped ridge regression. That is, let X be the stimulus features derived from our topic model and let Y_v be the measured BOLD response for a given voxel v. For each voxel, we found linear weights β_v by optimizing

$$\min_{\beta_v}(Y_v - X\beta_v) + \lambda||\beta_v||_2 \quad (1)$$

where $||\cdot||_2$ denotes the L_2-norm and λ is a regularization parameter.

3.3 Skewness as a Marker of Functional Selectivity

With β_v computed for every voxel, we used it to determine which brain voxels are highly selective for a small number of topics. To do this, we measured the voxelwise Pearson skewness of β_v. Intuitively, Pearson skewness is high when most of the weight in β_v is allocated to a small number of its elements. These highly-skew weights are more likely to be driven by the existence or nonexistence of a narrow number of topics in a given context. As functional selectivity is just the property of being selective for a narrow number of topics, high-skew voxels are by definition highly functionally-selective.

With highly-selective voxels identified, we segmented them into local clusters based on their cortical proximity. Contiguous sets of voxels of high skewness were grouped into proposed ROIs. For a given region $\mathcal{R}$, the weights β_v corresponding to the voxels in that region are then averaged and we observe topics with the highest weights in the averaged $\beta_{\mathcal{R}}$. If those topics shared a semantic category (for instance, if they are all "number words"),

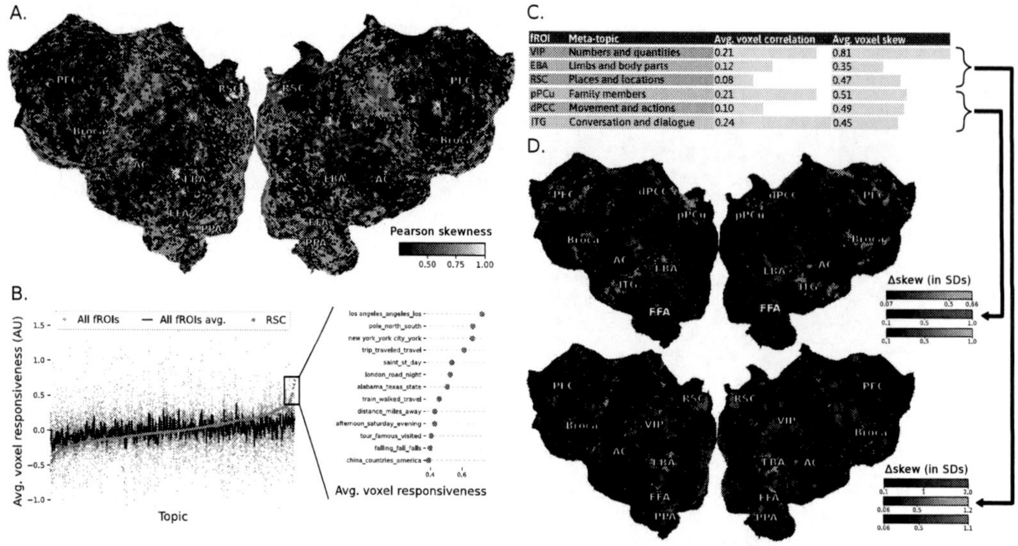

Figure 2: **Analyzing Functional Selectivity** (A) A cortical flatmap of voxels with high functional-selectivity using our skewness metric. The ventral visual stream has the highest overall functional-selectivity, whereas the frontal lobe has comparatively lower selectivity. (B) Individual topic responsiveness, according to our linear mapping β is visualized for the retrosplenial cortex. Most of the skewness in the distribution is derived from topics relating to location or time. Responses to these topics are substantially higher for RSC than other semantic categories. (C) Average voxel correlations and skewnesses for several fROIs are shown. Corresponding meta-topics are determined via post-hoc analysis of the most prominent topics. (D) Regions selective for the assorted meta-topics are visualized according to their relative selectivity. Voxels are colored according to how much omitting that set of meta-topics reduces overall skewness in that voxel. *Bottom:* Visualizes more novel, more poorly understood selectivities derived from our method. Meta-topics in (D) are colored according to the legend in (C).
Top: Visualizes well-understood semantic functional selectivities.

we concluded that the corresponding ROI is functionally selective for that category.

To map the putative functional organization of a semantic category or meta-topic, we prompted an LLM (GPT-4) (OpenAI, 2023) to select the top 6% of topics from the list of generated topics that semantically aligned most with the provided meta-topic. These output topics were checked for correctness and the top 20 (~4%) topics were selected. Voxel-wise, Z-scored Pearson skewness was then recalculated with and without the chosen topics. Since the average voxel had a z-scored skewness of zero, voxels selective for the meta-topic have high skew magnitudes when the meta-topic topics are included, but regress to zero once the topics were removed. The difference between the z-scored skews is the number of standard deviations from the mean skew that the meta-topic provides for the voxel.

We define the voxel-level Pearson skewness for any set of topic indices $\Omega \subseteq \{1, \ldots, T_n\}$ as

$$s_v(\Omega) = \frac{\sum_{i \in \Omega} \left(\beta_{v,i} - \bar{\beta}_v(\Omega)\right)^3}{\left(\sum_{i \in \Omega} \left(\beta_{v,i} - \bar{\beta}_v(\Omega)\right)^2\right)^{3/2}} \qquad (2)$$

where $\bar{\beta}_v(\Omega) = \frac{1}{|\Omega|} \sum_{i \in \Omega} \beta_{v,i}$.

After z-scoring these skewness values across voxels (so that the mean voxel has zero z-scored skewness), the contribution of a chosen meta-topic $\mathcal{M}$ is then

$$\Delta\text{skew}_v(\mathcal{M}) = Z\big(s_v(\Omega_{\text{all}})\big) - Z\big(s_v(\Omega_{\text{all}} \backslash \mathcal{M})\big), \qquad (3)$$

where $\Omega_{\text{all}} = \{1, \ldots, T_n\}$ is the full set of topics.

This skewness differential is used to measure the degree to which voxel v is selective for the selected meta-topic. If a voxel has high-initial skewness, and then that skewness is substantially reduced when topics from a given meta-topic are excluded, we conclude that that voxel is functionally selective for the associated meta-topic. The full pipeline for functional selectivity detection is depicted in **Figure 1**.

3.4 Analyzing Meta-topic Specificity

Following the application of our functional selectivity pipeline to our data, we observed a small number of regions with apparently strong semantic

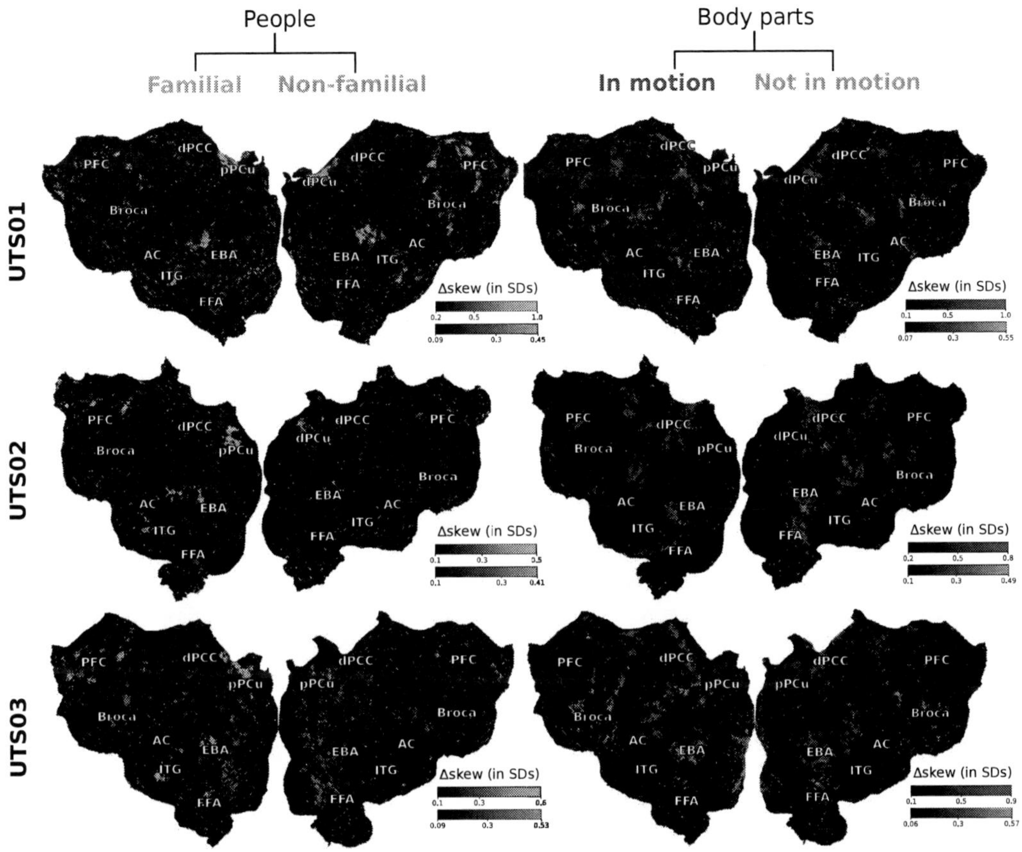

Figure 3: **Investigating Meta-topic Precision for Novel Regions** For each of our three subjects (*Top:* UTS01, *Center:* UTS02, *Bottom:* UTS03), we visualize the meta-topic selectivity of familial people vs. non-familial people (*Left*) and body parts in motion vs. not in motion (*Right*), In each case, we find that the selectivity of the corresponding region is precisely captured by the chosen meta-topic (i.e. familial people for pPCu; moving body parts for dPCC) and not its antithesis.

functional selectivity, according to our metric, that did not appear to have a strong basis in prior literature. To determine the meta-topic specificity these novel ROIs, we provided GPT-4 with a theme one level broader than the ROI's proposed meta-topic and analyzed the previously missed topics. For example, if an ROI is found selective for family members, we prompted GPT-4 to select the top 6% of topics that are most aligned with people but do not reference family. Analysis on the skewness differential was then repeated for the top 20 topics of this new, broader meta-topic. This process ensures that the meta-topic selected possesses the highest level of granularity for which that ROI is functionally selective.

3.5 Measuring Anatomical Consistency

To validate the generality of the anatomical observations made from the topic selectivity encoding models, we follow a methodology similar to that of Huth et al. (2016) in observing the semantic tiling of the cortex with respect to our topic space. In particular, we perform PCA along the topic axis of our linear mapping for one subject (UTS03) to get a set of orthogonal principal components that maximally explain the variance along that axis. We then project these components to the voxel space for every subject, by computing the dot product of the topic components with the specific linear encoding weights for that subject. The anatomical alignment of the resulting projection between subjects determines the degree to which observations derived from our topic encoding models are population trends.

4 Results

Figure 2 shows the results of applying our functional selectivity mapping protocol to a single subject from our fMRI dataset. Additional results for the other two subjects in our study are presented in Appendix A. Results are highly consistent across the subjects in our dataset, suggesting that the functional selectivities described here are population-level trends.

Figure 2a shows the voxels described as functionally selective according to our topic skewness metric. We find that many regions previously identified as functionally selective are correctly labeled as such by our skewness metric. The highest functional selectivity is observed along a band of the higher ventral visual stream, which includes regions like occipital place area, extrastriate body area, and borders interparietal sulcus. We observed comparatively smaller amounts of functional selectivity in regions outside the ventral visual stream, such as the prefrontal cortex. This may suggest that the presence of local visual representations is a strong driver of selectivity, supporting grounding theories of cognition (Barsalou, 2008) that suggest that neural representations are "grounded" in sensorimotor information. Additionally, the result replicates prior work suggesting a visio-semantic alignment that occurs at the border of visual cortex (Popham et al., 2021).

Figure 2b demonstrates the process of isolating the functional selectivity of one such ROI through the example of a set of voxels located in RSC. We replicate the established result that this ROI is highly selective for "place semantics", as suggested by prior literature (Mitchell et al., 2018). Most topics with the highest weight on these voxels are semantically associated with locations, travel, or temporal concepts. The top three topics for this set of voxels (*New York, North/South Pole, Los Angeles*) are all prominent geographical locations. We additionally note a further time-semantics component to some of the most selective topics (e.g. *afternoon, night, day*), suggesting that RSC is further implicated in the processing of temporal information, not just spatial information. Additional analysis of the temporal profiles of the topics suggests that this is not due to place- and time-related topics co-occurring naturally in the stimuli, but instead due to separate and independent effects for both meta-topics. (Appendix Figure 7 and Appendix Table 1).

Figure 2c further shows this process applied to six selected fROIs, with the meta-topics associated with their functional selectivities. Average predictive performance and voxel skew for the voxels in these regions are also shown. All selected regions have high skewness and most have high prediction performance relative to the average cortical voxel. Meta-topic descriptions are consistent with prior literature, and we correctly identify the functional selectivity of regions such as extrastriate body area (EBA), ventral interparietal area (VIP) and parahippocampal place area (PPA). It is noteworthy that while selectivity in areas like EBA has been established previously using visual contrasts, our method replicates these findings purely from linguistic input, further supporting those claims in a modality distinct from prior work.

Figure 2d shows the cortex-wide meta-topic selectivity for the concepts of three previously-established functionally-selective regions: RSC, EBA and VIP. We find several other less well-described functional selectivity regions, such as an area near inferior temporal gyrus (ITG) cortex that is selective for "conversation" words, an area in posterior precuneus (pPCu) that is selective for "family"-related words, and an area that is selective for words describing movement or physical actions of body parts, which is located in dorsal posterior cingulate cortex (dPCC). Voxels are colored according to how much that voxel's skewness would change if the corresponding meta-topic's weights were removed.

Given that we found the existence of these newer regions surprising owing to their unusual specificity, we examined the degree to which the descriptors of newly described regions were precise. For the posterior precuneus and dorsal cingulate ROIs, **Figure 3** looks at the effect of subtly altering the meta-topic we have associated with each region. Remarkably, we find that for pPCu, topic selectivity is no longer observed in the region when we choose a meta-topic of "non-familial" people. Similarly, the dorsal cingulate is not selective for body part actions that do not involve active movement. These effects are consistent across all 3 subjects in our study, further supporting the claim that these descriptors are indeed accurate summaries of the semantic functional selectivity of these regions. We believe these results strongly warrant further investigation given their surprising consistency and specificity.

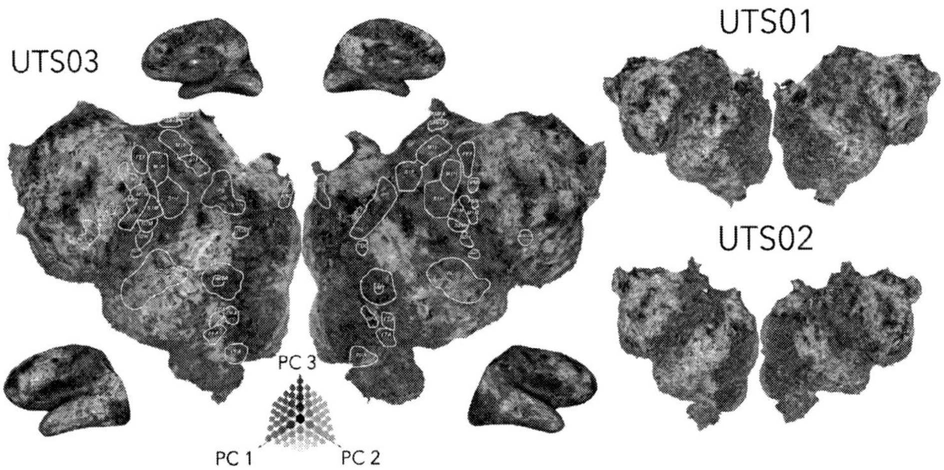

Figure 4: **Population-level Topic Selectivity** For each of our three subjects, the top 3 principal components of the topic model space for UTS03 are computed and then projected into the respective voxel space using the linear encoding model weights. The final projection is plotted, where each color channel denotes a single principal component from the topic space (*Red:* PC1, *Green:* PC2, *Blue:* PC3). We see largely consistent anatomical alignment across subjects, suggesting that topic-level selectivity generalizes to population-level trends.

Finally, we analyzed whether the weights from our topic encoding models were largely subject-specific, or generalized across the population. **Figure 4** shows the result of the principal component analysis of our topic encoding models. We see strong anatomical alignment across subjects, with especially prominent laterality patterns. For example, linear combination of PC1 and PC2 (*yellow*) is more observable in left temporal cortex, whereas a linear combination of PC1 and PC3 (*pink*) is more observable in right temporal cortex. Most importantly, this strong anatomical alignment across three subjects provides good support for the claim that the topic encoding models are largely consistent across individuals and are therefore not heavily influenced by subject-level differences.

5 Discussion and Limitations

Unlike today's computers, which are no more than collections of billions of identical and functionally equivalent transistors, the brain is no computational monolith. Despite this well-known fact, remarkably little effort has gone into designing methods to automatically detect and characterize this functional selectivity, especially in the realm of language semantics. To this day, functional selectivity is primarily analyzed through painstaking and tedious "contrast studies" in which subjects are exposed to carefully curated experiments, in order to narrow down the functional selectivity of a region. Here, we show that by utilizing modern machine learning techniques, we can detect and analyze functional selectivity in a vacuum.

Replicating prior studies (Mitchell et al., 2018; Burles et al., 2017; Astafiev et al., 2004), our results show many regions of the brain are highly selective for specific semantic categories, such as places, conversations, or body parts. We further explore evidence for functional selectivity of less well-understood regions like posterior precuneus and dorsal posterior cingulate cortex, showing that they are selective for the highly specific concepts of family members and movement-based actions respectively. We find this surprising, but are able to show that this selectivity is consistent across subjects and actually requires this level of specificity. We show that functional selectivity is most heavily distributed along the ventral visual stream, but is also present to a lesser degree in areas such as prefrontal cortex. The functional selectivity we detect tends to be more biased toward concrete concepts over abstract ones, suggesting that more abstract concepts are less likely to have uniquely specialized regions. Nevertheless, this ongoing work has several limitations. Firstly, the proximity-based process of clustering voxels into fROIs is still rudimentary and could be supplemented with a more nuanced approach that directly takes into account similarity in voxel weights. Next, the meta-topic classification that is currently performed by an LLM could be subject to additional validation on its agreement with human classification. Further work should also be pursued into understanding individual subject-level differences in functional selectivity to determine the degree to which these observations hold across the population. The relative data-efficiency of our method could provide a more fruitful perspective into these differences across subjects.

What can functional selectivity tell us about the nature of human intelligence? We often find that, outside of the ventral visual stream, most functional selectivity is closely related to the non-semantic role of adjacent regions. For example, the semantic selectivities of dPCu (movement and actions) and ITG (conversations) are closely associated with their non-semantic roles (motor planning and auditory processing). We find such "functional coincidences" to be persuasive evidence in support of cognitive grounding, the notion that cognitive representations are "ultimately grounded in bodily, affective, perceptual, and motor processes" (Pezzulo et al., 2013), rather than "computation on amodal symbols in a modular system" (Barsalou, 2008). In a model of intelligence based on grounded cognition, functionally-selective regions would likely benefit from their proximity to areas specialized in related low-level processes. Further research into the mapping of functional selectivity could one day help to reveal the underlying organizational drivers of cortical structure.

Acknowledgments

This work is based on work done during the 2024 Telluride Neuromorphic Cognition Engineering Workshop, sponsored by the NSF. Additional funding was provided by the National Institutes of Health (NIH-NIDCD), the Dingwall Foundation, and a grant from Marie Josee and Henry R. Kravis. We thank Alexander Huth and Nicole Dumont for their insightful feedback and assistance during this project.

References

Richard Antonello, Chandan Singh, Shailee Jain, Aliyah Hsu, Jianfeng Gao, Bin Yu, and Alexander Huth. 2024. A generative framework to bridge data-driven models and scientific theories in language neuroscience. *arXiv preprint arXiv:2410.00812*.

Richard Antonello, Javier S Turek, Vy Vo, and Alexander Huth. 2021. Low-dimensional structure in the space of language representations is reflected in brain responses. *Advances in Neural Information Processing Systems*, 34.

Richard Antonello, Aditya Vaidya, and Alexander G. Huth. 2023. Scaling laws for language encoding models in fmri. *Preprint*, arXiv:2305.11863.

Serguei V Astafiev, Christine M Stanley, Gordon L Shulman, and Maurizio Corbetta. 2004. Extrastriate body area in human occipital cortex responds to the performance of motor actions. *Nature neuroscience*, 7(5):542–548.

Lawrence W Barsalou. 2008. Grounded cognition. *Annu. Rev. Psychol.*, 59(1):617–645.

Ford Burles, Edward Slone, and Giuseppe Iaria. 2017. Dorso-medial and ventro-lateral functional specialization of the human retrosplenial complex in spatial updating and orienting. *Brain structure & function*, 222:1481–1493.

Beatriz Calvo-Merino, Cosimo Urgesi, Guido Orgs, Salvatore M Aglioti, and Patrick Haggard. 2010. Extrastriate body area underlies aesthetic evaluation of body stimuli. *Experimental brain research*, 204:447–456.

Charlotte Caucheteux, Alexandre Gramfort, and Jean-Rémi King. 2023. Evidence of a predictive coding hierarchy in the human brain listening to speech. *Nature Human Behaviour*, pages 1–12.

Daniel D. Dilks, Joshua B. Julian, Alexander M. Paunov, and Nancy Kanwisher. 2013. The occipital place area is causally and selectively involved in scene perception. *Journal of Neuroscience*, 33:1331–1336.

Russel A. Epstein. 2005. The cortical basis of visual scene processing. *Visual Cognition*, 12:954–978.

Russell Epstein and Nancy Kanwisher. 1998. A cortical representation of the local visual environment. *Nature*, 392:598–601.

Evelina Fedorenko, Michael K Behr, and Nancy Kanwisher. 2011. Functional specificity for high-level linguistic processing in the human brain. *Proceedings of the National Academy of Sciences*, 108(39):16428–16433.

Maarten Grootendorst. 2020. Keybert: Minimal keyword extraction with bert.

Maarten Grootendorst. 2022. Bertopic: Neural topic modeling with a class-based tf-idf procedure. *arXiv preprint arXiv:2203.05794*.

R.J. Howard, M. Brammer, I. Wright, P.W. Woodruff, E.T. Bullmore, and S. Zeki. 1996. A direct demonstration of functional specialization within motion-related visual and auditory cortex of the human brain. *Current Biology*, page 1015–1019.

Alexander G Huth, Wendy A De Heer, Thomas L Griffiths, Frédéric E Theunissen, and Jack L Gallant. 2016. Natural speech reveals the semantic maps that tile human cerebral cortex. *Nature*, 532(7600):453–458.

Shailee Jain and Alexander Huth. 2018. Incorporating context into language encoding models for fmri. In *Advances in Neural Information Processing Systems*, volume 31. Curran Associates, Inc.

Joshua B Julian, Jack Ryan, Roy H Hamilton, and Russell A Epstein. 2016. The occipital place area is causally involved in representing environmental boundaries during navigation. *Current Biology*, 26(8):1104–1109.

Frederik S Kamps, Joshua B Julian, Jonas Kubilius, Nancy Kanwisher, and Daniel D Dilks. 2016. The occipital place area represents the local elements of scenes. *Neuroimage*, 132:417–424.

Amanda LeBel, Lauren Wagner, Shailee Jain, Aneesh Adhikari-Desai, Bhavin Gupta, Allyson Morgenthal, Jerry Tang, Lixiang Xu, and Alexander G Huth. 2022. A natural language fmri dataset for voxelwise encoding models. *bioRxiv*, pages 2022–09.

Joel Z Leibo, Qianli Liao, Fabio Anselmi, and Tomaso Poggio. 2015. The invariance hypothesis implies domain-specific regions in visual cortex. *PLoS Computational Biology*, 10.

Leland McInnes, John Healy, and Steve Astels. 2017. hdbscan: Hierarchical density based clustering. *Journal of Open Source Software*, 2(11):205.

Anna S Mitchell, Rafal Czajkowski, Ningyu Zhang, and Andrew J D Jeffery, Kate adn Nelson. 2018. Retrosplenial cortex and its role in spatial cognition. *Brain and neuroscience advances*, 2.

Tom M Mitchell, Svetlana V Shinkareva, Andrew Carlson, Kai-Min Chang, Vicente L Malave, Robert A Mason, and Marcel Adam Just. 2008. Predicting human brain activity associated with the meanings of nouns. *science*, 320(5880):1191–1195.

OpenAI. 2023. Gpt-4 system card.

Daniela Perani, Maria Cristina Saccuman, Paola Scifo, Danilo Spada, Guido Andreolli, Rosanna Rovelli, Cristina Baldoli, and Stefan Koelsch. 2010. Functional specializations for music processing in the human newborn brain. *Proceedings of the National Academy of Sciences*, 107(10):4758–4763.

Giovanni Pezzulo, Lawrence W Barsalou, Angelo Cangelosi, Martin H Fischer, Ken McRae, and Michael J Spivey. 2013. Computational grounded cognition: a new alliance between grounded cognition and computational modeling. *Frontiers in psychology*, 3:612.

Sara F Popham, Alexander G Huth, Natalia Y Bilenko, Fatma Deniz, James S Gao, Anwar O Nunez-Elizalde, and Jack L Gallant. 2021. Visual and linguistic semantic representations are aligned at the border of human visual cortex. *Nature neuroscience*, 24(11):1628–1636.

Aman B. Saleem, E. Mika Diamanti, Julien Fournier, Kenneth D. Harris, and Matteo Carandini. 2018. Coherent encoding of subjective spatial position in visual cortex and hippocampus. *Nature*, 562:124–127.

Chandan Singh, Aliyah R Hsu, Richard Antonello, Shailee Jain, Alexander G Huth, Bin Yu, and Jianfeng Gao. 2023. Explaining black box text modules in natural language with language models. *arXiv preprint arXiv:2305.09863*.

John C Taylor, Alison J Wiggett, and Paul E Downing. 2007. Functional mri analysis of body and body part representations in the extrastriate and fusiform body areas. *Journal of neurophysiology*, 98(3):1626–1633.

Mari Tervaniemi, Anu Kujala, Kimmo Alho, Juha Virtanen, Risto J Ilmoniemi, and Risto Näätänen. 1999. Functional specialization of the human auditory cortex in processing phonetic and musical sounds: a magnetoencephalographic (meg) study. *Neuroimage*, 9(3):330–336.

Danhong Wang, Randy L Buckner, and Hesheng Liu. 2014. Functional specialization in the human brain estimated by intrinsic hemispheric interaction. *Journal of Neuroscience*, 34(37):12341–12352.

Tony W Wilson, Max J Kurz, and David J Arpin. 2014. Functional specialization within the supplementary motor area: a fnirs study of bimanual coordination. *NeuroImage*, 85:445–450.

Karl Zilles and Katrin Amunts. 2015. Anatomical basis for functional specialization. *fMRI: From nuclear spins to brain functions*, pages 27–66.

A Supplementary subject data

Here we reproduce Figure 2 for the other two subjects that we examined. We observe similar selectivity patterns throughout the cortex.

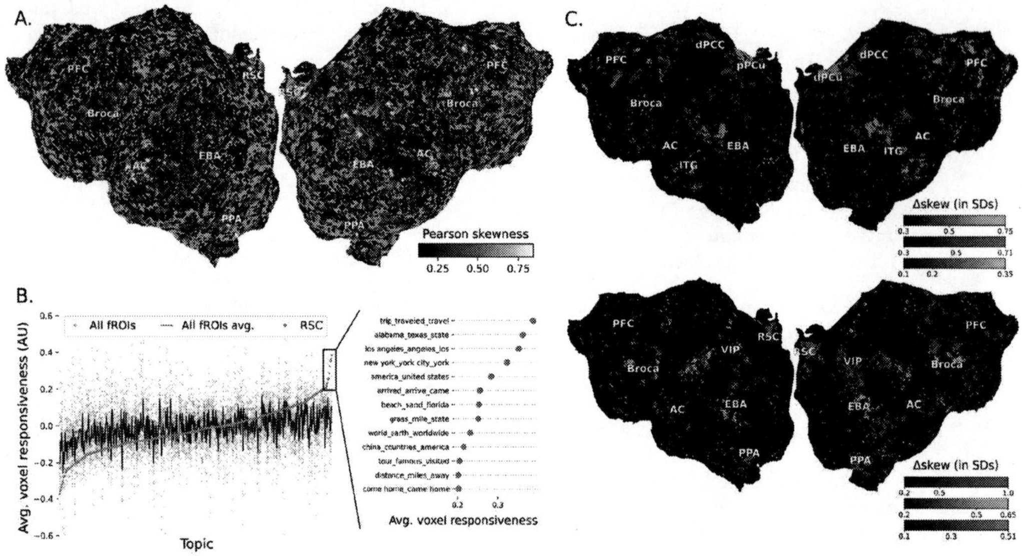

Figure 5: Replication of Figure 2 for UTS01. The same meta-topics and color key are used for (C) as in Figure 2D.

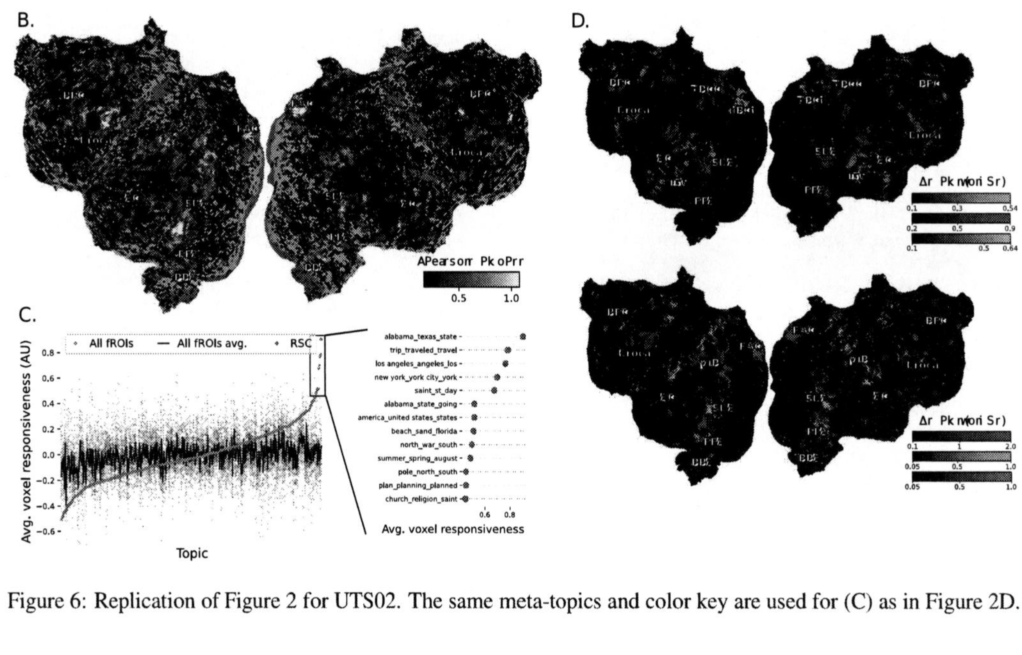

Figure 6: Replication of Figure 2 for UTS02. The same meta-topics and color key are used for (C) as in Figure 2D.

B Meta-topic data

The 20 topics that comprise each meta-topic are listed in Figure 8. This includes the six meta-topics that relate to an ROI ('numbers and quantities', 'limbs and body parts', 'places and locations', 'family members', 'movement and actions' and 'conversation and dialogue') and the two broader-level meta-topics that were used to determine ROI specificity in Section 3.4 ('people excluding family' and 'body parts without movement').

To test whether topics within a meta-topic tended to be predicted at similar timepoints in each story, we calculated pair-wise correlations between all 463 topics based on their probability scores per TR. To minimize the effect of noise from low-probability scores, only the top 10% of scores within each TR were used in this calculation while the bottom 90% were set to zero. Then, maximum-distance hierarchical clustering on pairwise correlations was used to group the topics into 102 clusters. Figure 7 shows these pair-wise correlations, with the topics reordered to visualize the clusters in their hierarchical order.

This data was used to determine whether the co-existence of more than one topic theme in an ROI's apparent topic selectivity is likely due to an actual functional selectivity, or an artifact of topic co-expression in the same sentences in the story data. For example, the data suggests RSC to be indeed functionally selective for both temporal topics (cluster 22) and geographical topics (clusters 71 and 92), as the inter-cluster correlations for cluster 22 are significantly lower than the intra-cluster correlations (Figure 7 and Table 1).

Figure 8 shows the correlation matrix subsetted to display values relevant to the listed meta-topic topics only. The involvement of many different clusters within each meta-topic similarly suggests our results on ROI functional selectivity (Figures 2 and 3) to not be heavily dependent on topic co-expression.

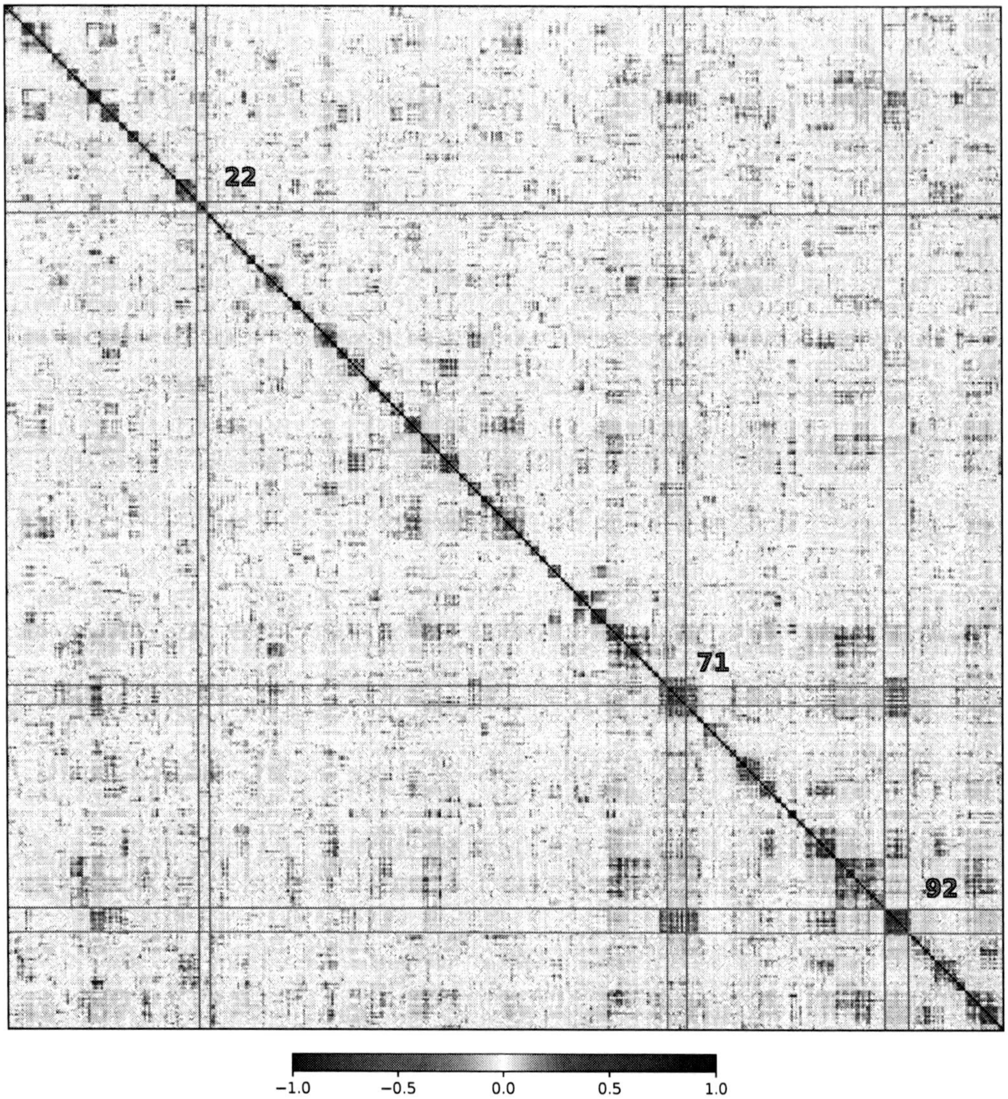

Figure 7: Biclustering results on the 463 topics of the final topic model. The x- and y-axis are symmetrical, with each row and column organized in hierarchical order following maximum-distance clustering. Clusters highlight topics that tend to occur near each other in time (i.e. occur within the same sentence) in the story data. Three clusters that contain the top RSC topics shown in Figure 2B have been highlighted in *red*, and the topics contained listed under Table 1.

Cluster	Topics
22	afternoon_saturday_evening lights_light_bright sleep_sleeping_slept wake_terrifying_right clock_morning_time
71	trip_traveled_travel come home_came home_home camp_park_meet london_road_night escort_father_family staying_stayed_stay ticket_tickets_flight funeral_celebrating_family train_walked_travel
92	new york_york city_york los angeles_angeles_los distance_miles_away alabama_texas_state north_war_south beach_sand_florida america_united states_states streets_east_street pole_north_south grass_mile_state alabama_state_going

Table 1: List of topics contained in the clusters labeled in Figure 7.

Figure 8: The topics comprising each meta-topic and their pairwise correlation scores. X-axis and y-axis labels are symmetrical. White borders and topic colors show the different cluster groups. Correlation scores were calculated by comparing the prediction profiles of each topic over all TRs.

"Is There Anything Else?": Examining Administrator Influence on Linguistic Features from the Cookie Theft Picture Description Cognitive Test

Changye Li[1], Zhecheng Sheng[2], Trevor Cohen[1], and Serguei Pakhomov[2]

[1]University of Washington
[2]University of Minnesota
[1]{changyel, cohenta}@uw.edu
[2]{sheng136, pakh0002}@umn.edu

Abstract

Alzheimer's Disease (AD) dementia is a progressive neurodegenerative disease that negatively impacts patients' cognitive ability. Previous studies have demonstrated that changes in naturalistic language samples can be useful for early screening of AD dementia. However, the nature of language deficits often requires test administrators to use various speech elicitation techniques during spontaneous language assessments to obtain enough propositional utterances from dementia patients. This could lead to the "observer's effect" on the downstream analysis that has not been fully investigated. Our study seeks to quantify the influence of test administrators on linguistic features in dementia assessment with two English corpora the "Cookie Theft" picture description datasets collected at different locations and test administrators show different levels of administrator involvement. Our results show that the level of test administrator involvement significantly impacts observed linguistic features in patient speech. These results suggest that many of significant linguistic features in the downstream classification task may be partially attributable to differences in the test administration practices rather than solely to participants' cognitive status. The variations in test administrator behavior can lead to systematic biases in linguistic data, potentially confounding research outcomes and clinical assessments. Our study suggests that there is a need for a more standardized test administration protocol in the development of responsible clinical speech analytics frameworks.[1]

1 Introduction

Alzheimer's Disease (AD) dementia is a neurodegenerative disease that causes progressive decline in cognitive function. Even though AD currently has no cure, a timely diagnosis is imperative to alleviate negative consequences of delayed or absent diagnosis including emergency events, family strife, and exposure to scam artists praying on the vulnerable (Stokes et al., 2015). Changes in naturalistic language samples collected from individuals at high-risk for dementia have been identified as one of the early signs of AD (Almor et al., 1999; Blanken et al., 1987; Bucks et al., 2000), showing its potential as an early screening tool. However, analyzing speech samples is labor-intensive and time-consuming. Contemporary studies predominately focus on automated prediction and detection of such changes with language models with considerable success in distinguishing the speech of dementia patients and healthy controls (for recent reviews, see Shi et al. (2023); Ding et al. (2024)). Despite these advances, this line of research often faces the limited data availability. As noted in Shi et al. (2023), the majority of prior work focuses on analyzing naturalistic speech samples using the transcripts of "Cookie Theft" picture description cognitive task produced by English-speaking cohorts in the Pitt corpus (Becker et al., 1994).

While several prior studies have focused on connected speech from non-English speaking participants (e.g., French (Rousseaux et al., 2010b), Spanish (Custodio et al., 2020), and German (Weiner et al., 2016)), a very limited discussion has been held in prior literature on the influence of test administrators. Similarly, methods for data collection, such as optimal sample duration, distance to the microphone, and presence of background noise, have not been standardized (Seyed Ahmad Sajjadi and Nestor, 2012). In addition, the impaired communication ability of people with dementia (Ash et al., 2006; Hier et al., 1985; Rousseaux et al., 2010a) creates additional barriers for their caregivers (Eggenberger et al., 2012; Banovic et al., 2018). This could also extend to neuropsychological assessment batteries such as picture description tasks, which are used extensively by speech-

[1]Our code is available at https://github.com/LinguisticAnomalies/turns

Proceedings of the Workshop on Cognitive Modeling and Computational Linguistics, pages 91–103
May 3, 2025 ©2025 Association for Computational Linguistics

language pathologists in the management of clients with language disorders, including aphasia and dementia (Cummings, 2019; Berube et al., 2019). Prior works have demonstrated that test administrators often perform a variety of speech elicitation techniques to extract additional propositions from aphasic patients (Menn and Obler, 1989; Caplan and Hanna, 1998). As a number of studies have argued in favor of a similarity of linguistic behavior in patients with dementia and aphasia (Gewirth et al., 1984; Nicholas et al., 1985; Blanken et al., 1987; Gumus et al., 2024), similar elicitation strategies may be employed when collecting speech samples from dementia patients. This could lead to the "observer effect" (Labov, 1973) in feature values as many distinct linguistic features are sensitive to the length of the text sample. A previous study (Petti et al., 2023) demonstrated that sample length is important for extracting the various language features of AD by analyzing the speech samples (e.g., public interviews, talk shows and public speeches) from cognitively healthy public figures and those diagnosed with AD dementia. However, this previous study did not address the influence of interviewers and their speech elicitation techniques on collected speech. The impact of test administrators/interviewers and the resulting reliability of linguistic features in clinical settings also remains understudied. This less-discussed gap is particularly concerning given the potential for these factors to introduce systematic biases in the assessment of cognitive decline.

To address this limitation, our study seeks to quantify the influence of test administrators on speech collected with the "Cookie Theft" picture description task. Specifically, we analyze the quantity and distribution of part-of-speech (POS) tags in task transcripts collected from participants residing in two distinct United States locations: Pennsylvania and Wisconsin. We anticipate that test administrators employ significantly more interactions to elicit speech from dementia patients compared to healthy controls, which may contribute to patients with dementia producing linguistic patterns found to be associated with dementia, such as increased use of repetitions (Hier et al., 1985), higher pronoun usage (Almor et al., 1999), and elevated lexical frequency (Bucks et al., 2000) when compared to healthy controls. We analyze the Pitt corpus and the Wisconsin Longitudinal Study (WLS) (Herd et al., 2014) datasets from the Dementia Bank. Both employ the "Cookie Theft" picture

Figure 1: The "Cookie Theft" picture description stimuli.

description task from the Boston Diagnositc Aphasia Examination (Goodglass and Kaplan, 1983). We aim to quantify the extent to which the linguistic features commonly attributed to dementia patients may be artifacts of the data collection and test administration process.

The contributions of this work can be summarized as follows: a) we examine patterns in how test administrator involvement may relate to linguistic features observed in patient speech and their association with dementia vs. control classification; and b) our analyses raise questions about how variations in test administrator behavior might interact with linguistic patterns in clinical assessments. These observations point to opportunities for future research to investigate the role of test administration in linguistic analyses and clinical assessments.

2 Related Work

Verbal production tasks are common neuropsychological assessments for measuring language and executive retrieval functions, with the category fluency task being one of the most widely utilized in clinical settings. In this task, participants are asked to generate exemplars of specific semantic categories – such as animals or food – in a given time. While the category fluency task has demonstrated the diagnostic utility for AD screening (Monsch et al., 1992; Cerhan et al., 2002), these assessments are typically conducted in controlled clinical settings and often require longitudinal observation before a final diagnosis can be made. Such controlled testing environments can be insensitive to naturalistic language patterns (Sabat, 1994) and may miss early signs of linguistic deficits that manifest in daily communications (Crockford and Lesser, 1994). In contrast, spontaneous speech has proven to be a valuable source of information for assessing an individual's cognitive state (Bucks et al., 2000).

The "Cookie Theft" picture description task (Figure 1) is designed to elicit speech samples in pathological cohorts. Participants are asked to describe everything they observe in a picture where two children collaborate to secretly take cookies from a high cupboard shelf, while their mother is preoccupied washing dishes. Previous studies using *statistical* analyses have demonstrated many linguistic anomalies associated with AD progression, such as increased use of repetitions (Hier et al., 1985), higher pronoun usage (Almor et al., 1999), and elevated lexical frequency (Bucks et al., 2000; Cummings, 2019) compared to healthy controls. Supervised machine/deep learning methods, including transformer-based (Vaswani et al., 2017) neural language models can learn to distinguish subtle linguistic characteristics between dementia patients and healthy controls with impressive classification performance (for a review , see Ding et al. (2024)). However, such models bring an additional challenge – often the best-performing models (i.e., neural language models) are least transparent, and the less-accurate models (i.e., statistical models) are easier to explain. Limited interpretability could obscure the bias, which is particularly concerning in clinical artificial intelligence development (Reddy, 2022).

Building upon the previous findings that longer speech is important to extract distinguishable linguistic features (Petti et al., 2023) and interaction patterns between speakers are predictive of the downstream classification task (Farzana and Parde, 2022), we build statistical models to investigate the role of test administrator behavior in the manifestation of linguistic markers associated with dementia. We show that the level of test administrator's engagement significantly impacts the linguistic features observed in the patients' speech.

3 Method

3.1 Data

We use two publicly available datasets resulting from deploying the "Cookie Theft" picture description task during data collection: a) the Pitt corpus[2] and b) the WLS[3] corpus. The Pitt corpus includes recordings and corresponding transcripts from 319 participants. 102 out of 319 participants were classified as control subjects and 204 participants as patients categorized with any AD-related label. Specifically, we restricted the original Pitt corpus to a subset of 169 patients with an assignment of probable AD dementia and 99 healthy controls, resulting in 214 and 182 transcripts for AD patients and healthy controls, respectively.

The WLS is a large-scale, extended longitudinal study of a random sample of 10,317 men and women who graduated from Wisconsin high schools in 1957. The WLS participants were interviewed up to 6 times between 1957 and 2011. Several nueropsychological tests, including letter fluency task and category fluency task were administered in both 2004 and 2011. The "Cookie Theft" picture description task was introduced in 2011. While the WLS participants were interviewed with Telephone Interview for Cognitive Status-modified (TICS-m) for a clinical proxy diagnosis in 2020, we decide to follow a prior study (Guo et al., 2021) to build a "noisy" label with statistically determined age- and education-adjusted thresholds of 16, 14, and 12 for participants in < 60, 60-79, and > 79 age ranges for the category fluency score, respectively. This addresses a critical temporal aspect in AD assessment, particularly given the 9-year gap between speech data collection and clinical assessment in the WLS dataset, contrasting with the Pitt corpus where participants were diagnosed at the time of speech collection. In supporting this approach, the category fluency task, administered concurrently with the "Cookie Theft" picture description task in the WLS corpus, has demonstrated the diagnostic utility on discriminating AD patients and healthy controls, with sensitivity of 0.88 and specificity of 0.96 (Canning et al., 2004). Additionally, the number of WLS participants who completed both the cognitive tests and follow-up clinical interview remained particularly small ($<$ 35 labeled dementia patients), potentially limiting the statistical power of our study.

As a result, we restrict the original WLS dataset to a total of 1,169 participants (1,017 healthy controls and 152 dementia cased patients) who a) agreed to participant in the "Cookie Theft" picture description task and category fluency test in 2011; b) had not been diagnosed with a mental illness at the time of interview; and c) did not previously have a stroke at the time of the interview. Given the fact that the Pitt corpus contains dementia labels obtained from clinical assessments conducted concurrently with the picture description task, we

[2]https://dementia.talkbank.org/access/English/Pitt.html

[3]https://dementia.talkbank.org/access/English/WLS.html

Characteristics		Pitt		WLS	
		Control	Dementia	Control	Dementia
Gender (%)	Female	57 (59.4)	99 (68.3)	523 (51.4)	63 (41.4)
	Male	39 (40.6)	46 (31.7)	494 (48.6)	89 (58.6)
# of transcripts		182	214	1017	152
Age (mean (SD))		64.1 (7.9)	71.5 (8.63)	70.30 (4.14)	70.20 (5.75)
Education (mean (SD))		13.9 (2.4)	12.3 (2.8)	13.77 (3.01)	12.64 (2.16)

Table 1: Basic characteristics of the Pitt corpus and the WLS corpus before propensity score matching.

consider this to be an example of dementia *detection*. In contrast, the WLS dataset represents the case of dementia *prediction*. Data characteristics are provided in Table 1.

3.2 Preprocessing

We perform transcript pre-processing using TRESTLE (**T**oolkit for **R**eproducible **E**xecution of **S**peech **T**ext and **L**anguage **E**xperiments) (Li et al., 2023) for both participants and test administrators. Specifically, we remove non-ASCII characters, unintelligible words, and non-speech artifacts event descriptions or gestures. We also retain the utterances from participants in a relatively "raw" state, in which we preserve repetitions, invited interruptions, and speech repairs (self-revisions).

3.3 Topics Analysis

We segment the utterances from test administrators into individual sentences and remove the duplicates to establish a clean dataset for analysis. These utterances are then clustered based on frequency in each diagnostic group to understand the predominant conversation topics.

3.4 Linguistic feature extraction

Following the established evidence (Bucks et al., 2000; Almor et al., 1999; Hier et al., 1985; Cummings, 2019; Blanken et al., 1987), we focus our the analysis of part-of-speech (POS) tags, lexical frequency (LF), and type-to-token ratio (TTR) on utterances from participants in the Pitt and WLS corpora. We extract the counts of each POS tag for each transcript using spaCy[4] with RoBERTa (Liu et al., 2019) as the base model[5]. The log LF of each transcript is calculated using the $\text{SUBTLEX}_{\text{us}}$ corpus (Brysbaert and New, 2009). Tokens that do not appear in the $\text{SUBTLEX}_{\text{us}}$ corpus are removed as out-of-vocabulary items. TTR quantifies lexical diversity in speech samples, calculated as the proportion of unique words to total words in the transcript. We also count the number of clauses in each transcript. In this study, we define a clause as a syntactic unit centered around a verb that expresses a proposition. As a proxy of syntactic complexity (Caplan and Hanna, 1998), clause count has been shown to be a sensitive linguistic feature for detecting dementia from spoken samples (Seyed Ahmad Sajjadi and Nestor, 2012; Pakhomov et al., 2011).

Additionally, we define *turn* as the number of utterances from either participants (denoted as `par_turns`) or test administrators (denoted as `inv_turns`) in each transcript. We extract the number of turns from test administrators from transcripts for follow-up propensity score matching (PSM).

3.5 Propensity score matching

Propensity score matching (PSM) (Austin, 2011) is a statistical matching method to estimate the effect of a treatment by accounting for the covariates that predict receiving the treatment. PSM assigns a propensity score, which is the probability of treatment assignment conditional on the observed covariates. This conditional probability, serving as a balancing score, matches each individual in the treatment group to an individual in the control group in controlled experiments.

Luz et al. (2020) introduces the AD Recognition through Spontaneous Speech (ADReSS) Challenge, providing researchers with the first available benchmark that is acoustically pre-processed and balanced in terms of age and gender, both of which are risk factors for AD (Ruitenberg et al., 2001; van der Flier and Scheltens, 2005). However, it does not take into account the following possible confounding factors: a) education level, (lower education level is a risk factor of dementia later in

[4]https://spacy.io/

[5]See Table 3 in Appendix for the full list of POS tags analyzed in this study.

life and contributes to the lower linguistic ability) (Snowdon et al., 1996; Ngandu et al., 2007; Nguyen et al., 2016; Caamaño-Isorna et al., 2006); and b) the influence of test administrators, who may perform a variety of speech elicitation techniques to extract enough propositions from patients (Menn and Obler, 1989; Caplan and Hanna, 1998) in a constrained task, such as the "Cookie Theft" picture description task.

To address these concerns, we match the Pitt and the WLS corpora on: a) years of education received, and b) the number of turns from test administrators using PSM. This resulted in a balanced Pitt corpus with 167 transcripts for both dementia patients and healthy controls, and a balanced WLS corpus containing 152 transcripts for both dementia patients and healthy controls.

3.6 Statistical models

We apply z-score normalization on the POS tags, lexical frequency and TTR extracted from each transcript and treat the number of turns from test administrators as the random effects. We split the original and the matched Pitt corpus into 70/30 training/test split. We fit a generalized linear mixed models on the *matched* Pitt training split where we treat the number of turns from test administrators (`inv_turns`) as random effects. Our preliminary results show that fitting such a model for *matched* WLS data results in singularity (i.e., the random effects of `inv_turns` variance-covariance matrix is of *less than full rank*). Therefore we decide to fit generalized linear model on the WLS corpus. In addition, we compare the interaction model (models with interaction terms between `inv_turns` and each linguistic feature) and naïve models (models without interaction terms) and apply backward selection using Akaike's Information Criteria (AIC) (Akaike, 1998). AIC is an information-theoretic approach that estimates the distance between candidate models and the true model on a log-scale, which selects a parsimonious approximating model for the observed data. Our preliminary results show that interaction models achieve better fit with lower AIC. We then continue our analysis with the resulting interaction model for Pitt corpus ($\mathcal{M}_{\text{pitt}}$) and WLS corpus ($\mathcal{M}_{\text{wls}}$).

We also perform cross validation on each dataset to test for internal validity. Specifically, we assess the classification performance of $\mathcal{M}_{\text{pitt}}$ on both the matched Pitt test split and the matched WLS corpus and $\mathcal{M}_{\text{wls}}$ on the matched Pitt test split, respectively.

4 Results

The results of PSM for the Pitt and the WLS corpus can be found in Table 4 and Table 5 in Appendix, respectively. We observed that many linguistic features preserved imbalance even after PSM, with standardized mean difference (SMD) > 0.1 (Zhang et al., 2019). It should be noted that SMD does not indicate the differences in the direction of the scale (Chandler et al., 2019) (i.e., cannot substitute the p-value from significance testing). We also observed that the WLS participants obtained a higher level of education than the Pitt participants (one-sided Wilcoxon rank sum test p-value < 0.001). These observations suggest that additional, potentially unaccounted-for variability may be influencing the results. Thus we proceeded with further quantitative and qualitative analyses.

4.1 Topics analysis

We found that test administrators' utterances usually cover the following topics: a) initiation of the task (e.g., "and there's a picture" and "what's going on in this picture"); b) acknowledgment of progress (e.g., "okay"); c) speech elicitation (e.g., "anything else", "if you see anything else" and "is there anything else"); and d) ending the task (e.g., "alright", "thank you", "that's fine" and "good"). For the Pitt corpus, test administrators said "anything else?" more frequently to dementia patients (18 times) than to healthy controls (10 times). In contrast, the WLS test administrators used the same level of speech elicitation for both groups (dementia patients: 2 times; healthy controls: 2 times).

4.2 Test administrator interaction styles

We observed a moderate negative correlation (Spearman's $\rho = -0.481$) between the number of turns used by Pitt test administrators and participants' Mini-Mental State Examination (MMSE) scores. Pitt test administrators interacted more with dementia patients who had lower MMSE scores, likely in an effort to elicit sufficient speech for analysis. As shown in Table 2, Pitt test administrators used 3 more turns on dementia patients compared to healthy controls whereas the WLS test administrators uses similar number of turns on both diagnostic groups.

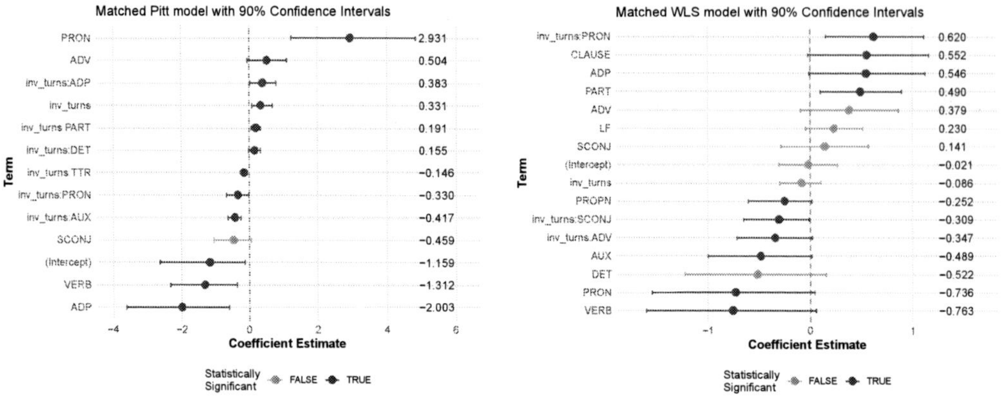

(a) The coefficients of $\mathcal{M}_{\text{pitt}}$ after backward selection with AIC (b) The coefficients of $\mathcal{M}_{\text{wls}}$ after backward selection with AIC

Figure 2: The estimated coefficients and the corresponding 90% confidence intervals of $\mathcal{M}_{\text{pitt}}$ and $\mathcal{M}_{\text{wls}}$. The blue points and ranges indicate that the confidence interval does not cross zero, suggesting the estimate is statistically significant, whereas the dark gray points and ranges indicate that the confidence interval crosses zero, suggesting the estimate is not statistically significant.

Dataset/Condition			Participants' turns (mean (SD))	Test administrators' turns (mean (SD))
Pitt	Before matching	Control	13.55 (6.04)	3.16 (1.77)
		Dementia	13.54 (6.98)	6.10 (4.48)
	After matching	Control	13.44 (5.97)	3.34 (1.73)
		Dementia	12.38 (5.60)	4.38 (1.85)
WLS	Before matching	Control	14.39 (7.91)	0.75 (1.53)
		Dementia	11.97 (7.04)	0.82 (1.79)
	After match	Control	13.80 (7.76)	0.82 (1.62)
		Dementia	11.97 (7.04)	0.82 (1.79)

Table 2: The number of turns from participants and test administrators in the Pitt and the WLS corpus, before and after matching.

4.3 Quantifying the administrator effect

The Pitt model As shown in Figure 2(a), we found that the number of test administrators' turns remain positive and significant ($\beta = 0.331$, p-value < 0.05) in the $\mathcal{M}_{\text{pitt}}$, suggesting that a more interactive test administrator dynamic is associated with a higher probability of developing dementia. We also observed that pronoun usage ($\beta = 2.93$, p-value $<$ 0.001) showed a strong positive association with a higher probability of developing dementia. Interestingly, we observed significant interactions between test administrators' turns and various linguistic features, including TTR ($\beta = -0.146$, p-value $<$ 0.001), the usage of pronoun usage ($\beta = -0.330$, p-value < 0.05), auxiliary ($\beta = -0.417$, p-value < 0.001), adposition ($\beta = 0.382$, p-value < 0.05), and particle ($\beta = 0.191$, p-value < 0.001).

The WLS model As showed in Figure 2(b), we observed fewer significant predictors in $\mathcal{M}_{\text{wls}}$. Interestingly, we observed that, while the usage of pronoun ($\beta = -0.76$, p-value <0.1) showed significantly negative association with having a dementia diagnosis, its interactions terms with the number of test administrators' turns demonstrated an *opposite* directional effects ($\beta = 0.620$, p-value < 0.05).

The predicted effects of the interaction terms As shown in Figure 3(a), we observed that $\mathcal{M}_{\text{pitt}}$ predicts a dramatic increase in the probability of having a dementia diagnosis from 0.1 to 0.8 as conversations went longer for participants who used lower level of pronoun during the test. For participants with average pronoun usage (at mean, shown in green), $\mathcal{M}_{\text{pitt}}$ maintained consistent predicted probabilities of having a dementia diagnosis throughout all conversation lengths. Conversely, participants with high pronoun usage showed an initial high probability of approximately 0.8 for have a dementia diagnosis in shorter conversations, which gradually decreased to 0.7 as conversation went longer. As we observed in Figure 3(b), participants with lower TTR (shown in red) had an increasing probability of having a dementia diagnosis as the number of turns from test administrators increased, rising dramatically from around 0.5 to nearly 0.95 over 10 turns. Notably, participants with higher TTR (shown in blue) showed a contrasting pattern - their probability of having

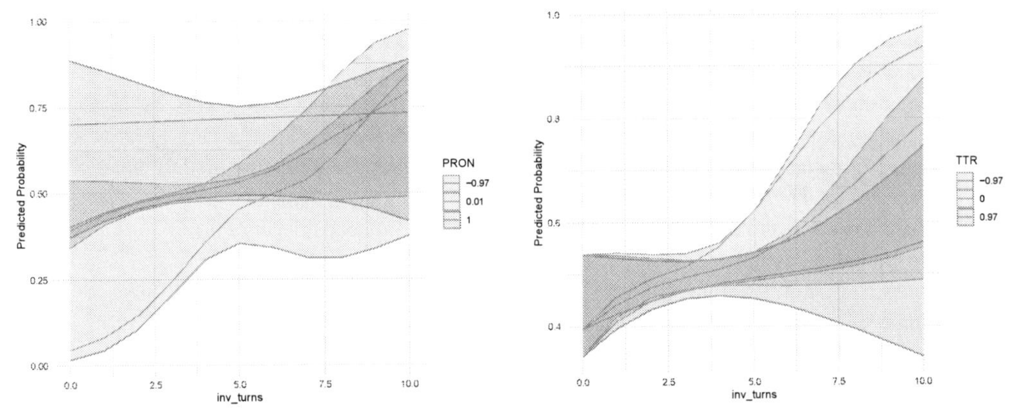

(a) The effect of the interaction term between pronoun usage and inv_turns

(b) The effect of the interaction term between TTR and inv_turns

Figure 3: The predicted values and confidence intervals of the interaction terms between linguistic markers and inv_turns. The level of usage are denoted in color, where red indicates the lower usage (1 SD below the mean), green indicates the average usage, and blue indicates higher usage (1 SD above the mean). The x-axis indicates the number of turns from test administrators.

a dementia diagnosis actually decreased slightly as conversations went longer, dropping from 0.5 to 0.35. Furthermore, we found that the predictive probabilities of pronoun usage and TTR varies systematically with inv_turns. Collectively, Figure 3 suggests an interesting diagnostic transition: at a lower level of test administrator involvement (inv_turns ≤ 3, typical for healthy controls), pronoun usage provides greater diagnostic utility; at moderate involvement (inv_turns ≈ 4, typical for matched dementia patients), both features offer complementary values; while at a higher involvement levels ((inv_turns ≥ 6, typical for dementia patients before PSM), TTR becomes the dominant discriminative marker. This suggests that different linguistic features gain or lose diagnostic utility depending on the degree of administrator involvement.

4.4 Cross validation: classification performance

$\mathcal{M}_{\text{pitt}}$ achieved accuracy of 0.67, precision of 0.69, recall of 0.56, and F_1 score of 0.62 on the matched Pitt test split, respectively. Interestingly, $\mathcal{M}_{\text{pitt}}$ did not generalize well to the original WLS corpus, reaching accuracy of 0.59, precision of 0.13, recall of 0.38, and F_1 score of 0.19, respectively. $\mathcal{M}_{\text{pitt}}$ performed similarly on the matched WLS corpus, reaching accuracy of 0.50, precision of 0.50, recall of 0.38, and F_1 score of 0.43, respectively. $\mathcal{M}_{\text{wls}}$ also generalized poorly to the matched Pitt corpus, with accuracy of 0.55, precision of 0.54, recall of 0.47, and F_1 score of 0.50 on the matched Pitt test split.

5 Discussion

Our key findings are as follows. First, we show that many linguistic features previously studied in AD dementia progression appear to vary with level of test administrator involvement. Second, the observed variability between two corpora underscores the importance of considering administrator behavior as a potential confounding variable in linguistic analyses of clinical populations. These findings collectively suggest that some of the linguistic features commonly observed in dementia patients may be affected by the data collection processes rather than cognitive decline alone.

The observation of interactive test administrator dynamics in the Pitt corpus is consistent with prior work (Menn and Obler, 1989; Caplan and Hanna, 1998), which report that the test administrator needs to induce *enough* propositional utterances from participants in the constrained task such as the "Cookie Theft" picture description task. However, it is often noted that dementia patients are incapable of producing complex utterances due to the progression of the disease. As such, an interactive test administrator dynamic may lead to overestimation of a patients' linguistic ability in some cases.

Our results further suggest that these interaction patterns influence downstream dementia classification, which is consistent with a prior work (Farzana and Parde, 2022). Our study further quantifies the influence of test administrator behavior, demonstrating how the varying levels of investigator involvement between groups may confound our interpretation of linguistic markers as diagnostic indicators. Our results highlight the need to interpret linguistic markers not as isolated indicators, but as features embedded within an interactive context that includes test administrators' role in shaping the discourse. Further research design might benefit from explicitly accounting for and potentially controlling test administrator involvement when developing screening criteria based on linguistic features.

Our findings suggest a nuanced relationship between linguistic markers, administrator interaction patterns, and their predictability for cognitive decline. The consistently high predicted probability of a higher probability of developing dementia for participants with elevated pronoun usage (shown by the stable high probabilities in the blue line in Figure 3(a)) supports existing literature on pronoun over-usage (Almor et al., 1999; Jarrold et al., 2014; Cummings, 2019) as a linguistic marker of cognitive decline. However, our results also indicate that this relationship may be masked or amplified by test administrators' interaction styles, as evidenced by varying predicted probability trajectories across different conversation lengths. Similarly, while the observed TTR patterns also align with previous findings (Hier et al., 1985) that lower lexical diversity indicates cognitive decline, the dramatic increase in predicted probability for participants with lower TTR during longer conversations suggests that the established observations might be influenced by the test administrators' interaction patterns, suggests that these established linguistic markers may be partially attributable to differences in the test administration practices rather than the true construct measures of cognitive decline.

The disparities of classification performance of two models – $\mathcal{M}_{\text{pitt}}$ for *detecting* AD dementia, and $\mathcal{M}_{\text{wls}}$ for *predicting* dementia – confirms the often-observed challenges of developing robust and generalizable models for dementia detection and prediction. While $\mathcal{M}_{\text{pitt}}$ demonstrated moderate performance on its test split, it generalized poorly on the WLS corpus where precision and F_1 score dropped dramatically. $\mathcal{M}_{\text{pitt}}$'s slight improvement in performance on the matched vs. original WLS corpus suggests that the PSM may somewhat mitigate the confounding effect, but not fully resolve the cross-corpus and cross-task generalization issues. Similarly, $\mathcal{M}_{\text{wls}}$ showed limited generalization on the Pitt corpus. This consistent underperformance across corpora suggests the significant challenge of creating models that can *reliably* detect or predict dementia. Our results also suggest the need of considering corpus- and population-specific characteristics in the model development. Factors such as demographic differences, test administrating styles, and the temporal aspect of dementia progression (i.e., detection vs. prediction) may contribute to the observed lack of cross-corpus and cross-task generalizability.

The variability between two corpora suggests that some linguistic markers previously attributed to dementia may be specific to certain data collection protocols rather than universal linguistic anomalies associated with the disease's progression. $\mathcal{M}_{\text{pitt}}$ demonstrates reasonable performance on its own test split, suggesting that within a single dataset, certain linguistic patterns may indeed be indicative of cognitive decline after controlling for the influence of test administrators. However, its substantially degraded performance on the WLS corpus points out a critical issue: linguistic markers that appear robust within one population may not translate effectively to another. This lack of cross-corpus generalizability persists when we validate $\mathcal{M}_{\text{wls}}$ on the Pitt corpus - the performance of $\mathcal{M}_{\text{wls}}$ actually worsens on the matched Pitt test split. These findings collectively suggest that the linguistic anomalies associated with AD progression may be highly context-dependent, influenced by factors such as data collection protocols, test administrator dynamics, and population-specific characteristics. This indicates the need for caution when interpreting linguistic markers of cognitive decline, developing specialized neural language models, and validating findings across diverse datasets and populations.

While the speech samples produced by population with high clinical risks are scarce, incorporating text corpora drawn from different sources (also known as confounding by provenance) presents both opportunities and challenges for detecting linguistic anomalies in AD dementia. Previous studies demonstrate that treating the provenance of a transcript (i.e., Pitt vs. WLS) as a secondary target for prediction (Guo et al., 2021) and data augmentation (Liu et al., 2021; Bertini et al., 2022; Duan et al., 2023, *inter alia*) could lead to performance improvements. However, our results suggest the need for extra caution in such applications. These disparities suggest these approaches, if not carefully implemented, may introduce additional confounding variables rather than identifying true indicators of cognitive impairment. As such, the observed lack of cross-corpus and cross-task generalizability may explain why fine-tuned neural language models generalize less-than-ideal to other speech samples produced by populations at high clinical risk (Li et al., 2022; Farzana and Parde, 2023).

While the automated analysis of spoken language produced by population with high clinical risk remains a valuable component of early-screening cognitive assessment, the observed influence of test administrator dynamics on AD-related linguistic anomalies calls for a re-evaluation of current methods. Researchers and clinicians should exercise caution when interpreting the linguistic features of the "Cookie Theft" picture description task, as they may be partially artifacts of the data collection itself. Our results call for a standardized test administration to minimize the variability in administrator engagement, and the need for population- and language-specific norms for assessments.

6 Conclusion

Our study explored the relationship between test administrator involvement and linguistic features in dementia assessments using the "Cookie Theft" picture description task. The patterns we observed raise questions about how established linguistic features might be shaped by the dynamics of test administration alongside cognitive status. Our study brings the potential benefits of considering administrator behavior in future development of clinical speech analytics frameworks.

Limitations

The work presented here has several limitations. While our analysis identifies significant correlations between the test administrator interactions and linguistic features, we should note that our study design does not establish a direct causal link. Future experimental studies with standardized administrator protocols would be necessary to establish such a link. Second, the size of the datasets used in this study is considerably small, which is a common concern in this line of research (Petti et al., 2020). Moreover, all datasets used in this study are in American English, and many participants are representative of White, non-Hispanic American residents, which certainly limits the generalizability to other languages and ethnic groups. In this study, we only focus on analyzing POS tags for both datasets, which is a limited feature set for detecting cognitive impairment. Future studies should explore comprehensive linguistic and acoustic features (i.e., Fraser et al. (2015)) to establish a more definitive measurement of the effects of test administrator engagement. We acknowledge that there are linguistic differences between the two corpora studied in this work (Johnstone et al., 2015), which may affect the comparability of results across datasets. We should also note that while category fluency task has demonstrates the clinical utility for dementia screening; it is, however, not a complete clinical diagnosis, which may not capture the full spectrum of cognitive decline and could potentially lead to misclassification of some participants.

Acknowledgement

Research reported in this publication was supported by the National Library of Medicine of the National Institutes of Health under award number R01 LM014056-02S1, and the National Institute on Aging of the National institutes of Health under award number AG069792.

References

Hirotogu Akaike. 1998. Information theory and an extension of the maximum likelihood principle. In *Selected papers of hirotugu akaike*, pages 199–213. Springer.

Amit Almor, Daniel Kempler, Maryellen C MacDonald, Elaine S Andersen, and Lorraine K Tyler. 1999. Why do alzheimer patients have difficulty with pronouns?

working memory, semantics, and reference in comprehension and production in alzheimer's disease. *Brain and language*, 67(3):202–227.

S. Ash, P. Moore, S. Antani, G. McCawley, M. Work, and M. Grossman. 2006. Trying to tell a tale. *Neurology*, 66(9):1405–1413.

Peter C. Austin. 2011. An introduction to propensity score methods for reducing the effects of confounding in observational studies. *Multivariate Behavioral Research*, 46(3):399–424.

Silva Banovic, Lejla Junuzovic Zunic, and Osman Sinanovic. 2018. Communication difficulties as a result of dementia. *Materia socio-medica*, 30(3):221.

James T. Becker, François Boiler, Oscar L. Lopez, Judith Saxton, and Karen L. McGonigle. 1994. The Natural History of Alzheimer's Disease: Description of Study Cohort and Accuracy of Diagnosis. *Archives of Neurology*, 51(6):585–594.

Flavio Bertini, Davide Allevi, Gianluca Lutero, Laura Calzà, and Danilo Montesi. 2022. An automatic alzheimer's disease classifier based on spontaneous spoken english. *Computer Speech & Language*, 72:101298.

Shauna Berube, Jodi Nonnemacher, Cornelia Demsky, Shenly Glenn, Sadhvi Saxena, Amy Wright, Donna C Tippett, and Argye E Hillis. 2019. Stealing cookies in the twenty-first century: Measures of spoken narrative in healthy versus speakers with aphasia. *American journal of speech-language pathology*, 28(1S):321–329.

Gerhard Blanken, Jürgen Dittmann, J-Christian Haas, and Claus-W Wallesch. 1987. Spontaneous speech in senile dementia and aphasia: Implications for a neurolinguistic model of language production. *Cognition*, 27(3):247–274.

Marc Brysbaert and Boris New. 2009. Moving beyond kučera and francis: A critical evaluation of current word frequency norms and the introduction of a new and improved word frequency measure for american english. *Behavior research methods*, 41(4):977–990.

Romola S Bucks, Sameer Singh, Joanne M Cuerden, and Gordon K Wilcock. 2000. Analysis of spontaneous, conversational speech in dementia of alzheimer type: Evaluation of an objective technique for analysing lexical performance. *Aphasiology*, 14(1):71–91.

Francisco Caamaño-Isorna, Montserrat Corral, Agustín Montes-Martínez, and Bahi Takkouche. 2006. Education and dementia: a meta-analytic study.

SJ Duff Canning, L Leach, D Stuss, L Ngo, and SE14981170 Black. 2004. Diagnostic utility of abbreviated fluency measures in alzheimer disease and vascular dementia. *Neurology*, 62(4):556–562.

David Caplan and Joy E. Hanna. 1998. Sentence production by aphasic patients in a constrained task. *Brain and Language*, 63(2):184–218.

Jane H Cerhan, Robert J Ivnik, Glenn E Smith, Eric C Tangalos, Ronald C Petersen, and Bradley F Boeve. 2002. Diagnostic utility of letter fluency, category fluency, and fluency difference scores in alzheimer's disease. *The Clinical Neuropsychologist*, 16(1):35–42.

Jacqueline Chandler, Miranda Cumpston, Tianjing Li, Matthew J Page, and VJHW Welch. 2019. Cochrane handbook for systematic reviews of interventions. *Hoboken: Wiley*.

Catherine Crockford and Ruth Lesser. 1994. Assessing functional communication in aphasia: Clinical utility and time demands of three methods. *International Journal of Language & Communication Disorders*, 29(2):165–182.

Louise Cummings. 2019. Describing the cookie theft picture: Sources of breakdown in alzheimer's dementia. *Pragmatics and Society*, 10(2):153–176.

Nilton Custodio, Lissette Duque, Rosa Montesinos, Carlos Alva-Diaz, Martin Mellado, and Andrea Slachevsky. 2020. Systematic review of the diagnostic validity of brief cognitive screenings for early dementia detection in spanish-speaking adults in latin america. *Frontiers in Aging Neuroscience*, 12.

Kewen Ding, Madhu Chetty, Azadeh Noori Hoshyar, Tanusri Bhattacharya, and Britt Klein. 2024. Speech based detection of alzheimer's disease: a survey of ai techniques, datasets and challenges. *Artificial Intelligence Review*, 57(12):1–43.

Junwen Duan, Fangyuan Wei, Jin Liu, Hongdong Li, Tianming Liu, and Jianxin Wang. 2023. CDA: A contrastive data augmentation method for Alzheimer's disease detection. In *Findings of the Association for Computational Linguistics: ACL 2023*, pages 1819–1826, Toronto, Canada. Association for Computational Linguistics.

Eva Eggenberger, Katharina Heimerl, and Michael I. Bennett. 2012. Communication skills training in dementia care: a systematic review of effectiveness, training content, and didactic methods in different care settings. *International Psychogeriatrics*, 25:345 – 358.

Shahla Farzana and Natalie Parde. 2022. Are interaction patterns helpful for task-agnostic dementia detection? an empirical exploration. In *Proceedings of the 23rd Annual Meeting of the Special Interest Group on Discourse and Dialogue*, pages 172–182, Edinburgh, UK. Association for Computational Linguistics.

Shahla Farzana and Natalie Parde. 2023. Towards domain-agnostic and domain-adaptive dementia detection from spoken language. In *Proceedings of the 61st Annual Meeting of the Association for Computational Linguistics (Volume 1: Long Papers)*, pages 11965–11978, Toronto, Canada. Association for Computational Linguistics.

Kathleen C Fraser, Jed A Meltzer, and Frank Rudzicz. 2015. Linguistic features identify alzheimer's disease in narrative speech. *Journal of Alzheimer's disease*, 49(2):407–422.

Letitia R Gewirth, Andrea G Shindler, and Daniel B Hier. 1984. Altered patterns of word associations in dementia and aphasia. *Brain and Language*, 21(2):307–317.

Harold Goodglass and Edith Kaplan. 1983. *Boston diagnostic aphasia examination booklet*. Lea & Febiger.

Melisa Gumus, Morgan Koo, Christa M. Studzinski, Aparna Bhan, Jessica Robin, and Sandra E. Black. 2024. Linguistic changes in neurodegenerative diseases relate to clinical symptoms. *Frontiers in Neurology*, 15.

Yue Guo, Changye Li, Carol Roan, Serguei Pakhomov, and Trevor Cohen. 2021. Crossing the "cookie theft" corpus chasm: applying what bert learns from outside data to the adress challenge dementia detection task. *Frontiers in Computer Science*, 3:642517.

Pamela Herd, Deborah Carr, and Carol Roan. 2014. Cohort Profile: Wisconsin longitudinal study (WLS). *International Journal of Epidemiology*, 43(1):34–41.

Daniel B Hier, Karen Hagenlocker, and Andrea Gellin Shindler. 1985. Language disintegration in dementia: Effects of etiology and severity. *Brain and language*, 25(1):117–133.

William Jarrold, Bart Peintner, David Wilkins, Dimitra Vergryi, Colleen Richey, Maria Luisa Gorno-Tempini, and Jennifer Ogar. 2014. Aided diagnosis of dementia type through computer-based analysis of spontaneous speech. In *Proceedings of the Workshop on Computational Linguistics and Clinical Psychology: From Linguistic Signal to Clinical Reality*, pages 27–37, Baltimore, Maryland, USA. Association for Computational Linguistics.

Barbara Johnstone, Daniel Baumgardt, Maeve Eberhardt, and Scott Kiesling. 2015. *Pittsburgh speech and Pittsburghese*, volume 11. Walter de Gruyter GmbH & Co KG.

William Labov. 1973. *Sociolinguistic patterns*. 4. University of Pennsylvania press.

Changye Li, David Knopman, Weizhe Xu, Trevor Cohen, and Serguei Pakhomov. 2022. GPT-D: Inducing dementia-related linguistic anomalies by deliberate degradation of artificial neural language models. In *Proceedings of the 60th Annual Meeting of the Association for Computational Linguistics (Volume 1: Long Papers)*, pages 1866–1877, Dublin, Ireland. Association for Computational Linguistics.

Changye Li, Weizhe Xu, Trevor Cohen, Martin Michalowski, and Serguei Pakhomov. 2023. Trestle: Toolkit for reproducible execution of speech, text and language experiments. *AMIA Summits on Translational Science Proceedings*, 2023:360.

Yinhan Liu, Myle Ott, Naman Goyal, Jingfei Du, Mandar Joshi, Danqi Chen, Omer Levy, Mike Lewis, Luke Zettlemoyer, and Veselin Stoyanov. 2019. Roberta: A robustly optimized bert pretraining approach. *ArXiv*, abs/1907.11692.

Zhaoci Liu, Zhiqiang Guo, Zhenhua Ling, and Yunxia Li. 2021. Detecting alzheimer's disease from speech using neural networks with bottleneck features and data augmentation. In *ICASSP 2021 - 2021 IEEE International Conference on Acoustics, Speech and Signal Processing (ICASSP)*, pages 7323–7327.

Saturnino Luz, Fasih Haider, Sofia de la Fuente, Davida Fromm, and Brian MacWhinney. 2020. Alzheimer's Dementia Recognition Through Spontaneous Speech: The ADReSS Challenge. In *Proc. Interspeech 2020*, pages 2172–2176.

Lise Menn and Loraine K Obler. 1989. Cross-language data and theories of agrammatism. In *Agrammatic aphasia*, pages 1369–1389. John Benjamins.

Andreas U Monsch, Mark W Bondi, Nelson Butters, David P Salmon, Robert Katzman, and Leon J Thal. 1992. Comparisons of verbal fluency tasks in the detection of dementia of the alzheimer type. *Archives of neurology*, 49(12):1253–1258.

Tiia Ngandu, Eva von Strauss, E-L Helkala, B Winblad, A Nissinen, J Tuomilehto, H Soininen, and M Kivipelto. 2007. Education and dementia: what lies behind the association? *Neurology*, 69(14):1442–1450.

Thu T Nguyen, Eric J Tchetgen Tchetgen, Ichiro Kawachi, Stephen E Gilman, Stefan Walter, Sze Y Liu, Jennifer J Manly, and M Maria Glymour. 2016. Instrumental variable approaches to identifying the causal effect of educational attainment on dementia risk. *Annals of epidemiology*, 26(1):71–76.

Marjorie Nicholas, Loraine K. Obler, Martin L. Albert, and nancy helm estabrooks. 1985. Empty speech in alzheimer's disease and fluent aphasia. *Journal of speech and hearing research*, 28 3:405–10.

Serguei Pakhomov, Dustin Chacon, Mark Wicklund, and Jeanette Gundel. 2011. Computerized assessment of syntactic complexity in alzheimer's disease: a case study of iris murdoch's writing. *Behavior research methods*, 43:136–144.

Ulla Petti, Simon Baker, and Anna Korhonen. 2020. A systematic literature review of automatic alzheimer's disease detection from speech and language. *Journal of the American Medical Informatics Association*, 27(11):1784–1797.

Ulla Petti, Simon Baker, Anna Korhonen, and Jessica Robin. 2023. How Much Speech Data Is Needed for Tracking Language Change in Alzheimer's Disease? A Comparison of Random Length, 5-Min, and 1-Min Spontaneous Speech Samples. *Digital Biomarkers*, 7(1):157–166.

Sandeep Reddy. 2022. Explainability and artificial intelligence in medicine. *The Lancet Digital Health*, 4(4):e214–e215.

Marc Rousseaux, Amandine Sève, Marion Vallet, Florence Pasquier, and Marie Anne Mackowiak-Cordoliani. 2010a. An analysis of communication in conversation in patients with dementia. *Neuropsychologia*, 48(13):3884–3890.

Marc Rousseaux, Amandine Sève, Marion Vallet, Florence Pasquier, and Marie Anne Mackowiak-Cordoliani. 2010b. An analysis of communication in conversation in patients with dementia. *Neuropsychologia*, 48(13):3884–3890.

Annemieke Ruitenberg, Alewijn Ott, John C. van Swieten, Albert Hofman, and Monique M.B. Breteler. 2001. Incidence of dementia: does gender make a difference? *Neurobiology of Aging*, 22(4):575–580.

Steven R Sabat. 1994. Language function in alzheimer's disease: a critical review of selected literature. *Language & Communication*, 14(4):331–351.

Michal Tomek Seyed Ahmad Sajjadi, Karalyn Patterson and Peter J. Nestor. 2012. Abnormalities of connected speech in semantic dementia vs alzheimer's disease. *Aphasiology*, 26(6):847–866.

Mengke Shi, Gary Cheung, and Seyed Reza Shahamiri. 2023. Speech and language processing with deep learning for dementia diagnosis: A systematic review. *Psychiatry Research*, 329:115538.

David A Snowdon, Susan J Kemper, James A Mortimer, Lydia H Greiner, David R Wekstein, and William R Markesbery. 1996. Linguistic ability in early life and cognitive function and alzheimer's disease in late life: Findings from the nun study. *Jama*, 275(7):528–532.

Laura Stokes, Helen Combes, and Graham Stokes. 2015. The dementia diagnosis: a literature review of information, understanding, and attributions. *Psychogeriatrics*, 15(3):218–225.

Wiesje M van der Flier and Philip Scheltens. 2005. Epidemiology and risk factors of dementia. *Journal of Neurology, Neurosurgery & Psychiatry*, 76(suppl 5):v2–v7.

Ashish Vaswani, Noam Shazeer, Niki Parmar, Jakob Uszkoreit, Llion Jones, Aidan N Gomez, Ł ukasz Kaiser, and Illia Polosukhin. 2017. Attention is all you need. In *Advances in Neural Information Processing Systems*, volume 30. Curran Associates, Inc.

Jochen Weiner, Christian Herff, and Tanja Schultz. 2016. Speech-based detection of alzheimer's disease in conversational german. In *Interspeech 2016*, pages 1938–1942.

Zhongheng Zhang, Hwa Jung Kim, Guillaume Lonjon, Yibing Zhu, et al. 2019. Balance diagnostics after propensity score matching. *Annals of translational medicine*, 7(1).

Appendix

POS tags	**Name**
ADJ	Adjective
ADP	Adposition
ADV	Adverb
AUX	Auxiliary
CCONJ	Coordinating conjunction
DET	Determiner
INTJ	Interjection
NOUN	Noun
PART	Particle
PRON	Pronoun
PROPN	Proper noun
SCONJ	subordinating conjection
VERB	Verb

Table 3: The Universal POS tags

Features	Before matching				After matching			
	Level	Control	Dementia	SMD	Level	Control	Dementia	SMD
Number of transcripts (n)		182	214			167	167	
Education (mean (SD))		13.92 (2.42)	12.28 (2.81)	0.629		13.66 (2.24)	12.53 (2.93)	0.434
Age (mean (SD))		64.08 (7.91)	71.51 (8.63)	0.897		64.27 (7.85)	71.46 (8.63)	0.871
Gender (%)	Female	114 (62.6)	147 (68.7)	0.128	Female	104 (62.3)	116 (69.5)	0.152
	Male	68 (37.4)	67 (31.3)		Male	63 (37.7)	51 (30.5)	
PRON (mean (SD))		15.03 (9.85)	17.18 (12.36)	0.193		14.72 (9.48)	15.59 (10.80)	0.086
PROPN (mean (SD))		0.12 (0.51)	0.25 (0.65)	0.227		0.13 (0.53)	0.14 (0.46)	0.024
NOUN (mean (SD))		24.93 (13.94)	19.41 (11.06)	0.439		24.57 (13.96)	19.37 (10.88)	0.416
ADJ (mean (SD))		4.06 (3.52)	3.21 (3.47)	0.243		3.88 (3.38)	3.16 (3.48)	0.211
ADV (mean (SD))		3.91 (3.75)	5.43 (5.03)	0.342		3.81 (3.79)	4.65 (3.95)	0.217
CLAUSE (mean (SD))		20.13 (9.22)	20.43 (11.00)	0.030		19.72 (8.92)	18.87 (9.21)	0.093
AUX (mean (SD))		13.18 (6.36)	11.66 (7.09)	0.224		13.02 (6.32)	11.22 (6.55)	0.281
VERB (mean (SD))		16.81 (8.17)	15.70 (8.79)	0.131		16.49 (7.94)	15.00 (8.06)	0.186
ADP (mean (SD))		11.58 (7.22)	9.29 (6.32)	0.338		11.35 (7.05)	9.50 (6.40)	0.274
DET (mean (SD))		16.65 (9.07)	13.73 (7.97)	0.342		16.40 (9.01)	13.79 (8.05)	0.306
PUNCT (mean (SD))		24.41 (10.80)	23.96 (12.13)	0.040		24.23 (10.67)	22.23 (9.90)	0.195
CCONJ (mean (SD))		5.68 (4.28)	5.84 (4.15)	0.038		5.59 (4.20)	5.85 (4.21)	0.063
PART (mean (SD))		2.77 (2.25)	3.21 (2.74)	0.174		2.59 (2.11)	3.09 (2.50)	0.214
SCONJ (mean (SD))		1.63 (2.46)	1.27 (1.78)	0.171		1.58 (2.46)	1.18 (1.72)	0.189
INTJ (mean (SD))		5.16 (4.02)	6.21 (6.83)	0.187		5.07 (3.97)	5.66 (4.61)	0.138
LF (mean (SD))		8.16 (0.36)	8.36 (0.47)	0.479		8.15 (0.37)	8.30 (0.45)	0.358
TTR (mean (SD))		0.33 (0.05)	0.31 (0.06)	0.373		0.34 (0.05)	0.32 (0.06)	0.286
par_turns (mean (SD))		13.55 (6.04)	13.54 (6.98)	0.003		13.44 (5.97)	12.38 (5.60)	0.183
inv_turns (mean (SD))		3.16 (1.77)	6.10 (4.48)	0.863		3.33 (1.73)	4.38 (1.85)	0.589
mmse (mean (SD))		29.13 (1.11)	18.54 (5.11)	2.864		29.08 (1.13)	19.50 (4.50)	2.920

Table 4: The differences of linguistic features before/after matching on the Pitt corpus

Features	Before matching				After matching			
	Level	Control	Dementia	SMD	Level	Control	Dementia	SMD
Number of transcripts (n)		1017	152			152	152	
Education (mean (SD))		13.77 (3.01)	12.64 (2.16)	0.431		12.62 (2.18)	12.64 (2.16)	0.006
Age (mean (SD))		70.30 (4.14)	70.20 (5.75)	0.021		70.81 (3.77)	70.20 (5.75)	0.126
PRON (mean (SD))		15.20 (9.93)	11.16 (8.05)	0.447		14.37 (8.91)	11.16 (8.05)	0.377
AUX (mean (SD))		10.76 (6.63)	7.81 (5.48)	0.485		9.75 (6.25)	7.81 (5.48)	0.330
VERB (mean (SD))		16.82 (9.08)	12.71 (7.19)	0.502		15.25 (7.91)	12.71 (7.19)	0.336
ADP (mean (SD))		11.53 (6.74)	8.57 (5.71)	0.474		10.07 (5.77)	8.57 (5.71)	0.262
DET (mean (SD))		16.99 (9.87)	12.22 (7.23)	0.551		15.03 (8.00)	12.22 (7.23)	0.368
NOUN (mean (SD))		29.00 (16.89)	22.38 (13.71)	0.430		26.86 (14.61)	22.38 (13.71)	0.316
PUNCT (mean (SD))		26.61 (13.24)	21.68 (11.74)	0.393		25.47 (11.87)	21.68 (11.74)	0.321
CCONJ (mean (SD))		5.47 (4.83)	3.43 (3.62)	0.478		5.02 (4.99)	3.43 (3.62)	0.365
ADJ (mean (SD))		3.89 (3.75)	2.30 (2.37)	0.509		3.02 (2.93)	2.30 (2.37)	0.272
PART (mean (SD))		2.83 (2.46)	2.40 (2.14)	0.186		2.63 (2.25)	2.40 (2.14)	0.105
SCONJ (mean (SD))		1.55 (1.92)	0.90 (1.36)	0.390		1.38 (1.60)	0.90 (1.36)	0.324
ADV (mean (SD))		4.06 (3.98)	2.93 (3.41)	0.305		3.77 (3.60)	2.93 (3.41)	0.240
INTJ (mean (SD))		1.88 (2.91)	1.50 (2.58)	0.139		1.99 (2.80)	1.50 (2.58)	0.181
LF (mean (SD))		8.06 (0.43)	8.05 (0.44)	0.033		8.02 (0.42)	8.05 (0.44)	0.057
TTR (mean (SD))		0.35 (0.06)	0.37 (0.07)	0.303		0.36 (0.06)	0.37 (0.07)	0.189
CLAUSE (mean (SD))		21.01 (10.44)	17.21 (9.26)	0.385		19.81 (9.14)	17.21 (9.26)	0.282
PROPN (mean (SD))		0.07 (0.36)	0.02 (0.18)	0.170		0.14 (0.55)	0.02 (0.18)	0.288
par_turns (mean (SD))		14.39 (7.91)	11.97 (7.04)	0.323		13.88 (6.68)	11.97 (7.04)	0.278
inv_turns (mean (SD))		0.75 (1.53)	0.82 (1.79)	0.044		0.77 (1.25)	0.82 (1.79)	0.034

Table 5: The differences of linguistic features before/after matching on the WLS dataset

Cross-Framework Generalizable Discourse Relation Classification Through Cognitive Dimensions

Yingxue Fu
School of Computer Science
University of St Andrews, Scotland, UK
fuyingxue321@gmail.com

Abstract

Existing discourse corpora annotated under different frameworks adopt distinct but somewhat related taxonomies of relations. How to integrate discourse frameworks has been an open research question. Previous studies on this topic are mainly theoretical, although such research is typically performed with the hope of benefiting computational applications. In this paper, we show how the proposal by Sanders et al. (2018) based on the Cognitive approach to Coherence Relations (CCR) (Sanders et al., 1992, 1993) can be used effectively to facilitate cross-framework discourse relation (DR) classification. To address the challenges of using predicted UDims for DR classification, we adopt the Bayesian learning framework based on Monte Carlo dropout (Gal and Ghahramani, 2016) to obtain more robust predictions. Data augmentation enabled by our proposed method yields strong performance (55.75 for RST and 55.01 for PDTB implicit DR classification in macro-averaged F1). We compare four model designs and analyze the experimental results from different perspectives. Our study shows an effective and cross-framework generalizable approach for DR classification, filling a gap in existing studies.[1]

1 Introduction

Discourse coherence relates to the way that a monologue or dialogue is organized so that it is a coherent entity, instead of a random collection of clauses or sentences. As such, coherence represents an important aspect of text quality (Webber and Joshi, 2012). Various studies have shown the benefits of incorporating discourse-level information or coherence-related training objectives in NLP tasks, such as text generation (Bosselut et al., 2018), language modelling (Iter et al., 2020; Lee et al., 2020; Stevens-Guille et al., 2022), and summarization (Xu et al., 2020).

Discourse-level analysis is typically concerned with discourse relations (Rutherford and Xue, 2015). These relations describe the links with which two segments are associated with each other and they form an integral part of discourse theories including the Rhetorical Structure Theory (RST) (Mann and Thompson, 1988) and D-LTAG (Webber, 2004), which is the theoretical foundation for the PDTB framework, named after the Penn Discourse Treebank (PDTB) (Prasad et al., 2008; Webber et al., 2019). As discourse annotation is a demanding task and different discourse theories provide distinctive but often not incompatible perspectives of discourse modelling, the integration of different discourse theories has been a topic of interest for a long time (Hovy and Maier, 1992; Bunt and Prasad, 2016; Benamara and Taboada, 2015; Sanders et al., 2018; Chiarcos, 2014).

The UniDim proposal (Sanders et al., 2018), which originates from the Cognitive approach to Coherence Relations (CCR) (Sanders et al., 1992, 1993), is shown to be relatively successful in mapping PDTB and RST relations (Demberg et al., 2019). With this approach, a set of unifying dimensions (henceforth UDims) serve as *interlingua*, and relations under different frameworks can be decomposed and compared through the intermediary of it. For example, the RST relation *Contrast* can be decomposed as *negative* (at the polarity dimension, henceforth *pol*), *additive* (at the basic operation dimension, henceforth *bop*), *not applicable (NA)* (at the implication order dimension, henceforth *imp*), *objective/subjective* (at the source of coherence dimension, henceforth *soc*), and *under-specified* (at the temporality dimension, henceforth *temp*), while *Contrast* in PDTB is represented by *negative* (*pol*), *additive* (*bop*), *NA* (*imp*), *objective* (*soc*), and *under-specified* (*temp*). It is clear that the two relations are quite similar but the RST *Contrast* relation may include subjective cases (we refer those inter-

[1] Code will be released here.

Proceedings of the Workshop on Cognitive Modeling and Computational Linguistics, pages 104–134
May 3, 2025 ©2025 Association for Computational Linguistics

ested to Appendix A for the meaning of UDims, and Appendix B and Appendix C for a better understanding of how the relations in RST and PDTB are analyzed in terms of the UDims).

Previous studies (Roze et al., 2019; Fu, 2023; Varghese et al., 2023) demonstrate the possibility of incorporating these dimensions in discourse relation (henceforth DR) classification tasks. Varghese et al. (2023) use UDims as features for implicit DR classification, with a focus on leveraging label similarities to improve the performance of a classifier on this task. Roze et al. (2019) adopt a pipeline approach, where separate classifiers are trained for the UDims and the predicted UDims are mapped to the sense hierarchy of PDTB 2.0. As the performance on UDim classification is low, when the predicted UDims are used together to identify a sense label, the accuracy is much lower than training a classifier for DRs directly, without involving UDims. Meanwhile, the mappings are not unambiguous even between gold UDims and sense labels. The same combination of UDims can be mapped to different sense labels and the same sense labels can have different UDim representations.[2] The third challenge is that the distributions of UDims and DRs are generally imbalanced.

The study by Roze et al. (2019) shows an example of leveraging UDims in analyzing challenges of DR classification, but with their approach, UDims cannot be used effectively for DR classification tasks due to reasons discussed above. In contrast, Fu (2023) demonstrates that high performance can be achieved when gold UDims are employed for DR classification across different discourse frameworks, but the performance gains rely on availability of gold UDims, which is not feasible in realistic settings. In this study, we explore several ways of applying UDims in DR classification, and the results suggest that simply incorporating objectives of UDim classification can improve the performance on DR classification, which may be considered as empirical evidence for the correlation between UDims and DRs. However, we also notice that model performance is not a simple reflection of the relationship between UDims and DRs, for instance, a temporal relation does not necessarily have the lowest recognition accuracy when the temporal dimension is not considered in the training process, which is consistent with the findings shown in Fu (2023). In addition, we conduct experiments on using RST and PDTB data together, and the results reveal that PDTB explicit relation data is useful for data augmentation for both RST and PDTB implicit DR classification tasks.

Our contributions can be summarized as follows:

- We propose a method based on Monte Carlo (MC) dropout (Gal and Ghahramani, 2016) to enable UDims to be applied to DR classification tasks under different frameworks, which fills a gap in existing studies (Roze et al., 2019; Fu, 2023).
- We show how UDims can be used to bridge DR classification tasks under different discourse frameworks.
- We conduct analysis of different model designs and model performance on specific relations.

2 Related Work

2.1 Cross-Framework DR Classification

Discourse connective prediction is considered a potentially effective auxiliary task for both RST DR classification (Yu et al., 2022; Yung et al., 2019) and PDTB DR classification (Qin et al., 2017; Shi and Demberg, 2019; Jiang et al., 2021; Liu and Strube, 2023). Motivated by the high performance on PDTB explicit DR classification, researchers try to convert PDTB implicit DR classification into explicit DR classification by predicting discourse connectives first. As RST does not make a clear distinction between implicit and explicit DRs in annotation, this approach is less frequently utilized for RST.

To address the challenge of limited training data for RST parsing, Braud et al. (2016) utilize multi-task learning to benefit from supervision of related tasks such as PDTB DR classification. As RST elementary discourse units (EDUs) and PDTB arguments are determined based on different criteria, they have to make adjustments to PDTB data and use sentences rather than manually annotated

[2]For example, the pattern *pos* (positive in polarity), *cau* (causal in basic operation), *NS* (under-specified in implication order), *obj* (objective in source of coherence), *NS* (under-specified in temporality), *non-specificity* (encoded by "-"), *non-alternative* ("-"), *non-conditional* ("-") and *non-goal-oriented* ("-") has two sense labels *Cause* and *Explanation* in the training set of RST, and the RST *Evaluation* relation has four patterns of UDim combinations: *pos, NS, NS, sub NS*,+, -, -, - (580 instances); *pos, add, NA, sub, NS*, +, -, -, - (272 instances); *pos, cau, bas, sub, NS*, +, -, -, - (8 instances); and *pos, cau, non-b, sub, NS*, +, -, -, - (2 instances) (see Appendix D for a full list of unique mapping patterns between UDims and DRs for RST and Appendix E for PDTB 3.0).

arguments in their experiments and ignore intra-sentential PDTB relations. Multi-task learning is also adopted in Liu et al. (2016) for PDTB implicit DR classification, where RST DR classification is treated as an auxiliary task. It shows that RST DR classification improves performance on the classification of some of PDTB Level-1 implicit DRs.

2.2 The UniDim Proposal

Under the TextLink Action, which aims at unifying existing linguistic resources on discourse structure, Sanders et al. (2018) propose a set of unifying dimensions (UDims) as an interface for different discourse frameworks to be related with each other. The UDims originate from four cognitive primitives—*basic operation*, *source of coherence*, *order of segments* (called *implication order* in Sanders et al. (2018)) and *polarity*, which are used to define coherence relations in Sanders et al. (1992), where a different approach towards representing discourse relations is taken, namely, the Cognitive approach to Coherence Relations (CCR). Compared with RST and PDTB, the CCR approach treats discourse relations as cognitive entities that can be analyzed from different dimensions, and a relation is thus described from four dimensions, such as *causal, objective, basic order, positive*, rather than with a single label, such as *Cause* in RST. Each of these dimensions functions as an attribute that has a number of possible values, for example, the *polarity* dimension allows for distinction between *positive*, *negative* or *under-specified*.

To make the taxonomy more expressive, additional dimensions are added, including *temporality*, and *specificity*, *lists* and *alternatives* for additive relations, and *conditionals* and *goal-orientedness* for causal relations. Recall that *additive* and *causal* are values under the source of coherence dimension. With these UDims, DRs from different discourse frameworks can be decomposed and compared systematically.

Demberg et al. (2019) try to validate existing proposals for mapping DRs of different discourse frameworks, and the results of their data-driven investigation exhibit higher consistency with the results obtained with the UniDim proposal, compared with the OLiA reference model (Chiarcos, 2014) and the ISO standard proposal (Bunt and Prasad, 2016).

3 Our Method

We focus on RST DR classification and PDTB implicit DR classification in this study. However, the method is generalizable, not limited to the two discourse frameworks.

3.1 UDim Extraction

Since existing discourse corpora, such as the RST Discourse Treebank (RST-DT) (Carlson et al., 2001) and PDTB, do not contain annotations of UDims, we adopt the rule-based method in Fu (2023) to obtain gold UDim values for each of the relation instances first. For RST-DT, with annotations of end labels (the original 78 relations) and nuclearity information, the mapping rules shown in Appendix B allow us to obtain UDim values. For PDTB, as the actual linear order of arguments in the original text is needed to determine values of *implication order* while the assignment of arguments does not simply follow the linear order, we first write a script to determine the linear order of arguments, and with the annotation of end labels, the mapping rules shown in Appendix C can be used to derive UDim values for each instance.

3.2 Cascaded Classifier

Given that UDims are originally intended to be used as a platform-agnostic interlingua of DRs, a natural approach is to combine all the data and train classifiers for UDims and map the predicted UDims to DRs of different discourse frameworks, based on knowledge of how UDim combinations are mapped to DRs (Appendix B and Appendix C), which is analogous to training a "universal classifier" of DRs. This approach is adopted by Roze et al. (2019), but only on PDTB 2.0, and the results are much lower than training a simple classifier for DRs directly. Moreover, Fu (2023) shows that combining PDTB and RST data does not improve the performance over using PDTB data alone for UDim classification. Therefore, instead of only using the predicted UDims for identifying DRs with a rule-based method, we deem it necessary to add DR classification as a training objective, thus forming a cascaded classifier. While this step may compromise the "universality" of the intended use of UDims, it is a necessary procedure to obtain better performance on DR classification. Figure 1 illustrates the model design.

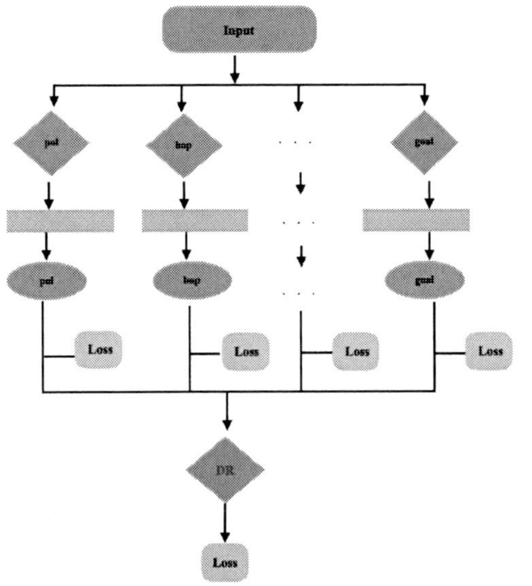

Figure 1: Cascaded classifier for DR classification. The losses in orange boxes are to be minimized. The green bars represent embedding layers. As is shown here, the input is not used for DR classification directly, which distinguishes this approach from the methods discussed in section 3.3.

3.3 Input+UDim for DR Classification

We investigate another set of methods, where the input is used for both UDim classification and DR classification. The intuition is that predicted UDims are not robust enough to be used as the only signal for DR classification, and they are better treated as attributes. Section 3.3.2 shows different model designs with this approach.

3.3.1 UDim Classification

For an input sequence X_i in a dataset with size N, i.e., $\{X_i\}_{i=1}^{N}$, X_i is formed by a pair of arguments of lengths m and n, respectively, i.e., $X_i = A_1^{(1)}$ ... $A_m^{(1)}$, $A_1^{(2)}$ ... $A_n^{(2)}$. We use a pre-trained language model as the input encoder f_{enc}. Special tokens are to be inserted based on the requirements of the chosen encoder, and X_i is typically padded to a fixed length. In our experiments, the two arguments are padded separately at the ends. The representation h of the preprocessed input sequence, denoted as $\widetilde{X_i}$, can be obtained from the encoder:

$$h = f_{enc}(\widetilde{X_i}) \tag{1}$$

A three-layer feed-forward network g, comprising a fully connected layer, a LeakyReLU activation function, followed by a dropout layer, is applied to transform h to a lower dimensional space before it is passed for UDim classification:

$$h_{UDim} = g(h) \tag{2}$$

UDims are not independent. For example, the *implication order* dimension is only applicable to causal relations, which are a category under the *basic operation* dimension. Therefore, the *basic operation* dimension functions as a parent of the *implication order* dimension. This parenthood relationship between UDims can be understood from the description of UDims in Appendix A.

Inspired by the method proposed by Gerych et al. (2021), which leverages class dependencies and conditions the prediction of child classes on the prediction of their parents, we exploit knowledge about the relationship between UDims to improve the performance on UDim classification. For instance, the embedding vector of the predicted *basic operation* dimension $E(\hat{y}_{bop})$ will be passed as features to the classification head of the *implication order* dimension, f_{impl}:

$$\tilde{y}_{impl} = softmax(f_{impl}(h_{UDim} \oplus E(\hat{y}_{bop}))) \tag{3}$$

Equation 3 shows how the prediction of the *implication order* dimension can be obtained, where $\oplus$ denotes concatenation operation.

An argmax function is required to obtain a discrete value from the predicted probability distribution, so that $E(\hat{y}_{UDim})$ can be obtained from embedding layers and passed as features for the classification of another related UDim or DR. However, this operation is non-differentiable and the training signal of one UDim cannot backpropagate to the training of the related UDims or from DRs to UDims. Therefore, we adopt the Gumbel-Softmax function (Jang et al., 2016), which is a differentiable approximation to the argmax function:

$$y_i = \frac{\exp((\log(p_i) + g_i)/\tau)}{\sum_{j=1}^{k} \exp((\log(p_j) + g_j)/\tau)} \tag{4}$$

where p_i represents a class probability for a categorical variable with k possible outcomes. $g_i ... g_k$ are i.i.d samples drawn from a Gumbel(0, 1) distribution, which can be sampled by drawing $\mu \sim$ Uniform(0, 1) and $g = -\log(-\log(\mu))$.

3.3.2 DR Classification

Similar to UDim classification, a three-layer feed-forward network ϕ is applied to h before it is passed for DR classification:

$$h_{DR} = \phi(h) \tag{5}$$

We experiment with four ways of leveraging UDims in the DR classification task:

1. *TrainonGoldTestonPred*: During training, gold UDims are used and their embeddings are concatenated with h_{DR} for DR classification, so that the model learns the relationship between the input and the UDims and the target DR labels. During inference time, the embeddings of the predicted UDims are used. This is where we differ from Fu (2023), where gold UDims are still used during inference time.

2. *InputDimCat*: During both training and testing, the embeddings of predicted UDims are used, which are concatenated with h_{DR}.

3. *InputDimAtt*: During both training and testing, the embeddings of predicted UDims are combined with h_{DR} via an attention mechanism based on scaled dot product (Vaswani et al., 2017).

4. *InputForRelCls*: The hypothesis is that due to the close relationship between UDims and DRs, if the model is trained on UDim classification tasks, the performance on DR classification may be improved, even without using the predicted UDims as features, forming a scenario of multi-task learning.

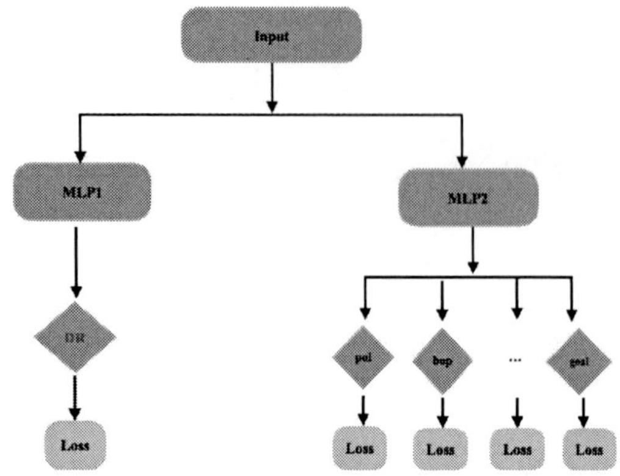

Figure 2: Model design for *InputForRelCls*. The losses in orange boxes are to be minimized.

Figure 2 shows the model design for *InputForRelCls*, which is also employed in the experiments on data augmentation, thus illustrated here to facilitate understanding.

Preliminary experiments show that directly using predicted UDims as features yields mixed results. This could be attributed to the utilization of *predicted* UDims, where the classification errors of these UDims might introduce noise, and combined use of these predicted UDims exacerbates uncertainty in the DR classification task. To address this challenge, the MC dropout method is employed.

3.3.3 MC Dropout

Due to the property of learning a distribution over model parameters, Bayesian networks represent a natural choice for uncertainty estimation. However, traditional Bayesian methods typically come with large computational costs, and for transformer-based models, the computational costs can be prohibitive. Gal and Ghahramani (2016) introduce the MC dropout method to tackle the challenge of uncertainty estimation in deep neural networks. Different from the standard dropout method, dropout is activated during inference time. The MC dropout method represents a lightweight Bayesian approximation.

For an input representation from the previous layer h_{i-1}, the output representation h_i of the i_{th} layer is determined with:

$$h_i = \sigma(h_{i-1}, \mathbf{W}_i, \mathbf{M}_i) \tag{6}$$

where $\mathbf{W}_i$ denotes weights of the i_{th} layer, and $\mathbf{M}_i$ is a masking matrix, with its entries being sampled from a Bernoulli distribution, and the probability of being zero is the dropout probability p. σ denotes the activation function of this layer.

For a model with l layers, the model weights ω can be expressed as a set of weight matrices for each layer: $\omega = \{\mathbf{W}_i\}_{i=1}^{l}$. With MC dropout, during inference, one can sample T sets of ω for T stochastic forward passes and the mean predicted distribution is obtained by averaging over the T passes:

$$p(y'|\mathbf{x}, \mathbf{X}, \mathbf{Y}) = \frac{1}{N}\sum_{t=1}^{T} p(y'|\mathbf{x}, [\mathbf{W}_i^t, \mathbf{M}_i^t], \ldots, [\mathbf{W}_l^t, \mathbf{M}_l^t]) \tag{7}$$

The variance can be used as an indicator of model uncertainty. As indicated by Shelmanov et al. (2021), applying MC dropout to all the dropout layers of a transformer model yields better performance for uncertainty estimation. Even though our focus is not uncertainty estimation, the MC dropout method can be used conveniently to approximate the results of an ensemble model and we can use mean predictive distribution over multiple runs for UDim and DR classification.

3.4 Data Augmentation

Although RST and PDTB adopt different criteria for determining discourse units/arguments of DRs, data from both frameworks can be used together for UDim classification. For example, for RST DR classification, PDTB data (explicit, implicit, or both) can be used for training the model on UDim classification. Increased data amount and more diversified training data might increase model robustness in UDim classification, which may improve model performance on DR classification. Fig 3 shows a diagram of the data augmentation method.

3.5 Training

Cross-entropy loss is used for model training. Model losses for UDim classification and DR classification are added:

$$\mathcal{L}_{total} = \mathcal{L}_{UDims} + 2.0 * \mathcal{L}_{DR} \tag{8}$$

Note that there are multiple UDims involved in the experiments, even though the loss term shows them collectively as $\mathcal{L}_{UDims}$. In order to guide the model training towards DR classification, we increase the weight for DR classification loss.

4 Experiments

4.1 Data Preprocessing

The experiments on RST are carried out on RST-DT and the experiments on PDTB are performed on PDTB 3.0. As we follow the mainstream practice of preprocessing on the two corpora, the details are shown in Appendix F.

Since PDTB 3.0 contains a much larger number of articles, data amount differences between RST and PDTB may have a confounding effect in our experiments on data augmentation, because if the master task has a smaller data amount, the model may be trained to be biased towards the data of auxiliary tasks and the performance may decrease when evaluation is performed on the test set of the master task. Therefore, we try to increase the data amount for RST by back-translating data of the training set (English→French→English, translated by Google Translate), thus doubling the training data amount for RST and narrowing the data amount differences between RST, PDTB explicit relations and PDTB implicit relations. In addition, we exclude the UDim *list*, following Fu (2023), and merge sub-categories under *specificity*, making *specificity* a binary attribute, similar to *alternative*, *conditional* and *goal-orientedness*, which is also the approach adopted in Roze et al. (2019).

UDims (*abb.*)	Values	Parent
polarity(*pol*)	NS, positive, negative	-
basic operation(*bop*)	NS, additive, causal	-
source of coherence(*soc*)	NS, objective, subjective	-
implication order(*imp*)	NS, NA, basic, non-basic	bop
temporality(*temp*)	NS, anti-chronological, chronological, synchronous	-
specificity(*spec*)	specificity, non-specificity	bop
alternative(*alt*)	alternative, non-alternative	bop
conditional(*con*)	conditional, non-conditional	bop
goal-orientedness(*goal*)	goal-oriented, non-goal-oriented	bop

Table 1: UDims used in the experiments. Their abbreviations used in the paper are shown in the brackets in italics. "-" in the last column suggests that no parent passing is performed for the classification of this UDim.

Table 1 shows all the UDims used in the experiments, their abbreviations, and possible values. The parents of UDims, which are used in the method described by equation 3, are included in the last column. Appendix G shows statistics of UDims in the training sets of RST and PDTB implicit and explicit relation data, and Appendix H shows label frequency of the training sets for reference.

4.2 Implementation Details

We use the pre-trained RoBERTa$_{\text{BASE}}$ model (Liu et al., 2019) from the Transformers library (Wolf et al., 2020) as the input encoder. The embeddings of the UDims are derived from embedding layers, which are configured with learnable parameters, and the embedding vectors are initialized from uniform distributions. Hyper-parameter settings are attached in Appendix I.

Baseline The baseline is thus DR classification based on the input, involving no utilization of UDims. To ensure fair comparison, we also apply MC dropout to the baseline models, i.e., the pre-trained RoBERTa$_{\text{BASE}}$ model, and run the same

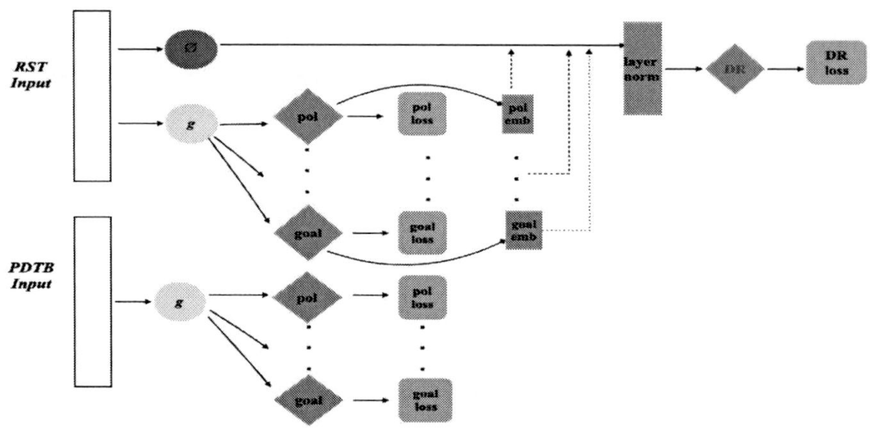

Figure 3: Data augmentation with PDTB data and the final task is RST DR classification. As we explore different ways of leveraging predicted UDims, the embeddings of the UDims are not necessarily fed as features to the DR classification task, hence represented with dashed arrow lines. The losses shown in orange boxes are to be minimized through model training for all the four methods.

number of passes to obtain the mean predictive distribution.

5 Results

We select models based on their performance measured by F1 in DR classification, and thus, they do not necessarily perform the best in terms of accuracy or in UDim classification. The Stuart-Maxwell test (Stuart, 1955; Maxwell, 1970) is used, and all the results are statistically significant (Appendix J).

5.1 DR Classification

Table 2 shows the results for RST DR classification. The best performance is achieved with *TrainonGoldTestonPred*, followed by *InputForRelCls*. In both cases, the predicted UDims are not used as features for DR classification during training. Compared with the baseline method, the models are trained for UDim classification. The results support our hypothesis that because of the association between UDims and DRs, training the model on UDim classification tasks can improve performance on DR classification.

Table 3 shows the results for PDTB implicit DR classification. A performance drop compared with the baseline is visible with the approach *TrainonGoldTestonPred*. As shown in Sanders et al. (2018,

Model	F1	Acc
Baseline	53.72	65.56
TrainonGoldTestonPred	**55.21**	66.27
InputDimCat	54.49	66.16
InputDimAtt	54.65	66.27
InputForRelCls	54.89	**66.32**

Table 2: Results for RST DR classification (The best-performing system, HITS, in DISRPT 2023 (Braud et al., 2023) achieves 50.96 in macro-averaged F1 on this corpus. As data augmentation is performed in our experiments and the preprocessing steps are different, the results are not directly comparable but shown here for reference.)

Model	F1	Acc
Baseline	52.36	60.47
TrainonGoldTestonPred	51.80	59.09
InputDimCat	52.82	**61.43**
InputDimAtt	52.93	60.67
InputForRelCls	**53.44**	60.26

Table 3: Results for PDTB implicit DR classification. Previous results on this task include 54.92 in macro-averaged F1 reported in Liu and Strube (2023), 57.62 in Long and Webber (2022) and 52.16 in Wu et al. (2023).

Model	F1	Acc
InputForRelCls	54.89	66.32
InputForRelCls+PDTBExpl	55.28	**65.72**
InputForRelCls+PDTBTotal	**55.75**	65.61
InputForRelCls+PDTBImpl	54.57	65.02

Table 4: Results for RST DR classification with data augmentation. *Baseline* refers to the approach without using UDims in training and testing in Table 2. *PDTB-Expl*, *PDTBImpl* and *PDTBTotal* denote PDTB explicit relation data, implicit relation data and the combination of both parts, respectively.

Model	F1	Acc
InputForRelCls	53.44	60.26
InputForRelCls+RST	52.12	61.02
InputForRelCls+PDTBExpl	**55.01**	61.22
InputForRelCls+PDTBExpl&RST	53.05	**61.70**

Table 5: Results for PDTB implicit DR classification with data augmentation from RST data (*+RST*), from PDTB explicit relation data (*+PDTBExpl*) and from both (*+PDTBExpl&RST*).

p.52, section 5.3), implicit relations pose a challenge for the UniDim proposal, and it is likely that model performance on UDim classification is not high, when the model is trained on PDTB implicit relation data, causing a large discrepancy between training and inference time, which may result in a performance drop with *TrainonGoldTestonPred* here.

5.2 Data Augmentation

Based on the results for DR classification, we focus on the *InputForRelCls* method in this set of experiments.

Table 4 shows the results for RST DR classification under augmentation with different types of PDTB data. As is shown, data augmentation improves F1 score, but an increase in F1 does not necessarily lead to higher accuracy, which is not rare for classification on imbalanced data, suggesting that the model is trained to distinguish smaller classes. Data augmentation with total PDTB data yields the highest performance, which is expected. However, it is noticeable that adding PDTB implicit relation data causes a performance drop. This might be attributed to the high ambiguity in representing implicit relations with UDims discussed in Sanders et al. (2018).

Table 5 shows the results for PDTB implicit DR classification under augmentation with different types of data. Our method does not outperform the hierarchical sense classification method used in Long and Webber (2022) but the performance is slightly higher than that shown in Liu and Strube (2023), the best-performing method with the connective-insertion approach for converting PDTB implicit DR classification into explicit DR classification, and Wu et al. (2023), which is the SOTA performance with prompt learning.

As is shown in Table 5, adding PDTB explicit DR data is the most helpful form of data augmentation for both *InputForRelCls* and *InputDimAtt*, but adding RST data causes performance drops, possibly due to the high dissimilarity between RST data and PDTB implicit relation data.

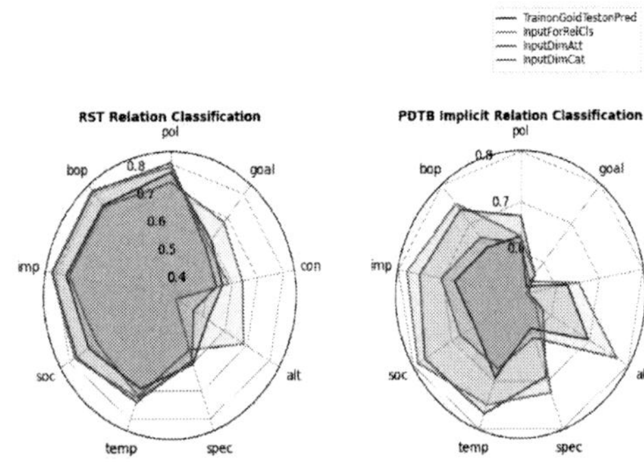

Figure 4: Correlation between DR classification loss and UDim classification losses for RST and PDTB. The abbreviations of the UDims have been explained in Table 1, and the scales represent the Pearson correlation coefficient scores. Note that the areas of different models cannot be compared between RST and PDTB, since the scales on the two plots are arranged in different ways to suit the range of the real data.

5.3 Results on Cascaded Classifier

This approach does not perform well on DR classification, but it represents a possible direction for exploration with UDims. Therefore, preliminary results are attached in Appendix K for comparison.

6 Analysis

6.1 Analysis of Different Model Designs

We examine the four approaches discussed in section 3.3.2. Losses at each training step are collected, and Pearson correlation coefficients are computed between the DR classification loss and the UDim classification losses for each model. The results are shown in Figure 4. The full results on UDim classification are shown in Appendix L for reference.

As is clear from Figure 4, for RST DR classification, the models show high correlation between DR classification and the classification of five major UDims, including *pol*, *bop*, *imp*, *soc* and *temp*, while correlation with the other UDims is not prominent. The pattern with *InputDimAtt* is different, where correlation with the UDims is basically evenly distributed, except for the smaller value at *spec*, which might be attributed to importance weighting with the attention mechanism.

For PDTB implicit DR classification, different models show divergence in their correlation strengths with different UDims. In the case of the best performing model *InputForRelCls*, the correlation with *pol* is low but the correlation with *spec* is high. We find that the performance of the model on the classification of *pol* is relatively low, and this could be a reason why the model learns to rely less on this UDim. Similar to the patterns for RST, apart from the five major UDims, the other UDims do not show high correlation with the target DR classification task, but in *TrainonGoldTestonPred* and *InputDimAtt*, relatively high correlation with *con* and *alt* in particular, is observable. The performance with *TrainonGoldTestonPred* is lower than the baseline and we can see that the total area of correlation for this model is the smallest. With *InputDimAtt*, the association area is also small, which may suggest that the attention mechanism gives more weight to h_{DR} than the predicted UDims.

6.2 Ablation Studies

Ablation studies are performed on *InputForRelCls*. Table 6 shows the UDims that, when removed, cause the lowest F1 for each DR. The full results are shown in Appendix M (RST) and Appendix N (PDTB).

RST DR	UDim
Background	*temp*
Cause	*bop*
Comparison	*spec*
Condition	*spec*
Contrast	*pol*
Elaboration	*goal*
Enablement	*alt*
Evaluation	*bop*
Explanation	*temp*
Joint	*spec*
Manner-Means	*imp*
Summary	*alt*
Temporal	*alt*
Textual-Organization	*alt*
Topic-Change	*goal*
Topic-Comment	*goal*

PDTB DR	UDim
Asynchronous	*con*
Cause	*alt*
Cause+Belief	*alt*
Concession	*goal*
Condition	*goal*
Conjunction	*soc*
Contrast	*goal*
Equivalence	*bop*
Instantiation	*pol*
Level-of-Detail	*goal*
Manner	*temp*
Purpose	*pol*
Substitution	*alt*
Synchronous	*temp*

Table 6: UDims that cause the lowest F1 for each relation. *Cause+Belief* forms a special case, where removing the UDim yields the highest performance, while removing the remaining UDims results in 0.00 for this relation.

It can be seen that the performance on some relations is consistent with the assumption about the relationship between DRs and UDims. For example, for RST, the correlation betwen *Background* and the *temp* dimension is expected. Similarly, *Cause* is indeed closely related to the *bop* dimension, which primarily distinguishes between additive and causal relations. For PDTB, the correlation between UDims and DRs is reflected in the results on *Substitution* and *Synchronous*. However, there are multiple cases when a discourse relation is not affected the most by the UDim that is supposed to be significant for it, such as RST *Condition*, which is not strongly related to *con*, but to *spec*, and *Elaboration*, which is not affected by *spec* the most, but by *goal*. Similar to what is shown in Fu (2023), model performance is not a simple reflection of the association between DRs and UDims, and it is influenced by data distributions, especially when distributions of DR and UDims are heavily imbalanced.

7 Conclusion

We propose a cross-framework generalizable approach for DR classification based on the UniDim proposal, which allows cross-framework data augmentation. With data augmentation, we obtain strong performance in macro-averaged F1 for DR classification (55.75 for RST and 55.01 for PDTB implicit DR classification). Our experiments suggest that training the model with objectives of UDim classification helps the model in DR classification, and adding PDTB explicit DR data is helpful for both RST and PDTB implicit DR classification. Our analysis shows that most of the model designs rely on five UDims, including *pol*, *bop*, *imp*, *soc* and *temp*, although differences between models are also observable. Furthermore, model performance is not a simple reflection of the expected correlation between UDims and DRs, and it is likely to be influenced by varied amounts of data for different classes. Although the present study does not involve other frameworks, such as SDRT, the proposed approach is not specific to any framework, as long as the original sense labels and rules of converting them to UDims are known.

8 Limitations

With our approach, multiple runs have to be performed during inference time, even though the number of model parameters is not increased. On the other hand, this fact justifies the choice of using results obtained from a seemingly single run of the models, which actually involves multiple runs based on the the principle of MC dropout.

Another limitation is that in the experiments on using UDims for DR classification (without data augmentation), the improvement over the baseline is not large. However, we believe this is understandable, as more tasks are involved in the experiments (classification of nine UDims), but the data amount remains the same as the baseline, which only involves DR classification.

Compared with the upper limit of using gold UDims in DR classification, there is still a large gap. Although the UDims may be easier to understand for human annotators than the relation taxonomies employed in RST and PDTB, the performance with automatic means to predict UDims still has a large room for improvement. It remains to be tested if the difficulty in predicting these UDims forms the underlying cause for the challenges of DR classification.

We have to stress that it is beyond our scope to elaborate on the meaning of UDims and how DRs are decomposed into the combination of UDims, which falls under the CCR framework for discourse analysis. Moreover, comparison with other proposals for integrating discourse relations of different frameworks, such as the OLiA reference model and the ISO standard proposal, will be a beneficial complement to the current research. However, it is conceivable that different proposals would require different algorithmic designs to achieve good results. The current research is built on existing studies, and comparing with other proposals in computational experiments requires much more effort than the current submission can cover, and therefore, we leave it to future work.

Lastly, we are aware that discourse parsing is more than DR classification, but discourse structure is not considered in the proposed approach, similar to the focus of the work by Braud et al. (2024).

9 Ethics Statement

We do not foresee any ethical concerns with this study.

References

Farah Benamara and Maite Taboada. 2015. Mapping different rhetorical relation annotations: A proposal. In *Proceedings of the Fourth Joint Conference on Lexical and Computational Semantics*, pages 147–152, Denver, Colorado. Association for Computational Linguistics.

Antoine Bosselut, Asli Celikyilmaz, Xiaodong He, Jianfeng Gao, Po-Sen Huang, and Yejin Choi. 2018. Discourse-aware neural rewards for coherent text generation. In *Proceedings of the 2018 Conference of the North American Chapter of the Association for Computational Linguistics: Human Language Technologies, Volume 1 (Long Papers)*, pages 173–184, New Orleans, Louisiana. Association for Computational Linguistics.

Chloé Braud, Yang Janet Liu, Eleni Metheniti, Philippe Muller, Laura Rivière, Attapol Rutherford, and Amir Zeldes. 2023. The DISRPT 2023 shared task on elementary discourse unit segmentation, connective detection, and relation classification. In *Proceedings of the 3rd Shared Task on Discourse Relation Parsing and Treebanking (DISRPT 2023)*, pages 1–21, Toronto, Canada. The Association for Computational Linguistics.

Chloé Braud, Barbara Plank, and Anders Søgaard. 2016. Multi-view and multi-task training of RST discourse parsers. In *Proceedings of COLING 2016, the 26th International Conference on Computational Linguistics: Technical Papers*, pages 1903–1913, Osaka, Japan. The COLING 2016 Organizing Committee.

Chloé Braud, Amir Zeldes, Laura Rivière, Yang Janet Liu, Philippe Muller, Damien Sileo, and Tatsuya Aoyama. 2024. DISRPT: A multilingual, multi-domain, cross-framework benchmark for discourse processing. In *Proceedings of the 2024 Joint International Conference on Computational Linguistics, Language Resources and Evaluation (LREC-COLING 2024)*, pages 4990–5005, Torino, Italia. ELRA and ICCL.

Harry Bunt and Rashmi Prasad. 2016. ISO DR-Core (ISO 24617-8): Core concepts for the annotation of discourse relations. In *Proceedings 12th Joint ACL-ISO Workshop on Interoperable Semantic Annotation (ISA-12)*, pages 45–54.

Lynn Carlson, Daniel Marcu, and Mary Ellen Okurovsky. 2001. Building a discourse-tagged corpus in the framework of Rhetorical Structure Theory. In *Proceedings of the Second SIGdial Workshop on Discourse and Dialogue*.

Christian Chiarcos. 2014. Towards interoperable discourse annotation. discourse features in the ontologies of linguistic annotation. In *Proceedings of the Ninth International Conference on Language Resources and Evaluation (LREC'14)*, pages 4569–4577, Reykjavik, Iceland. European Language Resources Association (ELRA).

Vera Demberg, Merel CJ Scholman, and Fatemeh Torabi Asr. 2019. How compatible are our discourse annotation frameworks? Insights from mapping RST-DT and PDTB annotations. *Dialogue & Discourse*, 10(1):87–135.

Yingxue Fu. 2023. Discourse relations classification and cross-framework discourse relation classification through the lens of cognitive dimensions: An empirical investigation. In *Proceedings of the 6th International Conference on Natural Language and Speech Processing (ICNLSP 2023)*, pages 21–42, Online. Association for Computational Linguistics.

Yarin Gal and Zoubin Ghahramani. 2016. Dropout as a Bayesian approximation: Representing model uncertainty in deep learning. In *International Conference on Machine Learning*, pages 1050–1059. PMLR.

Walter Gerych, Tom Hartvigsen, Luke Buquicchio, Emmanuel Agu, and Elke A Rundensteiner. 2021. Recurrent bayesian classifier chains for exact multi-label classification. *Advances in Neural Information Processing Systems*, 34:15981–15992.

Xavier Glorot and Yoshua Bengio. 2010. Understanding the difficulty of training deep feedforward neural networks. In *Proceedings of the thirteenth international conference on artificial intelligence and statistics*, pages 249–256. JMLR Workshop and Conference Proceedings.

Eduard H Hovy and Elisabeth Maier. 1992. Parsimonious or profligate: how many and which discourse structure relations? Technical report, UNIVERSITY OF SOUTHERN CALIFORNIA MARINA DEL REY INFORMATION SCIENCES INST.

Dan Iter, Kelvin Guu, Larry Lansing, and Dan Jurafsky. 2020. Pretraining with contrastive sentence objectives improves discourse performance of language models. In *Proceedings of the 58th Annual Meeting of the Association for Computational Linguistics*, pages 4859–4870, Online. Association for Computational Linguistics.

Eric Jang, Shixiang Gu, and Ben Poole. 2016. Categorical reparameterization with gumbel-softmax. In *International Conference on Learning Representations*.

Yangfeng Ji and Jacob Eisenstein. 2014. Representation learning for text-level discourse parsing. In *Proceedings of the 52nd Annual Meeting of the Association for Computational Linguistics (Volume 1: Long Papers)*, pages 13–24, Baltimore, Maryland. Association for Computational Linguistics.

Yangfeng Ji and Jacob Eisenstein. 2015. One vector is not enough: Entity-augmented distributed semantics for discourse relations. *Transactions of the Association for Computational Linguistics*, 3:329–344.

Congcong Jiang, Tieyun Qian, Zhuang Chen, Kejian Tang, Shaohui Zhan, and Tao Zhan. 2021. Generating pseudo connectives with MLMs for implicit discourse relation recognition. In *PRICAI 2021: Trends in Artificial Intelligence: 18th Pacific Rim International Conference on Artificial Intelligence, PRICAI 2021, Hanoi, Vietnam, November 8–12, 2021, Proceedings, Part II 18*, pages 113–126. Springer.

Najoung Kim, Song Feng, Chulaka Gunasekara, and Luis Lastras. 2020. Implicit discourse relation classification: We need to talk about evaluation. In *Proceedings of the 58th Annual Meeting of the Association for Computational Linguistics*, pages 5404–5414, Online. Association for Computational Linguistics.

Haejun Lee, Drew A. Hudson, Kangwook Lee, and Christopher D. Manning. 2020. SLM: Learning a discourse language representation with sentence unshuffling. In *Proceedings of the 2020 Conference on Empirical Methods in Natural Language Processing (EMNLP)*, pages 1551–1562, Online. Association for Computational Linguistics.

Wei Liu and Michael Strube. 2023. Annotation-inspired implicit discourse relation classification with auxiliary discourse connective generation. In *Proceedings of the 61st Annual Meeting of the Association for Computational Linguistics (Volume 1: Long Papers)*, pages 15696–15712, Toronto, Canada. Association for Computational Linguistics.

Yang Liu, Sujian Li, Xiaodong Zhang, and Zhifang Sui. 2016. Implicit discourse relation classification via multi-task neural networks. In *Proceedings of the AAAI Conference on Artificial Intelligence*, volume 30.

Yinhan Liu, Myle Ott, Naman Goyal, Jingfei Du, Mandar Joshi, Danqi Chen, Omer Levy, Mike Lewis, Luke Zettlemoyer, and Veselin Stoyanov. 2019. RoBERTa: A robustly optimized bert pretraining approach. *arXiv preprint arXiv:1907.11692*.

Wanqiu Long and Bonnie Webber. 2022. Facilitating contrastive learning of discourse relational senses by exploiting the hierarchy of sense relations. In *Proceedings of the 2022 Conference on Empirical Methods in Natural Language Processing*, pages 10704–10716, Abu Dhabi, United Arab Emirates. Association for Computational Linguistics.

Ilya Loshchilov and Frank Hutter. 2018. Decoupled weight decay regularization. In *International Conference on Learning Representations*.

William C Mann and Sandra A Thompson. 1988. Rhetorical structure theory: Toward a functional theory of text organization. *Text*, 8(3):243–281.

Albert Ernest Maxwell. 1970. Comparing the classification of subjects by two independent judges. *The British Journal of Psychiatry*, 116(535):651–655.

Adam Paszke, Sam Gross, Francisco Massa, Adam Lerer, James Bradbury, Gregory Chanan, Trevor Killeen, Zeming Lin, Natalia Gimelshein, Luca Antiga, et al. 2019. PyTorch: An imperative style, high-performance deep learning library. *Advances in Neural Information Processing Systems*, 32.

Rashmi Prasad, Nikhil Dinesh, Alan Lee, Eleni Miltsakaki, Livio Robaldo, Aravind Joshi, and Bonnie Webber. 2008. The Penn Discourse TreeBank 2.0.

In *Proceedings of the Sixth International Conference on Language Resources and Evaluation (LREC'08)*, Marrakech, Morocco. European Language Resources Association (ELRA).

Lianhui Qin, Zhisong Zhang, Hai Zhao, Zhiting Hu, and Eric Xing. 2017. Adversarial connective-exploiting networks for implicit discourse relation classification. In *Proceedings of the 55th Annual Meeting of the Association for Computational Linguistics (Volume 1: Long Papers)*, pages 1006–1017, Vancouver, Canada. Association for Computational Linguistics.

Charlotte Roze, Chloé Braud, and Philippe Muller. 2019. Which aspects of discourse relations are hard to learn? primitive decomposition for discourse relation classification. In *Proceedings of the 20th Annual SIGdial Meeting on Discourse and Dialogue*, pages 432–441, Stockholm, Sweden. Association for Computational Linguistics.

Attapol Rutherford and Nianwen Xue. 2015. Improving the inference of implicit discourse relations via classifying explicit discourse connectives. In *Proceedings of the 2015 Conference of the North American Chapter of the Association for Computational Linguistics: Human Language Technologies*, pages 799–808, Denver, Colorado. Association for Computational Linguistics.

Ted JM Sanders, Vera Demberg, Jet Hoek, Merel CJ Scholman, Fatemeh Torabi Asr, Sandrine Zufferey, and Jacqueline Evers-Vermeul. 2018. Unifying dimensions in coherence relations: How various annotation frameworks are related. *Corpus Linguistics and Linguistic Theory*.

Ted JM Sanders, Wilbert PM Spooren, and Leo GM Noordman. 1992. Toward a taxonomy of coherence relations. *Discourse processes*, 15(1):1–35.

Ted JM Sanders, Wilbert PM Spooren, and Leo GM Noordman. 1993. Coherence relations in a cognitive theory of discourse representation.

Artem Shelmanov, Evgenii Tsymbalov, Dmitri Puzyrev, Kirill Fedyanin, Alexander Panchenko, and Maxim Panov. 2021. How certain is your Transformer? In *Proceedings of the 16th Conference of the European Chapter of the Association for Computational Linguistics: Main Volume*, pages 1833–1840, Online. Association for Computational Linguistics.

Wei Shi and Vera Demberg. 2019. Learning to explicitate connectives with Seq2Seq network for implicit discourse relation classification. In *Proceedings of the 13th International Conference on Computational Semantics - Long Papers*, pages 188–199, Gothenburg, Sweden. Association for Computational Linguistics.

Symon Stevens-Guille, Aleksandre Maskharashvili, Xintong Li, and Michael White. 2022. Generating discourse connectives with pre-trained language models: Conditioning on discourse relations helps reconstruct the PDTB. In *Proceedings of the 23rd Annual Meeting of the Special Interest Group on Discourse and Dialogue*, pages 500–515, Edinburgh, UK. Association for Computational Linguistics.

Alan Stuart. 1955. A test for homogeneity of the marginal distributions in a two-way classification. *Biometrika*, 42(3/4):412–416.

Nobel Varghese, Frances Yung, Kaveri Anuranjana, and Vera Demberg. 2023. Exploiting knowledge about discourse relations for implicit discourse relation classification. In *Proceedings of the 4th Workshop on Computational Approaches to Discourse (CODI 2023)*, pages 99–105.

Ashish Vaswani, Noam Shazeer, Niki Parmar, Jakob Uszkoreit, Llion Jones, Aidan N Gomez, Łukasz Kaiser, and Illia Polosukhin. 2017. Attention is all you need. *Advances in Neural Information Processing Systems*, 30.

Bonnie Webber. 2004. D-ltag: extending lexicalized tag to discourse. *Cognitive Science*, 28(5):751–779.

Bonnie Webber and Aravind Joshi. 2012. Discourse structure and computation: Past, present and future. In *Proceedings of the ACL-2012 Special Workshop on Rediscovering 50 Years of Discoveries*, pages 42–54, Jeju Island, Korea. Association for Computational Linguistics.

Bonnie Webber, Rashmi Prasad, Alan Lee, and Aravind Joshi. 2019. The Penn Discourse Treebank 3.0 annotation manual. *Philadelphia, University of Pennsylvania*.

Thomas Wolf, Lysandre Debut, Victor Sanh, Julien Chaumond, Clement Delangue, Anthony Moi, Pierric Cistac, Tim Rault, Remi Louf, Morgan Funtowicz, Joe Davison, Sam Shleifer, Patrick von Platen, Clara Ma, Yacine Jernite, Julien Plu, Canwen Xu, Teven Le Scao, Sylvain Gugger, Mariama Drame, Quentin Lhoest, and Alexander Rush. 2020. Transformers: State-of-the-art natural language processing. In *Proceedings of the 2020 Conference on Empirical Methods in Natural Language Processing: System Demonstrations*, pages 38–45, Online. Association for Computational Linguistics.

Hongyi Wu, Hao Zhou, Man Lan, Yuanbin Wu, and Yadong Zhang. 2023. Connective prediction for implicit discourse relation recognition via knowledge distillation. In *Proceedings of the 61st Annual Meeting of the Association for Computational Linguistics (Volume 1: Long Papers)*, pages 5908–5923, Toronto, Canada. Association for Computational Linguistics.

Jiacheng Xu, Zhe Gan, Yu Cheng, and Jingjing Liu. 2020. Discourse-aware neural extractive text summarization. In *Proceedings of the 58th Annual Meeting of the Association for Computational Linguistics*, pages 5021–5031, Online. Association for Computational Linguistics.

Nan Yu, Meishan Zhang, Guohong Fu, and Min Zhang. 2022. RST discourse parsing with second-stage

EDU-level pre-training. In *Proceedings of the 60th Annual Meeting of the Association for Computational Linguistics (Volume 1: Long Papers)*, pages 4269–4280, Dublin, Ireland. Association for Computational Linguistics.

Frances Yung, Vera Demberg, and Merel Scholman. 2019. Crowdsourcing discourse relation annotations by a two-step connective insertion task. In *Proceedings of the 13th Linguistic Annotation Workshop*, pages 16–25, Florence, Italy. Association for Computational Linguistics.

A UDims

Table 7 provides an overview of UDims used in the paper.

UDims (*abb.*)	Possible Values (*abb.*)	Explanations	Examples
polarity (*pol*)	positive(*pos*)	A relation is characterized by a *positive* polarity if the propositions P and Q, expressed by S_1 and S_2, respectively, have the same logical polarity and support each other.	[We like the garden]$_{S_1}$ because [it is pretty.]$_{S_2}$
	negative(*neg*)	A relation is of a *negative* polarity if the relation involves juxtaposition of $\neg P$ and P or $\neg Q$ and Q in two segments.	[The university library was closed]$_{S_1}$ although [students wanted more space for study.]$_{S_2}$
	NS	-	-
basic operation (*bop*)	additive(*add*)	If two segments are just loosely connected and only a conjunction relation $P \wedge Q$ can be inferred, the relation is additive.	[She is a painter]$_{S_1}$ and [her studio is a few blocks away.]$_{S_2}$
	causal(*cau*)	A causal relation means that two segments are strongly connected and typically, an implication relationship $P \rightarrow Q$ can be inferred.	[He immigrated to the US,]$_{S_1}$ because [his natural parents were believed to live there.]$_{S_2}$
	NS	-	-
source of coherence (*soc*)	objective(*obj*)	A relation is objective if two segments are connected because of their propositional content, and the relation holds because the connection is coherent based on world knowledge.	[It was dark outside,]$_{S_1}$ so [he lit up a candle.]$_{S_2}$
	subjective(*sub*)	A relation is subjective if the speaker's reasoning or the pragmatic effect of the relation is prominent.	[Smoking is unhealthy]$_{S_1}$ and [we should limit it.]$_{S_2}$
	NS	-	-
implication order (*imp*)	NA	This dimension distinguishes between *non-basic* and *basic* implication orders for causal relations, and it does not apply to additive relations, which are generally symmetric.	-
	basic(*bas*)	For a causal relation characterized by $P \rightarrow Q$, if S_1 expresses P and S_2 expresses Q (S_1 and S_2 are in linear order), then this relation is in basic implication order.	Because [he received a warning message,]$_{S_1}$ [he did not attend the conference.]$_{S_2}$
	non-basic(*non-b*)	In contrast to the case of basic implication order, if S_2 actually expresses P while S_1 expresses Q, this relation is in non-basic implication order.	[He did not attend the conference,]$_{S_1}$ because [he received a message telling him not to go.]$_{S_2}$
	NS	-	-
temporality (*temp*)	anti-chronological (*anti*)	If the events in two segments are not in their temporal order of occurrence, then the relation is anti-chronological.	[He went home in a low mood.]$_{S_1}$ [He had a fight with a customer and was fired.]$_{S_2}$
	chronological (*chron*)	If the events described in two segments happen in temporal order, then the relation is chronological.	[She had been stuck in a traffic jam,]$_{S_1}$ so [she was late for the opening ceremony.]$_{S_2}$
	synchronous (*sync*)	Synchronous relations are those temporal relations that feature simultaneous occurrence of events.	[The children were playing in the park]$_{S_1}$ while [their parents were chatting away.]$_{S_2}$
	NS	non-temporal relations or ambiguous cases	-

specificity (*spec*)	specificity(+)	RST and PDTB contain some relations that describe the specificity property, such as *Example*, *Definition* and *Elaboration* in RST, and *Equivalence*, *Instantiation* and *Level-of-Detail* in PDTB.	[In this light, the comparative advantages of legislative law-making become clear:]$_{S_1}$ [(1) Before it acts, the legislature typically will hear the views of representatives of all those affected by its decision, not just the immediate parties before the court; and (2) the legislature can frame "bright line" standards that create less uncertainty than the fact-bound decisions of courts.]$_{S_2}$ (wsj_2059)
	non-specificity(-)	This dimension is only applicable to additive relations. Therefore, causal relations and additive relations that do not have the property of denoting specificity are assigned the label *non-specificity*.	-
alternative (*alt*)	alternative(+)	This dimension distinguishes relations that feature two semantically alternative arguments, such as *Disjunction* in RST, and *Disjunction* and *Substitution* in PDTB.	[make their fans cheer again]$_{S_1}$ or [recapture the camaraderie of seasons past]$_{S_2}$ (wsj_0214)
	non-alternative(-)	This dimension is only applicable to additive relations. Therefore, causal relations and additive relations that do not have the property of denoting alternative propositions are assigned the label *non-alternative*.	-
conditional (*con*)	conditional(+)	Based on Sanders et al. (2018), this dimension is added to account for conditional relations, such as *Condition* in RST and PDTB, which is not possible based only on CCR dimensions (*pol*, *bop*, *soc* and *imp*).	[he will relinquish the government's so-called golden share in the company]$_{S_1}$ as long as [Jaguar shareholders agree.]$_{S_2}$ (wsj_0224)
	non-conditional(-)	This dimension is only applicable to causal relations. Therefore, additive relations and causal relations that do not have the property of being conditional are assigned the label *non-conditional*.	-
goal-orientedness (*goal*)	goal-oriented(+)	Based on Sanders et al. (2018), this dimension is added to account for relations that feature intentional and goal-oriented actions, such as *Enablement* and *Manner-Means* in RST and *Purpose* and *Manner* in PDTB.	[to clear the way]$_{S_1}$ so [the playing field is level between all contestants.]$_{S_2}$ (wsj_0224)
	non-goal-oriented(-)	This dimension is only applicable to causal relations. Therefore, additive relations and causal relations that do not have the goal-oriented property are assigned the label *non-goal-oriented*.	-

Table 7: UDims used in the experiments. Their abbreviations in this study are shown in parentheses in italics. The explanation and examples are mostly taken from Fu (2023), except for *spec*, *alt*, *con* and *goal*, which are additional dimensions deemed necessary in Sanders et al. (2018) to account for some relations in RST, PDTB and SDRT.

B Mapping Between RST Relations and UDims

Table 8 shows the mapping between RST relations and UDims, which is originally given in Sanders et al. (2018).

Class	End label	Nuc.	N-S	pol	bop	imp	soc	temp	other
Background	Background	Mono	N-S	pos/neg	add	N.A.	obj	anti/N.A.	
	Background	Mono	S-N	pos/neg	add	N.A.	obj	chron/N.A.	
	Circumstance	Mono		pos/neg	add	N.A.	obj	syn/N.A.	
Cause	Cause	Mono	N-S	pos	cau	bas	obj	chron	
	Cause	Mono	S-N	pos	cau	non-b	obj	anti	
	Cause-result	Multi		pos	cau	bas/non-b	obj	chron/anti	
	Result	Mono	N-S	pos	cau	non-b	obj	anti	
	Result	Mono	S-N	pos	cau	bas	obj	chron	
	Consequence-n	Mono	N-S	pos	cau	non-b	obj	anti	
	Consequence-n	Mono	S-N	pos	cau	bas	obj	chron	
	Consequence-s	Mono	N-S	pos	cau	bas	obj	chron	
	Consequence-s	Mono	S-N	pos	cau	non-b	obj	anti	
	Consequence	Multi		pos	cau	bas/non-b	obj	chron/anti	
Comparison	Comparison	Both		pos	add	N.A.	obj/sub	N.A.	
	Preference	Mono		neg	add	N.A.	obj/sub	N.A.	
	Analogy	Both		pos	add	N.A.	sub	N.A.	
	Proportion	Multi		pos	add/cau	any	obj/sub	any	
Conditional	Condition	Mono	N-S	pos/neg	cau	non-b	obj/sub	anti/N.A.	conditional
	Condition	Mono	S-N	pos/neg	cau	bas	obj/sub	chron/N.A.	conditional
	Hypothetical	Mono	N-S	pos	cau	non-b	sub	N.A.	conditional
	Hypothetical	Mono	S-N	pos	cau	bas	sub	N.A.	conditional
	Contingency	Mono	N-S	pos/neg	cau	non-b	obj	anti	conditional
	Contingency	Mono	S-N	pos/neg	cau	bas	obj	chron	conditional
	Otherwise	Mono	N-S	neg	cau	bas	obj/sub	chron/N.A.	conditional
	Otherwise	Multi		neg	cau	bas	obj/sub	chron/N.A.	conditional
Contrast	Contrast	Multi		neg	add	N.A.	obj/sub	any	
	Concession	Mono	N-S	neg	cau	non-b	obj/sub	anti/N.A.	
	Concession	Mono	S-N	neg	cau	bas	obj/sub	chron/N.A.	
	Antithesis	Mono		neg	add/cau	any	obj/sub	any	
Elaboration	El.-additional	Mono		pos	add	N.A.	obj/sub	N.A.	
	El.-gen.-spec.	Mono		pos	add	N.A.	obj/sub	N.A.	specificity
	El.-part-whole	Mono		pos	add	N.A.	obj	N.A.	specificity
	El.-process-step	Mono		pos	add	N.A.	obj	N.A.	specificity
	El.-object-attr.	Mono		pos	add	N.A.	obj	N.A.	specificity
	El.-set-member	Mono		pos	add	N.A.	obj	N.A.	spec.-ex.
	Example	Mono		pos	add	N.A.	obj	N.A.	spec.-ex.
	Definition	Mono		pos	add	N.A.	obj	N.A.	specificity
Enablement	Purpose	Mono	N-S	pos	cau	bas	obj/sub	chron/N.A.	goal
	Purpose	Mono	S-N	pos	cau	non-b	obj/sub	anti/N.A.	goal
	Enablement	Mono	N-S	pos	cau	non-b	obj/sub	anti/N.A.	goal
	Enablement	Mono	S-N	pos	cau	bas	obj/sub	chron/N.A.	goal
Evaluation	Evaluation	Both		pos	add/cau	any	sub	N.A.	specificity
	Interpretation	Both		pos	add/cau	any	sub	N.A.	specificity
	Conclusion	Mono	N-S	pos	cau	bas	sub	N.A.	specificity
	Conclusion	Mono	S-N	pos	cau	non-b	sub	N.A.	specificity
	Conclusion	Multi		pos	cau	bas/non-b	sub	N.A.	specificity
	Comment	Mono		pos	add	N.A.	sub	N.A.	specificity
Explanation	Evidence	Mono	N-S	pos	cau	non-b	sub	anti	
	Evidence	Mono	S-N	pos	cau	bas	sub	chron	
	Exp.-argument.	Mono	N-S	pos	cau	non-b	obj	anti	
	Exp.-argument.	Mono	S-N	pos	cau	bas	obj	chron	
	Reason	Mono	N-S	pos	cau	non-b	obj	anti	
	Reason	Mono	S-N	pos	cau	bas	obj	chron	
	Reason	Multi		pos	cau	bas/non-b	obj	chron/anti	
Joint	List	Multi		pos	add	N.A.	obj/sub	syn/chron/N.A.	list
	Disjunction	Multi		pos/neg	add	N.A.	obj/sub	syn/N.A.	alternative
Summary	Summary	Mono		pos	add	N.A.	obj	N.A.	specificity
	Restatement	Mono		pos	add	N.A.	obj	N.A.	spec.-equiv.
Temporal	Temp.-before	Mono	N-S	pos	add	N.A.	obj	chron	
	Temp.-before	Mono	S-N	pos	add	N.A.	obj	anti	
	Temp.-after	Mono	N-S	pos	add	N.A.	obj	anti	
	Temp.-after	Mono	S-N	pos	add	N.A.	obj	chron	
	Temp.-same-time	Both		pos	add	N.A.	obj	syn	
	Sequence	Multi		pos	add	N.A.	obj	chron	
	Inverted-seq.	Multi		pos	add	N.A.	obj	anti	
Manner-Means	Means	Mono	N-S	pos	cau	non-b	obj	anti	
	Means	Mono	S-N	pos	cau	bas	obj	chron	goal
Topic-Comment	Problem-sol.-n	Mono	N-S	pos	cau	non-b	obj/sub	anti/N.A.	goal
	Problem-sol.-n	Mono	S-N	pos	cau	bas	obj/sub	chron/N.A.	goal
	Problem-sol.-s	Mono	N-S	pos	cau	bas	obj/sub	chron/N.A.	goal
	Problem-sol.-s	Mono	S-N	pos	cau	non-b	obj/sub	anti/N.A.	goal
	Problem-sol.	Multi		pos	cau	bas/non-b	obj/sub	achron/anti/N.A.	goal

Table 8: Mapping between RST relations and UDims.

C Mapping Between PDTB Relations and UDims

Table 9 shows the mapping between relations in PDTB 3.0 and UDims. As the mapping given in Sanders et al. (2018) is between relations in PDTB 2.0 and UDims, we adopt the mapping table in Fu (2023).

Class_type	End label	A1-A2	pol	bop	imp	soc	temp	other
Temporal								
Synchronous			pos	add	N.A.	obj	sync	
Asynchronous	Precedence	A1-A2	pos	add	N.A.	obj	chron	
	Precedence	A2-A1	pos	add	N.A.	obj	anti	
	Succession	A1-A2	pos	add	N.A.	obj	anti	
	Succession	A2-A1	pos	add	N.A.	obj	chron	
Contingency								
Cause	Reason	A1-A2	pos	cau	non-b	obj	anti	
	Reason	A2-A1	pos	cau	bas	obj	chron	
	Result	A1-A2	pos	cau	bas	obj	chron	goal
	Result	A1-A2	pos	cau	bas	obj	chron	goal
	NegResult		neg	cau	bas	obj	chron	
Cause+Belief	Reason+Belief	A1-A2	pos	cau	non-b	sub	NS	
	Reason+Belief	A2-A1	pos	cau	bas	sub	NS	
	Result+Belief	A1-A2	pos	cau	bas	sub	NS	
	Result+Belief	A2-A1	pos	cau	non-b	sub	NS	
Cause +SpeechAct	Reason+SpeechAct	A1-A2	pos	cau	non-b	sub	NS	
	Reason+SpeechAct	A2-A1	pos	cau	bas	sub	NS	
	Result+SpeechAct	A1-A2	pos	cau	bas	sub	NS	
	Result+SpeechAct	A2-A1	pos	cau	non-b	sub	NS	
Purpose	arg1-as-goal	A1-A2	pos	cau	non-b	obj/sub	NS	goal
	arg1-as-goal	A2-A1	pos	cau	bas	obj/sub	NS	goal
	arg2-as-goal	A1-A2	pos	cau	bas	sub	NS	goal
Condition	arg1-as-cond	A1-A2	pos	cau	bas	obj/sub	NS	conditional
	arg1-as-cond	A2-A1	pos	cau	non-b	obj/sub	NS	conditional
	arg2-as-cond	A1-A2	pos	cau	non-b	obj/sub	NS	conditional
	arg2-as-cond	A2-A1	pos	cau	bas	obj/sub	NS	conditional
Condition +SpeechAct			pos	cau	bas	sub	NS	conditional
Negative -Condition	arg1-as-negcond	A1-A2	neg	cau	bas	sub	NS	conditional
	arg1-as-negcond	A2-A1	neg	cau	non-b	sub	NS	conditional
	arg2-as-negcond	A1-A2	neg	cau	non-b	sub	NS	conditional
	arg2-as-negcond	A2-A1	neg	cau	bas	sub	NS	conditional
Negative- Condition+ SpeechAct			neg	cau	bas	sub	NS	conditional
Comparison								
Concession	arg1-as-denier	A1-A2	neg	cau	non-b	obj/sub	NS	
	arg1-as-denier	A2-A1	neg	cau	bas	obj/sub	NS	
	arg2-as-denier	A1-A2	neg	cau	bas	obj/sub	NS	
	arg2-as-denier	A2-A1	neg	cau	non-b	obj/sub	NS	
Concession +SpeechAct			neg	cau	bas	sub	NS	
Contrast			neg	add	NA	obj	NS	
Similarity			pos	add	NA	obj	NS	
Expansion								
Conjunction			pos	add	NA	obj/sub	NS	
Disjunction			neg	add	NA	obj/sub	NS	alternative
Equivalence			pos	add	NA	obj/sub	NS	
Exception	arg1-as-excpt		neg	add	NA	obj/sub	NS	
	arg2-as-excpt		neg	add	NA	obj/sub	NS	
Instantiation	arg1-as-instance		pos	add	NA	obj/sub	NS	specificity
	arg2-as-instance		pos	add	NA	obj/sub	NS	specificity
Level-of-detail	arg1-as-detail		pos	add	NA	obj/sub	NS	specificity
	arg2-as-detail		pos	add	NA	obj/sub	NS	specificity
Manner	arg1-as-manner	A1-A2	pos	add	NA	obj/sub	NS	specificity
	arg2-as-manner		pos	add	NA	obj/sub	NS	specificity
Substitution	arg1-as-subst	A1-A2	neg	cau	bas	obj/sub	NS	
	arg1-as-subst	A2-A1	neg	cau	non-b	obj/sub	NS	
	arg2-as-subst	A1-A2	neg	cau	non-b	obj/sub	NS	
	arg2-as-subst	A2-A1	neg	cau	bas	obj/sub	NS	

Table 9: Mapping of sense labels of PDTB 3.0 to UniDim dimensions.

D Unique Mapping Between UDims and DRs in RST-DT

Table 10 shows unique patterns in the mapping between UDims and DRs in the training set of RST-DT. The last column shows the count of a pattern.

NS	NS	NS	NS	NS	-	-	-	-	Manner-Means	130
NS	NS	NS	NS	NS	-	-	-	-	Textual-organization	234
NS	NS	NS	NS	NS	-	-	-	-	Topic-Change	322
NS	NS	NS	NS	NS	-	-	-	-	Topic-Comment	112
NS	add	NA	NS	NS	-	+	-	-	Joint	34
NS	add	NA	obj	NS	-	-	-	-	Background	1328
NS	cau	bas	NS	NS	-	-	+	-	Condition	186
NS	cau	bas	obj	chron	-	-	+	-	Condition	14
NS	cau	non-b	NS	NS	-	-	+	-	Condition	150
NS	cau	non-b	obj	anti	-	-	+	-	Condition	26
neg	NS	NS	NS	NS	-	-	-	-	Contrast	556
neg	add	NA	NS	NS	-	-	-	-	Comparison	16
neg	add	NA	NS	NS	-	-	-	-	Contrast	588
neg	cau	bas	NS	NS	-	-	+	-	Condition	26
neg	cau	bas	NS	NS	-	-	-	-	Contrast	294
neg	cau	non-b	NS	NS	-	-	-	-	Contrast	106
pos	NS	NS	sub	NS	+	-	-	-	Evaluation	580
pos	add	NA	NS	NS	+	-	-	-	Elaboration	620
pos	add	NA	NS	NS	-	-	-	-	Comparison	368
pos	add	NA	NS	NS	-	-	-	-	Elaboration	5816
pos	add	NA	NS	NS	-	-	-	-	Joint	2898
pos	add	NA	obj	NS	+	-	-	-	Elaboration	4686
pos	add	NA	obj	NS	+	-	-	-	Summary	300
pos	add	NA	obj	anti	-	-	-	-	Temporal	124
pos	add	NA	obj	chron	-	-	-	-	Temporal	410
pos	add	NA	obj	syn	-	-	-	-	Temporal	220
pos	add	NA	sub	NS	+	-	-	-	Evaluation	272
pos	add	NA	sub	NS	+	-	-	-	Topic-Comment	4
pos	add	NA	sub	NS	-	-	-	-	Comparison	24
pos	cau	NS	NS	NS	-	-	-	-	Topic-Comment	82
pos	cau	NS	obj	NS	-	-	-	-	Cause	136
pos	cau	NS	obj	NS	-	-	-	-	Explanation	10
pos	cau	bas	NS	NS	-	-	-	+	Enablement	814
pos	cau	bas	NS	NS	-	-	-	+	Topic-Comment	14
pos	cau	bas	obj	chron	-	-	-	+	Manner-Means	18
pos	cau	bas	obj	chron	-	-	-	-	Cause	594
pos	cau	bas	obj	chron	-	-	-	-	Explanation	76
pos	cau	bas	sub	NS	+	-	-	-	Evaluation	8
pos	cau	bas	sub	NS	-	-	+	-	Condition	18
pos	cau	bas	sub	chron	-	-	-	-	Explanation	2
pos	cau	non-b	NS	NS	-	-	-	+	Enablement	76
pos	cau	non-b	obj	anti	-	-	-	-	Cause	264
pos	cau	non-b	obj	anti	-	-	-	-	Explanation	1018
pos	cau	non-b	obj	anti	-	-	-	-	Manner-Means	154
pos	cau	non-b	sub	NS	+	-	-	-	Evaluation	2
pos	cau	non-b	sub	NS	-	-	+	-	Condition	54
pos	cau	non-b	sub	anti	-	-	-	-	Explanation	278

Table 10: Unique patterns of the mapping between UDims and DRs in the training set of RST-DT.

Table 11 shows unique patterns in the mapping between UDims and DRs in the test set of RST-DT.

NS	NS	NS	NS	NS	-	-	-	-	Manner-Means	9
NS	NS	NS	NS	NS	-	-	-	-	Textual-organization	9
NS	NS	NS	NS	NS	-	-	-	-	Topic-Change	13
NS	NS	NS	NS	NS	-	-	-	-	Topic-Comment	15
NS	add	NA	NS	NS	-	+	-	-	Joint	6
NS	add	NA	obj	NS	-	-	-	-	Background	111
NS	cau	bas	NS	NS	-	-	+	-	Condition	24
NS	cau	bas	obj	chron	-	-	+	-	Condition	1
NS	cau	non-b	NS	NS	-	-	+	-	Condition	15
NS	cau	non-b	obj	anti	-	-	+	-	Condition	2
neg	NS	NS	NS	NS	-	-	-	-	Contrast	46
neg	add	NA	NS	NS	-	-	-	-	Comparison	2
neg	add	NA	NS	NS	-	-	-	-	Contrast	64
neg	cau	bas	NS	NS	-	-	-	-	Contrast	28
neg	cau	non-b	NS	NS	-	-	-	-	Contrast	8
pos	NS	NS	NS	NS	-	-	-	-	Comparison	2
pos	NS	NS	sub	NS	+	-	-	-	Evaluation	46
pos	add	NA	NS	NS	+	-	-	-	Elaboration	77
pos	add	NA	NS	NS	-	-	-	-	Comparison	24
pos	add	NA	NS	NS	-	-	-	-	Elaboration	381
pos	add	NA	NS	NS	-	-	-	-	Joint	206
pos	add	NA	obj	NS	+	-	-	-	Elaboration	338
pos	add	NA	obj	NS	+	-	-	-	Summary	32
pos	add	NA	obj	anti	-	-	-	-	Temporal	11
pos	add	NA	obj	chron	-	-	-	-	Temporal	37
pos	add	NA	obj	syn	-	-	-	-	Temporal	25
pos	add	NA	sub	NS	+	-	-	-	Evaluation	34
pos	add	NA	sub	NS	-	-	-	-	Comparison	1
pos	cau	NS	NS	NS	-	-	-	-	Topic-Comment	5
pos	cau	NS	obj	NS	-	-	-	-	Cause	13
pos	cau	NS	obj	NS	-	-	-	-	Explanation	1
pos	cau	bas	NS	NS	-	-	-	+	Enablement	43
pos	cau	bas	NS	NS	-	-	-	+	Topic-Comment	4
pos	cau	bas	obj	chron	-	-	-	+	Manner-Means	2
pos	cau	bas	obj	chron	-	-	-	-	Cause	44
pos	cau	bas	obj	chron	-	-	-	-	Explanation	2
pos	cau	non-b	NS	NS	-	-	-	+	Enablement	3
pos	cau	non-b	obj	anti	-	-	-	-	Cause	25
pos	cau	non-b	obj	anti	-	-	-	-	Explanation	95
pos	cau	non-b	obj	anti	-	-	-	-	Manner-Means	16
pos	cau	non-b	sub	NS	-	-	+	-	Condition	6
pos	cau	non-b	sub	anti	-	-	-	-	Explanation	12

Table 11: Unique patterns of UDims and DRs in the test set of RST-DT.

E Unique Mapping Between UDims and Implicit DRs in PDTB 3.0

Table 12 shows unique patterns in the mapping between UDims and implicit DRs in the training set of PDTB 3.0.

pol.	bop.	imp.	soc.	temp.	spec.	alt.	con.	goal	DR	frequency
NS	NS	NS	NS	NS	-	-	-	-	Asynchronous	12
NS	NS	NS	NS	NS	-	-	-	-	Cause	220
NS	NS	NS	NS	NS	-	-	-	-	Cause+Belief	21
NS	NS	NS	NS	NS	-	-	-	-	Concession	7
NS	NS	NS	NS	NS	-	-	-	-	Condition	14
NS	NS	NS	NS	NS	-	-	-	-	Level-of-detail	5
NS	NS	NS	NS	NS	-	-	-	-	Manner	3
NS	NS	NS	NS	NS	-	-	-	-	Purpose	453
NS	NS	NS	NS	NS	-	-	-	-	Substitution	3
neg	add	NA	obj	NS	-	-	-	-	Contrast	607
neg	cau	bas	obj/sub	NS	-	-	-	-	Concession	1123
neg	cau	non-b	obj/sub	NS	-	-	-	-	Concession	34
neg	cau	non-b	obj/sub	NS	-	-	-	-	Substitution	275
pos	add	NA	obj	anti	-	-	-	-	Asynchronous	122
pos	add	NA	obj	chron	-	-	-	-	Asynchronous	851
pos	add	NA	obj	sync	-	-	-	-	Synchronous	325
pos	add	NA	obj/sub	NS	+	-	-	-	Instantiation	1117
pos	add	NA	obj/sub	NS	+	-	-	-	Level-of-detail	2488
pos	add	NA	obj/sub	NS	+	-	-	-	Manner	188
pos	add	NA	obj/sub	NS	-	-	-	-	Conjunction	3562
pos	add	NA	obj/sub	NS	-	-	-	-	Equivalence	252
pos	cau	bas	obj	chron	-	-	-	+	Cause	2074
pos	cau	bas	obj	chron	-	-	-	-	Cause	92
pos	cau	bas	obj/sub	NS	-	-	+	-	Condition	29
pos	cau	bas	obj/sub	NS	-	-	-	+	Purpose	1
pos	cau	bas	sub	NS	-	-	-	+	Purpose	647
pos	cau	bas	sub	NS	-	-	-	-	Cause+Belief	54
pos	cau	non-b	obj	anti	-	-	-	-	Cause	2083
pos	cau	non-b	obj/sub	NS	-	-	+	-	Condition	109
pos	cau	non-b	obj/sub	NS	-	-	-	+	Purpose	1
pos	cau	non-b	sub	NS	-	-	-	-	Cause+Belief	82

Table 12: Unique patterns of UDims and implicit DRs in the training set of PDTB 3.0.

Table 13 shows unique patterns in the mapping between UDims and implicit DRs in the test set of PDTB 3.0.

Table 14 shows unique patterns in the mapping between UDims and DRs in the training set of explicit data.

pol.	bop.	imp.	soc.	temp.	spec.	alt.	con.	goal	DR	frequency
NS	NS	NS	NS	NS	-	-	-	-	Asynchronous	3
NS	NS	NS	NS	NS	-	-	-	-	Cause	20
NS	NS	NS	NS	NS	-	-	-	-	Cause+Belief	1
NS	NS	NS	NS	NS	-	-	-	-	Concession	1
NS	NS	NS	NS	NS	-	-	-	-	Condition	1
NS	NS	NS	NS	NS	-	-	-	-	Instantiation	1
NS	NS	NS	NS	NS	-	-	-	-	Manner	1
NS	NS	NS	NS	NS	-	-	-	-	Purpose	33
NS	NS	NS	NS	NS	-	-	-	-	Substitution	1
neg	add	NA	obj	NS	-	-	-	-	Contrast	53
neg	cau	bas	obj/sub	NS	-	-	-	-	Concession	88
neg	cau	non-b	obj/sub	NS	-	-	-	-	Concession	9
neg	cau	non-b	obj/sub	NS	-	-	-	-	Substitution	25
pos	add	NA	obj	anti	-	-	-	-	Asynchronous	9
pos	add	NA	obj	chron	-	-	-	-	Asynchronous	93
pos	add	NA	obj	sync	-	-	-	-	Synchronous	35
pos	add	NA	obj/sub	NS	+	-	-	-	Instantiation	123
pos	add	NA	obj/sub	NS	+	-	-	-	Level-of-detail	208
pos	add	NA	obj/sub	NS	+	-	-	-	Manner	16
pos	add	NA	obj/sub	NS	-	-	-	-	Conjunction	236
pos	add	NA	obj/sub	NS	-	-	-	-	Equivalence	30
pos	cau	bas	obj	chron	-	-	-	+	Cause	200
pos	cau	bas	obj	chron	-	-	-	-	Cause	11
pos	cau	bas	obj/sub	NS	-	-	+	-	Condition	4
pos	cau	bas	sub	NS	-	-	-	+	Purpose	56
pos	cau	bas	sub	NS	-	-	-	-	Cause+Belief	8
pos	cau	non-b	obj	anti	-	-	-	-	Cause	175
pos	cau	non-b	obj/sub	NS	-	-	+	-	Condition	10
pos	cau	non-b	sub	NS	-	-	-	-	Cause+Belief	6

Table 13: Unique patterns of UDims and implicit DRs in the test set of PDTB 3.0.

pol.	bop.	imp.	soc.	temp.	spec.	alt.	con.	goal	DR	frequency
NS	NS	NS	NS	NS -	-	-	-	Purpose	4	
neg	add	NA	obj	NS	-	-	-	-	Contrast	846
neg	add	NA	obj/sub	NS	-	+	-	-	Disjunction	228
neg	cau	bas	obj/sub	NS	-	-	-	-	Concession	3449
neg	cau	bas	obj/sub	NS	-	-	-	-	Substitution	55
neg	cau	non-b	obj/sub	NS	-	-	-	-	Concession	237
neg	cau	non-b	obj/sub	NS	-	-	-	-	Substitution	123
pos	add	NA	obj	anti	-	-	-	-	Asynchronous	737
pos	add	NA	obj	chron	-	-	-	-	Asynchronous	869
pos	add	NA	obj	sync	-	-	-	-	Synchronous	1492
pos	add	NA	obj/sub	NS	+	-	-	-	Instantiation	241
pos	add	NA	obj/sub	NS	+	-	-	-	Level-of-detail	187
pos	add	NA	obj/sub	NS	+	-	-	-	Manner	227
pos	add	NA	obj/sub	NS	-	-	-	-	Conjunction	6756
pos	cau	bas	obj	chron	-	-	-	+	Cause	374
pos	cau	bas	obj	chron	-	-	-	-	Cause	173
pos	cau	bas	obj/sub	NS	-	-	+	-	Condition	415
pos	cau	bas	obj/sub	NS	-	-	-	+	Purpose	3
pos	cau	bas	sub	NS	-	-	-	+	Purpose	202
pos	cau	non-b	obj	anti	-	-	-	-	Cause	907
pos	cau	non-b	obj/sub	NS	-	-	+	-	Condition	693
pos	cau	non-b	obj/sub	NS	-	-	-	+	Purpose	92

Table 14: Unique patterns of UDims and DRs in the training set of explicit data, shown here as supplementary material for the experiments on data augmentation.

F Preprocessing

The experiments on RST are carried out on RST-DT. We follow the gold division of the corpus for training and test sets and take 20% from the training set for validation. We utilize the preprocessing method by Ji and Eisenstein (2014) and binarize the RST trees in order to obtain pairs of discourse units linked by DRs. The 78 relations are mapped to 18 broad classes based on the template in Braud et al. (2016), but as *Same-Unit* and *Attribution* are not covered in Sanders et al. (2018), the two relations are excluded in our experiments, leaving a set of 16 RST relations.

The experiments on PDTB are performed on PDTB 3.0. We follow the data split used in Ji and Eisenstein (2015), i.e., sections 2-20 for training, sections 0-1 for validation, and sections 21-22 for testing, and discard DRs with fewer than 100 instances to alleviate data imbalance, as proposed in Kim et al. (2020), leaving 14 senses from Level-2 (L2) of the sense hierarchy.

G Statistics of UDims

We follow the format of the graph in Roze et al. (2019).

Figure 5 shows statistics of UDims for the training set of RST-DT.

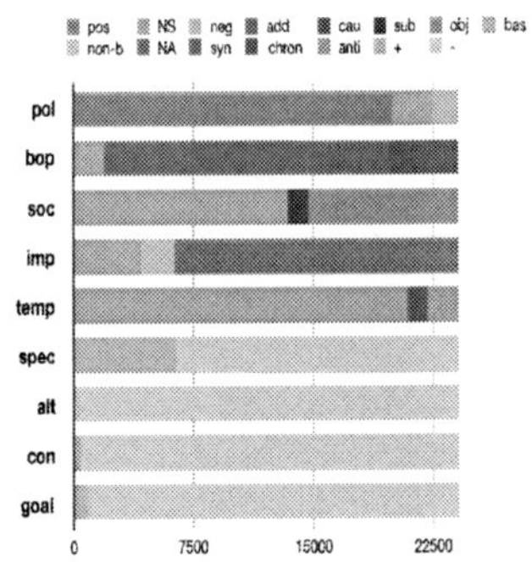

Figure 5: Statistics of UDims for the training set of RST-DT.

Figure 6 shows statistics of UDims for the training set of PDTB implicit relation data.

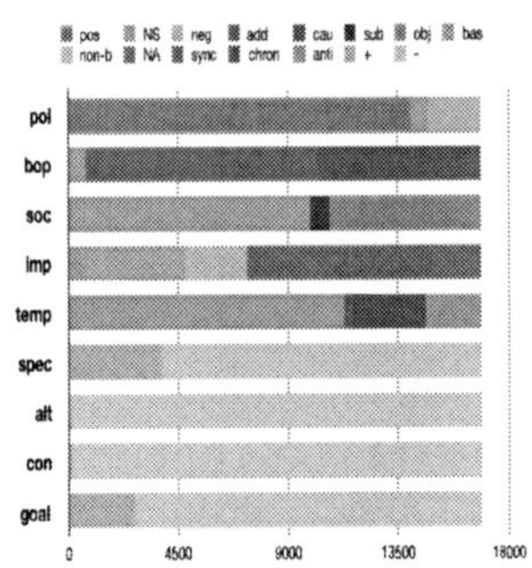

Figure 6: Statistics of UDims for the training set of PDTB implicit relation data.

H Label Frequency for Training Sets of RST and PDTB Implicit Relations

Table 15 shows label frequency in the training set of RST.

Label	Frequency
Explanation	1384
Manner-Means	302
Summary	300
Elaboration	11122
Contrast	1544
Evaluation	862
Joint	2932
Background	1328
Topic-Comment	212
Enablement	890
Cause	994
Condition	474
Topic-Change	322
Textual-Organization	234
Temporal	754
Comparison	408

Table 15: Label frequency in the training set of RST.

Table 16 shows label frequency in the training set of PDTB implicit relations.

Label	Frequency
Level-of-Detail	2493
Conjunction	3562
Concession	1164
Cause	4469
Instantiation	1117
Equivalence	252
Substitution	278
Asynchronous	985
Synchronous	325
Cause+Belief	157
Purpose	1102
Manner	191
Contrast	607
Condition	152

Table 16: Label frequency in the training set of PDTB implicit relations.

I Hyper-parameter Settings

The arguments of the input sequences are padded to a fixed length of 250 tokens, and all the model parameters are initialized with the Xavier uniform initialization (Glorot and Bengio, 2010). The output sizes of the feed-forward networks g and ϕ described in section 3.3.1 and section 3.3.2 are both set to 128 through manual tuning. The dropout probability is kept at 0.2 for all the experiments. In line with MC dropout, we keep all the dropout layers active during inference time, and run the model for UDim classification three times and obtain the average predictive distributions. The UDim embeddings are set with a dimension size of 100 in all the experiments, except for *InputDimCat* in section 3.3.2, where the dimension sizes of the UDim embeddings are set to be 2 * number of values, which we find sufficient through experimentation. Similarly, we also run the DR classifier three times and obtain the average predictive distribution. The batch size is set to the largest value that the GPU machine can accommodate.

The model learning rate is set to $1e-5$ and it is trained for a maximum of 30 epochs, with an early-stopping scheme monitoring performance improvement for DR classification on the validation set with a threshold of 7 epochs. The AdamW optimizer (Loshchilov and Hutter, 2018) is used and a warmup ratio of 0.06 is set for the scheduler. A weight decay of 0.1 is applied, and gradients are clipped to a maximum of 1.0. The implementation is based on the PyTorch machine learning framework (Paszke et al., 2019). A single A5000 GPU with a capacity of 24GB is used for all the experiments.

J Statistical Significance Test for Model Results

The saved models are used to predict DR sense labels on the test set of RST or PDTB, and different models are compared pairwise, in line with Stuart-Maxwell test.

Table 17 shows Stuart-Maxwell test of statistical significance of results for RST.

Model A	Model B	Difference	p-value
RST baseline	*InputForRelCls*	31.53487265756919	0.007444391838374066
RST baseline	*InputDimCat*	64.59896992698941	4.0166800266956324e-08
RST baseline	*InputDimAtt*	107.31845836146087	5.266424736880601e-16
RST baseline	*TrainonGoldTestonPred*	63.96165551732709	5.19121909560304e-08
InputForRelCls	*InputDimCat*	43.01215622117389	0.00015676857689742404
InputForRelCls	*InputDimAtt*	134.2049214835401	3.1837974277302182e-21
InputForRelCls	*TrainonGoldTestonPred*	57.65006061709332	6.363774121513998e-07
InputDimCat	*InputDimAtt*	178.08228924962432	5.7895617480969986e-30
InputDimCat	*TrainonGoldTestonPred*	75.50117669436882	4.596013953778202e-10
InputDimAtt	*TrainonGoldTestonPred*	90.04348995437392	9.735088746634535e-13

Table 17: Statistical significance test for results of RST models. Compared with the baseline, all the model results are statistically significant.

Table 18 shows Stuart-Maxwell test of statistical significance of results for PDTB implicit DR classification.

Model A	Model B	Difference	p-value
PDTB impl baseline	*InputForRelCls*	96.37746867104653	8.322748692517058e-15
PDTB impl baseline	*InputDimCat*	97.67850546549909	4.6673553418486555e-15
PDTB impl baseline	*InputDimAtt*	35.46139837486632	0.0007189097931712012
PDTB impl baseline	*TrainonGoldTestonPred*	106.07628543197474	1.0923958667709962e-16
InputForRelCls	*InputDimCat*	98.47524634808387	3.2737145426570587e-15
InputForRelCls	*InputDimAtt*	154.30765485412508	2.788891357957465e-26
InputForRelCls	*TrainonGoldTestonPred* 95.28342048662472	1.3526258777197362e-14	
InputDimCat	*InputDimAtt*	108.8129041233804	3.1898108418072124e-17
InputDimCat	*TrainonGoldTestonPred*	155.30024500712676	1.7579323354258866e-26
InputDimAtt	*TrainonGoldTestonPred*	136.33343659405318	1.1401098443142066e-22

Table 18: Statistical significance test for results of PDTB models. As is shown, all the model results are statistically significant.

K Detailed Results for Cascaded Classifier

This part involves two experiments. To get an estimate of the upper limit of only using UDims for DR classification, we experiment with using a single MLP to predict DRs based on gold UDims (*MLPGoldUDims*), which represents an upper limit of the approach of *universal classifier*.

The second experiment simulates the cascaded classifier, where UDim classification is performed first and predicted UDims are used for DR classification. In this experiment, input is only used for UDim classification and the predicted UDims are combined via an attention mechanism for DR classification. The training objective is to minimize losses of DR classification and UDim classification.

Table 19 shows the results, indicating a large gap between using predicted UDims (*UDimAtt*, i.e. using attention of embeddings of predicted UDims) and gold UDims (*MLPGoldUDims*) for DR classification.

	F1	Acc.
RST(*MLPGoldUDims*)	56.55	79.60
RST(*UDimAtt*)	32.24	55.50
PDTB impl.((*MLPGoldUDims*)	73.00	85.79
PDTB impl.(*UDimAtt*)	41.69	56.21

Table 19: Results on cascaded classification of UDims and DRs. *UDimAtt* denotes combining predicted UDims with an attention mechanism, which performs better than simple concatenation of predicted UDims here.

Table 20 shows the detailed performance on DR classification for RST, based on the cascaded classifier.

	precision	recall	f1	frequency
Background	44.44	36.04	39.80	111
Cause	36.36	24.39	29.20	82
Comparison	0.00	0.00	0.00	29
Condition	76.09	72.92	74.47	48
Contrast	68.32	75.34	71.66	146
Elaboration	59.42	82.79	69.19	796
Enablement	62.96	73.91	68.00	46
Evaluation	30.14	27.50	28.76	80
Explanation	37.42	55.45	44.69	110
Joint	37.50	1.42	2.73	212
Manner-Means	0.00	0.00	0.00	27
Summary	0.00	0.00	0.00	32
Temporal	65.96	42.47	51.67	73
Textual-Organization	33.33	11.11	16.67	9
Topic-Change	13.79	30.77	19.05	13
Topic-Comment	0.00	0.00	0.00	24

Table 20: Detailed results of RST DR classification with the cascaded classifier.

Table 21 shows test performance on UDim classification for RST, with the cascaded classifier based on *UDimAtt*.

Model	pol F1	bop F1	impl F1	soc F1	temp F1	spec F1	alt F1	con F1	goal F1	pol acc	bop acc	impl acc	soc acc	temp acc	spec acc	alt acc	con acc	goal acc
UDimAtt	74.66	58.44	55.41	63.02	48.16	83.09	83.29	88.85	84.52	88.36	78.56	77.15	74.48	86.89	86.13	99.84	98.91	98.31

Table 21: Results for UDim classification on RST for the cascaded classifier based on *UDimAtt*

Table 22 shows the detailed performance on DR classification for PDTB implicit relation data, based on the cascaded classifier.

Table 23 shows test performance on UDim classification for PDTB implicit relation data, with the cascaded classifier based on *UDimAtt*.

L Full Results for UDim Classification on RST and PDTB

Table 24 shows test performance on UDim classification for RST.

Table 25 shows test performance on UDim classification for PDTB implicit DRs.

	precision	recall	f1	frequency
Asynchronous	65.00	74.29	69.33	105
Cause	71.71	63.05	67.10	406
Cause+Belief	00.00	00.00	00.00	15
Concession	59.38	58.16	58.76	98
Condition	77.78	46.67	58.33	15
Conjunction	47.63	68.22	56.10	236
Contrast	55.36	58.49	56.88	53
Equivalence	00.00	00.00	00.00	30
Instantiation	00.00	00.00	00.00	124
Level-of-detail	40.00	58.65	47.56	208
Manner	00.00	00.00	00.00	17
Purpose	79.05	93.26	85.57	89
Substitution	42.11	61.54	50.00	26
Synchronous	66.67	22.86	34.04	35

Table 22: Detailed results of PDTB implicit DR classification with the cascaded classifier.

Model	pol F1	bop F1	impl F1	soc F1	temp F1	spec F1	alt F1	con F1	goal F1	pol acc	bop acc	impl acc	soc acc	temp acc	spec acc	alt acc	con acc	goal acc
UDimAtt	68.62	68.97	66.46	71.28	64.66	82.55	100.00	84.66	80.80	87.51	78.65	76.32	76.87	80.44	87.58	100.00	99.52	89.29

Table 23: Results for UDim classification on PDTB implicit relation data for the cascaded classifier based on *UDimAtt*

Model	pol F1	bop F1	impl F1	soc F1	temp F1	spec F1	alt F1	con F1	goal F1	pol acc	bop acc	impl acc	soc acc	temp acc	spec acc	alt acc	con acc	goal acc
TrainonGold TestonPred	73.65	57.78	57.06	60.69	47.18	82.50	64.22	87.82	85.16	87.43	78.45	77.53	73.78	88.79	85.91	99.73	98.91	98.37
InputDimCat	75.33	57.72	56.88	62.57	48.43	82.64	79.95	89.30	83.52	88.41	78.13	77.64	74.48	87.49	86.02	99.78	98.97	98.20
InputDimAtt	74.09	59.02	56.32	60.85	45.42	82.72	74.95	88.42	86.15	87.60	77.86	76.71	75.46	87.21	86.40	99.78	98.86	98.48
InputFor RelCls	73.19	60.34	58.33	61.39	46.41	82.53	83.29	88.36	85.16	87.54	78.84	78.13	75.14	87.00	86.45	99.84	98.91	98.37

Table 24: Results for UDim classification on RST.

Model	pol F1	bop F1	impl F1	soc F1	temp F1	spec F1	alt F1	con F1	goal F1	pol acc	bop acc	impl acc	soc acc	temp acc	spec acc	alt acc	con acc	goal acc
TrainonGold TestonPred	66.84	66.41	63.50	69.61	58.10	81.42	100.00	84.66	77.10	86.55	75.77	72.82	74.95	76.53	87.17	100.00	99.52	87.17
InputDimCat	68.59	69.71	66.43	72.12	60.72	82.46	100.00	81.68	79.84	87.71	77.97	74.74	76.53	79.75	87.37	100.00	99.45	88.81
InputDimAtt	69.03	68.40	65.66	74.24	59.93	80.16	100.00	77.10	81.08	88.95	77.49	74.19	77.08	77.21	85.86	100.00	99.31	89.09
InputFor RelCls	66.27	65.25	62.48	70.66	58.76	82.10	100.00	84.66	78.92	86.41	75.77	73.03	75.22	77.97	87.71	100.00	99.52	88.81

Table 25: Results for UDim classification on PDTB implicit relation data.

M Ablation Studies for RST

Table 26 presents results of ablation studies for RST DR classification.

DR	UDim	P.	R.	F1
Background	*-pol*	44.55	44.14	44.34
	-bop	48.28	37.84	42.42
	-imp	48.89	39.64	43.78
	-soc	44.55	40.54	42.45
	-temp	45.65	37.84	41.38
	-spec	45.26	38.74	41.75
	-alt	43.56	39.64	41.51
	-con	41.07	41.44	41.26
	-goal	42.86	43.24	43.05
Cause	*-pol*	42.86	21.95	29.03
	-bop	33.33	25.61	28.97
	-imp	34.92	26.83	30.34
	-soc	32.00	29.27	30.57
	-temp	35.82	29.27	32.21
	-spec	38.71	29.27	33.33
	-alt	34.25	30.49	32.26
	-con	36.67	26.83	30.99
	-goal	35.29	29.27	32.00
Comparison	*-pol*	52.00	44.83	48.15
	-bop	54.17	44.83	49.06
	-imp	51.61	55.17	53.33
	-soc	66.67	41.38	51.06
	-temp	52.17	41.38	46.15
	-spec	47.62	34.48	40.00
	-alt	50.00	41.38	45.28
	-con	58.33	48.28	52.83
	-goal	46.43	44.83	45.61
Condition	*-pol*	82.50	68.75	75.00
	-bop	87.50	72.92	79.55
	-imp	80.00	75.00	77.42
	-soc	80.43	77.08	78.72
	-temp	73.47	75.00	74.23
	-spec	77.27	70.83	73.91
	-alt	83.72	75.00	79.12
	-con	80.95	70.83	75.56
	-goal	76.09	72.92	74.47
Contrast	*-pol*	68.75	67.81	68.28
	-bop	75.89	73.29	74.56
	-imp	78.57	67.81	72.79
	-soc	73.76	71.23	72.47
	-temp	73.15	74.66	73.90
	-spec	75.19	68.49	71.68
	-alt	75.36	71.23	73.24
	-con	72.41	71.92	72.16
	-goal	78.79	71.23	74.82
Elaboration	*-pol*	71.61	83.67	77.17
	-bop	71.84	83.67	77.31
	-imp	72.23	82.04	76.82
	-soc	70.75	84.80	77.14
	-temp	73.66	81.16	77.23
	-spec	73.77	81.28	77.35
	-alt	73.36	84.05	78.34
	-con	76.74	81.66	79.12
	-goal	74.91	78.77	76.79
Enablement	*-pol*	71.43	76.09	73.68
	-bop	77.27	73.91	75.56
	-imp	72.00	78.26	75.00
	-soc	73.91	73.91	73.91
	-temp	68.63	76.09	72.16
	-spec	64.41	82.61	72.38
	-alt	66.67	78.26	72.00
	-con	75.00	78.26	76.60
	-goal	74.00	80.43	77.08
Evaluation	*-pol*	39.68	31.25	34.97
	-bop	38.89	26.25	31.34
	-imp	41.67	31.25	35.71
	-soc	36.62	32.50	34.44
	-temp	42.00	26.25	32.31
	-spec	36.84	35.00	35.90
	-alt	44.90	27.50	34.11
	-con	40.58	35.00	37.58
	-goal	33.33	35.00	34.15
Explanation	*-pol*	50.55	41.82	45.77
	-bop	46.85	47.27	47.06
	-imp	51.16	40.00	44.90
	-soc	48.19	36.36	41.45
	-temp	43.30	38.18	40.58
	-spec	54.00	49.09	51.43
	-alt	50.00	44.55	47.12
	-con	49.49	44.55	46.89
	-goal	38.69	48.18	42.91

Joint	*-pol*	67.10	73.11	69.98
	-bop	69.12	70.75	69.93
	-imp	65.97	74.06	69.78
	-soc	70.98	64.62	67.65
	-temp	63.60	75.00	68.83
	-spec	63.60	71.70	67.41
	-alt	70.51	72.17	71.33
	-con	64.43	76.89	70.11
	-goal	67.26	71.70	69.41
Manner-Means	*-pol*	75.00	44.44	55.81
	-bop	75.00	44.44	55.81
	-imp	71.43	37.04	48.78
	-soc	68.75	40.74	51.16
	-temp	66.67	44.44	53.33
	-spec	73.68	51.85	60.87
	-alt	65.00	48.15	55.32
	-con	57.14	44.44	50.00
	-goal	72.22	48.15	57.78
Summary	*-pol*	65.00	40.62	50.00
	-bop	66.67	43.75	52.83
	-imp	80.00	50.00	61.54
	-soc	80.00	37.50	51.06
	-temp	85.71	37.50	52.17
	-spec	75.00	46.88	57.69
	-alt	61.90	40.62	49.06
	-con	68.18	46.88	55.56
	-goal	71.43	46.88	56.60
Temporal	*-pol*	65.22	41.10	50.42
	-bop	66.04	47.95	55.56
	-imp	54.29	52.05	53.15
	-soc	66.67	41.10	50.85
	-temp	54.69	47.95	51.09
	-spec	68.52	50.68	58.27
	-alt	59.18	39.73	47.54
	-con	61.22	41.10	49.18
	-goal	72.97	36.99	49.09
Textual-Organization	*-pol*	66.67	88.89	76.19
	-bop	63.64	77.78	70.00
	-imp	72.73	88.89	80.00
	-soc	66.67	88.89	76.19
	-temp	72.73	88.89	80.00
	-spec	66.67	88.89	76.19
	-alt	57.14	88.89	69.57
	-con	66.67	88.89	76.19
	-goal	66.67	88.89	76.19
Topic-Change	*-pol*	62.50	38.46	47.62
	-bop	46.15	46.15	46.15
	-imp	38.46	38.46	38.46
	-soc	57.14	30.77	40.00
	-temp	45.45	38.46	41.67
	-spec	41.67	38.46	40.00
	-alt	62.50	38.46	47.62
	-con	50.00	38.46	43.48
	-goal	36.36	30.77	33.33
Topic-Comment	*-pol*	45.45	20.83	28.57
	-bop	37.50	25.00	30.00
	-imp	41.18	29.17	34.15
	-soc	46.67	29.17	35.90
	-temp	40.00	25.00	30.77
	-spec	46.67	29.17	35.90
	-alt	52.94	37.50	43.90
	-con	40.00	41.67	40.82
	-goal	31.58	25.00	27.91

Table 26: Ablation studies for RST, based on *InputForRelCls*. The lowest F1 scores are shown in blue, although there are cases when the differences between values are quite small.

N Ablation Studies for PDTB Implicit DR Classification

Table 27 presents results of ablation studies for PDTB implicit DR classification.

DR	UDim	P.	R.	F1
	-pol	63.11	61.90	62.50
	-bop	74.73	64.76	69.39
	-imp	66.04	66.67	66.35
	-soc	56.15	69.52	62.13
Asynchronous	*-temp*	68.09	60.95	64.32
	-spec	65.35	62.86	64.08
	-alt	63.55	64.76	64.15
	-con	59.65	64.76	62.10
	-goal	64.15	64.76	64.45
	-pol	66.58	66.26	66.42
	-bop	64.99	69.95	67.38
	-imp	64.93	67.49	66.18
	-soc	64.49	60.84	62.61
Cause	*-temp*	65.30	66.75	66.02
	-spec	69.83	59.85	64.46
	-alt	69.28	56.65	62.33
	-con	65.26	64.78	65.02
	-goal	71.64	59.11	64.78
	-pol	11.11	06.67	08.33
	-bop	00.00	00.00	00.00
	-imp	00.00	00.00	00.00
	-soc	09.09	06.67	07.69
Cause+Belief	*-temp*	00.00	00.00	00.00
	-spec	00.00	00.00	00.00
	-alt	10.71	20.00	13.95
	-con	00.00	00.00	00.00
	-goal	20.00	06.67	10.00
	-pol	58.54	48.98	53.33
	-bop	63.41	53.06	57.78
	-imp	58.43	53.06	55.61
	-soc	66.22	50.00	56.98
Concession	*-temp*	57.14	53.06	55.03
	-spec	50.00	62.24	55.45
	-alt	55.45	57.14	56.28
	-con	70.77	46.94	56.44
	-goal	59.15	42.86	49.70
	-pol	77.78	46.67	58.33
	-bop	81.82	60.00	69.23
	-imp	80.00	53.33	64.00
	-soc	81.82	60.00	69.23
Condition	*-temp*	83.33	66.67	74.07
	-spec	77.78	46.67	58.33
	-alt	87.50	46.67	60.87
	-con	77.78	46.67	58.33
	-goal	71.43	33.33	45.45
	-pol	56.68	66.53	61.21
	-bop	53.31	71.61	61.12
	-imp	54.58	63.14	58.55
	-soc	50.48	67.37	57.71
Conjunction	*-temp*	55.16	65.68	59.96
	-spec	53.77	69.49	60.63
	-alt	50.31	69.49	58.36
	-con	51.44	68.22	58.65
	-goal	49.46	77.54	60.40
	-pol	61.11	41.51	49.44
	-bop	43.64	45.28	44.44
	-imp	48.84	39.62	43.75
	-soc	55.56	47.17	51.02
Contrast	*-temp*	60.53	43.40	50.55
	-spec	52.17	45.28	48.48
	-alt	52.50	39.62	45.16
	-con	45.83	41.51	43.56
	-goal	42.59	43.40	42.99
	-pol	29.73	36.67	32.84
	-bop	33.33	03.33	06.06
	-imp	25.93	23.33	24.56
	-soc	18.42	23.33	20.59
Equivalence	*-temp*	28.00	23.33	25.45
	-spec	22.22	13.33	16.67
	-alt	40.00	20.00	26.67
	-con	18.52	33.33	23.81
	-goal	29.73	36.67	32.84
	-pol	80.25	52.42	63.41
	-bop	71.15	59.68	64.91
	-imp	81.61	57.26	67.30
	-soc	80.49	53.23	64.08
Instantiation	*-temp*	74.51	61.29	67.26
	-spec	71.03	61.29	65.80
	-alt	75.53	57.26	65.14
	-con	79.57	59.68	68.20
	-goal	64.89	68.55	66.67

Level-of-Detail	*-pol*	46.62	59.62	52.32
	-bop	51.47	50.48	50.97
	-imp	49.79	57.21	53.24
	-soc	49.32	51.92	50.59
	-temp	49.79	55.77	52.61
	-spec	49.43	62.02	55.01
	-alt	47.39	56.73	51.64
	-con	55.61	54.81	55.21
	-goal	52.38	47.60	49.87
Manner	*-pol*	66.67	47.06	55.17
	-bop	69.23	52.94	60.00
	-imp	80.00	47.06	59.26
	-soc	100.00	47.06	64.00
	-temp	63.64	41.18	50.00
	-spec	80.00	47.06	59.26
	-alt	72.73	47.06	57.14
	-con	66.67	47.06	55.17
	-goal	68.75	64.71	66.67
Purpose	*-pol*	86.87	96.63	91.49
	-bop	91.40	95.51	93.41
	-imp	88.54	95.51	91.89
	-soc	90.53	96.63	93.48
	-temp	89.47	95.51	92.39
	-spec	92.47	96.63	94.51
	-alt	87.00	97.75	92.06
	-con	93.41	95.51	94.44
	-goal	92.39	95.51	93.92
Substitution	*-pol*	40.74	42.31	41.51
	-bop	50.00	50.00	50.00
	-imp	45.45	38.46	41.67
	-soc	48.00	46.15	47.06
	-temp	41.38	46.15	43.64
	-spec	47.83	42.31	44.90
	-alt	45.00	34.62	39.13
	-con	51.85	53.85	52.83
	-goal	50.00	53.85	51.85
Synchronous	*-pol*	46.67	20.00	28.00
	-bop	45.00	25.71	32.73
	-imp	44.44	22.86	30.19
	-soc	47.62	28.57	35.71
	-temp	22.22	11.43	15.09
	-spec	64.29	25.71	36.73
	-alt	30.77	22.86	26.23
	-con	43.75	20.00	27.45
	-goal	43.75	20.00	27.45

Table 27: Ablation studies for PDTB implicit DR classification, based on *InputForRelCls*. Similar to RST, lowest F1 scores are shown in blue, with the exception of *Cause+Belief*, for which removing the majority of UDims yields 00.00.

Distinct social-linguistic processing between humans and large audio-language models: Evidence from model-brain alignment

Hanlin Wu[1] **Xufeng Duan**[1] **Zhenguang G. Cai**[1,2]
[1]Department of Linguistics and Modern Languages, The Chinese University of Hong Kong
[2]Brain and Mind Institute, The Chinese University of Hong Kong
hanlin.wu@link.cuhk.edu.hk

Abstract

Voice-based AI development faces unique challenges in processing both linguistic and paralinguistic information. This study compares how large audio-language models (LALMs) and humans integrate speaker characteristics during speech comprehension, asking whether LALMs process speaker-contextualized language in ways that parallel human cognitive mechanisms. We compared two LALMs' (Qwen2-Audio and Ultravox 0.5) processing patterns with human EEG responses. Using surprisal and entropy metrics from the models, we analyzed their sensitivity to speaker-content incongruency across social stereotype violations (e.g., a man claiming to regularly get manicures) and biological knowledge violations (e.g., a man claiming to be pregnant). Results revealed that Qwen2-Audio exhibited increased surprisal for speaker-incongruent content and its surprisal values significantly predicted human N400 responses, while Ultravox 0.5 showed limited sensitivity to speaker characteristics. Importantly, neither model replicated the human-like processing distinction between social violations (eliciting N400 effects) and biological violations (eliciting P600 effects). These findings reveal both the potential and limitations of current LALMs in processing speaker-contextualized language, and suggest differences in social-linguistic processing mechanisms between humans and LALMs.

1 Introduction

Humans are remarkably adept at extracting speaker characteristics from vocal cues. Within milliseconds of hearing a voice, listeners can perceive a speaker's gender, age, health condition, personality traits, and other socio-demographic attributes (Lavan et al., 2024). The perceived speaker attributes then form a critical context for language comprehension, shaping how linguistic input is processed and interpreted (Wu and Cai, 2024a). For example, when we hear someone say "The first time I got *pregnant* I had a hard time," it is straightforward when coming from a female speaker but would be puzzling if a man were to say it.

Electroencephalography (EEG) studies show that when people hear sentences containing speaker incongruencies—such as "The first time I got *pregnant...*" spoken by a man (violating biological knowledge) or "I like to get *manicures...*" spoken by a man (violating gender stereotypes)—their brain responses diverge from speaker-congruent conditions, showing an N400 effect (Martin et al., 2016; Van Berkum et al., 2008; Van den Brink et al., 2012) or a P600 effect (Lattner and Friederici, 2003; Foucart et al., 2015). These neural responses show that speaker characteristics actively shape the real-time processing of spoken language.

The human capacity for speaker-contextualized language processing has recently been explained through a rational inference framework (Wu and Cai, 2024b). This framework proposes that humans engage in rational inference during real-time language comprehension—a process where listeners actively reason about the most likely interpretation given both linguistic input and speaker characteristics. Using social-stereotype violation (e.g., men getting manicures) and biological-knowledge violation (e.g., men getting pregnant) as test cases, they showed that when encountering speaker-content mismatches that violate social stereotypes, listeners can still arrive at a "literal" interpretation through effortful integration with their social knowledge, reflected in N400 effects. However, when faced with biological impossibilities, listeners rationally infer potential errors in the input and engage in error correction processes, manifested as P600 effects.

Recent advances in large language models (LLMs) have demonstrated increasing capabilities in contextual understanding (Zhu et al., 2024) and multimodal processing (Wang et al., 2024; Zhang et al., 2024). While initially focused on text, these models have expanded into multimodal tasks, show-

Proceedings of the Workshop on Cognitive Modeling and Computational Linguistics, pages 135–143
May 3, 2025 ©2025 Association for Computational Linguistics

ing remarkable abilities in integrating inputs from diverse modalities like vision and speech. This evolution has led to the development of large audio-language models (LALMs) that can process audio inputs, including speaker characteristics, acoustic features, along with other contextual information.

The integration of LLMs into audio processing has progressed through several stages (Peng et al., 2024). Early attempts focused on incorporating Transformer architectures into traditional speech models, as exemplified by HuBERT's self-supervised learning on unlabeled speech data (Hsu et al., 2021). More recent approaches have shifted toward direct audio processing with LLMs by mapping audio features to tokens, not only for higher computational efficiency but also enabling richer paralinguistic processing through end-to-end multimodal integration (e.g., Chu et al., 2024).

This paradigm shift has produced models that are capable of increasingly complex tasks: AudioPaLM can preserve speaker voice characteristics during speech processing and generation (Rubenstein et al., 2023), SALMONN can perform audio-based storytelling and speech-audio co-reasoning (Tang et al., 2023), and Qwen2-Audio can explicitly identify speaker demographics and emotions (Chu et al., 2024). These emerging abilities raise questions about whether LALMs process speaker-contextualized language in ways that parallel human cognitive mechanisms.

As these models are increasingly deployed in interactive settings where they must interpret and respond to diverse speakers, understanding their social-linguistic processing has both theoretical and practical implications. On the one hand, comparing LALMs with human processing can provide insights into models' emergent cognitive mechanisms, an approach that has been widely used with deep neural networks (AlKhamissi et al., 2024, 2025; Schrimpf et al., 2018); on the other hand, identifying divergences between human and model processing helps pinpoint potential limitations in current architectures or training method, suggesting directions for developing more natural human-AI interactions.

To this end, we utilize computational metrics that have been shown to capture humans' real-time language processing. Specifically, surprisal (Hale, 2001; Levy, 2008), which reflects the unpredictability of a word given its context, has been linked to increased processing effort and has been shown to predict reading times (Smith and Levy, 2013) and N400 amplitudes (Krieger et al., 2024; Salicchi and Hsu, 2025). Entropy, which captures the uncertainty within the probability distribution of upcoming stimuli, was suggested to be associated with P600 amplitudes (Salicchi and Hsu, 2025).

In this research, we investigate whether LALMs align with human cognitive mechanisms in social-linguistic processing. We use the EEG data from Wu and Cai (2024b) as a benchmark of human processing and examine: a) whether LALMs align with humans in perceiving speaker characteristics and use them to guide real-time language processing; b) whether LALMs align with humans in the specific mechanism in processing speaker-content relationships.

2 Method

2.1 Human EEG data

The human data were EEG responses to speech stimuli from native Mandarin Chinese speakers. The study employed a 2×2 factorial design crossing Congruency (speaker-congruent vs. speaker-incongruent) with Type (social vs. biological). Congruency was manipulated by matching or mismatching speaker characteristics with the sentence content, while Type distinguished between violations of social stereotypes and biological knowledge. The experimental materials consisted of 80 self-referential sentences (each with a speaker-congruent and a speaker-incongruent audio version) in Mandarin Chinese, with speaker characteristics varying along gender and age dimensions (Table 1). All sentence audios were generated using text-to-speech technique with consistent acoustic properties.

The EEG data were collected from 60 participants while they listened to these sentences. A region of interest of 59 central-posterior sites was selected, and trial-level amplitudes were averaged across these sites before being further averaged over 300-600 ms (N400) and 600-1000 ms (P600) post-critical word onset. Their results revealed that social incongruency elicited a long-lasting N400 effect (across the 300-600-ms and the 600-1000-ms time windows), while biological incongruency elicited a P600 effect (600-1000 ms).

2.2 LALM metrics

We collected the computational metrics from two LALMs: Qwen2-Audio 7B Instruct (Chu et al., 2024) and Ultravox 0.5 8B (www.ultravox.ai). We

Category	Example	English translation
SM	在工作单位我一般都是穿西服打领带。	At the workplace I usually wear a suit and a tie.
SF	这个周末我要先去做美甲然后理发。	This weekend I'm going to get a manicure and then a haircut.
SA	我最近上班压力太大需要休息。	I've been working too hard lately and I need a break.
SC	他把我的玩具抢走了我要去找妈妈告状。	He took my toys away from me and I'm going to tell mummy about it.
BM	我需要定期去医院检查前列腺的健康状况。	I need to go to the hospital to check my prostate on a regular basis.
BF	我第一次怀孕的时候过得很艰难。	The first time I got pregnant I had a hard time.
BA	我发现我脸上的老年斑越来越多了我正在寻找新的治疗方法。	I noticed that I'm getting more and more age spots on my face and I am looking for new treatments.
BC	我在等我的乳牙掉下来然后我要把它扔到房顶上。	I'm waiting for my milk tooth to fall out and then I'm going to throw it on the roof.

Table 1: Examples of Stimuli used in Wu and Cai (2024b) with English translations. SM: socially congruent with male speakers; SF: socially congruent with female speakers; SA: socially congruent with adult speakers; SC: socially congruent with child speakers; BM: biologically congruent with male speakers; BF: biologically congruent with female speakers; BA: biologically congruent with adult speakers; BC: biologically congruent with child speakers. Critical words are underscored.

obtained the surprisal and entropy of the critical word through a sentence continuation task where we inputted the audio sentences that were cut short at the critical word following a text-based instruction to guide the model to continue the audio sentence by outputting text (see Appendix for prompts).

Surprisal was computed as the negative log probability of the target word given its context:

$$S(w_t) = -\log_2 P(w_t|C) \quad (1)$$

Where w_t represents the target word (i.e., the critical word that distinguishes speaker-congruent and -incongruent conditions); C represents the context before the target word, including the text-based instruction and the audio sentence; $P(w_t|C)$ was the word probability. For words containing multiple tokens, we calculated the joint probability at the token level.

Entropy was calculated over the probability distribution of the model's predictions at the target word position:

$$H(w_t) = -\sum P(w_x|C) \log_2 P(w_x|C) \quad (2)$$

Where w_x represents possible continuations. For words containing multiple tokens, we calculated the sum of the entropy for each token in the word. To test the generalizability across languages, we additionally created an English version of each sentence by translation and adaptation. The English audio was generated using the same standard as the Chinese audio. Metrics were collected for both the original Chinese stimuli and their English translations to test cross-linguistic generalization. We also collected these metrics from the text-based stimuli (the text transcription of those audio sentences) to serve as the baseline.

3 Results

We examined the model-brain alignment from two perspectives. First, we examined whether the LALM response patterns resembled humans by replicating the analyses in the human study on LALM data. Second, we examined whether LALM responses could predict human brain responses by including LALM metrics as additional predictors for the human brain responses. For all analyses, we used linear mixed-effects (LME) modeling with maximal random-effect structure determined by forward model comparison (α = 0.2, Matuschek et al., 2017). For surprisal and entropy analyses, we used item-level data and included the random effect of Item; for model-EEG alignment analyses, we used trial-level data and included the random effects of both Participant and Item.

3.1 Surprisal (Qwen2-Audio)

To test whether surprisal metric replicated the human brain pattern, we conducted LME analyses with Congruency (congruent = -0.5, incongruent = 0.5) and Type (social = -0.5, biological = 0.5) as interacting fixed effects, along with text-based surprisal as control, and showed a significant main effect of Congruency (β = 0.41, SE = 0.19, t = 2.12, p = .037) and text-based surprisal (β = 3.97, SE = 0.30, t = 13.17, p < .001), suggesting that

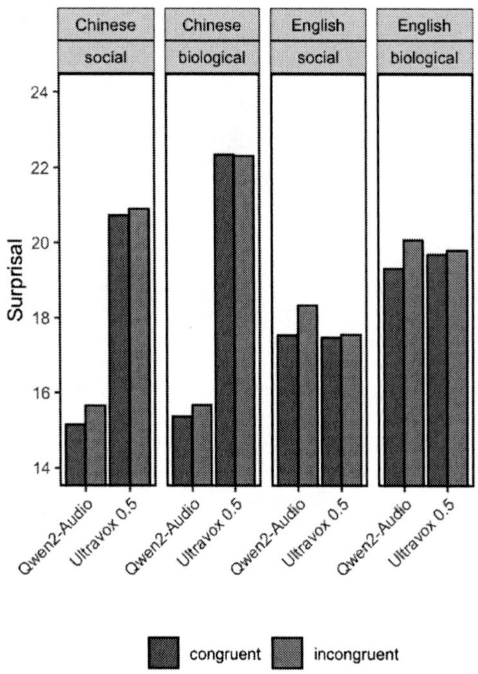

Figure 1: Surprisal values from Qwen2-Audio and Ultravox 0.5 models for speaker-congruent (blue) and speaker-incongruent (red) utterances, shown separately for social and biological conditions in Chinese and English.

the LALM model was sensitive to speaker-content incongruency regardless of violation type. The critical interaction between Congruency and Type was absent (β = -0.20, SE = 0.38, t = -0.52, p = .602), suggesting that unlike humans, the model processed social and biological violations similarly. The same pattern was replicated in English materials, as there was a significant main effect of Congruency (β = 0.73, SE = 0.20, t = 3.55, p < .001) and text-based surprisal (β = 3.89, SE = 0.32, t = 12.14, p < .001), while the interaction between Congruency and Type was absent (β = -0.17, SE = 0.41, t = -0.42, p = .678).

3.2 Surprisal (Ultravox 0.5)

Unlike Qwen2-Audio, the results for Ultravox 0.5 only showed a significant main effect of text-based surprisal (β = 4.09, SE = 0.36, t = 11.32, p < .001) for Chinese materials, while the main effect of Congruency (β = 0.07, SE = 0.08, t = 0.85, p = .399) or the interaction between Congruency and Type was absent (β = -0.20, SE = 0.16, t = -1.23, p = .222), suggesting that this model might not be sensitive to speaker-content relationships. The same pattern was shown in English materials, as there was a significant main effect of text-based surprisal (β = 2.41, SE = 0.42, t = 5.71, p < .001), and no main effect of Congruency (β = 0.05, SE = 0.10, t = 0.44, p = .663) or interaction between Congruency and Type (β = -0.05, SE = 0.21, t = -0.26, p = .799).

3.3 Entropy (Qwen2-Audio)

To test whether entropy metric replicated the human brain pattern, we conducted LME analyses with Congruency and Type as interacting fixed effects, along with text-based entropy as control, and showed that there was only a significant main effect of text-based entropy (β = 10.27, SE = 0.36, t = 28.49, p < .001) for Chinese materials. Neither the main effect of Congruency (β = -0.09, SE = 0.15, t = -0.61, p = .546) nor the interaction between Congruency and Type (β = -0.17, SE = 0.30, t = -0.55, p = .582) reached significance, suggesting that the model's uncertainty in prediction was primarily driven by the linguistic properties of the input rather than speaker-content relationships. The same pattern was shown in English materials, as the main effect of text-based entropy emerged (β = 8.71, SE = 0.42, t = 20.89, p < .001), while the main effect of Congruency (β = -0.04, SE = 0.17, t = -0.21, p = .836) and the interaction between Congruency and Type remained absent (β = -0.37, SE = 0.34, t = -1.07, p = .289).

3.4 Entropy (Ultravox 0.5)

The pattern observed in Qwen2-Audio was replicated with Ultravox 0.5, as there was only a significant main effect of text-based entropy (β = 9.50, SE = 0.23, t = 41.77, p < .001) for Chinese materials. Neither the main effect of Congruency (β = -0.01, SE = 0.02, t = -0.48, p = .630) nor the interaction between Congruency and Type (β = 0.04, SE = 0.05, t = 0.90, p = .369) reached significance. This pattern was further replicated with English materials, as there was only a significant main effect of text-based entropy (β = 3.63, SE = 0.70, t = 5.22, p < .001). Neither the main effect of Congruency (β = -0.03, SE = 0.04, t = -0.64, p = .526) nor the interaction between Congruency and Type (β = -0.05, SE = 0.08, t = -0.63, p = .531) reached significance.

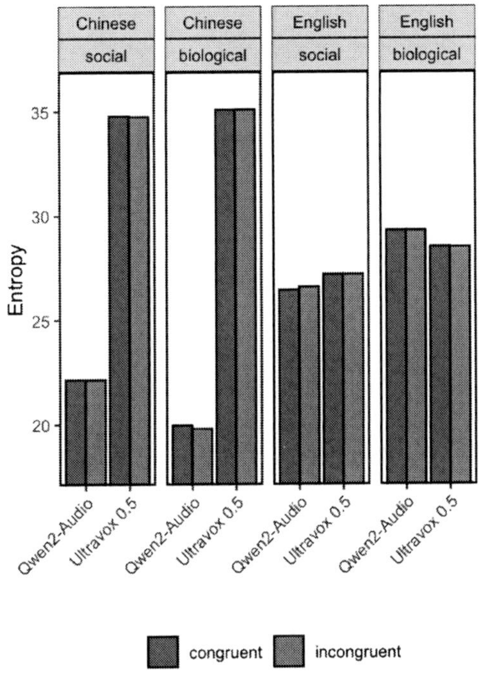

Figure 2: Entropy values from Qwen2-Audio and Ultravox 0.5 models for speaker-congruent (blue) and speaker-incongruent (red) utterances, shown separately for social and biological conditions in Chinese and English.

3.5 Surprisal-EEG alignment (Qwen2-Audio)

To test whether Surprisal could predict EEG response and whether the prediction varied across conditions, we added Surprisal (a scaled continuous variable) as a fixed effect interacting with Congruency and Type to the original LME analyses of EEG amplitude in Wu and Cai (2024a). For 300-600 ms, the results revealed a significant main effect of Surprisal (β = -0.50, SE = 0.16, t = -3.12, p = .002), while it did not interact with Congruency (β = 0.15, SE = 0.26, t = 0.57, p = .574), Type (β = 0.18, SE = 0.32, t = 0.56, p = .579), or the interaction between Congruency and Type (β = 0.17, SE = 0.52, t = 0.34, p = .736). For 600-1000 ms, there was no main effect of Surprisal (β = -0.22, SE = 0.18, t = -1.21, p = .229), or interaction with Congruency (β = 0.23, SE = 0.30, t = 0.76, p = .447), Type (β = 0.53, SE = 0.36, t = 1.50, p = .138), or three-way interaction with Congruency and Type (β = -0.09, SE = 0.60, t = -0.16, p = .877). These results suggested that surprisal significantly predicted N400 responses in a condition-independent manner, while it did not contribute to P600 responses.

3.6 Surprisal-EEG alignment (Ultravox 0.5)

For 300-600 ms, the results revealed a marginally significant main effect of Surprisal (β = -0.33, SE = 0.18, t = -1.79, p = .078), while it did not interact with Congruency (β = 0.33, SE = 0.28, t = 1.16, p = .250), Type (β = 0.23, SE = 0.37, t = 0.62, p = .539), or the interaction between Congruency and Type (β = -0.34, SE = 0.56, t = -0.60, p = .548). For 600-1000 ms, there was no main effect of Surprisal (β = 0.26, SE = 0.20, t = 1.26, p = .212), or its interaction with Congruency (β = 0.19, SE = 0.32, t = 0.61, p = .544), Type (β = 0.46, SE = 0.38, t = 1.22, p = .227), or the three-way interaction with Congruency and Type (β = -0.31, SE = 0.63, t = -0.49, p = .626). These results suggested that unlike Qwen2-Audio, Ultravox 0.5's surprisal did not reliably predict either N400 or P600 responses, despite showing a trend predicting N400.

3.7 Entropy-EEG alignment (Qwen2-Audio)

To test whether Entropy can predict EEG response and whether the prediction varied across conditions, we added Entropy (a scaled continuous variable) as a fixed effect interacting with Congruency and Type. The results revealed no significant main effect of Entropy (300-600 ms: β = -0.19, SE = 0.17, t = -1.14, p = .259; 600-1000 ms: β = 0.02, SE = 0.18, t = 0.12, p = .907), or interaction with Congruency (300-600 ms: β = 0.34, SE = 0.26, t = 1.31, p = .193; 600-1000 ms: β = -0.05, SE = 0.30, t = -0.18, p = .861), Type (300-600 ms: β = 0.44, SE = 0.34, t = 1.29, p = .202; 600-1000 ms: β = 0.36, SE = 0.37, t = 0.98, p = .333), or the three-way interaction with Congruency and Type (300-600 ms: β = -0.64, SE = 0.52, t = -1.24, p = .220; 600-1000 ms: β = -0.59, SE = 0.60, t = -0.98, p = .329). These results suggested that the model's predictive uncertainty did not predict human neural responses for either N400 or P600.

3.8 Entropy-EEG alignment (Ultravox 0.5)

The results revealed no significant main effect of Entropy in the N400 time window (300-600 ms: β = 0.04, SE = 0.18, t = 0.20, p = .844), but a marginal main effect in the P600 time window (600-1000 ms: β = 0.31, SE = 0.18, t = 1.76, p = .083). There were no significant interactions with Congruency (300-600 ms: β = 0.32, SE = 0.25, t = 1.28,

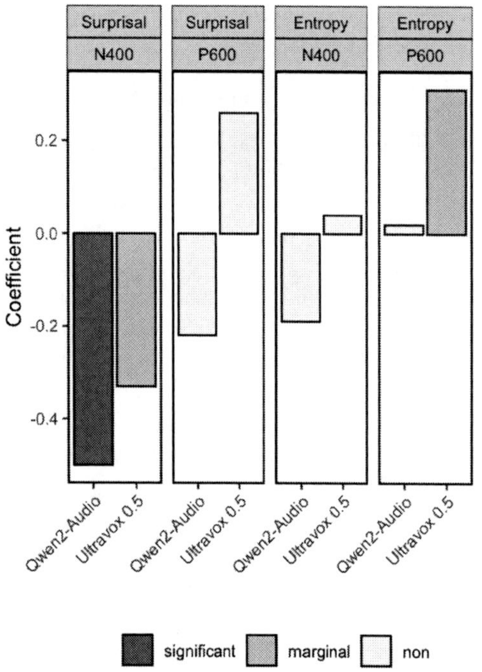

Figure 3: Main effect coefficients of Surprisal and Entropy on N400 and P600 amplitudes from LME analyses. Dark blue indicates a significant effect, light blue indicates marginal effects, and alice blue indicates non-significant effects for Qwen2-Audio and Ultravox 0.5 models.

p = .204; 600-1000 ms: β = 0.27, SE = 0.30, t = 0.89, p = .375), Type (300-600 ms: β = 0.11, SE = 0.34, t = 0.33, p = .744; 600-1000 ms: β = 0.17, SE = 0.36, t = 0.48, p = .633), or the three-way interaction with Congruency and Type (300-600 ms: β = -0.48, SE = 0.50, t = -0.96, p = .340; 600-1000 ms: β = -0.27, SE = 0.60, t = -0.45, p = .652). These results suggested that, similar to Qwen2-Audio, the model's predictive uncertainty did not strongly predict human neural responses for either N400 or P600, though there was a trend for higher entropy to predict larger P600 amplitudes.

4 Discussion

Our results revealed varying degrees of alignment between humans and LALMs in the social-linguistic processing of speech. Qwen2-Audio showed sensitivity to speaker-content incongruency through increased surprisal for incongruent utterances and significantly predicted human N400 responses. In contrast, Ultravox 0.5 showed no sensitivity to speaker-content relationships in its surprisal patterns and did not reliably predict human neural responses, despite showing a trend for N400.

Moreover, neither model showed human-like distinctions between social and biological violations, and both models' predictive uncertainty (entropy) was primarily driven by linguistic properties rather than speaker-content relationships and generally did not predict human neural responses, though Ultravox 0.5 showed a marginal trend for higher entropy predicting larger P600 amplitudes.

The distinct neural signatures for social versus biological violations in humans likely reflect different cognitive mechanisms. As Wu and Cai (2024b) suggested, social violations may be processed through semantic integration where linguistic content and speaker characteristics are integrated with prior knowledge about social roles and stereotypical behaviors, leading to N400 effects. In contrast, biological violations may trigger error detection and correction processes that attempt to resolve the physical impossibility, resulting in P600 effects. This distinction reflects rationality in human cognition.

Unlike humans who engage in active reanalysis when encountering biological impossibilities (reflected in the P600), current LALMs operate through single-pass forward prediction without mechanisms for backtracking or reanalysis. This may relate to the fact that current LLMs are typically trained to predict tokens one at a time, optimizing for local coherence rather than longer-range consistency. While some models are beginning to explore multi-token prediction windows (Gloeckle et al., 2024; Liu et al., 2024) that could theoretically capture longer-range dependencies and support reanalysis-like processes, most still lack similar mechanisms.

An open question is the precise mechanism by which LALMs utilize speaker information in their predictions. Unlike humans who readily identify speaker characteristics from voice and use this information to guide comprehension, it remains unclear whether LALMs explicitly represent speaker identity (e.g., assigning a gender category to a voice) or simply learn statistical associations between acoustic features and linguistic content. This distinction has implications for understanding both model processing and human cognition. For humans, the N400 and P600 effects depend on correctly identifying speaker characteristics and applying relevant world knowledge. If LALMs do not explicitly represent speaker identity but still show some degree of sensitivity to speaker-content relationships, this would suggest that explicit categorization may not be necessary for content prediction, though it might be essential for the rational inference processes that humans employ when resolving incongruencies. Future research could probe this question by examining model representations of speaker characteristics and their relationship to linguistic predictions.

Lastly, our findings also raise ethical considerations regarding LALMs' gender (and age) bias, which has been widely shown in LLMs (Kotek et al., 2023; Zhao et al., 2024). The observation that Qwen2-Audio showed increased surprisal for gender-nonconforming utterances indicates that it might have internalized societal gender stereotypes during training. While such sensitivity may facilitate natural interactions with humans, it also risks perpetuating harmful stereotypes if deployed in applications that influence decision-making or content generation.

In conclusion, we show that LALMs can potentially detect speaker-content violations and predict human N400 responses, but this capability varies between models. While Qwen2-Audio showed some level of alignment with human processing, neither Qwen2-Audio nor Ultravox 0.5 captured the human-like rational inference (as reflected by the distinction between social and biological violations), suggesting potential limitations in current LALM architectures or LLM architectures in general regarding real-time error analysis mechanisms.

5 Limitations

Several limitations of the current study should be acknowledged. First, our analyses focused on only two LALMs with a relatively small set of stimuli, which may not be representative of all current audio-language models or the full range of potential speaker-content relationships. A larger-scale investigation would better characterize the variation in speaker-content processing capabilities across different model architectures and training paradigms. Additionally, While surprisal and entropy are established metrics that have been linked to N400 and P600 responses respectively, they may be insufficient to capture the full range of processing distinctions that humans exhibit. Future research could explore alternative metrics such as analyzing activation patterns in different model layers, or utilizing representation similarity analysis between model embeddings and neural data. Finally, we only examined models' "static" responses to speaker characteristics, whereas humans show dynamic adaptation to individual speakers over increasing contexts (Grant et al., 2020). Human listeners rapidly adjust their predictions based on a speaker's established patterns—for example, becoming less surprised by stereotype-incongruent statements from a speaker who consistently violates stereotypes. This adaptive processing, which involves updating speaker models in real-time and adjusting predictions accordingly (Wu et al., 2025), represents an aspect of human language processing that our current single-utterance design cannot capture. Future work should examine how LALMs' predictions evolve across multiple utterances from the same speaker to better assess their capability for speaker-specific adaptation.

References

Badr AlKhamissi, Greta Tuckute, Antoine Bosselut, and Martin Schrimpf. 2024. The llm language network: A neuroscientific approach for identifying causally task-relevant units. *arXiv preprint arXiv:2411.02280*.

Badr AlKhamissi, Greta Tuckute, Yingtian Tang, Taha Binhuraib, Antoine Bosselut, and Martin Schrimpf. 2025. From language to cognition: How llms outgrow the human language network. *arXiv preprint arXiv:2503.01830*.

Yunfei Chu, Jin Xu, Qian Yang, Haojie Wei, Xipin Wei, Zhifang Guo, Yichong Leng, Yuanjun Lv, Jinzheng He, Junyang Lin, et al. 2024. Qwen2-audio technical report. *arXiv preprint arXiv:2407.10759*.

Alice Foucart, Xavier Garcia, Meritxell Ayguasanosa, Guillaume Thierry, Clara Martin, and Albert Costa. 2015. Does the speaker matter? online processing of semantic and pragmatic information in l2 speech comprehension. *Neuropsychologia*, 75:291–303.

Fabian Gloeckle, Badr Youbi Idrissi, Baptiste Rozière, David Lopez-Paz, and Gabriel Synnaeve. 2024. Better & faster large language models via multi-token prediction. *arXiv preprint arXiv:2404.19737*.

Angela Grant, Sarah Grey, and Janet G van Hell. 2020. Male fashionistas and female football fans: Gender stereotypes affect neurophysiological correlates of semantic processing during speech comprehension. *Journal of Neurolinguistics*, 53:100876.

John Hale. 2001. A probabilistic earley parser as a psycholinguistic model. In *Second meeting of the north american chapter of the association for computational linguistics*.

Wei-Ning Hsu, Benjamin Bolte, Yao-Hung Hubert Tsai, Kushal Lakhotia, Ruslan Salakhutdinov, and Abdelrahman Mohamed. 2021. Hubert: Self-supervised speech representation learning by masked prediction of hidden units. *IEEE/ACM transactions on audio, speech, and language processing*, 29:3451–3460.

Hadas Kotek, Rikker Dockum, and David Sun. 2023. Gender bias and stereotypes in large language models. In *Proceedings of the ACM collective intelligence conference*, pages 12–24.

Benedict Krieger, Harm Brouwer, Christoph Aurnhammer, and Matthew W Crocker. 2024. On the limits of llm surprisal as functional explanation of erps. In *Proceedings of the Annual Meeting of the Cognitive Science Society*, volume 46.

Sonja Lattner and Angela D Friederici. 2003. Talker's voice and gender stereotype in human auditory sentence processing–evidence from event-related brain potentials. *Neuroscience letters*, 339(3):191–194.

Nadine Lavan, Paula Rinke, and Mathias Scharinger. 2024. The time course of person perception from voices in the brain. *Proceedings of the National Academy of Sciences*, 121(26):e2318361121.

Roger Levy. 2008. Expectation-based syntactic comprehension. *Cognition*, 106(3):1126–1177.

Aixin Liu, Bei Feng, Bing Xue, Bingxuan Wang, Bochao Wu, Chengda Lu, Chenggang Zhao, Chengqi Deng, Chenyu Zhang, Chong Ruan, et al. 2024. Deepseek-v3 technical report. *arXiv preprint arXiv:2412.19437*.

Clara D Martin, Xavier Garcia, Douglas Potter, Alissa Melinger, and Albert Costa. 2016. Holiday or vacation? the processing of variation in vocabulary across dialects. *Language, Cognition and Neuroscience*, 31(3):375–390.

Hannes Matuschek, Reinhold Kliegl, Shravan Vasishth, Harald Baayen, and Douglas Bates. 2017. Balancing type i error and power in linear mixed models. *Journal of memory and language*, 94:305–315.

Jing Peng, Yucheng Wang, Yu Xi, Xu Li, Xizhuo Zhang, and Kai Yu. 2024. A survey on speech large language models. *arXiv preprint arXiv:2410.18908*.

Paul K Rubenstein, Chulayuth Asawaroengchai, Duc Dung Nguyen, Ankur Bapna, Zalán Borsos, Félix de Chaumont Quitry, Peter Chen, Dalia El Badawy, Wei Han, Eugene Kharitonov, et al. 2023. Audiopalm: A large language model that can speak and listen. *arXiv preprint arXiv:2306.12925*.

Lavinia Salicchi and Yu-Yin Hsu. 2025. Not every metric is equal: Cognitive models for predicting n400 and p600 components during reading comprehension. In *Proceedings of the 31st International Conference on Computational Linguistics*, pages 3648–3654.

Martin Schrimpf, Jonas Kubilius, Ha Hong, Najib J Majaj, Rishi Rajalingham, Elias B Issa, Kohitij Kar, Pouya Bashivan, Jonathan Prescott-Roy, Franziska Geiger, et al. 2018. Brain-score: Which artificial neural network for object recognition is most brainlike? *BioRxiv*, page 407007.

Nathaniel J Smith and Roger Levy. 2013. The effect of word predictability on reading time is logarithmic. *Cognition*, 128(3):302–319.

Changli Tang, Wenyi Yu, Guangzhi Sun, Xianzhao Chen, Tian Tan, Wei Li, Lu Lu, Zejun Ma, and Chao Zhang. 2023. Salmonn: Towards generic hearing abilities for large language models. *arXiv preprint arXiv:2310.13289*.

Jos JA Van Berkum, Danielle Van den Brink, Cathelijne MJY Tesink, Miriam Kos, and Peter Hagoort. 2008. The neural integration of speaker and message. *Journal of cognitive neuroscience*, 20(4):580–591.

Daniëlle Van den Brink, Jos JA Van Berkum, Marcel CM Bastiaansen, Cathelijne MJY Tesink, Miriam Kos, Jan K Buitelaar, and Peter Hagoort. 2012. Empathy matters: Erp evidence for inter-individual differences in social language processing. *Social cognitive and affective neuroscience*, 7(2):173–183.

Shuqi Wang, Xufeng Duan, and Zhenguang Cai. 2024. A multimodal large language model "foresees" objects based on verb information but not gender. In *Proceedings of the 28th Conference on Computational Natural Language Learning*, pages 435–441.

Hanlin Wu and Zhenguang G Cai. 2024a. Speaker effects in spoken language comprehension. *arXiv preprint arXiv:2412.07238*.

Hanlin Wu and Zhenguang G Cai. 2024b. When a man says he is pregnant: Erp evidence for a rational account of speaker-contextualized language comprehension. *arXiv preprint arXiv:2409.17525*.

Hanlin Wu, Xiaohui Rao, and Zhenguang G Cai. 2025. Probabilistic adaptation of language comprehension for individual speakers: Evidence from neural oscillations. *arXiv preprint arXiv:2502.01299*.

Duzhen Zhang, Yahan Yu, Jiahua Dong, Chenxing Li, Dan Su, Chenhui Chu, and Dong Yu. 2024. Mm-llms: Recent advances in multimodal large language models. *arXiv preprint arXiv:2401.13601*.

Jinman Zhao, Yitian Ding, Chen Jia, Yining Wang, and Zifan Qian. 2024. Gender bias in large language models across multiple languages. *arXiv preprint arXiv:2403.00277*.

Yilun Zhu, Joel Ruben Antony Moniz, Shruti Bhargava, Jiarui Lu, Dhivya Piraviperumal, Site Li, Yuan Zhang, Hong Yu, and Bo-Hsiang Tseng. 2024. Can large language models understand context? *arXiv preprint arXiv:2402.00858*.

A Appendix: prompts for sentence continuation task

A.1 Qwen2-Audio

Chinese materials (audio)

System: 你是一个实验中的参与者，你需要仔细听下面的录音。

User: 请补全录音中的句子，例如‘我喜欢吃‘，你可以回答‘苹果‘。直接回答补充的内容，不要说其他内容。录音：

User: (audio)

English materials (audio)

System: You are a participant in an experiment, you need to listen carefully to the following recording.

User: Please complete the sentence from the recording, for example if you hear 'I like to eat', you can answer 'apples'. Just answer with the completing content, don't say anything else. Recording:

User: (audio)

Chinese materials (text)

System: 你是一个实验中的参与者，你需要认真完成下面的任务。

User: 请补全以下句子。例如，‘我喜欢吃‘，你可以回答‘苹果‘，直接回答补充的内容，不要说其他内容。句子：(text)

English materials (text)

System: You are a participant in an experiment, you need to complete the following task carefully. User: Please complete the following sentence. For example, 'I like to eat', you can answer 'apples'. Just answer with the completing content, don't say anything else. Sentence: (text)

A.2 Ultravox 0.5

Chinese materials (audio)

System: 请补全录音中的句子，例如'我喜欢吃'，你可以回答'苹果'。直接回答补充的内容，不要说其他内容。(audio)

English materials (audio)

System: Please complete the sentence from the recording. For example, if you hear 'I like to eat', you can answer 'apples'. Just answer with the completing content, don't say anything else. (audio)

Chinese materials (text)

System: 请补全以下句子。例如，'我喜欢吃'，你可以回答'苹果'。直接回答补充的内容，不要说其他内容。句子：(text)

English materials (text)

System: Please complete the following sentence. For example, if you hear 'I like to eat', you can answer 'apples'. Just answer with the completing content, don't say anything else. Sentence: (text)

SPACER: A Parallel Dataset of *S*peech *P*roduction *A*nd *C*omprehension of *E*rror *R*epairs

Shiva Upadhye* **Jiaxuan Li*** **Richard Futrell**
{shiva.upadhye, jiaxuan.li, rfutrell}@uci.edu
Department of Language Science
University of California, Irvine
**equal contribution*

Abstract

Speech errors are a natural part of communication, yet they rarely lead to complete communicative failure because both speakers and comprehenders can detect and correct errors. Although prior research has examined error monitoring and correction in production and comprehension separately, integrated investigation of both systems has been impeded by the scarcity of parallel data. In this study, we present *SPACER*, a parallel dataset that captures how naturalistic speech errors are corrected by both speakers and comprehenders. We focus on single-word substitution errors extracted from the Switchboard corpus, accompanied by speaker's self-repairs and comprehenders' responses from an offline text-editing experiment. Our exploratory analysis suggests asymmetries in error correction strategies: speakers are more likely to repair errors that introduce greater semantic and phonemic deviations, whereas comprehenders tend to correct errors that are phonemically similar to more plausible alternatives or do not fit into prior contexts. Our dataset [1] enables future research on integrated approaches toward studying language production and comprehension.

1 Introduction

Production errors are common in naturalistic speech; however, they rarely lead to a complete breakdown in communication, as interlocutors are able to monitor, detect, and repair errors in real-time. For this reason, characterizing the process of error correction has remained a shared goal of both language comprehension and production research.

Comprehenders process errors by integrating perceived linguistic input with prior context and expectations, and might arrive at an interpretation different from the literal meaning of the linguistic input (Ferreira et al., 2002; Ferreira and Stacey, 2000; Dempsey et al., 2023; Bader and Meng, 2018; Levy et al., 2009; Gibson et al., 2013). One possible mechanism is that they perform rational inference over the perceived errors (Levy et al., 2009; Levy, 2008; Gibson et al., 2013; Futrell et al., 2020; Ryskin et al., 2018; Poppels and Levy, 2016; Zhang et al., 2023). When the perceived form is incongruent with prior context or similar to a more plausible alternative, comprehenders might override the literal input and reconstruct an alternative interpretation.

In language production research, speech errors have played a crucial role in shaping our understanding of the cognitive machinery of production, including the role of online control (Fromkin and Fromkin, 1973; Levelt, 1983; Dell, 1986). Numerous studies analyzing the temporal and distributional properties of speech errors have found evidence of a two-stage monitoring and correction process, which operates first on internal representations and then on the articulated linguistic signal (Levelt, 1983; Blackmer and Mitton, 1991; Hartsuiker and Kolk, 2001; Nooteboom and Quené, 2017). Although the mechanism of monitoring has remained a point of contention in the literature (Levelt, 1999; Nozari et al., 2011; Hickok et al., 2011; Roelofs, 2020; Gauvin and Hartsuiker, 2020), accounts of repair processing have posited sustained competition between activated representations and selection control as potential mechanisms of correction (Hartsuiker and Kolk, 2001; Nozari et al., 2016; Nooteboom and Quené, 2019; Gauvin and Hartsuiker, 2020).

Much of our understanding of speakers and comprehenders' error correction strategies comes from research traditions that have made limited contact with each other. In particular, existing datasets or experimental paradigms focus solely on corrective behavior in the *absence* of an interlocutor. However, in a communicative context, speaker choices may exhibit a balance between ease of production

[1] The dataset and code are available at: https://github.com/goldengua/SPACER-CMCL

Proceedings of the Workshop on Cognitive Modeling and Computational Linguistics, pages 144–154
May 3, 2025

and communicative efficiency (Ferreira and Dell, 2000; Jaeger and Levy, 2006; Jaeger, 2010; Koranda et al., 2018; Goldberg and Ferreira, 2022; Futrell, 2023). For example, speakers may preemptively hyperarticulate words to improve comprehensibility (Aylett and Turk, 2004; Arnold et al., 2012; Meinhardt et al., 2020) or modulate the acoustic characteristics of their speech in response to listener feedback (Pate and Goldwater, 2015; Buz et al., 2016). Comprehension can be talker-specific as well: comprehenders can tailor their expectations to the speaker (Ryskin et al., 2020) and adapt their error correction strategies accordingly (Futrell and Gibson, 2017; Brehm et al., 2019).

In this study, we present a parallel dataset of Speech Production and Comprehension Error Repairs (*SPACER*) that captures how naturalistic speech errors are corrected by speakers and comprehenders. First, we compiled a corpus of naturalistic utterances with single-word substitution errors and repairs, as well as utterances that are not corrected by speakers. These utterances were then presented to comprehenders in a web-based text editing experiment, where each case is annotated by four to six comprehenders. Our dataset contains 1056 instances of naturalistic speaker's utterances as well 5808 comprehenders' responses to speaker's initial utterances. We also provide an exploratory analysis on how well comprehender's error correction behavior can be predicted by lexical properties of speaker's error and repairs, and vice versa. Our results suggest that asymmetries between error correction behaviors by comprehenders and speakers might be related to interaction between the two modes. The dataset offers resources to build experimental and computational work that bridges comprehension and production and informs how interaction affects strategic cue weighting in error monitoring.

2 Dataset

We focus on how comprehenders engage with utterances that may or may not have been corrected by a speaker in their original context. Figure 1 illustrates the design of the dataset. We assume that both the speaker and the comprehender can perform error correction, and we remain agnostic to the mechanism that accomplishes this process. Suppose a speaker produces an initial utterance (... *people don't want the heat of the northeast*), which may contain an error, or non-optimal choice of words. The speaker can monitor the initial utterance and *may* correct *heat* into *cold*. After receiving the initial utterance, comprehenders engage in an interpretation process, where the final response might not be the same as the literal meaning of the initial utterance.

The development of this dataset involved a two-step process. First, we identified and extracted utterances with and without word substitutions and overt repairs from the Switchboard corpus (Godfrey et al., 1992) of spontaneous speech. Subsequently, these utterances were presented as stimuli to participants in a web-based correction experiment. Hence, for each utterance, this dataset provides a speaker's final production along with a group of comprehenders' annotations. The two stages of this process are detailed below.

2.1 Naturalistic Speaker Correction Data

We identify and extract stimuli for the correction experiment from Switchboard NXT annotations (Calhoun et al., 2010), a subset of the Switchboard corpus that provides gold-standard disfluency annotations generated by human raters. While words in the corpus are annotated as *fluent*, *reparandum*, and *repair*, the *reparandum* label encompasses a variety of disfluencies such as filled pauses, false starts, repetitions, and substitutions. We programmatically identify substitutions using the following criteria. First, we only consider utterances with an equal number of *reparandum* and *repair* annotations to filter out instances where the speaker's utterance plan may have undergone structural revisions. Next, we focused on utterances where (i) the word labeled *reparandum* (bolded) was immediately followed by a **non-identical** word that was labeled *repair* (underlined; see 1) or where (ii) the speaker repeated the *reparandum* sequence almost verbatim except for a single-word change (2). Finally, we eliminated instances where the *reparandum* was either a filled pause, false start, repetition, or a contracted form [2].

1. I I think that might be **talking** <u>referring</u> to uh something kind of uh alternative to the draft you know

2. So until I see the entire quote old guard of the Soviet **military** of the Soviet <u>government</u>

[2]We eliminate instances of contractions such as *I've* since they are reduced forms of multiword expressions such as *I have*

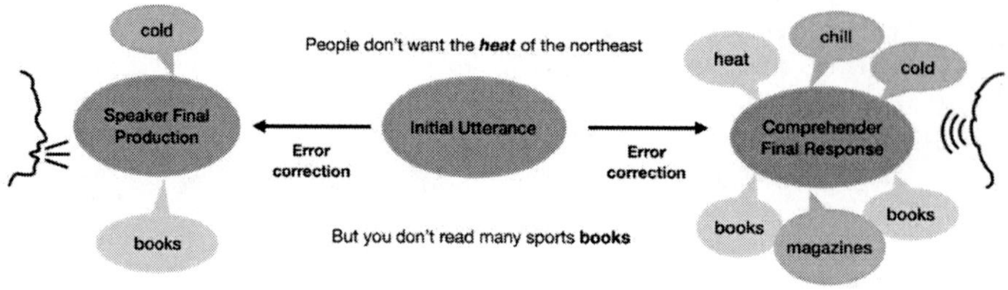

Figure 1: An illustration of the dataset design. Suppose a speaker produces an initial utterance. Both the speaker and the comprehender may engage in error monitoring and correction processes, resulting in speaker final production and comprehender final response being either the same as the initial utterance (represented in gray bubbles) or different from it (represented in green bubbles). Each utterance is annotated by four to six comprehenders.

> completely roll over and disappear preferably buried I still consider them a threat

For utterances with multiple substitutions and repairs, we generate variants of the original utterance with each containing only one reparandum-repair position (see Appendix A for examples).

Finally, the selected utterances were screened for inappropriate content by three human annotators. This process yielded a total of 576 distinct utterance frames that featured errors repaired by the speaker (henceforth, *speaker corrected* or **SC** utterances). Furthermore, we also included 480 sentences from the same corpus that did not feature any overt repair made by the speaker (henceforth, *speaker uncorrected* or **SU** utterances; see Fig. 2).

2.2 Correction Experiment

We conducted human error correction experiments to understand how selected utterances are corrected during comprehension. 66 native English speakers participated in the experiment. Participants were recruited online via Prolific and compensated at $16/hr. The experiment takes around 30 minutes.

The stimuli consisted of 1056 initial utterances, which included both the SC (*speaker corrected*) and SU (*speaker uncorrected*) utterances. We distributed the 1056 selected utterances into 12 lists. Each list contains 48 SC utterances and 40 SU utterances. Each list is annotated by four to six subjects.

The subjects are presented with initial utterances along with proceeding context, and are instructed to check the quality of the last sentence from speech transcriptions and make necessary corrections by replacing the erroneous word with a more appropriate choice (Fig. 3). They also received explicit instruction to avoid insertion or deletion of word(s) (see Appendix B for the detailed instructions provided to participants).

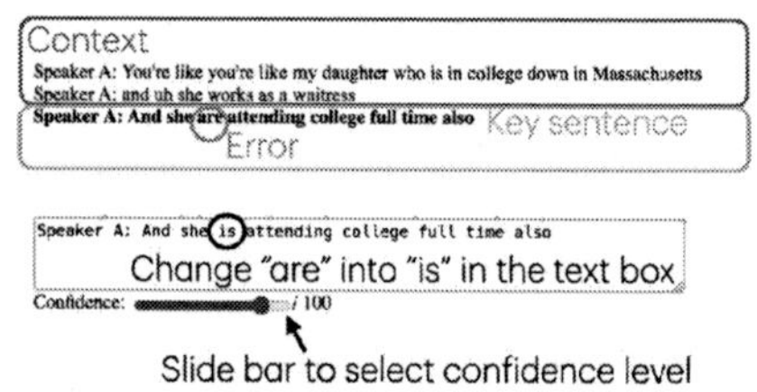

Figure 3: An illustration of comprehension experiment. A comprehender is presented with the *key sentence* together with preceding *context*. The comprehender is instructed to make necessary edits in the textbox and slide bar to indicate their confidence level.

We exclude subjects that made less than two corrections throughout the experiment ($N = 3$), and subjects who did not move confidence bars ($N = 3$). After subject exclusion, 528 trials were further removed because they contain word insertion or deletion, resulting in 5808 responses with either one or no substitution.

3 Analysis

3.1 Descriptive summary

As shown in Table 1, our dataset contain a total of 1056 initial utterances, where 576 initial utterances have been corrected by speakers (SC utterances). Each initial utterance is annotated by four to six comprehenders, yielding a total of 5808 responses with either one or no substitution. 34.7% of trials were corrected by the comprehender.

We focus on the items that are corrected by speakers (SC), and analyzed lexical properties of the critical target that has undergone correction (*error*) and its corresponding corrected form (*re-*

Speaker Uncorrected (SU)

Well when they meant the topic you know of what's wrong with the public schools my first impulse was it isn't really what's wrong with the public schools

Speaker Corrected (SC)

I don't think we've missed a fish store on the entire east → northeast coast of the United States

Like all these people are just standing → sitting around just going you know like what shall we do

Comprehender Uncorrected (CU)

Like all these people are just standing around just going you know like what shall we do

Comprehender Corrected (CC)

I don't think we've missed a fish → tourist store on the entire east coast of the United States

Well when they meant the topic you know of what's wrong with the public schools my first impulse → impression was it isn't really what's wrong with the public schools

Figure 2: Examples of *speaker uncorrected* (SU), *speaker corrected* (SC), *comprehender uncorrected* (CU), and *comprehender corrected* (CC) utterances in the SPACER dataset. Words highlighted in red were initially produced a speaker and later corrected. Words highlighted in green are corrections made by either the speaker in the original context or by a participant in the comprehension experiment. A grey highlight indicates that the word was not corrected by the participant. Note that for each SU and SC utterance, there may be up to four responses, which we classify as either CC or CU responses depending on whether or not the participant made a correction in their response.

	Comprehender		
	Corrected	Uncorrected	Total
Speaker Corrected	1437	1731	3168
Speaker Uncorrected	578	2062	2640
Total	2015	3793	5808

Table 1: Instances of *speaker corrected* and *speaker uncorrected* utterances that were corrected or remained uncorrected by participants in the correction experiment

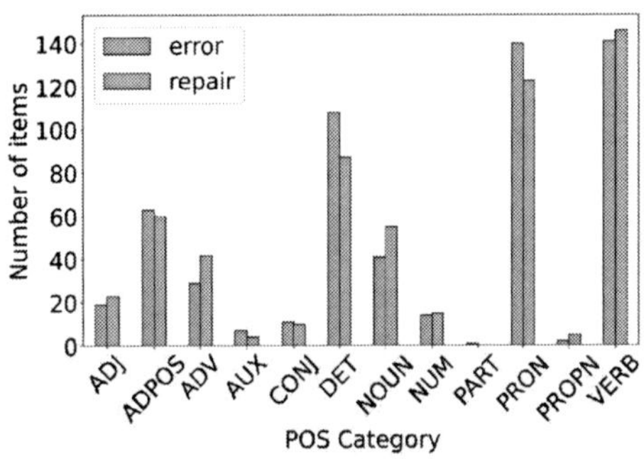

Figure 4: The POS categories of speaker-produced errors and corresponding repairs in *speaker corrected* utterances.

pair). We first analyzed the part-of-speech (POS) categories of the critical words (error and repair). Figure 4 shows the distribution of part-of-speech categories for speaker initial produced errors and the corresponding repairs. The errors and repairs vary by POS category, with determiners (DET), pronouns (PRON), and verbs (VERB) exhibiting the highest frequency of both errors and repairs, whereas auxiliaries (AUX), particles (PART), and proper nouns (PROPN) show relatively fewer occurrences.

We further analyzed how the POS categories of speaker-produced errors would affect comprehender's error correction behavior. Figure 5 shows the number of corrected and uncorrected responses given speaker-produced errors with different part-of-speech (POS) categories. The results suggest variation in comprehenders' tendency to correct errors depending on the POS category of the presented errors, with higher correction rates for determiners (DET), verbs (VERB), and pronouns (PRON).

We examined how often comprehenders corrected errors in speaker-corrected versus speaker-uncorrected utterances. Figure 6 presents the proportion of corrected and uncorrected responses across items in the *speaker uncorrected* items (top panel) and *speaker corrected* items (bottom panel). A higher proportion of items were corrected in the *speaker corrected* items than in *speaker uncorrected* items. While initial utterances that are corrected by speakers are also more likely to be corrected by comprehenders, there is great variation between items.

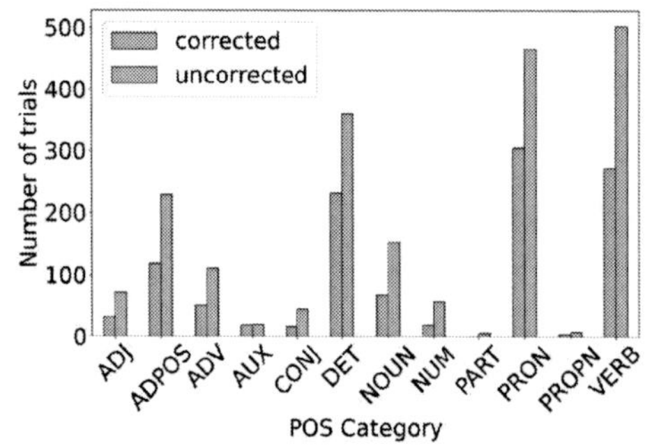

Figure 5: The number of corrected and uncorrected responses across different part-of-speech (POS) categories of presented errors in the *speaker corrected* utterances.

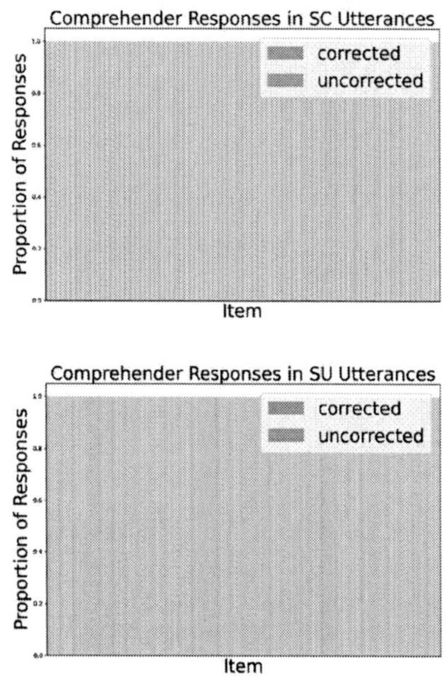

Figure 6: The proportion of corrected and uncorrected responses for each item in the *speaker corrected* condition (top) and *speaker uncorrected* condition (bottom). Each bar represents an individual item, with corrected responses shown in teal and uncorrected in gray.

3.2 Inter-rater agreement

Figure 7 shows the number of corrected and uncorrected responses by each subject. There is variability across subjects, with some participants correcting a substantial proportion of responses while others made few or no corrections. The average Cohen's Kappa across all lists is 0.213, indicating fair agreement between subjects. Figure 8 displays pairwise agreement scores between subjects across all items (distributed in 12 lists). This suggests that while some systematic agreement is present, variability in responses remains substantial.

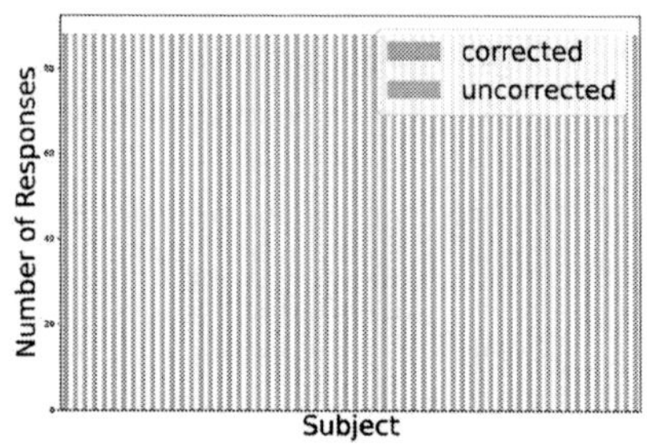

Figure 7: The number of corrected and uncorrected responses for each subject, sorted by the number of corrected responses.

3.3 Computational Metrics

For words that are corrected by either a speaker or a comprehender and their corresponding corrected counterparts, we calculated the following computational metrics: word predictability, word frequency in SUBTLEXus (Brysbaert and New, 2009), word length, semantic and phonemic distance between the initial word and the corrected word. We define word predictability as the log probability of the target word given proceeding context, which we estimated from a pre-trained GPT-2 (small, uncased) transformer language model (Radford et al., 2019; Misra, 2022). The semantic distance is calculated using the cosine distance between GloVe word embeddings (Pennington et al., 2014). To compute the phonemic distance, we first convert the words to their corresponding IPA forms using the Carnegie Mellon Pronouncing Dictionary, and subsequently compute the Levenshtein edit distance between these forms.

4 Exploratory Analysis: Modeling Corrections

The dataset could provide opportunities for the investigation of asymmetric strategies on error correction during language production and comprehension. We present an exploratory analysis that examines the parallels between speaker and comprehender corrections. In particular, we ask (i) whether the lexical properties of the speaker's error and repair are predictive of a comprehender's decision to correct and (ii) whether comprehender's responses over the perceived initial utterance are

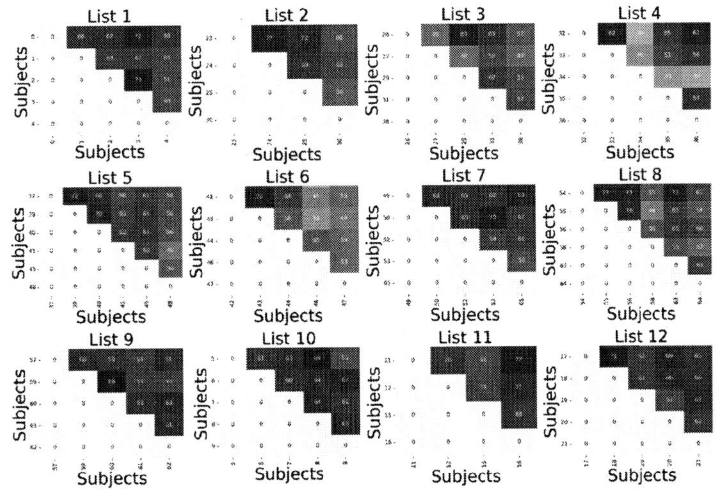

Figure 8: Pairwise agreement scores between subjects across 12 different lists of items.

predictive of the speaker's decision to repair. We model both these choices as functions of the relative **frequency** and **predictability** of the initially produced/perceived word and target correction, as well as the **phonemic** and **semantic** distance between these forms.

4.1 Speaker Model

A significant challenge in modeling whether or not a speaker has made correction in naturalistic contexts is that instances where a speaker *could* have made a correction but decided not to can only be reliably and accurately determined in highly controlled production studies. Here, we use comprehender corrections to approximate instances where a correction *could* have been made by the speaker. We make this assumption for two reasons. First, comprehender repairs give us a distribution over possible speaker repairs and *may* include the true repair. Furthermore, we assume that the speaker may be incentivized to correct when she believes there is a greater discrepancy between the speaker's intended and comprehender's inferred meaning respectively.

Consider the following corrections made by the original speaker and three of the comprehenders in the experiment. Based on observed corrections, we define a **critical window** at the position where either a speaker or a comprehender has made a correction.

3. *Speaker Corrected*: Well we also in this area seem to have a lot of retirees people who don't want the heat of Florida but don't want the cold of the northeast

4. *Comprehender Corrected* #1: Well we also in this area seem to have a lot of retirees people who don't want the heat of Florida but don't want the cold of the northeast

5. *Comprehender Corrected* #2: Well we also in this area seem to have a lot of retirees people who don't want the heat of Florida but don't want the chill of the northeast

6. *Comprehender Corrected* #3: Well we also in this area seem to have a lot of retired people who don't want the heat of Florida but don't want the heat of the northeast

For each critical window, we compute the difference in frequency, predictability, phonemic, and semantic representations of the speaker's initial production (e.g., *heat* or *retirees*) and the various comprehender responses in those positions (e.g., *chill* or *cold* in response to *heat* and *retired* in response to *retirees*). We develop the following maximally-converging mixed-effects logistic regression model (Barr et al., 2013) to predict correction decisions in speakers:

```
SpeakerCorrected ~ ΔLogProbability + ΔFrequency + Semantic Distance + Phonemic Distance + 1|item + 1|critical window
```

where Δ denotes the *difference* between the frequency and log probability of the speaker's initial production and the comprehender's response. We included random intercepts for item and critical window to account for the participant-level variability at each correction site. We set `SpeakerCorrected` $= 1$ for critical windows where the speaker did, in fact, make a repair (for example, 3–5). For all other instances, `SpeakerCorrected` $= 0$ (for example, 6).

4.2 Comprehender Model

When modeling comprehenders' corrections, we restrict the analysis to *speaker corrected* utterances. In particular, we only consider critical windows defined by the speaker's repair (3–5), thus excluding responses such as (6). We compare the word in the critical window in comprehender's final response (*chill* or *cold*) with the word in the perceived initial utterance (*heat*), and annotate it as *corrected* or *uncorrected*. We use the same metrics (relative frequency, predictability, semantic, and phonemic distance), which we calculate over the critical word in the initial utterance (*heat*) and the repair in speaker's final production (*cold*), to predict whether a comprehender will make a correction in their final response.

We then use the following parallel model to predict correction decisions in comprehenders:
`ComprehenderCorrected` $\sim$ `ΔLogProbability + ΔFrequency + Semantic Distance + Phonemic Distance + 1|item + 1|critical window + 1|subject`

4.3 Results

The results from the mixed-effects models reveal key asymmetries in how speakers and comprehenders decide to correct errors, with distinct influences from predictability, frequency, phonemic form, and semantic features. Model coefficients are summarized in Figure 9.

In the speaker model, the correction behavior is a function of the initially produced/perceived word and the comprehender's final response. When the log probability difference between the comprehender's final inferred response and their initial perceived word is higher, a speaker is less likely to self-correct ($\beta = -0.260, SE = 0.04, p < 0.01$). This suggests that if comprehenders could recover the intended meaning from the perceived erroneous form, the speaker is less likely to intervene. Additionally, greater semantic distance between the comprehender's initial perception and their final response increases the likelihood of correction ($\beta = 0.227, SE = 0.08, p < 0.05$), indicating that speakers are more likely to correct when their utterance creates a significant meaning deviation. Phonemic distance exhibits a similar effect, with greater phonemic dissimilarity between the comprehender's perceived word and the corrected form leading to a higher probability of correction ($\beta = 0.270, SE = 0.05, p < 0.001$). Word frequency does not significantly impact speaker correction behavior ($\beta = -0.05, SE = 0.04, p = 0.21$), suggesting that lexical frequency alone is not a primary driver of corrective processes in production.

In contrast, the comprehenders' corrections are based on the difference between the speaker's erroneous production and their intended repair. Unlike speakers, comprehenders are more likely to correct when the speaker's repair has a much higher log probability than the produced error, as indicated by a significant positive effect of log probability difference ($\beta = 0.278, SE = 0.07, p < 0.01$). This suggests that comprehenders rely more heavily on contextual expectations when detecting errors and overriding them. While semantic distance also increases the likelihood of correction ($\beta = 0.139, SE = 0.07, p < 0.05$), its effect is weaker compared to speakers, implying that comprehenders may is less sensitive to semantic deviations. Crucially, phonemic distance has the opposite effect in comprehension compared to production: while speakers are more likely to correct errors when phonemic distance is large, comprehenders exhibit reduced correction likelihood as phonemic distance increases ($\beta = -0.404, SE = 0.08, p < 0.001$), suggesting the comprehenders are more likely to correct errors that are phonemically similar to the intended meaning. As in the speaker model, frequency does not significantly influence comprehender corrections ($\beta = 0.0068, SE = 0.007, p = 0.92$).

5 Discussion

In this study, we develop *SPACER*, a parallel dataset of speech errors and repairs, which is designed to examine how speakers and comprehenders engage in error correction. We identified naturally occurring speech errors and repairs from speech corpus, and used web-based experiments to examine how speech errors are detected and corrected by comprehenders. We conducted exploratory analysis on the asymmetries of error correction strategies between production and comprehension. Specifically, we used linear models to predict whether lexical properties of speaker-produced

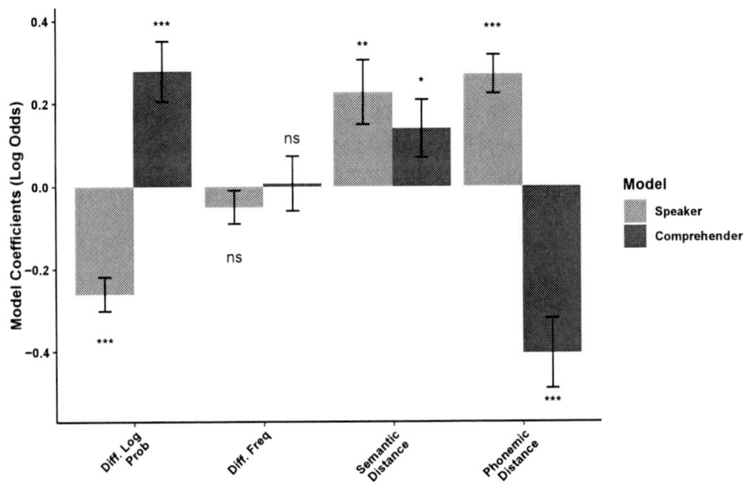

Figure 9: Model coefficients from speaker and comprehender logistic regression models. Error bars denote standard error. Significance: *** ($p < 0.001$), ** ($p < 0.01$), * ($p < 0.05$), *ns* ($p > 0.05$)

errors and repairs are predictive of how the errors would be corrected by comprehenders, and whether comprehender's error correction could inform the speaker's self-repair. Our analysis show asymmetries between error correction by speakers and comprehenders.

Our dataset links production and comprehension and enables a principled comparison between the two modes. Previous studies have largely examined production and comprehension of errors separately (Ryskin et al., 2018; Dell, 1986; Levelt, 1983; Blank et al., 2018), making it difficult to assess whether and how these processes might share underlying principles. Our dataset bridges the gap by examining how speakers and comprehenders make choices about error correction on the *same* utterance. This parallel structure enables integrated analysis of correction strategies in production and in comprehension, providing a valuable resource for future studies.

Our exploratory analysis reveals key asymmetries in how speakers and comprehenders engage in error correction. Comprehenders are likely to correct errors that are phonemically similar to a more plausible alternative, or when the error is not supported by contextual cues. Speakers, on the other hand, are more likely to self-correct errors that might not be recoverable for comprehenders. The asymmetries might imply potential interplay between comprehension and production, arising from differing demands of the two modalities: while speakers correct their own speech to ensure communicative clarity given the message that they know they want to communicate, comprehenders may be able to use predictability and form-based cues to successfully recover the intended word. The inverse effects of phonemic distance in our models —where comprehenders correct more when errors are phonemically similar to an alternative, while speakers correct more when errors are phonemically distant from the intended meaning – suggest that interlocutors may engage in complementary error correction strategies. Future work can leverage *SPACER* for more principled computational models that simulate error correction as a rational inference process over various linguistic constraints and cues.

6 Limitations

The dataset is restricted to single-word substitution errors and does not include other common types of speech error such as insertions, deletions, and transpositions. While this allows for a controlled investigation of the error correction process, it may not capture other types of errors and correction strategies in naturalistic communication. Future work could expand SPACER to include a broader range of error types to better understand the full spectrum of production and comprehension repair mechanisms.

A key challenge when studying how speakers may adapt their correction strategies in naturalistic contexts is that the intended lexical target is often difficult to determine. In other words, while speech error corpora provide *positive* examples of speaker corrections, they do not provide instances of *negative* examples i.e., where a speaker *could* have made a repair, but opted against it. Our corpus approach allows us to locate speech errors that have been overtly repaired, but we do not have access to speaker's true communicative goal to identify uncorrected speech errors. We used the distribution of comprehender corrections as an approximation for speaker's communicative goal, to identify errors that could have been corrected by the speaker but were left uncorrected. We acknowledge that the approximation may be different from the speaker's intended meaning.

We used a web-based experiment to investigate how utterances are interpreted and corrected by comprehenders. There are several differences between our experiment and real-time language comprehension. First, comprehenders were presented with the full key sentence, whereas listeners do not have access to the entire utterance at once. Second, comprehenders are given unlimited time to make corrections. In contrast, real-time comprehension is constrained by limited cognitive and processing resources. Third, the text-based presentation method does not provide prosodic and phonetic cues. Comprehenders might rely on disfluencies and pauses to detect errors. Finally, it bears mentioning that the speaker and comprehender corrections are situated in entirely different contexts, separated by both time and space.

7 Acknowledgements

We thank the anonymous reviewers at CMCL, members of the QuantLang Lab at UC Irvine and TedLab at MIT, and the audience at Human Sentence Processing (HSP 2023), Society for Computation in Linguistics (SCiL 2023), and California Meeting on Psycholinguistics (CAMP 2024) for their valuable feedback on previous iterations of this work.

References

Jennifer E Arnold, Jason M Kahn, and Giulia C Pancani. 2012. Audience design affects acoustic reduction via production facilitation. *Psychonomic bulletin & review*, 19:505–512.

Matthew Aylett and Alice Turk. 2004. The smooth signal redundancy hypothesis: A functional explanation for relationships between redundancy, prosodic prominence, and duration in spontaneous speech. *Language and speech*, 47(1):31–56.

Markus Bader and Michael Meng. 2018. The misinterpretation of noncanonical sentences revisited. *Journal of Experimental Psychology: Learning, Memory, and Cognition*, 44(8):1286.

Dale J. Barr, Roger Levy, Christoph Scheepers, and Harry J. Tily. 2013. Random effects structure for confirmatory hypothesis testing: Keep it maximal. *Journal of Memory and Language*, 68(3):255–278.

Elizabeth R Blackmer and Janet L Mitton. 1991. Theories of monitoring and the timing of repairs in spontaneous speech. *Cognition*, 39(3):173–194.

Helen Blank, Marlene Spangenberg, and Matthew H Davis. 2018. Neural prediction errors distinguish perception and misperception of speech. *Journal of Neuroscience*, 38(27):6076–6089.

Laurel Brehm, Carrie N Jackson, and Karen L Miller. 2019. Speaker-specific processing of anomalous utterances. *Quarterly Journal of Experimental Psychology*, 72(4):764–778.

Marc Brysbaert and Boris New. 2009. Moving beyond kučera and francis: A critical evaluation of current word frequency norms and the introduction of a new and improved word frequency measure for american english. *Behavior research methods*, 41(4):977–990.

Esteban Buz, Michael K Tanenhaus, and T Florian Jaeger. 2016. Dynamically adapted context-specific hyper-articulation: Feedback from interlocutors affects speakers' subsequent pronunciations. *Journal of memory and language*, 89:68–86.

Sasha Calhoun, Jean Carletta, Jason M. Brenier, Neil Mayo, Dan Jurafsky, Mark Steedman, and David Ian Beaver. 2010. The nxt-format switchboard corpus: a rich resource for investigating the syntax, semantics, pragmatics and prosody of dialogue. *Language Resources and Evaluation*, 44:387–419.

Gary S Dell. 1986. A spreading-activation theory of retrieval in sentence production. *Psychological review*, 93(3):283.

Jack Dempsey, Anna Tsiola, Suphasiree Chantavarin, Fernanda Ferreira, and Kiel Christianson. 2023. Nonce word evidence for the misinterpretation of implausible events. *Journal of Cognitive Psychology*, 35(5):526–544.

Fernanda Ferreira, Karl GD Bailey, and Vittoria Ferraro. 2002. Good-enough representations in language comprehension. *Current directions in psychological science*, 11(1):11–15.

Fernanda Ferreira and Janis Stacey. 2000. The misinterpretation of passive sentences. *Manuscript submitted for publication*. Publisher: Citeseer.

Victor S Ferreira and Gary S Dell. 2000. Effect of ambiguity and lexical availability on syntactic and lexical production. *Cognitive psychology*, 40(4):296–340.

Victoria Fromkin and Victoria Fromkin. 1973. *Speech errors as linguistic evidence*. Mouton The Hague.

Richard Futrell. 2023. Information-theoretic principles in incremental language production. *Proceedings of the National Academy of Sciences*, 120(39):e2220593120.

Richard Futrell and Edward Gibson. 2017. L2 processing as noisy channel language comprehension. *Bilingualism: Language and Cognition*, 20(4):683–684.

Richard Futrell, Edward Gibson, and Roger P. Levy. 2020. Lossy-context surprisal: An information-theoretic model of memory effects in sentence processing. *Cognitive science*, 44(3):e12814.

Hanna S Gauvin and Robert J Hartsuiker. 2020. Towards a new model of verbal monitoring. *Journal of Cognition*, 3(1).

Edward Gibson, Leon Bergen, and Steven T. Piantadosi. 2013. Rational integration of noisy evidence and prior semantic expectations in sentence interpretation. *Proceedings of the National Academy of Sciences*, 110(20):8051–8056.

John J Godfrey, Edward C Holliman, and Jane McDaniel. 1992. Switchboard: Telephone speech corpus for research and development. In *Acoustics, speech, and signal processing, ieee international conference on*, volume 1, pages 517–520. IEEE Computer Society.

Adele E Goldberg and Fernanda Ferreira. 2022. Good-enough language production. *Trends in Cognitive Sciences*, 26(4):300–311.

Robert J Hartsuiker and Herman HJ Kolk. 2001. Error monitoring in speech production: A computational test of the perceptual loop theory. *Cognitive psychology*, 42(2):113–157.

Gregory Hickok, John Houde, and Feng Rong. 2011. Sensorimotor integration in speech processing: computational basis and neural organization. *Neuron*, 69(3):407–422.

T Jaeger and Roger Levy. 2006. Speakers optimize information density through syntactic reduction. *Advances in neural information processing systems*, 19.

T Florian Jaeger. 2010. Redundancy and reduction: Speakers manage syntactic information density. *Cognitive psychology*, 61(1):23–62.

Mark Koranda, Martin Zettersten, and Maryellen C MacDonald. 2018. Word frequency can affect what you choose to say. In *CogSci*.

W Levelt. 1999. Producing spoken language. *The neurocognition of language*, pages 83–122.

Willem JM Levelt. 1983. Monitoring and self-repair in speech. *Cognition*, 14(1):41–104.

Roger Levy. 2008. A noisy-channel model of human sentence comprehension under uncertain input. In *Proceedings of the 2008 conference on empirical methods in natural language processing*, pages 234–243.

Roger Levy, Klinton Bicknell, Tim Slattery, and Keith Rayner. 2009. Eye movement evidence that readers maintain and act on uncertainty about past linguistic input. *Proceedings of the National Academy of Sciences*, 106(50):21086–21090.

Eric Meinhardt, Eric Baković, and Leon Bergen. 2020. Speakers enhance contextually confusable words. In *Proceedings of the 58th annual meeting of the association for computational linguistics*, pages 1991–2002.

Kanishka Misra. 2022. minicons: Enabling flexible behavioral and representational analyses of transformer language models. *arXiv preprint arXiv:2203.13112*.

Sieb Nooteboom and Hugo Quené. 2019. Temporal aspects of self-monitoring for speech errors. *Journal of Memory and Language*, 105:43–59.

Sieb G Nooteboom and Hugo Quené. 2017. Self-monitoring for speech errors: Two-stage detection and repair with and without auditory feedback. *Journal of Memory and Language*, 95:19–35.

Nazbanou Nozari, Gary S Dell, and Myrna F Schwartz. 2011. Is comprehension necessary for error detection? a conflict-based account of monitoring in speech production. *Cognitive psychology*, 63(1):1–33.

Nazbanou Nozari, Michael Freund, Bonnie Breining, Brenda Rapp, and Barry Gordon. 2016. Cognitive control during selection and repair in word production. *Language, cognition and neuroscience*, 31(7):886–903.

John K Pate and Sharon Goldwater. 2015. Talkers account for listener and channel characteristics to communicate efficiently. *Journal of Memory and Language*, 78:1–17.

Jeffrey Pennington, Richard Socher, and Christopher D Manning. 2014. Glove: Global vectors for word representation. In *Proceedings of the 2014 conference on empirical methods in natural language processing (EMNLP)*, pages 1532–1543.

Till Poppels and Roger Levy. 2016. Structure-sensitive noise inference: Comprehenders expect exchange errors. In *CogSci*.

Alec Radford, Jeffrey Wu, Rewon Child, David Luan, Dario Amodei, Ilya Sutskever, et al. 2019. Language models are unsupervised multitask learners. *OpenAI blog*, 1(8):9.

Ardi Roelofs. 2020. On (correctly representing) comprehension-based monitoring in speaking: Rejoinder to nozari (2020). *Journal of Cognition*, 3(1).

Rachel Ryskin, Richard Futrell, Swathi Kiran, and Edward Gibson. 2018. Comprehenders model the nature of noise in the environment. *Cognition*, 181:141–150.

Rachel Ryskin, Shukhan Ng, Katherine Mimnaugh, Sarah Brown-Schmidt, and Kara D Federmeier. 2020. Talker-specific predictions during language processing. *Language, cognition and neuroscience*, 35(6):797–812.

Yuhan Zhang, Rachel Ryskin, and Edward Gibson. 2023. A noisy-channel approach to depth-charge illusions. *Cognition*, 232:105346.

A Example items and illustration of the pre-processing pipeline

- Original utterance: it depends on whether **you** whether <u>we</u> figure that we have a defense oriented military or an **aggressive** <u>aggression</u> oriented military

- Frame 1: it depends on whether **you** whether <u>we</u> figure that we have a defense oriented military or an aggression oriented military

- Frame 2: it depends on whether we figure that we have a defense oriented military or an **aggressive** <u>aggression</u> oriented military

B Instructions and prompts provided to participants in the web-based editing experiment

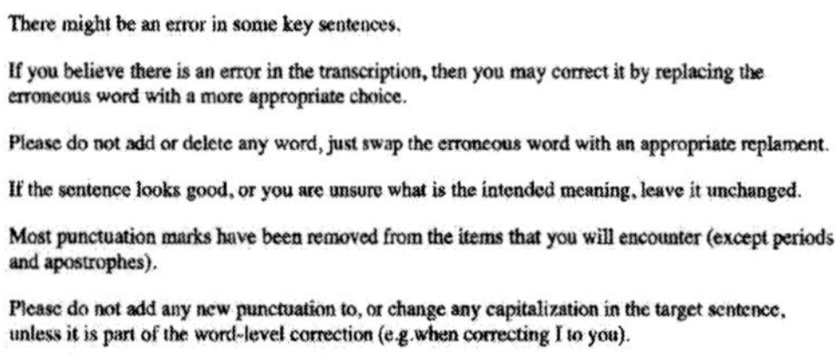

Figure 10: Instructions provided to participants at the beginning of the error correction experiment.

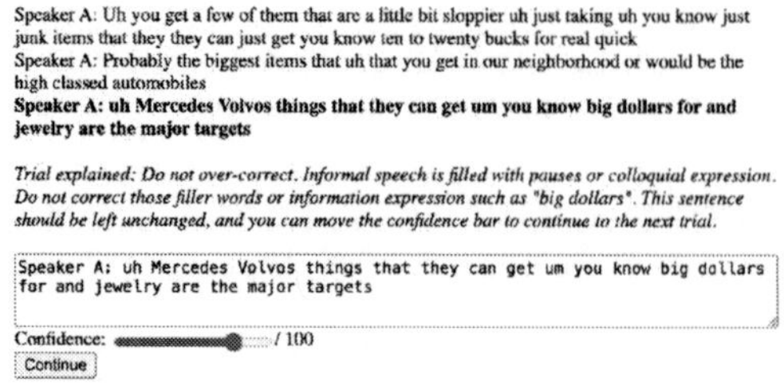

Figure 11: Sample practice trial with feedback to ensure familiarization with the above instructions.

Are Larger Language Models Better at Disambiguation?

Ziyuan Cao
Department of Linguistics
The Ohio State University
cao.1610@osu.edu

William Schuler
Department of Linguistics
The Ohio State University
schuler.77@osu.edu

Abstract

Humans deal with temporary syntactic ambiguity all the time in incremental sentence processing. Sentences with temporary ambiguity that causes processing difficulties, often reflected by increase in reading time, are referred to as garden-path sentences. Garden-path theories of sentence processing attribute the increases in reading time to the reanalysis of the previously ambiguous syntactic structure to make it consistent with the new disambiguating text. It is unknown whether transformer-based language models successfully resolve the temporary ambiguity after encountering the disambiguating text. We investigated this question by analyzing completions generated from language models for a type of garden-path sentence with ambiguity between a complement clause interpretation and a relative clause interpretation. We found that larger language models are worse at resolving such ambiguity.

1 Introduction

Linguistic analysis of neural language models suggests that pre-trained language models capture the syntax of natural languages (Hewitt and Manning, 2019) and represent the incremental syntactic processing states similar to those of humans (Marvin and Linzen, 2018; Futrell et al., 2019). People experience processing difficulties while they encounter a continuation of a sentence that conforms to the less likely interpretation of the previously ambiguous syntactic structure. Such processing difficulties, called garden path effects, can be observed in eye-tracking and self-paced reading experiments as increases in reading time for the disambiguating continuation (Frazier and Rayner, 1982; Christianson et al., 2001). Through the surprisal theory (Hale, 2001; Levy, 2008), prior studies observed garden path effects in autoregressive language models (van Schijndel and Linzen, 2018; Futrell et al., 2019). However, it is unclear whether autoregressive language models finally resolve the temporary syntactic ambiguity after being exposed to the disambiguating text.

We probed the incremental syntactic representations of language models by analyzing their completions of garden-path prefixes. We used a set of garden-path sentences that were originally curated to study the garden-path effect in humans (Altmann et al., 1992). We chose this set of garden-path sentences since completions of this set of sentences generated by language models seem to be indicative of their incremental syntactic representations. In other words, the completions generated by a language model can be used to probe whether the language model successfully resolves the temporary syntactic ambiguity after they have seen the disambiguating text.

We gathered 30 garden-path sentences from Altmann et al. (1992) and modified some of them to make each of them have a similar form. We evaluated autoregressive language models of five families on whether each of them successfully resolve the temporary ambiguity in each of the 30 garden-path sentences. For each model, we sampled 50 completions and used a dependency parser to judge whether each completion is grammatically correct. Aggregating those judgments, we found that larger language models are worse at resolving temporary ambiguities. A follow-up experiment based on models' preference between two possible continuations of garden path prefixes showed the same trend with weaker significance. Overall, this paper provides evidence that larger language models are worse at recovering from syntactic ambiguity, suggesting that they are not maintaining explicit syntactic structures.

2 Related Work

Multiple studies have found that larger language models are not always better. From a behavioral perspective, a recent inverse scaling challenge col-

Proceedings of the Workshop on Cognitive Modeling and Computational Linguistics, pages 155–164
May 3, 2025

lected and reported a diverse set of tasks which the larger language models show worse performance (McKenzie et al., 2023). Most tasks reported are not about fundamental linguistic capabilities. For example, one of the tasks involves redefining particular symbols and evaluating whether language models recognize the redefinition. Another study looked at how BERT-style models understand garden path sentences via auxiliary question answering tasks and found that BERT-style models do not perform better than humans on question answering accuracy despite being bidirectional (Irwin et al., 2023).

From a cognitive modeling perspective, it was shown that surprisals from larger and more capable (measured by perplexity) language models are worse at predicting human reading time of naturally occurring texts due to their superhuman capabilities of predicting rare words. (Oh and Schuler, 2023; Oh et al., 2024). It was also shown that surprisals from neural language models cannot entirely explain human syntactic processing difficulties (van Schijndel and Linzen, 2020; Arehalli et al., 2022; Huang et al., 2024). The lack of explanatory power, however, is not compared among models of different sizes.

Several works have looked at how language models handle ambiguity. Aina and Linzen (2021) studied whether language models recognize structural ambiguities by analyzing completions from the models. However, it did not focus on comparing models of varying sizes. Hanna and Mueller (2024) investigated how language models process garden-path sentences with mechanistic interpretation. Irwin et al. (2023); Li et al. (2024); Amouyal et al. (2025) investigated how language models process garden-path sentences with question answering. However, those work only looked at how language models process garden-path sentences indirectly through comprehension questions.

3 Experiment 1: Probing for Syntactic Representation by Completions

The purpose of this experiment is to compare how language models of different sizes resolve temporary syntactic ambiguity. We chose garden path sentences where the completions generated by a language model are indicative of its incremental syntactic representation. The original material was collected by Altmann et al. (1992) to investigate the effect of referential context on sentence processing.

An example garden path sentence of our evaluation set is

(1) The householder told the builder that he had arranged to pay that the bill was fair.

Until one encounters *that the bill*, the sentence is ambiguous. The segment of text, *that he had arranged to pay*, can be interpreted as either a relative clause or a (partial) sentential complement clause. After one encounters *that the bill*, this ambiguity can be resolved. At this point, the relative clause interpretation is the only consistent interpretation. Increase in reading time was observed for the disambiguating region, *that the bill*, in the garden path sentence compared to that of a non-ambiguous control (Altmann et al., 1992). Garden path theories predict that one will adopt the sentential complement interpretation at first (Frazier and Rayner, 1982). It attributes the increase in reading time to the reanalysis of structure after one encounters the disambiguating texts. However, it is possible that language models are led down the garden path and don't resolve the ambiguity even after encountering the disambiguating region.

To find out whether a language model resolves the temporary ambiguity, consider the disambiguated prefix,

(2) The householder told the builder that he had arranged to pay that the bill ...

If a language model successfully resolves the temporary ambiguity, it should recognize that *the bill* is the subject of a clause that serves as the complement of the predicate *told*. On the other hand, if a language model fails to resolve the ambiguity, the model often incorrectly treats *the bill* as the complement of *pay* and it may generate ungrammatical completions without a complete sentential complement. An example ungrammatical completions generated by a language model is

(3) * The householder told the builder that he had arranged to pay that the bill in two weeks.

Therefore the completions generated by language models can serve as a probe for the incremental syntactic representation of the language models.

Materials We gathered 30 sentences from Altmann et al. (1992) and transformed them into a similar form such that each sentence contains a temporary syntactic ambiguity between a relative

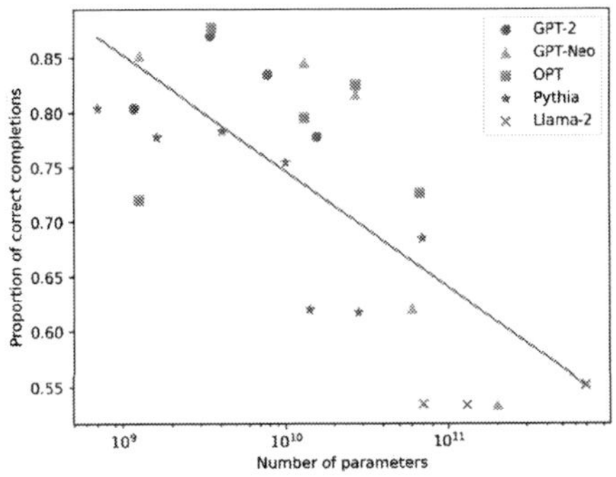

Figure 1: The proportion of grammatical completions for models of different sizes. It shows a log-linear relationship between the model's size and proportion of grammatical completions. A permutation test (10,000 samples) shows that the negative slope is significant ($p < 0.005$).

clause interpretation and a complement clause interpretation and the disambiguating region starts with a noun phrase (e.g., *the bill*) which is the subject for another clause. We provided the disambiguated prefixes of a similar form as that of Example 2 to the language model. The full prefixes can be found the in appendix A.

Evaluation For each prefix, we sampled 50 completions (with temperature = 1) from language models with different sizes in five model families, including GPT-2 (Radford et al., 2019), GPT-Neo (Black et al., 2021, 2022), OPT (Zhang et al., 2022), Pythia (Biderman et al., 2023), and Llama-2 (Touvron et al., 2023). We measured how well each model resolves the ambiguity by the proportion of grammatical completions that it generated. To judge whether a completion is grammatical, we can look at whether the model's completion treats the noun phrase at the end of the prefix as the subject of a complete clause. We automatically analyzed the structure of the part of the sentence after the second complementizer *that* using the spaCy dependency parser (Honnibal and Johnson, 2015). If the noun phrase in the disambiguating region is annotated as the subject of a clause, we know that the completion is grammatical. On the other hand, if it is annotated as the root of the tree, we know that the completion is ungrammatical. We observed that the dependency parser correctly discriminates between the two cases for 98 out of 100 sampled model completions. Note that this automatic labeling scheme may produce false positives since a completion may still be ungrammatical even if the noun phrase in the disambiguating region is treated as the subject of the complement clause. However, we observed that this rarely happens on our test sentences and it can only underestimate the proportion of ungrammatical completions.

Result We calculated the accuracy of each model as the proportion of completions that are grammatical. The accuracy of each language model is shown in Figure 1. The line fit shows a trend that larger models are worse at generating grammatical completions. A permutation test was conducted to determine the significance of the slope. Each simulation was constructed by randomly permuting the sample completions among all different models. A permutation test of 10,000 simulation shows that the negative slope is highly significant ($p < 0.005$).

Discussion The result that larger language models are worse at resolving temporary syntactic ambiguities is at first surprising. It contradicts the perceived general trend that larger language models have better linguistic capabilities (though see Oh and Schuler (2023); Oh et al. (2024)).

This result, however, does not imply that smaller language models are better at resolving temporary ambiguities. It is possible that smaller language models focus on the more recent information while completing a prefix. In contrast, larger language models may rely on the broader context and treat the disambiguating texts as a text error. The next experiment investigates this hypothesis using a modified set of sentences used in experiment 1.

4 Experiment 2

A follow-up experiment was conducted to test whether larger language models are more likely to treat the local contradicting information as a text error compared to smaller language models. To test this, we present the model a set of prefixes with text errors near the end. The following is one example of such prefixes,

(4) * The householder had arranged to pay that the bill ...

This prefix is constructed by removing the main predicate with the ambiguous relative clause from the same stimulus used in experiment 1. Note that there is no obvious grammatical completion of Example 4. If it is the case that smaller language

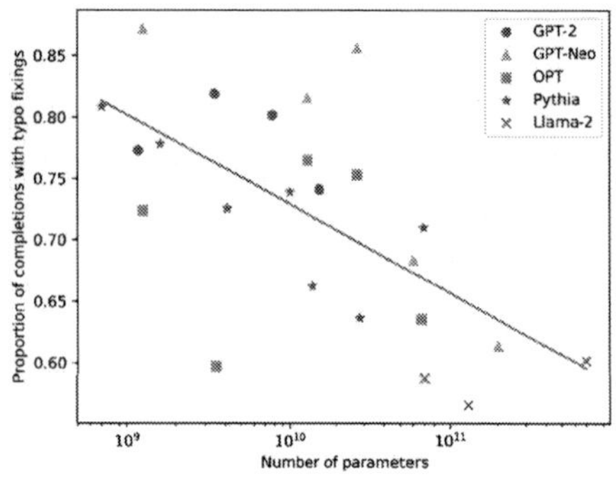

Figure 2: This figure shows the tendency of different models on recognizing text errors. Larger language models tend to treat the local contradicting information as text errors while smaller language models tend to ignore the broader context.

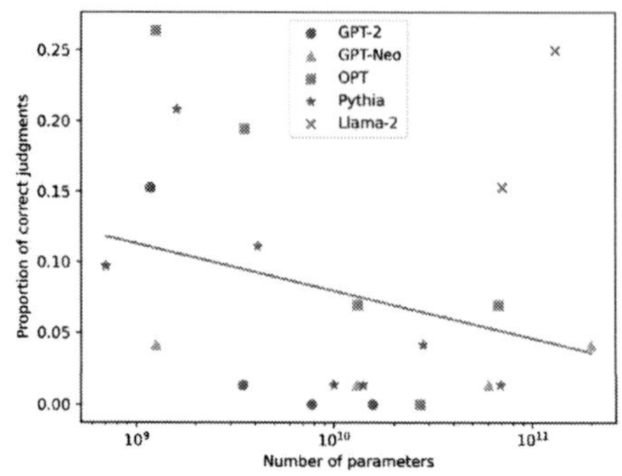

Figure 3: Proportion of correct judgments for models of different sizes.

models are more likely to focus on the more recent information but larger language models tend to focus on the broader context, the smaller models will complete the prefix as if *the bill* is a subject that starts a clause and the larger models will complete the prefix as if *that the bill* is a text error. Here's one example completion which indicates that the language model treats the end of the prefix as a text error as if the word "that" was not in the sentence,

(5) * The householder had arranged to pay that the bill to the landlord.

Similar to experiment 1, we used the completions generated by a language model to probe for the model's representation of the prefix.

Materials We modified the 30 sentences used in experiment 1 to make each of them have a similar form as example 4. Each sentence contains a text error with a duplicate determiner.

Evaluation Similar to experiment 1, for each model and each prefix, we sampled 50 completions. To distinguish whether the model treats the duplicate determiners as a text error, we used the spaCy dependency parser to recognize whether the noun phrase at the end of the prefix is the root of the dependency tree. We aggregated all the completions generated by the language model to calculate the proportion of the completions where the duplicate determiners are recognized as a typo.

Result As shown in Figure 2, larger models are more likely to recognize the duplicate determiners as a text error and complete as if only one determiner exists while smaller models are more likely to ignore the earlier part of the prefix and complete it as if the noun phrase at the end is the start of a clause.

5 Experiment 3: Probing for Syntactic Representation by Targeted Evaluation

The method used in experiment 1 can reveal whether language models resolve the ambiguity between the relative clause interpretation and the sentential clause interpretation. However, it is not clear how it can be applied to investigate language models' representation of other types of ambiguities. In this experiment, we used syntactic judgment of language models to probe how they represent garden path prefixes. Consider a pair of prefixes that only differ in the last token, such as,

(6) David's father told the builder that David's mother had arranged to pay that the bills were fair and was proud of himself/*herself.

If the language model successfully discards the sentential clause interpretation, it should prefer *himself* over *herself.* Therefore language models preference on such pairs of prefixes can shed light on whether they disambiguate garden path prefixes.

Materials We gathered 36 sentences with ambiguity between a relative clause interpretation and a sentential clause interpretation from Altmann et al. (1992). We manipulated the gender of the subject of the matrix clause and that of the subject of the relative clause and append *and was proud of* *himself/herself* at the end of each sentence. This resulted in 72 pairs of sentences. One of the sentence in each pair indicates successful disambiguation and the other sentence indicates incorrect representation. The complete set of test sentences is in Appendix B.

Result As shown in Figure 3, we observed a trend that larger language models produce fewer correct judgments. A permutation test shows a weak significance of this trend ($p < 0.1$).

6 Conclusion

By analyzing completions of garden-path sentences generated by language models and examining the preference of language models on a set of pairs of garden path sentences, we showed that larger language models are worse at resolving temporary syntactic ambiguities. This challenges the view that neural language models maintain explicit syntactic structure during their incremental processing of language.

7 Limitations

We only investigated models' behavior on limited types of garden-path sentences since it is not obvious how completions of other types of garden-path sentences can tell us whether the model successfully resolves the ambiguity. Also, we only investigated language models' behavior in English. In experiment 3, we noticed that the two Llama-2 variants have comparable performance as the smaller GPT2 variants and OPT variants. It is possible that the trend is reversed for models that are larger than the ones we tested with. We leave it for future work.

References

Laura Aina and Tal Linzen. 2021. The language model understood the prompt was ambiguous: Probing syntactic uncertainty through generation. In *Proceedings of the Fourth BlackboxNLP Workshop on Analyzing and Interpreting Neural Networks for NLP*, pages 42–57, Punta Cana, Dominican Republic. Association for Computational Linguistics.

Gerry T. M. Altmann, Alan Garnham, and Yvette Dennis. 1992. Avoiding the garden path: Eye movements in context. *Journal of Memory and Language*, 31:685–712.

Samuel Joseph Amouyal, Aya Meltzer-Asscher, and Jonathan Berant. 2025. When the lm misunderstood the human chuckled: Analyzing garden path effects in humans and language models. *arXiv preprint arXiv:2502.09307*.

Suhas Arehalli, Brian Dillon, and Tal Linzen. 2022. Syntactic surprisal from neural models predicts, but underestimates, human processing difficulty from syntactic ambiguities. In *Proceedings of the 26th Conference on Computational Natural Language Learning (CoNLL)*, pages 301–313, Abu Dhabi, United Arab Emirates (Hybrid). Association for Computational Linguistics.

Stella Biderman, Hailey Schoelkopf, Quentin Gregory Anthony, Herbie Bradley, Kyle O'Brien, Eric Hallahan, Mohammad Aflah Khan, Shivanshu Purohit, USVSN Sai Prashanth, Edward Raff, et al. 2023. Pythia: A suite for analyzing large language models across training and scaling. In *International Conference on Machine Learning*, pages 2397–2430. PMLR.

Sid Black, Stella Biderman, Eric Hallahan, Quentin Anthony, Leo Gao, Laurence Golding, Horace He, Connor Leahy, Kyle McDonell, Jason Phang, et al. 2022. Gpt-neox-20b: An open-source autoregressive language model. *arXiv preprint arXiv:2204.06745*.

Sid Black, Leo Gao, Phil Wang, Connor Leahy, and Stella Biderman. 2021. Gpt-neo: Large scale autoregressive language modeling with mesh-tensorflow.

Kiel Christianson, Andrew Hollingworth, John F. Halliwell, and Fernanda Ferreira. 2001. Thematic roles assigned along the garden path linger. *Cognitive Psychology*, 42:368–407.

Lyn Frazier and Keith Rayner. 1982. Making and correcting errors during sentence comprehension: Eye movements in the analysis of structurally ambiguous sentences. *Cognitive Psychology*, 14:178–210.

Richard Futrell, Ethan Wilcox, Takashi Morita, Peng Qian, Miguel Ballesteros, and Roger Levy. 2019. Neural language models as psycholinguistic subjects: Representations of syntactic state. In *Proceedings of the 2019 Conference of the North American Chapter of the Association for Computational Linguistics: Human Language Technologies, Volume 1 (Long and Short Papers)*, pages 32–42, Minneapolis, Minnesota. Association for Computational Linguistics.

John Hale. 2001. A probabilistic earley parser as a psycholinguistic model. In *North American Chapter of the Association for Computational Linguistics*.

Michael Hanna and Aaron Mueller. 2024. Incremental sentence processing mechanisms in autoregressive transformer language models. *arXiv preprint arXiv:2412.05353*.

John Hewitt and Christopher D. Manning. 2019. A structural probe for finding syntax in word representations. In *North American Chapter of the Association for Computational Linguistics*.

Matthew Honnibal and Mark Johnson. 2015. An improved non-monotonic transition system for dependency parsing. In *Conference on Empirical Methods in Natural Language Processing*.

Kuan-Jung Huang, Suhas Arehalli, Mari Kugemoto, Christian Muxica, Grusha Prasad, Brian Dillon, and Tal Linzen. 2024. Large-scale benchmark yields no evidence that language model surprisal explains syntactic disambiguation difficulty. *Journal of Memory and Language*, 137:104510.

Tovah Irwin, Kyra Wilson, and Alec Marantz. 2023. Bert shows garden path effects. In *Conference of the European Chapter of the Association for Computational Linguistics*.

R. Levy. 2008. Expectation-based syntactic comprehension. *Cognition*, 106:1126–1177.

Andrew Li, Xianle Feng, Siddhant Narang, Austin Peng, Tianle Cai, Raj Sanjay Shah, and Sashank Varma. 2024. Incremental comprehension of garden-path sentences by large language models: Semantic interpretation, syntactic re-analysis, and attention. *arXiv preprint arXiv:2405.16042*.

Rebecca Marvin and Tal Linzen. 2018. Targeted syntactic evaluation of language models. In *Proceedings of the 2018 Conference on Empirical Methods in Natural Language Processing*, pages 1192–1202, Brussels, Belgium. Association for Computational Linguistics.

Ian R. McKenzie, Alexander Lyzhov, Michael Martin Pieler, Alicia Parrish, Aaron Mueller, Ameya Prabhu, Euan McLean, Aaron Kirtland, Alexis Ross, Alisa Liu, Andrew Gritsevskiy, Daniel Wurgaft, Derik Kauffman, Gabriel Recchia, Jiacheng Liu, Joe Cavanagh, Max Weiss, Sicong Huang, The Floating Droid, Tom Tseng, Tomasz Korbak, Xudong Shen, Yuhui Zhang, Zhengping Zhou, Najoung Kim, Sam Bowman, and Ethan Perez. 2023. Inverse scaling: When bigger isn't better. *Trans. Mach. Learn. Res.*, 2023.

Byung-Doh Oh and William Schuler. 2023. Why does surprisal from larger transformer-based language models provide a poorer fit to human reading times? *Transactions of the Association for Computational Linguistics*, 11:336–350.

Byung-Doh Oh, Shisen Yue, and William Schuler. 2024. Frequency explains the inverse correlation of large language models' size, training data amount, and surprisal's fit to reading times. *ArXiv*, abs/2402.02255.

Alec Radford, Jeffrey Wu, Rewon Child, David Luan, Dario Amodei, Ilya Sutskever, et al. 2019. Language models are unsupervised multitask learners. *OpenAI blog*, 1(8):9.

Hugo Touvron, Louis Martin, Kevin Stone, Peter Albert, Amjad Almahairi, Yasmine Babaei, Nikolay Bashlykov, Soumya Batra, Prajjwal Bhargava, Shruti Bhosale, et al. 2023. Llama 2: Open foundation and fine-tuned chat models. *arXiv preprint arXiv:2307.09288*.

Marten van Schijndel and Tal Linzen. 2018. Modeling garden path effects without explicit hierarchical syntax. *Cognitive Science*.

Marten van Schijndel and Tal Linzen. 2020. Single-stage prediction models do not explain the magnitude of syntactic disambiguation difficulty. *Cognitive science*, 45 6:e12988.

Susan Zhang, Stephen Roller, Naman Goyal, Mikel Artetxe, Moya Chen, Shuohui Chen, Christopher Dewan, Mona Diab, Xian Li, Xi Victoria Lin, et al. 2022. Opt: Open pre-trained transformer language models. *arXiv preprint arXiv:2205.01068*.

A Stimuli for experiment 1

1 The householder told the builder that he had arranged to pay that the bill

2 The woman told the policeman that she had been trying to avoid that the arrestment

3 The student told the tutor that she had consulted that the professor

4 The doctor told the patient that she had been ready to examine that the X ray

5 The captain told the colonel that he had contacted that the commander

6 The manager told the woman that he was confident about that the project

7 The minister told the councilor that he had agreed to see that the proposal

8 The bank manager told the woman that he had misunderstood that the situation

9 The driving instructor told the woman that he had been impressed by that her skill

10 The solicitor told the woman that he had doubts about that the validity

11 The headmistres told the boy that she was worried about that his behavior

12 The sales assistant told the man that she had dealt with that the faults

13 The journalist told the woman that he had been working with that the next issue

14 The doctor told the woman that he was worried about that the health condition

15 The electrician told the man that he was impressed by that his explanation

16 The teacher told the father that she was shocked by that his attitude

17 The musician told the guitarist that he was impressed by that the play

18 The auctioneer told the woman that he had just sold a painting for that the price

19 The politician told the journalist that he agreed with that the deal

20 The Queen Mother told the comedian that she was amused by that the show

21 The film director told the actress that he had heard of that her accomplishments

22 The baker told the old lady that he had been baked a cake for that the party

23 The couple told the boy that they had brought a gift for that their child

24 The photographer told the model that he had taken bad photos of that the pose

25 The social worker told the father that she was horrified by that his attitude

26 The ski instructor told the girl that he was happy with that her performance

27 The patient told the nurse that he was complaining about that the chest pain

28 The young boy told the girl that he was frightened of that his classmate

29 The man told the policewoman that he had been talking to that the young girl

30 The antique dealer told the woman that he was talking to that another dealer

B Stimuli for experiment 3

1 John's mother told the builder that John's father had arranged to pay that the bills were very fair and was proud of **herself**/himself

2 John's mother told the tutor that John's father had consulted that the projects had been boring and was proud of **herself**/himself

3 John's mother told the policewomen that John's father had been talking to that the incidents were terrifying and was proud of **herself**/himself

4 John's mother told the patient that John's father had some good news about that the X ray images were clear and was proud of **herself**/himself

5 John's mother told the colonel that John's father had contacted that the enemies were now advancing and was proud of **herself**/himself

6 John's mother told the man that John's father had been insulted by to take a running jump and was proud of **herself**/himself

7 John's mother told the woman that John's father was confident about to return in a fortnight and was proud of **herself**/himself

8 John's mother told the councillor that John's father had agreed to see to submit further details and was proud of **herself**/himself

9 John's mother told the policeman that John's father had been trying to avoid to contact the lawyer and was proud of **herself**/himself

10 John's mother told the woman that John's father had misunderstood to repeat the last question and was proud of **herself**/himself

11 John's mother told the officer that John's father had been meeting that gradually things were changing and was proud of **herself**/himself

12 John's mother told the woman that John's father had been impressed by to ensure she drove with care and was proud of **herself**/himself

13 John's mother told the woman that John's father had doubts about to confirm the new statement and was proud of **herself**/himself

14 John's mother told the boy that John's father was worried about to concentrate on his homework and was proud of **herself**/himself

15 John's mother told the man that John's father had dealt with that the faults would be repaired and was proud of **herself**/himself

16 John's mother told the woman that John's father had been working with to outline the next case and was proud of **herself**/himself

17 John's mother told the woman that John's father was worried about to be positive about the illness and was proud of **herself**/himself

18 John's mother told the woman that John's father was impressed by to explain it all to her friend and was proud of **herself**/himself

19 John's mother told the father that John's father was shocked by that his attitude was appalling and was proud of **herself**/himself

20 John's mother told the guitarist that John's father was impressed by to audition again on Friday and was proud of **herself**/himself

21 John's mother told the wife that John's father was worried about to come and visit more often and was proud of **herself**/himself

22 John's mother told the woman that John's father had risked his life for to install a smoke detector and was proud of **herself**/himself

23 John's mother told the woman that John's father had just sold a painting for to give him the fee and was proud of **herself**/himself

24 John's mother told the man that John's father was pleased to see to order another coffee and was proud of **herself**/himself

25 John's mother told the journalist that John's father agreed with to write a report on the subject and was proud of **herself**/himself

26 John's mother told the comedian that John's father was amused by to impersonate the other guests and was proud of **herself**/himself

27 John's mother told the actress that John's father had heard of to audition for the next film and was proud of **herself**/himself

28 John's mother told the old lady that John's father had baked a cake for to pay the bill on Saturday and was proud of **herself**/himself

29 John's mother told the boy that John's father had brought a gift for to share it with his friend and was proud of **herself**/himself

30 John's mother told the woman that John's father wanted to go with to meet her outside the museum and was proud of **herself**/himself

31 John's mother told the woman that John's father was talking to that the chairs were exquisite and was proud of **herself**/himself

32 John's mother told the model that John's father had taken bad photos of to pose again the next day and was proud of **herself**/himself

33 John's mother told the father that John's father was horrified by to change his attitude and was proud of **herself**/himself

34 John's mother told the girl that John's father was happy with to try a more difficult slope and was proud of **herself**/himself

35 John's mother told the nurse that John's father was complaining about to treat her with more care and was proud of **herself**/himself

36 John's mother told the girl that John's father was frightened of to bully someone her own age and was proud of **herself**/himself

37 John's father told the builder that John's mother had arranged to pay that the bills were very fair and was proud of **himself**/herself

38 John's father told the tutor that John's mother had consulted that the projects had been boring and was proud of **himself**/herself

39 John's father told the policewomen that John's mother had been talking to that the incidents were terrifying and was proud of **himself**/herself

40 John's father told the patient that John's mother had some good news about that the X ray images were clear and was proud of **himself**/herself

41 John's father told the colonel that John's mother had contacted that the enemies were now advancing and was proud of **himself**/herself

42 John's father told the man that John's mother had been insulted by to take a running jump and was proud of **himself**/herself

43 John's father told the woman that John's mother was confident about to return in a fortnight and was proud of **himself**/herself

44 John's father told the councillor that John's mother had agreed to see to submit further details and was proud of **himself**/herself

45 John's father told the policeman that John's mother had been trying to avoid to contact the lawyer and was proud of **himself**/herself

46 John's father told the woman that John's mother had misunderstood to repeat the last question and was proud of **himself**/herself

47 John's father told the officer that John's mother had been meeting that gradually things were changing and was proud of **himself**/herself

48 John's father told the woman that John's mother had been impressed by to ensure she drove with care and was proud of **himself**/herself

49 John's father told the woman that John's mother had doubts about to confirm the new statement and was proud of **himself**/herself

50 John's father told the boy that John's mother was worried about to concentrate on his homework and was proud of **himself**/herself

51 John's father told the man that John's mother had dealt with that the faults would be repaired and was proud of **himself**/herself

52 John's father told the woman that John's mother had been working with to outline the next case and was proud of **himself**/herself

53 John's father told the woman that John's mother was worried about to be positive about the illness and was proud of **himself**/herself

54 John's father told the woman that John's mother was impressed by to explain it all to her friend and was proud of **himself**/herself

55 John's father told the father that John's mother was shocked by that his attitude was appalling and was proud of **himself**/herself

56 John's father told the guitarist that John's mother was impressed by to audition again on Friday and was proud of **himself**/herself

57 John's father told the wife that John's mother was worried about to come and visit more often and was proud of **himself**/herself

58 John's father told the woman that John's mother had risked her life for to install a smoke detector and was proud of **himself**/herself

59 John's father told the woman that John's mother had just sold a painting for to give him the fee and was proud of **himself**/herself

60 John's father told the man that John's mother was pleased to see to order another coffee and was proud of **himself**/herself

61 John's father told the journalist that John's mother agreed with to write a report on the subject and was proud of **himself**/herself

62 John's father told the comedian that John's mother was amused by to impersonate the other guests and was proud of **himself**/herself

63 John's father told the actress that John's mother had heard of to audition for the next film and was proud of **himself**/herself

64 John's father told the old lady that John's mother had baked a cake for to pay the bill on Saturday and was proud of **himself**/herself

65 John's father told the boy that John's mother had brought a gift for to share it with his friend and was proud of **himself**/herself

66 John's father told the woman that John's mother wanted to go with to meet him outside the museum and was proud of **himself**/herself

67 John's father told the woman that John's mother was talking to that the chairs were exquisite and was proud of **himself**/herself

68 John's father told the model that John's mother had taken bad photos of to pose again the next day and was proud of **himself**/herself

69 John's father told the father that John's mother was horrified by to change his attitude and was proud of **himself**/herself

70 John's father told the girl that John's mother was happy with to try a more difficult slope and was proud of **himself**/herself

71 John's father told the nurse that John's mother was complaining about to treat him with more care and was proud of **himself**/herself

72 John's father told the girl that John's mother was frightened of to bully someone her own age and was proud of **himself**/herself

Towards a Bayesian hierarchical model of lexical processing

Cassandra L. Jacobs
Department of Linguistics
State University of New York at Buffalo
Buffalo, NY, USA
cxjacobs@buffalo.edu

Morgan Grobol
MoDyCo
Université Paris Nanterre
Nanterre, France
lgrobol@parisnanterre.fr

Abstract

In cases of pervasive uncertainty, cognitive systems benefit from heuristics or committing to more general hypotheses. Here we present a hierarchical cognitive model of lexical processing that synthesizes advances in early rational cognitive models with modern-day neural architectures. Probabilities of higher-order categories derived from vector representations extracted from the middle layers of an encoder language model have predictive power in accounting for several reading measures for both predicted and unpredicted words and influence even early first fixation duration behavior. The results suggest that lexical processing can take place within a latent, but nevertheless discrete, space in cases of uncertainty.

1 Introduction

Skilled readers are able to quickly and accurately leverage real-world and linguistic knowledge to understand texts. Lexical and syntactic factors strongly influence the speed and accuracy of sentence processing (Levy, 2008; Brennan and Hale, 2019). In addition to factors such as lexical frequency, word length, and syntactic processes, there is also lexico-semantic structure in language as it unfolds in time. Such higher-order abstractions are posited to be advantageous for any cognitive system to track (Kwisthout et al., 2017), such as anticipating or quickly integrating the semantic category that a word belongs to into one's understanding of a sentence (Federmeier and Kutas, 1999; Roland et al., 2012).

Despite clear macro structure in the predictability of individual words (e.g., the mention of *couch* versus *sofa*), it has been less clear how semantic structure influences reading times. The present paper aims to account for such macro structure and better understand how the semantic predictability of words shapes reading behavior. We quantify this structure using Bayesian Gaussian mixture models trained over embeddings of cloze responses, which we apply to a standardized dataset of reading times with associated predictability norms. Then, we obtain "semantic" estimates using cluster probabilities derived from the above Bayesian Gaussian mixture modeling process, which we incorporate into models of "early" predictive processing measures of reading times and a later, a more "semantic" reading time measure.

2 A hierarchical model of reading times

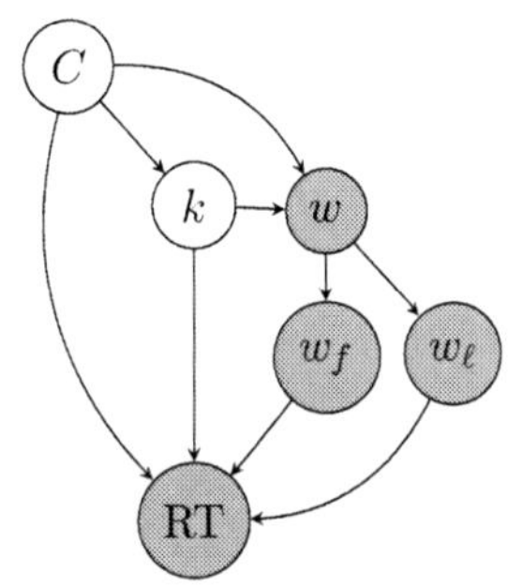

Figure 1: Our hierarchical model relating linguistic variables to reading time. C is the context (potentially including extralinguistic components), k a semantic cluster, w the observed word and w_f and w_ℓ its frequency and length respectively, RT is a measure of reading time such as fixation go-pass duration (FGPD) ; arrows denote random variable dependencies ; shaded variables are observable, unshaded ones are latent/unobserved.

Reading times partially reflect the contextual or conditional probability of a linguistic event (such as a word or syntactic structure), in that low-probability events are correlated with longer reading times (e.g., de Varda et al., 2024; Shain et al., 2024). Since the advent of neural language models, researchers have taken a strongly lexical approach to these analyses, though there is a growing appreciation that estimates of a word or syntactic structure's probability in context do not tell the full story

Proceedings of the Workshop on Cognitive Modeling and Computational Linguistics, pages 165–171
May 3, 2025 ©2025 Association for Computational Linguistics

about what makes written language easier or harder to read (Gruteke Klein et al., 2024). Reliance on lexical estimates of predictability may over-estimate the uncertainty of the linguistic future (Kwisthout et al., 2017) and thus under-estimate the importance of higher-order prediction and over-estimate processing difficulty (Ozaki et al., 2024). For example, a comprehender may make more general linguistic predictions (e.g., the CAT concept) or more specific ones (e.g., "oriental longhair"; Degen et al., 2020; Roland et al., 2012; Federmeier and Kutas, 1999). We present a clustering method that estimates these higher-order, lexico-semantic hypothesis spaces K, which we demonstrate provides additional predictive power in explaining reading times beyond word-level information alone. Quantifying higher-order structure ties the modern lexical approach to hierarchical Bayesian processing models and early surprisal approaches (e.g., Levy, 2008). We outline such a model in Figure 1.

3 Applying cloze data to the study of rational language comprehension

Accounting for hierarchical processing in reading requires suitable resources for estimating these hierarchical categories. While the contemporary approach to estimating lexical predictability overwhelmingly relies on language model surprisal, human beings and language models do not align make the same prediction (Smith and Levy, 2011). We aggregate cloze production data (Taylor, 1953) into quasi-semantic clusters using Bayesian Gaussian mixture modeling. We focus on the Provo Corpus, in which participants read an incomplete text and guessed the identity of the next word for each word in a sentence ("serial cloze"; Luke and Christianson, 2016, 2018; Lowder et al., 2018), which is one of the only parallel datasets with reading time and cloze production statistics.

In the Provo corpus, college-age American English speaking participants incrementally guessed the identity of each non-initial word w_i for every preamble $p = w_1 \dots w_{i-1}$ in order. The resulting cloze corpus consists of 41 236 unique continuations across 2398 unique preambles, from a collection of 55 short, multi-sentence web texts. Cloze probabilities are defined as follows:

$$P(\text{word} \mid p) = \frac{\text{count}(\text{word} \cap p)}{\text{count}(p)}$$

The Provo corpus also includes reading time data for each of these texts from 84 participants from the same population. We focus on two reading time measures for their relative cognitive transparency and to minimize the number of statistical comparisons (Von der Malsburg and Angele, 2017): first fixation duration (FFD) and first go-past duration (FGPD). FFD is often conceptualized as reflecting early-stage visual processes while FGPD is thought to reflect additional time for semantic integration. Both FFD and FGPD measures are sensitive to quantitative indicators of lexical and syntactic predictability (Staub, 2015).

4 Clustering model

We model semantic predictability using a Dirichlet process mixture (Antoniak, 1974) of Gaussians trained with variational inference (Blei and Jordan, 2006) on the set $E \subset \mathbb{R}^d$ of token embeddings of participants' best guesses in a serial cloze task. More precisely: we model E as a sample drawn from a weighted sum of d-dimensional multivariate Gaussian variables k_i (components) $\sum_i \pi_i k_i$. This can be reformulated as a two-step process of first sampling one component k from a set K, then sampling an embedding from k. If we identify each component with the set of the embeddings it generated, K can then be seen as a clustering of E, which can be approximated by estimating a probability distribution over components $P(e \in k)$ for each embedding $e \in E$ and assigning e to its maximum-likelihood component $\text{argmax}_{k \in K} P(e \in k)$.

The number of unique word forms in a cluster (of approximately 36 000 completions) ranged from 1 to 1534, showing substantial skew with a mean/median/mode of 128/5/2 words per cluster. Clustering results in a drop in uncertainty during naturalistic reading that reduces the complexity of the prediction process by lowering the size of the hypothesis space from that of the whole vocabulary $|V|$ to an average of $|K| + \mathbb{E}[|k|]$, making it a more tractable (and therefore more plausible) problem for readers to solve. We demonstrate an example case in Figure 2. More details of our implementation can be found at the `clamp` repository github page.[1]

Part-of-speech labels are strong predictors of clusters, with further subcategorizations being evident by assessing the component words for each cluster. The resulting clusters partially encode part-of-speech, with cluster agreement index (Rabbany and Zaïane, 2017) of 0.42 between part-of-speech

[1] https://github.com/calicolab/clamp

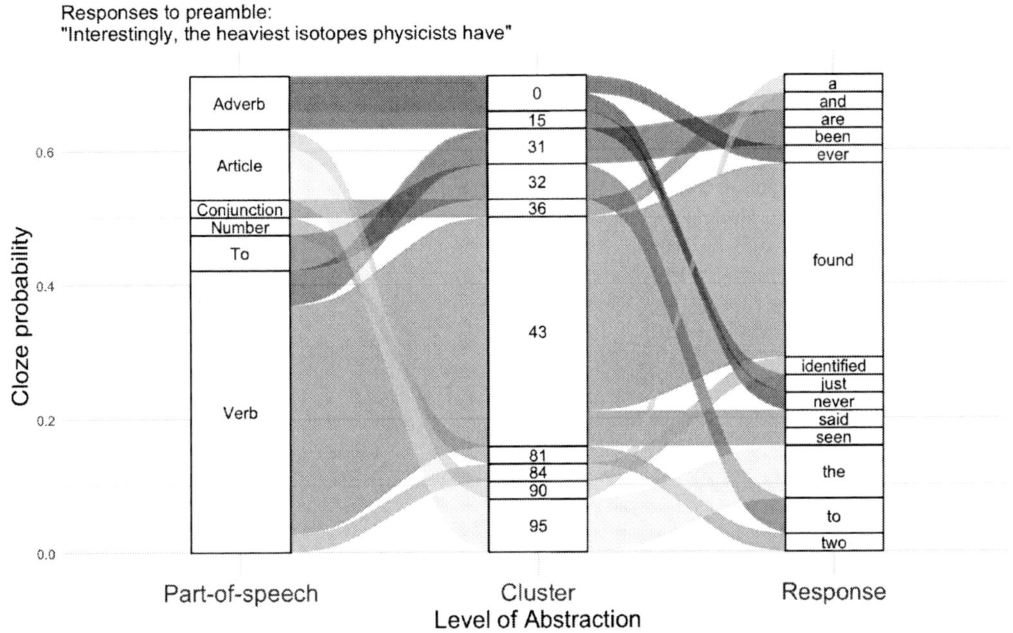

Figure 2: Word and POS repartition by cluster for responses to the preamble "Interestingly, the heaviest isotopes physicists have...". Plot made using ggalluvial (Brunson, 2020).

labels and our clustering. We present a visualization of cluster structure by word and by POS for a single preamble in Figure 2.

In contrast to lexical approaches and in keeping with the hierarchical nature of prediction (Kwisthout et al., 2017), out-of-sample words (i.e., words with a cloze probability of 0 that are the empirical next word in a sentence) may also attain a non-zero probability, which we explore in the next section.[2]

5 Predicting reading times

Hierarchical prediction mechanisms empower readers to make less precise predictions in cases of uncertainty, and result in greater ease of processing even at early stages (Kwisthout et al., 2017). We clustered human responses in the cloze (next-word prediction) portion of the Provo corpus by extracting their contextual representations from the hidden layers of RoBERTa (Liu et al., 2019). As described above, we apply Bayesian Gaussian mixture models and interpret the resulting clusters as approximations of higher-order lexico-semantic categories.

[2]In principle, it is possible to leverage the uncertainty in a mixture model's assignment of a data point to clusters. In practice, most embeddings are assigned to a cluster with probability 1 due to properties of the embedding space that make lexical representations highly distinct from each other.

In that setting, the probability of a cluster C for a given preamble p is the sum of the cloze probabilities (eq. 3) of its elements:

$$P(C \mid p) = \sum_{\text{word} \in C} P(\text{word} \mid p, C)$$

We constructed linear mixed effects models of FFD and FGPD measures for words in the Provo corpus that were either responses produced in the cloze task ($P(\text{word} > 0$; *guessed*; Table 1) or were not observed (*unguessed*; Table 2). Such cases are precisely where we would expect uncertainty to promote maintaining a general hypothesis rather than a very specific one about upcoming words (Bannon et al., 2024; Kwisthout et al., 2017; Giulianelli et al., 2024).

Following Luke and Christianson (2016), we include several basic predictors to model reading times for each word — log word frequency, word number, sentence number, word length, LSA Context Score, and cloze probability (where applicable) to the base model with maximal random intercepts and slopes. LSA Context Score was defined as the fit between the empirical next word and the surrounding context using a cosine similarity distance metric, which was reported to significantly influence processing in Luke and Christianson (2016).

Coefficient	β	E	t	p	β	E	t	p
Intercept	−0.02	0.04	−0.64	n.s.	0.01	0.03	0.26	n.s.
Cluster Probability	−0.03	0.01	−3.35	***	−0.02	0.01	−2.36	*
Word frequency	−0.05	0.03	−1.73	.	—	—	—	—
Sentence Number	−0.01	0.01	−1.23	n.s.	0.02	0.01	1.85	.
Word in Sentence	−0.02	0.01	−1.78	.	0.01	0.01	1.04	n.s.
Word Length	0.18	0.03	7.20	***	0.04	0.02	2.60	**
LSA Context Score	−0.01	0.01	−1.07	n.s.	−0.02	0.01	−1.84	.

Table 1: Linear mixed effects model for FGPD for words with non-zero cloze probability. Singularity issues affecting model convergence led to the removal of the word frequency term from the FFD model. . represents $p < 0.1$; ** $p < 0.01$; *** $p < 0.001$.

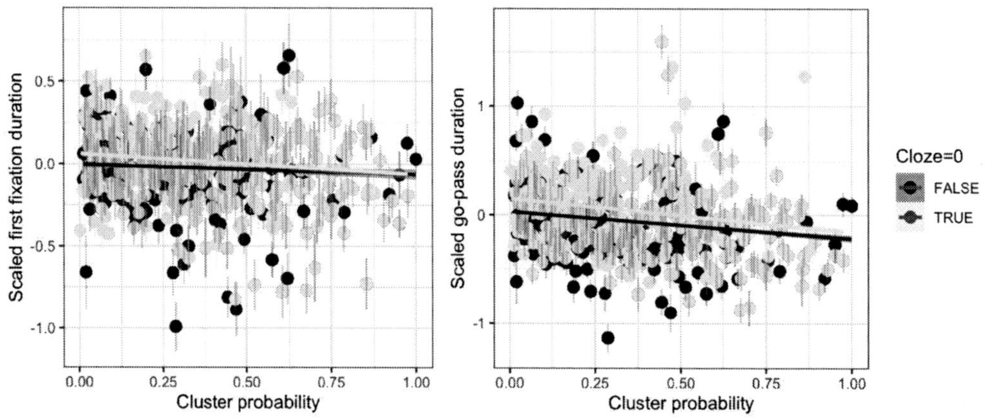

Figure 3: First fixation duration (FFD) and go-pass duration (FGPD) as a function of cluster probability for words that were guessed in the cloze norms. Cluster probability has a facilitative effect on both word types for both eyetracking measures.

Our analyses focus on FGPD and FFD specifically.

We tested for the importance of the Cluster Probability measure $P(C \mid p)$ through model comparison against a base model that did not include Cluster Probability as a predictor. Including Cluster Probability in the model resulted in significant improvements in ΔLL via a likelihood ratio test for all measures and datasets. All models showed the same pattern, such that next words belonging to higher-probability clusters were read more quickly, for both early visual stages (FFD) and higher order semantic stages (FGPD) and for guessed and unguessed words. For words that were guessed, cloze probability did not significantly predict either gaze measure and was thus excluded from the final model.

Furthermore, for such zero-cloze probability words, the effect of Cluster Probability on FPGD was larger (Satterwhaite $t(640) = -4.37$) than the effect of lexical frequency ($t(440) = 3.85$) for words that had zero-probability cloze but non-zero probability of that cluster. We visualize this relationship for FGPD in Figure 3 and present the results for zero-cloze FFDs in Table 2.

6 Related work

We are not the first to cluster language model representations. Others modeled semantic processing in analyses of reading times, typically comparing static word vectors for next words against prior context with cosine similarity (e.g., Luke and Christianson, 2016; Staub et al., 2015) or, more recently, used such similarities as a smoothing factor for surprisal distributions —slightly improving surprisal theory fits to reading time measures (Meister et al., 2024). Gaussian processes are particularly common in cognitive modeling of linguistic category learning (Kleinschmidt and Jaeger, 2015; Toscano

Coefficient	β	E	t	p	β	E	t	p
Intercept	−0.03	0.04	−0.72	n.s.	−0.01	0.03	−0.27	n.s.
Cluster Probability	−0.04	−0.01	−4.37	***	−0.03	0.01	−3.29	**
Word frequency	−0.08	−0.02	−3.85	***	−0.06	0.02	−3.45	***
Sentence Number	−0.05	0.01	−4.09	***	—	—	—	—
Word in Sentence	−0.01	0.01	−0.93	n.s.	—	—	—	—
Word Length	0.19	0.02	9.67	< .001	0.02	0.02	1.12	n.s.
LSA Context Score	−0.02	0.01	−1.72	.	−0.01	0.01	−1.38	n.s.

Table 2: Linear mixed effects model for FGPD for words with 0 cloze probability but non-zero cluster probability. Backwards elimination from the FFD model recommended removal of other control variables. . represents $p < 0.1$; ** $p < 0.01$; *** $p < 0.001$.

and McMurray, 2010). Modeling semantics using Dirichlet distributions (as in topic modeling Blei and Jordan, 2006) has also proven successful in modeling human semantic memory (Steyvers et al., 2006).

Other work in computational psycholinguistics has tested whether language processing involves a semantic comparison between alternatives in contextual language space (Giulianelli et al., 2023). We believe the current proposal that readers represent semantics as scalar, but nevertheless quasi-discrete, categories is a novel synthesis of these areas. The present results support the proposal that efficient, rational language processing can be achieved by combining levels of granularity of linguistic predictions.

7 Conclusion

Here we presented a hierarchical cognitive model of lexical processing that synthesizes early rational cognitive models with modern-day neural architectures. We argue that language model representations can be combined with human cloze data to infer higher-order structure. Cluster probabilities had predictive power in accounting for several reading measures for both predicted and unpredicted words and influence even early first fixation duration behavior. The results suggest that lexical processing can take place at a featural level in cases of uncertainty (Federmeier and Kutas, 1999; Roland et al., 2012; Kwisthout et al., 2017).

8 Limitations

This work is meant as a proof of concept for a hierarchical model of lexical processing and the use of transformer language models as predictors of reading times, not only through next-word probabilities, but also through their internal contextual representations of words. This study is by no mean exhaustive, and further replications and refinements using other datasets should be undertaken in the future using a wider variety of datasets.

Our work did not explore the potential semantic capacity of next word prediction-based language models. We did not consider larger models, nor simpler ones. We did not vary the number of clusters or manipulate the hyperparameters we used for the mixture model; future work should determine the optimal number of clusters.

The cloze norms and the eye tracking data here are relatively limited compared to real-world reading. The data are limited to American English which makes asking questions about other phenomena (e.g., morphosyntactic processing) more challenging. The data were gathered from highly literate populations at a prestigious university in the United States and are not representative of all people. Many individuals vary substantially in their language experience and this variability, which shapes processing fluency (e.g., Breen et al., 2024).

Some believe that lexicalized language model probabilities are the best probabilistic predictor of reading time and neural data (Shain et al., 2024), though this claim may not hold for all types of stimuli (de Varda et al., 2024; Szewczyk and Federmeier, 2022). Perhaps more pertinently, the use of surprisal as a measure of linguistic predictability is not central to our question; we demonstrated that cloze responses are highly structured and that modeling this structure accounts even for early language processing dynamics. Future work should examine how to automate the discovery of semantic probabilities using language models directly.

The appropriateness of modeling LLM embeddings as samples drawn from a mixture of multivariate Gaussians has not – to our knowledge – been extensively studied. The semantic structure of cloze responses can be approached from several angles, ranging from ontologies such as WordNet (Miller, 1995), to feature sets (Turton et al., 2020), to representing words by their distributional semantics, the approach we take here. However, the clustering results presented here are suggestive of meaningful distributional sub-structure, and could in principle be replicated by many other clustering algorithms, such as k-means or agglomerative clustering.

References

Charles E. Antoniak. 1974. Mixtures of Dirichlet Processes with Applications to Bayesian Nonparametric Problems. *The Annals of Statistics*, 2(6):1152–1174.

Julie Bannon, Tamar H Gollan, and Victor S Ferreira. 2024. Is predicting during language processing worth it? effects of cloze probability and semantic similarity on failed predictions. *Journal of Experimental Psychology: Learning, Memory, and Cognition*.

David M. Blei and Michael I. Jordan. 2006. Variational inference for Dirichlet process mixtures. *Bayesian Analysis*, 1(1):121–143.

Mara Breen, Julie Van Dyke, Jelena Krivokapić, and Nicole Landi. 2024. Prosodic features in production reflect reading comprehension skill in high school students. *Journal of Experimental Psychology: Learning, Memory, and Cognition*.

Jonathan R Brennan and John T Hale. 2019. Hierarchical structure guides rapid linguistic predictions during naturalistic listening. *PloS one*, 14(1):e0207741.

Jason Cory Brunson. 2020. ggalluvial: Layered grammar for alluvial plots. *Journal of Open Source Software*, 5(49):2017.

Andrea Gregor de Varda, Marco Marelli, and Simona Amenta. 2024. Cloze probability, predictability ratings, and computational estimates for 205 english sentences, aligned with existing eeg and reading time data. *Behavior Research Methods*, 56(5):5190–5213.

Judith Degen, Robert D Hawkins, Caroline Graf, Elisa Kreiss, and Noah D Goodman. 2020. When redundancy is useful: A bayesian approach to "overinformative" referring expressions. *Psychological Review*, 127(4):591.

Kara D Federmeier and Marta Kutas. 1999. A rose by any other name: Long-term memory structure and sentence processing. *Journal of Memory and Language*, 41(4):469–495.

Mario Giulianelli, Andreas Opedal, and Ryan Cotterell. 2024. Generalized measures of anticipation and responsivity in online language processing. In *Findings of the Association for Computational Linguistics: EMNLP 2024*, pages 11648–11669.

Mario Giulianelli, Sarenne Wallbridge, and Raquel Fernández. 2023. Information value: Measuring utterance predictability as distance from plausible alternatives. In *Proceedings of the 2023 Conference on Empirical Methods in Natural Language Processing*, pages 5633–5653, Singapore. Association for Computational Linguistics.

Keren Gruteke Klein, Yoav Meiri, Omer Shubi, and Yevgeni Berzak. 2024. The effect of surprisal on reading times in information seeking and repeated reading. In *Proceedings of the 28th Conference on Computational Natural Language Learning*, pages 219–230, Miami, FL, USA. Association for Computational Linguistics.

Dave F Kleinschmidt and T Florian Jaeger. 2015. Robust speech perception: recognize the familiar, generalize to the similar, and adapt to the novel. *Psychological review*, 122(2):148.

Johan Kwisthout, Harold Bekkering, and Iris Van Rooij. 2017. To be precise, the details don't matter: On predictive processing, precision, and level of detail of predictions. *Brain and Cognition*, 112:84–91.

Roger Levy. 2008. Expectation-based syntactic comprehension. *Cognition*, 106(3):1126–1177.

Yinhan Liu, Myle Ott, Naman Goyal, Jingfei Du, Mandar Joshi, Danqi Chen, Omer Levy, Mike Lewis, Luke Zettlemoyer, and Veselin Stoyanov. 2019. Roberta: A robustly optimized bert pretraining approach. *Preprint*, arXiv:1907.11692.

Matthew W Lowder, Wonil Choi, Fernanda Ferreira, and John M Henderson. 2018. Lexical predictability during natural reading: Effects of surprisal and entropy reduction. *Cognitive Science*, 42:1166–1183.

Steven G. Luke and Kiel Christianson. 2016. Limits on lexical prediction during reading. *Cognitive Psychology*, 88:22–60.

Steven G. Luke and Kiel Christianson. 2018. The Provo Corpus: A large eye-tracking corpus with predictability norms. *Behavior Research Methods*, 50(2):826–833.

Clara Meister, Mario Giulianelli, and Tiago Pimentel. 2024. Towards a similarity-adjusted surprisal theory. In *Proceedings of the 2024 Conference on Empirical Methods in Natural Language Processing*, pages 16485–16498, Miami, Florida, USA. Association for Computational Linguistics.

George A. Miller. 1995. WordNet: a lexical database for English. *Commun. ACM*, 38(11):39–41.

Satoru Ozaki, Aniello De Santo, Tal Linzen, and Brian Dillon. 2024. CCG parsing effort and surprisal jointly predict RT but underpredict garden-path effects. *Proceedings of the Society for Computation in Linguistics (SCiL)*, pages 362–364.

Reihaneh Rabbany and Osmar Zaïane. 2017. A General Clustering Agreement Index: For Comparing Disjoint and Overlapping Clusters. *Proceedings of the AAAI Conference on Artificial Intelligence*, 31(1).

Douglas Roland, Hongoak Yun, Jean-Pierre Koenig, and Gail Mauner. 2012. Semantic similarity, predictability, and models of sentence processing. *Cognition*, 122(3):267–279.

Cory Shain, Clara Meister, Tiago Pimentel, Ryan Cotterell, and Roger Levy. 2024. Large-scale evidence for logarithmic effects of word predictability on reading time. *Proceedings of the National Academy of Sciences*, 121(10):e2307876121.

Nathaniel Smith and Roger Levy. 2011. Cloze but no cigar: The complex relationship between cloze, corpus, and subjective probabilities in language processing. In *Proceedings of the Annual Meeting of the Cognitive Science Society*, volume 33.

Adrian Staub. 2015. The effect of lexical predictability on eye movements in reading: Critical review and theoretical interpretation. *Language and Linguistics Compass*, 9(8):311–327.

Adrian Staub, Margaret Grant, Lori Astheimer, and Andrew Cohen. 2015. The influence of cloze probability and item constraint on cloze task response time. *Journal of Memory and Language*, 82:1–17.

Mark Steyvers, Thomas L Griffiths, and Simon Dennis. 2006. Probabilistic inference in human semantic memory. *Trends in Cognitive Sciences*, 10(7):327–334.

Jakub M. Szewczyk and Kara D. Federmeier. 2022. Context-based facilitation of semantic access follows both logarithmic and linear functions of stimulus probability. *Journal of Memory and Language*, 123:104311.

Wilson L. Taylor. 1953. "Cloze Procedure": A New Tool for Measuring Readability. *Journalism Quarterly*, 30(4):415–433.

Joseph C Toscano and Bob McMurray. 2010. Cue integration with categories: Weighting acoustic cues in speech using unsupervised learning and distributional statistics. *Cognitive Science*, 34(3):434–464.

Jacob Turton, David Vinson, and Robert Smith. 2020. Extrapolating binder style word embeddings to new words. In *Proceedings of the Second Workshop on Linguistic and Neurocognitive Resources*, pages 1–8, Marseille, France. European Language Resources Association.

Titus Von der Malsburg and Bernhard Angele. 2017. False positives and other statistical errors in standard analyses of eye movements in reading. *Journal of Memory and Language*, 94:119–133.

Modeling Chinese L2 Writing Development: The LLM-Surprisal Perspective

Jingying Hu[1], Yan Cong[1,2]
[1] Department of Linguistics, Purdue University
[2] School of languages and cultures, Purdue University
{hu880, cong4}@purdue.edu

Abstract

LLM-surprisal is a computational measure of how unexpected a word or character is given the preceding context, as estimated by large language models (LLMs). This study investigated the effectiveness of LLM-surprisal in modeling second language (L2) writing development, focusing on Chinese L2 writing as a case to test its cross-linguistical generalizability. We selected three types of LLMs with different pretraining settings: a multilingual model trained on various languages, a Chinese-general model trained on both Simplified and Traditional Chinese, and a Traditional-Chinese-specific model. This comparison allowed us to explore how model architecture and training data affect LLM-surprisal estimates of learners' essays written in Traditional Chinese, which in turn influence the modeling of L2 proficiency and development. We also correlated LLM-surprisals with 16 classic linguistic complexity indices (e.g., character sophistication, lexical diversity, syntactic complexity, and discourse coherence) to evaluate its interpretability and validity as a measure of L2 writing assessment. Our findings demonstrate the potential of LLM-surprisal as a robust, interpretable, cross-linguistically applicable metric for automatic writing assessment and contribute to bridging computational and linguistic approaches in understanding and modeling L2 writing development. All analysis scripts are available at https://github.com/JingyingHu/ChineseL2Writing-Surprisals.

1 Introduction

The rapid development of large language models (LLMs) has opened new avenues for modeling second language acquisition (SLA) and quantifying interlanguage systems. Among these, LLM-derived surprisal (hereafter LLM-surprisal), an information-theoretic measure, has shown strong potential for quantifying linguistic unpredictability across different contexts.

LLM-surprisal has been widely used in psycholinguistics studies to model human language comprehension (Wilcox et al., 2023; Huber et al., 2024). Recent research has highlighted its potential in modeling second language (L2) writing development. For example, Cong (2025) found that LLM-surprisal is potentially linked to L2 writing naturalness and can effectively capture lexical diversity and syntactic complexity in English L2 writing. As such, LLM-surprisal shows promise as a holistic metric for evaluating English L2 writing proficiency.

Despite these findings, the cross-linguistic generalizability of LLM-surprisal remains underexplored, particularly in typologically distant languages such as Chinese. The linguistic complexities that LLM-surprisal captures in Chinese L2 writing may differ from those observed in Cong's (2025) studies on English L2 writing. Therefore, a closer investigation of these differences is crucial not only for validating the cross-linguistic applicability of LLM-surprisal but also for understanding what specific linguistic features LLM-surprisal measures in the Chinese L2 writing context.

LLMs have recently demonstrated impressive language understanding and generation abilities, but their performance can vary across model architecture, scale, and training data. Notably, most mainstream LLMs are trained predominantly on English or other high-resource languages, raising concerns about their efficacy in low-resource settings or typologically diverse language contexts. Among these, Traditional Chinese texts remain particularly underrepresented due to their non-Latin script and limited presence in large-scale training corpora. This study also examined how different types of LLM (multilingual, Chinese-

Proceedings of the Workshop on Cognitive Modeling and Computational Linguistics, pages 172–183
May 3, 2025

general, and Traditional-Chinese-specific language models) process Traditional Chinese written texts, contributing to broader discussions on multilingual LLM performance in low-resource settings.

To summarize, the present study investigates the potential of LLM-derived surprisal as a robust and cross-linguistically applicable metric for L2 writing assessment, addressing the following research questions:

(1) **Cross-linguistic efficacy of LLM-surprisal in L2 writing assessment**
Can LLM-surprisal differentiate proficiency levels in Chinese L2 writing, thereby supporting its validity as a cross-linguistic metric for L2 writing evaluation?

(2) **The efficacy of multilingual LLMs in low-resource language settings**
If so, how do three types of LLMs, which vary in the scale of their training data on Traditional Chinese, differ in their ability to evaluate Chinese L2 writing?

(3) **LLM-surprisal's interpretability in the Chinese L2 context**
What aspects of linguistic complexity are captured by LLM-surprisal in Chinese L2 writing, and how do they differ from those captured in English L2 writing assessment?

For **RQ1**, we hypothesize that LLM-surprisal can differentiate different proficiency levels in Chinese L2 writing. That is, advanced-level essays tend to exhibit lower LLM-surprisal scores than beginner-level ones, as higher proficiency is associated with more natural and predictable language production.

For **RQ2**, among three LLMs examined, we hypothesize that the LLM pre-trained on Traditional Chinese-specific data will outperform both multilingual and general Chinese LLMs in modeling Chinese L2 writing development, due to its language-specific optimizations.

For **RQ3**, unlike classic complexity indices, which focus on specific aspects of language, we hypothesize that LLM-surprisal can capture the multidimensional nature of linguistic complexity in Chinese L2 writing. Building on prior work in English L2 research (Cong, 2025; Tang, 2024), we hypothesize that LLM-surprisal also captures lexical and syntactic complexity in the context of Chinese L2 writing assessment. Moreover, it may further capture character-level and discourse-level features, given the typological differences between Chinese and English.

The significance of this study lies in both its theoretical and practical contributions. By validating the effectiveness of LLM-surprisal in Chinese L2 writing, this study not only introduces a new potential quantitative metric for the automated writing assessment system for Chinese but also provides empirical evidence supporting the cross-linguistic applicability of surprisal as a universal and robust metric for L2 writing assessment. Additionally, by analyzing what linguistic complexity LLM-surprisal specifically measures in Chinese L2 writing, this study further improves the interpretability of LLM-surprisal in modeling L2 acquisition. Practically, the study provides insights into how LLMs can be applied in SLA research, particularly in selecting models for low-resource languages like Traditional Chinese.

2 Related Work

2.1 LLM-surprisal and multilingual LLMs

Mathematically, LLM-surprisal is defined as the negative log-probability of a word given its preceding context as computed by LLMs (Misra, 2022). LLM-surprisal has shown a strong correlation with **human language comprehension**, with higher LLM-surprisal indicating greater processing difficulty. Behavioral studies found that the higher LLM-surprisal predicts longer reading times, as cognitive load increases when processing less predictable input (Goodkind & Bicknell, 2018; Rethi, 2021). Neurocognitive further supports this relationship: words with higher surprisal elicit larger N400 amplitudes or increased P600 responses, both of which are neural markers of processing difficulty (Aurnhammer et al., 2021; Li et al., 2024).

The application of LLM-surprisal has also been extended to evaluate **human language production.** Recent studies suggest that LLM-surprisal has merged as a promising metric for assessing both writing quality and language proficiency among English L2 learners. Tang (2024) analyzed essays written by English L2 learners and found that as proficiency increases, learners convey more informative content while maintaining lower levels of unpredictability in their writing, as measured by entropy and LLM-surprisal respectively. Cong's (2025) study also confirmed LLM-surprisal's predictive power in tracking English L2 writing development, showing that it numerically represents the interplay between syntactic complexity and lexical diversity in English L2 interlanguage development.

However, the robustness of LLM-surprisal as a metric for assessing Chinese L2 writing quality has not been sufficiently investigated. Furthermore, the typological difference between English and Chinese raises critical questions about whether LLM-surprisal captures comparable dimensions of linguistic complexity in Chinese L2 contexts. This dual gap highlights the need to examine both LLM-surprisal's cross-linguistic validity and its capacity to capture language-specific features in non-English settings.

The choice of LLM is important, as the effectiveness of LLM-surprisal is contingent upon the underlying language model's performance. Higher quality language models can produce more accurate surprisal estimates, which in turn better predict human behavior (Hao et al., 2020; Oh, 2023). A key consideration in LLM selection is whether to use a multilingual or monolingual model, yet previous studies have reported mixed findings. While some studies suggest that English-centric multilingual LLMs perform robustly across languages (Nguyen et al., 2023; Joshi et al., 2024; Kargaran et al., 2024), Xu et al. (2023) found that multilingual LLMs rely on translation-like behavior for cross-linguistic generalization, which may introduce biases in language-specific tasks. Moreover, multilingual LLMs tend to perform significantly better on high-resource languages, particularly those using Latin scripts, but struggle with low-resource languages and complex linguistic structures (Alam et al., 2024; Shu et al., 2024).

Based on these findings, and given that Traditional Chinese is a low-resource language in LLM training, it remains unclear how multilingual, Chinese-general, and Traditional Chinese-specific LLM differ in their ability to capture Traditional Chinese linguistic complexity or to provide more reliable surprisal estimates. Addressing these gaps is critical for understanding the applicability of LLM-surprisal in assessing Chinese L2 writing.

2.2 Classic linguistics indices in assessing Chinese L2 writing development

Previous studies on Chinese L2 writing assessment primarily focus on syntactic and lexical complexity indices. Early Chinese L2 studies adapted T-unit analysis from English, but Jin (2007) found it ineffective for distinguishing proficiency levels due to Chinese's topic-prominent structure. As an alternative, Jin (2007) proposed the Terminal Topic-Comment Unit (TTCU), which was later validated as a more effective measure (Jiang, 2013; Yu, 2021). Recent research has shifted from large-grained to more fine-grained syntactic analysis. At the level of phraseological complexity, Lu & Wu (2022) identified noun-phrase complexity as a stronger predictor of L2 Chinese writing quality, while Hu et al. (2022) highlighted the importance of word-combination-based measures. Hao et al. (2024) found that fine-grained syntactic indices more effectively predicted Chinese L2 writing quality than large-grained ones.

Lexical complexity indices have also been widely used in Chinese L2 writing evaluation. For example, Wang (2017) found that lexical errors, the number of unique word types, and the use of high-frequency words were effective indicators of the writing performance of Chinese learners.

It is worth noting that *Chinese Proficiency Grading Standards for International Chinese Language Education* (2021) (hereafter referred to as the *Grade Standard*), which defines the characters, vocabulary, and syntactic structures that Chinese learners at each proficiency level are expected to master, provides an effective tool for measuring Chinese L2 writing complexity. For example, Wang et al. (2022) used advanced-level vocabulary and grammar items from the *Grade Standard* to assess lexical and grammatical sophistication in Chinese L2 writing. They found that the use of advanced-level vocabulary and grammatical structure was strongly correlated with learner proficiency.

Despite these findings, few studies have focused on lexical semantic diversity and its role in tracking Chinese L2 writing development. Different from lexical diversity measured by TTR (the ratio of unique word types of total words), lexical semantic diversity is a computationally derived measure of the variability in a word's meaning across different contexts (Hoffman et al., 2012). A word with a high semantic diversity value indicates that it appears across more varied, semantically distinct contexts. Berger et al. (2017) found that advanced learners of English have greater lexical semantic diversity values in their language production, suggesting they can use words across many semantic diverse contexts.

Taken together, various linguistics complexity indices were used to characterize Chinese L2 learners' writing development, which provides a strong foundation for testing the reliability and validity of the new indices. Among the classic indices, the role of *Grade Standard* and lexical semantic diversity needs to be further investigated. Moreover, while much attention has been given to lexical, phrasal, and sentence-level complexity in Chinese L2 writing, relatively little is known about whether discourse-level features can effectively distinguish different proficiency levels. LLM-surprisal, which captures both the local and global unpredictability and naturalness based on prior context information, holds the potential to fill this gap by evaluating L2 quality at the discourse level or textual level that spans across a larger context.

Furthermore, previous studies have emphasized the need for assessment metrics that are sensitive to Chinese-specific linguistic properties. Unlike English, a subject-prominent language, Chinese is a topic-prominent and pro-drop language, allowing subject omission in the discourse (Li and Thompson, 1976; Liu, 2010). Chinese also has a logographic writing system, where each character represents a morpheme or meaning unit, in contrast to English's alphabetic system (Wang, 2015). Additionally, Chinese lacks rich inflectional morphology found in English and instead relies on aspect markers and contextual cues (Klein et al., 2000). These typological differences not only set Chinese apart from English but also shape how Chinese L2 learners implicitly organize their writings across lexical, syntactic, and discourse levels.

Therefore, this study applied LLM-surprisal to Chinese L2 writing to examine its predictive power in assessing writing proficiency and its ability to capture Chinese-specific typological features. Additionally, we examined the interpretation of LLM-surprisal in the Chinese L2 writing context, and how this may differ from its established interpretations in English L2 assessment.

3 Method

3.1 Dataset

We used the publicly available TOCFL Learner dataset[1] (Lee et al., 2018), which collected written essays from the standardized Test of Chinese as a Foreign Language. This dataset includes 2,837 essays written by learners from 46 different L1 backgrounds, covering proficiency levels A2 to C1, as defined by the CEFR framework. Although each essay was originally scored on a 0-5-point scale by at least two Chinese teachers, only essays that scored above 3, which is indicative of sufficient proficiency to meet the passing grade, were included in this dataset.

In the present study, we selected 65 essays from each CEFR level (A2, B1, B2, C1) to ensure balanced comparisons across proficiency groups. These essays were also carefully matched based on their scores and the learners' L1 backgrounds (see Appendix A for details). Given that LLM-surprisal can be influenced by text length, we also explicitly controlled for essay length in the experiment, with each essay containing approximately 200 Chinese characters. After applying these controls, we compiled a balanced dataset of 260 Traditional Chinese essays for subsequent analysis.

3.2 LLM-surprisals calculation

LLMs-surprisals were calculated as shown below in (1) (Misra, 2022; Cong, 2025).

$$surprisal(w_t) = -logP\ (w_t|(w_{1\ldots t-1}) \quad (1)$$

In order to answer whether LLM-surprisal can effectively distinguish different proficiency levels in Chinese L2 writing, we calculated mean LLM-surprisal scores for each essay. Specifically, we first computed character-wise surprisal within each essay, and the surprisal scores of all characters were summed and then divided by the essay length (total number of characters). We hypothesize that low surprisal, as an indicator of low unpredictability, is associated with advanced learner's writing, given that as proficiency increases, proficient learners tend to produce natural writings in their L2.

Three transformer-based language models were selected to calculate the LLM-surprisal scores:

1) *bigscience/bloom-7b1* (Le Scao et al., 2023), a large-scale multilingual model trained on 45 natural languages with 7.07 billion parameters;

2) *hfl/chinese-llama-2-7b* (Cui et al., 2023), a pre-trained transformer model trained on both simplified and traditional Chinese language with 7 billion parameters;

3) *Taiwan-LLM-7B-v2.1-chat* (Lin and Chen, 2023), an LLM exclusively tailored for Traditional Chinese with 7 billion parameters, with an emphasis on linguistic norms specific to Taiwan.

[1] https://github.com/NYCU-NLP/TOCFL

These selections enable us to compare how model architecture and training data of LLM affect their ability to model (Traditional) Chinese L2 writing, especially in the low-resource language setting. All selected LLMs are publicly available on HuggingFace (https://huggingface.co/). We utilized minicons (Misra, 2022) to conduct a systematic evaluation of different LLMs' behavior.

3.3 Classic Chinese complexity indices

To tease apart what aspects of L2 Chinese the LLM-indices can characterize, and to examine the reliability and validity of the LLM-surprisal, we selected 16 well-established Chinese complexity indices, including character, lexicon, syntax, clause, discourse coherence, and text length indices. These indices have been validated in previous Chinese L2 writing research and have also been incorporated into different linguistic complexity calculation tools (Cui et al., 2022; Sung et al., 2016). We used L2C-Rater (Wang & Hu, 2021) and CTAP for Chinese (Cui et al., 2022) to calculate these complexity indices. Additionally, we correlated these indices with LLM-surprisal to better understand what aspects of linguistic complexity are captured by LLM-surprisal in Chinese L2 essays.

We first calculated **the cohesive complexity**: first personal pronouns per token. As a pro-drop and topic-prominent language, Chinese allows the omission of subject pronouns when they can be inferred from context (Li & Thompson, 1989), a phenomenon known as zero anaphora. At the discourse level, this feature results in fewer overt first-person pronouns compared to non-pro-drop languages, which rely on pronoun retention to maintain coherence. Therefore, the appropriate use of first-person pronouns, particularly the management of pronoun dropping and retention, serves as a crucial indicator of learners' grammatical knowledge and their mastery of Chinese-specific discourse conventions. Moreover, it also allows us to examine whether LLM-surprisal is sensitive to discourse-level cohesive complexity.

Given the Chinese L2 context, we also included the **character, lexical, and syntactical sophistication indices based on the *Grade Standard***, which provides a standardized metric for assessing the difficulty of Chinese characters, words, and grammatical structure for Chinese L2 learners. Higher levels indicate greater complexity or difficulty. For each essay, we calculated the average levels of characters, average levels of words, and average levels of grammar. Advanced Chinese learners are expected to produce writings with higher average levels in all three dimensions.

In addition to lexical sophistication, we included **lexical semantic diversity,** following Cong (2025). We used the semantic diversity norms established by Chang & Lee (2018), which provide a semantic diversity value for each Chinese character. By mapping each character in the essays to its corresponding value using a dictionary-based approach, we calculated the mean lexical semantic diversity for each essay. Higher lexical semantic diversity is expected to be observed in advanced learners' essays due to their ability to utilize diverse contextual words.

For **clausal complexity**, we calculated four important phrases per simple clause: coordinate phrases, noun phrases, prepositional phrases, and verb phrases. Additionally, syntactical indices such as mean dependency distance and the height of the highest parse tree were also included to measure **syntactical complexity**. Moreover, we included **text length indices** such as mean length of sentences, clauses, and T-units, as well as the number of clauses per sentence, and number of T-units per sentence to measure sentence production complexity. We expect that advanced Chinese learners show higher values for these clausal, syntactical, and text length indices in their essays.

4 Results

Statistical analyses were conducted in R (R Core Team, 2023). The results of the Shapiro–Wilk test and Levene's test on all dependent variables suggested that the data violates the assumptions (normality and homogeneity of variance) for parametric tests. Therefore, we used non-parametric statistical tests throughout the paper. The alpha level is 0.05.

4.1 LLM-surprisal's efficiency in modeling Chinese L2 writing development

In order to answer whether LLM-surprisal can differentiate proficiency levels in Chinese L2 writing, we conducted three separate Kruskal-Wallis tests to examine the differences in LLM-surprisal across different proficiency levels. Effect sizes for the statistical tests are reported in Table 1.

The result showed significant differences in LLM-surprisal scores across proficiency levels for all three LLMs (Bloom: $\chi2=33.39$, $p<.000$,

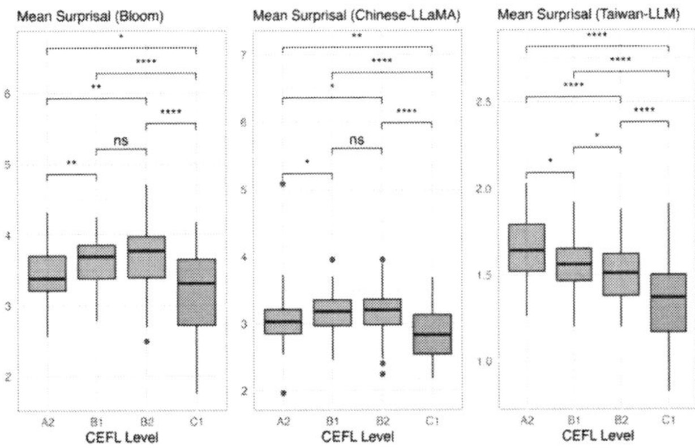

Figure 1: Paired comparisons across four proficiency levels (A2–C1). Significance notation: $*p < 0.05$; $**p < 0.01$; $****p < 0.0001$; ns: $p > 0.05$.

$\eta 2$=0.12; Chinese-LLaMA: $\chi 2$=32.4, p<.000, $\eta 2$=0.12; Taiwan-LLM: $\chi 2$=62.81, p<.000, $\eta 2$=0.23), indicating that LLM-surprisal is effective in distinguishing between L2 proficiency levels. Among the three LLMs, Taiwan-LLM demonstrated the largest effect size, suggesting its greater sensitivity to proficiency differences.

As a post-hoc analysis, to identify the specific proficiency levels at which the LLM-surprisal indices become informative, we conducted Mann-Whitney U tests on LLM-surprisal scores between adjacent proficiency levels. The results are visualized in Figure 1. Detailed descriptive statistics can be found in Appendix B.

LLM-surprisal scores calculated by Bloom and Chinese-LLaMA showed a similar trend across different proficiency levels. That is, as proficiency levels increase from A2 to B2 level, the mean LLM-surprisal scores slightly increase. However, no statistically significant difference was found in LLM-surprisal scores between the B1 and B2 levels (p > .05). Notably, the C1 level showed significantly lower LLM-surprisal scores than the other proficiency levels. In summary, LLM-surprisal scores calculated by Bloom and Chinese-LLaMA exhibited less distinct separation between adjacent levels, but both confirmed that advanced Chinese learners produce essays with the lowest LLM-surprisal score.

Taiwan-LLM showed the most consistent LLM-surprisal trends across proficiency levels, with surprisal scores decreasing significantly as proficiency increased. All pairwise comparisons were statistically significant (p < .05). These results support our hypothesis. That is, Taiwan-LLM can capture the surprisal scores difference across all proficiency levels. In other words, Taiwan-LLM is more sensitive to the subtle variations in learner writing at different proficiency stages.

In summary, these findings confirm that LLM-surprisal effectively differentiates proficiency levels in Chinese L2 writing, supporting its cross-linguistic applicability despite typological differences between Chinese and English. Across three LLMs, essays written by advanced Chinese learners (C1) consistently exhibited the lowest surprisal scores. On the other hand, Taiwan-LLM outperformed both Bloom and Chinese-LLaMA, given that it shows the largest effect size in the Kruskal-Wallis tests and demonstrated a more distinct separation between adjacent proficiency levels.

4.2 Interpreting LLM-surprisal in Chinese L2 writing context

To further validate the effectiveness of LLM-surprisal and identify which aspects of linguistic complexity it captures in Chinese L2 writing, we conducted a correlation analysis between LLM-surprisal scores and 16 classic complexity indices.

Table 1 provides the results of Kruskal–Wallis tests on three LLM-surprisal indices and 16 classic linguistic complexity indices. We found that most classic indices showed generally stronger effects than the new LLM-surprisal indices, suggesting that the classic complexity measures at the levels of characters, lexicon, phrases, coherence, syntax, and text length remain robustly informative in indexing Chinese L2 writing development.

Figure 2 shows a heatmap visualization of Spearman's rank correlations between LLM-surprisal scores and 16 classic complexity indices.

	Index	χ^2 (3)	Sig	Eta2
LLM-surprisal scores	Bloom surprisal	33.392	0.000	0.119
	Chinese-LLaMA surprisal	32.397	0.000	0.115
	Taiwan-LLM surprisal	62.808	0.000	0.234
Classic index: cohesive complexity	First Personal Pronouns per Token	94.124	0.000	0.356
Classic index: character	Average Character Levels	159.049	0.000	0.610
Classic indices: lexicon	Lexical Semantic Diversity	98.308	0.000	0.372
	Average Word Levels	165.828	0.000	0.636
Classic indices: clausal complexity	Coordinate Phrases per Simple Clause	70.698	0.000	0.264
	Noun Phrases per Simple Clause	77.881	0.000	0.293
	Prepositional Phrases per Simple Clause	29.662	0.000	0.104
	Verb Phrases per Simple Clause	30.388	0.000	0.107
Classic indices: syntactic complexity	Mean Dependency Distance	69.672	0.000	0.260
	The Height of the Highest Parse Tree	46.281	0.000	0.169
	Average Grammatical Levels	9.317	0.025	0.025
Classic indices: text length	Mean Length of Sentences	112.998	0.000	0.430
	Mean Length of Clauses	92.557	0.000	0.350
	Mean Length of T-Units	132.487	0.000	0.506
	Number of Clauses per Sentence	59.361	0.000	0.220
	Number of T-Units per Sentence	20.253	0.000	0.067

Table 1: Efficacy comparisons between the classic and the LLM-Surprisal indices in modeling Chinese L2 writing proficiency and development.

At **the discourse coherence level**, all LLM-surprisal scores were positively correlated with first personal pronouns per token, indicating that essays with lower surprisal scores tend to have fewer first personal pronouns per token, that is, less first personal pronouns repetition in the essay.

At **the character level**, all LLM-surprisals were strongly negatively correlated with average character levels, indicating that essays with lower mean surprisal scores had higher average character levels. Taiwan-LLM surprisal showed the strongest correlation coefficient, which means Taiwan-LLM is more effective at capturing character complexity than the other two LLMs.

At **the lexicon level**, all LLM-surprisals were strongly negatively correlated with average word levels and lexical semantic diversity, indicating that essays with higher mean surprisal scores had higher average word levels and higher lexical semantic diversity. Taiwan-LLM also showed the highest correlation coefficient here.

Notably, only Taiwan-LLM surprisal scores correlated with **clausal, syntactic, and sentence complexity indices**. First, Taiwan-LLM surprisal scores were strongly negatively correlated with prepositional phrases per simple clause, noun phrases per simple clause, and coordinate phrases per simple clause. That indicated that essays with lower mean surprisal scores had more complex phrases per clause. Second, Taiwan-LLM surprisal scores were strongly negatively correlated with mean dependency distance and the height of the highest parse tree, indicating that essays with lower surprisal scores exhibited higher syntactic complexity. Third, Taiwan-LLM surprisal scores also strongly negatively correlated with the mean length of sentence, clause, and T-units, as well as number of clauses per sentence.

We also found strong positive correlations within LLMs-surprisal scores. That is not surprising, since they are all transformer-based decoder models and share the core architecture. Besides that, Taiwan-LLM showed a higher correlation coefficient with Chinese-LLaMa than with Bloom. The stronger correlation may be attributed to the overlapping Traditional Chinese training data within these two Chinese LLMs.

Taken together, LLM-surprisal can capture linguistic complexity at the levels of coherence, characters, lexicon, phrases, syntax, and text length in Chinese L2 writing.

5 Conclusions and Discussions

In this study, we attempted to answer whether LLM-surprisal can serve as an effective and interpretable metric for L2 writing assessment across languages, and whether multilingual LLMs can effectively handle low-resource languages, such as traditional Chinese text.

Consistent with our hypothesis, we found that LLM-surprisal can effectively differentiate essays written by Chinese L2 learners across different proficiency levels. Specifically, advanced Chinese L2 learners exhibit lower surprisal values in their essays compared to less proficient learners. In line with Cong's (2025) work on English L2 writing, the present study demonstrates that LLM-surprisal is also effective in a typologically distinct language, such as Chinese, thereby further supporting its cross-linguistic robustness as a measure of

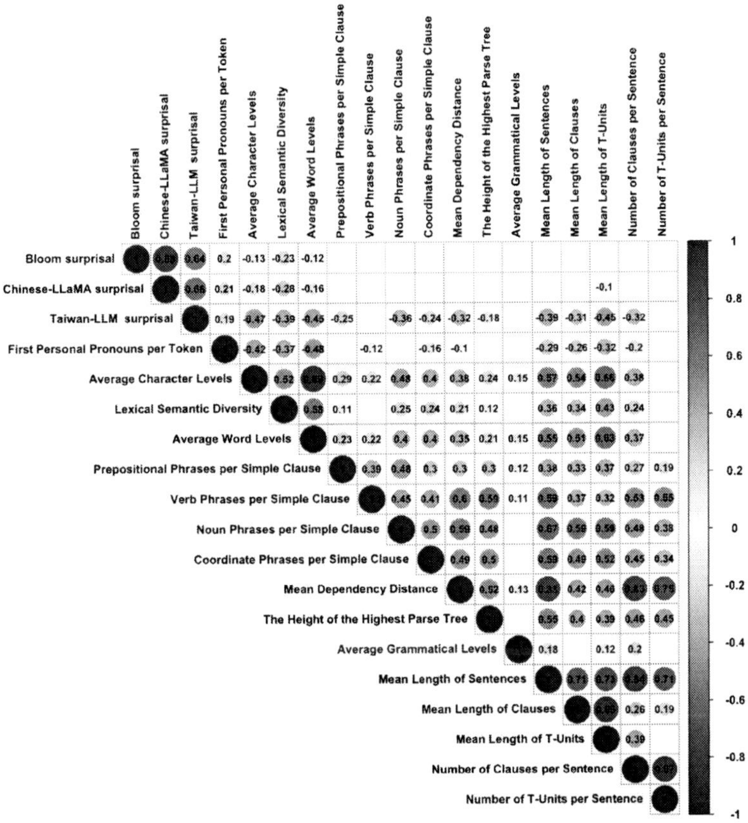

Figure 2: Correlations coefficients heatmap of LLMs-surprisals and 16 selected classic linguistic complexity indices. Darker colors indicate stronger correlations. Insignificant cells are left blank.

linguistic proficiency. These findings align with previous studies that demonstrated the cross-linguistic universality of surprisal effects in naturalistic reading (Wilcox et al., 2023; Xu et al., 2023). Extending this line of work, the present study broadens the application of LLM-surprisal by applying it to modeling language production, particularly within the contexts of automated L2 writing assessment and L2 acquisition modeling. In sum, this study highlights the potential of LLM-surprisal as a universal and effective metric for modeling human language behavior across both receptive (comprehension) and productive (writing) modalities.

Could the cross-linguistic efficacy of LLM-surprisal lie in its ability to capture multiple dimensions of linguistic complexity, including language-specific features? L2 learners' writing development is complex and encompasses multiple facets of language complexity. Cong's (2025) study on English L2 writing showed that LLM-surprisal functions as an integrated measure, capturing both lexical diversity and syntactic complexity. We speculate that LLM-surprisal may serve as a proxy for evaluating both linguistic complexity and the naturalness of learners' essays in the Chinese L2 writing context. Our correlation analysis indicated that LLM-surprisal computed by Taiwan-LLM significantly showed a significant correlation with a wide range of linguistic complexity indices (see Figure 2), suggesting its capacity to model language complexity at the character, lexical, syntactic, clausal, sentential, and discourse levels. In other words, while LLM-surprisal can capture similar linguistic complexities in both English and Chinese L2 contexts, it also uniquely showed sensitivity to certain characteristics specific to Chinese, such as character complexity and cohesive complexity. For example, we found that essays with lower surprisal scores exhibit reduced usage of first-person pronouns, a characteristic of pro-drop languages such as Chinese where subject pronouns can be omitted when implied by the context. Therefore, this study suggests that LLM-surprisal can capture the appropriate use of first-person pronouns following Chinese-specific discourse coherence conventions.

With the rapid development of LLMs, it has become increasingly important to understand how multilingual LLMs and monolingual LLMs differ in their performance across tasks. Previous studies showed mixed findings on whether multilingual or monolingual language models perform better (Goyal et al., 2020; Rönnqvist et al., 2019; Kargaran et al., 2024). In the present study, we utilized three different LLMs (Bloom, Chinese-LLaMa, Taiwan-LLM) to calculate the mean surprisal scores of each essay written in Traditional Chinese. The three LLMs feature different architectural designs and were trained on progressively larger Traditional Chinese data, allowing us to further investigate LLM's performance in low-resource languages. Among the tested models, Taiwan-LLM exhibited the best performance, characterized by the largest effect sizes, clear distinctions between different proficiency levels, and strong correlations with multiple classic language complexity indices. In contrast with Chinese-general LLM, Taiwan-LLM is trained on Traditional Chinese data with diverse textual sources, and can better capture linguistic features in the Chinese learners' essays written in Traditional Chinese. In short, LLM selection is indeed crucial for low-resource languages, as the performance of these models heavily depends on the availability and quality of training data specific to such languages. Our findings highlight that monolingual LLMs outperformed multilingual LLMs in the low-resource language setting.

Why does the Taiwan-LLM outperform the other two models? The strong performance of the Taiwan-LLM may initially raise concerns about potential data overlap or overfitting, especially given its pretraining on traditional Chinese texts. However, we argue that the observed outstanding performance cannot be fully attributed to such data familiarity. Our correlation analysis provides evidence that the LLM-surprisal estimates reflect more than mere memorization of surface patterns. Specifically, Taiwan-LLM surprisal scores showed significant correlations with a broad range of linguistic complexity indices, including lexical diversity, syntactic depth, and discourse coherence. These correlations suggest that the model captures meaningful structural and functional aspects of language that are relevant to L2 proficiency, rather than simply reproducing patterns from potentially familiar training data. In this sense, Taiwan-LLM's strongest performance likely reflects a genuine sensitivity to various linguistic complexity indices of proficient writing, thereby reinforcing the interpretability and potential utility of LLM-surprisal in L2 assessment contexts.

This study has important implications in different aspects. First, this study introduces, validates, and demystifies LLM-surprisal as a novel and robust tool for analyzing linguistic complexity in Chinese L2 writing. Given its powerful ability to capture Chinese-specific features, this study expands our methodological toolkit for automatic Chinese L2 essay scoring or writing assessment. This study also advances computational approaches to modeling L2 acquisition and human language behavior. We not only demonstrate LLM-surprisal's cross-linguistic utility in modeling language production but also provide insights into the role of LLM architecture and training data in modeling linguistic complexity in the low-resource language setting.

6 Limitations

This study provides new insights into LLM-surprisal as a cross-linguistic metric for L2 writing assessment. However, several limitations should be acknowledged. First, the number of essays per proficiency level is limited. The writing genres were also not well-controlled. This is attributed to the inherent design of the Test of Chinese as a Foreign Language (TOCFL). This standardized test assigns different genres to different proficiency levels, for example, practical messages and picture-based storytelling at A2, functional writing and letters at B1–B2, and argumentative or report-style essays at C1. Genre variability may introduce differences in rhetorical structure, topical content, and linguistic features, potentially confounding the relationship between LLM-surprisal and proficiency, as different genres have distinct lexical and syntactic characteristics. Although our results showed the robust effectiveness of LLM-surprisal in evaluating L2 essay proficiency with a broad spectrum of genres, the nature of the dataset and the variability of writing tasks in this study restrict our ability to isolate genre-specific effects. Future research should investigate the impact of genre by analyzing essays from a single genre across multiple proficiency levels and using larger, more balanced datasets

We maintain that our correlation analysis provides an approach to unpack LLM-surprisal, improving LLMs' interpretability and transparency in L2 modeling. While the Taiwan-LLM demonstrated particularly strong performance, questions about the potential overlap between its training data and the learner essays remain outside the scope of our current investigation. Future studies should evaluate model performance on out-of-domain writing samples and systematically investigate how different pretraining corpora influence surprisal estimates. In addition, fine-tuning multilingual models on controlled datasets may help disentangle the effects of language exposure, model architecture, and data familiarity in surprisal-based assessments.

Another limitation lies in our exclusive focus on written text, which leaves open questions about how LLM-surprisal operates in spoken or multimodal L2 contexts. LLM-surprisal can also be measured at phoneme or utterance level. Previous studies have shown that disfluencies tend to occur before high-surprisal and syntactically complex elements (Dammalapati et al., 2021), and words with higher surprisal are associated with longer articulation durations (Lazic et al., 2025). Future studies should explore the applicability of surprisal in L2 spoken data and the effectiveness of LLM-surprisal on automatic phonetic evaluation of L2 speech.

Acknowledgments

Special thanks to Elaine J. Francis for her kind support. We appreciate anonymous reviewers' constructive and helpful comments. This project is supported by the School of Interdisciplinary Studies, Purdue University.

References

Alam, F., Chowdhury, S. A., Boughorbel, S., & Hasanain, M. (2024, March). LLMs for low-resource languages in multilingual, multimodal, and dialectal settings. *Proceedings of the 18th Conference of the European Chapter of the Association for Computational Linguistics: Tutorial Abstracts*, 27–33.

Aurnhammer, C., Delogu, F., Schulz, M., Brouwer, H., & Crocker, M. (2021). Retrieval (N400) and integration (P600) in expectation-based comprehension. *PLOS ONE, 16*(9), e0257430. https://doi.org/10.1371/journal.pone.0257430

Berger, C. M., Crossley, S. A., & Kyle, K. (2017). Using novel word context measures to predict human ratings of lexical proficiency. *Journal of Educational Technology & Society, 20*(2), 201-212.

Chang, Y. N., & Lee, C. Y. (2018). Semantic ambiguity effects on traditional Chinese character naming: A corpus-based approach. *Behavior Research Methods, 50*(6), 2292–2304.

Cong, Y. (2025). Demystifying large language models in second language development research. *Computer Speech & Language, 89*, 101700.

Cui, Y., Zhu, J., Yang, L., Fang, X., Chen, X., Wang, Y., & Yang, E. (2022, June). CTAP for Chinese: A linguistic complexity feature automatic calculation platform. *Proceedings of the 13th Language Resources and Evaluation Conference*, 5525–5538.

Cui, Y., Yang, Z., & Yao, X. (2023). Efficient and effective text encoding for Chinese LLAMA and Alpaca. *arXiv preprint arXiv:2304.08177.*

Dammalapati, S., Rajkumar, R., Ranjan, S., & Agarwal, S. (2021, February). Effects of duration, locality, and surprisal in speech disfluency prediction in English spontaneous speech. In *Proceedings of the Society for Computation in Linguistics 2021* (pp. 91-101).

Goyal, N., Khandelwal, K., Goyal, N., Chaudhary, V., Wenzek, G., Guzmán, F., ... & Stoyanov, V. (2020). Unsupervised cross-lingual representation learning at scale. *Proceedings of the 58th Annual Meeting of the Association for Computational Linguistics*. https://doi.org/10.18653/v1/2020.acl-main.747

Goodkind, A., & Bicknell, K. (2018, January). Predictive power of word surprisal for reading times is a linear function of language model quality. *Proceedings of the 8th Workshop on Cognitive Modeling and Computational Linguistics (CMCL 2018)*, 10–18.

Hao, Y., Mendelsohn, S., Sterneck, R., Martinez, R., & Frank, R. (2020). Probabilistic predictions of people perusing: Evaluating metrics of language model performance for psycholinguistic modeling. *arXiv preprint arXiv:2009.03954.*

Hao, Y., Wang, X., Bin, S., Yang, Q., & Liu, H. (2024). How syntactic complexity indices predict Chinese L2 writing quality: An analysis of unified dependency syntactically-annotated corpus. *Assessing Writing*, 61, 100847.

Hoffman, P., Lambon Ralph, M. A., & Rogers, T. T. (2013). Semantic diversity: A measure of semantic ambiguity based on variability in the contextual usage of words. *Behavior Research Methods, 45*(3), 718–730.

Hu, R., Wu, J., & Lu, X. (2022). Word-combination-based measures of phraseological diversity, sophistication, and complexity and their relationship to second language Chinese proficiency and writing quality. *Language Learning, 72*(4), 1128–1169.

Huber, E., Sauppe, S., Isasi-Isasmendi, A., Bornkessel-Schlesewsky, I., Merlo, P., & Bickel, B. (2024). Surprisal from language models can predict ERPs in processing predicate-argument structures only if enriched by an Agent Preference principle. *Neurobiology of Language, 5*(1), 167–200.

Jiang, W. (2013). Measurements of development in L2 written production: The case of L2 Chinese. *Applied Linguistics, 34*(1), 1–24.

Jin, H. G. (2007). Syntactic maturity in second language writings: A case of Chinese as a foreign language (CFL). *Journal of the Chinese Language Teachers Association, 42*(1), 27.

Joshi, R., Singla, K., Kamath, A., Kalani, R., Paul, R., Vaidya, U., ... & Long, E. (2024). Adapting multilingual LLMs to low-resource languages using continued pre-training and synthetic corpus. *arXiv preprint arXiv:2410.14815.*

Kargaran, A. H., Modarressi, A., Nikeghbal, N., Diesner, J., Yvon, F., & Schütze, H. (2024). MEXA: Multilingual evaluation of English-centric LLMs via cross-lingual alignment. *arXiv preprint arXiv:2410.05873.*

Klein, W., Li, P., & Hendriks, H. (2000). Aspect and assertion in Mandarin Chinese. *Natural Language & Linguistic Theory, 18*(4), 723–770.

Lazic, J., & Vujnovic, S. (2025). Influence of the Surprisal Power Adjustment on Spoken Word Duration in Emotional Speech in Serbian. SSRN. https://ssrn.com/abstract=5102491

Le Scao, T., Fan, A., Akiki, C., Pavlick, E., Ilić, S., Hesslow, D., ... & Al-Shaibani, M. S. (2023). Bloom: A 176B-parameter open-access multilingual language model.

Lee, L. H., Tseng, Y. H., & Chang, L. P. (2018, May). Building a TOCFL learner corpus for Chinese grammatical error diagnosis. *Proceedings of the Eleventh International Conference on Language Resources and Evaluation (LREC 2018).*

Li, C. N., & Thompson, S. A. (1989). *Mandarin Chinese: A functional reference grammar.* University of California Press.

Li, C., & Thompson, S. (1976). Subject and topic: A new typology of language. In C. Li (Ed.), *Subject and topic* (pp. 457–489). Academic Press.

Li, J., & Futrell, R. (2024). Decomposition of surprisal: Unified computational model of ERP components in language processing. *arXiv preprint arXiv:2409.06803.*

Liu, H. (2010). Dependency direction as a means of word-order typology: A method based on dependency treebanks. *Lingua, 120*(6), 1567–1578.

Lin, Y. T., & Chen, Y. N. (2023). Taiwan llm: Bridging the linguistic divide with a culturally aligned language model. *arXiv preprint arXiv:2311.17487.*

Lu, X., & Wu, J. (2022). Noun-phrase complexity measures in Chinese and their relationship to L2 Chinese writing quality: A comparison with topic–comment-unit-based measures. *The Modern Language Journal, 106*(1), 267–283.

Center for Language Education and Cooperation, China's Ministry of Education. (2021). *Chinese Proficiency Grading Standards for International Chinese Language Education.* Higher Education Press

Misra, K. (2022). minicons: Enabling flexible behavioral and representational analyses of transformer language models. *arXiv preprint arXiv:2203.13112.*

Nguyen, X. P., Aljunied, S. M., Joty, S., & Bing, L. (2023). Democratizing LLMs for low-resource languages by leveraging their English dominant abilities with linguistically-diverse prompts. *arXiv preprint arXiv:2306.11372.*

Oh, B. (2023). Transformer-based language model surprisal predicts human reading times best with about two billion training tokens. https://doi.org/10.18653/v1/2023.findings-emnlp.128

R Core Team. (2023). *R: A language and environment for statistical computing.* R Foundation for Statistical Computing. https://www.R-project.org/

Rathi, N. (2021, June). Dependency locality and neural surprisal as predictors of processing difficulty: Evidence from reading times. *Proceedings of the Workshop on Cognitive Modeling and Computational Linguistics*, 171–176.

Rönnqvist, S., Kanerva, J., Salakoski, T., & Ginter, F. (2019). Is multilingual BERT fluent in language generation? *arXiv preprint arXiv:1910.03806.*

Shu, P., Chen, J., Liu, Z., Wang, H., Wu, Z., Zhong, T., ... & Liu, T. (2024). Transcending language boundaries: Harnessing LLMs for low-resource language translation. *arXiv preprint arXiv:2411.11295.*

Sung, Y. T., Chang, T. H., Lin, W. C., Hsieh, K. S., & Chang, K. E. (2016). CRIE: An automated analyzer for Chinese texts. *Behavior Research Methods, 48*, 1238–1251.

Tang, Z., & van Hell, J. G. (2024). Learning to Write Rationally: How Information Is Distributed in Non-

Native Speakers' Essays. *arXiv preprint arXiv:2411.03550.*

Wang, Y. (2017). The Correlation between Lexical Richness and Writing Score of CSL Learner—the Multivariable Linear Regression Model and Equation of Writing Quality. *Applied Linguistics*, (2), 93-101

Wang, H., Cheng, Y., & Hu, X. (2022). A dynamic development study of CSL writing quality based on lexical features and grammatical patterns. *TCSOL studies*, (2), 20-31

Wang, Y., & Hu, R. (2021). A prompt-independent and interpretable automated essay scoring method for Chinese second language writing. In *Chinese Computational Linguistics* (pp. 450–470). Springer. https://doi.org/10.1007/978-3-030-84186-7_30

Hu, R., Wu, J., &, Lu, X. (2022). Word-Combination-Based Measures of Phraseological Diversity, Sophistication, and Complexity and Their Relationship to Second Language Chinese Proficiency and Writing Quality. *Language Learning, 72*(4), 1128-1169.

Wang, M., Li, C., & Lin, C. (2015). The contributions of segmental and suprasegmental information in reading Chinese characters aloud. Plos One, 10(11), e0142060. https://doi.org/10.1371/journal.pone.0142060

Wilcox, E. G., Pimentel, T., Meister, C., Cotterell, R., & Levy, R. P. (2023). Testing the predictions of surprisal theory in 11 languages. *Transactions of the Association for Computational Linguistics, 11*, 1451–1470.

Xu, W., Chon, J., Liu, T., & Futrell, R. (2023, December). The linearity of the effect of surprisal on reading times across languages. In Findings of the Association for Computational Linguistics: EMNLP 2023 (pp. 15711-15721).

Yu, Q. (2021). An organic syntactic complexity measure for the Chinese language: The TC-unit. *Applied Linguistics, 42*(1), 60-92.

Appendix A. L1 Backgrounds Distribution of L2 Learners in the Writing Dataset

L1 of L2 Learners	Number of Essays per Level	Total number of essays	Percentage of Dataset
English	18	72	27.69%
Vietnamese	14	56	21.54%
Japanese	13	52	20.00%
Korean	9	36	13.85%
Indonesian	6	24	9.23%
French	2	8	3.08%
Hungarian	1	4	1.54%
Russian	1	4	1.54%
Swedish	1	4	1.54%

Appendix B. Summary of LLM-Surprisal Scores, Mean (SD) for Chinese L2 Essays across Four CEFR Proficiency Levels

	Bloom	Chinese-LLaMA	Taiwan-LLM
A2	3.45(0.37)	3.06 (0.39)	1.64 (0.18)
B1	3.63(0.33)	3.16 (0.28)	1.59 (0.17)
B2	3.67(0.45)	3.18 (0.35)	1.51 (0.17)
C1	3.17(0.62)	2.85 (0.38)	1.34 (0.25)

Beyond Binary Animacy: A Multi-Method Investigation of LMs' Sensitivity in English Object Relative Clauses

Yue Li[1], Yan Cong[1,2], Elaine J. Francis[1]
[1]Department of Linguistics, Purdue University
[2]School of Languages and Cultures, Purdue University
{li4207, cong4, ejfranci}@purdue.edu

Abstract

Animacy is a well-documented factor affecting language production, but its influence on Language Models (LMs) in complex structures like Object Relative Clauses (ORCs) remains underexplored. This study examines LMs' sensitivity to animacy in English ORC structure choice (passive vs. active) using surprisal-based and prompting-based analyses, alongside human baselines. In surprisal-based analysis, DistilGPT-2 best mirrored human preferences, while GPT-Neo and BERT-base showed rigid biases, diverging from human patterns. Prompting-based analysis expanded testing to GPT-4o-mini, Gemini models, and DeepSeek-R1, revealing GPT-4o-mini's stronger human alignment but limited animacy sensitivity in Gemini models and DeepSeek-R1. Some LMs exhibited inconsistencies between analyses, reinforcing that prompting alone is unreliable for assessing linguistic competence. Corpus analysis confirmed that training data alone cannot fully explain animacy sensitivity, suggesting emergent animacy-aware representations. These findings underscore the interaction between training data, model architecture, and linguistic generalization, highlighting the need for integrating structured linguistic knowledge into LMs to enhance their alignment with human sentence processing mechanisms.

1 Introduction

Animacy belongs to a set of semantic factors known to affect language production due to its centrality in human communication (Cooper and Ross, 1975). Previous studies have found that the animacy status of nouns affects how structures are formed. Specifically, one commonly investigated structure is object relative clauses (ORC). Many studies found that ORCs with animate head nouns are more likely to be produced in the passive structure instead of the active structure (e.g., Gennari et al., 2012; Humphreys et al., 2016; Wu et al., 2022). For example, English speakers overwhelmingly prefer passive structures like (1-a) in Table 1 over their active counterparts (1-b), whereas in describing an inanimate target, (1-c) and (1-d) are equally probable.

The concept of animacy—distinguishing between living and non-living entities—is rooted in human beings' perceptual, cognitive, and linguistic development (Gelman, 1981; Leslie, 1994; Rakison and Poulin-Dubois, 2001). However, transformer-based pre-trained language models (LMs) learn solely from text, raising the question of whether they exhibit human-like sensitivity to animacy when processing complex syntactic structures like ORCs, or if their behavior differs due to their text-based learning paradigm.

Recent studies have begun exploring this question, finding that while some LMs demonstrate sensitivity to animacy constraints, this varies across models (Hanna et al., 2023; Kauf et al., 2023; Yun et al., 2023), leaving open the question of whether LMs encode animacy as an abstract linguistic feature or simply reflect statistical patterns in text. Particularly relevant to the current study, Yun et al. (2023) reported ChatGPT-3.5's higher probability of generating active ORCs when the head noun was inanimate and the agent noun was animate than when both were animate. However, their study did not fully control for all possible animacy configurations of head and agent nouns. And the rapid advancement of LMs highlights the need for continued research to refine our understanding of their linguistic processing.

To address the gap, we use psycholinguistically guided minimal pairs to systematically test how animacy influences active vs. passive ORC structure choice across a full list of animacy conditions: AA (animate head noun + animate agent), IA (inanimate head noun + animate agent), AI (animate head noun + inanimate agent), and II (inanimate head noun + inanimate agent). This approach allows

Proceedings of the Workshop on Cognitive Modeling and Computational Linguistics, pages 184–196
May 3, 2025

No.	Cond.	Head Noun	Agent Noun	Structure	Example
(1-a)	AA	animate	animate	passive	*the man who's being punched by the woman*
(1-b)	AA	animate	animate	active	*the man that the woman is punching*
(1-c)	IA	inanimate	animate	passive	*the sandbag that's being punched by the woman*
(1-d)	IA	inanimate	animate	active	*the sandbag that the woman is punching*

Table 1: Sample ORCs varied by head noun animacy.

us to determine whether LMs replicate humanlike animacy effects or diverge from human processing, providing insight into the role of animacy in LMs' ORC structure selection.

2 Related Works

2.1 Animacy in object relative clauses

One of the widely studied structures affected by animacy in psycholinguistics is the object relative clause (ORC): the animacy status of nouns involved in the ORC was found to affect whether the ORC is produced in passive or active structures in many languages (e.g., Gennari et al., 2012; Hsiao and MacDonald, 2016; Rodrigo et al., 2018; Wu et al., 2022). Specifically, the passive ORC is strongly preferred when both the head noun and the agent noun are animate (Condition AA), but this preference diminishes when the head noun is inanimate and the agent noun remains animate (Condition IA).

One explanation for the preference for passive ORCs is the animacy-based accessibility mechanism (Gordon et al., 2001), which suggests that animate nouns are conceptually salient and more likely to take the subject role in ORCs, leading to a passive preference (J. K. Bock and Warren, 1985). Alternatively, the similarity-based competition mechanism (K. Bock et al., 1992; McDonald et al., 1993) argues that two animate nouns (e.g., *man* and *woman* in Table 1) create higher cognitive load than inanimate-animate pair (e.g., *sandbag* and *woman*) due to conceptual competition in working memory. To ease this load, speakers prefer passives, which postpone the agent noun (Gennari et al., 2012). While both mechanisms predict animacy effects on ORC structure choice, they differ in their explanations for the passive preference in animate-head ORCs. However, past studies have only tested two (AA, IA: Gennari et al., 2012; Hsiao and MacDonald, 2016; Humphreys et al., 2016; Wu et al., 2022) or three (AA, IA, AI: Rodrigo et al., 2018) conditions, leaving gaps in understanding the full scope of animacy effect.

Which structure would speakers prefer when producing ORCs with inanimate head nouns and inanimate agents (condition II)? Would they equally choose passive or active because there are no animate head nouns urgently in need of a subject role? Or would they still strongly favor passives because due to the cognitive load imposed by competition between two similar inanimate nouns? Due to the lack of studies incorporating all four animacy conditions, the relationship between animacy status and ORC structure preference is not clear. This gap extends beyond psycholinguistics to LMs, as investigating animacy-driven structure choices in LMs can provide insights into whether they reflect human-like processing or rely on different underlying mechanisms. Conversely, exploring these patterns in LMs may also offer predictions about what to expect in the underexplored conditions, guiding future psycholinguistic research. To bridge these gaps, the current study first exposes human participants to all four animacy conditions to establish a baseline. This not only fills a critical gap in psycholinguistics but also lays the groundwork for evaluating LMs' animacy-sensitivity in making syntactic decisions in the following steps.

2.2 Animacy in LMs

The role of animacy in language modeling has been a topic of interest in computational linguistics. Early work by Elman (1990) showed that a simple recurrent network trained on synthetic language data formed distinct clusters for animate and inanimate entities, suggesting that basic LMs developed animacy-sensitive representations.

More recent studies have examined how animacy is integrated into broader linguistic behavior in LMs. Kauf et al. (2023) found that LMs exhibit sensitivity to animacy as it relates to selectional constraints, indicating that animacy is integrated into their broader event knowledge. Hanna et al. (2023) found that LMs can infer animacy from contextual cues and adjust their processing accordingly, though not always to the same extent as humans.

Several studies have also explored how animacy affects syntactic structure choice. Futrell and Levy (2018) found that recurrent neural network language models (RNN LMs) learn animacy as an abstract feature that influences word order, though its effect was weaker and less consistent than other factors like constituent length. In a more targeted investigation, Yun et al. (2023) prompted GPT-3.5 with sentence fragments and observed significantly more active ORCs when the head noun was inanimate than when it was animate, suggesting that animacy influences structural choices in LMs. Papadimitriou (2024) found that animacy is a strong predictor of subjecthood in mBERT's embedding space: animate nouns were more likely to be classified as agents, even when controlling for syntactic role. This finding supports the idea that LMs encode subjectivity in gradient and functionally-driven ways, with animacy as a core dimension.

Building on this line of research, our study goes beyond the typical binary manipulation of head noun animacy in ORC configurations. We introduce a four-way animacy design that systematically varies both head noun and agent animacy across conditions (AA, IA, AI, II). Our investigation consists of three complementary experiments: (1) surprisal-based analysis, (2) training corpus examination, and (3) direct prompting-based analysis. Our goal is to determine whether LMs show animacy sensitivity in ORC processing, and if so, whether their animacy effects reflect an emergent linguistic pattern or are merely artifacts of training data biases. We hypothesize that (1) LMs will exhibit systematic surprisal-based animacy effects, but with model variations, (2) corpus distributions alone will not fully account for LMs' structure choices, and (3) prompting analysis will reveal animacy-driven patterns in ORC selection for some LMs, if not all.

3 Psycholinguistic Data

Design Fruitful previous studies, including Gennari and MacDonald (2009) with 82 native English speakers, Montag and MacDonald (2015) with 30, and Humphreys et al. (2016) with 16, have consistently found that animacy affects the choice between passive and active ORCs, particularly in Conditions AA and IA, using similar picture-based elicitation tasks. In the current study, we used 20 illustrated scenes created with Procreate and supplemented with licensed clip art (See Appendix A for an example). Each scene depicted four distinct events, all involving the same action (e.g., hitting, pulling, pushing, chasing, lifting), varying by the animacy of the agent and patient: AA: Animate Agent – Animate Patient (e.g., a woman lifting a boy); IA: Animate Agent – Inanimate Patient (e.g., a woman lifting a box); AI: Inanimate Agent – Animate Patient (e.g., balloons lifting a boy); II: Inanimate Agent – Inanimate Patient (e.g., balloons lifting a box). We also included 50 filler scenes depicting unrelated events (e.g., riding bikes, playing cards), designed to elicit a range of structures including simple and subject relative clauses. Participants viewed the images and responded to questions. Their choice of active or passive relative clause structure was analyzed. As a proof-of-concept psycholinguistic study, five adult native English speakers each produced twenty responses. Their structure choices were coded accordingly. This preliminary study establishes a human baseline for evaluating LM behavior, as no prior work has systematically investigated all four animacy configurations of ORCs.

Result Our preliminary results align with previous research in two key ways: (1) a general preference for passives overall (Gennari et al., 2012; Montag et al., 2017), and (2) higher passive usage in AA and AI compared to IA (e.g., Humphreys et al., 2016; Rodrigo et al., 2018). As shown in Figure 1, passive structures were strongly preferred in AA (96%) over IA (63%), with a significant difference ($B = 2.69$, $p = 0.02*$) confirmed by binomial mixed-effects logistic regression. AI also showed a high passive rate (95%), comparable to AA, consistent with findings by Rodrigo et al. (2018) in Spanish and Japanese. Our study further provides new insights into the II condition. While II did not differ significantly from other conditions ($p > 0.5$), its passive rate (82%) was noticeably higher than IA (63%), suggesting that even without an animate noun, similarity-based competition between two inanimates may still promote passive use.

These results reinforce the complex role of animacy in ORC structure choice. The strong passive preference in AA and AI aligns with the expectation that animate head nouns favor the subject position, making passivization the preferred structure (Gennari et al., 2012; Rodrigo et al., 2018). The IA condition, which lacks both an animate

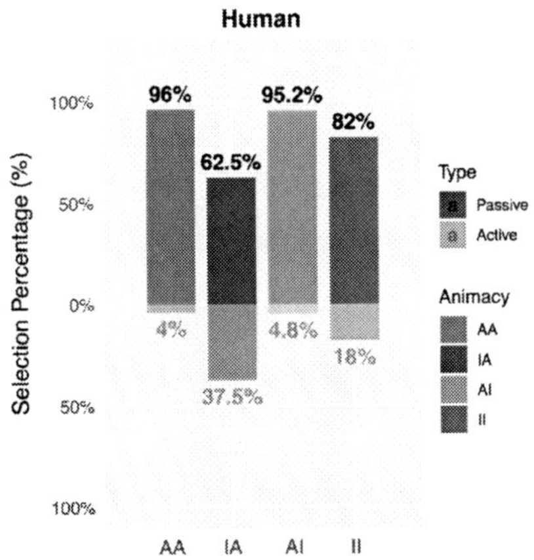

Figure 1: Human responses: ORC structure choice by animacy condition. AA represents ORCs with animate head noun and animate agent; IA: inanimate head noun, animate agent; AI: animate head noun, inanimate agent; II: inanimate head noun and agent.

head noun and animacy congruence, showed the lowest passive preference, suggesting that the absence of these factors results in weaker motivation for passivization. The II condition, despite the absence of an animate noun, exhibited a higher passive rate than IA, suggesting that *similarity-based competition* may still influence structure choice even among inanimate referents. While we acknowledge the limitations of our sample size[1], the clear alignment of our findings with prior research and the observed significant effects suggest that animacy effects in ORC processing extend beyond a simple binary contrast and involve a more complex interaction between competition and accessibility mechanisms.

4 LMs and Experiments

4.1 Surprisal-based analysis

Dataset Following our psycholinguistic paradigm and previous research (e.g., Gennari and MacDonald, 2009; Humphreys et al., 2016), we designed experimental English prompt minimal pairs (Cong, 2022), each consisting of a written *context story* and a pair of *target sentences*. Expanding on our psycholinguistics experiment, we developed a set of 384 prompt pairs, with 96 pairs per animacy condition. Each pair includes both a passive ORC target sentence and its active counterpart. For instance, in Table 2, the target sentences (passive: "*The baby that is held by the father is crying*"; active: "*The baby that the father holds is crying*") both serve as grammatically valid answers to the final question in the *context story*. We hypothesize that LMs will select different target sentences depending on the animacy condition, despite potential variations due to model differences.

Experimental Design and LMs We evaluated the performance of various LMs on ORCs' structure choice: DistilGPT-2 (Sanh et al., 2019), GPT-Neo (Black et al., 2021; Gao et al., 2020), BERT-large-uncased (Devlin et al., 2018), and the BERT-base-uncased (Devlin et al., 2018). See Table 3 for summary. These differences, including size, architecture (masked vs. causal), and training data diversity, are likely to influence how each LM processes syntactic structure and animacy-sensitive patterns, and thus are important for interpreting model–human comparisons.

In the current analysis, the preference for a particular answer is measured by the *surprisal score* of each target sentence given by LMs (Cong et al., 2023; Hale, 2001; Michaelov and Bergen, 2022). For GPT-type LMs, surprisal was calculated as the negative log probability of the word given left context (Levy, 2013). We computed the *surprisal score* at the sentence level. When the LMs tokenizer splits the target in more than one token, we take the average of the *surprisal score* of its subtokens (See Appendix B for out-of-vocabulary (OOV) ratios by animacy condition for each LM). For BERT-type models, which are bidirectional and trained via a masked language modeling objective, *surprisal* was calculated as the sum of the negative log probabilities of each word, conditioned on both its preceding and following context—normalized by the total number of tokens in the sentence. This sentence-level *surprisal* aligns with BERT's bidirectional training: unlike autoregressive models that rely solely on left context, denoising autoencoding models like BERT and RoBERTa are explicitly trained to make word predictions based on both left and right contexts. Our *surprisal* calculation for BERT therefore mirrors its underlying architecture and learning objective, supporting a more principled comparison with GPT-style models. To keep consistency in operation, we used minicons (Misra, 2022) for both BERT and GPT-type LMs, specifically the scorer module for the masked language models such as BERT (i.e., the scorer.MaskedLMScorer class), and standard au-

[1]Our ongoing psycholinguistic research with 35 participants replicates these findings. Details will be published in a forthcoming paper.

Context Story	Structure	Target Sentence
There are two babies, a mother, and a father in the scene. The father holds the crying baby. The mother holds the smiling baby. Which baby is crying?	Passive	The baby that *is held by the father* is crying.
	Active	The baby that *the father holds* is crying.

Table 2: Example prompt pair for surprisal analysis.

Model	Arch.	Size	Training Data
BERT-base	masked	110M	BooksCorpus, Wikipedia
BERT-large	masked	340M	BooksCorpus, Wikipedia
DistilGPT-2	causal	82M	OpenWebText
GPT-Neo	causal	1.3B	The Pile

Table 3: Summary of LMs used in the surprisal-based analysis.

toregressive language models such as DistilGPT-2 (i.e., the scorer.IncrementalLMScorer class). When the passive structure in a prompt pair receives a lower mean surprisal score than its active counterpart, we coded the outcome variable *choose-psv* as 1, otherwise as 0.

For statistical analysis, binomial logistic mixed-effects model was fitted for each LM with *choose-psv* as the dependent variable, Animacy as the main predictor (categorical). The random-effects structure included only Items. The LME4 package in R (Bates, 2014) was used for statistics modeling. Post-hoc comparisons were conducted with the *emmeans* package (Lenth, 2019), applying *Tukey* adjustments for pairwise comparisons. Our implementation is available on our Github page.

Results Figure 2 shows structure selection rates by animacy for each LM, with darker bars indicating passive selection and lighter bars representing active selection. Several key patterns emerged. First, different LMs exhibited distinct structural biases: BERT-large ($B = 0.79$, $p < 0.001$), BERT-base ($B = 2.71$, $p < 0.001$), and DistilGPT-2 ($B = 0.92$, $p < 0.001$) showed overall strong passive preference, whereas GPT-Neo significantly favored actives across conditions, shown by its significant negative intercept ($B = -0.78$, $p < 0.01$).

Next, for each LM, the results (see Figure 2) showed significant animacy effects for BERT-large ($p < 0.001$), DistilGPT-2 ($p < 0.01$), and GPT-Neo ($p < 0.001$), while BERT-base did not reach significance ($p = 0.06$). BERT-large showed significantly lower passive selection rates in IA and AI conditions compared to AA and II, suggesting that BERT-large is less likely to choose passives when the head noun and agent differ in animacy features.

DistilGPT-2 chose significantly fewer passives in IA, indicating an increased selection for actives when the head noun is animate and the agent is inanimate. GPT-Neo, unlike other models, showed a stronger passive preference in IA compared to AI and II. BERT-base, due to its exceptionally high passive selection rates across all conditions, did not exhibit significant effect of animacy.

To evaluate the alignment between LMs and human responses, we conducted Pearson correlation analyses and RMSE (Root Mean Square Error) calculations between each LM's passive selection rates and human data. The results reported DistilGPT-2's highest Pearson correlation ($r = 0.98$) and lowest RMSE (0.14), suggesting closer alignment with human patterns. GPT-Neo showed the lowest Pearson correlation ($r = -0.66$) and highest RMSE (0.55), indicating its substantial divergence from human patterns. Figure 3 visualizes passive selection rates across animacy conditions for each LM, with the red line representing human response patterns from psycholinguistic data. The figure further highlights DistilGPT-2's closer alignment to human behavior (navy blue line), while GPT-Neo exhibits the greatest divergence (light blue line).

4.2 OpenWeb corpus analysis

While surprisal-based experiment found varying degrees of animacy sensitivity in LMs, an open question remains: Is this sensitivity an emergent linguistic property or merely a reflection of the distribution in the training data? Specifically, do LMs assign surprisal scores based on inherent animacy effects, or are these scores simply mirroring the animacy-driven distribution of ORCs in the training data?

Method To address this question, we exam-

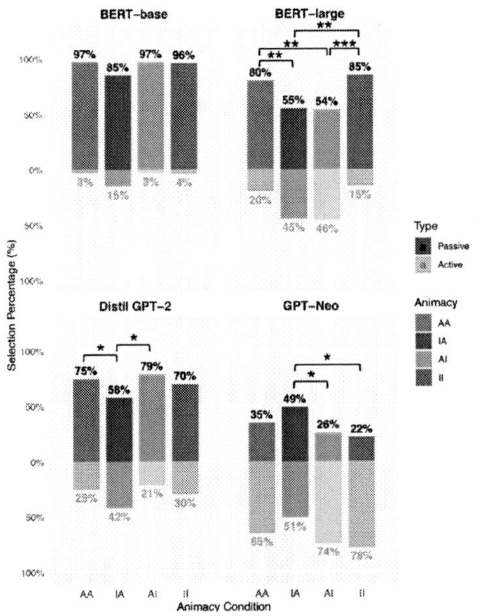

Figure 2: Structure selection rate by animacy and LM according to surprisal-based analysis.

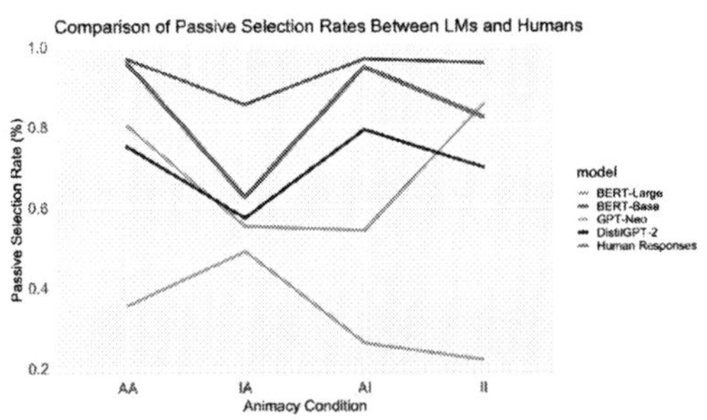

Figure 3: Passive selection pattern comparison between LMs and human data.

ined the structural distribution of active and passive ORCs across animacy conditions in the OpenWeb corpus (Gokaslan and Cohen, 2019), an open-source reproduction of OpenAI's WebText dataset, which was used to train GPT-2. We randomly selected over 8,000 sentences from the corpus and used a custom syntactic parsing pipeline using SpaCy to automatically extract sentences containing ORCs. The extraction procedure identified ORCs based on the presence of a head noun, an embedded verb phrase, and an agent noun—accounting for both overt and omitted relative pronouns. Manual examination of the automatically identified ORCs was conducted and only those with correct annotations were retained. Each validated ORC was then categorized as active or passive, and the animacy status of both the head noun and agent noun was annotated. This allowed us to quantify the frequency of active and passive ORC structures across different animacy conditions.

Then, we conducted Pearson correlation tests to assess whether the ORC distribution in OpenWeb alone could account for the animacy-driven ORC patterns found in human responses, to identify which LMs' surprisal scores best aligned with human responses, and to determine whether incorporating corpus data could enhance the explanatory power of LMs in modeling human behavior.

Results Only 1.34% of our examined sentences were found to contain a complete ORC. As shown in Table 4, these ORCs are skewed toward actives (71.03%) over passives (28.97%) and are imbalanced by animacy, with IA conditions dominating (66.36%). Particularly, active IA ORCs alone account for 53.27% of all ORCs, suggesting a pronounced structural bias in the training corpus. In contrast, AA and AI conditions are rare, comprising only 4.67% and 1.87% of the total ORCs, respectively.

Struct.	AA (%)	IA (%)	AI (%)	II (%)	Sum (%)
Passive	0.93	13.08	0.93	14.02	28.97
Active	3.74	53.27	0.93	13.08	71.03
Total	4.67	66.36	1.87	27.10	100

Table 4: ORCs found in OpenWeb sample grouped by animacy and structure.

Pearson correlation tests (Table 5) indicate that corpus data alone has low predictive power for both human responses ($R^2 = 0.12$, $p = 0.66$) and DistilGPT-2's surprisal values ($R^2 = 0.26$, $p = 0.49$). While the corpus shows moderate predictive power for GPT-Neo ($R^2 = 0.78, p = 0.12$), the negative correlation ($r = -0.89$) suggests that GPT-Neo follows an opposite trend from corpus-based distributions.

Among the four tested LMs (DistilGPT2, GPT-Neo, BERT-large, and BERT-base), DistilGPT2 accounted for the highest variance in human responses ($R^2 = 0.96, p = 0.02$), explaining 95.6% of the variance with statistical significance. Adding OpenWeb further increased the explained variance to 98.7%, but the lack of significance suggests that the combined model did not outperform DistilGPT-2 alone. The other three LLMs showed weaker alignment with human behavior. GPT-Neo exhibited strong divergence, as indicated by its negative estimates and low R^2 values, suggesting an opposite structure preference. BERT-large explained only 9% of the variance (not significant), indicating it is a weak predictor of human responses. BERT-base captured 88.4% of the variance but was not significant, and incorporating OpenWeb did not improve its predictive power.

4.3 Prompting-based analysis

LMs To further strengthen our investigation, we conducted a supplementary analysis using prompt engineering. In addition to the four previously examined LMs, we included four recent state-of-the-art models: GPT-4o-mini (Achiam et al., 2023), Gemini-1.5-flash (Team et al., 2023), Gemini-2.0-flash, and DeepSeek-R1 (Guo et al., 2025). This analysis used the same dataset as the surprisal analysis, which consists of 384 context stories paired with sentences containing passive and active ORCs.

Method Each LM was prompted to select the more appropriate syntactic structure based on the given context. The structured prompt explicitly instructed the model as follows: *"Read the following context carefully, which includes a short story and a question at the end. Two possible answers are provided. Your task is to choose the answer that sounds most natural to a native English speaker. Please respond with either "1" for the first option (Passive) or "2" for the second option (Active)".*

Same as surprisal-based analysis, LMs' choice was recorded as 1 for *passive* and 0 for *active* in the variable *choose-psv* for each trial. The passive selection rate was calculated as the proportion of trials in which the model selected *passive* within each animacy condition.

For model comparison, we computed Pearson correlation, MSE and RMSE. Pearson correlation evaluates the linear relationship, while RMSE quantifies the average deviation of model predictions from human responses, with lower values indicating better fit. Together, these measures provide a comprehensive evaluation of how closely or differently each LM perform compared to human.

Design Considerations While our human experiment used picture-based elicitation (See Appendix A for an example), we opted for a controlled, text-based prompting design in this analysis. This choice was made to avoid confounds introduced by image recognition and visual reasoning, which current LMs may not reliably handle in a standardized way. Instead, we used context stories that mirrored the structural and referential properties of the original visual stimuli, allowing us to isolate syntactic preference.

That said, a potential alternative design could involve describing the visual scene and posing a direct question (e.g., "Who is wearing red?"), then analyzing the model's free-text response. Such a design could more closely simulate the referential pressure that led to ORC production in humans and may be explored in future work.

Results As shown in Figure 4, the structure choices made by different LMs in the prompt engineering experiment show great variation. Several noticeable patterns emerged. First, BERT models (BERT-large, BERT-base) exhibit limited variation in response, overwhelmingly favoring passive ORCs (near 100%) across all conditions. Gemini models (Gemini-1.5-flash, Gemini-2.0-flash), on the other hand, strongly prefer actives, with Gemini-2.0-flash selecting active ORCs in nearly 100% of all conditions. Both model families seem to lack human-like variation in structure choice. GPT models (DistilGPT2, GPT-Neo, GPT-4o-mini) and DeepSeek-R1 show more variation. ANOVA analysis confirms significant differences among LMs compared to human responses ($df = 8$, $p < 0.001$). Post-hoc tests indicate that while all LMs deviate from human responses to some extent, GPT-4o-mini exhibits the smallest difference ($diff. = 0.19, p = 0.01$).

Model evaluation (see Figure 5) showed GPT-4o-mini as the top performer, with the highest correlation to human data ($estimate = 0.98$), highest explained variance ($R^2 = 96.4\%$), and lowest RMSE ($estimate = 0.21$). BERT models (especially BERT-base) performed the worst, as they explained almost no variance in human data and had weak correlations. DistilGPT2 and GPT-Neo showed moderate alignment, indicating they capture some trends but weren't very strong predictors. Gemini models and DeepSeekR1 performed inconsistently, they had low variance explained and high RMSE, suggesting they aren't reliable in matching human responses.

5 Discussion

5.1 LMs show animacy sensitivity with model-specific variations

Our surprisal-based and prompting-based analyses revealed LMs' varying sensitivity to animacy in

	R^2	Adjusted R^2	F-statistic	p-value
	How Corpus Explains Human Responses			
OpenWeb (corpus)	0.12	-0.33	0.26	0.66
	How Corpus Explains GPT Models			
DistilGPT-2	0.26	-0.12	0.69	0.49
GPT-Neo	0.78	0.67	7.13	0.12
	How LMs Explain Human Responses			
DistilGPT-2	0.96	0.93	42.93	0.02*
DistilGPT-2 + OpenWeb	0.99	0.96	37.11	0.12
GPT-Neo	0.44	0.16	1.58	0.34
GPT-Neo + OpenWeb	0.72	0.15	1.26	0.53
BERT(large)	0.09	-0.36	0.20	0.70
BERT(large) + OpenWeb	0.18	-1.43	0.12	0.90
BERT(base)	0.88	0.83	15.29	0.06
BERT(base) + OpenWeb	0.93	0.80	6.95	0.26

Table 5: Regression results: corpus vs. LMs and human ORC structure choice.

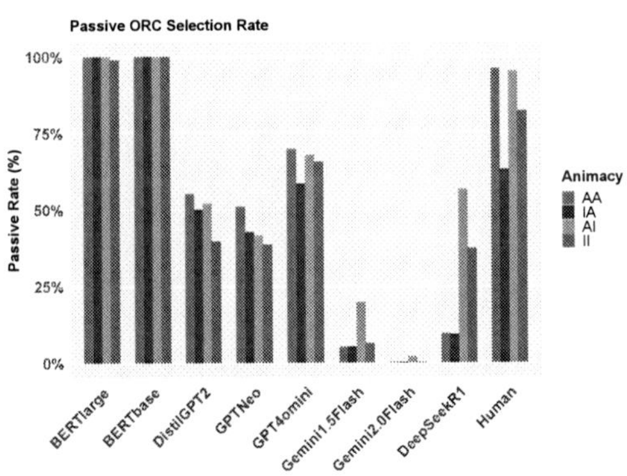

Figure 4: Passive selection rate by animacy and LM in prompting-based analysis

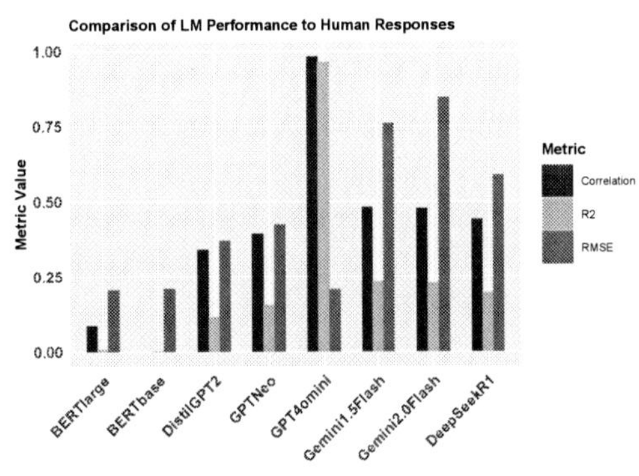

Figure 5: Evaluation of LMs' performance by human responses in prompting-based analysis

ORC structure choice, aligning with Hanna et al. (2023). The surprisal-based analysis reveals that DistilGPT-2's lower passive selection rate in IA compared to AA and AI aligns well with human data and psycholinguistic predictions (Gennari et al., 2012; Hsiao and MacDonald, 2016). According to the similarity-based competition mechanism (Gennari et al., 2012), passives should be more frequent in animacy-congruent conditions (AA and II). Among the tested LMs, only BERT-large followed this expected pattern, while BERT-base consistently over-selected passives, diverging from human data. Similar to Ettinger (2020), we report greater sensitivity of BERT-large to linguistic constraints than BERT-base. GPT-Neo showed a general preference for actives but unexpectedly showed its highest passive rate in IA, contradicting human data and psycholinguistic theories.

Some LMs performed inconsistently across prompting- and surprisal-based analyses. DistilGPT-2 and BERT-large performed poorly in prompting, explaining only 11.55% and 0.75% of human variance, respectively, likely due to fundamental task differences. As Hu and Levy (2023) pointed out, prompting is not a substitute for direct probability measurements in LMs, and results may vary within the same LM.

Among the four newly tested LMs in prompting-based analysis, GPT-4o-mini best mirrored human patterns, despite an overall lower rate of passive selection. In contrast, Gemini models (Gemini-1.5-Flash and Gemini-2.0-Flash) showed minimal variation across animacy conditions, suggesting that their internal representations likely do not align with established linguistic theories (Cong, 2024). Gemini-2.0-Flash, in particular, overwhelmingly favored active structures ($\sim$100%), justifying its choices by claiming actives sound more direct and natural in English, whereas passives feel overly formal. DeepSeek-R1 exhibited structural variation across animacy conditions but in a theoretically ungrounded way. While psycholinguistic studies consistently report higher passive rates in AA than IA (Gennari et al., 2012; Hsiao and MacDonald, 2016), DeepSeek-R1 showed little distinction between these conditions, deviating from both human behavior and psycholinguistic predictions.

5.2 Training data alone fails to explain animacy sensitivity in LMs

Our analysis of ORC distribution in OpenWeb suggests that training data alone is a weak predictor of LMs' structure choices, as reflected in surprisal results. While training data influences LM behavior (Chai et al., 2024), it fails to fully account for observed animacy effects, challenging the idea that these effects stem solely from training biases. Instead, our findings suggest that some LMs, particularly DistilGPT-2 (surprisal-based) and GPT-4o-mini (prompting-based), develop emergent animacy sensitivity beyond exposure, aligning with human data and psycholinguistic predictions (Gennari et al., 2012; Hsiao and MacDonald, 2016), despite training corpus' limited explanatory power. DistilGPT-2 alone explains 95.6% of the variance in human responses, indicating that its animacy sensitivity cannot be attributed to corpus distributions alone.

That said, the predominance of active ORCs in IA conditions in the corpus may still contribute to LMs' preference for active structures in these cases. This pattern is consistent with Roland et al. (2007), they also found higher percentage of active ORCs in IA conditions compared to AA in both the Brown corpus (IA: 53%, AA: 25%) and the Switchboard corpus (IA: 69%, AA: 9%). Our corpus analysis revealed an even stronger dominance of active ORCs in IA conditions, reinforcing the influence of corpus-based biases.

Ultimately, while corpus distributions shape structure choices to some extent, they fail to explain the deeper, human-like patterns observed in surprisal-based and prompting-based analyses. The strong alignment between certain LMs and human responses suggests that animacy sensitivity in LMs arises from more than just statistical learning—it may reflect deeper linguistic generalization.

5.3 Optimize LMs with psycholinguistic knowledge

Despite carefully controlled input pairs and explicit instructions, many LMs failed to capture human-like animacy effects, with only a few demonstrating satisfactory sensitivity. Gemini-1.5-Flash, Gemini-2.0-Flash, DeepSeek-R1, and GPT-Neo showed little alignment with human patterns.

It is likely that these LMs struggle with the syntactic-semantic interface required for ORC structure choice processing, particularly when two structures convey the same meaning. Their training on large, diverse datasets may not emphasize fine-grained semantic features that guide human sentence processing. Future LM development and optimization could benefit from explicit integration of semantic and syntactic knowledge and targeted training on animacy effects and structural dependencies. Moving beyond surface-level pattern recognition towards deeper linguistic representation would improve LMs' alignment with human-like reasoning and formal (psycho-)linguistic theories.

6 Conclusion

To conclude, we found that LMs exhibited animacy sensitivity, though the extent varied across models, as reflected in their ORC structure choices. While some models aligned closely with human data, others diverged significantly, highlighting variation in how LMs process animacy in syntactic structures. DistilGPT-2 and GPT-4o-mini showed the strongest alignment, while Gemini models, DeepSeek-R1, and GPT-Neo failed to capture animacy effects meaningfully.

While training data influences LM behavior to some extent, it does not fully explain their animacy sensitivity, suggesting that some models develop emergent linguistic generalizations beyond mere statistical learning. To improve LMs' alignment with human cognition, future development should integrate psycholinguistic insights, refine semantic-syntactic training, and move beyond surface-level pattern learning. Strengthening linguistic representations will inspire the development of psychologically plausible models.

Limitations

While this study offers valuable insights into LMs' sensitivity to animacy in English ORC structure choice, several limitations remain.

Our current surprisal analysis computed average surprisal across tokens at the sentence level. While this approach simplifies comparison across sentence types, future work could adopt additive surprisal values, which better reflect joint probabilities over token sequences. Moreover, exploring surprisal at more localized levels—such as word- or phrase-level surprisal given left context—may better align with psycholinguistic processing and production (for this, we thank our anonymous reviewer for the suggestion). In addition, analyzing surprisal using a binary outcome variable (*choose-psv*) was conducted to mirror human production, but using raw surprisal differences as the dependent measure could potentially yield additional insights. This is an alternative analysis that can be done in future work to identify more fine-grained distinctions in model preferences.

Our psycholinguistic proof-of-concept study involved a limited number of human participants. While our findings are consistent with prior literature documenting animacy effects—particularly in AA, IA, and AI conditions—a larger sample size would strengthen empirical comparisons with LMs. Furthermore, in this project, we did not collect separate animacy norming data for our stimuli, which could improve future experimental control and interpretation in the future.

Our corpus analysis used a representative sample of the OpenWeb corpus to approximate natural distributional patterns, but it does not reconstruct LMs' full pretraining data. Broader corpus comparisons and controlled datasets would offer a more robust estimate of the linguistic patterns LMs are exposed to.

Lastly, although not the focus of the current work, future studies could incorporate layer-wise probing to explore whether animacy effects arise during lexical encoding, syntactic composition, or higher-level integration processes.

Acknowledgments

This project was supported by Purdue-internal funding sources, including the Ross-Lynn Research Scholar Fund, the College of Liberal Arts PROMISE Award, the School of Interdisciplinary Studies, the Department of Linguistics, and the Department of English. We also gratefully acknowledge external support from the 2023 Gorilla and Prolific Grant. We thank the Gilbreth Cluster at the Rosen Center for Advanced Computing (RCAC), Purdue University, for providing GPU computational resources; Gorilla Experiment Builder for the implementation of the psycholinguistic experiment. We also thank our research assistants—Marley Mack, Golsa Khodadadi, and Yongjia Deng—for their help with data collection in psycholinguistic experiment; the members of Purdue Experimental Linguistics Lab—Shaohua Fang, Vanessa Sheu, Jingying Hu, and Kyle Swanson—for their valuable feedback throughout the development of this project. We thank Yue Li's dissertation committee members—Alejandro Cuza, John Sundquist, and Mariko Wei—for their guidance and support. Finally, we gratefully thank three anonymous reviewers for their detailed feedback on the psycholinguistic experiment as well as the three LM analyses, which improved the clarity and quality of the paper. All codes and materials for this project are available on our OSF page and GitHub repository.

References

Achiam, J., Adler, S., Agarwal, S., Ahmad, L., Akkaya, I., Aleman, F. L., Almeida, D., Altenschmidt, J., Altman, S., Anadkat, S., et al. (2023). Gpt-4 technical report. *arXiv preprint arXiv:2303.08774*.

Bates, K. (2014). Empathy or entertainment? the form and function of violent crime narratives in early-nineteenth century broadsides. *Law, Crime Hist.*, *4*, 1.

Black, S., Gao, L., Wang, P., Leahy, C., & Biderman, S. (2021). Gpt-neo: Large scale autoregressive language modeling with mesh-tensorflow. *If you use this software, please cite it using these metadata*, *58*, 2.

Bock, J. K., & Warren, R. K. (1985). Conceptual accessibility and syntactic structure in sentence formulation. *Cognition*, *21*(1), 47–67.

Bock, K., Loebell, H., & Morey, R. (1992). From conceptual roles to structural relations: Bridging the syntactic cleft. *Psychological review*, *99*(1), 150.

Chai, Y., Liu, Q., Wang, S., Sun, Y., Peng, Q., & Wu, H. (2024). On training data influence of gpt models. https://arxiv.org/abs/2404.07840

Cong, Y. (2022). Psycholinguistic diagnosis of language models' commonsense reasoning. *Proceedings of the first workshop on com-*

monsense representation and reasoning (CSRR 2022), 17–22.

Cong, Y. (2024). Manner implicatures in large language models. *Scientific Reports*, *14*(1), 29113.

Cong, Y., Chersoni, E., Hsu, Y.-Y., & Lenci, A. (2023). Are language models sensitive to semantic attraction? a study on surprisal. *Proceedings of the 12th Joint Conference on Lexical and Computational Semantics (* SEM 2023)*, 141–148.

Cooper, W. E., & Ross, J. R. (1975). World order. *Papers from the parasession on functionalism*, *11*, 63–111.

Devlin, J., Chang, M.-W., Lee, K., & Toutanova, K. (2018). Bert: Pre-training of deep bidirectional transformers for language understanding. *arXiv preprint arXiv:1810.04805*.

Elman, J. L. (1990). Finding structure in time. *Cognitive science*, *14*(2), 179–211.

Ettinger, A. (2020). What bert is not: Lessons from a new suite of psycholinguistic diagnostics for language models. *Transactions of the Association for Computational Linguistics*, *8*, 34–48.

Futrell, R., & Levy, R. P. (2018). Do rnns learn human-like abstract word order preferences? *arXiv preprint arXiv:1811.01866*.

Gao, L., Biderman, S., Black, S., Golding, L., Hoppe, T., Foster, C., Phang, J., He, H., Thite, A., & Nabeshima, N. (2020). The pile: An 800gb dataset of diverse text for language modeling. *arXiv preprint arXiv:2101.00027*.

Gelman, R. (1981). The development of thoughts about animate and inanimate objects: Implications for research in social cognition. *The development of social cognition in children*.

Gennari, S. P., & MacDonald, M. C. (2009). Linking production and comprehension processes: The case of relative clauses. *Cognition*, *111*(1), 1–23.

Gennari, S. P., Mirković, J., & MacDonald, M. C. (2012). Animacy and competition in relative clause production: A cross-linguistic investigation. *Cognitive psychology*, *65*(2), 141–176.

Gokaslan, A., & Cohen, V. (2019). Openwebtext corpus.

Gordon, P. C., Hendrick, R., & Johnson, M. (2001). Memory interference during language processing. *Journal of experimental psychology: learning, memory, and cognition*, *27*(6), 1411.

Guo, D., Yang, D., Zhang, H., Song, J., Zhang, R., Xu, R., Zhu, Q., Ma, S., Wang, P., Bi, X., et al. (2025). Deepseek-r1: Incentivizing reasoning capability in llms via reinforcement learning. *arXiv preprint arXiv:2501.12948*.

Hale, J. (2001). A probabilistic earley parser as a psycholinguistic model. *Second meeting of the north american chapter of the association for computational linguistics*.

Hanna, M., Belinkov, Y., & Pezzelle, S. (2023). When language models fall in love: Animacy processing in transformer language models. *arXiv preprint arXiv:2310.15004*.

Hsiao, Y., & MacDonald, M. C. (2016). Production predicts comprehension: Animacy effects in mandarin relative clause processing. *Journal of Memory and Language*, *89*, 87–109.

Hu, J., & Levy, R. (2023). Prompting is not a substitute for probability measurements in large language models. https://arxiv.org/abs/2305.13264

Humphreys, G. F., Mirković, J., & Gennari, S. P. (2016). Similarity-based competition in relative clause production and comprehension. *Journal of Memory and Language*, *89*, 200–221.

Kauf, C., Ivanova, A. A., Rambelli, G., Chersoni, E., She, J. S., Chowdhury, Z., Fedorenko, E., & Lenci, A. (2023). Event knowledge in large language models: The gap between the impossible and the unlikely. *Cognitive Science*, *47*(11), e13386.

Lenth, R. (2019). Emmeans: Estimated marginal means, aka least-squares means. r package version 1.4. 3.01.

Leslie, A. M. (1994). Tomm, toby, and agency: Core architecture and domain specificity. *Mapping the mind: Domain specificity in cognition and culture*, *29*, 119–48.

Levy, R. (2013). Memory and surprisal in human sentence comprehension. In *Sentence processing* (pp. 78–114). Psychology Press.

McDonald, J. L., Bock, K., & Kelly, M. H. (1993). Word and world order: Semantic, phonological, and metrical determinants of serial position. *Cognitive psychology*, *25*(2), 188–230.

Michaelov, J. A., & Bergen, B. K. (2022). Rarely a problem? language models exhibit inverse scaling in their predictions following few-type quantifiers. *arXiv preprint arXiv:2212.08700*.

Misra, K. (2022). Minicons: Enabling flexible behavioral and representational analyses of transformer language models. *arXiv preprint arXiv:2203.13112*.

Montag, J. L., & MacDonald, M. C. (2015). Text exposure predicts spoken production of complex sentences in 8-and 12-year-old children and adults. *Journal of Experimental Psychology: General*, *144*(2), 447.

Montag, J. L., Matsuki, K., Kim, J. Y., & MacDonald, M. C. (2017). Language specific and language general motivations of production choices: A multi-clause and multi-language investigation. *Collabra: Psychology*, *3*(1), 20.

Nair, S., & Resnik, P. (2023). Words, subwords, and morphemes: What really matters in the surprisal-reading time relationship? *arXiv preprint arXiv:2310.17774*.

Papadimitriou, I. V. (2024). *Jointly studying linguistic structure and language models: Methods for a bilateral science* [Doctoral dissertation, Stanford University].

Rakison, D. H., & Poulin-Dubois, D. (2001). Developmental origin of the animate–inanimate distinction. *Psychological bulletin*, *127*(2), 209.

Rodrigo, L., Igoa, J. M., & Sakai, H. (2018). The interplay of relational and non-relational processes in sentence production: The case of relative clause planning in japanese and spanish. *Frontiers in psychology*, *9*, 325103.

Roland, D., Dick, F., & Elman, J. L. (2007). Frequency of basic english grammatical structures: A corpus analysis. *Journal of memory and language*, *57*(3), 348–379.

Sanh, V., Debut, L., Chaumond, J., & Wolf, T. (2019). Distilbert, a distilled version of bert: Smaller, faster, cheaper and lighter. *arXiv preprint arXiv:1910.01108*.

Team, G., Anil, R., Borgeaud, S., Alayrac, J.-B., Yu, J., Soricut, R., Schalkwyk, J., Dai, A. M., Hauth, A., Millican, K., et al. (2023). Gemini: A family of highly capable multimodal models. *arXiv preprint arXiv:2312.11805*.

Wu, S. H., Henderson, L.-M., & Gennari, S. P. (2022). Animacy-induced conflict in sentence production and comprehension from late childhood to adolescence. *Journal of experimental child psychology*, *217*, 105350.

Yun, H., Yi, E., & Song, S. (2023). Exploring ai-generated english relative clauses in comparison to human production. *Journal of Cognitive Science*, *24*(4).

A Appendix: Psycholinguistic Experiment Procedure

Figure 6 presents an example trail from the elicitation task used in the psycholinguistic experiment. Participants viewed the image for 3 seconds before hearing a prompt question (e.g., "*Who wears red?*"). They then responded based on their observation of the scene. To encourage the production of ORCs without directly instructing participants, we told them their responses would help another participant identify characters or objects in the images. To prevent reliance on surface-level features like color (e.g., "red") or position (e.g., "on the left"), participants were informed that these features would change for the next group, while the actions would remain constant. This setup subtly prompted the use of ORCs by emphasizing actions as the most stable and reliable descriptors.

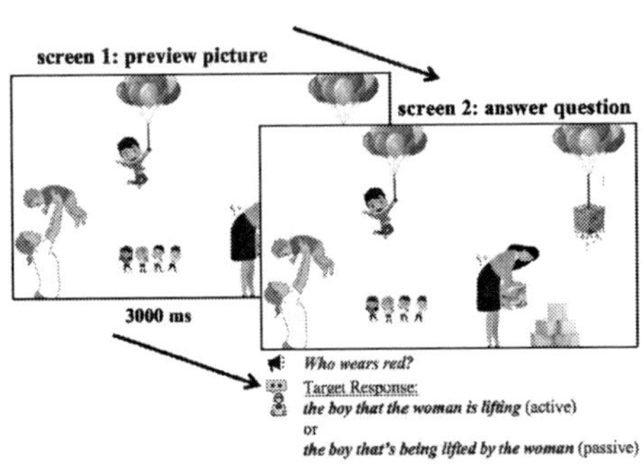

Figure 6: Sample stimulus image illustrating an ORC elicitation scenario

B Appendix: Surprisal-based analysis: out-of-vocabulary ratio

To ensure that surprisal differences across animacy conditions were not artifacts of tokenization, we examined the out-of-vocabulary (OOV) rates for each

LM by animacy condition. We acknowledge that word-level splits in subword tokenization may reduce the psycholinguistic validity of surprisal at the individual item level. However, Nair and Resnik (2023) found that BPE surprisal retains predictive power when comparing condition-level means—a pattern directly relevant to our study design, and that BPE-based models like GPT-2 still yield reliable surprisal–reading time correlations at the aggregate level.

Figure 7 shows the OOV percentage across animacy condition within each LM in our surprisal-based analysis. We see that OOV rates within each LM were quite consistent across animacy conditions. For example, BERT models ranged from 19.6% (AA) to 21.5% (II), while GPT models ranged from 33.9% (IA) to 36.5% (AI/II) (Distil GPT2 and GPT neo, BERT-base and BERT-large were combined due to the same OOV score). This stability across conditions suggests that differences in surprisal are unlikely to be driven by variability in tokenization. Thus, while GPT-based models naturally exhibit higher OOV due to their subword vocabularies, the uniformity of these rates across animacy conditions allows for meaningful interpretation of surprisal trends in line with the broader goals of our study.

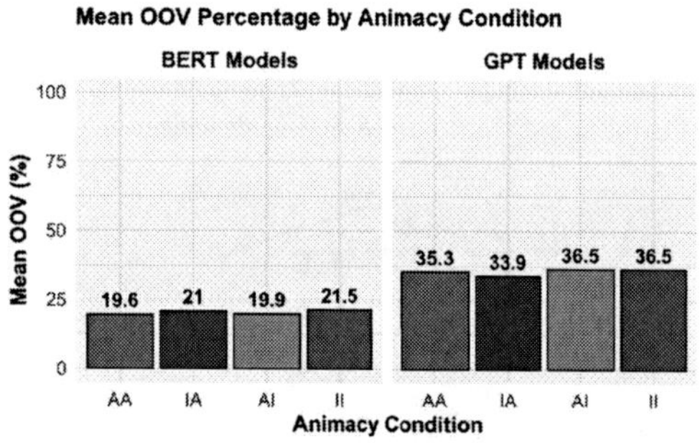

Figure 7: OOV by animacy by LM

An Empirical Study of Language Syllabification using Syllabary and Lexical Networks

Rusali Saha
Texas A&M University
rs0921@tamu.edu

Yannick Marchand
Faculty of Computer Science
Department of Pyschology and Neuroscience
Dalhousie University
marchand@cs.dal.ca

Abstract

Language syllabification is the separation of a word into written or spoken syllables. The study of syllabification plays a pivotal role in morphology and there have been previous attempts to study this phenomenon using graphs or networks. Previous approaches have claimed through visual estimation that the degree distribution of language networks follows the Power Law distribution, however, there have not been any empirically grounded metrics to determine the same. In our study, we implement two kinds of language networks, namely, syllabary and lexical networks, and investigate the syllabification of four European languages: English, French, German and Spanish using network analysis and examine their small-world, random and scale-free nature. We additionally empirically prove that contrary to claims in previous works, although the degree distribution of these networks appear to follow a power law distribution, they are actually more in agreement with a log-normal distribution, when a numerically grounded curve-fitting is applied. Finally, we explore how syllabary and lexical networks for the English language change over time using a database of age-of-acquisition rating words. Our analysis further shows that the preferential attachment mechanism appears to be a well-grounded explanation for the degree distribution of the syllabary network.

1 Introduction

A graph is a mathematical structure that is defined by a set of vertices (or nodes) that are potentially connected by edges (or links). In the last two decades, the formal study of graphs as well as their applications have received tremendous attention from the scientific community resulting in an exponential growth of academic publications.

The rapid rise of this field of research stems from the synergy of two main factors. First, this discipline benefited from the definition and characterization of special networks such as small-world networks (Watts and Strogatz, 1998) and scale-free networks (Barabási and Albert, 1999; Albert et al., 1999). Second, the amount of digital data has doubled in size every year (Lv et al., 2017), resulting in significant developments in associating various aspects of languages with graph-based approaches (Todorovska et al., 2023; Quispe et al., 2021; Liang et al., 2019).

In this work, we investigate the use of social networks in the context of syllabification. Syllabification has been used to study the division of a word into its constituent syllables and units of pronunciation. The syllable constitutes the key building block in phonetics (Laver, 1994) and in phonological theory (Fudge, 1969; Hooper, 1972; Selkirk, 1982). It aids word modelling in automatic speech and concatenative synthesis (Marchand and Damper, 2007). For instance, Müller, Möbius, and Prescher (2000, p.225) (Müller et al., 2000) write "syllable structure represents valuable information for pronunciation systems." In morphology, syllabification is also critical to understanding word formation as well as subsequent morphological changes (Ding et al., 2019). Furthermore, syllabification has greatly contributed to the comprehension of language acquisition (Langus et al., 2017), as it helps identify the pronunciation and rhythm of words. In our work, we study syllabification using network analysis, a powerful framework for revealing structural patterns that traditional linguistic methods may overlook.

Our work explores syllable networks and lexical networks in four European languages: English, French, German and Spanish. We quantitatively examine the organization of syllables and lexicons in the languages using network analysis. We have concerns that the visual estimation of log plots for degree distribution patterns is inadequate for identifying power law. Thus, we perform a detailed empirical analysis of the degree distribution of our networks. Furthermore, we use the concept of age-

Proceedings of the Workshop on Cognitive Modeling and Computational Linguistics, pages 197–206
May 3, 2025

of-acquisition for different words, to investigate the phenomena of preferential attachment.

2 Previous Work

Syllabification using network science has been previously explored only in three languages. First, there have been efforts to develop networks of syllables for the Portuguese language (Soares et al., 2005) in which the nodes represented syllables, and corresponding edges represented the co-occurrence of syllables in words (i.e. the pair of syllables occurred together in at least one word). The authors used two datasets for their study: (1) a Portuguese dictionary with 22,064 words; and (2) the works of Machado de Assis (Caldwell, 1970). This work claimed the presence of a mechanism of preferential attachment to explain the structure of their syllabary networks. Their finding was based on log-log plots inspection of the degree distributions as well as the calculation of the power law exponent (i.e. $gamma$), whose value was compatible with the $gamma$ value range that is commonly found in this kind of network (Albert and Barabási, 2002).

Second, syllabic and graphemic (character) networks for two Chinese dictionaries have also been generated (Peng et al., 2008) previously: (1) a Putonghua dictionary (CEDICT) consisting of 21,727 multisyllabic words and 8,834 monosyllabic words; and (2) a Cantonese dictionary (CULEX) including 35,732 multisyllabic words and 5,737 monosyllabic words. Considering the segmental (base syllable) and supra-segmental (tone) features of a syllable, the authors developed three levels of syllable networks: base-syllable, tonal syllable, and Chinese-character levels. Upon visual inspection of log-log plots and comparison of $gamma$ values, it was suggested that the syllabary networks followed a power-law distribution. Upon analyzing the power law exponent of the networks, they found an increasing order in the values of gamma, thus inferring preferential attachment to be strong at the base level, stronger at the tonal level and strongest at the character level networks.

Lastly, Croatian syllabic networks have been developed (Ban et al., 2013) using two large corpora: (1) the Croatian Wikipedia; and (2) the composition of 3218 articles from Croatian blogs. They construct three co-occurrence syllable networks and one directed, weighted first-neighbour syllable (formed by connecting only neighbour syllables) network. Although a formal power law analysis was not done, the authors visualized a log-log plot for the degree distribution of the co-occurrence syllable networks to estimate a premise for power law distribution.

Considering these works, our work explores syllable networks in four main European languages: English, French, German and Spanish. In addition to syllabary networks, we also model lexical networks to reflect the importance of words in the *mental lexicon*, a concept central to psycholinguistics (e.g., Coltheart et al., 2001; Aitchison, 2012). We analyze our networks through the lens of random, small-world, and scale-free models to develop insights into the linguistic structure and cognitive processing. We also suspect that a visual inspection of log-log plots of degree distribution is insufficient to estimate the presence of a power law accurately. Instead, statistical measures like Maximum Likelihood Estimation (MLE) and goodness-of-fit tests prove to be more accurate (Goldstein et al., 2004; Clauset et al., 2009). Thus we conduct a more rigorous numerical analysis related to the degree distribution of our networks. Finally, we use a database of age-of-acquisition rating words to look into the hypothetical mechanism that is commonly used to explain a scale-free degree distribution, that is the preferential attachment (Barabási and Albert, 1999).

3 Languages and lexicons used

Four European languages (English, French, German, and Spanish) were chosen for the current work. These languages were selected due to the availability of lexicons containing marked syllable boundaries in both the spelling (written) and pronunciation (spoken) domains[1]. All these languages are from the Indo-European family and are divided between the Germanic (English and German) and Romance (French and Spanish) subgroups (Algeo and Butcher, 2013).

All entries of these lexicons which were non-words, incomplete, or contained non-alphabetic characters are excluded from the network analysis. Additionally, proper nouns as well as all instances of homophones and homographs were also removed except in cases where these entries existed only with the same syllable boundaries. In such cases, one copy of the word was kept.

[1]We used the same methodology for the two domains. Since the results were highly similar, we only report the ones that are related to the spelling domain for the sake of simplicity and readability.

4 Network Analysis

4.1 Construction

For each of the four languages under investigation, we have developed two ways to build and study the networks, namely a 'syllabary network' and a 'lexical network'. In the first representation, the nodes represent a word and two words are connected when they share at least one common syllable. In the second representation, the nodes represent each unique syllable of the language and a link is generated when two syllable nodes have at least one word in common. The dataset and code for this study are available here [2].

Figures 1 and 2 respectively show an example of lexical and syllabary network for the following short list of 8 English words: "*a–mi–a–bil–i–ty*", "*a–vail–a–ble*", "*bin*", "*cred–i–bil–i–ty*", "*in–cred–u–lous*", "*mile*", "*sim–i–lar–i–ty*", and "*sim–u–la–tion*" (the symbol '–' denotes a syllable boundary). For instance, within the lexical network, there is a link between the words "*credibility*" and "*incredulous*" as they share the same syllable, namely "*cred*". Similarly, within the syllabary network, the syllables "*vail*" and "*ble*" are connected as the word "*available*" contains them. The nodes that do not have any connections (i.e. their degree is zero) such as "*mile*" and "*bin*" are called *hermits*. Note that the largest connected subgraph is called the *giant component* whereas an *island* is defined as a connected subgraph that is not part of any larger connected subgraph.

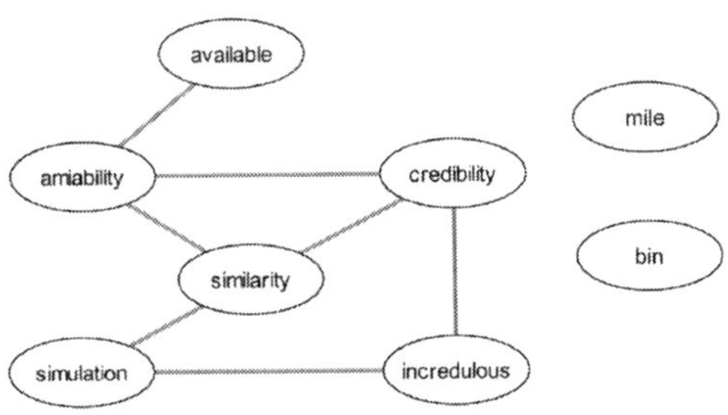

Figure 1: Example of an English lexical network

4.2 Key Properties

A network analysis was conducted by measuring a set of elementary characteristics known to formally define the main types of networks: random network (Erdős and Rényi, 1959), small-world network (Watts and Strogatz, 1998) and scale-free network (Barabási and Albert, 1999). These properties help us gain insights into the structure, cognitive efficiency and robustness of the language system. The following topological features were numerically evaluated:

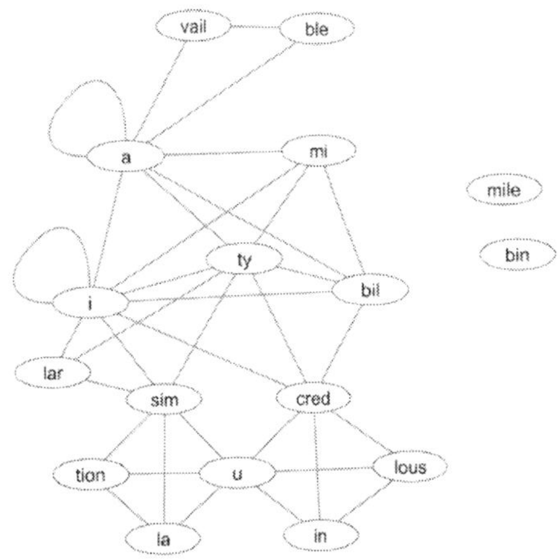

Figure 2: Example of an English syllabary network

Average Connectivity: This focuses on the degree of each node i in the network, denoted by k_i. It counts the average number of connections per node and indicates if our language networks are complex or not. If the number of nodes (N) is much larger than the average connectivity, $\langle k \rangle \ll N$, then the networks are complex by nature.

Density of a Network: Represents the proportion of possible relationships in the network that are present. It indicates the level of co-occurrences between the syllables and words. A lower density may potentially reflect phonotactic rules that restrict certain combinations.

Diameter of a Network: Defines the maximum distance between any two nodes in a network, reflecting overall connectivity, and how efficiently nodes are linked. A larger diameter for the lexical network indicates greater morphological diversity or isolated word groups. For the syllabary network, a larger diameter suggests a more fragmented structure, potentially due to rare or borrowed syllables.

Average Distance (or Average Path Length): Measures the average number of steps required to

[2] https://github.com/Rusali28/Network-analysis-syllabification-study

connect any two nodes in the network. A longer path length indicates a more fragmented language system with distinct syllable groups, thereby reflecting greater phonological diversity or complex word formation rules. A shorter length suggests that the syllables or lexicons are efficiently connected, thus speakers can easily transition between them during language processing. Small average distance (with high clustering) contributes as an indicator of small-world networks.

Average Clustering Coefficient: Measures the tendency of nodes to form tightly connected groups in the network. It determines how well a node's nearest neighbors are also connected to each other. High clustering coefficients for the lexical network suggest that words sharing syllables tend to form dense groups, reflecting phonotactic consistency and morphological relationships. High coefficients for the syllabary networks also indicate that frequently co-occurring syllables form dense clusters, revealing common phonological patterns. A high clustering coefficient is also a characteristic of small-world networks.

Distance of a Random Network (Erdös–Rényi Model): Same as the average distance. It is used to compare values with the lexical and syllabary networks, to identify their small-world nature.

Clustering Coefficient of a Random Network (Erdös–Rényi model): Similar to the average clustering coefficient. It is calculated to compare values with the lexical and syllabary networks, to identify their small-world nature.

4.3 Degree Distribution

The distribution of degree, denoted as *P(k)*, is used to measure the frequency of nodes in a network given a *k* connectivity. *P(k)* is a key metric for characterizing the structure of a network. For instance, scale-free networks have power-law distribution (Barabási and Albert, 1999) whereas random networks have Poisson-type distribution (Erdős and Rényi, 1959). To formally and adequately describe the degree distribution of the networks of our study, we used three main candidate models for curve fitting: power law distribution, lognormal distribution, and exponential distribution.

Power Law Distribution: Suggests that a small number of nodes have high connectivity, while the majority of other nodes have fewer connections. This structure is characteristic of scale-free networks, where frequently occurring syllables continue to gain more connections over time (growth driven by preferential attachment). If our networks follow a power law, it will indicate a pattern of hierarchical organization, where syllable usage is dominated by a few central syllables that appear in many words.

Lognormal Distribution: Suggests that, while some nodes may be highly connected, the distribution of connections is more balanced, with many nodes having moderate connectivity. Unlike a strict power law, it allows for a more gradual transition between high- and low-degree nodes. With respect to syllabification, this distribution implies that syllable connectivity is not only influenced by preferential attachment but also by phonotactic constraints and linguistic rules. This suggests that although some syllables are more common, their distribution is shaped by additional factors beyond just frequency-based reinforcement.

Exponential Distribution: Suggests that connections between nodes are relatively uniform, indicating that there are no highly dominant syllables or lexicons. This implies that syllable usage is almost random, without strong structural constraint or preferential growth. An exponential distribution in our networks will suggest that all syllables have almost equal probability of occurring in different words, which contradicts known linguistic patterns of syllable frequency and phonotactic constraints. Some previous studies (Vitevitch, 2009; Masucci and Rodgers, 2006) on language networks have suggested the presence of exponential degree distributions in certain conditions like highly restricted phonological systems. This model will help us verify whether syllabification networks follow a simple decay process rather than a structured process of phonology and lexical organization.

5 Results

Tables 1 show the results of the key properties for the lexical and syllabary networks, respectively. In both tables, the details of the largest connected component (i.e. giant component) are provided. The islands in our study represent small separate networks within the network consisting only of 2 to 3 nodes.

Figure 3: Word as node (lexical network).

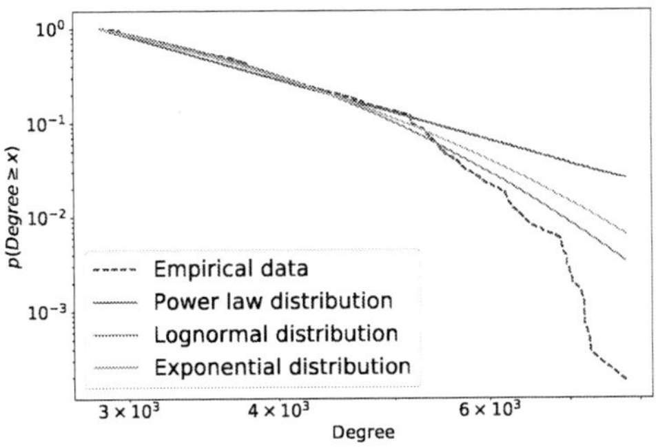

(a) English lexicon.

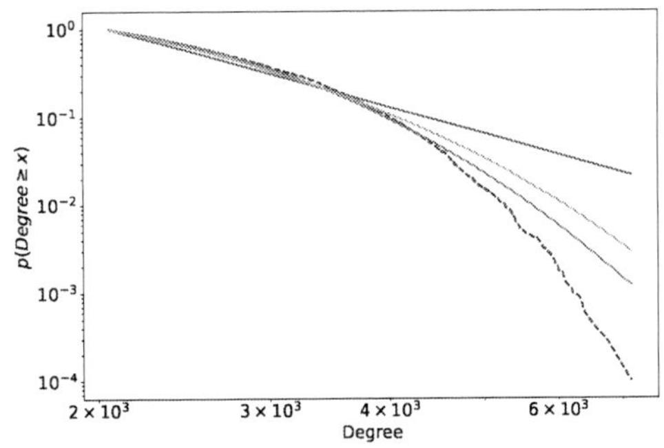

(b) French lexicon.

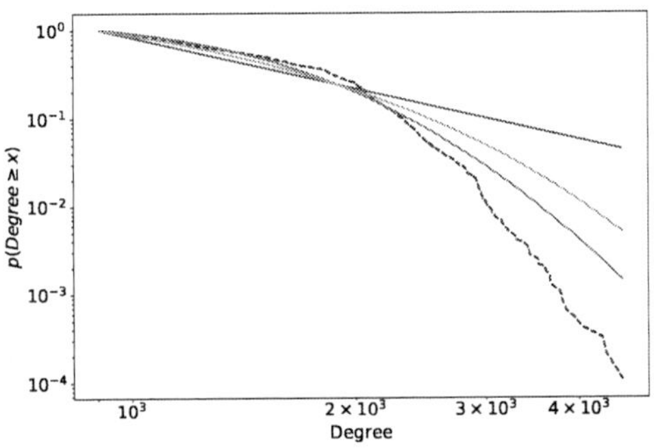

(c) German lexicon.

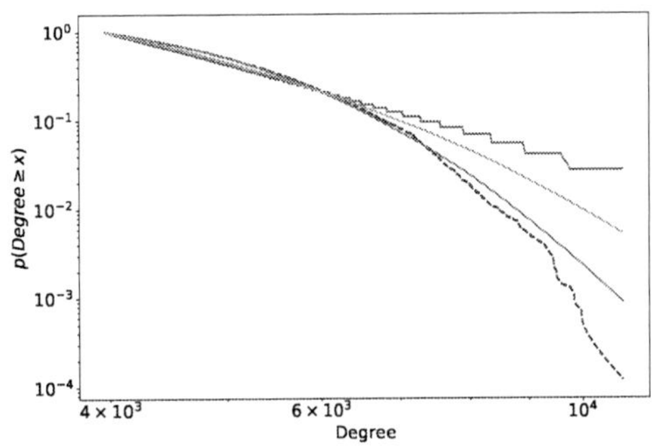

(d) Spanish lexicon.

Figure 4: Syllable as node (syllabary network).

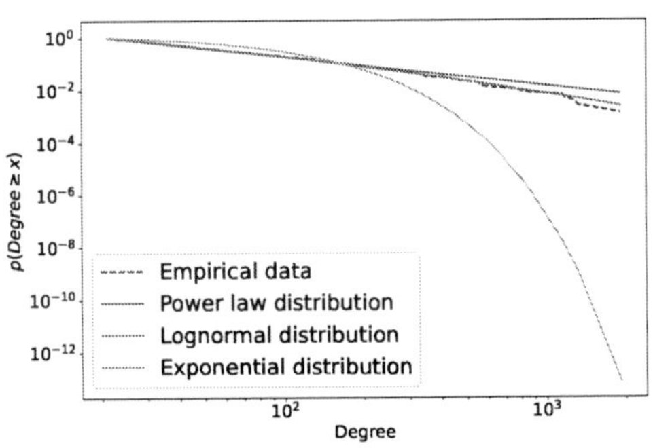

(a) English lexicon.

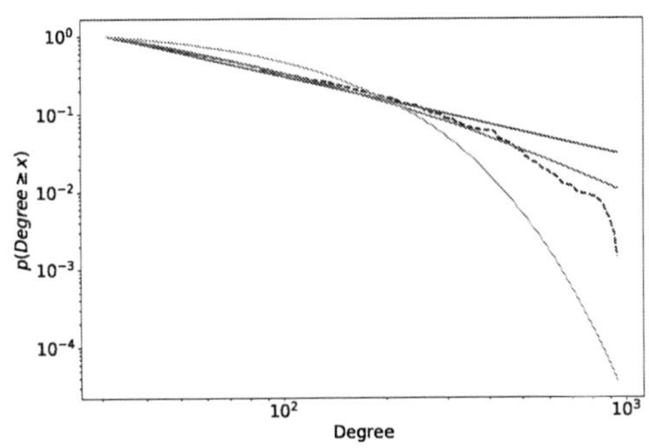

(b) French lexicon.

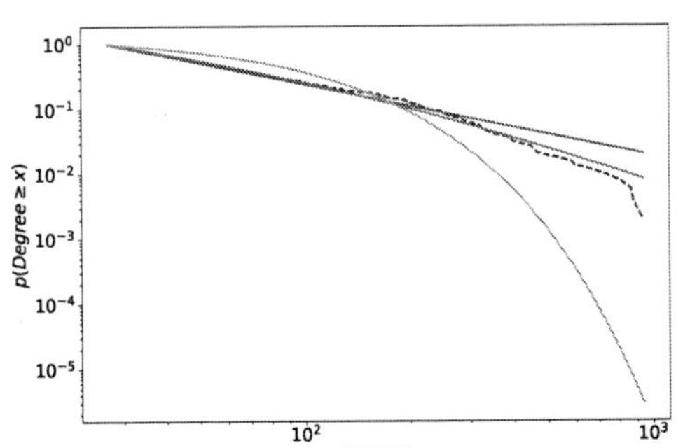

(c) German lexicon.

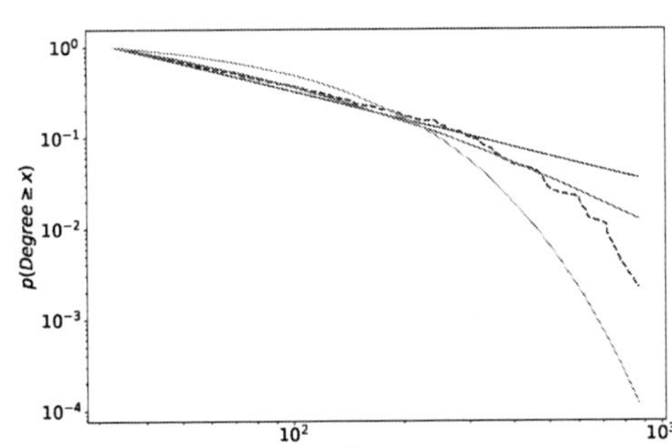

(d) Spanish lexicon.

Table 1: Values of the key properties for the lexical and syllabary networks.

Features	Lexical Networks				Syllabary Networks			
	English	French	German	Spanish	English	French	German	Spanish
Number of nodes	33,464	31,155	20,344	31,238	7,605	4,664	4,043	2,264
Number of islands	8	5	3	0	28	20	8	3
Number of hermits	1,245	297	84	95	1,225	282	79	93
Giant component								
Number of nodes	32,202	30,847	20,253	31,142	6,321	4,338	3,947	2,165
Number of links	20,352,425	24,235,869	9,676,660	46,186,583	44,698	53,430	35,868	34,945
Avg connectivity	1,216.4	1,555.8	951.3	2,957.1	14.1	24.6	18.2	32.3
Density	0.039	0.051	0.047	0.095	0.001	0.003	0.002	0.007
Avg distance	2.3	2.0	2.1	1.9	2.9	2.8	2.8	2.5
Diameter	9	7	7	5	10	8	7	6
Avg clustering coeff.	0.73	0.6	0.67	0.59	0.41	0.5	0.54	0.69

Table 2: Average distance and clustering coefficient for the lexical networks and their random counterparts.

Language	Lexical networks		Erdös–Rényi random networks	
	Average distance	Clustering coefficient	Average distance	Clustering coefficient
English	2.3	0.73	1.5	0.039
French	2.0	0.60	1.4	0.051
German	2.1	0.67	1.4	0.047
Spanish	1.9	0.59	1.3	0.095

The most striking difference between the four languages is the number of hermits elicited in the English language for the lexical network. It is about one order of magnitude larger than its counterparts. This finding reflects the fact that the English language has an unusually large number of loan words compared to other languages (e.g. "*zigzag*", "*seigneur*" are hermits because they are words whose syllables are unique). England being the subject to several invasions throughout its history, the English language ended up absorbing immense amounts of foreign vocabulary from Greek, Latin, Norman-French, Old French, Old Norse, and the Celtic languages as well as actively adopted words from around the parts of the world that used to be in the British Empire, and beyond (Bryson, 2001).

We observe that for all the networks, the average connectivity k satisfies the condition $\langle k \rangle \ll N$, indicating that the networks are sparse, an expected attribute for complex networks (Albert and Barabási, 2002). These results are in agreement with previous findings related to Portuguese (Soares et al., 2005), Chinese (Peng et al., 2008) and Croatian (Ban et al., 2013) language networks. Results from Tables 2 and 3 show that the networks have high clustering coefficient values when compared to corresponding Erdös–Rényi random (ER) networks whereas their average network distances are quite similar to the distances calculated for the ER random networks. Thus, our networks exhibit characteristics of small-world networks (i.e. high clustering coefficients and small average distances).

Of critical importance, we also numerically tested whether or not the empirical degree distribution of the networks was heavy-tailed by fitting three candidate distributions to the data : a power law distribution, a log-normal distribution, and an exponential distribution (Alstott et al., 2014). In the case of lexical networks, it is apparent from the four plots shown in Figure 3 that the log-normal distribution offers a better fit than the exponential model, which is not heavy-tailed. The values of the mean (μ) and standard deviation (σ) supporting the lognormal distribution are given in Table 4, for all the networks.

Concerning the syllable networks, Figure 4 shows that the degree distribution of those networks can be reasonably well modeled with a power law distribution. The associated γ values are displayed in Table 4 and are consistent with the values of γ generally observed in complex networks ($1 < \gamma < 3$). This finding is also comparable with values of complex networks that follow preferential attachment. In agreement with the study conducted by Broido and Clauset (Broido and Clauset, 2019), we also find that the lognormal distribution is a better fit for our networks than the power law distribution,

Table 3: Average distance and clustering coefficient for the syllabary networks and their random counterparts.

Language	Syllabary networks		Erdös–Rényi random networks	
	Average distance	Clustering coefficient	Average distance	Clustering coefficient
English	2.9	0.41	3.3	0.002
French	2.8	0.50	2.6	0.006
German	2.8	0.54	2.9	0.005
Spanish	2.5	0.69	2.2	0.014

Table 4: Parameters of lognormal distribution and power law distribution.

Language	English		French		German		Spanish	
Nodes of the network	Words	Syllables	Words	Syllables	Words	Syllables	Words	Syllables
Gamma (γ)	4.6	2.1	4.1	2.0	2.9	2.1	4.8	2.0
Best fit	Linear	Linear	Linear	Linear	Linear	Linear	Linear	Linear
μ	7.99	-8.80	7.65	0.94	7.20	-4.76	8.38	1.14
σ	0.32	3.35	0.40	2.04	0.45	2.04	0.28	2.02

even if the latter can be seen at first sight as a good fitting curve.

To further strengthen our empirical evaluation of the network's degree distribution, we perform the degree distribution fit using the two-parameter Zipf-Mandelbrot law and compare the fit against the lognormal distribution. To determine which distribution fits the best, we measure the goodness of fit using Akaike Information Criterion (AIC) and Bayesion Information Criterion (BIC). The results from Table 5 show that for both the lexical and syllabary networks, the AIC and BIC values for the lognormal distribution are lower than those for the Zipf-Mandelbrot model. Thus, these results further indicate that the lognormal distribution consistently provides a better fit for our networks. These findings therefore suggest that syllable organization is shaped by a combination of preferential attachment, phonological constraints and linguistic rules rather than an unrestricted rich-get-richer mechanism.

6 Preferential Attachment and Age-of-Acquisition

The mechanism of preferential attachment helps to understand the growth of a complex network (Barabási and Albert, 1999; Hills et al., 2009). It is associated with the metaphoric "rich-get-richer" expression. Given a network with a pre-existing fixed number of nodes and edges, when a new node is introduced to the network, the existing nodes to which the new node will connect are selected by a preferential mechanism, i.e. the probability of selection is directly proportional to the degree of the pre-existing nodes. This means that nodes with larger degrees will have higher probabilities to attract new nodes and generate more edges, as the network evolves into a larger network with time (Barabási and Albert, 1999). Owing to preferential attachment, as well-connected nodes continue to accumulate more edges and nodes with time, this mechanism also proceeds to support the power law distribution (Stumpf and Porter, 2012), hence the scale-free nature of complex networks.

In this section, we explore the effects of an age of acquisition (AoA) database in an attempt to validate the theory of preferential attachment for the English language networks. Age of acquisition refers to the age range in which an individual acquires knowledge over certain aspects of language (e.g. vocabulary, grammar). Here, we focus on the age of acquisition of vocabulary using a dataset (Kuperman et al., 2012) of AoA ratings for 30,121 English content words including nouns, verbs, and adjectives.

We take this longitudinal vocabulary data to cumulatively construct syllabary and lexical networks over time. In other terms, a network at a time instant t is built from words known (i.e. acquired) at time t and all the proceeding words before t. Going through the AoA database, we generate 23 networks, one for each year starting from 4 to 25 years old. We perform two measures on these longitudinal networks. The first measure is the size of the networks, that is, the number of nodes in the networks. It corresponds to the measure of vocabulary size for the lexical networks and the number of syllables (an index of flexibility in word combination) for the syllabary networks. Figure 5a shows that the rate of syllabary development is slower than the lexical one. Both trajectories reach

Table 5: AIC and BIC values for Lognormal and Zipf distributions in lexical and syllabary Networks.

Features	Lexical Networks				Syllabary Networks			
	English	**French**	**German**	**Spanish**	**English**	**French**	**German**	**Spanish**
AIC (lognormal)	91599.64	163654.51	139663.52	147018.4	7832.26	7381.2	5329.9	4731.59
AIC (zipf)	361063.23	341027.47	199321.54	374468.74	21798.45	15072.72	13185.03	7604.13
BIC (lognormal)	91612.88	163668.97	139677.82	147032.51	7841.54	7390.33	5338.44	4739.82
BIC (zipf)	361088.49	341052.51	199345.30	374493.79	21818.73	15091.88	13203.88	7621.18

Figure 5: Longitudinal analysis.

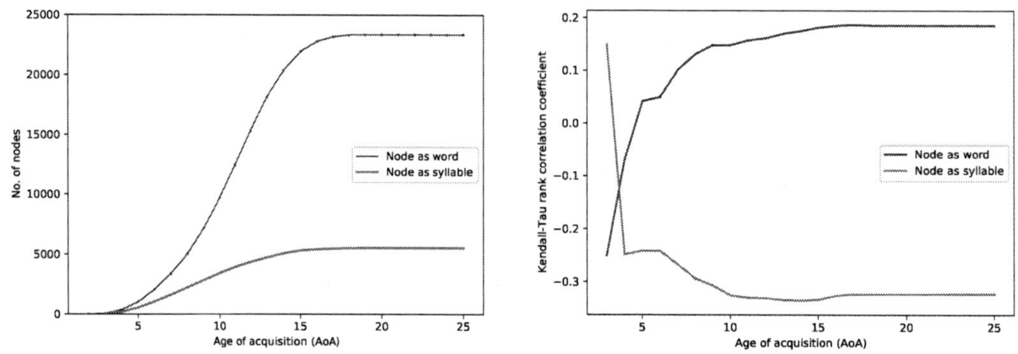

(a) Network size over time.

(b) Kendall's Tau correlation over time.

a plateau in adolescence with, at this time, a pool of about 5,000 syllables to assemble over 20,000 words.

For the second measure, we use a correlational analysis, in which the network growth allows us to assess the hypothesis of a preferential attachment. If preferential attachment[3] plays a role in shaping the English networks, then a negative relationship should be found between the AoA and degree. The first syllables that individuals acquire in earlier years should indeed be more connected over time than those learnt later in life. Figure 5b shows the Kendall's Tau correlation coefficient (Kendall, 1938) between degree and age of acquisition over time. This correlation coefficient was chosen since it is a non-parametric correlation measure that does not assume a linear relationship, thus making it more suitable for studying degree distributions, which are often skewed and not normally distributed. It provides a more robust measure of association, as opposed to the Pearson correlation coefficient (Anscombe, 1973). It can be seen that the degree and AoA of the syllabary network have a negative relationship that amplifies over time, thus supporting the theory of preferential attachment. As the age increases, newly acquired syllables tend to connect more likely to highly connected existing syllables. For the lexical network, the situation is reversed: the Kendall's Tau correlation coefficient elicits a positive correlation, reflecting different growth dynamics. As some new words are learnt over time, all their syllabic sub-parts are more likely to be linked to an existing stock of syllables. This highlights the importance of frequently used syllables, in their role as anchors in vocabulary expansion over time. The dual pattern indicates the contribution of broader linguistic constraints in shaping the overall network structure.

7 Conclusion

We used network science to study the syllabification of the English, French, German and Spanish languages. We built syllabary networks in which nodes and links constitute syllables and words, respectively. Furthermore, to acknowledge the ubiquitous prevalence of the mental lexicon in the language sciences, we also generated and studied the properties of lexical networks in which the roles are reversed, namely nodes and links act for words and syllables, respectively. By studying the two types of networks, our study acknowledges the role of syllables in influencing word formation, as well

[3]As previously mentioned, even if a lognormal distribution is a better fit to model our networks, preferential attachment may still influence local network growth, especially in early language acquisition. Thus, power law distribution is still a reasonable fit.

as the role of words in structuring how syllables interact within the lexicon. Thus, we attempt to capture both the phonological and lexical network dynamics.

All these networks exhibited small-world properties, having high clustering coefficients and small average distances when compared to their corresponding random networks. Previous studies on syllabary networks related to Portuguese, Chinese and Croatian languages, have all assumed that they are scale-free as their degree distribution looked as to follow a power law. However, this statement was mostly based on visual inspection. When an analysis of degree distribution is conducted under more rigorous circumstances using curve fitting, the results show that all our networks' degree distributions are consistently better modelled with a log-normal distribution. Our finding is in line with a few studies that have questioned and rebutted the claim of previously reported scale-free networks (e.g. Clauset et al., 2009; Broido and Clauset, 2019).

Finally, unlike earlier studies on syllabification that all dealt with static networks, we examined the English networks from a dynamic perspective using longitudinal data from the database of age-of-acquisition rating words. This approach allowed us to validate the preferential attachment mechanism for the syllabary network. Although our analysis shows that syllabification networks are better described by a lognormal distribution rather than a strict power law, this does not rule out preferential attachment as a contributing mechanism (Hills et al., 2009; Vitevitch, 2008). We find that preferential attachment can still operate locally in early network growth. This implies that language network growth is influenced by both preferential attachment and additional linguistic constraints, like phonological and morphological structures.

These findings in our work have important implications for linguistic modeling. Considering phonotactic constraints and linguistic rules have a role to play in the networks, models of lexical evolution must account for structured constraints beyond simple preferential attachment. Furthermore, cross-linguistic comparisons of degree distributions could further help us understand how these constraints vary across mutliple languages, thereby providing deeper insights into the universality of phonological organization.

8 Limitations

While our study provides new insights into syllabification networks, we address a few limitations in this section. First, the focus of our study is limited to four Indo-European languages. This generates a scope for cross-linguistic validation with typologically diverse languages, with different structures (e.g. Turkish, Finnish). Second, while our results demonstrate that a lognormal distribution better models the degree distribution than power law, we still observe reasonable behaviour with respect to power law as well. Future work could explore alternative mixture models to refine this finding. Third, while we confirm that preferential attachment influences network growth, our study does not quantify its relative impact compared to linguistic constraints like phonotactic rules, morphological constraints, cognitive biases, etc. A quantitative comparison of these factors could provide deeper insights into their contributions.

References

Jean Aitchison. 2012. *Words in the mind: An introduction to the mental lexicon*. John Wiley & Sons.

Réka Albert and Albert-László Barabási. 2002. Statistical mechanics of complex networks. *Reviews of modern physics*, 74(1):47.

Réka Albert, Hawoong Jeong, and Albert-László Barabási. 1999. Diameter of the world-wide web. *Nature*, 401(6749):130–131.

John Algeo and Carmen A Butcher. 2013. *The origins and development of the English language*. Cengage Learning.

Jeff Alstott, Ed Bullmore, and Dietmar Plenz. 2014. powerlaw: a python package for analysis of heavy-tailed distributions. *PloS one*, 9(1):e85777.

Francis J Anscombe. 1973. Graphs in statistical analysis. *The american statistician*, 27(1):17–21.

Kristina Ban, Ivan Ivakić, and Ana Meštrović. 2013. A preliminary study of croatian language syllable networks. In *2013 36th International Convention on Information and Communication Technology, Electronics and Microelectronics (MIPRO)*, pages 1296–1300. IEEE.

Albert-László Barabási and Réka Albert. 1999. Emergence of scaling in random networks. *Science*, 286(5439):509–512.

Anna D Broido and Aaron Clauset. 2019. Scale-free networks are rare. *Nature Communications*, 10(1):1017.

Bill Bryson. 2001. *The Mother Tongue: English and How it Got that Way*. William Morrow Paperbacks.

Helen Caldwell. 1970. *Machado de Assis: the Brazilian master and his novels*, volume 2. Univ of California Press.

Aaron Clauset, Cosma Rohilla Shalizi, and Mark EJ Newman. 2009. Power-law distributions in empirical data. *SIAM Review*, 51(4):661–703.

Max Coltheart, Kathleen Rastle, Conrad Perry, Robyn Langdon, and Johannes Ziegler. 2001. Drc: a dual route cascaded model of visual word recognition and reading aloud. *Psychological Review*, 108(1):204.

Chenchen Ding, Hnin Thu Zar Aye, Win Pa Pa, Khin Thandar Nwet, Khin Mar Soe, Masao Utiyama, and Eiichiro Sumita. 2019. Towards burmese (myanmar) morphological analysis: Syllable-based tokenization and part-of-speech tagging. *ACM Transactions on Asian and Low-Resource Language Information Processing (TALLIP)*, 19(1):1–34.

Paul Erdős and Alfréd Rényi. 1959. On random graphs. *Publicationes Mathematicae*, 6:290–297.

Erik C Fudge. 1969. Syllables. *Journal of Linguistics*, 5(2):253–286.

Michel L Goldstein, Steven A Morris, and Gary G Yen. 2004. Problems with fitting to the power-law distribution. *The European Physical Journal B-Condensed Matter and Complex Systems*, 41:255–258.

Thomas T Hills, Mounir Maouene, Josita Maouene, Adam Sheya, and Linda Smith. 2009. Longitudinal analysis of early semantic networks: Preferential attachment or preferential acquisition? *Psychological Science*, 20(6):729–739.

Joan B Hooper. 1972. The syllable in phonological theory. *Language*, pages 525–540.

Maurice G Kendall. 1938. A new measure of rank correlation. *Biometrika*, 30(1/2):81–93.

Victor Kuperman, Hans Stadthagen-Gonzalez, and Marc Brysbaert. 2012. Age-of-acquisition ratings for 30,000 english words. *Behavior Research Methods*, 44(4):978–990.

Alan Langus, Jacques Mehler, and Marina Nespor. 2017. Rhythm in language acquisition. *Neuroscience & Biobehavioral Reviews*, 81:158–166.

John Laver. 1994. *Principles of phonetics*. Cambridge university press.

Wei Liang, Guanrong Chen, and Zihan Zhang. 2019. Adjacency spectra of chinese character co-occurrence networks in different historical periods. *Physica A: Statistical Mechanics and its Applications*, 536:122541.

Zhihan Lv, Houbing Song, Pablo Basanta-Val, Anthony Steed, and Minho Jo. 2017. Next-generation big data analytics: State of the art, challenges, and future research topics. *IEEE Transactions on Industrial Informatics*, 13(4):1891–1899.

Yannick Marchand and Robert I Damper. 2007. Can syllabification improve pronunciation by analogy of english? *Natural Language Engineering*, 13(1):1–24.

A. P. Masucci and G. J. Rodgers. 2006. Network properties of written human language. *Physical Review E*, 74(2):026102.

Karin Müller, Bernd Möbius, and Detlef Prescher. 2000. Inducing probabilistic syllable classes using multivariate clustering. In *Proceedings of the 38th Annual Meeting of the Association for Computational Linguistics*, pages 225–232.

Gang Peng, James W Minett, and William S-Y Wang. 2008. The networks of syllables and characters in chinese. *Journal of Quantitative Linguistics*, 15(3):243–255.

Laura VC Quispe, Jorge AV Tohalino, and Diego R Amancio. 2021. Using virtual edges to improve the discriminability of co-occurrence text networks. *Physica A: Statistical Mechanics and its Applications*, 562:125344.

Elisabeth Selkirk. 1982. The syllable. *The structure of phonological representations*, 2:337–383.

M Medeiros Soares, Gilberto Corso, and LS Lucena. 2005. The network of syllables in portuguese. *Physica A: Statistical Mechanics and its Applications*, 355(2-4):678–684.

Michael PH Stumpf and Mason A Porter. 2012. Critical truths about power laws. *Science*, 335(6069):665–666.

Ana Todorovska, Hristijan Peshov, Ivan Rusevski, Irena Vodenska, Lubomir T Chitkushev, and Dimitar Trajanov. 2023. Using ml and explainable ai to understand the interdependency networks between classical economic indicators and crypto-markets. *Physica A: Statistical Mechanics and its Applications*, page 128900.

Michael S Vitevitch. 2008. What can graph theory tell us about word learning and lexical retrieval?

Michael S. Vitevitch. 2009. What can network science tell us about phonological similarity? *Speech Communication*, 51(1):5–13.

Duncan J Watts and Steven H Strogatz. 1998. Collective dynamics of 'small-world'networks. *Nature*, 393(6684):440–442.

Creolization versus code-switching: An agent-based cognitive model for bilingual strategies in language contact

Charles Torres
University of California, Irvine
charlt4@uci.edu

Weijie Xu
University of California, Irvine
weijie.xu@uci.edu

Yanting Li
University of California, Irvine
yantil5@uci.edu

Richard Futrell
University of California, Irvine
rfutrell@uci.edu

Abstract

Creolization and code-switching are closely related contact-induced linguistic phenomena, yet little attention has been paid to the connection between them. In this paper, we propose an agent-based cognitive model which provides a linkage between these two phenomena focusing on the statistical regularization of language use. That is, we identify that creolization as a conventionalization process and code-switching as flexible language choice can be optimal solutions for the same cognitive model in different social environments. Our model postulates a social structure of bilingual and monolingual populations, in which a set of agents seek for optimal communicative strategy shaped by multiple cognitive constraints. The simulation results show that our model successfully captures both phenomena as two ends of a continuum, characterized by varying degrees of regularization in the use of linguistic constructions from multiple source languages. The model also reveals a subtle dynamic between social structure and individual-level cognitive constraints.

1 Introduction

Creolization and code-switching, despite being two distinct linguistic phenomena, share notable similarities in many aspects. For example, both occur in a social situation that involves language contact, where multiple linguistic communities encounter and engage in communication; both involve speakers processing linguistic signals encoded in different languages; and, most importantly, both result in utterances with a mixture of linguistic representations from multiple source languages.

However, creolization and code-switching are often studied with different theoretical and empirical focus (Muysken, 2013). Creolization, on one hand, is often treated as a population-level phenomenon, drawing attention primarily from historical and sociolinguists whose main goal is to depict the change and evolution of linguistic representations as a function of social movements (Thomason and Kaufman, 1988; Mufwene, 2011).[1] On the other hand, research on code-switching leans towards the individual level, with joint force from psycho- and contact linguistics to understand the psychological mechanism adopted by bilingual speakers (Green and Abutalebi, 2013; Green and Wei, 2014) as well as the grammatical and structural configurations constraining code-switching (Myers-Scotton, 1997; Muysken, 2000; Poplack, 1980).

In the current study, we aim to bring together these two closely related phenomena, focusing on the statistical aspect of language use (Bybee, 2006; Reali and Griffiths, 2009). In short, our use of the term *creolization* mainly focuses on its convention-formation nature, while the use of the term *code-switching* mainly focuses on the flexibility of language choice. In this sense, we consider creolization and code-switching as two ends of a continuum, varying in the degree of statistical regularization in the use of linguistic constructions from multiple source languages. Crucially, we identify that creolization as a conventionalization process and code-switching as flexible language choice can be optimal solutions for the same cognitive model in different social environments. [2]

[1]There are certainly different levels of explanations in creole studies (e.g., individual strategies, the role of the inductive bias in L1 acquisition, etc.). However, many studies conceptualize *creoles* (and other similar communicative systems, e.g., pidgins) as new languages/linguistic systems, which implies certain degree of conventionalization that is only meaningful at the population or subcommunity level.

[2]Our use of the term creolization here presupposes the answer to a theoretical question that is still under debate, in particular whether creolization is a distinct process or whether it is fundamentally similar to other forms of language change (Jourdan, 2021; Mufwene, 2004; McWhorter, 1998). By referring to a mix of constructions drawn from multiple languages as 'creolization', we follow recent work which eschews pidginization as a step in creolization. However, this debate between pidginization and creolization is beyond the scope of the current study: our model can be applied to other frameworks. The optimal codes we identify could be construed as operating during pidginization or any process where new signals are con-

Proceedings of the Workshop on Cognitive Modeling and Computational Linguistics, pages 207–218
May 3, 2025

Through an agent-based cognitive model, we aim to provide a linkage between creolization as a population-level process and code-switching as an individual-level effect. Our model postulates a social structure of bilingual and monolingual populations, in which a set of agents engage in communication with each other. For each agent, their communicative strategy is shaped by multiple cognitive constraints. Specifically, each agent seeks to minimize their cognitive effort while maintaining the communicative success with their partner, a computational problem that we implement information-theoretically.

To preview the results, our model successfully captures both creolization and code-switching on the continuum of statistical regularization. Specifically, our model shows that when bilinguals put more cognitive effort in tracking their partner's identity and develop a partner-specific communicative strategy, they can rely on a simpler strategy per partner, leading to creolization as a conventionalization process. In contrast, when bilinguals put less effort into partner tracking, they will have to use a strategy that is more uncertain, leading to code-switching. Moreover, our model reveals a subtle dynamic between the social structure and the individual-level cognitive constraints: more intensive contact within the bilingual population is more likely to lead to creolization, but only when the bilingual agent puts enough effort into developing a partner-specific communicative strategy.

2 Background

A creole is a fully developed natural language with native speakers, often found to emerge in communities with intensive multilingual contact (e.g., colonies) as a strategy to address the need to communicate among speakers of different languages (Mufwene, 2004; Thomason and Kaufman, 1988). How creoles emerge is still an ongoing debate. McWhorter (1998) believes that creole is a special synchronically definable typological class that emerges from pidgins. However, opponents including Mufwene see creoles as more of a sociohistorical construct—they are just contact-heavy vernaculars of their lexifiers (i.e., the language from which the lexicon of a creole is primarily drawn) (Mufwene, 1996, 2004). Under this view, the constructions of a creole reflect features of the various source languages in contact as a result of a selection process. That is, from the combined "feature pool" of source languages, individuals select features for the creation of the new language. Such idiolectal selections then gradually converge through negotiation and compromise during communications, allowing the language to evolve into a new communal system that is unique enough from all source languages (Mufwene, 2002, 2004). In this paper, we adopt this "feature pool" viewpoint, and we model the bilingual strategy in language contact as a selection process from the pool of linguistic constructions from source languages.

Another contact-induced phenomenon in bilingual communication is code-switching, which unlike creolization, gives the speaker freedom to choose constructions from multiple languages during language production. According to Green and Abutalebi (2013), code-switching can happen in three interaction contexts: (1) single-language, where one language is used in one environment (e.g. at work) and the other in a second distinct environment (e.g. at home); (2) dual-language, where both languages are used but typically with different speakers; and 3) dense code-switching, where speakers switch languages within a single utterance, or even adapt words morphologically from one language in the context of the other. Later, Green and Wei (2014) proposed a control process model of code-switching, where the above interaction contexts determine whether the two languages are competitive (as in the single- and dual-language contexts) or cooperative (as in the dense code-switch context). If the two languages are competitive, cognitive efforts are needed to suppressed the non-target language, preventing it from entering into planning. If, however, the two languages are cooperative, neither needs to be suppressed. Speakers can choose whichever available construction that is most appropriate on the basis of semantic, syntactic and collocational considerations.

Conceptually, we view the key difference between creolization and code-switching as a matter of the degree of regularization with regard to the usage of linguistic constructions (Mufwene, 2020). At the one end is creolization, where linguistic constructions are used in a highly conventionalized way although the speakers are at the disposal of a repertoire of constructions from multiple source languages. That is, given a specific intended meaning, native speakers of a creole will agree on the

ventionalized. Meanwhile, the term code-switching might also have a different emphasis here than in many code-switching studies. We use this term to indicate the freedom to choose between languages when conveying a certain meaning.

construction to be used to express that meaning. At the other end is code-switching. Although bilinguals of the same languages may share some intuitions about where a switch can happen within a sentence, possibly due to some grammatical constraints (Poplack, 1980; Muysken, 2000), it will not be surprising at all if they choose different constructions and switching points to express the same intended meaning.

3 Modeling Framework

Through an agent-based model of bilingual strategies in a language contact scenario, we explore how creolization and code-switching are optimal solutions to a cognitive constraint problem within the bilingual population at two ends of a continuum which varies the regularization of linguistic constructions from multiple source languages.[3] Our model has two components. First, there is a **social structure** consisting of bilingual and monolingual populations, and a set of agents communicate with each other within this social structure. Second, at the individual level, each agent follows a communicative policy that is shaped by multiple cognitive constraints.

3.1 Communication within a social structure

There are two languages L_{A} and L_{B} in our toy scenario, and they share a discrete common meaning space $\mathcal{M}$. Each language consists of a disjoint set of $|\mathcal{M}|$ possible constructions (representing words, morphemes, syntactic patterns, and other strategies languages may use to convey meaning) for these meanings, $\mathcal{C}_{\mathrm{A}}$ and $\mathcal{C}_{\mathrm{B}}$. Therefore, there are $2|\mathcal{M}|$ constructions in total, forming a joint construction space for the entire society $\mathcal{C}_{\mathrm{A+B}} = \mathcal{C}_{\mathrm{A}} \cup \mathcal{C}_{\mathrm{B}}$.

In a communicative event, a speaker agent a_i, first comes up with an intended meaning $m \in \mathcal{M}$. Then, they select a construction $c \in \mathcal{C}$ to realize the intended meaning and send it to the listener agent a_j. The agent a_i's selection of construction c given meaning m follows a **communicative policy**, which is a probability distribution $p(c \mid m, a_j)$ to produce construction c given meaning m for listener a_j. In general, the goal of the sender in each communication is to choose a construction c in a way that helps the receiver a_j reconstruct the meaning m from it.

Figure 1 shows the social structure of a language

[3]Code for this model is available at `https://github.com/cj-torres/creolization-codeswitching`.

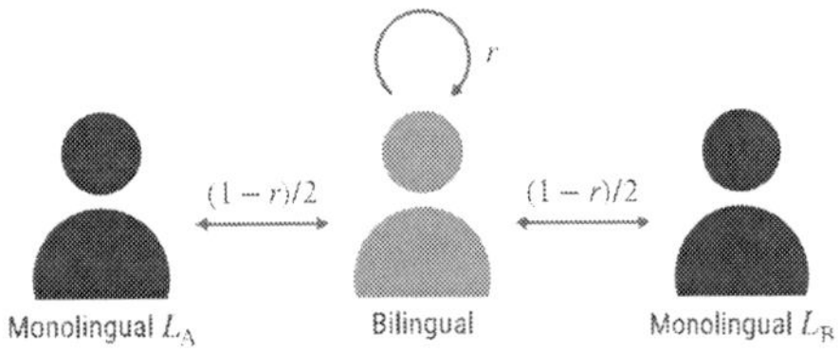

Figure 1: The social structure in a language contact scenario. A bilingual agent (in the middle) communicates both with monolingual agents (on the sides) and with other agents from the same bilingual population. The arrows represent the communication pathway along with the intensity of contact for each pathway.

contact scenario that defines the dynamics between agents. It consists of three agents, corresponding to three linguistic communities[4]: (1) two separate monolingual agents, one speaking L_{A} and the other L_{B}, and (2) a bilingual agent, which speaks both languages. For monolingual agents, given an intended meaning, they can only select a construction from their corresponding language, that is, either $c \in \mathcal{C}_{\mathrm{A}}$ or $c \in \mathcal{C}_{\mathrm{B}}$. For the bilingual agent, it can select constructions from the joint set of both languages $c \in \mathcal{C}_{\mathrm{A+B}}$.

The arrows in Figure 1 represent the dynamic of interaction among the three linguistic communities.[5] First, the bilingual speakers communicate among themselves, with the proportion of communicative events, or contact intensity, being r. Second, the bilingual agent communicates with each monolingual agent separately, with $(1-r)/2$ representing the intensity of contact, that is, the proportion of communicative events that the bilingual agent has with the corresponding monolingual agent.[6] There is no direct communication between the two monolingual agents in this social structure.

[4]In the current version of our model, we assume the homogeneity within each community, in the sense that each individual within a community follows the same cognitive model and the same dynamic of interaction. Therefore, each community is represented as only one agent in our model.

[5]For simplicity, we assume that the communicative policy of monolingual groups remains stable and is not influenced by bilingual speakers, although this is not necessarily the case in a real language contact scenario (Thomason and Kaufman, 1988). Therefore, we only focused on the evolution of communicative policy within the bilingual group, without specifying any interaction within each monolingual group.

[6]Again, for simplicity, we assume that the intensity of contact with each monolingual group is equal, but our model is capable of accommodating unequal intensity as well.

3.2 Cognitive model for communicative policy

The cognitive model specifies at the individual level the communicative policy of the bilingual agent. This policy is subject to multiple competing constraints, and the goal of the agent is to search for an optimal policy striking a balance among these constraints. In this section, we first give a conceptual overview of these constraints and how they shape our individual-level cognitive model. We then turn to the mathematical formalization of our model.

3.2.1 Conceptual Overview

The fitness of the communicative policy is governed by two primary constraints. The first one is **communicative success**. That is, when encoding an intended meaning, the speaker should choose a construction such that their communicative partner can reconstruct the intended meaning based on the construction they receive. The second constraint is **cognitive effort**. A policy that involves more complicated decision-making processes may be more costly, inducing greater demand for working memory and cognitive control, and therefore will be less favored due to the limited cognitive resources that agent is equipped with.

The constraint of cognitive effort can be further decomposed into two components, namely, **partner tracking** and **construction selection**. The idea behind partner tracking is that the communicative policy needs to be partner-specific (Hawkins et al., 2023; Kleinschmidt and Jaeger, 2015). This means that the speaker should adopt a distinct policy based on the identity of the specific partner they interact with. Such a partner-specific policy is especially important for the bilingual population in a language contact scenario, since the policy effective for monolingual speakers of L_{A} does not work on monolingual speakers of L_{B}. In addition to keeping track of the partner's identity, the second part of the cognitive effort results from construction selection. Specifically, given a communicative partner, the agent needs to select a specific construction to encode the intended meaning. Higher uncertainty in selecting the appropriate construction increases the cognitive demand for decision-making (Hick, 1952; Kuperberg and Jaeger, 2016; Fan, 2014; Zénon et al., 2019; Zheng and Meister, 2025). If the agent can consistently rely on a specific construction to convey a particular meaning to a given partner, the selection process becomes more automatic, thus reducing cognitive effort.

Importantly, in policies that achieve a constant level of communicative success, partner tracking and construction selection compete with each other for limited cognitive resources during bilingual-to-bilingual communication, resulting in a trade-off between the two.[7]

For the communication with monolinguals, bilinguals always need to track the monolingual's identity to select an appropriate construction under the pressure for communicative success. Moreover, communication with different monolinguals results in exposure to a mixed selection of constructions from both languages, leading to a marginal distribution with an irreducible amount of uncertainty.

For the communication between bilinguals, since they know both languages, language choice does not affect communication success anymore, and a trade-off between partner tracking and construction selection now occurs. When agents attempt to minimize attention to partner identity they will revert to policies which reflect a mix of the languages they've been exposed to when they can do so without impacting communicative success. However, a mixture of L_{A} and L_{B} has a high uncertainty over construction selection since constructions from both languages are valid for each meaning. Attempting to reduce this uncertainty in all policies means that bilinguals must devise a third, separate, conventionalized communication system with one another. This creation of a conventional system means the bilinguals must be attentive of construction selection even among each other, thus increasing the load on partner tracking.

Therefore, partner tracking and construction selection are in a trade-off in the bilingual-to-bilingual policies: increasing effort in partner tracking reduces the effort needed to address the uncertainty in construction selection, and vice versa. Given this trade-off, no policy can simultaneously minimize both partner tracking and construction selection while maintaining communicative success. Instead, the agent needs to figure out an optimal balance.

To sum up, at the individual level, the communicative policy followed by an agent is under the constraints of communicative success and cognitive effort, with latter being further decomposed

[7] There is actually also a trade-off between cognitive effort and communicative success, such that a policy that achieves higher communicative success may require greater cognitive effort. However, this trade-off is not the main focus of the current investigation, and the constraint of communicative success, given our setup, primarily impacts how the bilingual agent speaks with monolinguals (see Appendix B).

into partner tracking and construction selection. To find an optimal policy, the agent seeks to minimize the cognitive effort by striking a balance between the effort for partner tracking and the effort for construction selection.

3.2.2 Mathematical Formalization

For each listener agent a and meaning m, a speaker agent has a policy $p(c \mid m, a)$. As mentioned above, we are interested in a tradeoff between partner tracking and construction selection while ensuring communicative success. We model this with the following objective function to be minimized for the communicative policy for speaker agent a^*, consisting of three terms reflecting partner tracking, construction selection, and communicative success:

$$\begin{aligned} \mathcal{J}_{a^*} = & \underbrace{\mathop{\mathbb{E}}_{a,m}\left[\sum_c p(c \mid m, a) \log \frac{p(c \mid m, a)}{p(c \mid m)}\right]}_{\text{partner tracking; } I(a;c \mid m)} \\ & + \alpha \underbrace{\mathop{\mathbb{E}}_{a,m}\left[\sum_c p(c \mid m, a) \log \frac{1}{p(c \mid m, a)}\right]}_{\text{construction selection; } H(c \mid m, a)} \\ & + \beta \underbrace{\mathop{\mathbb{E}}_{a,m}\left[\sum_c p(c \mid m, a) \log \frac{1}{q_a(m \mid c, a^*)}\right]}_{\text{communicative success; } \mathcal{L}(p)}, \end{aligned} \quad (1)$$

where q_a is the decoder policy for the listener agent a used with speaker agent a^* derived from its encoder via Bayes' rule.[8] The scalar α governs the tradeoff between the two components of cognitive effort: partner tracking and construction selection. The relative weight of cognitive effort compared to communicative success is governed by scalar parameter β. However, we are not primarily interested in the behavior of these interactions, so for our purposes β will remain fixed at a value ensuring that communication systems bilinguals share with monolinguals do not degrade. More information on this choice can be found in Appendix B.

Here in Equation 1 we have used information-theoretic quantities $I(a; c \mid m)$ and $H(c \mid m, a)$ to represent cognitive effort. This is in line with recent work in neuroscience, cognitive science, and psycholinguistics which has constrained the complexity of policies in this way (Tishby and Polani, 2011; van Dijk and Polani, 2013; Genewein et al., 2015; Zaslavsky et al., 2018; Gershman, 2020; Futrell, 2021; Lai and Gershman, 2021; Futrell, 2023).

The first term of Equation 1 is the mutual information between the variable a and the variable c given m or $I(a; c \mid m)$. It represents how much information an agent must use about its interlocutors in determining which constructions c to select given its policy. The second term in Equation 1 is the conditional entropy $H(c \mid m, a)$, a value which represents, among other things, the uncertainty inherent in the distribution $p(c \mid m, a)$. The final term $\mathcal{L}(p)$ represents the communicative success expected given policy p.

What we will seek to answer in this investigation is how this policy varies with respect to α between 0 and 1. The behavior on the extremes are relatively easy to predict. For $\alpha = 0$, the objective reduces to

$$\mathcal{J}_{a^*} = I(a; c \mid m) + \beta\mathcal{L}(p), \quad (2)$$

and we would predict speakers will attempt to choose policies that are close to the marginal distribution $p(c \mid m)$, that is, a policy which does minimal partner tracking to achieve the desired level of communicative success. For $\alpha = 1$ we instead get

$$\begin{aligned} \mathcal{J}_{a^*} &= I(a; c \mid m) + H(c \mid m, a) + \beta\mathcal{L}(p) \\ &= H(c \mid m) + \beta\mathcal{L}(p), \end{aligned} \quad (3)$$

which means that speakers choose as deterministic a policy as possible when $\mathcal{L}(p)$ is not impacted (see Appendix A for the full derivation of Equation 3). At these extreme ends we will see that social demography does not matter. However, we will also see that for intermediate values of α, the speaker's policy is heavily mediated by the social structure of their environment.

4 Procedure

With the agent communication structures and objective functions defined we are able to calculate optimal policies using gradient descent. We investigate whether the resulting policies that bilinguals share with each other entrench constructions from one or the other language, or whether the policies show freedom to choose between constructions from L_A and L_B. The former resembles creolization in the feature pool model, where bilinguals select mixes of features from both languages (Mufwene, 2004). The latter resembles code-switching, with agents

[8] For monolinguals the encoder is fixed as language L_A or L_B and does not update (see Figure 2 for a depiction of these policies).

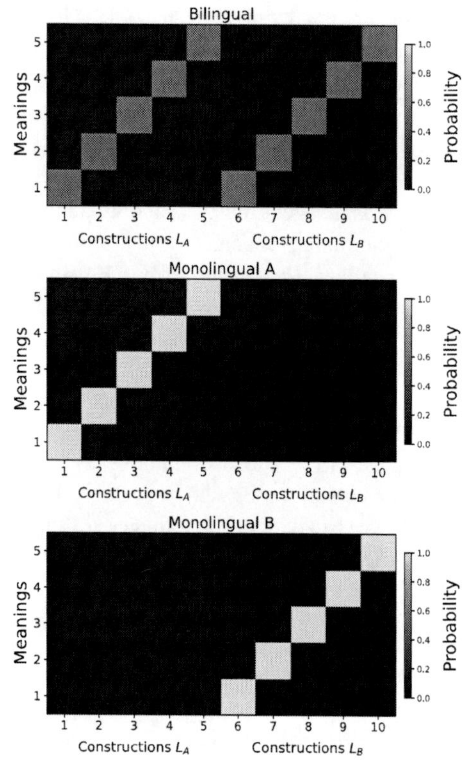

Figure 2: Model initialization: all bilingual agents are initialized to perform code-switching, where the agent has equal probability to choose constructions from L_{A} or L_{B} given a meaning m. Monolingual agents are initialized to use only one language.

being able to freely use constructions from either language. We assume for sake of simplicity that the monolingual populations are so large that they resist changing in response to contact, but we leave the bilingual population policies free to update.

Model initialization. We set the number of meanings $|\mathcal{M}|$ to 5. Three agents are initialized: the monolingual L_{A} speakers, the monolingual L_{B} speakers, and the bilingual speakers. Monolingual speakers were initialized with language policies reflecting their language, either L_{A} or L_{B}, which were disjoint mappings from meanings to constructions. Bilingual speakers were initialized with mappings reflecting a uniform mixure of L_{A} and L_{B}. We show initializations for bilingual and monolingual agents in Figure 2.

Model training. During training, the bilingual agent's language policies were updated using gradient descent. Training was performed for five different values of $\alpha \in \{0.0, 0.25, 0.5, 0.75, 1.0\}$ and for five different values of $r \in \{0.1, 0.3, 0.5, 0.7, 0.9\}$. β was kept constant at a value of 10.0. Training was performed until successive improvements of the loss due to gradient descent were less than 10^{-4}.

5 Result

Our model successfully captures both creolization and code-switching, as we explain below. Figure 3 shows the optimal bilingual-to-bilingual communicative policies with varying α and bilingual-to-bilingual contact intensity r.[9] Figure 4 shows the overall cognitive effort in communicative policies, again with varying α and r. We now highlight three critical findings in our model result.

Effect of uncertainty in construction selection. First, the model result shows that as the bilingual agents prioritize partner tracking (i.e., lowering α), they become more likely to adopt code-switching as their optimal communicative policy, such that the constructions from both source languages L_{A} and L_{B} are kept active for each meaning (as seen in panels from the top rows in Figure 3). In contrast, when the bilingual agents prioritize minimizing construction selection costs (i.e., increasing α), they are more likely to develop creolization within the bilingual population: for each meaning, only one construction from either L_{A} or L_{B} is selected deterministically, resulting in a highly conventionalized use of linguistic constructions (as seen in panels from the bottom rows in Figure 3).

Effect of contact intensity. We also observed that higher contact intensity within the bilingual population leads to increased creolization. As shown in Figure 3, when r increases (indicating stronger contact among bilinguals), the optimal policy usually assigns the full—or nearly full—probability mass to a single construction. In other words, for each meaning a convention is established using source constructions from either L_A or L_B. To illustrate why this is the case we analyzed the effects of choosing constructions from L_A over L_B in conveying a single meaning m_i for varying levels of r and α. The results can be seen in Figure 4. The effect of variable r on policy optima is clearer in these charts: as r increases, the optimal policy with respect to cognitive effort gradually moves

[9]As mentioned above, β was set such that bilingual-to-monolingual communication was always accurate. However, to see how these policies appear after training, and to see the effect of varying β on them, see Appendix B.

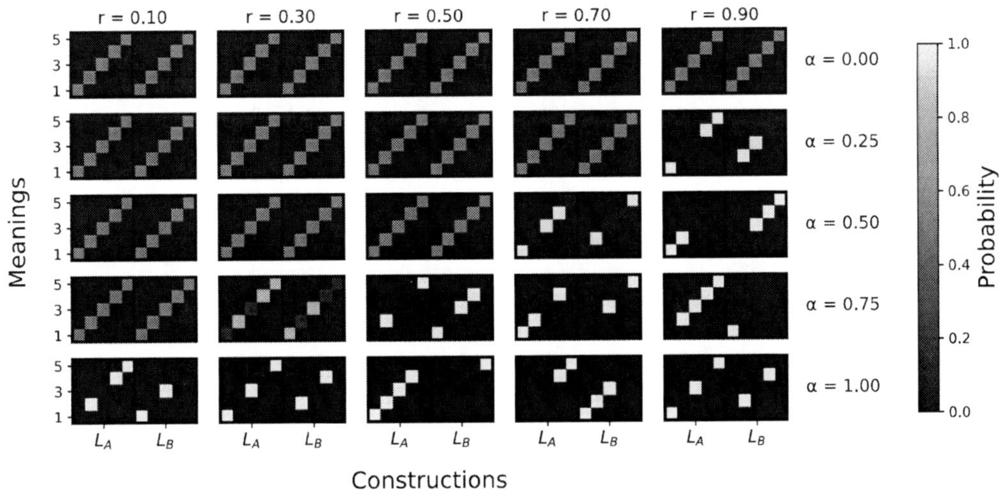

Figure 3: Optimal communicative policies $p(c \mid m)$ for bilingual agents speaking to bilingual agents, as a function of (1) the penalty α applied to the uncertainty of construction selection, and (2) the contact intensity r within the bilingual population (as opposed to bilingual-to-monolingual contact). Code-switching corresponds to a communicative policy that probabilistically alternates between the languages L_{A} and L_{B}, as found at $\alpha = 0.0$ (top row). Creolization corresponds to a policy that combines constructions from the two languages, but where the outputs are deterministic, as found at $\alpha = 1.0$ (bottom row). For intermediate values of the uncertainty penalty α, the outcome (code-switching vs. creolization) is determined by the contact intensity r.

away from an equal probability of using either language towards the highly conventionalized use of one language for a given meaning (i.e., moving away from the middle point to the sides).

For all values of α we see another general effect: higher r, which means less monolingual contact, leads to lower possible cognitive costs. Such a result can be explained by Green and Wei (2014)'s model: when the contact with monolingual population is weak, bilinguals are less likely to encounter single- and/or dual-language contexts, where cognitive control is needed to suppress the non-target language.

When $\alpha = 0$ or $\alpha = 1$, no effect of contact intensity. Our result also reveals an interaction between the bilingual-to-bilingual contact intensity and α, a model parameter that represents how the two sub-components of the cognitive constraint are prioritized. As shown in Figure 4, the contact intensity only influences optima when $0 < \alpha < 1$. When $\alpha = 0$, the bilingual population always adopts code-switching as their optimal policy regardless of their internal contact intensity. On the other hand, when $\alpha = 1$, the optimal policy is always creolization.[10] Counterintuitive as it may seem at first glance, this dynamic suggests that, on the one hand, in order for creolization to emerge, the bilingual agent must put enough effort to develop a somewhat partner-specific policy (i.e., $\alpha > 0$), regardless of the bilingual-to-monolingual contact intensity. On the other hand, in order to derive code-switching, that is, to keep the representation from both languages active for bilingual communication, the bilingual agent must to some extent ignore partner identity and put at least some effort to address a more uncertain selection over constructions (i.e., $\alpha < 1$), regardless of the bilingual-to-monolingual contact intensity.

6 Discussion

This paper presents an agent-based cognitive model aiming to capture two common phenomena in bilingual language use, namely creolization and code-switching, as two ends of a continuum of varying regularization. We set up the stage for our modeling in a language contact scenario with bilingual agents communicating among themselves and with mono-

[10]Technically, the value of α can go beyond 1. However, the result of $\alpha > 1$ will be qualitatively the same as when $\alpha = 1$, with creolization being the optimal strategy.

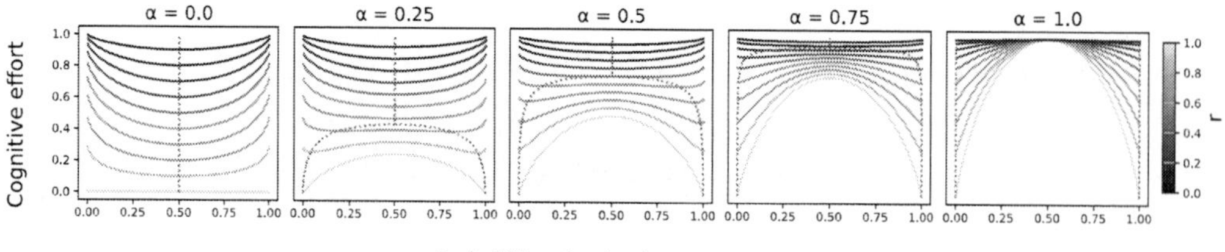

Figure 4: Cognitive effort in communicative policies for a random meaning and its two candidate constructions, with varying penalty α applied to the uncertainty of construction selection. Cognitive effort is calculated as the sum of partner tracking and the uncertainty in construction selection (i.e., the first two terms in the objective function given by Equation 1). Each line within each panel shows how the choice to use constructions from L_{A} versus L_{B} (x axis) affects the overall optimality of the cognitive effort (y axis), given the contact intensity r within the bilingual population (line color). Optimal solutions with minimal cognitive effort for each r are shown as red dotted lines. These optima were calculated for 1000 values of $r \in [0.0, 1.0)$, with only $r \in \{0.0, 0.1, ..., 0.8, 0.9\}$ shown here for ease of visualization.

lingual agents of two different languages. Within the model, the bilingual agent's communicative policy is constrained by communicative success and cognitive effort, with the latter pressure further breaking down into partner tracking and construction selection subcomponents. The bilingual agent is trained with the goal of striking a balance among these constraints by updating their language policies using gradient descent. We find that the optimal solution—creolization versus code-switching—varies with the contact intensity bilinguals have with monolinguals, but the effect varies by relative importance of the cognitive effort subcomponents.

The reason for the transition in bilingual-to-bilingual communication policies from code-switching to creolization as a function of contact intensity can be seen in Figure 4, which shows how the choice of meaning–construction mapping affects the cognitive effort (the sum of partner tracking and construction selection in Equation 1). At extremum $\alpha = 0.0$, the optima (indicated by a red line) all lie at the .5 mark, meaning that the optimal strategy to choose a construction given meaning is always an even probability between L_{A} and L_{B}, that is, a code-switching strategy. However, as α increases, a bifurcation in optima appears for critical bilingual population values. This bifurcation corresponds to the bilingual-to-bilingual contact intensity at which bilingual speakers can reduce cognitive effort by entrenching the use of L_{A} or L_{B} at the exclusion of the other. As α rises, so does this critical contact intensity value until $\alpha = 1.0$, where code-switching is never cognitively preferred. In reality, of course, both conventionalization and flexible use of constructions are observed in bilingual communities, and the critical question is more about which strategy is preferred under which condition. Therefore, we expect the actual value of α, if we are able to fit our model on some form of empirical data, would lie between these two extreme values.

From the perspective of code-switching, our model of bilingual strategy shares similarities with some other models previously proposed in the literature, especially the one in Green and Abutalebi (2013). Specifically, the model in their work tracks how different social contexts change the mode of control bilinguals may apply. Such a context-dependent control echos the partner-tracking component in our model, in the sense that the identity of communicative partner forms one aspect of the contextual information which the bilingual speaker depends on to select their optimal policy. Despite this similarity, our model differs from many others in that we aim to capture the phenomenon at a different timescale. That is, for our model, it characterizes the optimal strategy of code-switching at the population level. In contrast, many studies in the existing code-switching literature focus on the communicative strategy within each individual communicative event (e.g., the processing of a single sentence), and they often look into what specific conditions within that communicative event (e.g., grammatical configurations, processing mode, etc.) trigger or allow code-switching. This is an important question that the current study has left unaddressed, and is worth investigating in future extensions of our model.

From the perspective of creolization, unlike code-switching, the phenomenon is typically approached with a highlight on the special role of inductive bias during the language acquisition in children. The learning process in adults, in contrast, was not at the center of theoretical focus in the literature, or at least has been viewed as only playing a secondary role. Certainly, our model by no means aims to downplay the significant role of children's language acquisition in creole genesis. However, our result also suggests that, at least under certain cognitive pressures and social circumstances, creolization seems to be inevitable even though the model does not specify any acquisition process for inter-generational transmission, which is a setup typically considered pidginization. In fact, more and more psycholinguistics research have proposed that the learning mechanism in children may not be fundamentally different from the one in adults (Chang et al., 2006, 2000). It is therefore crucial to ask to what extent the effect of children's acquisition bias on creolization is fundamentally different from the effect of adults' imperfect learning, and to what extent the empirical difference between the two observed in the literature is a qualitative versus a quantitative one.

One thing which remains unaddressed is the possible typological differences creoles display (McWhorter, 1998). This is outside the scope of this model due to the model's very simple nature. Our own model assumes no preference between constructions, such that constructions from either language are equally likely to be selected by bilinguals in creolization. In other words, the model incorporates no inductive biases with respect to constructions. Explaining the common traits of creoles—for example the loss of gender and case—may require resorting to a more detailed characterization of the learnability and inductive bias of certain linguistic features, which is more sophisticated than our model can provide. To what degree creoles are typologically unique is still a matter of heated debate. We do not intend this work to stake any claim on this matter.

7 Conclusion

We successfully provide a cognitive model which when paired with the correct social environment can explain both code-switching and creolization as behavioral optima among bilinguals for certain parameterizations. How to fit such parameterizations to real bilingual behavior, or whether a single parameterization exists remain open questions. Is there a single value for α or is it dependent on other factors? This remains to be seen.

Limitations

Our model makes a number of assumptions that might seem unrealistic. We aim to address some of these in future work, but some are inherent to attempting to explain such a complex phenomenon using such a simple model.

Among the inherent assumptions are that both languages share a discrete common meaning space $\mathcal{M}$, and a discrete message space. Constructions are also considered independent of one another. Neither of these are realistic assumptions, but addressing them directly would introduce substantial complexity to the model for unclear gain and so is not yet a priority.

However, we seek to address some limitations in the future. One is that we model communities as homogeneous. In reality bilingual communities exhibit heterogeneity, with different bilinguals having different levels of proficiency in each language and maybe different cognitive resources and therefore different preferred strategies (α). Modeling this is a priority for future work and will involve changes to the social network.

The second major limitation we hope to address with future work is the communicative policy of monolingual groups, which is currently assumed to remain stable. This is also not realistic. Language contact, even of a more moderate kind, can lead to the creation of *sprachbunds* with large regions of shared linguistic features. This may be addressable in future work with a more detailed social network, as with the case of heterogeneity. However, without any source of innovation, we should expect that a community where all policies update should eventually converge to a common policy.

References

Joan Bybee. 2006. From usage to grammar: The mind's response to repetition. *Language*, pages 711–733.

Franklin Chang, Gary S Dell, and Kathryn Bock. 2006. Becoming syntactic. *Psychological Review*, 113(2):234.

Franklin Chang, Gary S Dell, Kathryn Bock, and Zenzi M Griffin. 2000. Structural priming as implicit learning: A comparison of models of sentence production. *Journal of Psycholinguistic Research*, 29:217–230.

Jin Fan. 2014. An information theory account of cognitive control. *Frontiers in Human Neuroscience*, 8:680–696.

Richard Futrell. 2021. An information-theoretic account of semantic interference in word production. *Frontiers in Psychology*, 12:672408.

Richard Futrell. 2023. Information-theoretic principles in incremental language production. *Proceedings of the National Academy of Sciences*, 120(39):e2220593120.

Tim Genewein, Felix Leibfried, Jordi Grau-Moya, and Daniel Alexander Braun. 2015. Bounded rationality, abstraction, and hierarchical decision-making: An information-theoretic optimality principle. *Frontiers in Robotics and AI*, 2:27.

Samuel J Gershman. 2020. Origin of perseveration in the trade-off between reward and complexity. *Cognition*, 204:104394.

David W Green and Jubin Abutalebi. 2013. Language control in bilinguals: The adaptive control hypothesis. *Journal of Cognitive Psychology*, 25(5):515–530.

David W Green and Li Wei. 2014. A control process model of code-switching. *Language, Cognition and Neuroscience*, 29(4):499–511.

Robert D Hawkins, Michael Franke, Michael C Frank, Adele E Goldberg, Kenny Smith, Thomas L Griffiths, and Noah D Goodman. 2023. From partners to populations: A hierarchical Bayesian account of coordination and convention. *Psychological Review*, 130(4):977.

W. E. Hick. 1952. On the rate of gain of information. *Quarterly Journal of Experimental Psychology*, 4(1):11–26.

Christine Jourdan. 2021. Pidgins and creoles: Debates and issues. *Annual Review of Anthropology*, 50(Volume 50, 2021):363–378.

Dave F Kleinschmidt and T Florian Jaeger. 2015. Robust speech perception: recognize the familiar, generalize to the similar, and adapt to the novel. *Psychological Review*, 122(2):148.

Gina R Kuperberg and T Florian Jaeger. 2016. What do we mean by prediction in language comprehension? *Language, Cognition and Neuroscience*, 31(1):32–59.

Lucy Lai and Samuel J Gershman. 2021. Policy compression: An information bottleneck in action selection. In *Psychology of Learning and Motivation*, volume 74, pages 195–232. Elsevier.

John H McWhorter. 1998. Identifying the creole prototype: Vindicating a typological class. *Language*, pages 788–818.

Salikoko S Mufwene. 1996. The founder principle in creole genesis. *Diachronica*, 13(1):83–134.

Salikoko S Mufwene. 2002. Competition and selection in language evolution. *Selection*, 3(1):45–56.

Salikoko S Mufwene. 2004. *The ecology of language evolution*. Cambridge University Press.

Salikoko S Mufwene. 2011. Creolization is a social, not a structural, process. In *Degrees of Restructuring in Creole Languages*, pages 65–84. John Benjamins Publishing Company.

Salikoko S Mufwene. 2020. Language shift. *The International Encyclopedia of Linguistic Anthropology. Edited by James Stanlaw. JohnWiley & Sons, Inc. DOI*, 10:9781118786093.

Pieter Muysken. 2000. *Bilingual Speech: A Typology of Code-Mixing*. Cambridge University Press.

Pieter Muysken. 2013. Language contact outcomes as the result of bilingual optimization strategies. *Bilingualism: Language and Cognition*, 16(4):709–730.

Carol Myers-Scotton. 1997. *Duelling languages: Grammatical structure in codeswitching*. Oxford University Press.

Shana Poplack. 1980. Sometimes I'll start a sentence in spanish y termino en espanol: toward a typology of code-switching. *Linguistics*, 18:581–618.

Florencia Reali and Thomas L Griffiths. 2009. The evolution of frequency distributions: Relating regularization to inductive biases through iterated learning. *Cognition*, 111(3):317–328.

Sarah Grey Thomason and Terrence Kaufman. 1988. *Language contact, creolization, and genetic linguistics*. Univ of California Press.

Naftali Tishby and Daniel Polani. 2011. Information theory of decisions and actions. In *Perception–Action Cycle*, pages 601–636. Springer.

Sander G. van Dijk and Daniel Polani. 2013. Informational constraints-driven organization in goal-directed behavior. *Advances in Complex Systems*, 16(2–3):1350016.

Noga Zaslavsky, Charles Kemp, Terry Regier, and Naftali Tishby. 2018. Efficient compression in color naming and its evolution. *Proceedings of the National Academy of Sciences*, 115(31):7937–7942.

Alexandre Zénon, Oleg Solopchuk, and Giovanni Pezzulo. 2019. An information-theoretic perspective on the costs of cognition. *Neuropsychologia*, 123:5–18.

Jieyu Zheng and Markus Meister. 2025. The unbearable slowness of being: Why do we live at 10 bits/s? *Neuron*, 113(2):192–204.

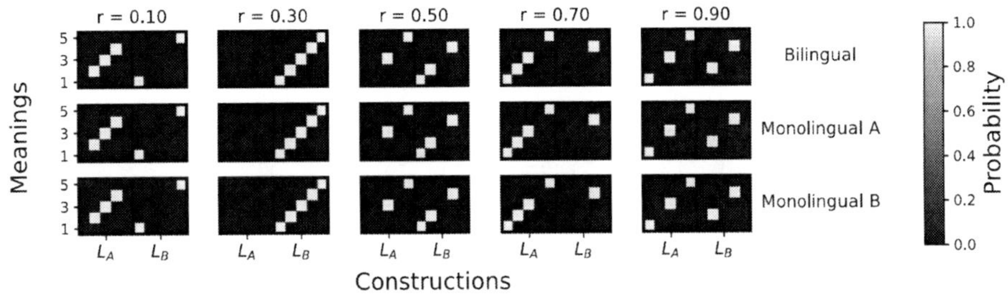

Figure 5: Optimal policies ($\beta = 0.01$) of the bilingual agent when communicating with different types of partners.

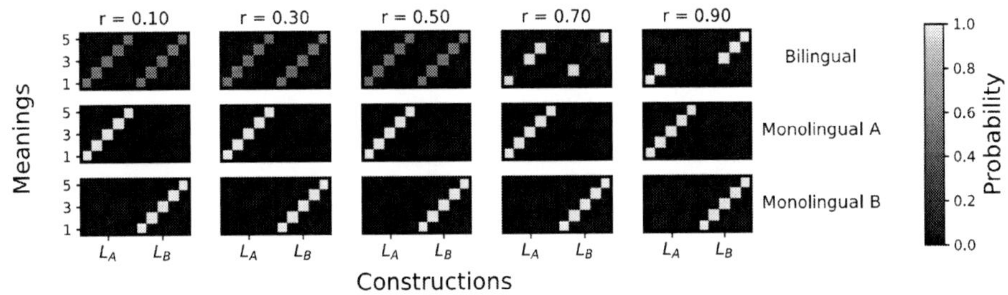

Figure 6: Optimal policies ($\beta = 10$) of the bilingual agent when communicating with different types of partners.

A Deriving Equation 3

Unlike in the $\alpha = 0$ case it might not be immediately obvious how setting $\alpha = 1$ results in Equation 1 becoming Equation 3 and so we figured it would be reasonable to devote a little space explaining why this happens. In fact, it is easiest to see why this is the case by merging the first two terms in Equation 1. If we do that, we get the condensed version

$$\mathcal{J}_{a^*} = \mathop{\mathbb{E}}_{a,m}\left[\sum_c p\left(c|m,a\right)\log\frac{p\left(c|m,a\right)^{1-\alpha}}{p\left(c|m\right)}\right] + \beta \mathop{\mathbb{E}}_{a,m}\left[\sum_c p\left(c|m,a\right)\log\frac{1}{q_a\left(m|c,a^*\right)}\right], \tag{4}$$

which we get by moving the α parameter inside of the log terms. Doing this makes it obvious that when $\alpha = 1$ the objective function is given as:

$$\mathcal{J}_{a^*} = \mathop{\mathbb{E}}_{a,m}\left[\sum_c p\left(c|m,a\right)\log\frac{1}{p\left(c|m\right)}\right] + \beta \mathop{\mathbb{E}}_{a,m}\left[\sum_c p\left(c|m,a\right)\log\frac{1}{q_a\left(m|c,a^*\right)}\right], \tag{5}$$

with the first term now becoming the expected value of a cross-entropy term. In fact, this can be reduced further. If we take the expectation of the first term with respect to a we get

$$\mathcal{J}_{a^*} = \underbrace{\mathop{\mathbb{E}}_{m}\left[\sum_c p\left(c|m\right)\log\frac{1}{p\left(c|m\right)}\right]}_{H(c|m)} + \beta \mathop{\mathbb{E}}_{a,m}\left[\sum_c p\left(c|m,a\right)\log\frac{1}{q_a\left(m|c,a^*\right)}\right], \tag{6}$$

since the various $p(a)$ will sum to 1 and the terms inside the first log do not depend on a. This means the first term is the conditional entropy $H\left(c \mid m\right)$.

B The effects of β

We stated above that the trade-off between cognitive effort and communicative success (manipulated through β in Equation 1) was not of primary interest in the current study. This is because, although including a pressure for communicative success is necessary to get the results we do, the manipulation of the term β, given our setup, primarily impacts how the bilingual agent speaks with monolinguals. For low β their accuracy with monolinguals does not matter, and with any $\alpha \neq 0$ the pressure to decrease entropy results in bilingual agent communication policies drifting off L_{A} and

L_{B} with their monolingual interlocutors the majority of the time. In other words, the consequences of entropy-reduction (creolization) become the only observed effect.

A demonstration of this phenomenon can be seen in Figure 5 and Figure 6, which show the optimal policies of bilingual speakers when interacting with different types of communicative partners. For both figures, we fix $\alpha = 0.5$, with r varying in the columns. We set $\beta = 0.01$ in Figure 5 and $\beta = 10$ in Figure 6. When β is low ($\beta = 0.01$), all policies used by the bilingual agent collapse into a single one regardless of the type of their communicative partner. When β is high ($\beta = 10$), the bilingual agent use separate policies corresponding to different types agent populations, and only innovate the linguistic system when interacting with another bilingual. Monolingual policies remain accurate only when β is high enough, and when β is set in this manner the monolingual policies remain accurate for all values of α.

When *Men Bite Dogs*: Testing Good-Enough Parsing in Turkish with Humans and Large Language Models

Onur Keleş
Department of Linguistics
Boğaziçi University
onur.keles1@bogazici.edu.tr

Nazik Dinçtopal Deniz
Department of Foreign Language Education
Boğaziçi University
nazik.dinctopal@bogazici.edu.tr

Abstract

This paper investigates good-enough parsing in Turkish by comparing human self-paced reading performance to the surprisal and attention patterns of three Turkish Large Language Models (LLMs), GPT-2-Base, GPT-2-Large, and LLaMA-3. The results show that Turkish speakers rely on good-enough parsing for implausible but grammatically permissible sentences (e.g., interpreting sentences such as 'the man bit the dog' as 'the dog bit the man'). Although the smaller LLMs (e.g., GPT-2) were better predictors of human RTs, they seem to have relied more heavily on semantic plausibility than humans. Comparably, larger LLMs (e.g., LLaMA-3) tended to make more probabilistic parsing based on word order, exhibiting less *good-enough* parsing behavior. Therefore, we conclude that LLMs take syntactic and semantic constraints into account when processing thematic roles, but not to the same extent as human parsers.

Introduction

Human language comprehension is rapid and incremental, in which listeners or readers build up provisional interpretations of sentences *on the fly*. However, a growing body of work suggests that these interpretations can occasionally be shallow or incomplete, leading to syntactic misanalyses. *Good-enough parsing* (Ferreira et al., 2002; Ferreira and Patson, 2007; Christianson et al., 2001), argues that language comprehension sometimes relies on heuristics guided by real world knowledge and may not engage in detailed syntactic analyses. That is, a sentence, such as 'the dog was bitten by the man' can be interpreted as 'the dog bit the man.' Such errors are more prevalent when the event described is highly plausible in one particular direction (e.g., 'dogs biting people'), but is reversed in a sentence, such as 'the dog was bitten by the man' especially in noncanonical syntactic structure like passive constructions due to the conflict between real world knowledge and syntactic structure (Ferreira, 2000).

To our knowledge, *good-enough parsing* has not been examined in Turkish, a language that encodes key thematic roles through overt morphosyntactic marking that can potentially influence such misinterpretations. A passive construction, for instance, is marked not only by a syntactic operation (e.g., *Move-Merge* in generative approaches) but also through morphosyntactic operations on the verb (e.g., the passivizing suffix *-Il-*).

This paper investigates if Turkish speakers are prone to *good-enough parsing* effects and if Turkish LLMs, which are hitherto unexplored in the context of psycholinguistics, also exhibit these effects. Specifically, we investigate the extent to which Turkish speakers and Turkish LLMs use syntactic detail and real world plausibility in their processing of active and passive constructions.

To address these questions, we employed (i) a Self-Paced Reading (SPR) experiment with native Turkish speakers, using sentences adapted from Ferreira (2000) and (ii) computational simulations with three Turkish LLMs (GPT-2-Base, GPT-2-Large, and LLaMA-3). By comparing human reading times and model-based surprisal measures, along with each model's relative attention to morphological cues, we aim to show how factors like animacy, semantic plausibility, morphosyntax, and model capacity jointly shape the likelihood of *good-enough* interpretations in Turkish.

Psycholinguistics and LLMs

Recent studies have leveraged LLMs to explore how well they capture processing patterns in humans (Salicchi et al., 2023; Marvin and Linzen, 2018; Goldberg, 2019; Wilcox et al., 2023a; Wang et al., 2024). Surprisal is often used as a predictor of human reading times, showing strong correla-

Proceedings of the Workshop on Cognitive Modeling and Computational Linguistics, pages 219–231
May 3, 2025 ©2025 Association for Computational Linguistics

tions across languages and sentence types (Wilcox et al., 2023a; Oh and Schuler, 2022; Nair and Resnik, 2023). In particular, it has been claimed that processing difficulty at a word reflects how unexpected that word is, given prior context. LLMs have also been tested with respect to their ability to detect event plausibility in English (Pedinotti et al., 2021; Kauf et al., 2024). For example, Kauf et al. (2023) highlight that current LLMs can infer thematic relations and can recognize events more consistently that are truly impossible (e.g., 'the laptop bought the teacher') than those that are merely unlikely (e.g., 'the boy tutored the nanny'). Similarly, Amouyal et al. (2024) presented evidence that log probabilities from base and instruction-tuned models can be used as a proxy for human plausibility judgments, while Kauf et al. (2024) evaluated how these probabilities map onto graded semantic acceptability. Finally, Ettinger (2020) reported that although BERT can pick up on role reversal differences or identify thematic relations, its sensitivity is lower than that of human judgments. Together, these studies suggest that LLMs take into consideration the syntactic regularities and world knowledge, albeit not always matching the precise patterns found in human data and there seems to be variation among different models.

While most of the work on LLMs have centered on English, there is growing interest in multilingual settings and underrepresented languages, including Turkish. Recent work has tested Turkish LLMs for different linguistic tasks like indexical shift (Oğuz et al., 2024) and universal dependency annotation evaluation (Akkurt et al., 2024). However, as far as we are concerned, psycholinguistic evaluation in Turkish LLMs remains sparse. Our investigation therefore addresses a key gap by providing a direct comparison between human data and the predictions of autoregressive Turkish LLMs with differing sizes in an experiment designed to test *good-enough parsing* effects.

Methodology

Self-Paced Reading (SPR) Experiment

This experiment examined the predictions of *good-enough parsing* model (Ferreira and Patson, 2007) with native Turkish speakers. 26 native Turkish speakers ($M_{\text{age}} = 19$, all college students) participated in a word-by-word self-paced reading (SPR) experiment. The experimental sentences, exemplified in (1), were translated from the materials in Ferreira (2000) into Turkish and were slightly adapted to prevent ambiguity and ensure naturality (in (1) and elsewhere, PL: plural, ACC: accusative case, PST: past tense, PASS: passive voice, 1SG: first person singular marker).

(1) a. Köpek-ler adam-ı **ısır-dı** sanır-ım
dog-PL man-ACC bite-PST think-1SG
'I think the dogs bit the man.'

b. Adam-lar köpek tarafından **ısır-ıl-dı**
man-PL dog by bite-PASS-PST
sanır-ım
think-1SG
'I think the men were bitten by the dog.'

c. Adam-lar köpeğ-i **ısır-dı** sanır-ım
man-PL dog-ACC bite-PST think-1SG
'I think the men bit the dog.'

d. Köpek-ler adam tarafından **ısır-ıl-dı**
dog-PL man by bite-PASS-PST
sanır-ım
think-1SG
'I think the dogs were bitten by the man.'

e. **Question:** Is the event in the sentence plausible?

The experimental sentences manipulated syntactic structure as active voice as in (1a, c) or passive voice as in (1b, d), word order as non-reversed as in (1a, b) or reversed as in (1c, d). Half of the sentences had animate arguments which were reversible but *biased* as in 'the man bit the dog' and the other half had one animate one inanimate argument which were *irreversible* as in 'the chef wore the apron.' Reversing the arguments in the reversible set would result in permissible but unlikely events and the reversal of arguments in the irreversible set would cause semantic anomaly. A *symmetrical* set (e.g., 'the boy kissed the girl') was used as control in which the two arguments were equally likely to be agents. All sets had 21 experimental sentences. Each sentence ended with a content-neutral word[1] to prevent *wrap-up* effects. There were 21 sentences each in reversible and irreversible sets, with the four conditions manipulating syntactic structure (active, passive) and word order (reversed, non-reversed), totaling up to 42 experimental items. The experimental sentences were distributed across four reading lists counterbalancing for syntactic structure (active, passive) and word order (reversed, non-reversed). In each list, the experimental sentences were intermingled with 21 additional controls and six practice items.

The experiment was prepared on the PCIbex

[1]Words expressing epistemic modality like *perhaps, maybe, probably*.

experiment building software (Zehr and Schwarz, 2018)[2] and an online link to it was shared with the participants, who read, on their own computer, the sentences word-by-word moving from one word to the next with a key-press. Their task was to indicate, by clicking on two possible options presented under the sentence, if the sentence described a plausible event (see 1e). Accuracy of the response to the plausibility question, word reading time, and end-of-sentence plausibility decision time were measured.

LLM Experiments

Models In addition to Turkish speakers, we tested the predictions of the *good-enough parsing* model on three decoder-only Turkish LLMs using the same experimental item set. We used the base and large variant of the GPT-2 (Radford et al., 2019) trained on Turkish (Kesgin et al., 2024b) and a LLaMA-3 Turkish (Kesgin et al., 2024a), which is an adapted version of the LLaMA-3 model (Dubey et al., 2024) fine-tuned using a 30GB dataset of Turkish. The models used in this study shared the same architecture as autoregressive models trained for next token prediction to align well with the SPR task reported earlier, which tests incremental processing. However, these models differ in size and performance: GPT-2-Base Turkish has 124 million parameters, 12 layers, and 12 attention heads; GPT-2-Large Turkish, 774 million parameters, 36 layers, and 20 attention heads; LLaMA-3-8B Turkish, 8 billion parameters, 32 layers, and 32 attention heads. To compare with human word reading time, we calculated model surprisal for each word in each sentence. We also report a heatmap visualization of the model's attention to examine if it shifts based on the likelihood of the event.

Surprisal We simulated the incremental processing behavior of Turkish speakers as in the SPR task and estimated surprisal values for each word in the sentence to examine if model surprisal in Turkish could predict reading times. To do so, the experimental items were first tokenized using the byte-pair encoding (BPE) tokenizer (Sennrich, 2015), resulting in sub-word sequences. Each word w_i in the sentence was then incrementally presented to the model, conditioned on its preceding context $w_{1:i-1}$. Formally, surprisal $S(w_i)$ is defined as the negative log-probability of w_i given $w_{1:i-1}$:

$$S(w_i) = -\log P(w_i \mid w_{1:i-1}) \quad (1)$$

where $w_{1:i-1}$ represents the words preceding w_i. In practice, the first word w_1 has no context ($w_{1:0} = \emptyset$), the second word w_2 depends on w_1, the third word w_3 depends on w_1, w_2, and so on.

To account for sub-word segmentation, we aggregated the surprisal estimates of all the sub-words belonging to a single word (following Wilcox, 2020; Oh and Schuler, 2023, and others). If a word w is decomposed into sub-words $(s_1, s_2, \ldots, s_k)$, its word-level surprisal $S(w)$ is computed as the following:

$$S(w) = \sum_{i=1}^{k} S(s_i) \quad (2)$$

Attention weights Following Li et al. (2024)'s approach (also see Clark et al., 2019; Voita et al., 2019, for similar uses), we created a heatmap visualization of attention, which is a common strategy for probing model interpretability. In the transformer architecture (Vaswani et al., 2017), each layer contains multiple self-attention heads. These heads compute weighted dot products among token representations (query, key, value), allowing the model to capture a wide range of linguistic relationships. This way, we can try to understand what the model is attending to or *looking at* when processing a word w_i.

Our focus was the degree of attention to the post-position *tarafından* 'by', which introduces the agent in passive constructions in Turkish. For each condition, we computed (for all attention heads and layers) and subtracted the attention weights of the NP local to the post-position from the NP that is distant, which gives us how much more/less attention the two NPs received compared to each other. We then computed the difference between these relative attention patterns when word order was reversed and evaluated how reversing word order (i.e., the condition when event becomes less likely or impossible) affected these relative attention patterns. Increased attention toward the distant NP in the reversed condition may point to a less accurate interpretation (indicating that the sentence was processed in a *good-enough* manner), where the model relies more on semantic/real-world plausibility cues than on strict syntactic structure. Conversely, preference for the local NP would indicate that *tarafından* was successfully mapped to the correct agent phrase that it introduces (as in Figure 1).

[2]http://farm.pcibex.net

Figure 1: Possible model attention routes from the post-position *tarafından* 'by' and two noun phrases. A structural dependency between *tarafından* and the non-agentive distant NP is not possible in Turkish. The brown path indicates the correct dependency (resolved at the agent), whereas the blue path points to an incorrect dependency (resolved at the non-agent subject).

Results and Discussion

SPR Results

Accuracy Table 1 shows Turkish speakers' accuracy in their decisions. Following a strategy similar to Kauf et al. (2023), if speakers answered 'plausible' to reversed orders in biased and irreversible sets, we considered that response to be erroneous. For inference, we fit a mixed effect binomial model to Accuracy with Word Order (Reversed, Nonreversed), Structure (Active, Passive) as fixed effects using `lmer` (Bates et al., 2005) in R for biased and irreversible sets separately. Participants and Items were entered as random effects.

Overall, Turkish speakers were successful (with a mean accuracy of 90% or higher) in all conditions except for reversed sentences in the reversible (i.e., biased) condition. For these sentences, we observed an error rate of 25% for reversed constructions, where the reversed order had a significant negative effect on accuracy (*Odd Ratio* $= 0.11, p < .001$). There was no reliable difference in accuracy for active (30% error) and passive constructions (20% error) in the reversed condition (*Odd Ratio* $= 3.48, p = .13$). Reversing the word order did not result in a decrease in accuracy for irreversible sentences (*Odd Ratio* $= 5.39, p = 0.13$). We attribute this to a *good-enough parsing* effect present in the biased set, whereby participants mistakenly preferred the interpretation that was more in line with their real world knowledge, but not with the syntactic structure of the sentence.

This did not happen for the irreversible sentences, though, possibly because the presence of an inanimate entity was a strong cue for the correct structure. Note that *good-enough parsing* effects were observed in passive constructions in English (Ferreira, 2000). We attribute the comparable decrease in accuracy in passive constructions (compared to that in active counterparts) in Turkish to the semantic content that the 'by'-phrase has in Turkish. Unlike its English counterpart 'by', *tarafından* is a semantically transparent word carrying lexical content that could have provided additional cue to the correct parse. The observation of the decrease in accuracy in active sentences in Turkish (compared to the lack thereof in English) can be attributed to the relatively flexible word order in Turkish in which the order of agents and patients can change depending on the information structure of the sentence (İşsever, 2003).

Set	Word Order	Structure	Accuracy
Biased	Nonreversed	Active	96%
Biased	Nonreversed	Passive	99%
Biased	Reversed	Active	71%
Biased	Reversed	Passive	80%
Irreversible	Nonreversed	Active	97%
Irreversible	Nonreversed	Passive	92%
Irreversible	Reversed	Active	99%
Irreversible	Reversed	Passive	99%

Table 1: Turkish Speakers' Mean Accuracies on the Plausibility Task

Word reading time The RTs for each word can be examined in Figure 2. We fit a mixed effects regression model on the log-transformed RTs for the reversible and irreversible sets separately. Word Order (Reversed, Nonreversed), and Structure (Active, Passive) were fit as fixed effects and Participant and Item were random effects. In addition, all models also included Word Length, Previous Word Length, Region (Verbal, immediately Preverbal, Other) as additional predictors. All numeric factors were centered to prevent collinearity. The verb region had the highest RT in all conditions ($\beta = .23, p < .001$ for both sets). There was no significant interaction between Word Order and Region for the biased set ($\beta = -.05, p = .218$ for preverbal; $\beta = -.07, p = .07$ for verbal), meaning that reversal of the arguments did not yield an online surprisal effect for Turkish speakers.

However, both the verbal ($\beta = .12, p = .001$) and preverbal ($\beta = .04, p = .029$) regions had significantly increased RTs in the reversed condition when the events were irreversible (as in 'aprons wearing chefs'). This suggests that semantic anomaly was detected at the verbal and preverbal region. In the preverbal region, which corresponds to the direct object with accusative marking (e.g., *önlüğ-ü* 'apron-ACC') in active sentences and the post-position *tarafından* in passive

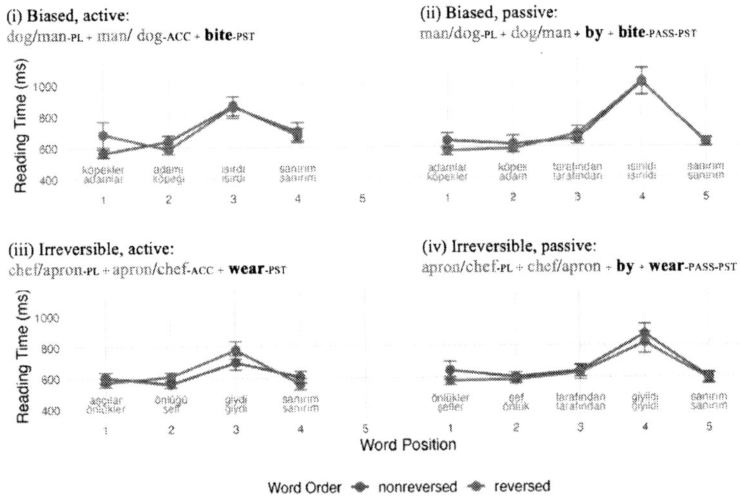

Figure 2: Word-by-word Reading Time (RT) in the Self-Paced Reading (SPR) Task by Set (Biased, Irreversible), Structure (Active, Passive), and Word Order (Reversed, Nonreversed).

sentences, participants encountered critical morphosyntactic/semantic cues that signaled the upcoming structure. In active sentences, the presence of accusative case-marking on an inanimate argument probably served as a strong predictive cue as to the theme/patient of the upcoming verb. Similarly, in passive sentences, encountering the agentive post-position *tarafindan* could have provided information about the upcoming passive verb. These morphosyntactic and semantic cues might have allowed the readers to construct syntactic and thematic dependencies before reaching the verb, where these predictions were ultimately resolved. This was not the case for biased sentences, in which both arguments were animate. This animacy information may have let readers to entertain both arguments as potential agents and patients.

Decision time Figure 3 shows the sentence-final decision times for each condition. We fit a mixed effects regression model to log-transformed decision times with Word Order (Reversed, Nonreversed) and Structure (Active, Passive) as fixed effects for each set. Participants and Items were random effects. Overall, in biased conditions, both in active and passive constructions, the participants took longer to decide in reversed conditions than in nonreversed conditions ($\beta = .18, p = .007$). In irreversible conditions, the opposite pattern was observed and the participants took less time to decide for reversed sentences ($\beta = -.014, p = .014$), and spent more time on sentences with a canonical word order.

Let us first consider the reversible condition. When one argument (e.g., 'the dog') is more likely to do an action (e.g., 'biting') than the other (e.g., 'the man'), reversing their order resulted in delay in decision times. Together with accuracy data (reduced accuracy in reversed than non-reversed conditions), we interpret this delay to *good-enough parsing* effects. Although the participants faced some processing difficulty due to the implausibility of the event (e.g., 'the man biting the dog'), some participants, to some extent, appear to have interpreted such sentences as their plausible counterparts (e.g., 'the dog biting the man'). The pattern in the irreversible conditions was not predicted but is explicable. In irreversible conditions, the agent (e.g., 'the chef') referred to an animate entity and the patient (e.g., 'the apron') was inanimate. Reversing their order was predicted to cause processing difficulty but it appears that the participants were quick to integrate the animacy information in their decisions and to detect the implausibility when the order of the arguments was reversed.

LLM Results

Surprisal The estimated surprisals from each of the three Turkish models are given in Figure 4. To investigate if the same critical regions resulted in difference in model surprisal, mixed effects linear models were fit for each model and for each set, resulting in 6 models. Word Length, Preceding

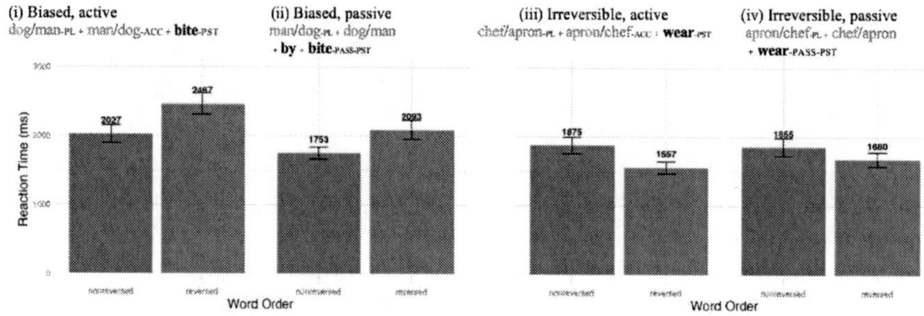

Figure 3: Semantic Plausibility Decision Time by Set (Biased, Irreversible), Structure (Active, Passive), and Word Order (Reversed, Nonreversed)

Word Length, Region (Verbal, Preverbal, Other), Word Order (Reversed, Nonreversed), and Structure (Active, Passive) were entered as fixed effects. Item was entered as a random effect. For the biased set, both variants of the GPT-2 (base and large) had only preverbal region significant in the passive voice when the arguments were reversed ($\beta = .37$, $p = .04$ for GPT-2-Base; $\beta = .28$, $p = .04$ for GPT-2-Large). In contrast, LLaMA-3 had significantly larger surprisal estimates only for the verb region in the reversed condition ($\beta = .42, p < .001$).

As to the irreversibles, the large and base variants of GPT-2 behaved almost identically except for the surprisal for the verbal region in the irreversible passive condition. Verbs that had reversed arguments in the passive voice had a larger surprisal estimate (p's $< .001$) than the non-reversed argument in GPT-2-Large. This means that the larger model was able to detect the semantic bias on both critical regions whereas GPT-2-Base did so only for the preverbal region with no significant effect of the verbal region ($\beta = .31, p = .07$). All critical regions significantly increased surprisal estimates in other conditions (p's $< .001$). In contrast, LLaMA-3 also yielded significantly larger surprisals for all conditions in the irreversible set (p's $< .005$).

Overall, LLaMA-3 demonstrated a broader sensitivity to structural and semantic cues compared to the GPT-2 family, particularly in irreversible sentences. In contrast, GPT-2 models showed sensitivity in specific regions (preverbal for the base model, and both preverbal and verbal for the larger variant). This suggests that LLaMA-3 might have better captured structural and semantic dependencies than the smaller models. Additionally, the differences in how GPT-2 variants process passive constructions with reversed arguments suggest that model size might be influencing the ability to integrate multiple linguistic cues in Turkish,[3] with the larger GPT-2 model estimating higher surprisal for both critical regions.

Predicting RTs We also tested if model surprisal predicted Turkish speakers' word RTs. For this, we added two additional predictors to the word reading time model described earlier. We added current word's w_i Surprisal and PrevSurprisal (which corresponds to the surprisal from the previous word w_{i-1} for potential spillover effects) following Wilcox et al. (2023b). Then, the baseline model and surprisal models were compared with a likelihood ratio test for each set. We found that the models that included surprisal as an additional predictor had significantly greater likelihood for both the biased ($\chi^2(3) = 28.94$, $p < .001$) and irreversible sets ($\chi^2(1) = 8.63$, $p < .01$). The general finding that surprisal predicts reading times is in line with observations from prior studies (Demberg and Keller, 2009; Shain et al., 2022; Wilcox et al., 2023b).

To investigate which of these language models best predict human RTs, we split the data by LLM and fit linear mixed-effects models, one for each LLM across the two sets. The surprisal derived from GPT-2-Large predicted the RTs at the critical region (the verb) ($\beta = .04, p < .001$). The surprisal of GPT-2-Base had some predictive power but it did not reach statistical significance ($\beta = .04, p = .09$). LLaMA-3 surprisal did not predict the RTs at the critical region ($\beta = .00, p = .759$) but it did predict the RTs at the region preceding the verb (at the accusative-marked NPs in the active condition and at the postposition 'by' in the passive condition) ($\beta = .03$, p < .002). Overall, these find-

[3]For comparison, see Appendix A for the surprisal estimates by the same models in English.

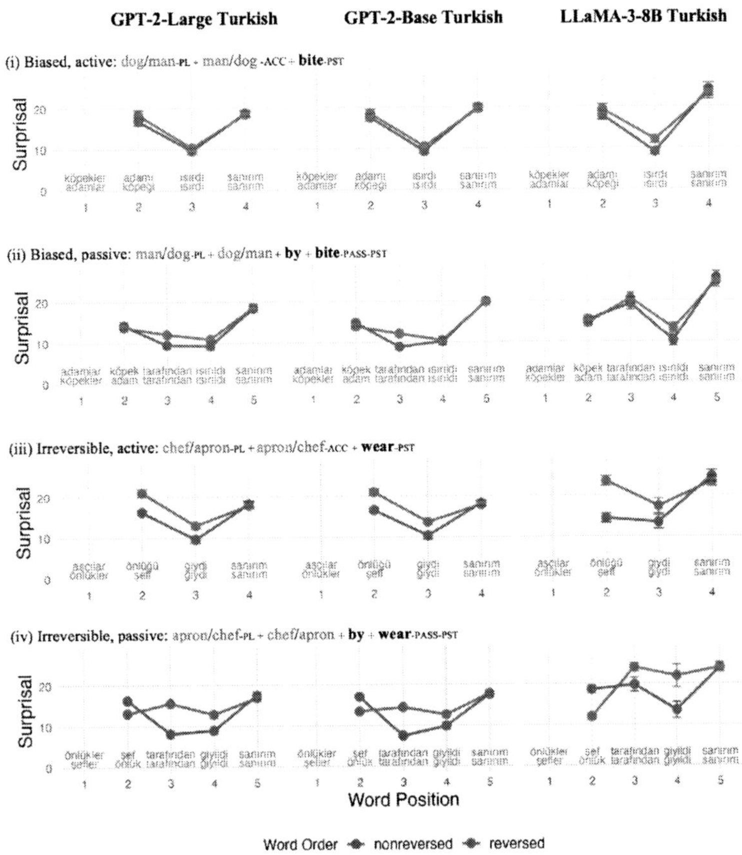

Figure 4: Replication of the SPR Task: Left-context Only Word-by-word Model Surprisal for GPT-2-Large Turkish, GPT-2-Base Turkish, LLaMA-3-8B Turkish by Set (Biased, Irreversible), Structure (Active, Passive), and Word Order (Reversed, Nonreversed).

ings indicate that the surprisal values from GPT-2 models (particularly the large variant) accounted for human RTs at the critical region better than those from LLaMA-3.

Attention weights Finally, we tested if models' attention patterns reflected sensitivity to argument structure, particularly in passive constructions with *tarafından* ('by') in Turkish. We focused on the attention weights from *tarafından* to its local, agent, NP and the more distant, patient, NP, comparing these patterns across canonical and reversed word orders. This analysis allowed us to examine whether the models correctly associated the agent marker with the more local and structurally correct NP, or if they showed increased attention to the distant NP in non-canonical orders, which might indicate shallower syntactic processing and more semantic or heuristic processing.

Figure 5 demonstrates the relative change in attention toward distant or local NP when the condition changed from non-reversed to reversed across all layers and attention heads. In other words, it shows us if the attention heads kept looking at the same NP or changed their attention weights in favor of either one of the two candidate NPs when the arguments were reversed. The red colors indicate change in attention in favor of the local NP, and the blue colors refer to a change in favor of the distant NP. A distant NP preference would imply that the model is associating *tarafından* more with the non-agent possibly because of a semantic intrusion.

For biased passive sentences (top row), GPT-2-Base showed mixed patterns with scattered attention shifts across layers and heads, while GPT-2-Large demonstrated more consistent but subtle changes (given the more faded colors) in attention distribution. LLaMA-3 exhibited the most uniform pattern, with minimal attention shifts between conditions. In irreversible passive constructions (bottom row), the patterns were more pronounced. In the GPT-2 models, there were increasing looks or sensitivity to the distant NP. While for the base model distant NP preference took place across different layers, for the large model it mainly occurred in the deeper layers, albeit less strongly.

LLaMA-3 maintained relatively stable attention patterns with only a few heads showing strong preferences for either NP. This suggests that LLaMA-3's processing of argument structure may be more immune to word order variations, particularly in syntactically constrained contexts. Deeper layers did not display significant attention shifts in either set. Furthermore, there was increasing attention weight at the local NP in the irreversible set. We infer that LLaMA-3 mostly did probabilistic and syntactically constrained processing, and presumably understood semantically implausible events with correct mapping of thematic relations. In contrast, both GPTs seem to have relied more on semantic cues and mapped *tarafindan* with the more plausible and animate NP in Turkish.[4]

General Discussion and Conclusion

Our findings offer converging evidence that Turkish speakers exhibit *good-enough parsing* effects, particularly for *biased* sentences in which real-world plausibility (e.g., 'dogs biting men' versus 'men biting dogs') competes with syntactic structure. The SPR experiment revealed that reversed sentences in the biased set generated a *good-enough parsing* effect, leading to increased error rates and slower plausibility decisions. However, this effect was greatly reduced in the irreversible events containing semantic anomaly. We conclude that the animacy cues help participants form accurate interpretations. Furthermore, all three autoregressive Turkish models (GPT-2-Base, GPT-2-Large, and LLaMA-3 Turkish) showed sensitivity to structural and semantic anomalies in their surprisal estimates. However, the larger GPT-2 model captured more linguistic cues than its smaller variant, and LLaMA-3 model appeared to be the most robust in assigning correct syntactic dependencies even under conditions of unlikely events. In addition, human reading times were significantly predicted by LLM-based surprisal, supporting earlier findings in the literature (Li et al., 2024; Wilcox, 2020). The surprisal analysis also revealed that GPT-2 better predicted human RTs than LLaMA-3. This finding aligns well with earlier observations made for English suggesting that smaller or mid-sized models (e.g., GPT-2 variants) can mirror human reading patterns (Oh and Schuler, 2023; Kuribayashi et al., 2023) more closely, in line with large-scale evidence for surprisal-based predictability effects (Shain et al., 2024). Moreover, attention weight analyses showed that GPT-2 models often shifted attention toward the more semantically plausible (but syntactically incorrect) noun phrase in reversed sentences, presumably reflecting good-enough heuristics across both biased and irreversible stimuli. Meanwhile, LLaMA-3 appeared more robust in capturing correct agent–patient mappings, which was more unlike the human data.

Crucially, Turkish speakers also relied on *good-enough parsing* strategies, but only for biased sentences, similar to the English speakers in Ferreira (2000). This may place their performance between the heuristic-driven patterns of the GPT-2 models and the more consistent syntactic mappings observed in LLaMA-3. GPT-2 models appear to rely more heavily on good-enough strategies than humans, whereas the attention patterns of LLaMA-3 suggest more syntactically detailed parsing. These results highlight the potential of LLMs as computational proxies for psycholinguistic phenomena and the need to incorporate semantic plausibility cues into neural parsing models. While human participants occasionally rely on shallow heuristics, larger models may attend to semantic and structural cues differently across representational scales. We conclude that both Turkish speakers and LLMs are sensitive to syntactic and semantic constraints, but differ in how they prioritize these linguistic cues.

These findings raise broader questions about the architecture of both human and model-based parsing. In the context of *good-enough* processing, transformer models appear to operate such that earlier layers capture syntax-level information and frequency-based cues, while deeper layers seem to encode information related to real world plausibility. (See similar observations for human sentence processing, not specifically in the context of *good-enough* parsing, e.g., Lowder and Gordon, 2015; and Frazier and Fodor, 1978.) The varia-

[4]For comparability, we also tested the attention weights of BERT and BERTurk (Schweter, 2020) (see Appendix B), bidirectional models for English and Turkish, respectively, and found similar changes in attention, but BERT (compared to BERTurk) had more shifts to the distant NP in the deeper layers, which might be related to the greater distance between the two NPs in English.

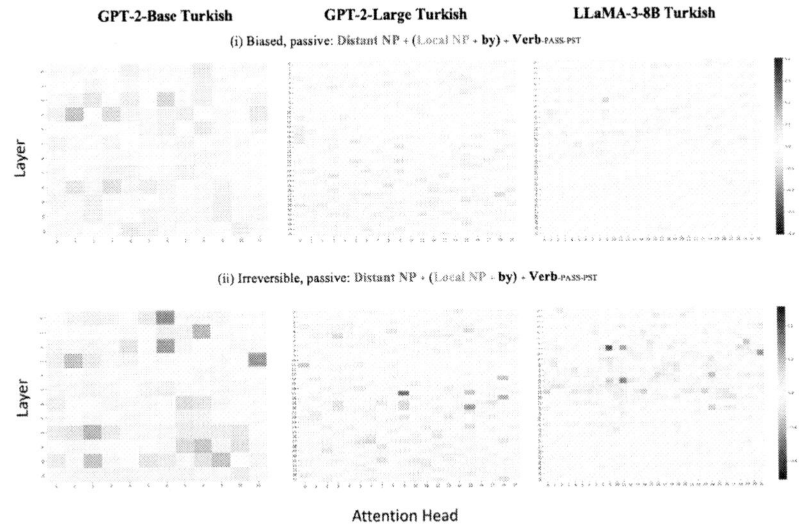

Figure 5: Attention difference between the NPs distant and local to the post-position (in Reversed - Non-reversed word order) for passive constructions. Results are shown for three Turkish LLMs: GPT-2-Base (12 layers, 12 heads), GPT-2-Large (36 layers, 20 heads), and LLaMA-3-8B (32 layers, 32 heads). Blue regions indicate stronger attention to Distant NP (incorrect dependency) in reversed word order, while red regions indicate stronger attention to Local NP (correct dependency. Top row shows differences for biased passive sentences, bottom row does so for irreversible passive sentences.

tion in attention across layers and heads further suggests that different layers may support distinct parsing functions. Future research can examine if a cascaded cue integration approach can be extended to *good-enough* processing in human sentence comprehension. These directions can help clarify how humans and LLMs balance shallow and syntactically-detailed processing.

Limitations and Future Research

We can acknowledge several limitations that require further exploration: (i) We relied on surprisal and attention analyses, but did not include broader generative tasks (e.g., full-sentence completions, direct plausibility ratings from the models). Also, instead of plausibility ratings, agent and patient matching tasks could be used to investigate *good-enough* parsing. Future work could integrate these methods to probe whether humans and LLMs interpret semantically implausible sentences accurately. (ii) Our experiments focused on decoder-only architectures (GPT-2 and LLaMA-3). Other decoder-models available in Turkish like Kanarya (Safaya et al., 2022) or alternative model families, such as T5-based architectures (e.g., TURNA, Uludoğan et al., 2024) and possibly multilingual models like mGPT (Shliazhko et al., 2023) and Aya (Üstün et al., 2024), might yield different patterns of surprisal or attention particularly for language comprehension tasks in Turkish. (iii) Finally, recent work (Giulianelli et al., 2024) has raised concerns about tokenization granularity and argued that token-level language models should ideally be (approximately) marginalized into character-level representations before being used in psycholinguistic studies. Since the current work relies on token-level surprisals, we acknowledge that this may introduce a degree of misalignment with human processing.

Acknowledgments

We would like to thank the anonymous reviewers for their constructive comments, Mehtap Güven Çoban for her contribution to the translations of the material, the participants of the SPR experiment for their time, Allison Dods and Ümit Atlamaz for valuable feedback on earlier versions of this work.

References

Furkan Akkurt, Onur Gungor, Büşra Marşan, Tunga Gungor, Balkiz Ozturk Basaran, Arzucan Özgür, and Susan Uskudarli. 2024. Evaluating the quality of a corpus annotation scheme using pretrained language models. In *Proceedings of the 2024 Joint International Conference on Computational Linguistics, Language Resources and Evaluation (LREC-COLING 2024)*, pages 6504–6514, Torino, Italia. ELRA and ICCL.

Samuel Joseph Amouyal, Aya Meltzer-Asscher, and Jonathan Berant. 2024. Large language models for psycholinguistic plausibility pretesting. *arXiv preprint arXiv:2402.05455*.

Douglas Bates et al. 2005. Fitting linear mixed models in r. *R news*, 5(1):27–30.

Kiel Christianson, Andrew Hollingworth, John F. Halliwell, and Fernanda Ferreira. 2001. Thematic Roles Assigned along the Garden Path Linger. *Cognitive Psychology*, 42(4):368–407.

Kevin Clark, Urvashi Khandelwal, Omer Levy, and Christopher D. Manning. 2019. What does bert look at? an analysis of bert's attention. *Preprint*, arXiv:1906.04341.

Vera Demberg and Frank Keller. 2009. A computational model of prediction in human parsing: Unifying locality and surprisal effects. In *Proceedings of the annual meeting of the cognitive science society*, volume 31. Issue: 31.

Abhimanyu Dubey, Abhinav Jauhri, Abhinav Pandey, Abhishek Kadian, Ahmad Al-Dahle, Aiesha Letman, Akhil Mathur, Alan Schelten, Amy Yang, Angela Fan, et al. 2024. The llama 3 herd of models. *arXiv preprint arXiv:2407.21783*.

Allyson Ettinger. 2020. What bert is not: Lessons from a new suite of psycholinguistic diagnostics for language models. *Transactions of the Association for Computational Linguistics*, 8:34–48.

Fernanda Ferreira. 2000. Syntactic Vulnerability and Thematic Misinterpretation. page 64.

Fernanda Ferreira, Karl GD Bailey, and Vittoria Ferraro. 2002. Good-enough representations in language comprehension. *Current directions in psychological science*, 11(1):11–15.

Fernanda Ferreira and Nikole D Patson. 2007. The 'good enough'approach to language comprehension. *Language and linguistics compass*, 1(1-2):71–83.

Lyn Frazier and Janet Dean Fodor. 1978. The sausage machine: A new two-stage parsing model. *Cognition*, 6(4):291–325. Publisher: Elsevier.

Mario Giulianelli, Luca Malagutti, Juan Luis Gastaldi, Brian DuSell, Tim Vieira, and Ryan Cotterell. 2024. On the proper treatment of tokenization in psycholinguistics. *arXiv preprint arXiv:2410.02691*.

Yoav Goldberg. 2019. Assessing bert's syntactic abilities. *Preprint*, arXiv:1901.05287.

Selçuk İşsever. 2003. Information structure in turkish: the word order–prosody interface. *Lingua*, 113(11):1025–1053.

Carina Kauf, Emmanuele Chersoni, Alessandro Lenci, Evelina Fedorenko, Anna A Ivanova, et al. 2024. Log probabilities are a reliable estimate of semantic plausibility in base and instruction-tuned language models. Association for Computational Linguistics (ACL).

Carina Kauf, Anna A. Ivanova, Giulia Rambelli, Emmanuele Chersoni, Jingyuan Selena She, Zawad Chowdhury, Evelina Fedorenko, and Alessandro Lenci. 2023. Event Knowledge in Large Language Models: The Gap Between the Impossible and the Unlikely. *Cognitive Science*, 47(11):e13386.

H Toprak Kesgin, M Kaan Yuce, Eren Dogan, M Egemen Uzun, Atahan Uz, Elif İnce, Yusuf Erdem, Osama Shbib, Ahmed Zeer, and M Fatih Amasyali. 2024a. Optimizing large language models for turkish: New methodologies in corpus selection and training. In *2024 Innovations in Intelligent Systems and Applications Conference (ASYU)*, pages 1–6. IEEE.

H Toprak Kesgin, M Kaan Yuce, Eren Dogan, M Egemen Uzun, Atahan Uz, H Emre Seyrek, Ahmed Zeer, and M Fatih Amasyali. 2024b. Introducing cosmosgpt: Monolingual training for turkish language models. *arXiv preprint arXiv:2404.17336*.

Tatsuki Kuribayashi, Yohei Oseki, and Timothy Baldwin. 2023. Psychometric predictive power of large language models. *arXiv preprint arXiv:2311.07484*.

Andrew Li, Xianle Feng, Siddhant Narang, Austin Peng, Tianle Cai, Raj Sanjay Shah, and Sashank Varma. 2024. Incremental comprehension of garden-path sentences by large language models: Semantic interpretation, syntactic re-analysis, and attention. *arXiv preprint arXiv:2405.16042*.

Matthew W Lowder and Peter C Gordon. 2015. Focus takes time: Structural effects on reading. *Psychonomic Bulletin & Review*, 22:1733–1738.

Rebecca Marvin and Tal Linzen. 2018. Targeted Syntactic Evaluation of Language Models. *arXiv preprint*. ArXiv:1808.09031 [cs].

Sathvik Nair and Philip Resnik. 2023. Words, Subwords, and Morphemes: What Really Matters in the Surprisal-Reading Time Relationship? In *Findings of the Association for Computational Linguistics: EMNLP 2023*, pages 11251–11260, Singapore. Association for Computational Linguistics.

Metehan Oğuz, Yusuf Umut Ciftci, and Yavuz Faruk Bakman. 2024. Do llms recognize me, when i is not me: Assessment of llms understanding of turkish indexical pronouns in indexical shift contexts. *arXiv preprint arXiv:2406.05569*.

Byung-Doh Oh and William Schuler. 2022. Entropy- and distance-based predictors from gpt-2 attention patterns predict reading times over and above gpt-2 surprisal. *arXiv preprint arXiv:2212.11185*.

Byung-Doh Oh and William Schuler. 2023. Why does surprisal from larger transformer-based language models provide a poorer fit to human reading times? *Transactions of the Association for Computational Linguistics*, 11:336–350.

Paolo Pedinotti, Giulia Rambelli, Emmanuele Chersoni, Enrico Santus, Alessandro Lenci, and Philippe Blache. 2021. Did the Cat Drink the Coffee? Challenging Transformers with Generalized Event Knowledge. *arXiv preprint*. ArXiv:2107.10922 [cs].

Alec Radford, Jeffrey Wu, Rewon Child, David Luan, Dario Amodei, Ilya Sutskever, et al. 2019. Language models are unsupervised multitask learners. *OpenAI blog*, 1(8):9.

Ali Safaya, Emirhan Kurtuluş, Arda Goktogan, and Deniz Yuret. 2022. Mukayese: Turkish NLP strikes back. In *Findings of the Association for Computational Linguistics: ACL 2022*, pages 846–863, Dublin, Ireland. Association for Computational Linguistics.

Lavinia Salicchi, Emmanuele Chersoni, and Alessandro Lenci. 2023. A study on surprisal and semantic relatedness for eye-tracking data prediction. *Frontiers in Psychology*, 14:1112365. Publisher: Frontiers.

Stefan Schweter. 2020. Berturk-bert models for turkish. *Zenodo*, 2020:3770924.

Rico Sennrich. 2015. Neural machine translation of rare words with subword units. *arXiv preprint arXiv:1508.07909*.

Cory Shain, Clara Meister, Tiago Pimentel, Ryan Cotterell, and Roger Levy. 2024. Large-scale evidence for logarithmic effects of word predictability on reading time. *Proceedings of the National Academy of Sciences*, 121(10):e2307876121.

Cory Shain, Clara Meister, Tiago Pimentel, Ryan Cotterell, and Roger Philip Levy. 2022. Large-scale evidence for logarithmic effects of word predictability on reading time. Publisher: PsyArXiv.

Oleh Shliazhko, Alena Fenogenova, Maria Tikhonova, Vladislav Mikhailov, Anastasia Kozlova, and Tatiana Shavrina. 2023. mgpt: Few-shot learners go multilingual. *Preprint*, arXiv:2204.07580.

Gökçe Uludoğan, Zeynep Yirmibeşoğlu Balal, Furkan Akkurt, Melikşah Türker, Onur Güngör, and Susan Üsküdarlı. 2024. Turna: A turkish encoder-decoder language model for enhanced understanding and generation. *arXiv preprint arXiv:2401.14373*.

Ahmet Üstün, Viraat Aryabumi, Zheng-Xin Yong, Wei-Yin Ko, Daniel D'souza, Gbemileke Onilude, Neel Bhandari, Shivalika Singh, Hui-Lee Ooi, Amr Kayid, et al. 2024. Aya model: An instruction finetuned open-access multilingual language model. *arXiv preprint arXiv:2402.07827*.

Ashish Vaswani, Noam Shazeer, Niki Parmar, Jakob Uszkoreit, Llion Jones, Aidan N. Gomez, \Lukasz Kaiser, and Illia Polosukhin. 2017. Attention is all you need. *Advances in neural information processing systems*, 30.

Elena Voita, David Talbot, Fedor Moiseev, Rico Sennrich, and Ivan Titov. 2019. Analyzing multi-head self-attention: Specialized heads do the heavy lifting, the rest can be pruned. *Preprint*, arXiv:1905.09418.

Daphne Wang, Mehrnoosh Sadrzadeh, Miloš Stanojević, Wing-Yee Chow, and Richard Breheny. 2024. How can large language models become more human? In *Proceedings of the Workshop on Cognitive Modeling and Computational Linguistics*, pages 166–176.

Ethan G Wilcox. 2020. On the predictive power of neural language models for human real-time comprehension behavior. *arXiv preprint arXiv:2006.01912*.

Ethan G Wilcox, Tiago Pimentel, Clara Meister, Ryan Cotterell, and Roger P Levy. 2023a. Testing the predictions of surprisal theory in 11 languages. *Transactions of the Association for Computational Linguistics*, 11:1451–1470.

Ethan G. Wilcox, Tiago Pimentel, Clara Meister, Ryan Cotterell, and Roger P. Levy. 2023b. Testing the predictions of surprisal theory in 11 languages. *Transactions of the Association for Computational Linguistics*, 11:1451–1470. Publisher: MIT Press One Broadway, 12th Floor, Cambridge, Massachusetts 02142, USA .

Jérémy Zehr and Florian Schwarz. 2018. PennController for Internet Based Experiments (IBEX).

A Model Surprisal in English

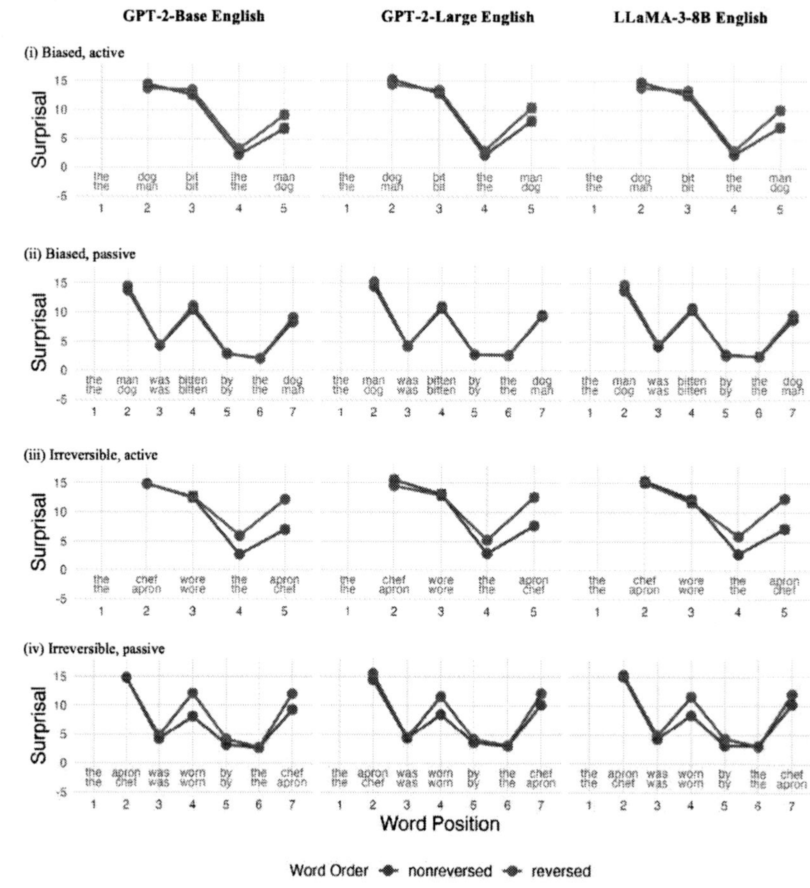

Figure 6: Word-by-word Model Surprisal for the English BERT and BERTurk (Turkish BERT) by Set (Biased, Irreversible), Structure (Active, Passive), and Word Order (Reversed, Nonreversed)

B Comparing English and Turkish: Encoder Model Attention

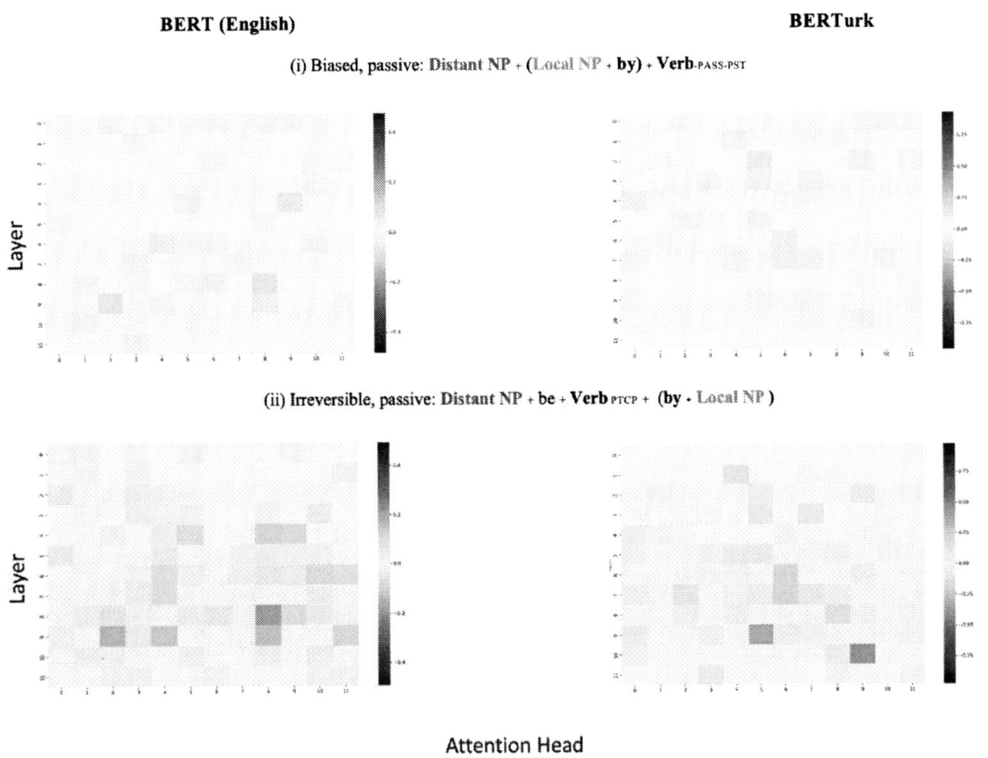

Figure 7: Attention difference between the NPs distant and local to the post-position (in Reversed - Non-reversed word order) for passive constructions, comparing the English BERT and BERTurk (Turkish BERT) (12 layers, 12 heads). Blue regions indicate stronger attention to Distant NP in reversed word order, while red regions indicate stronger attention to Local NP. Top row shows differences for biased passive sentences, bottom row does so for irreversible passive sentences.

Transformers Can Model Human Hyperprediction in Buzzer Quiz

Yoichiro Yamashita, Yuto Harada, Yohei Oseki
University of Tokyo
{yamashita-yoichiro416, harada-yuto, oseki}@g.ecc.u-tokyo.ac.jp

Abstract

Humans tend to predict the next words during sentence comprehension, but under unique circumstances, they demonstrate an ability for longer coherent word sequence prediction. In this paper, we investigate whether Transformers can model such hyperprediction observed in humans during sentence processing, specifically in the context of Japanese buzzer quizzes. We conducted eye-tracking experiments where the participants read the first half of buzzer quiz questions and predicted the second half, while we modeled their reading time using the GPT-2. By modeling the reading times of each word in the first half of the question using GPT-2 surprisal, we examined under what conditions fine-tuned language models can better predict reading times. As a result, we found that GPT-2 surprisal effectively explains the reading times of quiz experts as they read the first half of the question while predicting the latter half. When the language model was fine-tuned with quiz questions, the perplexity value decreased. Lower perplexity corresponded to higher psychometric predictive power; however, excessive data for fine-tuning led to a decrease in perplexity and the fine-tuned model exhibited a low psychometric predictive power. Overall, our findings suggest that a moderate amount of data is required for fine-tuning in order to model human hyperprediction.

1 Introduction

It is widely recognized that the probability of a word within a specific context (i.e., surprisal) affects the difficulty of processing during incremental human language comprehension (Hale, 2001; Levy, 2008). Based on this premise, researchers have compared a variety of language models in terms of how well their surprisal correlates with human reading behavior (Wilcox et al., 2020; Kuribayashi et al., 2021; Van Schijndel and Linzen, 2021).

However recent works found that this cannot be applied to very large language models, which provides a poorer fit to human reading times. Oh and Schuler (2023) argues that larger Transformer-based models 'memorize' sequences during training, and their surprisal estimates diverge from humanlike expectations.

In those studies on cognitive modeling, self-paced reading experiments and eye-movement corpora are employed to utilize data regarding human reading times (Kennedy et al., 2013; Asahara et al., 2016; Futrell et al., 2018; Goodkind and Bicknell, 2018; Yoshida et al., 2021). These corpora typically use newspaper and novel texts as material and measure the reading time required for participants to read and comprehend the text. These works have devoted much attention to understanding everyday sentence comprehension, particularly the prediction of the next word (Kuribayashi et al., 2021; Yoshida et al., 2021). In such typical sentence comprehension, psycholinguistics research has emphasized humans' use of contextual information to predict the next word while reading (Kutas and Hillyard, 1984; Altmann and Kamide, 1999; Kamide et al., 2003).

However, when comprehending a sentence under specialized conditions such as buzzer quizzes, humans can sometimes make predictions about the whole sentence that go beyond the next word prediction (hereafter referred to as "hyperprediction"). This phenomenon requires comprehenders to anticipate not only the next word but also the structure of subsequent sentences. Although hyperprediction is a highly advanced and complex aspect of human predictive processing it has attracted little attention so far and remains largely unexplored.

In this paper, we aim to fill this gap by evaluating the language models' capacity to model human predictive processes, particularly in tasks emphasizing hyperprediction in the context of a buzzer quiz. Buzzer quiz is a popular type of quiz

Proceedings of the Workshop on Cognitive Modeling and Computational Linguistics, pages 232–243
May 3, 2025 ©2025 Association for Computational Linguistics

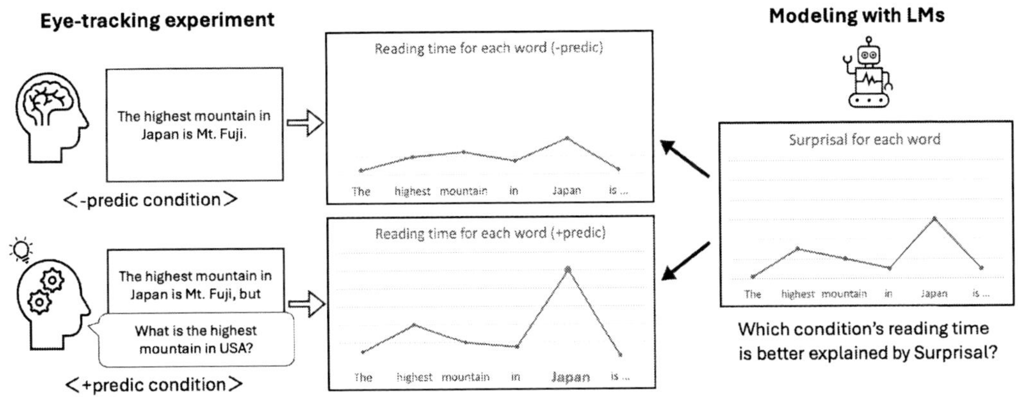

Figure 1: The process of the experiment. Human total reading time measured in the eye-tracking experiment was modeled with surprisal computed by pre-trained GPT-2 and fine-tuned GPT-2.

game (Tokuhisa, 2012), and buzzer quiz players are known to engage in this predictive process (Izawa, 2021).

It remains unclear whether human hyperprediction occurs in more natural reading behaviors beyond quiz settings. However, this study focuses specifically on buzzer quiz scenarios to first examine the extent to which language models can simulate human hyperprediction.

In summary, our key contributions are as follows:

- This paper studies data collected from native Japanese speakers, which complements most studies using data collected in western languages.
- Our results demonstrate that the GPT-2 can partially model human hyperprediction to some extent.
- Analyses on fine-tuning reveal that fine-tuned GPT-2 can model human hyperprediction more accurately.

2 Related work

2.1 Prediction in human sentence processing

Psycholinguistics research spanning several decades has consistently suggested that humans engage in predictive processes while comprehending sentences (Ehrlich and Rayner, 1981; Kutas and Hillyard, 1984; Altmann and Kamide, 1999; Kamide et al., 2003; Pickering and Garrod, 2013; Martin et al., 2018). Psycholinguists have employed diverse methodologies to explore human behavior in sentence comprehension. Altmann and Kamide (1999) and Kamide et al. (2003) employed the Visual World Paradigm and revealed that humans utilize contextual cues within sentences to predict upcoming words, such as direct objects or verbs. Additionally, many researchers conducted EEG experiments and demonstrated that encountering a word unrelated to the context elicits a large N400 response in readers, which is associated with a semantic gap between a word and its context (Kutas and Hillyard, 1984; Van Petten and Kutas, 1990; Frank et al., 2015). Moreover, the process of next-word prediction during human sentence processing has been investigated and recent research has highlighted the empoloyment of the speech production system in generating lexical predictions during sentence comprehension (Martin et al., 2018). These studies emphasize that humans utilize the preceding context as a crucial cue for predicting upcoming words.

However, humans demonstrate the ability to predict longer sequences of words in a special situation such as in a buzzer quiz (Izawa, 2021). Skilled quiz players can answer correctly by only listening to a few words of the question sentence. In this context, they are not only required to predict the next word but also anticipate the structure of the entire sentence.

This ability to make strong predictions during sentence comprehension is a crucial aspect of sentence processing, but it has received limited attention in previous research. Therefore, this study specifically focuses on human hyperprediction.

Question	Type
サッカーのコート で、 短い方の辺 は ゴールライン ですが、 長い方の辺 は 何でしょう？ football pitch on shorter side TOPIC goal line but, longer side TOPIC what? "On a football pitch, the shorter side is the goal line, but what is the longer side?"	**easy**
南アメリカ大陸 で 最も高い山 は アコンカグア ですが、 北アメリカ大陸 で 最も高い山 は 何でしょう？ South America in the highest peak TOPIC Aconcagua but, North America in the highest peak TOPIC what? "The highest mountain in South America is Aconcagua, but what is the highest mountain in North America?"	**easy**
アメリカ合衆国 の 国の花 は バラ ですが、 メキシコ合衆国 の 国の花 は 何でしょう？ the USA 's national flower TOPIC rose but, Mexico 's national flower TOPIC what? "The national flower of the United States of America is the rose, but what is the national flower of the United Mexican States?"	**difficult**
オーストラリア の 公用語 は 英語 ですが、 オーストリア の 公用語 は 何でしょう？ Australia 's language TOPIC English but, Austria 's language TOPIC what? "The official language of Australia is English, but what is the official language of Austria?"	**difficult**

Table 1: Examples of parallel quizzes. In each question, the words in red in the first half are contrasted with those in blue in the second half. The first and second quizzes are the **easy** type of parallel quizzes, and the third quiz is the **difficult** type.

2.2 Surprisal theory

Surprisal theory is a widely accepted concept in computational psycholinguistics, particularly in cognitive modeling research. As Eq. (1) shows, surprisal is calculated as the negative logarithm of the probability of a word or sequence of words occurring in a particular context.

$$Surprisal_{word} = -\log P(word|context) \quad (1)$$

This theory proposes that the processing difficulty of a word is determined by its predictability within its preceding context (Hale, 2001; Levy, 2008; Smith and Levy, 2013). Put simply, the easier a word is to predict, the lower the cognitive load associated with it. Surprisal serves as a measure of its processing difficulty. In order to evaluate "human-like" trends of the language models, studies have been conducted to compare the surprisal calculated by language models with data obtained from humans, such as eye movement and EEG (Fossum and Levy, 2012; Smith and Levy, 2013; Frank et al., 2015; Wilcox et al., 2020; Yoshida et al., 2021).

For example, Wilcox et al. (2020) and Goodkind and Bicknell (2018) compared various models by computing how well their next-word expectations predict human reading time behavior on naturalistic text corpora, and found that the lower perplexity of a model, the better its psychometric predictive power.

The previous research most closely related to our work is Kuribayashi et al. (2021). They used the Japanese eye-tracking corpus BCCWJ and found that lower perplexity in Japanese language models did not always lead to better psychometric predictive power. This contrasts with findings for English language models. We observe the same trend in this study on human hyperprediction.

Our work uses eye movement data following previous research. The surprisal calculated by the "human-like" language model is expected to correlate better with the human reading time of each word.

3 Buzzer quiz in Japanese

Buzzer quiz is a type of quiz where participants compete to answer questions quickly by buzzing in with a buzzer. In a buzzer quiz, a moderator or host reads out questions to the players. Each player is equipped with a buzzer and when players know the answer to a question, they buzz in to signal that they want to answer. The first person or team to buzz in gets the opportunity to answer the question.

While quiz players are listening to the question, they are said to predict the rest of the question sentence, not just the next word, but the entire sentence (Izawa, 2021). Typically, the players try to buzz the button even before the question is fully read.

In order to investigate human predictive processing when reading quiz questions, we experimented with *parallel quizzes*, which are typical among Japanese quizzes and where prediction is said to be important (Izawa, 2021). Parallel quizzes always have a consistent format as follows:

For A, $X(A) = x_a$, but what is $X(B)$?

The first half of the question sentence is the premise of the question and the second half is the main topic of the question, where B can be partially predicted from A.

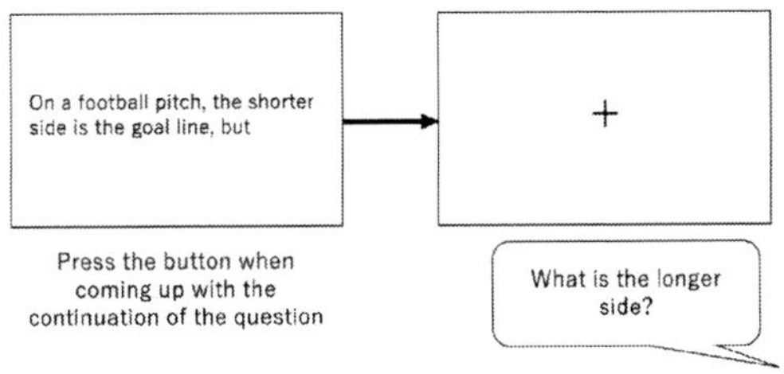

Figure 2: sentence-production task (**+predic**). Participants read the first half of a parallel quiz and predict what will follow. They orally answered the completion of the question in the second screen.

Table 1 shows examples of parallel quizzes, which contrast two elements in the first and second halves of the question text. In terms of the ease of predicting the second half of a question, parallel quizzes fall into two categories. The first and second questions of Table 1 are categorized as **easy** parallel quizzes, which can be answered by only listening to the first half of the question without listening to the second half. For example, the first parallel quiz on table 1 is about a football pitch. The first half of the question sentence explains the shorter edge of the pitch, then the quiz players can predict that the longer edge of the pitch will be contrasted and answer correctly (i.e., touchline) before the sentence is fully read. Skilled buzzer-quiz players can answer this kind of parallel quiz very quickly. On the other hand, in the third **difficult** parallel quiz, the country contrasted with the word "the United States of America" is not obvious, so it is difficult to perfectly predict the second half of the question.[1]

4 Experiment

Figure 1 illustrates the experimental procedure, wherein human reading time was measured through eye-tracking experiments. Subsequently, these data were modeled using surprisal computed by language models.

4.1 Eye-tracking experiment

We conducted an eye-tracking experiment to measure the time for reading and predicting parallel questions.

[1]One of the quiz players who participated in our experiment told that he was able to anticipate that the United Mexican States would be contrasted with the United States of America because the only two countries known as "United States" in the world are the USA and Mexico.

Participants We recruited 32 native Japanese speakers, aged 18 to 24. Among them, seven participants were classified as **experts** due to their previous involvement in quiz clubs during high school or university, where they regularly participated in buzzer quiz activities. The remaining 25 **novice** participants had no prior experience with such activities.

Before the experiment, each participant received detailed information about the study procedures and how their data would be used. Written consent to participate in the experiment was obtained from each participant.

Stimulus sentences In this experiment, we used parallel quiz questions as stimulus sentences. All of them were extracted from a corpus of Japanese buzzer quiz questions called JAQKET.

We classified the quiz questions into two categories, **easy** and **difficult**, following the classification criteria of Izawa (2021). [2] We prepared 20 **easy** parallel quizzes and 20 **difficult** quizzes. **Easy** questions are those in which reading the first half of the sentence clearly determines the continuation, either leading to a single plausible second half or a limited set of around two to three possible continuations. In contrast, **difficult** questions are those where predicting the second half is challenging, either because multiple continuations remain possible or because significant domain-specific knowledge is required to narrow down the possibilities.[3] Additionally, 40 random quiz sentences were added as fillers.

Tasks In this experiment, participants performed two types of tasks: a sentence-production task (**+predic**) and a sentence-comprehension task (**-predic**). These two tasks were shown to the participants in a randomized order.[4] In this experiment, the total reading time (TRT) of each word on the first screen was measured.

Figure 2 illustrates the process of a sentence-production task. Participants viewed the first half of a parallel quiz on the screen. They were instructed that even though there was no set time limit, they were encouraged to press the button as quickly as possible once they found an idea to continue the

[2]In this book, Japanese buzzer quiz questions are categorized into 25 patterns, and the classification of parallel quizzes is also discussed.

[3]These questions were selected from a wide range of genres to avoid bias.

[4]Each participant read 20 question sentences in **+predic** condition and the other 20 in **-predic** condition.

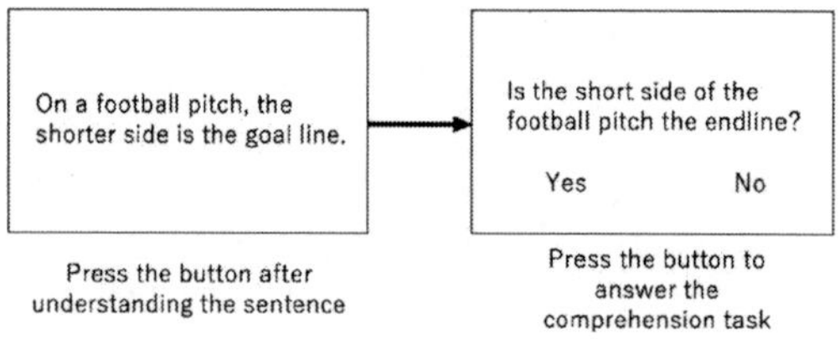

Figure 3: sentence-comprehension task (**-predic**). Participants read a sentence and answer a comprehension test on the following screen.

question.[5] After pressing the button, they answered aloud on the second screen.

Figure 3 depicts the procedure of the sentence-comprehension task. The first half of a quiz was displayed as a declarative sentence. The participants pressed the button after reading it and answered the comprehension test on the next screen.

Hypothesis In the -predic condition, participants were only required to comprehend the content of the sentence. In contrast, in the +predic condition, they were tasked not only with understanding the sentence but also with predicting its continuation. In the current experiment, under time pressure, words with longer reading times are expected to serve as key cues for predicting subsequent sentences. Consequently, we anticipated that a language model capable of simulating human reading times would assign greater informational content (and thus lower probabilities) to these cue words. Conversely, words that do not serve as cues for predicting the latter part of the sentence—those that participants would naturally expect to follow based on the context—should be assigned higher probabilities by the language model. For example, in Figure 1, the word "Japan," highlighted in red, is associated with longer reading time.

4.2 Language models

The surprisal for each subword was calculated using GPT-2 (Radford et al., 2019) published by rinna (Chou and Sawada, 2021) on Huggingface. Experiments were conducted using both the pre-trained model[6] and fine-tuned models.

The surprisal for the ith subword w_i is calculated based on the next-token probabilities $P(w_i|w_1, ..., w_{i-1})$ computed by the language models:

$$Surprisal_i = -\log P(w_i|w_1, ..., w_{i-1}) \quad (2)$$

Pre-trained GPT-2 GPT-2 calculated the surprisal for each subword in the sentence utilized in the eye-tracking experiment.

Fine-tuned GPT-2 We fine-tuned the GPT-2 with parallel quizzes extracted from resources such as JAQKET(Suzuki et al., 2020), QuizWorks[7], and Quiz-No-Mori[8]. These corpora include both datasets curated for academic research and question collections compiled by quiz enthusiasts.[9]

From these corpora, we extracted 4,100 parallel quizzes for fine-tuning. The dataset for fine-tuning was divided into 10 splits of increasing size, ranging from 10 to 4,100 data points(10, 100, 200, 300, 500, 700, 1,000, 1,500, 2,000, 4,100).[10] For each data size, we conducted fine-tuning five times using different seed values. The epoch number in training was set to ten for each fine-tuning. For conditions with 2,000 data points or fewer, the sentences used for fine-tuning were randomly selected. Importantly, none of the questions employed in the eye-tracking experiments were included in the fine-tuning data.

4.3 Evaluation metrics

Psychometric Predictive Power (PPP): The surprisal measure serves as a commonly utilized information-theoretic complexity metric. In essence, a model's ability to predict human reading behavior is often assessed by comparing the surprisal values computed by the model with the reading times of human participants. Higher correspondence between the trends of model-generated surprisals and human reading times indicates greater psychometric predictive power. Previous studies have evaluated the psychometric predictive power of language models by comparing the surprisal values generated by each model with human reading times.

In our eye-tracking experiment, we quantified the reading time for each character and computed

[5]This replicates the situation in quiz competitions, where participants must buzz in as quickly as possible.

[6]GPT-2 used in this experiment was rinna/japanese-gpt2-medium(`https://huggingface.co/rinna/japanese-gpt2-medium`). This model is published under MIT license.

[7]`https://quiz-works.com/`

[8]`https://quiz-schedule.info/quiz_no_mori/data/data.htm`

[9]The questions used in the eye-tracking experiment were excluded from the fine-tuning training data.

[10]The fine-tuning process with the full dataset size (4,100 data points) required approximately 15 minutes using a single NVIDIA Tesla T4 GPU.

the total reading time for each subword by summing the total reading times of all characters within the subword. As described in the Experiment section, in the +predic condition, longer reading times are expected for words that serve as cues for predicting subsequent sentences. If language models are capable of capturing human hyperprediction, they would be expected to assign high surprisal values to such keywords.

To examine the impact of surprisal on modeling human reading behavior, we employed a linear mixed-effects regression (Baayen et al., 2008) with the `lmer` function in the `lme4` package (Bates et al., 2015) in R (R Core Team, 2023). This model aimed to predict the total reading time (TRT) of each subword using the following formula:

$$\begin{aligned}\log(\texttt{TRT}) &\sim \texttt{surprisal} + \texttt{length} \\ &+ \texttt{is\_first} + \texttt{is\_last} + \texttt{lineN} \\ &+ \texttt{segmentN} + \texttt{log\_freq} \\ &+ \texttt{prev\_length} + \texttt{log\_freq\_prev} \\ &+ (1|\texttt{subject\_id}) + (1|\texttt{item\_id}) \quad (3)\end{aligned}$$

The detailed description of each variable is provided in table 3 in the Appendix.

The regression model included the surprisal factor with other baseline factors, which were previously examined in existing studies (Asahara et al., 2016; Wilcox et al., 2020; Kuribayashi et al., 2021; Yoshida et al., 2021). Factors found to be not significant ($p > 0.05$) for modeling reading time were excluded. The frequency (`freq`) of each subword was calculated based on the occurrences of each token within a corpus of 14 million paragraphs, extracted from Japanese Wikipedia.

To isolate the effect of surprisal on reading time modeling, we trained a baseline regression model without including surprisal information. Following the approach outlined by Wilcox et al. (2020), we computed the mean by-segment difference of log-likelihood between the model with surprisal values and the baseline model. This metric is referred to as ΔlogLik. A ΔlogLik score of zero indicates that surprisal from a language model is ineffective at all for reading time modeling. Conversely, a high ΔlogLik score suggests that the language model's surprisal values are effective for modeling reading time, indicating a high psychometric predictive power.

condition	#data points	ΔlogLik ($/10^5$)	p
-predic	7869	1.602	0.00390
+predic	8361	1.856	0.0215
+predic, novice	6351	1.801	0.00463
+predic, expert	2010	2.140	0.0131
+predic, easy	4579	2.390	0.0115
+predic, difficult	3782	1.912	0.0215

Table 2: PPP (i.e., ΔlogLik) for each condition of the pre-trained GPT-2. These values are the mean per-word ΔlogLik of the model on held-out test data, averaged over 10-fold cross-validation. "#data points" is the number of reading time annotations used in our experiments. p shows the p-values of paired permutation tests on 10 Δ logLik values of 10-fold cross-validation using broman package on R.

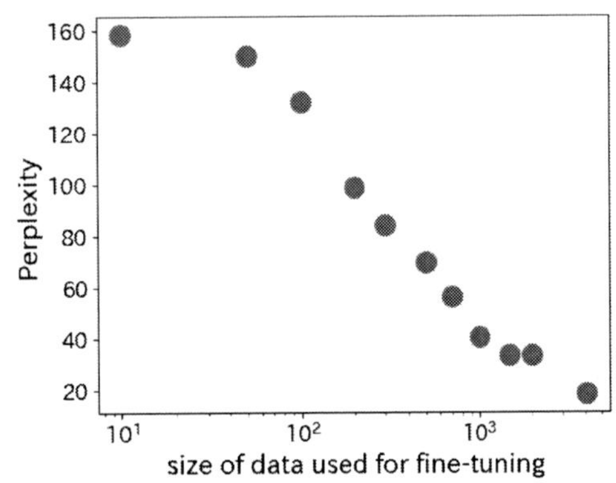

Figure 4: Relationship between the size of data used for fine-tuning (X-axis) and mean perplexity of the five fine-tuned models with different seeds (Y-axis). As the fine-tuning data set enlarges, a corresponding decrease in perplexity is observed.

Considering the low amount of data, we report mean per-word ΔlogLik of the model on held-out test data, averaged over 10-fold cross-validation as suggested by Wilcox et al. (2020).

Perplexity (PPL): In order to evaluate if fine-tuning enabled the language models to better predict the next word in parallel quizzes, we calculated the perplexity of each model. PPL is the inverse geometric mean of next-word probabilities $P(w_i|w_1, ..., w_{i-1})$ in a text that consists of N words $(w_1, w_2, ..., w_N)$, and it is a typical evaluation metric for unidirectional language models:

$$PPL = \prod_{i=0}^{N} P(w_i|w_1, ..., w_{i-1})^{-\frac{1}{N}} \quad (4)$$

A low perplexity (PPL) suggests that the language model effectively anticipates the next word based on its contextual information. The goal of training and fine-tuning language models is to minimize the perplexity computed by the model. In our experiments, we evaluated the perplexity of a language model using texts from the eye movement data, ensuring they do not overlap with the training dataset.

5 Results

5.1 GPT-2

Table 2 shows the psychometric predictive power (i.e., ΔlogLik) for each condition of the pre-trained GPT-2. In the +predic condition, the surprisal term was found to be significantly effective in the regression model ($p < 0.05$). In the sentence-production experiment (i.e., +predic condition), the participants read the first half of parallel quiz questions, and predicted what would follow. Therefore, these findings suggest that the pre-trained language model can effectively model the reading time associated with human hyperprediction when reading a parallel quiz question.

5.2 Fine-tuned GPT-2

Figure 5 illustrates the relationship between the size of the dataset used for fine-tuning and psychometric predictive power (ΔlogLik) of language models in +predic condition (i.e., sentence-production experiment). Each point represents a language model, with the Y-axis indicating the model's psychometric predictive power (higher scores indicate better performance) and the X-axis indicating the size of the dataset. The number of data points used for fine-tuning ranged from 10 to 4,100: 10, 100, 200, 300, 500, 700, 1,000, 1,500, 2,000, and 4,100. The plot for 10^0 represents the PPP value of the pre-trained model.

Blue points represent the modeling of the reading time for novice participants, while red points represent expert participants.

As Figure 4 shows, the perplexity tended to decrease as the number of data used for fine-tuning increased.

Novice participants Language models fine-tuned with parallel quiz questions exhibited higher psychometric predictive power values than the pre-trained model. Increasing the amount of data used for fine-tuning resulted in a smaller increase in psychometric predictive power.

The maximum value of psychometric predictive power was achieved with the language model fine-tuned with 1,500 sentences in the +predic, novice, easy condition and 1,000 sentences in the +predic, novice, difficult condition.

Expert participants The highest psychometric predictive power for the fine-tuned model, regardless of the number of data points used, was observed when expert participants read easy types of parallel quizzes (i.e., +predic, expert, easy condition). We believe that the high PPP values reflect the longer reading times for keywords of the question sentences in the +predic condition when experts read easy quiz questions.

In both easy and difficult conditions, the psychometric predictive power of fine-tuned models increased with the number of data points used for fine-tuning. The maximum psychometric predictive power was reached at 2,000 (+predic, expert, easy condition) or 1,500 data points (+predic, expert, difficult condition); however, beyond this threshold, a sharp decrease in psychometric predictive power was observed. Interestingly, across all four conditions, the peak psychometric predictive power did not coincide with the maximum quantity of training data.

6 Discussion

In this study, we focused on a phenomenon defined as hyperprediction, where humans are thought to predict not just the immediate next word, as is typically assumed during sentence comprehension, but also longer sequences of words and overall sentence structure. We utilized cognitive modeling techniques to examine if language models can capture this particular aspect of human prediction processing ability.

The pre-trained GPT-2 demonstrated its highest psychometric predictive power in the +predic, expert, easy condition, where human hyperprediction was expected to be most prominent. Conversely, it exhibited lower scores in the +predic, novice, difficult conditions, where hyperprediction was more challenging. Our findings suggest that even the pre-trained GPT-2 can partially capture human hyperprediction.

The surprisal from GPT-2 correlates better with the reading times of experts rather than novices, and with the +predic condition over the -predic condition. We consider that this result potentially implies the following: These results suggest that

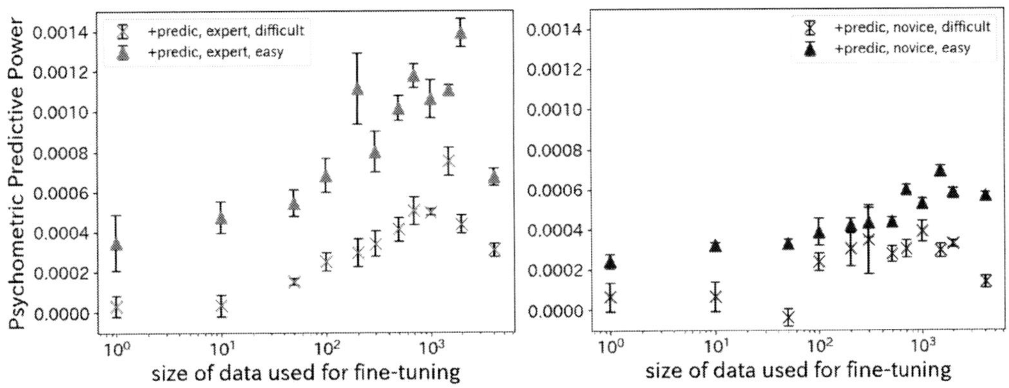

Figure 5: Relationship between the size of data used for fine-tuning (X-axis) and psychometric predictive power, i.e., ΔlogLik (Y-axis). Error bars are standard errors of by-fold mean ΔlogLik per token, using 10-fold cross-validation for five fine-tuned models with different seeds. The plot for 10^0 represents the PPP value of the pre-trained model.

the language processing of GPT-2 aligns more with the hyperprediction capabilities of experts, who excel at predicting longer word sequences, rather than the prediction processing of average humans during normal reading. This may also suggest that the reason language models such as GPT-2 don't replicate the average human behavior is that, at least in some instances, they emulate expert behavior.

Furthermore, if the language model's surprisal can successfully model human hyperprediction, this might suggest that when humans quickly answer questions in a buzzer quiz, they are not directly outputting the answer from a limited portion of the question. Instead, they may be anticipating the continuation of the question—much like how the language model operates—before providing their answer.

The fine-tuned models exhibited the highest psychometric predictive power in the +predic, expert, easy condition. This condition, characterized by participants' familiarity with parallel quizzes and their ease in making predictions, can be considered to reflect human hyperprediction. Language models demonstrated an ability to capture this aspect of human sentence processing.

As Figure 4 shows, the process of fine-tuning resulted in a decrease in perplexity, indicating that language models became more adept at predicting the next word in parallel quizzes. Specifically, when fine-tuned with 1,500 or 2,000 parallel quiz sentences or less, lower perplexity corresponded to higher psychometric predictive power, suggesting improved model performance.

However, the GPT-2 model fine-tuned with the most data did not necessarily exhibit the highest psychometric predictive power value. This could be attributed to the excessive data causing the model's surprisal to the sentence to decrease excessively. Consequently, the model may have failed to prioritize important words that typically require longer human reading time. This trend aligns with previous findings in Japanese language modeling research (Kuribayashi et al., 2021), which argue that lower perplexity does not always equate to human-like performance. A similar trend has been reported by Oh and Schuler (2023). They revealed that very large language models underestimated human processing difficulty. Our results align with these assertions.

7 Conclusion

This study investigated human hyperprediction in buzzer quizzes. Human hyperprediction during sentence processing involves not only predicting the next word, but also longer sequences of words and the overall structure of the sentence, which distinguishes it from regular prediction processing in sentence comprehension. In this study, we conducted experiments to test whether language models can capture this particular aspect of human predictive processing ability.

Our results showed that the pre-trained GPT-2 partially modeled human reading time while reading parallel quizzes, which suggested that language models can indeed capture aspects of human hyperprediction.

Furthermore, language models fine-tuned with parallel quizzes modeled human hyperprediction in buzzer quizzes better than the pre-trained GPT-2. Specifically, the highest predictive power was observed in conditions where hyperprediction would be most prominent (i.e., +predic, expert, and easy condition). Notably, fine-tuning resulted in a significant increase in predictive power values. However, excessive fine-tuning data (exceeding 1,500 or 2,000 data points) led to a decrease in perplexity and subsequently to reduced psychometric predictive power. This trend aligns with findings reported in previous work (Kuribayashi et al., 2021). Overall, our findings suggest that a moderate amount of data is required for fine-tuning in order to model human hyperprediction.

Limitations

In this study, we focused on hyperprediction during the reading of quiz questions and the subsequent prediction of their continuations. Hyperprediction in human sentence processing is particularly prominent in the context of buzzer quizzes. However, the occurrence of hyperprediction in more general sentence comprehension remains an open question for future investigation. Exploring other contexts in which hyperprediction may manifest is a promising direction for future research.

Our study focused on Japanese parallel quizzes and employed an eye-tracking experiment to measure the total reading time for each subword in parallel quiz questions. However, in buzzer quiz competitions, questions are typically orally read aloud. Players utilize intonation and prominence cues to consider the answer to the quiz, particularly in parallel quizzes where the moderator emphasizes the contrasted words in the first half of the question. Skilled players use phonological cues to anticipate the answer and buzz in as quickly as possible. Future research could explore incorporating these oral reading dynamics into language models.

Additionally, buzzer quiz players are influenced by various factors, including game rules and competitors' scores. Factors like strict penalties for wrong answers may lead players to hesitate to buzz in unless they reach a reliable prediction for the question's continuation. Conversely, players with lower scores may adopt a more aggressive approach, buzzing in even without full certainty about the answer. These varying confidence levels in predicting subsequent question text may differ from the prediction in the simplified situation of our eye-tracking experiment. Future studies can further explore these nuanced factors to gain a comprehensive understanding of quiz players' hyperprediction and the language model's ability to capture such hyperprediction.

Additionally, this eye-tracking experiment recruited a relatively small number of expert participants. There are 40 target items and 40 filler items, and given that the sentences are short, a total of 32 participants were few.

As for the statistical analysis, surprisal value was calculated for each subword. The GPT-2 tokenizer utilized in our experiment was trained using the Byte Pair Encoding (BPE) method. Consequently, since Japanese language is not written with a space between words, subwords that include a word boundary exist, resulting in reading time analyses based on subwords rather than individual words. For future work, training a tokenizer using a method that does not contain word boundaries within a single subword could allow for more cognitively valid analyses.

Ethical considerations

The eye-track experiment conducted in our work was approved by the research ethics committee of the university.

Buzzer quiz is a game of knowledge where participants may feel defeated if they are unable to answer a question. Prior to conducting the eye-tracking experiment, we emphasized to participants that the purpose of the experiment was not to assess their knowledge level. We made efforts to ensure that participants felt comfortable and performed naturally, without undue stress or pressure.

The data collected in this experiment included the timing of participants' button presses and the reading time of each word, calculated from their gaze location on the screen. These data were anonymized by assigning a random subject ID to each participant, thereby ensuring the separation of personal information from experimental data.

We aimed to ensure fair payment. As mentioned in the paper, our participants were recruited from the university and received compensation of 1,000 yen for their one-hour participation in the experiment. The compensation amount was determined following the university's guidelines.

Furthermore, in line with the ACL 2023 Policy on AI Writing Assistance, we utilized ChatGPT by OpenAI and Grammarly for writing assistance.

Acknowledgements

We are grateful to the members of the lab for their insightful advice. We would like to thank all the participants who joined our eye-tracking experiment.

This work was supported by JSPS KAKENHI Grant Number JPMJPR21C2, JP20H01254.

References

Gerry TM Altmann and Yuki Kamide. 1999. Incremental interpretation at verbs: Restricting the domain of subsequent reference. *Cognition*, 73(3):247–264.

Masayuki Asahara, Hajime Ono, and Edson T. Miyamoto. 2016. Reading-time annotations for "Balanced Corpus of Contemporary Written Japanese". In *Proceedings of COLING 2016, the 26th International Conference on Computational Linguistics: Technical Papers*, pages 684–694, Osaka, Japan. The COLING 2016 Organizing Committee.

R Harald Baayen, Douglas J Davidson, and Douglas M Bates. 2008. Mixed-effects modeling with crossed random effects for subjects and items. *Journal of memory and language*, 59(4):390–412.

Douglas Bates, Martin Mächler, Ben Bolker, and Steve Walker. 2015. Fitting Linear Mixed-Effects Models Using lme4. *Journal of Statistical Software*, 67(1):1–48.

Tennu Chou and Kei Sawada. 2021. Publishing pretrained GPT-2 in japanese natural language processing. *The Japanese Society for Artificial Intelligence, SLUD*, 93:169–170.

Susan F Ehrlich and Keith Rayner. 1981. Contextual effects on word perception and eye movements during reading. *Journal of verbal learning and verbal behavior*, 20(6):641–655.

Victoria Fossum and Roger Levy. 2012. Sequential vs. hierarchical syntactic models of human incremental sentence processing. In *Proceedings of the 3rd workshop on cognitive modeling and computational linguistics (CMCL 2012)*, pages 61–69.

Stefan L. Frank, Leun J. Otten, Giulia Galli, and Gabriella Vigliocco. 2015. The erp response to the amount of information conveyed by words in sentences. *Brain and Language*, 140:1–11.

Richard Futrell, Edward Gibson, Harry J. Tily, Idan Blank, Anastasia Vishnevetsky, Steven Piantadosi, and Evelina Fedorenko. 2018. The natural stories corpus. In *Proceedings of the Eleventh International Conference on Language Resources and Evaluation (LREC 2018)*, Miyazaki, Japan. European Language Resources Association (ELRA).

Adam Goodkind and Klinton Bicknell. 2018. Predictive power of word surprisal for reading times is a linear function of language model quality. In *Proceedings of the 8th workshop on cognitive modeling and computational linguistics (CMCL 2018)*, pages 10–18.

John Hale. 2001. A probabilistic Earley parser as a psycholinguistic model. In *Second Meeting of the North American Chapter of the Association for Computational Linguistics*.

Takushi Izawa. 2021. *Decomposition of Quiz Strategy*. Asahi Shimbun Publications.

Yuki Kamide, Gerry TM Altmann, and Sarah L Haywood. 2003. The time-course of prediction in incremental sentence processing: Evidence from anticipatory eye movements. *Journal of Memory and language*, 49(1):133–156.

Alan Kennedy, Joël Pynte, Wayne S Murray, and Shirley-Anne Paul. 2013. Frequency and predictability effects in the dundee corpus: An eye movement analysis. *Quarterly Journal of Experimental Psychology*, 66(3):601–618.

Tatsuki Kuribayashi, Yohei Oseki, Takumi Ito, Ryo Yoshida, Masayuki Asahara, and Kentaro Inui. 2021. Lower perplexity is not always human-like. In *Proceedings of the 59th Annual Meeting of the Association for Computational Linguistics and the 11th International Joint Conference on Natural Language Processing (Volume 1: Long Papers)*, pages 5203–5217, Online. Association for Computational Linguistics.

Marta Kutas and Steven A Hillyard. 1984. Brain potentials during reading reflect word expectancy and semantic association. *Nature*, 307(5947):161–163.

Roger Levy. 2008. Expectation-based syntactic comprehension. *Cognition*, 106(3):1126–1177.

Clara D. Martin, Francesca M. Branzi, and Moshe Bar. 2018. Prediction is production: The missing link between language production and comprehension. *Scientific Reports*.

Byung-Doh Oh and William Schuler. 2023. Transformer-based language model surprisal predicts human reading times best with about two billion training tokens. In *Findings of the Association for Computational Linguistics: EMNLP 2023*, pages 1915–1921, Singapore. Association for Computational Linguistics.

Martin J Pickering and Simon Garrod. 2013. An integrated theory of language production and comprehension. *Behavioral and brain sciences*, 36(4):329–347.

R Core Team. 2023. *R: A Language and Environment for Statistical Computing*. R Foundation for Statistical Computing, Vienna, Austria.

Alec Radford, Jeffrey Wu, Rewon Child, David Luan, Dario Amodei, Ilya Sutskever, et al. 2019. Language models are unsupervised multitask learners. *OpenAI blog*, 1(8):9.

Nathaniel J Smith and Roger Levy. 2013. The effect of word predictability on reading time is logarithmic. *Cognition*, 128(3):302–319.

Masatoshi Suzuki, Jun Suzuki, Koji Matsuda, Kyosuke Nishida, and Naoya Inoue. 2020. [JAQKET: Construction of a japanese qa dataset of quizzes] JAQKET: kuizu wo daizai ni shita nihon-go qa dataset no kouchiku (in japanese). *Proceedings of the Twenty-sixth Annual Meeting of the Association for Natural Language Processing*, pages 237–240.

Noriyasu Tokuhisa. 2012. *Citizen's Quiz 2.0*. Genron company limited.

Cyma Van Petten and Marta Kutas. 1990. Interactions between sentence context and word frequencyinevent-related brainpotentials. *Memory & cognition*, 18:380–393.

Marten Van Schijndel and Tal Linzen. 2021. Single-stage prediction models do not explain the magnitude of syntactic disambiguation difficulty. *Cognitive science*, 45(6):e12988.

Ethan Gotlieb Wilcox, Jon Gauthier, Jennifer Hu, Peng Qian, and Roger Levy. 2020. On the predictive power of neural language models for human real-time comprehension behavior.

Ryo Yoshida, Hiroshi Noji, and Yohei Oseki. 2021. Modeling human sentence processing with left-corner recurrent neural network grammars. In *Proceedings of the 2021 Conference on Empirical Methods in Natural Language Processing*, pages 2964–2973, Online and Punta Cana, Dominican Republic. Association for Computational Linguistics.

Factor name	Type	Description
surprisal	num	surprisal calculated by each language model
TRT	num	total reading time for each token
length	int	the number of characters
is_first	factor	the leftmost token within the line
is_last	factor	the rightmost token within the line
lineN	int	the serial number of the line where the token is displayed
segmentN	int	the serial number of the token within the line
log_freq	num	log of the frequency of the token
prev_length	int	length of the previous token
prev_freq	num	log_freq of the previous token
subject_id	factor	ID assigned to each participant
item_id	factor	ID assigned to each item

Table 3: Factors used in regression models.

n_layer	24
n_embd	1024
n_head	16
n_position	1024
vocab_size	32000

Table 4: Model architecture of GPT-2 we used in our work.

Optimizer	AdamW
Learning rate	5e-05
Number of epochs	10
Dropout rate	0.1
Batch size	1

Table 5: Hyperparameters for our fine-tuning.

A Factors used in regression model

Table3 shows the description of the factors used in our regression models. Factors found to be not significant ($p > 0.05$) for modeling reading time were excluded.

The frequency of a token (used in log_freq) was calculated using 14 million paragraphs extracted from Japanese Wikipadia.

B Model architecture

The model architecture of GPT-2 we used in our work is shown in Table4. The model is available on Hugging Face. [11]

C Hyperparameters

Hyperparameters for our work are shown in Table 5, which followed default settings.

[11] https://huggingface.co/rinna/japanese-gpt2-medium

What to Predict? Exploring How Sentence Structure Influences Contrast Predictions in Humans and Large Language Models

Shuqi Wang Xufeng Duan Zhenguang Cai
Department of Linguistics and Modern Languages, CUHK
{shuqiwang, xufeng.duan}@link.cuhk.edu.hk, zhenguangcai@cuhk.edu.hk

Abstract

This study examines how sentence structure shapes contrast predictions in both humans and large language models (LLMs). Using Mandarin ditransitive constructions — double object (DO, "She gave the girl the candy, but not...") vs. prepositional object (PO, "She gave the candy to the girl, but not...") as a testbed, we employed a sentence continuation task involving three human groups (written, spoken, and prosodically normalized spoken stimuli) and three LLMs (GPT-4o, LLaMA-3, and Qwen-2.5). Two principal findings emerged: (1) Although human participants predominantly focused on the theme (e.g., "the candy"), contrast predictions were significantly modulated by sentence structure—particularly in spoken contexts, where the sentence-final element drew more attention. (2) While LLMs showed a similar reliance on structure, they displayed a larger effect size and more closely resembled human spoken data than written data, indicating a stronger emphasis on linear order in generating contrast predictions. By adopting a unified psycholinguistic paradigm, this study advances our understanding of predictive language processing for both humans and LLMs and informs research on human–model alignment in linguistic tasks.

1 Introduction

Predictive processing is fundamental to how both humans and large language models (LLMs) handle language. When people read or listen, they continuously anticipate upcoming words and meanings, facilitating swift integration of new information and maintaining efficient comprehension (Altmann & Kamide, 1999; Christiansen & Chater, 2016; Clark, 2013; Kuperberg & Jaeger, 2016; Pickering & Gambi, 2018). Prediction also underlies language use in LLMs, as these models are explicitly designed to predict the next token in a sequence (Brown et al., 2020; Radford et al., 2018, 2019).

As a linguistic cue, **contrast** plays a key role by guiding attention toward the most distinctive or unexpected element in the context and prompting the prediction of an alternative (Repp, 2010; Rooth, 2016). Contrast often involves opposing or comparing one element to another of the same semantic type (Roberts, 2012). It is often signaled by a negation operator (e.g., "not") or discourse markers (e.g., "but"). Empirical findings indicate that human comprehenders are highly attuned to these cues. Upon encountering contrast markers, they actively anticipate an alternative that stands in contrast to a previously mentioned element (Carlson, 2014; Lowder & Ferreira, 2016).

A crucial question thus arises: which preceding element is being contrasted and which potential alternatives should be predicted? Contrast closely intersects with focus — the most emphasized or central constituent (Calhoun, 2009; Husband & Ferreira, 2016; Lowder & Gordon, 2015; Repp, 2010). Thus, the element chosen for contrast is often the sentence's focus. However, determining focus can become complicated in lengthy or structurally complex sentences. For instance, consider the ditransitive construction "She gave the girl the candy, not...". The focus—and therefore the contrast—could fall on the recipient ("the girl"), the theme ("the candy"), or the verb ("gave"). Depending on which element is in focus, comprehenders might predict contrasting recipients (e.g., "the father," "the boy"), contrasting themes (e.g., "the toy," "the cake"), or contrasting verbs (e.g., "bought," "made"). This is because **ditransitive structure** introduces multiple arguments and allows flexible constituent orders, complicating the task of pinpointing the focal element and thus the likely contrast (Paterson et al., 2007; Shyu, 2010).

This study thus uses ditransitive structure as a testbed for understanding how humans and LLMs

Proceedings of the Workshop on Cognitive Modeling and Computational Linguistics, pages 244–252
May 3, 2025

predict contrasts, and how sentence structure influences these predictions. Two primary constructions of the ditransitive pattern are the double object (DO) construction (e.g., "She bought the girl the candy") and the prepositional object (PO) construction (e.g., "She gave the candy to the daughter"). Critically, in Mandarin Chinese, these two constructions use the same set of segmental materials but in different orders (DO: 她送给了女孩糖果, literally "She gave to girl candy"; PO: 她送了糖果给女孩, literally "She gave candy to girl"), making them ideal for examining how linear arrangement affects focus and contrast.

Three main hypotheses address the potential locus of focus and, by extension, the nature of contrast predictions in ditransitive sentences:

1. The **Sentence-Final Hypothesis** posits that the focus tends to fall at the end of the sentence (Xu, 2004; Yan & Calhoun, 2020), predicting that DO sentences would contrast the theme (e.g., "not the candy") and PO sentences would contrast the recipient (e.g., "not the girl").
2. The **Thematic Hierarchy Hypothesis** proposes that focus falls on the element highest in the thematic hierarchy, namely the theme, which is more closely related to the verb (Shyu, 2010). Thus, both DO and PO constructions would yield the focus on the theme, leading to identical contrast predictions.
3. The **Verb-Dominant Hypothesis** claims that the verb or entire verb phrase is focused (Carlson, 2014; Roettger et al., 2021). In this scenario, both DO and PO constructions would lead comprehenders to predict a verb-related contrast (e.g., "not bought" or "not sang a song").

Notably, the latter two hypotheses predict similar outcomes for DO and PO forms, while the first emphasizes a structural effect tied to word order. Because written language is presented at once for readers, its linear-order impact may be weaker than in spoken language, where information unfolds sequentially (Ferreira & Anes, 1994), we employ both written and spoken stimuli in human experiments to determine whether modality modulates the influence of sentence structure on contrast prediction.

Taken together, this work aims to address two core questions:

1. How do humans predict contrasts in Mandarin ditransitive constructions and how does sentence structure modulate these predictions in both written and spoken contexts?
2. How do large language models predict contrasts in the same constructions, and how similar are these predictions to human behavior?

2 Methods

2.1 Design and Materials

We employed a sentence continuation task to examine how humans and LLMs predict and complete contrasts in ditransitive sentences. A total of 42 experimental items were created based on previous studies (Cai et al., 2013, 2022), each consisting of a ditransitive construction followed by a contrast marker. Each item appeared in two conditions: a DO construction (e.g., 她送给了女孩糖果，而不是…; "She gave the girl the candy, but not…") and a PO construction (e.g., 她送了糖果给女孩，而不是…; "She gave the candy to the girl, but not…"). We selected 14 ditransitive verbs (e.g., 买 'buy', 交 'hand', 借 'lend', 卖 'sell', 奖 'award', 带 'bring', 扔 'throw', 抛 'toss', 拿 'take', 捐 'donate', 让 'give away', 还 'return', 送 'send', 递 'pass'), each appearing in three items, yielding 42 experimental preambles.

To reduce participants' focus on contrast markers and maintain variety, we incorporated 90 filler sentences. Each filler contained different structures and a connective (e.g., "because," "so," "then"). This design aimed to ensure that participants engaged with the full range of sentence structures and did not develop a strategy specific to the contrast condition.

We used Microsoft Azure to generate spoken versions of the experimental items. Specifically, we selected a male adult speaker of simplified Mandarin ("Yunyang") at a speed of 0.75 and exported the files at 48 kHz. Two types of spoken stimuli were created: The first one is the original recording from Azure. These versions contained natural variations in sentence-final stress, such that DO sentences ended with a higher pitch and longer duration on the theme, whereas PO sentences ended with a higher pitch and longer duration on the recipient; The second type is the normalized recording, where segments from one condition were replaced with those from the other (counterbalanced between two conditions) and also added white noise to standardize duration. As a result, all segmental and suprasegmental features are the same in both conditions.

Our motivation for including these two types of spoken stimuli was twofold. First, the original version reflected more natural spoken processing, capturing how individuals predicted contrasts in everyday speech contexts. Second, the normalized version controlled for prosodic differences, allowing us to focus on the role of syntactic structure and word order in shaping contrast predictions.

2.2 Human experiments

2.2.1 Participants

A total of 164 native Mandarin speakers participated in this study, divided into three groups based on the type of stimuli they received: 52 for the written stimuli, 57 for the original spoken stimuli, and 55 for the normalized spoken stimuli. Following data screening (e.g., incomplete responses, procedural errors), we excluded some participants' responses. This resulted in 50 participants in the written group (27 females, 23 males; *M* age = 21.5), 50 participants in the original spoken group (17 females, 33 males; *M* age = 21.8), and 48 participants in the normalized spoken group (18 females, 30 males; *M* age = 21.3).

2.2.2 Procedure

All experiments were conducted online using Qualtrics (Qualtrics, 2024). Participants joined a Zoom session, shared their screen, and began the experiment while the researcher monitored their progress. This arrangement helped mitigate potential issues associated with online data collection, such as inattentiveness or lack of engagement. After providing informed consent, participants read on-screen instructions and examples explaining the sentence continuation task. They were asked to type the first, most natural completion that came to mind for each presented sentence preamble. Each stimulus was presented on a separate Qualtrics page.

Two lists of stimuli were created, with each item appearing in only one condition (DO or PO) in each list. Participants were randomly assigned to one of these lists. Upon completing the task, they provided demographic information and received a payment of 30 RMB in appreciation for their time.

2.3 LLMs Experiments

2.3.1 Models

We employed three LLMs in this study: OpenAI's GPT-4o (OpenAI, 2024), Meta's LLaMA-3 (Meta, 2024), and Alibaba's Qwen-2.5 (Yang et al., 2025). These models were chosen for three main reasons. First, they each represented state-of-the-art performance at the time of the study. Second, they allowed us to compare closed-source (GPT-4o) with open-weight (LLaMA-3 and Qwen-2.5) systems. Finally, we included English-dominant LLMs (GPT-4o and LLaMA-3) alongside a Chinese-dominant LLM (Qwen-2.5), ensuring coverage of different training backgrounds and linguistic emphases.

2.3.2 Procedure

We collected output from the three language models using an R package called "MacBehavior" (Duan et al., 2024), which was specifically developed for behavioral experimentation with large language models. The same stimuli given to human participants were presented to each model under a "one-trial-per-run" configuration. In this setup, each prompt–stimulus pair was input into the model in a new conversation, ensuring that no trial could be influenced by preceding prompts. The prompts mirrored the instructions given to human participants — "Please read the first half of a sentence and fill in the first word or phrase that comes to mind. Make the sentence complete, natural, and reasonable. The first half of the sentence is:". We conducted 50 sessions for each of the three LLMs, so each item received a total of 50 responses. This design roughly matched the sample size in the human experiments.

3 Analyses and results

3.1 Data coding

We employed the same coding scheme for both human and LLM continuations, categorizing responses into three main contrast types: (1) Theme Contrast (T): The continuation contrasts the theme (e.g., "the cake" in "She gave the girl the candy, but not the cake."). (2) Recipient Contrast (R): The continuation contrasts the recipient (e.g., "the boy"

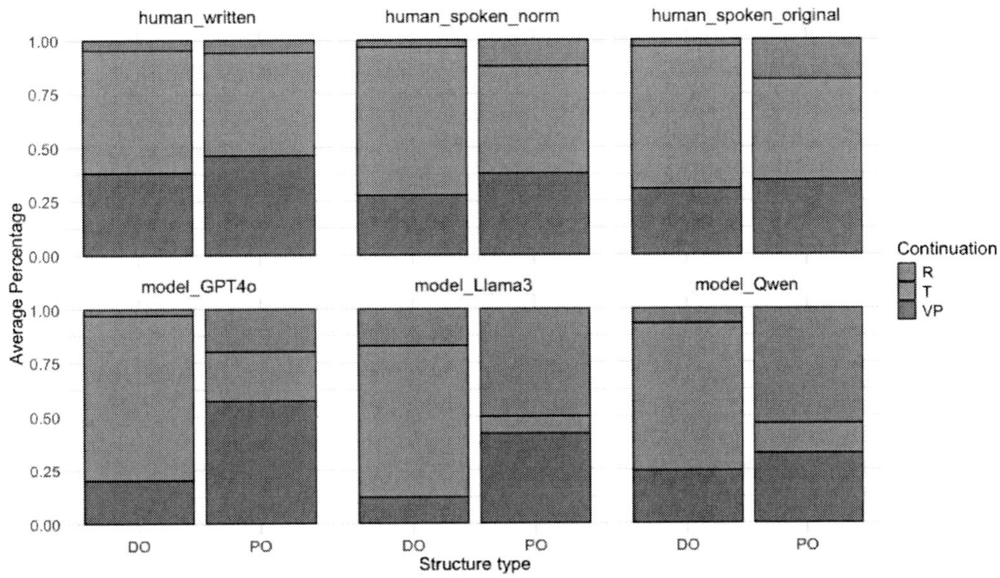

Figure 1 Average percentages of three types of continuations for ditransitive structures in human participants (top panel) and LLMs (bottom panel)

in "She gave the girl the candy, but not the boy."). (3) Verb or Verb Phrase Contrast (VP): The continuation contrasts the verb or verb phrase (e.g., "buy" or "sing a song" in "She gave the girl the candy, but didn't buy her one / sing a song to her.").

3.2 Statistical analysis

We adopted a three-step approach to analyze our data. First, we examined which continuation type was most prevalent across Mandarin ditransitive sentences. To this end, we performed a series of t-tests comparing the mean frequencies of these three contrast types. Second, to determine whether sentence structure significantly influenced contrast predictions, we conducted a linear mixed-effects model analysis. We began by aggregating responses by item, calculating the percentage of each continuation type for each item. We then performed a by-item analysis with structure type (DO vs. PO), continuation type (T, R and VP; With T as reference level), and group (humans vs. LLMs; Pairwise comparisons were conducted between each human modality and model, resulting in a total of nine comparisons) as fixed effects, and item as a random effect. Finally, to further assess how closely the LLM predictions aligned with human continuations (both written and spoken), we calculated Pearson correlations between the LLMs' aggregated prediction patterns and those in the human experiments. This approach allowed us to gauge the degree of similarity in contrast prediction patterns across the different groups.

3.3 Results

3.3.1 Human results

First, we performed the T-test to investigate which continuation type was the dominant. Across all three participant groups (written, original spoken, and normalized spoken), theme contrasts emerged as the most frequent continuation type, followed by verb contrasts and then recipient contrasts (see Figure 1). Specifically, in the written stimuli group, participants produced more theme ($M = 0.52$) than verb ($M = 0.42$) contrasts, $t(4183.5) = -6.56$, $p < .001$, while verb contrasts also exceeded recipient ($M = 0.05$, $t(2911.3) = 31.28$, $p < .001$). Similarly, in the original spoken stimuli group, theme ($M = 0.56$) contrasts were more frequent than verb ($M = 0.3274$) contrasts, $t(4169.4) = -15.88$, $p < .001$, and verb contrasts again exceeded recipient ($M = 0.11$), $t(3626.8) = 17.83$, $p < .001$. The normalized spoken stimuli showed the same pattern: theme ($M = 0.60$) contrasts dominated verb ($M = 0.32$) contrasts, $t(4006.3) = -18.82$, $p < .001$, which in turn were more frequent than recipient ($M = 0.08$) contrasts, $t(3219.7) = 19.92$, $p < .001$. Overall, these findings support the Thematic Hierarchy Hypothesis, suggesting that the theme is consistently viewed as the primary focal element for contrast in ditransitive constructions.

Second, the structure can modulate the contrast predictions in both written and spoken modalities. That is, in all three groups, the difference between recipient contrast and theme contrast was larger in the PO condition than in the DO condition (written stimuli group: $\beta = 0.10$, $SE = 0.02$, $t(164) = 5.82$, $p < .001$; original spoken stimuli group: $\beta = 0.35$, $SE = 0.02$, $t(164) = 15.25$, $p < .001$; normalized spoken stimuli group: $\beta = 0.28$, $SE = 0.03$, $t(205) = 8.49$, $p < .001$), as shown in the top panel of Figure 1. This pattern suggests a sentence-final bias in the focus locus and, consequently, in participants' contrast predictions—partially supporting the Sentence-Final Hypothesis.

Third, the modulation effect of structure is larger for spoken language than for written language (written vs. original spoken: $\beta = 0.25$, $SE = 0.03$, $t(410) = 7.68$, $p < .001$; written vs. normalized spoken: $\beta = 0.18$, $SE = 0.04$, $t(451) = 4.59$, $p < .001$), as shown in the top panel of Figure 1. These findings indicate that spoken language amplifies the impact of structural differences (DO vs. PO) on how listeners predict contrast, whereas this effect is comparatively reduced in written language. Moreover, the non-significant difference between original and normalized spoken data (original spoken vs. normalized spoken: $\beta = 0.07$, $SE = 0.04$, $t(451) = 1.688$, $p = .092$) suggests that prosody alone may not fully explain the stronger structure effect in speech; rather, linear-order presentation may heighten the prominence of sentence-final elements in spoken modalities.

3.3.2 Model Results

Similar to the human data, t-tests showed that theme contrast was the primary continuation type for all three models (GPT-4o, LLaMA-3, and Qwen-2.5). However, the relative ranking of verb phrase and recipient contrasts differed across models. In GPT-4o, theme contrast ($M = 0.50$) is greater than verb phrase contrast ($M = 0.39$), $t(4137.4) = -7.11$, $p < .001$, and verb phrase contrast exceeded recipient contrast ($M = 0.11$), $t(3548.1) = 21.67$, $p < .001$. In LLaMA-3, theme contrast ($M = 0.40$) surpassed recipient contrast ($M = 0.33$), $t(3733.6) = 4.49$, $p < .001$, and recipient exceeded verb phrase(M = 0.27), $t(3727.8) = -4.00$, $p < .001$. Finally, in Qwen-2.5, theme ($M = 0.42$) remained significantly higher than verb ($M = 0.28$), $t(4159.4) = -9.22$, $p < .001$, whereas the difference between verb and recipient ($M = 0.30$) was non-significant, $t(4192.2) = -1.46$, $p = .14$.

Similarly, the structure of the ditransitive sentences modulated contrast predictions in all three models. The difference between recipient contrast and theme contrast was significantly larger under PO constructions than under DO constructions for all three models (GPT-4o: $\beta = 0.71$, $SE = 0.06$, $t(164) = 12.01$, $p < .001$; LLaMA-3: $\beta = 0.96$, $SE = 0.06$, $t(164) = 17.10$, $p < .001$; Qwen-2.5: $\beta = 1.00$, $SE = 0.09$, $t(164) = 11.42$, $p < .001$), indicating that the models generated more theme contrasts in DO (than in PO) and more recipient contrasts in PO (than in DO). This aligns with the human pattern of sentence-final bias on contrast predictions.

3.3.3 Comparing Humans and Models

Having established that sentence structure influenced contrast predictions for both humans and models, we next examined whether the magnitude of this influence differed between the two groups. Across all comparisons, the three models exhibited a larger structural effect than their human counterparts, regardless of whether the human data were drawn from the written, original spoken, or normalized spoken conditions (GPT-4o vs. human: $\beta = 0.61$, $SE = 0.07$, $t(451) = 8.62$, $p < .001$ (written); $\beta = 0.36$, $SE = 0.07$, $t(451) = 4.85$, $p < .001$ (original spoken); $\beta = 0.43$, $SE = 0.08$, $t(451) = 5.50$, $p < .001$ (normalized spoken). LLaMA-3 vs. human: $\beta = 0.85$, $SE = 0.07$, $t(410) = 12.07$, $p < .001$ (written); $\beta = 0.61$, $SE = 0.07$, $t(410) = 8.60$, $p < .001$ (original spoken); $\beta = 0.67$, $SE = 0.07$, $t(410) = 9.10$, $p < .001$ (normalized spoken). Qwen-2.5 vs. human: $\beta = 0.90$, $SE = 0.10$, $t(410) = 8.83$, $p < .001$ (written); $\beta = 0.65$, $SE = 0.10$, $t(410) = 6.30$, $p < .001$ (original spoken); $\beta = 0.90$, $SE = 0.10$, $t(410) = 8.83$, $p < .001$ (normalized spoken)). These results indicate that all three models were more sensitive to structural differences between the DO and PO constructions than human participants. In other words, although humans and LLMs both adjust their contrast predictions based on sentence structure, the magnitude of this adjustment is notably larger in LLMs.

To assess the similarity of contrast prediction patterns between humans and LLMs, we computed Pearson correlations for each model and each type

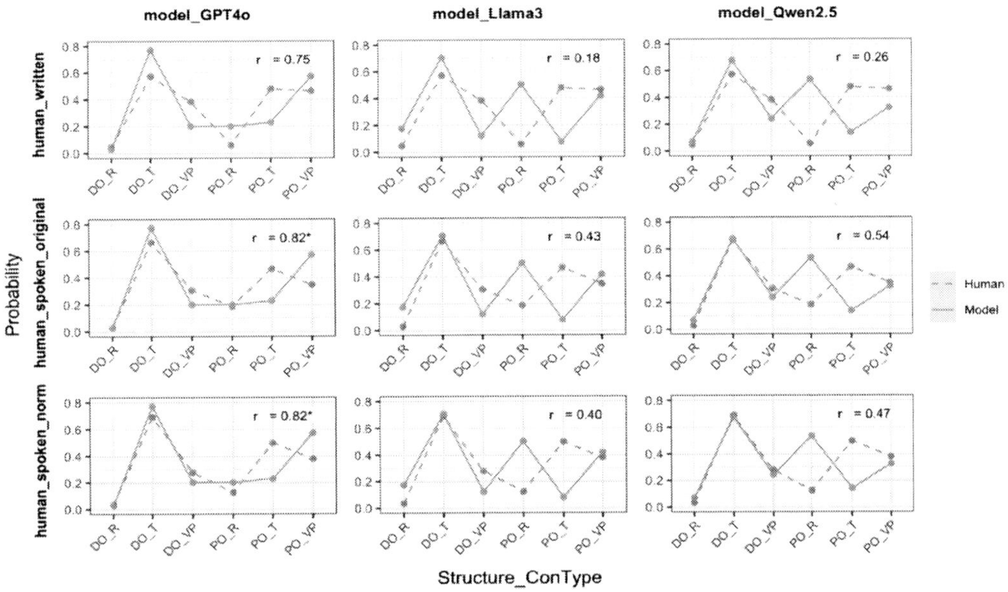

Figure 2 Human-model correlations in contrast predictions across structures and modalities. Each subplot compares a model's prediction probabilities (blue solid line) with human responses (red dashed line) under one of the three modality conditions (written, original spoken, or normalized spoken). The x axis combines structure type (DO, PO) and continuation type (R, T, VP), yielding six categories. The y axis indicates the probability of each category. Pearson correlation coefficients (r) show how closely each model align with human data.

of human data. As shown in Figure 2, two main findings emerged. First, GPT-4o showed the highest correlation with human data across all modalities, suggesting it was more human-like in its contrast predictions compared to LLaMA-3 or Qwen2.5. Second, all three models correlated more strongly with the spoken human data than with the written data, indicating that these models align better with the structure-incremental nature of speech (GPT-4o vs. human: r = 0.75, p = .083 (written); r = 0.82, p = <.05 (original spoken); r = 0.82, p = <.05 (normalized spoken). LLaMA-3 vs. human: r = 0.18, p = .734 (written); r = 0.43, p = .390 (original spoken); r = 0.39, p = .439 (normalized spoken) Qwen-2.5 vs. human: r = 0.26, p = .625 (written); r = 0.54, p = .263 (original spoken); r = 0.47, p = .351 (normalized spoken)).

4 Discussion

The present study investigated how humans and LLMs predict contrasts in Mandarin ditransitive constructions, focusing on whether sentence structure modulates these predictions and whether written or spoken modality influences the size of this structural effect. Our data revealed two primary results. First, for humans, although theme contrast was the most frequent continuation overall, sentence structure significantly modulated contrast predictions, with a stronger effect in spoken language than in written language. Second, LLMs showed an even stronger structure effect than humans, particularly GPT-4o, which most closely mirrored human data.

First, our data addressed a key theoretical linguistic question: which element in a Mandarin ditransitive sentence is in focus, thereby prompting contrast-based predictions? Human data showed that in both DO and PO constructions, the theme was consistently the focal element. This outcome aligns with the Thematic Hierarchy Hypothesis, which argues that the theme, closely tied to the verb, tends to be the default focus in ditransitive structures sentence (Shyu, 2010).

Critically, sentence structure also modulated how human participants predicted contrast in ditransitive structures. In the PO construction, there were more recipient contrasts predictions than in DO construction, because in PO construction (e.g., "she gave the candy to the daughter"), the recipient appears at the end of the sentence and thus draws more attention and induce more predictions that stand contrast with it. This finding partially supports the Sentence-Final Hypothesis (Xu, 2004;

Yan & Calhoun, 2020), which posits that focus naturally gravitates toward the last element in the sentence. Nevertheless, theme contrasts remained dominant across both DO and PO constructions, suggesting that linear order competes with overarching thematic structure in directing attention.

We further observed a difference between written and spoken modalities. In spoken language, participants exhibited a more pronounced effect of word order: sentence-final constituents in PO constructions attracted more recipient contrasts than in DO constructions. This enhanced contrast may stem from the incremental nature of speech (Ferreira & Anes, 1994), as listeners cannot revisit earlier segments and thus rely heavily on each new chunk of information. Interestingly, normalizing prosody did not attenuate the structural effect (i.e., no significant difference between original spoken group and normalized spoken group). While intonation can highlight final elements in Mandarin, our findings suggest that linear order alone can drive substantial focus-based predictions, emphasizing the importance of modality in shaping how comprehenders allocate attention.

Turning to LLMs, we found that each model exhibited a larger structural effect than any of the human groups. Similar to human participants, the models produced more contrasts on sentence-final arguments, but the magnitude of this tendency was amplified. Two factors may underlie this difference. First, transformer-based LLMs use positional embeddings to encode token order (Vaswani et al., 2017), which makes recently processed tokens more salient. This feature can mimic, yet also exaggerate, spoken-language emphasis on final constituents. Second, LLMs are trained with a next-token prediction objective on large text corpora, which could favor the final parts of a sequence, as the model aims to reduce prediction loss by paying attention to the most recent context. Our correlation analysis further revealed that all three LLMs resembled spoken human data more closely than written data, suggesting that next-token prediction architectures may align more naturally with the incremental processing profile of speech.

Together, these findings contribute to broader discussions about predictive processing in language. Although both humans and neural language models depend on anticipatory mechanisms (Brown et al., 2020; Pickering & Gambi, 2018), their respective mechanisms may diverge in how strongly they weight syntactic position over other linguistic cues. Our results also highlight that the models' predictive behavior bears closer resemblance to the incremental unfolding of speech than to the flexible reading patterns of silent text comprehension (Christiansen & Chater, 2016). Future research could employ more fine-grained methods (e.g., eye-tracking) and analyses (e.g., attention-weight examinations of LLMs) to investigate why humans and models display these similarities and discrepancies.

5 Conclusions

The current study employed a sentence continuation task to examine how humans and LLMs predict contrast in ditransitive sentences. Two main findings emerged: (1) theme contrasts were dominant for human participants, but sentence structure significantly modulated these contrasts—especially in spoken contexts; (2) LLMs showed stronger structural effects than humans, with GPT-4o aligning most closely with human data. This study highlights the interplay between syntactic structure and modality in guiding predictions in human language processing and offers a clearer lens into how humans and LLMs differ in their weighting sentence structure. By comparing the two groups in a straightforward task, this work offers practical insights for refining language models and yields theoretical implications for understanding predictive language processing across modalities.

Limitations

The first limitation is our reliance on the sentence continuation paradigm, which is offline and intermingles comprehension with production. Incorporating more online and time-sensitive methods like eye-tracking or neuroimaging methods could provide a clearer picture of when and how focus-based contrast predictions arise.

Moreover, although we sampled three prominent LLMs, the rapid evolution of language models suggests that further comparative studies would be valuable—particularly among systems trained mainly on Chinese text vs. models relying heavily on English corpora.

References

Altmann, G. T., & Kamide, Y. (1999). Incremental interpretation at verbs: Restricting the domain of subsequent reference. *Cognition, 73*(3), 247–264. https://doi.org/10.1016/S0010-0277(99)00059-1

Brown, T., Mann, B., Ryder, N., Subbiah, M., Kaplan, J. D., Dhariwal, P., Neelakantan, A., Shyam, P., Sastry, G., Askell, A., Agarwal, S., Herbert-Voss, A., Krueger, G., Henighan, T., Child, R., Ramesh, A., Ziegler, D., Wu, J., Winter, C., … Amodei, D. (2020). Language models are few-shot learners. In H. Larochelle, M. Ranzato, R. Hadsell, M. F. Balcan, & H. Lin (Eds.), *Advances in Neural Information Processing Systems* (Vol. 33, pp. 1877–1901). Curran Associates, Inc. https://proceedings.neurips.cc/paper/2020/hash/1457c0d6bfcb4967418bfb8ac142f64a-Abstract.html

Cai, Z. G., Pickering, M. J., & Sturt, P. (2013). Processing verb-phrase ellipsis in Mandarin Chinese: Evidence against the syntactic account. *Language and Cognitive Processes, 28*(6), 810–828. https://doi.org/10.1080/01690965.2012.665932

Cai, Z. G., Zhao, N., & Pickering, M. J. (2022). How do people interpret implausible sentences? *Cognition, 225*, 105101. https://doi.org/10.1016/j.cognition.2022.105101

Calhoun, S. (2009). What makes a word contrastive? Prosodic, semantic and pragmatic perspectives. *Where Prosody Meets Pragmatics: Research at the Interface, 8*, 53–78.

Carlson, K. (2014). Predicting contrast in sentences with and without focus marking. *Lingua, 150*, 78–91. https://www.sciencedirect.com/science/article/pii/S0024384114001624

Christiansen, M. H., & Chater, N. (2016). The Now-or-Never bottleneck: A fundamental constraint on language. *Behavioral and Brain Sciences, 39*, e62. https://doi.org/10.1017/S0140525X1500031X

Clark, A. (2013). Whatever next? Predictive brains, situated agents, and the future of cognitive science. *Behavioral and Brain Sciences, 36*(3), 181–204. https://doi.org/10.1017/S0140525X12000477

Duan, X., Li, S., & Cai, Z. G. (2024). MacBehaviour: An R package for behavioural experimentation on large language models. *Behavior Research Methods, 57*(1), 19. https://doi.org/10.3758/s13428-024-02524-y

Ferreira, F., & Anes, M. (1994). Why study spoken language? In M. A. Gernsbacher (Ed.), *Handbook of Psycholinguistics* (pp. 32–56). Academic Press. https://psycnet.apa.org/record/1994-97824-002

Husband, E. M., & Ferreira, F. (2016). The role of selection in the comprehension of focus alternatives. *Language, Cognition and Neuroscience, 31*(2), 217–235. https://doi.org/10.1080/23273798.2015.1083113

Kuperberg, G. R., & Jaeger, T. F. (2016). What do we mean by prediction in language comprehension? *Language, Cognition and Neuroscience, 31*(1), 32–59. https://doi.org/10.1080/23273798.2015.1102299

Lowder, M. W., & Ferreira, F. (2016). Prediction in the processing of repair disfluencies: Evidence from the visual-world paradigm. *Journal of Experimental Psychology: Learning, Memory, and Cognition, 42*(9), 1400–1416. https://doi.org/10.1037/xlm0000256

Lowder, M. W., & Gordon, P. C. (2015). Focus takes time: Structural effects on reading. *Psychonomic Bulletin & Review, 22*(6), 1733–1738. https://doi.org/10.3758/s13423-015-0843-2

Meta. (2024, April 18). *Introducing Meta Llama 3: The most capable openly available LLM to date*. https://ai.meta.com/blog/meta-llama-3/

OpenAI. (2024, May 13). *GPT-4o system card*. https://openai.com/index/gpt-4o-system-card/

Paterson, K. B., Liversedge, S. P., Filik, R., Juhasz, B. J., White, S. J., & Rayner, K. (2007). Focus Identification during Sentence Comprehension: Evidence from Eye Movements. *Quarterly Journal of Experimental Psychology, 60*(10), 1423–1445. https://doi.org/10.1080/17470210601100563

Pickering, M. J., & Gambi, C. (2018). Predicting while comprehending language: A theory and review. *Psychological Bulletin, 144*(10), 1002–1044. https://doi.org/10.1037/bul0000158

Qualtrics (Versions 09-2024). (2024). [Computer software]. Qualtrics.

Radford, A., Narasimhan, K., Salimans, T., & Sutskever, I. (2018). *Improving language understanding by generative pre-training*. https://www.mikecaptain.com/resources/pdf/GPT-1.pdf

Radford, A., Wu, J., Child, R., Luan, D., Amodei, D., & Sutskever, I. (2019). *Language models are unsupervised multitask learners*. https://insightcivic.s3.us-east-1.amazonaws.com/language-models.pdf

Repp, S. (2010). Defining 'contrast'as an information-structural notion in grammar. *Lingua, 120*(6), 1333–1345. https://doi.org/10.1016/j.lingua.2009.04.006

Roberts, C. (2012). Information Structure: Towards an integrated formal theory of pragmatics. *Semantics and Pragmatics, 5*, 6:1-69. https://doi.org/10.3765/sp.5.6

Roettger, T. B., Franke, M., & Cole, J. (2021). Positional biases in predictive processing of intonation. *Language, Cognition and Neuroscience*, *36*(3), 342–370. https://doi.org/10.1080/23273798.2020.1853185

Rooth, M. (2016). Alternative Semantics. In C. Féry & S. Ishihara (Eds.), *The Oxford Handbook of Information Structure* (p. 0). Oxford University Press. https://doi.org/10.1093/oxfordhb/9780199642670.013.19

Shyu, S.-I. (2010). Focus interpretation of zhi 'only' associated arguments in Mandarin triadic constructions. *Linguistics*, *48*(3). https://doi.org/10.1515/ling.2010.021

Xu, L. (2004). Manifestation of informational focus. *Lingua*, *114*(3), 277–299. https://doi.org/10.1016/S0024-3841(03)00031-7

Yan, M., & Calhoun, S. (2020). Rejecting false alternatives in Chinese and English: The interaction of prosody, clefting, and default focus position. *Laboratory Phonology*, *11*(1). https://doi.org/10.5334/labphon.255

Yang, A., Yang, B., Zhang, B., Hui, B., Zheng, B., Yu, B., Li, C., Liu, D., Huang, F., Wei, H., Lin, H., Yang, J., Tu, J., Zhang, J., Yang, J., Yang, J., Zhou, J., Lin, J., Dang, K., … Qiu, Z. (2025). *Qwen2.5 Technical Report* (No. arXiv:2412.15115). arXiv. https://doi.org/10.48550/arXiv.2412.15115

Investigating noun-noun compound relation representations in autoregressive large language models

Saffron Kendrick Mark Ormerod Hui Wang Barry Devereux

Queen's University Belfast, Northern Ireland
{skendrick01, mormerod01, h.wang, b.devereux}@qub.ac.uk

Abstract

This paper uses autoregressive large language models to explore at which points in a given input sentence the semantic information is decodable. Using representational similarity analysis and probing, the results show that autoregressive models are capable of extracting the semantic relation information from a dataset of noun-noun compounds. When considering the effect of processing the head and modifier nouns in context, the extracted representations show greater correlation after processing both constituent nouns in the same sentence. The linguistic properties of the head nouns may influence the ability of LLMs to extract relation information when the head and modifier words are processed separately. Probing suggests that Phi-1 and LLaMA-3.2 are exposed to relation information during training, as they are able to predict the relation vectors for compounds from separate word representations to a similar degree as using compositional compound representations. However, the difference in processing condition for GPT-2 and DeepSeek-R1 indicates that these models are actively processing the contextual semantic relation information of the compound.

1 Introduction

The popularity of transformer-based large language models (LLMs) has skyrocketed since the success of Vaswani (2017) with the attention mechanism and the conception of Bidirectional Encoders from Transformers (BERT) (Devlin et al., 2019). The attention-based architecture of LLMs allows them to carry out a wide variety of natural language processing (NLP) tasks, such as classification, sentiment analysis, translation and text generation.

Despite the positive reception and widespread implementation of LLMs, the internal processes of these complex models remain a key question within the fields of interpretable and explainable AI. In particular, the notion that state-of-the-art (SoTA) LLMs can process and understand word meaning in a similar way to natural language understanding remains an ongoing discussion (Bender and Koller, 2020; Piantadosi and Hill, 2022). This has inspired research into the syntactic and semantic capabilities of language models in an attempt to unify computational processes and human language processing.

The objective of this paper is to expand on the work of Ormerod et al. (2024) to investigate whether SoTA autoregressive models are capable of representing the semantic relation information of noun-noun compounds, and where in an input sequence the semantic information is decodable. The original framework uses representational similarity analysis (RSA) to compare the extracted token representations with two datasets of English noun-noun compounds. The token representations considered are suited for the bidrectional masked language models, however, autoregressive LLMs are unidirectional, meaning that they only rely on the previous inputs. Therefore, the experiments are adapted to incorporate a continuation word, taking the final head word and modifier token representations, and the token representation of the continuation word.

The models in this paper include RoBERTa (Liu et al., 2019), BERT-Japanese, GPT-2 (Radford et al., 2019), Phi-1 (Gunasekar et al., 2023), LLaMA-3.2 (Dubey et al., 2024), and DeepSeek-R1-Distill-Qwen-1.5B (DeepSeek-AI et al., 2025). BERT-Japanese acts as a control subject because it is not trained on English and therefore should not be able to decode the English semantic relation. RoBERTa is included as the top performing encoder model.

The results show that autoregressive models are capable of decoding the semantic relation information, with strongest correlation occurring from the final word token representations. The final head noun token also holds relation information, which may be accounted for by the level of concreteness

Proceedings of the Workshop on Cognitive Modeling and Computational Linguistics, pages 253–263
May 3, 2025 ©2025 Association for Computational Linguistics

of the head noun. However, the modifier word representations still contain some level of relation information, potentially reflecting frequency of relational information associated with specific modifier nouns in the training data. The models decode semantic information from the contextual representations, although Phi and LLaMA may learn information about coexisting compound relations during training as these models can predict relation information from individual word representations.

2 Background

The first transformer-based model, designed for a text translation task, consisted of six encoders and six decoders which were able to convert input sequences into output sequences. In the transformer, encoders are responsible for generating word embeddings which capture the content of an input, and positional encodings which provide information on the position of each token in the sequence. The multi-headed self-attention mechanism is a key part of the architecture which enables each encoder to focus on different parts of the input as it processes each token. Attention involves calculating the dot product of the query and key vectors, which indicates the level of emphasis that each word should place on other words. The attention weights are then passed through a softmax layer which gives a probability distribution that informs the model how much of each value representation to carry through to the next layer.

An alternative to the traditional BERT architecture, autoregressive decoder-based LLMs are unidirectional, which means that they rely on the previous input to predict the next token in the sequence. They are causal language models, consisting of stacks of decoder layers which take an input sequence and predict the next most likely term. These autoregressive models are often used for text generation and chatbots which are available to the public, thus it is crucial that their internal processes are investigated.

2.1 Probing LLMs

Probing is a technique commonly used within NLP interpretability to investigate whether the representations are able to capture certain information (Hewitt and Manning, 2019). Due to the complexity of blackbox models, probing methods are often extrinsic, post-hoc approaches. Classifiers are used to determine whether a model can successfully decode an abstract concept, although they do not provide causal information. For transformer models, probing often includes investigating the attention heads within the self-attention mechanism, embeddings, and token representations. Ju et al. (2024) used layer-wise probing to investigate how LLMs encode context, highlighting the emphasis that LLMs place on context knowledge in upper layers. This is supported by the work of Jawahar et al. (2019), using sentence-level probing to explore BERT's phrasal representations. They concluded that BERT encodes linguistic information including syntactic features in its middle layers and semantic features in the upper layers. Other probing studies have investigated function word comprehension, long-distance agreement, and other syntactic phenomena (Kim et al., 2019; Linzen and Baroni, 2021; Vulić et al., 2020). Probing proves to be a well-established method for exploring how LLMs are able to encode and decode semantic and syntactical information.

2.2 Conceptual combination

A major field of research that aims to bridge the gap between human language understanding and NLP focuses on the compositionality of words to form larger, meaningful phrases and sentences, a process known as conceptual combination. This process can be linked to concepts that are intersective, such as adjective-noun phrases that are overlaps of their constituent words, as well as noun-noun phrases which consist of a head noun and a modifier. A subset of noun-noun phrases can be considered lexical compounds, where they are highly idiomatised within language such that the combined meaning is not apparent from the meanings of the individual nouns themselves.

Early theories of intersective combination take inspiration from mathematical principles, proposing a fuzzy logic model that relies on a degree of overlap between two concepts. This early model led to the Selective Modification (Smith and Osherson, 1984; Smith et al., 1988) and Concept Specialisation models (Cohen and Murphy, 1984) which can be described as schema-based, where the head noun is represented by a set of empty slots and fillers, and its specialisation is determined by a modifier filling one or more of its slots. The dual-process model proposes a similar framework, however this model suggests three approaches to conceptual combination: relation-based, property-based, and a hybridisation of two concepts (Wisniewski, 1997). In this instance, relations are represented as slots within the schema of a head noun and when a modifier fills a slot, an appropriate relation is chosen. Building on the reasoning that relations drive conception, the Competition Among Relations in Nominals (CARIN) theory implies that the modifier representation contains knowledge of certain relations that are frequently used with the given modifier during conceptual combination, known as the relational distribution (Gagné, 2001).

2.3 Semantic properties of LLMs

Research into conceptual combination from a linguistic standpoint is far from complete, however early theories provide a starting point for probing LLMs to discern whether SoTA models extract meaningful representations about syntactic and semantic properties of language. In particular, insights into how LLMs handle complex linguistic structures can shed light on the internal mechanisms and how they relate to or deviate from human cognitive processes.

Conceptual combination in the context of NLP has primarily focused on using features to classify the relations between a head noun and a modifier word. Ó Séaghdha and Copestake (2008) adopted distributional kernels for three types of semantic classification, including the interpretation of compound nouns. For transformer-based language models, word embeddings have become an area of interest for probing the semantic capabilities. Peters et al. (2018) concluded that the complex architecture of transformers are capable of learning a hierarchy of linguistic features. Shwartz and Dagan (2019) evaluated both static and contextualised embeddings, concluding that contextualising improves performance, especially for recognising meaning shifts. Ettinger (2020) extracted word embeddings to assess phrasal similarity across layers of transformer models for two-word phrases, concluding that although models are able to represent individual word content, they struggle at representing the full compositional phrase meaning. Derby et al. (2021) investigated how the intermediate layer of long short-term memory (LSTM) models and transformers capture semantic knowledge, showing that transformers outperform LSTMs although both are able to retain semantic information after the target concept has been provided to the model.

Most recently, Coil and Shwartz (2023) investigated the interpretation and conceptualisation of noun-noun compounds on a supervised seq2seq model and GPT-3, an autoregressive LLM. They found that GPT-3 outperformed the seq2seq model when interpreting known compounds, however the LLM struggled to generalise to unseen, novel compounds. They suggested that GPT-3 relied heavily on memorisation to interpret previously seen compounds, leading to hallucinations when interpreting new compounds. Ormerod et al. (2024) focused on six encoder-based LLMs, including a multilingual model and a non-English monolingual model, to investigate whether LLMs are capable of representing the thematic relation shared between two constituent nouns within a compound. Their work highlighted the ability of BERT and RoBERTa to encode the thematic relation between the head and modifier, although they did not consider autoregressive models. Rambelli et al. (2024) also investigated the semantic relationships shared across compounds, using prompting and the Surprisal metric on a dataset of noun-noun compounds annotated with both semantic relations and concreteness ratings. Their results indicated that models identified semantic relations to varying degrees, influenced by the concreteness of a given compound. However, similar to Coil and Shwartz (2023), they found that LLMs were limited in their ability to generalise to novel compounds.

As an extension to Ormerod et al. (2024), this paper provides further support to the conclusions that autoregressive LLMs are able to extract implicit relation information after processing the full compound. Probing uses fine-grained relation information to explore the semantic information extracted from compounds at a higher level of granularity.

3 Data

Two datasets are used to explore the thematic relations of noun-noun compounds. The first dataset includes 300 English noun-noun compounds that are categorised into groups of 5 compounds (Gagné, 2001). Each group consists of a target compound, a compound with the same head noun and the same relation, a compound with the same head noun but a different relation, a compound with the same modifier word and the same relation, and a compound with the same modifier and a different relation. 60 groups of five compounds are constructed and a ground-truth representational dissimilarity matrix (RDM) is constructed to reflect whether or not pairs of compounds share the same thematic relation. Within each group of five compounds, there is one target compound, followed by four others that comply with the experimental conditions given in Table 1.

M	H	Experimental Condition
gas	lamp	Target
battery	lamp	Same H, same relation
cabin	lamp	Same H, different relation
gas	car	Same M, same relation
gas	hose	Same M, different relation

Table 1: Experimental conditions for each group of five noun-noun compounds used in the relation category RSA experiments, with the modifier (M) and the head noun (H).

The second dataset consists of 60 noun-noun compounds, where 34 participants were tasked with ranking the appropriateness of 18 possible relations for each compound (Devereux and Costello, 2005). This results in a dataset of 18-dimensional relation vectors. Compounds which are semantically linked, i.e. share the same thematic relation, tend to have similar relation vectors. This dataset provides a fine-grained representation of the semantic information for each compound, useful for probing the semantic capabilities of the LLMs.

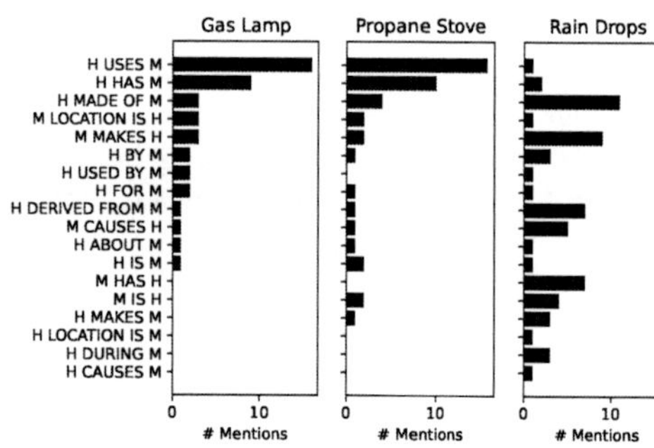

Figure 1: Sample relation vectors for three of the 60 compounds in the 60 compound dataset. Compounds GAS LAMP and PROPANE STOVE share similar relation vectors, when compared with RAIN DROPS (Devereux and Costello, 2005).

4 Experiments

The experimentation consists of two separate experiments, firstly using RSA to assess whether the token representations extracted layer-by-layer reflect the semantic relation information shared across the head and modifier of noun-noun compounds, and secondly using a linear probing classifier to discern whether the LLMs can successfully decode the thematic relation.

Experiment 1, also known as the relation category experiment, is designed to determine whether the relation between nouns influences the model's ability to distinguish between noun-noun compounds when presented in pairs. RSA, a technique commonly used in computational neuroscience, is useful for comparing disparate data sources by creating similarity matrices and analysing any shared structure, or lack of, by calculating the Pearson r correlation between the two matrices (Kriegeskorte et al., 2008). Experimental RDMs are constructed by calculating the cosine similarity of the extracted token representations, to compare with ground-truth RDMs which reflect whether two compounds share the same thematic relation (similar) or not (dissimilar), see Figure 2. The correlation indicates how strongly the extracted representations reflects the relation information represented by the ground-truth RDM, i.e. the category of relation for each compound.

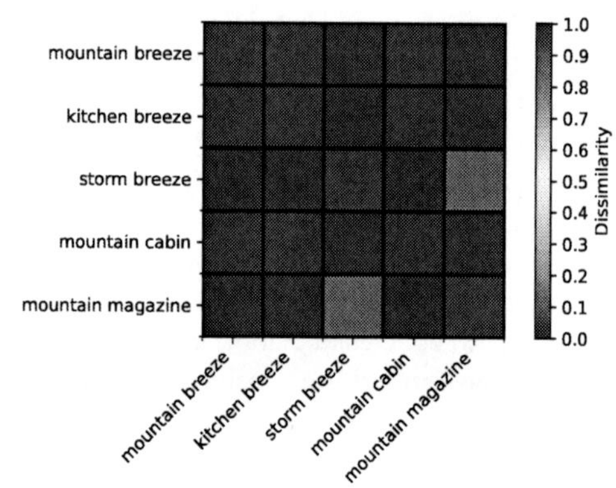

Figure 2: Ground-truth RDM, representing whether two compounds share the same thematic relation. The compounds that do not share either the same relation, head or modifier is not included in the Pearson r calculations (Ormerod et al., 2024).

This experiment also investigates the effect of considering the head and modifier in the same sentence, as opposed to considering each word separately. Higher correlation when the compound is processed together in the same sentence would indicate that the semantic relation information is represented by the models across the compound.

The second experiment, known as the compositional probe, applies a linear classifier to probe whether context is required in order to decode fine-grained relation information. The original framework set out by Mitchell and Lapata (2008) has been adapted for this probe experiment, where the 2-vs-2 testing framework is used to determine whether the extracted representations of pairs of compounds align more with ground-truth or with each other. Using the fine-grained 60-compound dataset, for each possible pair of compounds (out of a possible 1770), a linear regression model is trained on the mean-pooled representations for RoBERTa and BERT-Japanese, and the final word token representations of the remaining compounds for the autoregressive models to predict the 18-dimension relation vectors.

The regression model generates predictions $Y^{\tilde{i}}$ and $Y^{\tilde{j}}$ from Y^i and Y^j. A test is considered successful if it satisfies

$$\begin{aligned} \mathrm{dist}(Y^{\tilde{i}}, Y^{i}) + \mathrm{dist}(Y^{\tilde{j}}, Y^{j}) < \\ \mathrm{dist}(Y^{\tilde{i}}, Y^{j}) + \mathrm{dist}(Y^{\tilde{j}}, Y^{i}), \end{aligned} \quad (1)$$

where the distances are calculated as mean squared errors. Therefore, if the predicted vectors for i and j are closer to the true relation vectors for i and j, rather than the other way around, the test is marked as successful. The probing experiment considers two processing conditions, where the head and modifier word are processed together in context and where they are processed separately before being averaged. If the proportion of successful tests is high for the contextual processing condition, this would suggest that the models are actively processing the contextual composition of each compound, rather than relying on previously learned association information.

Four publicly available autoregressive models are used, including GPT-2-Small, Phi-1, LLaMA-3.2-3B, and DeepSeek-R1-Distill-Qwen-1.5B. All four models adopt different tokenisers to break down the input sequences into sub-units (tokens). DeepSeek is of particular interest as it adopts Mixture of Experts (MoE) approach, allowing it to predict multiple potential outputs simultaneously. For RoBERTa and BERT-Japanese, the input sequences are taken as the Gloss sentences from the dataset, e.g. "It is a MOUNTAIN STREAM." However, as the autoregressive models read from left to right, the input sequences include an additional continuation word so that the token representation can be extracted from the final word, e.g. "It is a MOUNTAIN STREAM *[and/but/that]*", where the average of applying each word is taken. When taking the processing condition into account, two separate sentences are used, each employing the head noun and modifier word, e.g. "It is a MOUNTAIN." and "It is a STREAM." Once again, for GPT, Phi, DeepSeek and LLaMA, the sentences include a continuation word.

4.1 Relation category RSA

Three experimental RDMs are constructed for each layer within the models by calculating the pairwise cosine similarity for the mean-pooled token representations, the head noun representations, and the modifier word representations for the BERT models. For the autoregressive models, the final head, final modifier, and final word representations are used. The Pearson r correlation between each experimental RDM and the ground-truth RDM is then plotted to show how well the extracted representations reflect the thematic relation of each compound, see Figure 3.

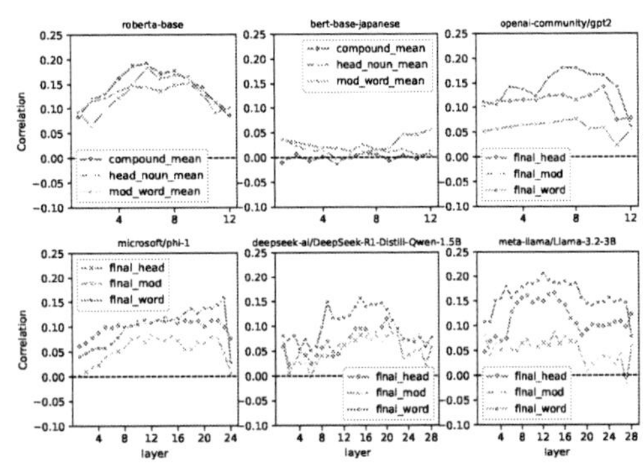

Figure 3: Results for the relation category RSA experiment (Section 4.1). The Pearson r correlation is calculated between the same thematic relation ground-truth RDM and experimental RDMs across all layers of six transformer models.

Figure 3 shows that all models, excluding BERT-Japanese, are capable of capturing the semantic relation information. As expected, the non-English model performs poorly, although the head and modifier representations produce higher correlation than the mean-pooled compound representations, suggesting that the separate representations may contribute to the thematic relation information.

For the autoregressive models, the final word representation produces the highest correlation to ground truth, followed by the final head noun representations. The correlation for the modifier word representation is non-zero, which may reflect statistical and semantic information about how modifier words are associated with thematic relations in the language data that the models have been exposed to during pre-training. The results for DeepSeek follow a similar trend to LLaMA, which could be due to the fact that DeepSeek-R1 is partly based on the LLaMA model. For all four autoregressive models, the correlation drops for the final word representations at the final layer.

4.2 Relation category RSA with processing condition

This is an extension of the previous experiment that considers whether context affects how well the models extract the thematic relation. Two experimental RDMs are constructed by comparing the cosine similarity of the mean-pooled token representations for BERT models, and the final word token representations for the four autoregressive models, of the compounds presented in context (the "Together" condition) and in separate sentences (the "Separate" condition). The results are presented in Figure 4.

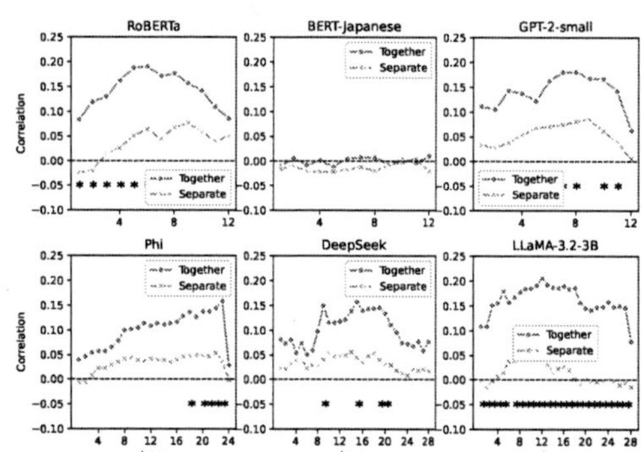

Figure 4: Results for the relation category RSA experiment with the processing condition (Section 4.2). The Pearson r correlation is taken between the same relation ground-truth RDM and the experimental RDMs of the mean-pooled and final word representations for the "Together" and "Separate" processing conditions. Asterisks reflect $p < 0.05$, i.e. under a paired t-test, the difference in correlation across processing conditions is statistically significant.

The "Together" processing condition consistently produces greater correlations when compared with the "Separate" condition, suggesting that GPT, Phi, DeepSeek and LLaMA represent the semantic relation information across the compound. In particular, after performing a paired t-test, the results are statistically significant across almost all layers for LLaMA, with statistically significant differences for GPT and DeepSeek across the middle layers, and Phi towards the later layers.

Processing the head and modifier words separately still alludes to some ability for the models to capture the relation information, which could be the result of the models taking into account the frequency of modifiers and head nouns coexisting with a particular relation during training.

For all models except BERT-Japanese, the gap between the correlations of each processing condition is most defined through the middle layers, supporting the results above that semantic information shared across the compound is encoded in the middle layers. Correlation for the "Separate" case for the autoregressive models falls almost to zero, implying that the token representations reflect very little semantic information in the final layers.

4.3 Compositional probe

The 2-vs-2 tests are performed pairwise to investigate whether context is required for decoding fine-grained semantic information.

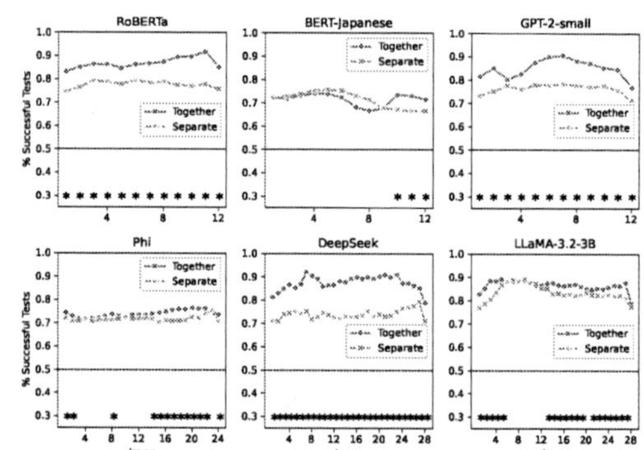

Figure 5: Results for the compositional probe experiment (Section 4.3). Proportion of successful tests out of 1770 tests, i.e. the models decode the thematic relation, using both the "Together" and "Separate" processing conditions. Asterisks signify tests for false-discovery, where $p < 0.05$, i.e. there is a significant difference between the number of successes across both processing conditions.

In Figure 5, the results for DeepSeek and GPT suggest that the models capture relation information in context, and contextual combination is responsible for creating representations that reflect the semantic information. However, there is little difference between the processing conditions for Phi and LLaMA, implying that the models are already aware of particular thematic relations and can identify these from the individual words.

In addition to the probing experiment, a false-discovery procedure is performed in order to account for statistical dependencies. These occurrences are marked as asterisks. The results for DeepSeek in particular show a large number of these tests across all layers, despite such a high proportion of successful tests.

5 Representations across layers

The experiments show that these models are capable of extracting semantic information, but in order to identify the points in the input sentences at which each model is able to decode the relation information, the correlation is plotted layer-wise against the input sentence.

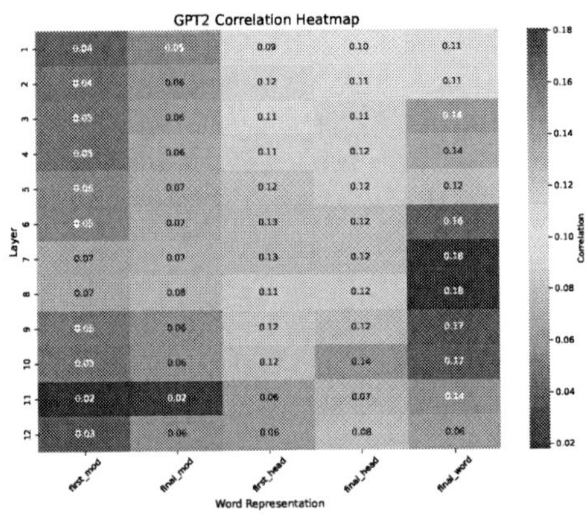

Figure 6: Correlation between the final word token representation RDM and the ground truth RDM across layers for GPT.

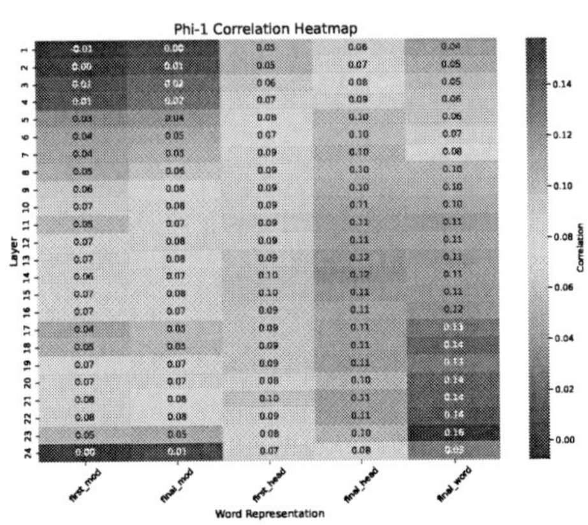

Figure 7: Correlation between the final word token representation RDM and the ground truth RDM across layers for Phi.

For GPT, Figure 6 shows that positive correlation begins at the first head token position. This implies that, once the model has been exposed to the full modifier word, it is capable of extracting a level of semantic relation information. The correlation is strongest in the middle and later layers for the final word representations, which aligns with the results from the relation category RSA experiment (Section 4.1).

Whilst there is a clear distinction between the modifier and head token correlations for GPT, the heatmap for Phi in Figure 7 shows that the modifier tokens do correlate to some extent with ground-truth, although this is not high at 0.08. Once again, the correlation is stronger towards the end of the input sequence, with the greatest correlation produced by the final word token representations.

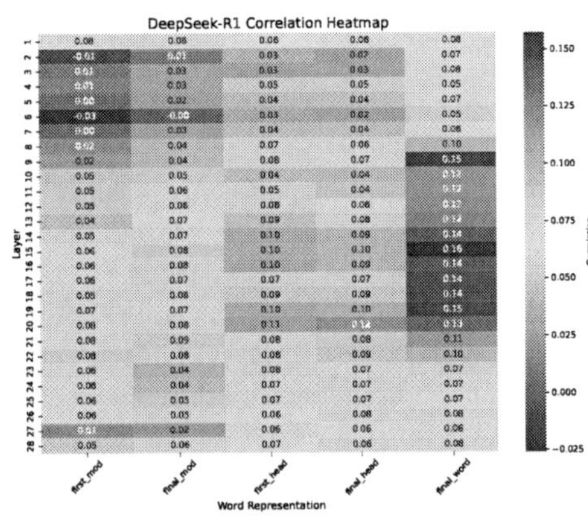

Figure 8: Correlation between the final word token representation RDM and the ground truth RDM across layers for DeepSeek.

For DeepSeek, the heatmap in Figure 8 shows that the modifier tokens may reflect some of the semantic relation information of the compounds. The correlation is most pronounced across the middle layers of the final word representation, before decreasing.

Similar to GPT, Figure 9 shows that the correlation for LLaMA begins to increase after the model has been presented with the full modifier. LLaMA achieves the highest correlation of 0.21 after processing the compound.

6 Discussion

The experimental results support the conclusions that transformer-based LLMs can retrieve the semantic relation information of noun-noun compounds. Intuitively, the averaged token representa-

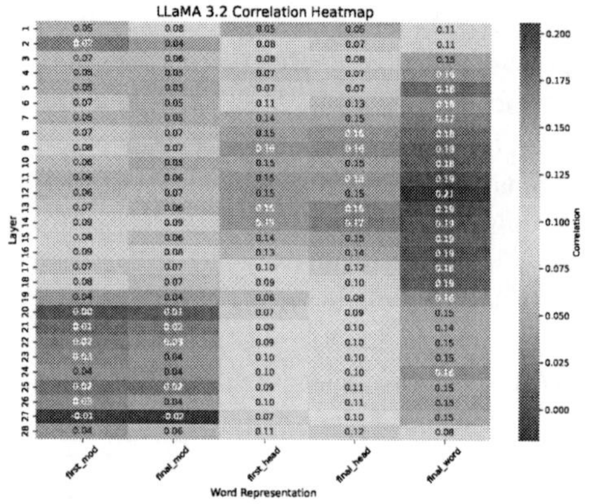

Figure 9: Correlation between the final word token representation RDM and the ground truth RDM across layers for LLaMA.

tion for the continuation words led to the greater correlation, which is to be expected as the autoregressive models will have processed the full compound. This result contradicts Ettinger (2020), who concluded that representations of two-word phrase embeddings do not reflect the semantic phrasal composition.

The head noun representations also correlate with the ground truth RDMs, suggesting some capability for the head nouns to store relational information. A possible explanation is the intrinsic semantic properties of the constituent nouns in the compounds, where head nouns reflect concrete concepts. From the fine-grained 60-compound dataset, the top mentioned relations include "H FOR M", "H MADE OF M", and "H USES M". These relations are more likely to be shared by at least one concrete noun (BREAKFAST SUGAR, HORSE STABLES, RAIN DROPS), compared with compounds that share less common relations such as "H DERIVED FROM M" or "M CAUSES H" (JOB ANXIETY, TAX PRESSURE, THERMAL TORTURE). Compounds which share the top mentioned relations are more likely to be tangible concepts in the real world, and thus require less context and inference than abstract themes. Conclusions from Rambelli et al. (2024) suggest that the linguistic property of concreteness may be, to some extent, responsible for the variation in success of LLMs interpreting compounds. The results here suggest that LLMs are leveraging the properties of the head nouns in order to represent relational information. When taking into account the processing condition of the head and modifier nouns (Section 4.2), the results for the "Separate" condition suggest that the constituent nouns may hold some level of relation information. In conjunction with the results that the head noun representations produce higher correlations, it is plausible that the properties of the head nouns contribute to the models' ability to reflect semantic information. The modifier token representations show slightly positive correlations, where the models are only exposed to the modifier word instead of the full compound. This result may support the CARIN model of conceptual combination which argues that modifiers contain a relational distribution and therefore more frequent modifiers can provide relational information. Models may learn relational distribution information from compounds processed during pre-training.

The results from Section 4.1 suggest that the four autoregressive models extract semantic information towards the middle and later layers, similar to the results that show BERT models encode the relation information in the middle layers. The correlation for LLaMA spikes in the early layers, whilst also producing peaks around the middle layers. After probing the layer-wise representations of LLaMA-2, Liu et al. (2024) found that the lower layers of the model are responsible for extracting lexical semantic information, and higher layers are better suited for predictive tasks. This resonates with the results from the relation category RSA experiment, where LLaMA produced high correlations for both the final head token and final word token representations between layers 6-18.

The decrease in correlation for autoregressive models in the final layers may be explained by Ethayarajh (2019), who concluded that GPT-2, as opposed to BERT, does not represent word meanings in the final layer. The vector space of embeddings appears to flatten, such that semantics, syntax and other linguistic properties of language are not reflected in the token representations extracted from the final layer. As a result, further fine-tuning for specific semantic tasks may be effective when focused on the middle layers of the transformer models.

DeepSeek is of particular interest as this model is a distilled LLM that uses MoE to generate predictions efficiently. The traditional transformer architecture is adapted by replacing feedforward networks (FFNs) with MoE layers (Dai et al., 2024). Each MoE is similar to a FFN in structure, and a number of experts are activated in parallel throughout the transformer when an input is being processed. This complex internal mechanism means that there may be subnetworks within the model that each contribute to the model's overall understanding. Contributions from a number of "experts" may result in the semantic relation information being decodable at early points in the input sequence, i.e. from the modifier representations. The distilled DeepSeek-R1 model is based on both LLaMA and Qwen, which could explain the similar correlation patterns for the relation category experiments.

7 Limitations and Future Work

The models included in this paper are all trained on the same scale of parameters (1-3B). Larger models may be explored to investigate the effect of the scale of pre-training, and whether a larger number of hidden dimension enhances or inhibits the extraction of meaningful representations. The datasets are also limited in size, with only 60 possible relation vectors available for probing. Whilst suitable for the size of the models being tested in this paper, investigating LLMs trained on billions of parameters and fine-tuned models would require larger datasets to account for potential noise and model sensitivity. Additionally, expanding the probing experiment to consider novel compounds would explore the generalisability of the findings.

These models were tested using their base configurations in order to explore their intrinsic semantic capabilities. For models such as Phi and LLaMA where little context required for decoding the relation in the probe experiment, fine-tuning could reveal contextual composition where the models can no longer rely on the relation information embedded during training.

Exploring the MoE architecture of DeepSeek could also reveal whether there are particular "experts" that are activated to extract semantic information, and whether these vary across layers or vary according to context. Understanding how DeepSeek dynamically selects experts during the processing of compounds may lead to further insights on subnetworks that exist within the network, and how they contribute to the success of the model interpreting relation information.

8 Conclusion

The main research question concerns whether autoregressive language models consisting of decoder-only layers are able to reflect the semantic relation information of noun-noun compounds, and which parts of the input sequences make the particular relation decodable. The RSA and probing results indicate that the LLMs successfully retrieve semantic information, with meaningful representations extracted after the models have been exposed to the full compound in context. Head noun token representations also reflect information about the thematic relation, which may be the result of the intrinsic concrete properties of the nouns. The modifier nouns show the potential for embedding relational information, however this may be explained by LLMs being exposed to compounds during training. For GPT and DeepSeek, probing reveals that they are actively processing the information stored across the compound in order to accurately predict the appropriate relation, whereas Phi and LLaMA appear to predict the relation just as well from the individual word representations.

References

E. M. Bender and A. Koller. 2020. Climbing towards NLU: On meaning, form, and understanding in the age of data. In *Proceedings of the 58th annual meeting of the association for Computational Linguistics*, pages 5185–5198.

B. Cohen and G. L. Murphy. 1984. Models of concepts. *Cognitive science*, 8(1):27–58.

A. Coil and V. Shwartz. 2023. From chocolate bunny to chocolate crocodile: Do language models understand noun compounds? In *Findings of the Association for Computational Linguistics: ACL 2023*, pages 2698–2710, Toronto, Canada. Association for Computational Linguistics.

D. Dai, C. Deng, C. Zhao, R. X. Xu, H. Gao, D. Chen, J. Li, W. Zeng, X. Yu, Y. Wu, et al. 2024. Deepseekmoe: Towards ultimate expert specialization in mixture-of-experts language models. *arXiv preprint arXiv:2401.06066*.

DeepSeek-AI, D. Guo, D. Yang, H. Zhang, and et al. 2025. Deepseek-r1: Incentivizing reasoning capability in llms via reinforcement learning. *Preprint*, arXiv:2501.12948.

S. Derby, P. Miller, and B. Devereux. 2021. Representation and pre-activation of lexical-semantic knowledge in neural language models. In *Proceedings of the Workshop on Cognitive Modeling and Computational Linguistics*, pages 211–221. Association for Computational Linguistics.

B. Devereux and F. Costello. 2005. Investigating the relations used in conceptual combination. *Artificial Intelligence Review*, 24:489–515.

J. Devlin, M. Chang, K. Lee, and K. Toutanova. 2019. BERT: Pre-training of deep bidirectional transformers for language understanding. *Preprint*, arXiv:1810.04805.

A. Dubey, A. Jauhri, A. Pandey, A. Kadian, A. Al-Dahle, A. Letman, A. Mathur, A. Schelten, A. Yang, A. Fan, et al. 2024. The llama 3 herd of models. *arXiv preprint arXiv:2407.21783*.

K. Ethayarajh. 2019. How contextual are contextualized word representations? comparing the geometry of BERT, ELMo, and GPT-2 embeddings. *CoRR*, abs/1909.00512.

A. Ettinger. 2020. What BERT is not: Lessons from a new suite of psycholinguistic diagnostics for language models. *Transactions of the Association for Computational Linguistics*, 8:34–48.

C. L. Gagné. 2001. Relation and lexical priming during the interpretation of noun–noun combinations. *Journal of Experimental Psychology: Learning, Memory, and Cognition*, 27(1):236.

S. Gunasekar, Y. Zhang, J. Aneja, C. C. T. Mendes, A. Del Giorno, S. Gopi, M. Javaheripi, P. Kauffmann, G. de Rosa, O. Saarikivi, et al. 2023. Textbooks are all you need. *arXiv preprint arXiv:2306.11644*.

J. Hewitt and C. D. Manning. 2019. A structural probe for finding syntax in word representations. In *Proceedings of the 2019 Conference of the North American Chapter of the Association for Computational Linguistics: Human Language Technologies, Volume 1 (Long and Short Papers)*, pages 4129–4138. Association for Computational Linguistics.

G. Jawahar, B. Sagot, and D. Seddah. 2019. What does BERT learn about the structure of language? In *ACL 2019-57th Annual Meeting of the Association for Computational Linguistics*, pages 3651—-3657. Association for Computational Linguistics.

T. Ju, W. Sun, W. Du, X. Yuan, Z. Ren, and G. Liu. 2024. How large language models encode context knowledge? a layer-wise probing study. *arXiv preprint arXiv:2402.16061*.

N. Kim, R. Patel, A. Poliak, A. Wang, P. Xia, T. R. McCoy, I. Tenney, A. Ross, T. Linzen, and B. Van Durme. 2019. Probing what different NLP tasks teach machines about function word comprehension. In *Proceedings of the Eighth Joint Conference on Lexical and Computational Semantics (SEM 2019)*, pages 235—-249. Association for Computational Linguistics.

N. Kriegeskorte, M. Mur, and P. A. Bandettini. 2008. Representational similarity analysis-connecting the branches of systems neuroscience. *Frontiers in systems neuroscience*, 2:249.

T. Linzen and M. Baroni. 2021. Syntactic structure from deep learning. *Annual Review of Linguistics*, 7(1):195–212.

Y. Liu, M. Ott, N. Goyal, J. Du, M. Joshi, D. Chen, O. Levy, M. Lewis, L. Zettlemoyer, and V. Stoyanov. 2019. Roberta: A robustly optimized BERT pretraining approach. *CoRR*, abs/1907.11692.

Z. Liu, C. Kong, Y. Liu, and M. Sun. 2024. Fantastic semantics and where to find them: Investigating which layers of generative llms reflect lexical semantics. *arXiv preprint arXiv:2403.01509*.

J. Mitchell and M. Lapata. 2008. Vector-based models of semantic composition. In *proceedings of ACL-08: HLT*, pages 236–244. Association for Computational Linguistics.

D. Ó Séaghdha and A. Copestake. 2008. Semantic classification with distributional kernels. In *Proceedings of the 22nd International Conference on Computational Linguistics (Coling 2008)*, pages 649–656. Association for Computational Linguistics.

M. Ormerod, J. M. del Rincón, and B. Devereux. 2024. How is a "kitchen chair" like a "farm horse"? Exploring the representation of noun-noun compound semantics in transformer-based language models. *Computational Linguistics*, 50(1):49–81.

M. E. Peters, M. Neumann, L. Zettlemoyer, and W.T. Yih. 2018. Dissecting contextual word embeddings: Architecture and representation. In *Proceedings of the 2018 Conference on Empirical Methods in Natural Language Processing*, pages 1499–1509. Association for Computational Linguistics.

S. T. Piantadosi and F. Hill. 2022. Meaning without reference in large language models. *arXiv preprint arXiv:2208.02957*.

A. Radford, J. Wu, R. Child, D. Luan, D. Amodei, and I. Sutskever. 2019. Language models are unsupervised multitask learners. *OpenAI*.

G. Rambelli, E. Chersoni, C. Collacciani, and M. Bolognesi. 2024. Can large language models interpret noun-noun compounds? a linguistically-motivated study on lexicalized and novel compounds. In *Proceedings of the 62nd Annual Meeting of the Association for Computational Linguistics (Volume 1: Long Papers)*, pages 11823–11835. Association for Computational Linguistics.

V. Shwartz and I. Dagan. 2019. Still a pain in the neck: Evaluating text representations on lexical composition. *Transactions of the Association for Computational Linguistics*, 7:403–419.

E. E. Smith and D. N. Osherson. 1984. Conceptual combination with prototype concepts. *Cognitive science*, 8(4):337–361.

E. E. Smith, D. N. Osherson, L. J. Rips, and M. Keane. 1988. Combining prototypes: A selective modification model. *Cognitive science*, 12(4):485–527.

A. Vaswani. 2017. Attention is all you need. In *Proceedings of the 31st International Conference on Neural Information Processing Systems*, pages 6000–6010.

I. Vulić, E. M. Ponti, R. Litschko, G. Glavaš, and A. Korhonen. 2020. Probing pretrained language models for lexical semantics. In *Proceedings of the 2020 Conference on Empirical Methods in Natural Language Processing (EMNLP)*, pages 7222–7240. Association for Computational Linguistics.

E. J. Wisniewski. 1997. When concepts combine. *Psychonomic bulletin & review*, 4:167–183.

Author Index